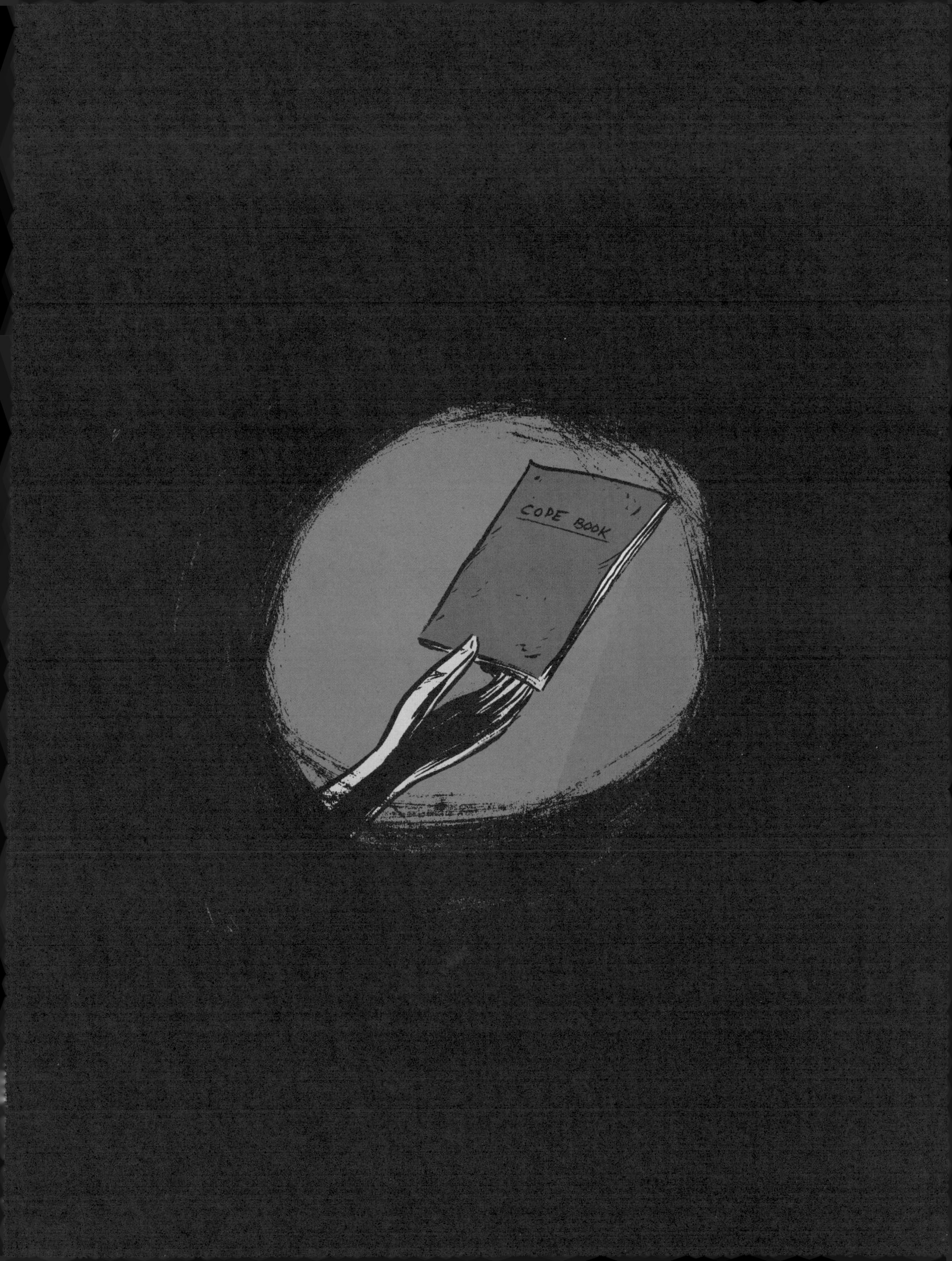
CODE BOOK

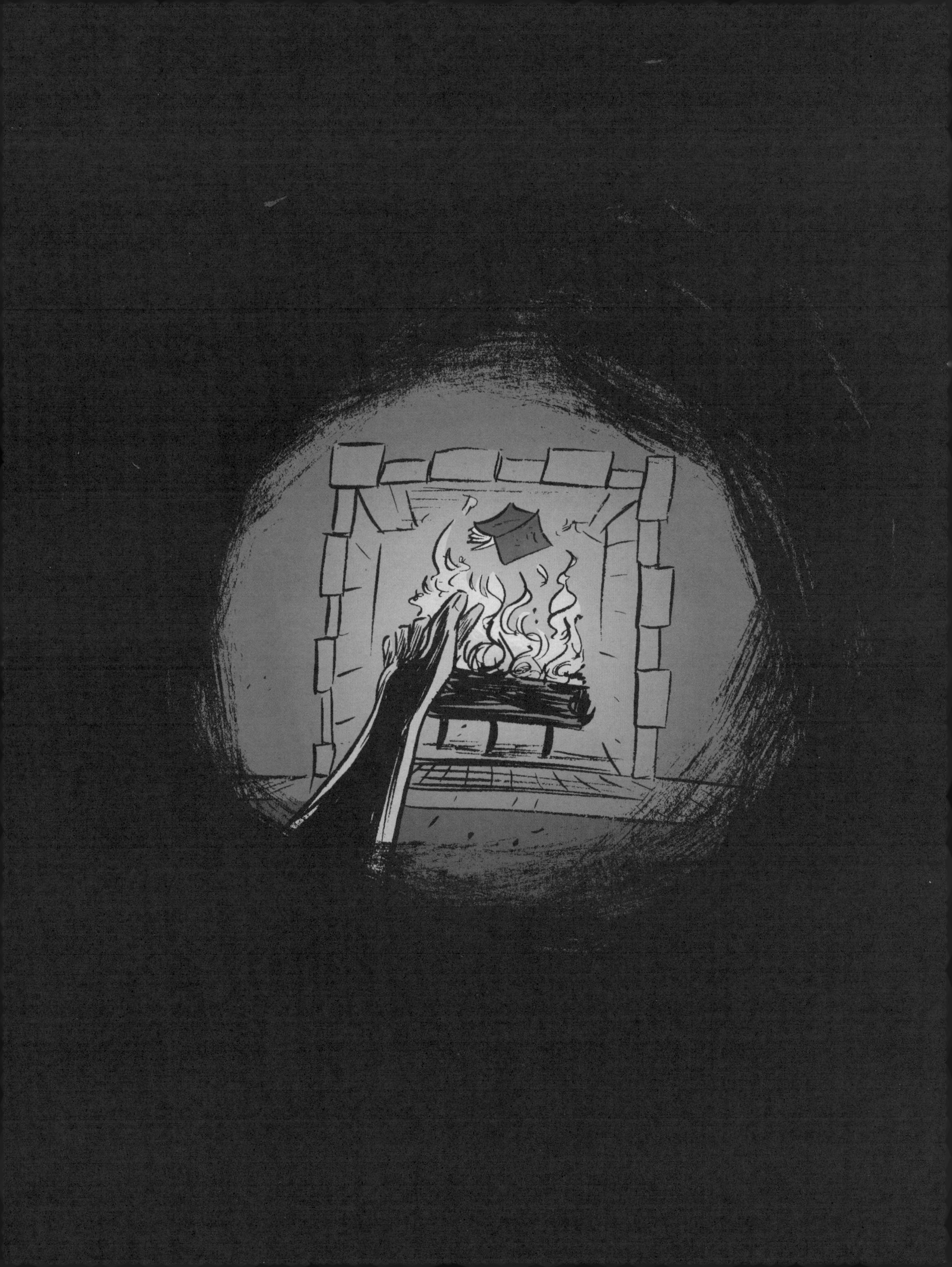

2 Sisters
A Super-Spy Graphic Novel

One-time Use Code

A–S	N–F
B–T	O–G
C–U	P–H
D–V	Q–I
E–W	R–J
F–X	S–K
G–Y	T–L
H–Z	U–M
I–A	V–N
J–B	W–O
K–C	X–P
L–D	Y–Q
M–E	Z–R

by Matt Kindt

Colors by Marie Enger

#41173

For secret
Ella as consp
Jean under sur
Kindt as guilty

...e the key to break the code,
...sit the super secret safehouse:
MattKindt.com

Published by Dark Horse Books
A division of Dark Horse Comics, Inc.
10956 SE Main Street
Milwaukie, OR 97222

Dark Horse Books, Dark Horse Comics, and the Dark Horse logo are registered trademarks of Dark Horse Comics, Inc.

DarkHorse.com

Publisher
Mike Richardson

Top Shelf Edition Editor
Chris Staros

Dark Horse Edition Editor
Brendan Wright

Assistant Editor
Ian Tucker

Book Designers
Matt Kindt with Jimmy Presler

Digital Art Technician
Jason Rickerd

Library of Congress Cataloging-in-Publication Data is available

First Dark Horse edition:
September 2015
10 9 8 7 6 5 4 3 2 1
ISBN 978-1-61655-721-8
Printed in China

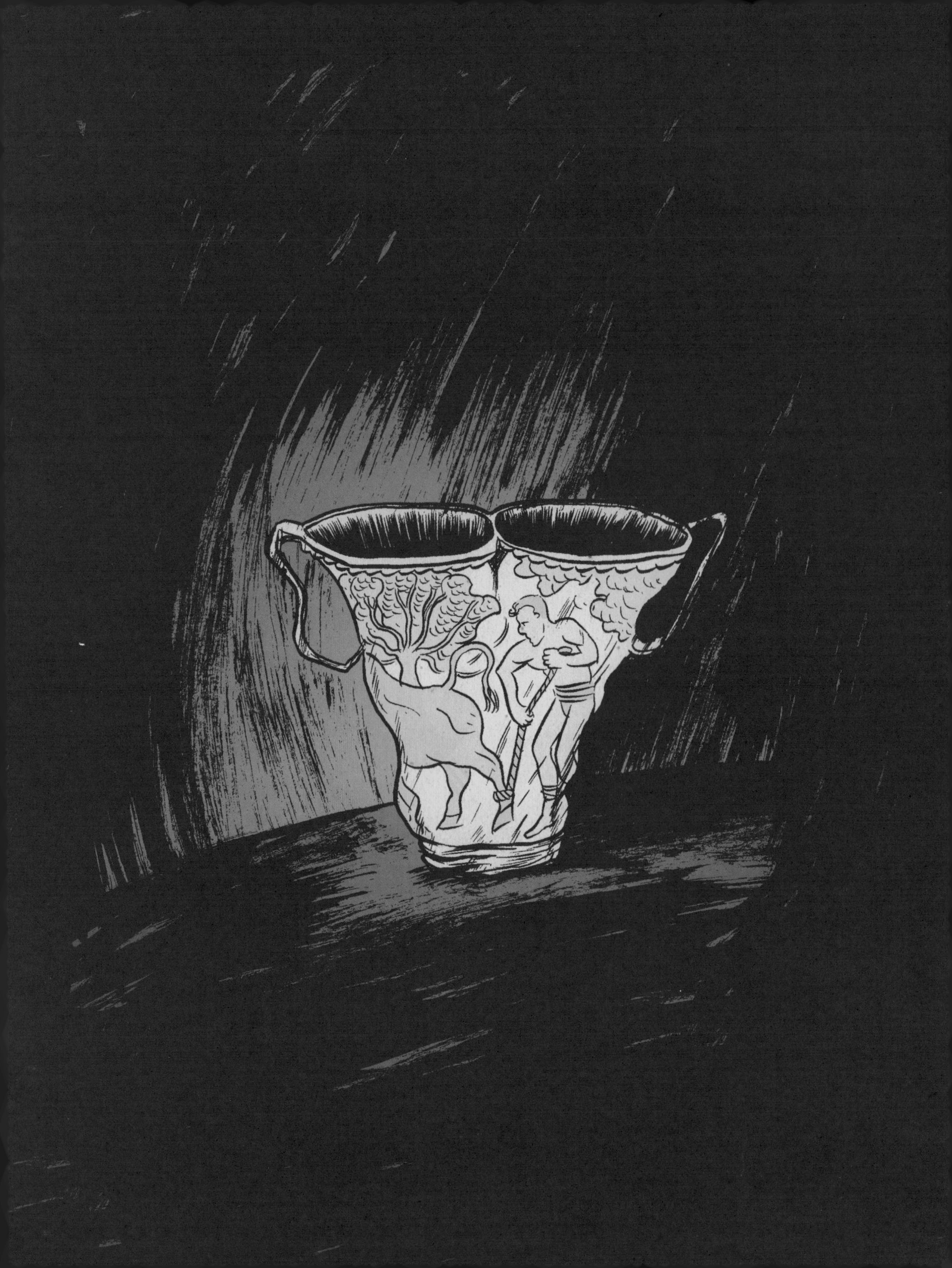

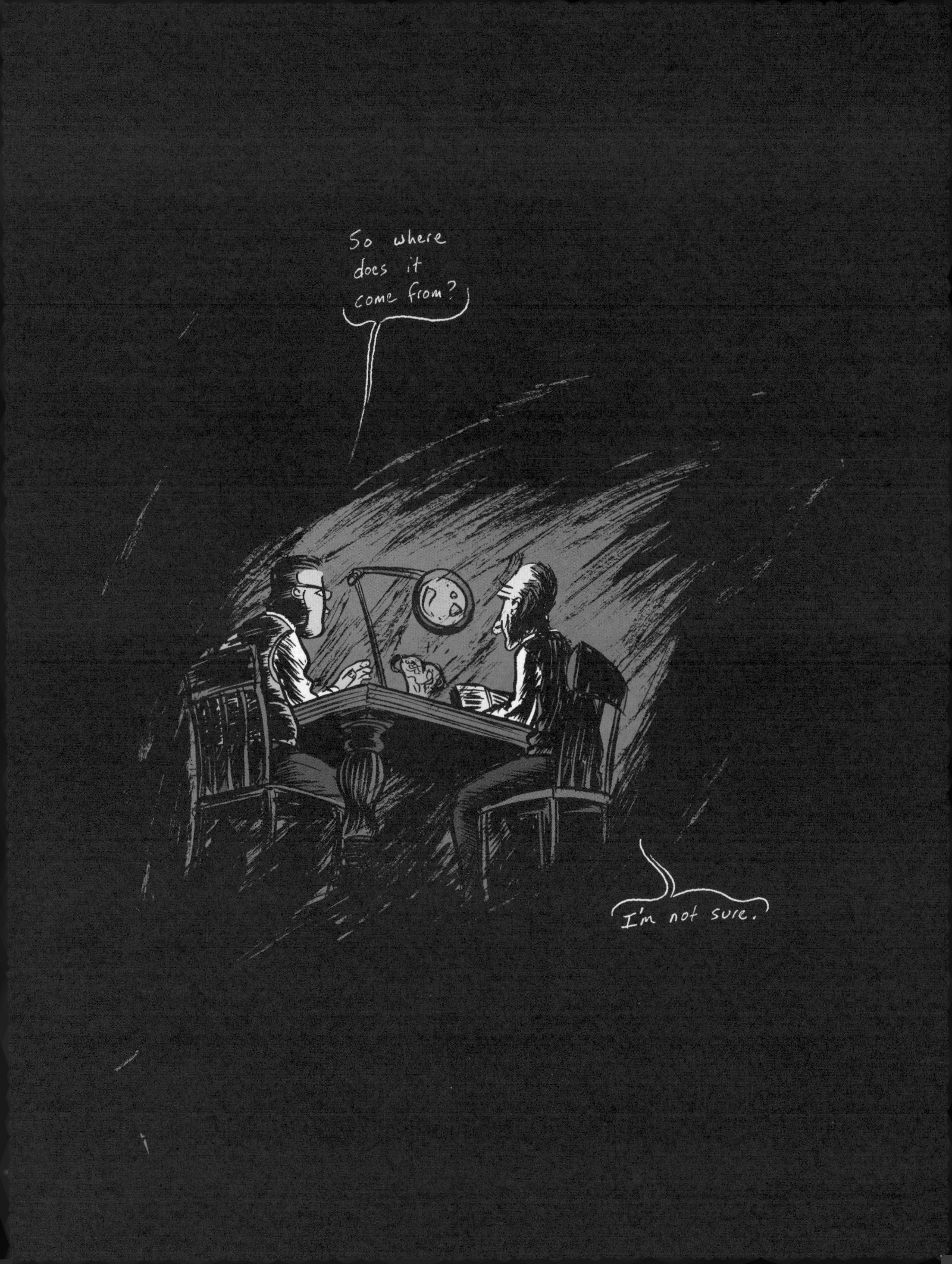
So where does it come from?
I'm not sure.

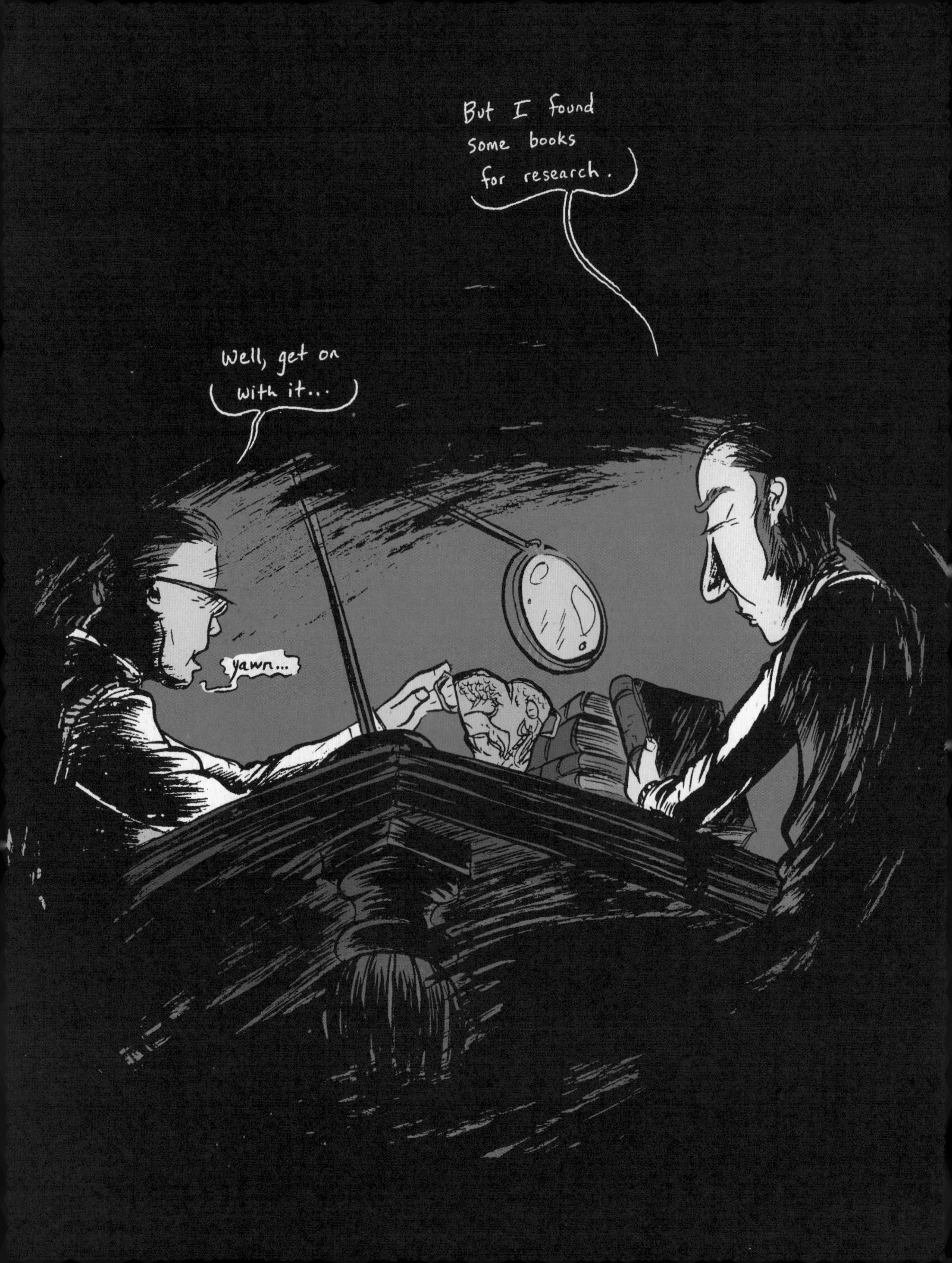
But I found some books for research.
Well, get on with it...
yawn...

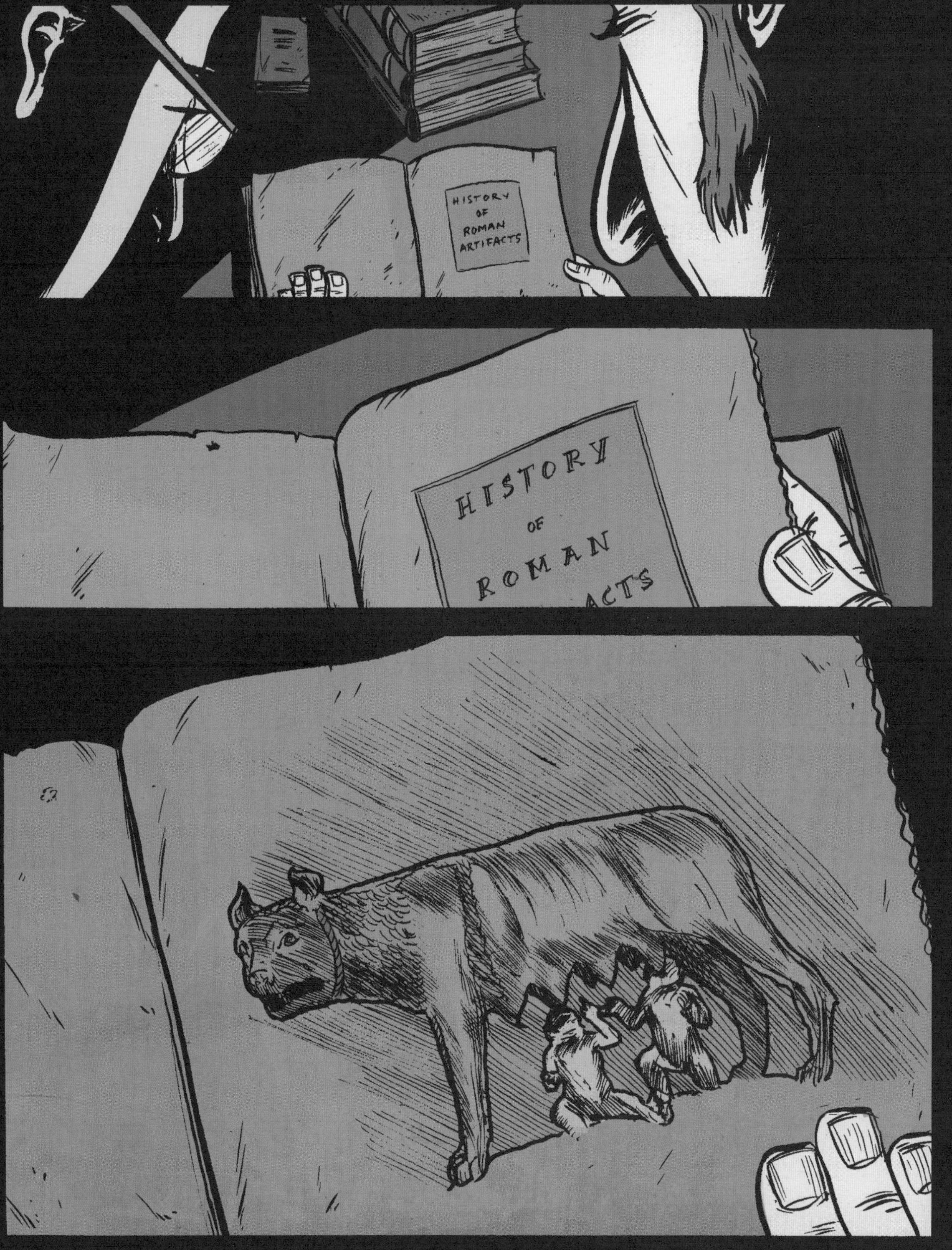
HISTORY OF ROMAN ARTIFACTS
HISTORY OF ROMAN

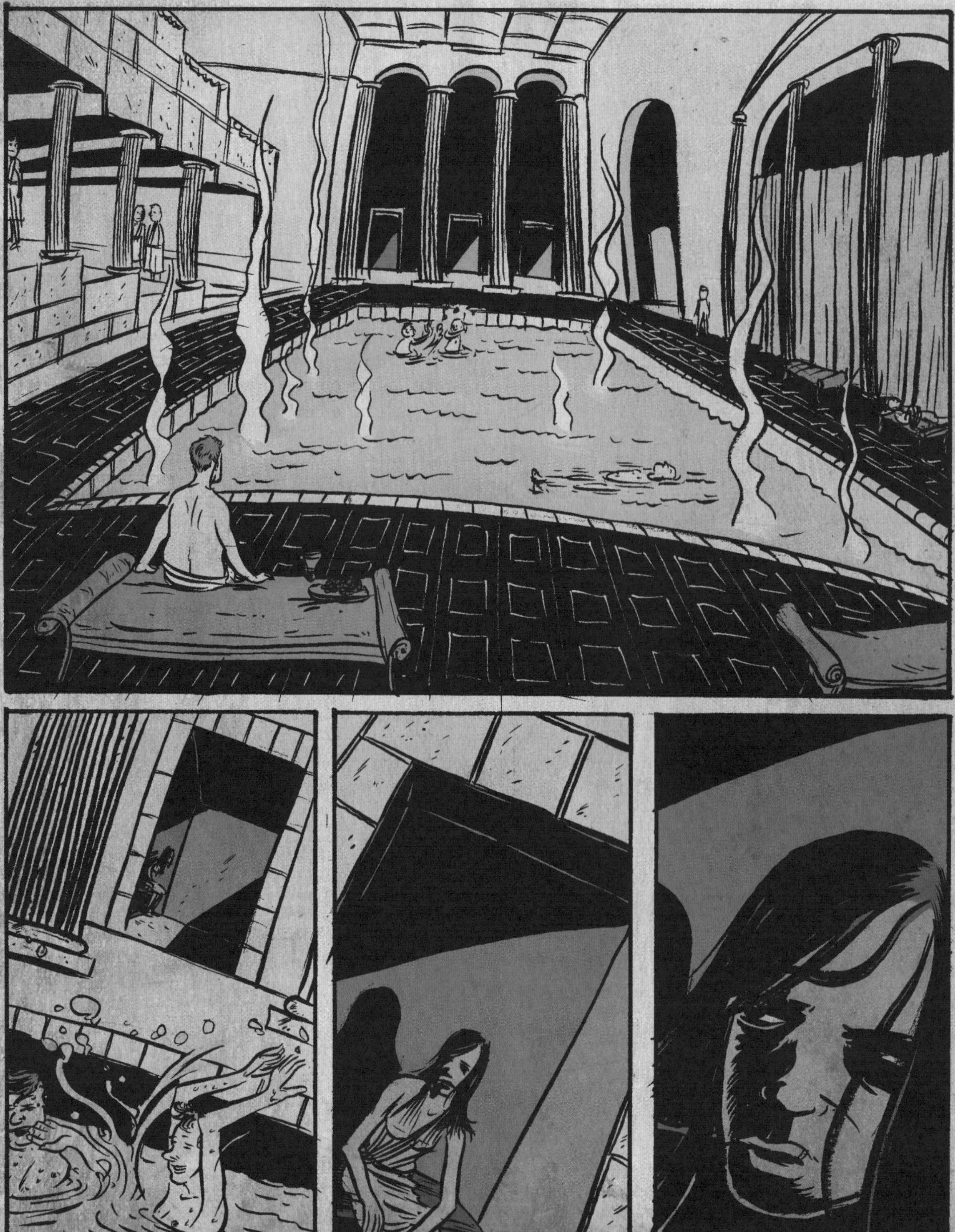

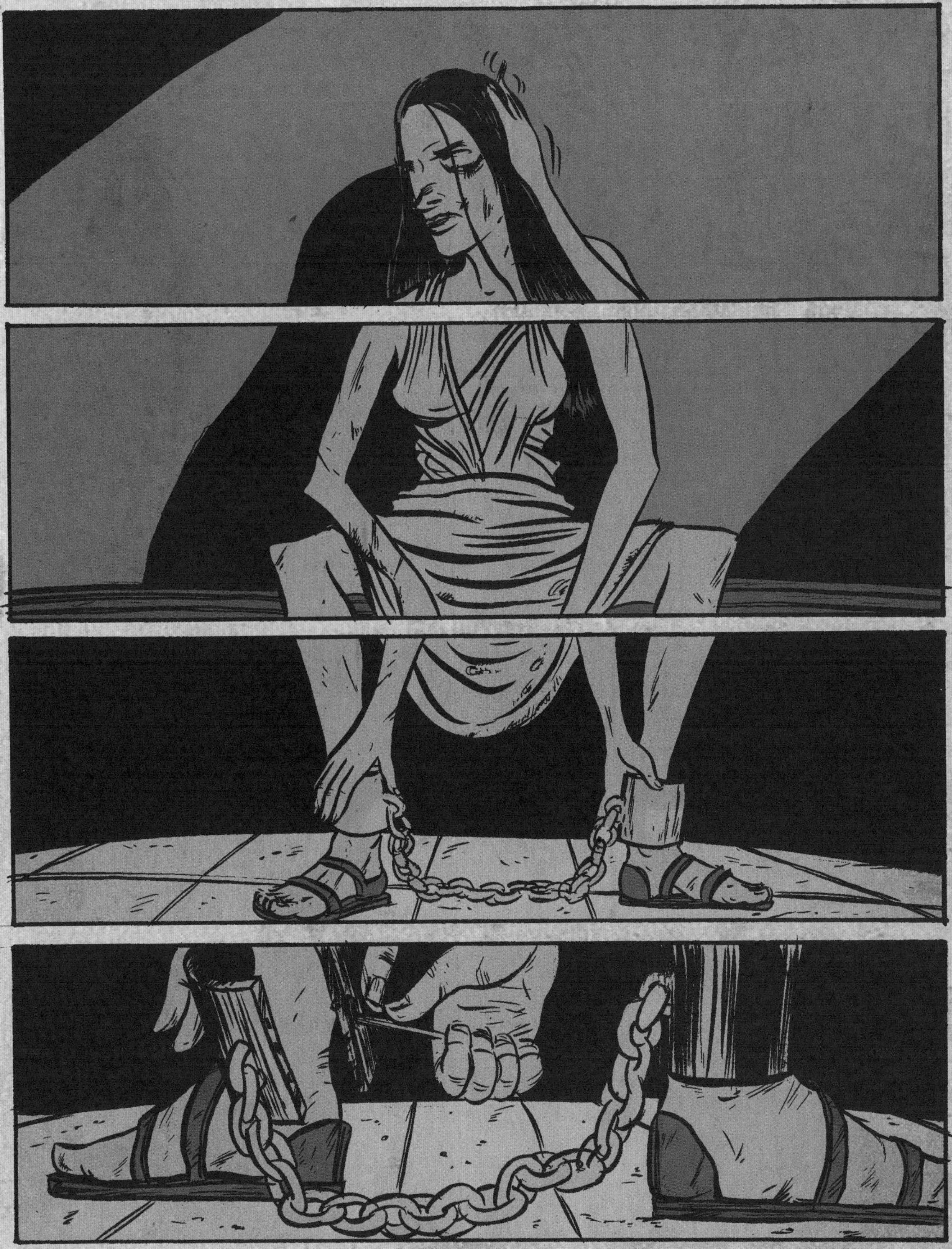

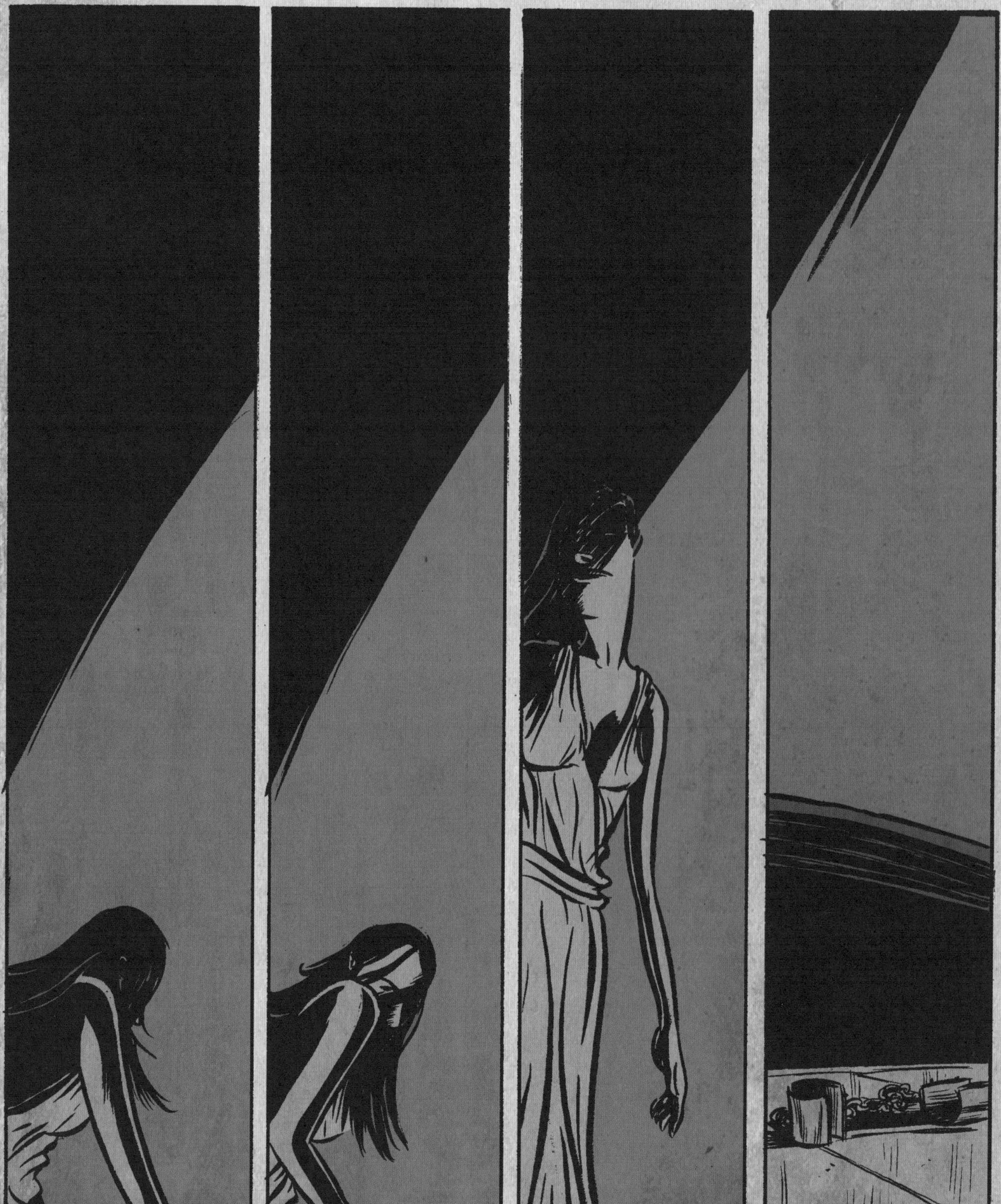

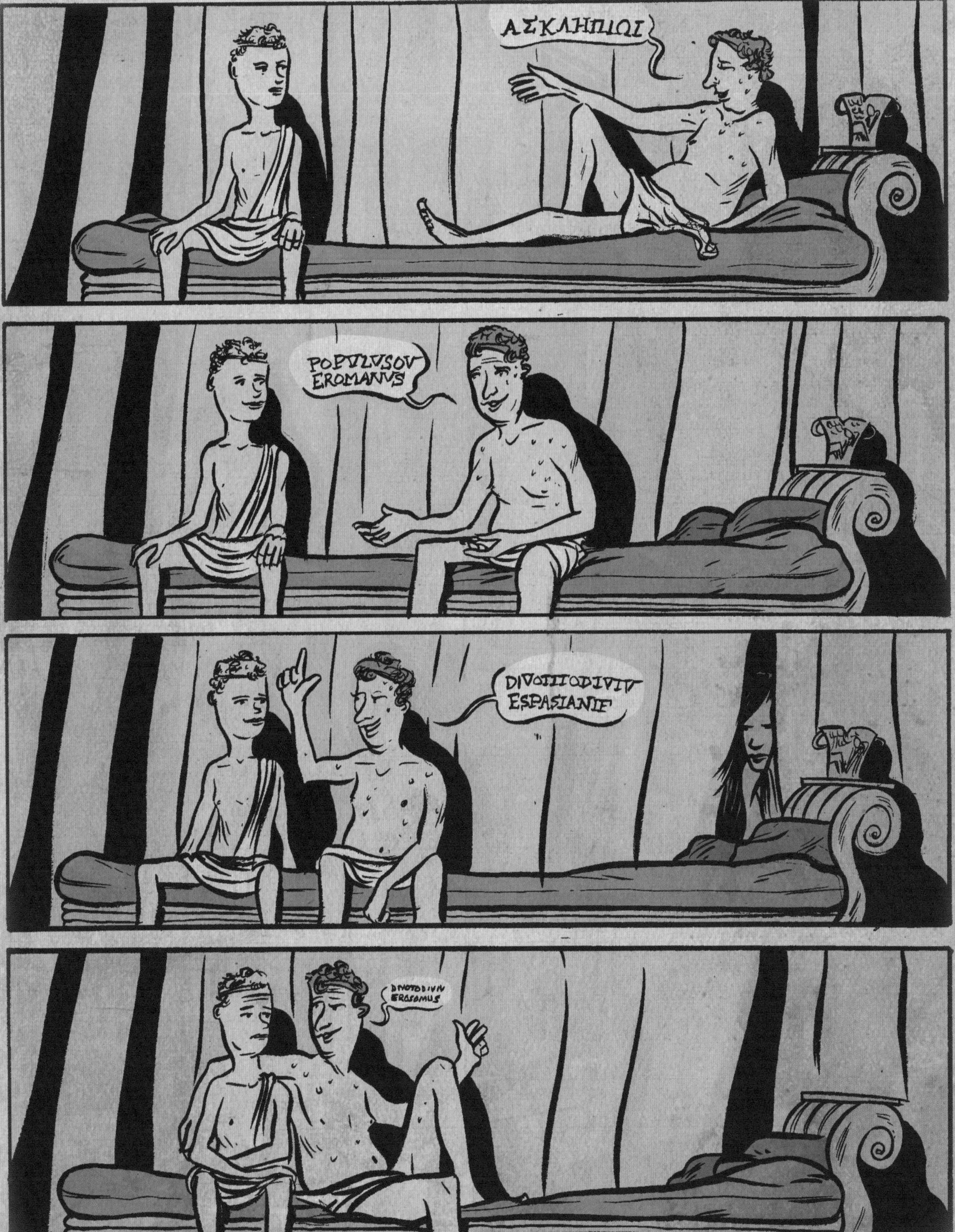
ΑΣΚΛΗΠΙΩΙ
POPVLVSQV
EROMANVS
DIVOTITODIVIV
ESPASIANIF
DIVOTODIVN
EROSOMUS

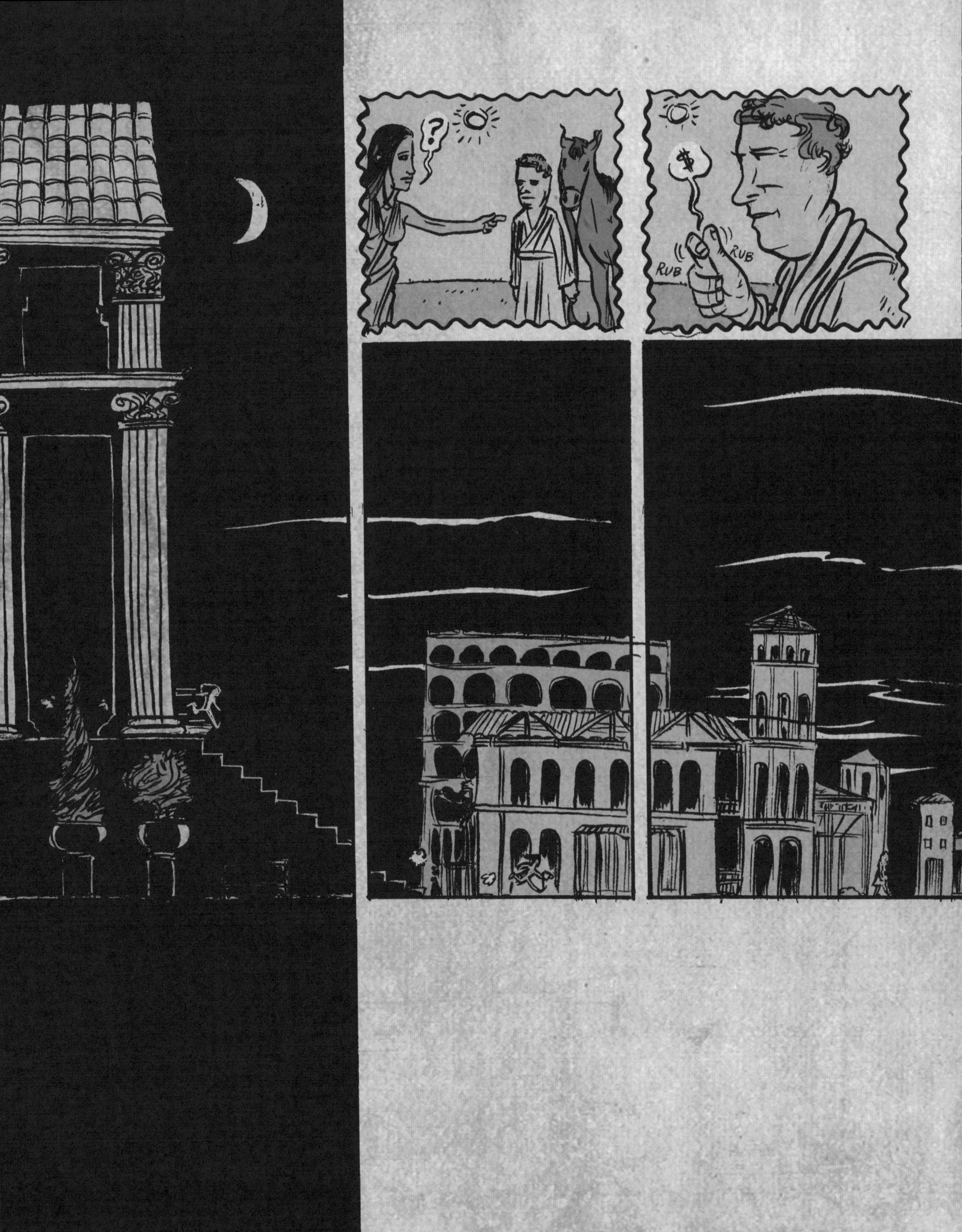
?
$
RUB
RUB

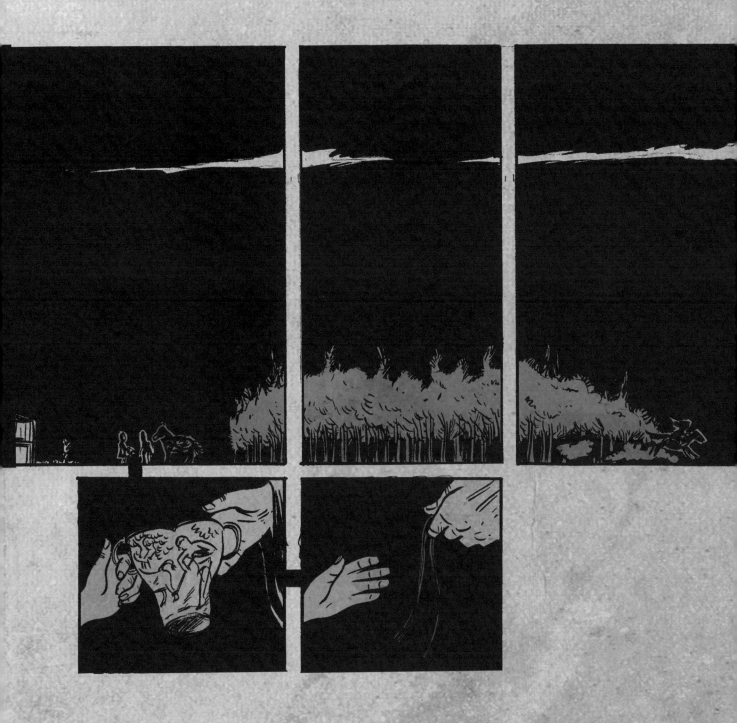

?
$$
Rub
Rub

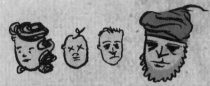

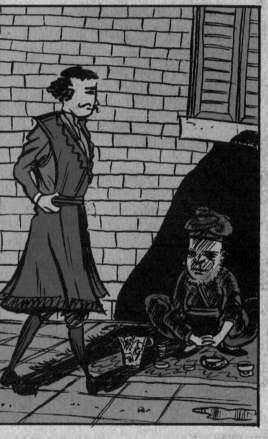

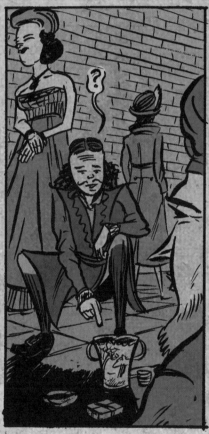

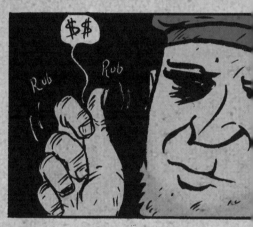

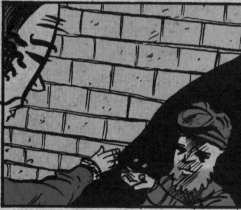

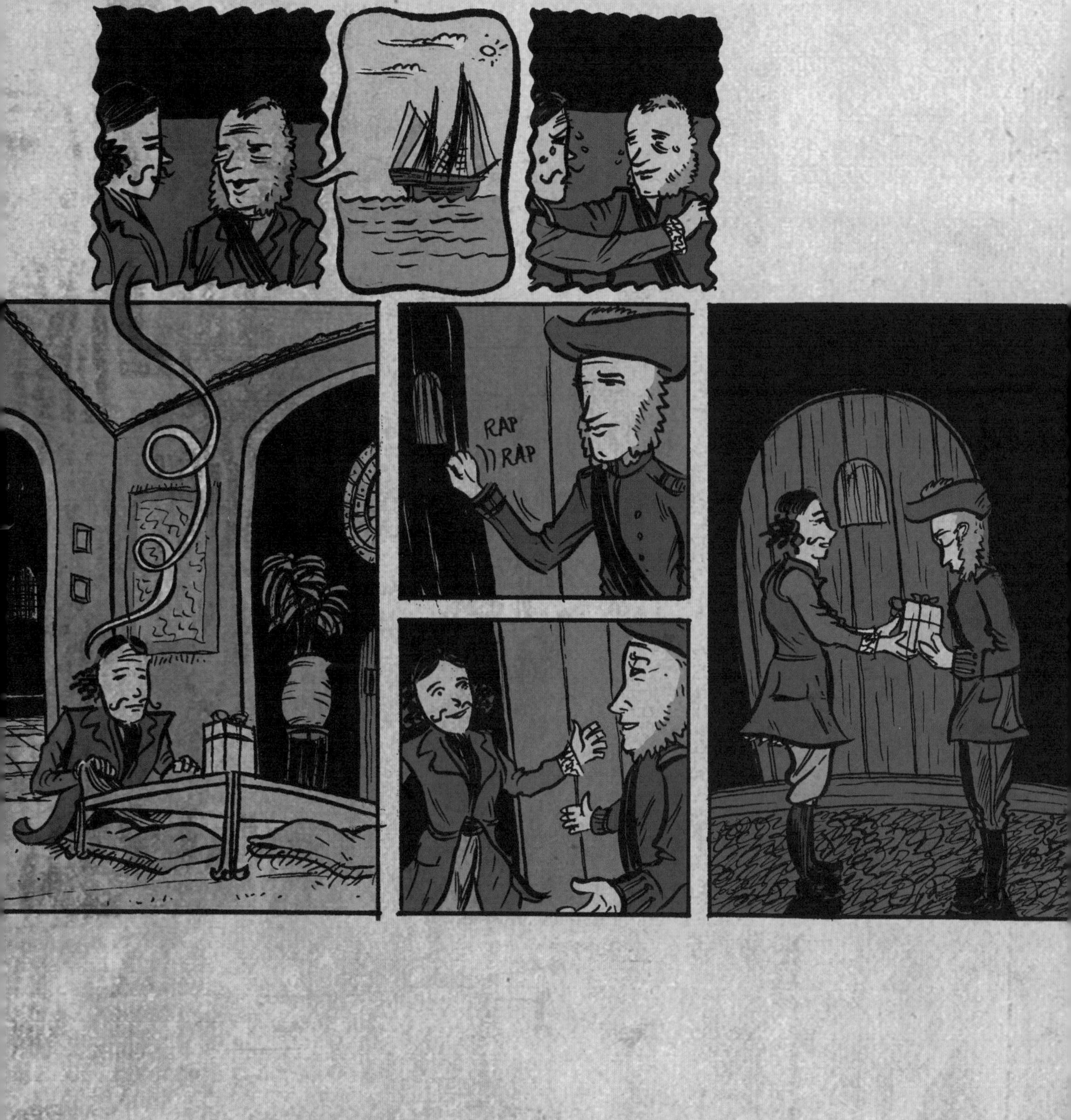
RAP
RAP

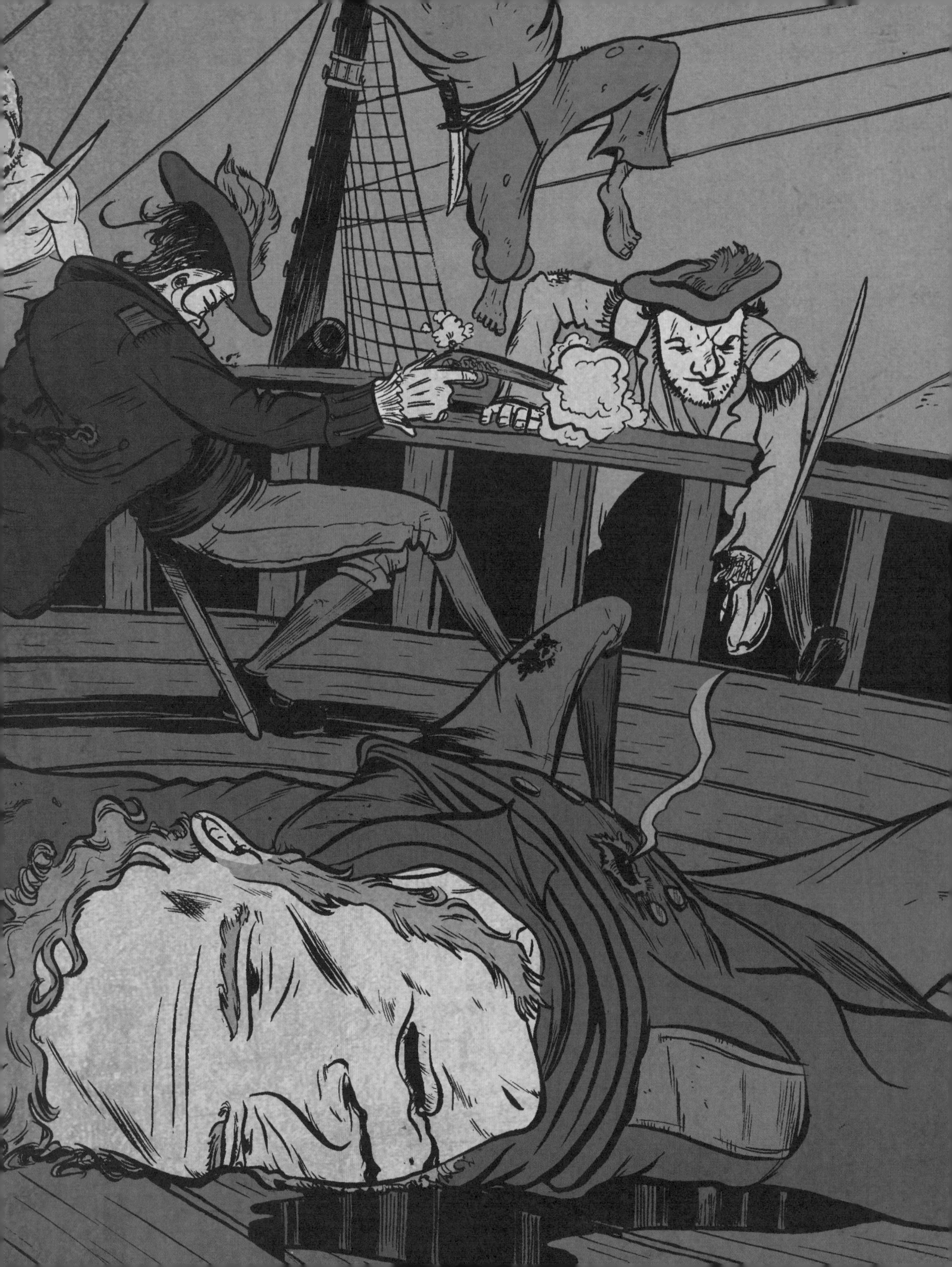

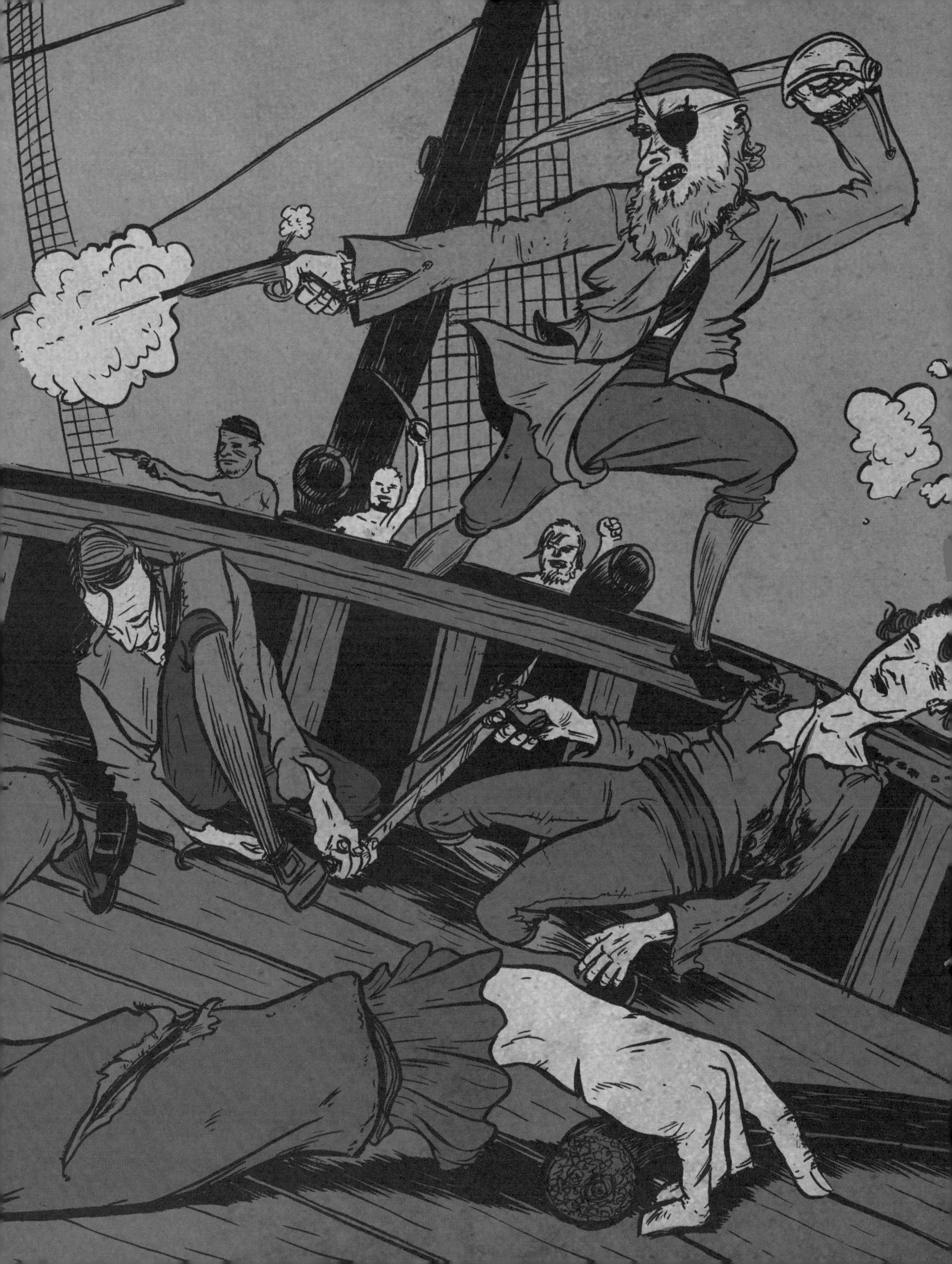

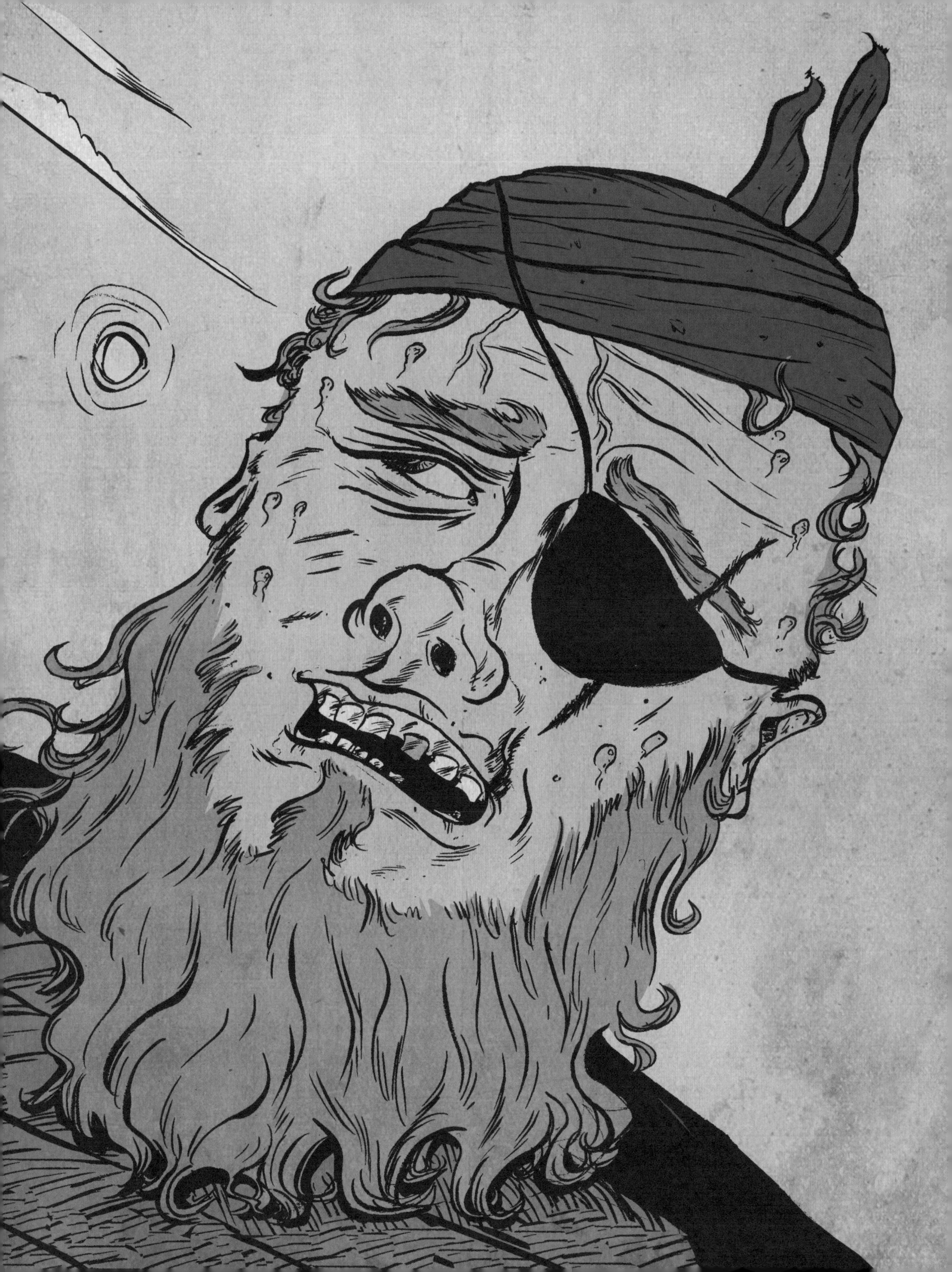

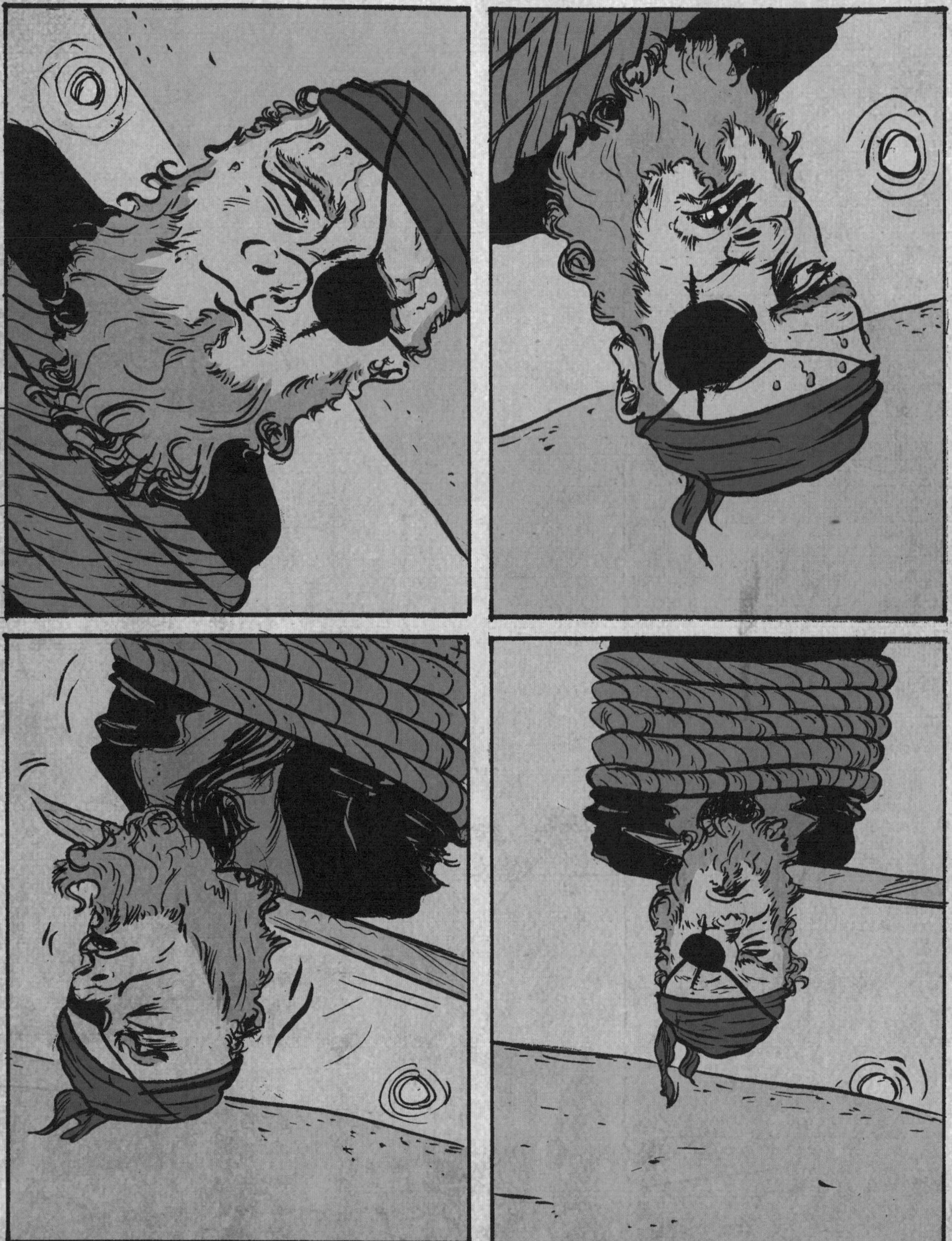

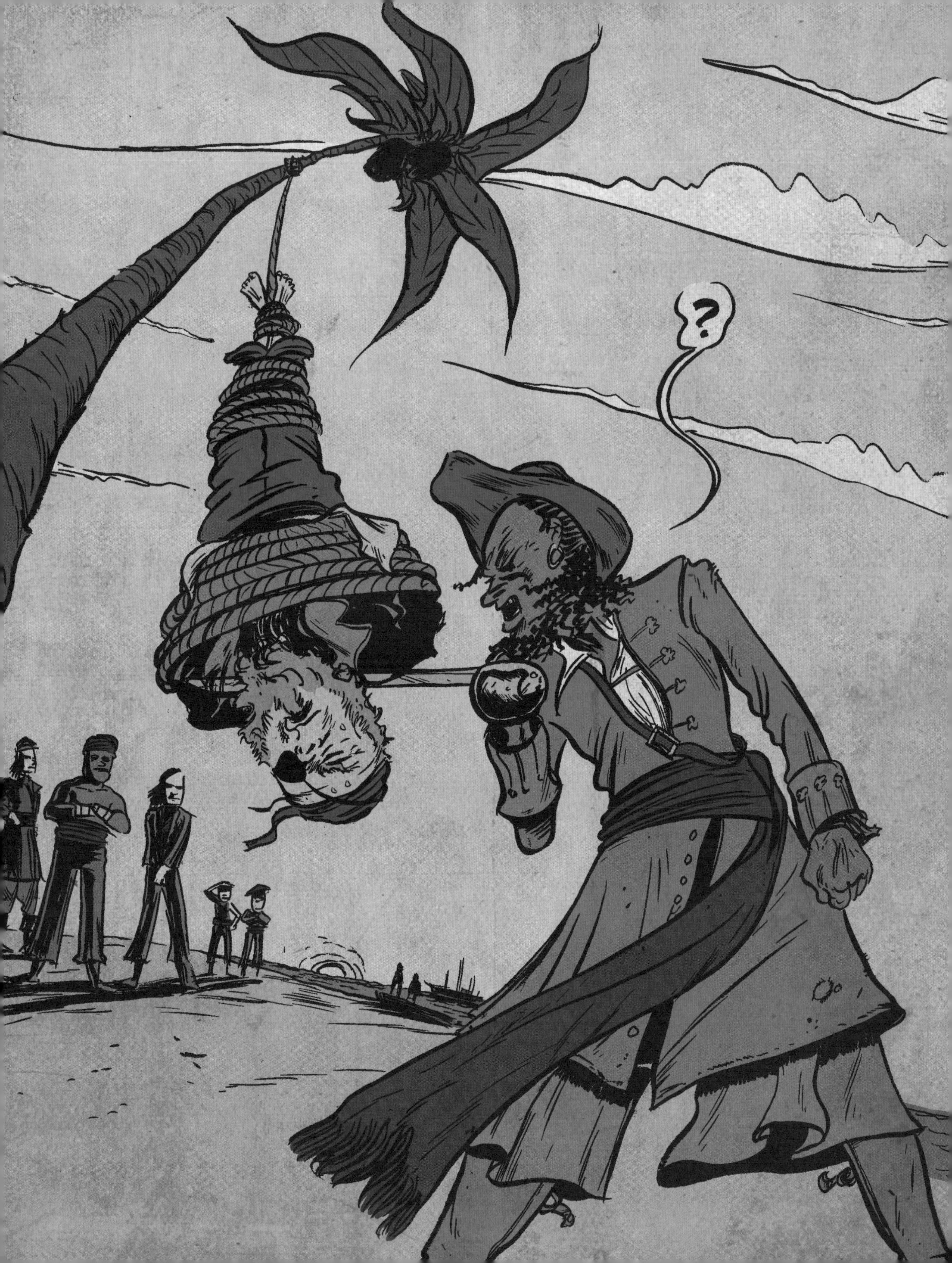
?

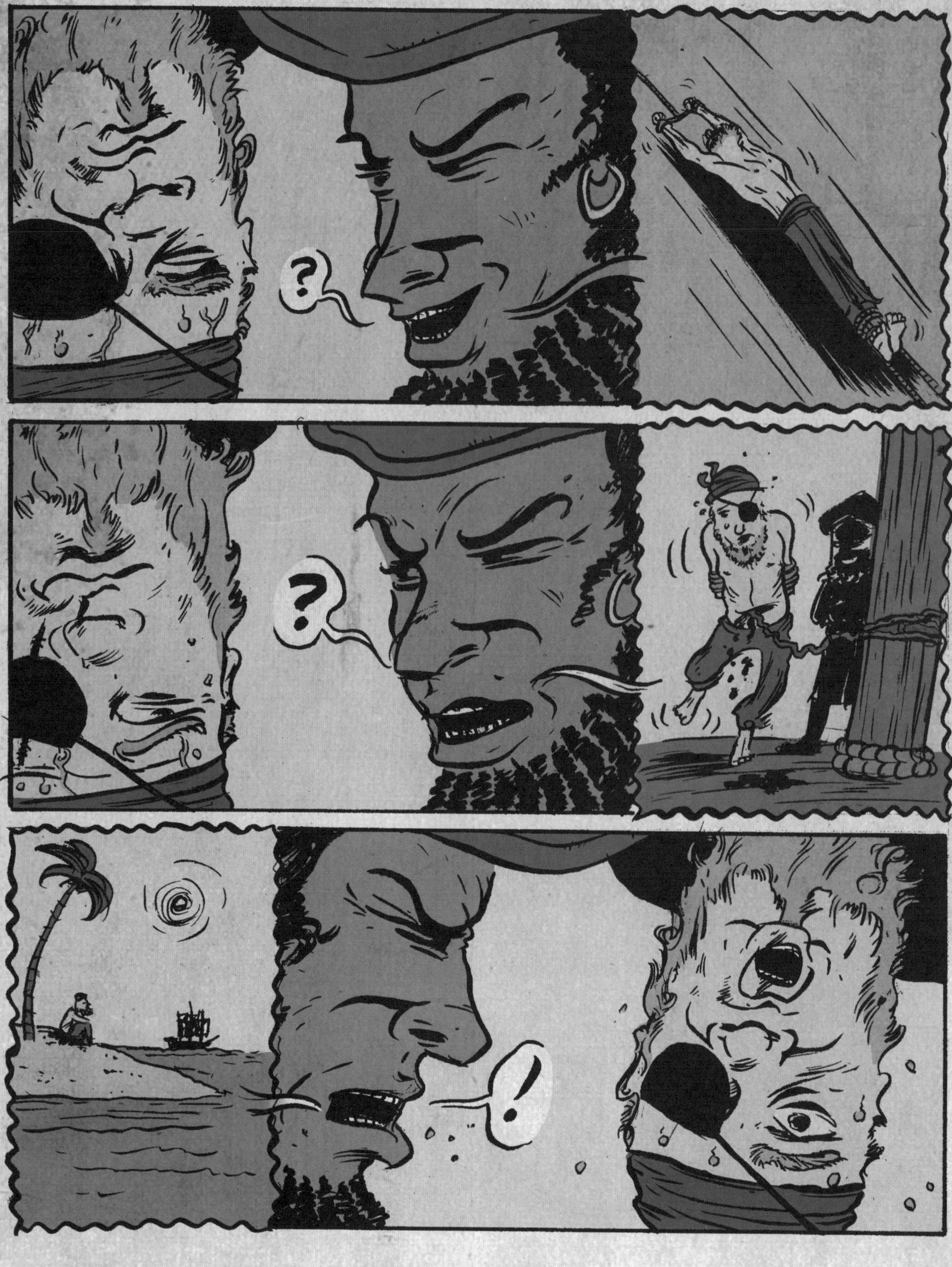
?
?
!

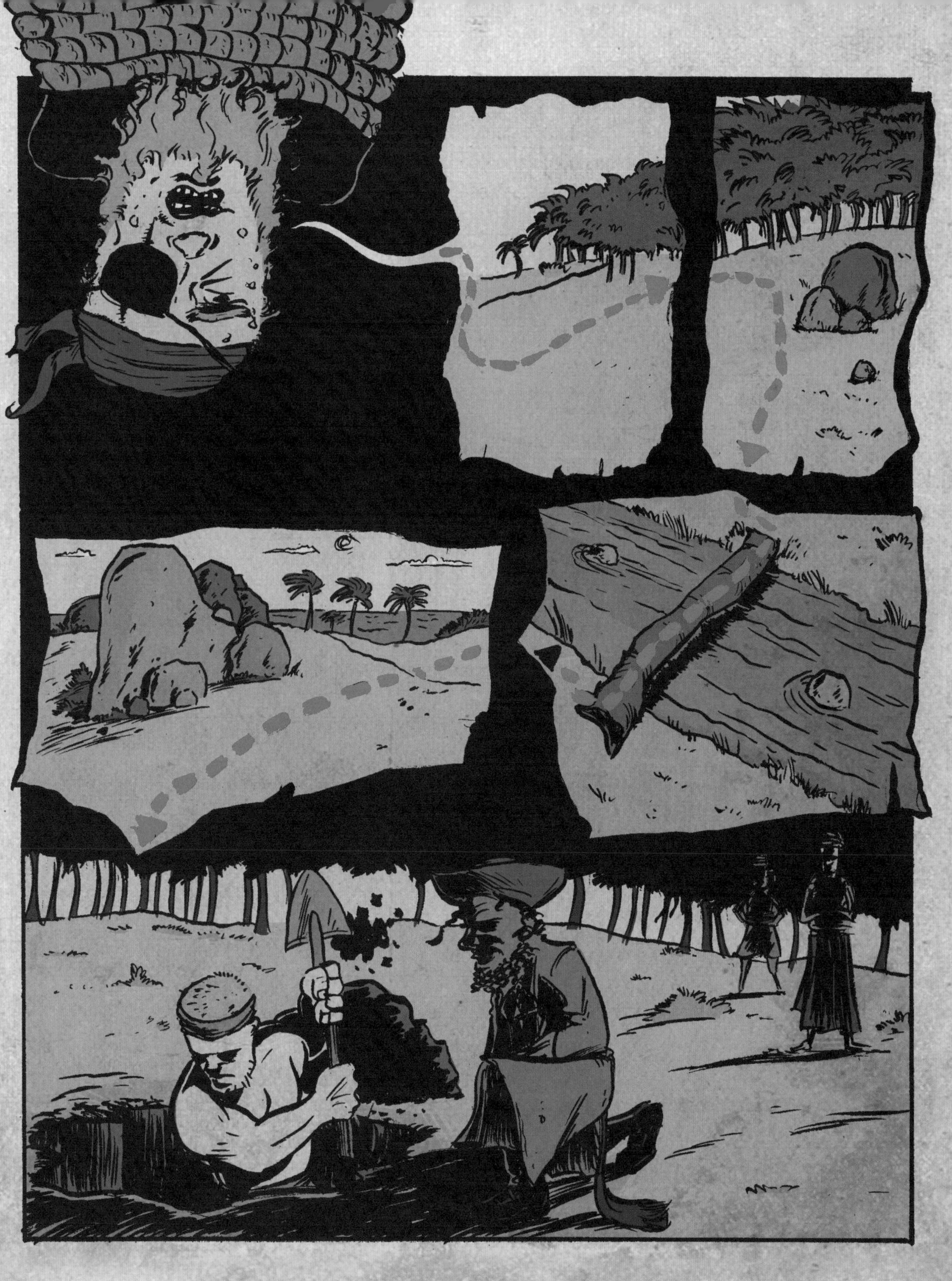

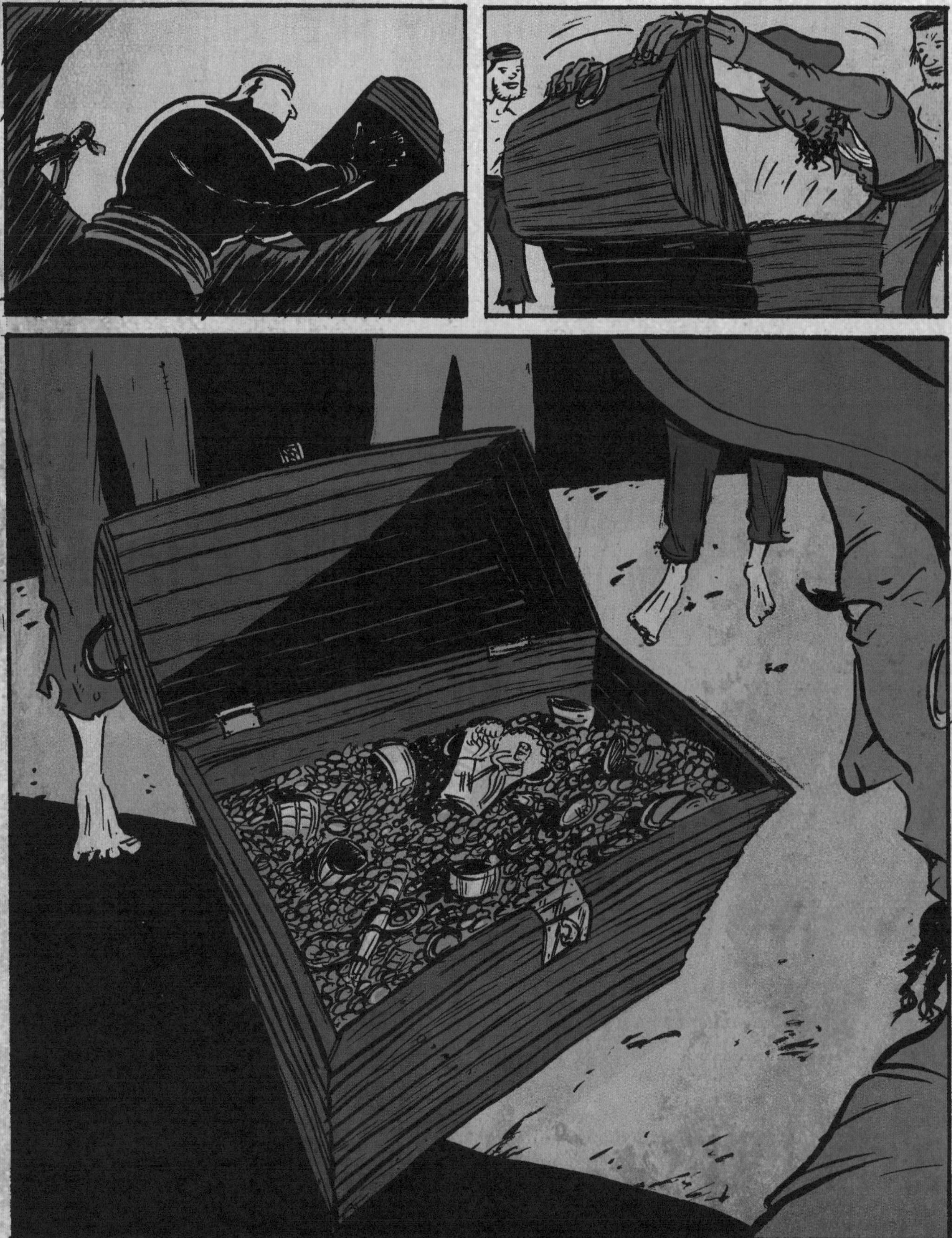

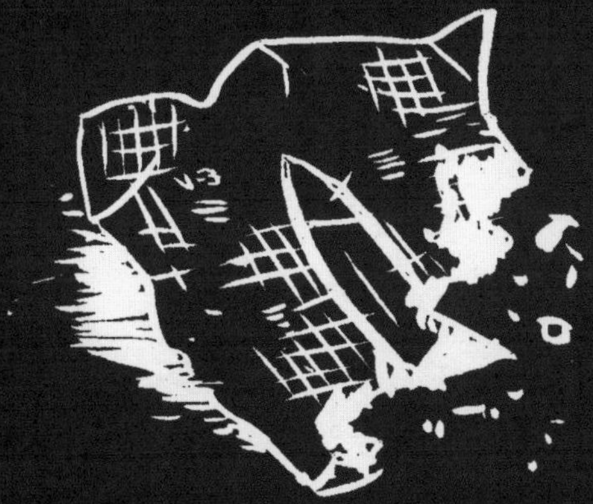
V3

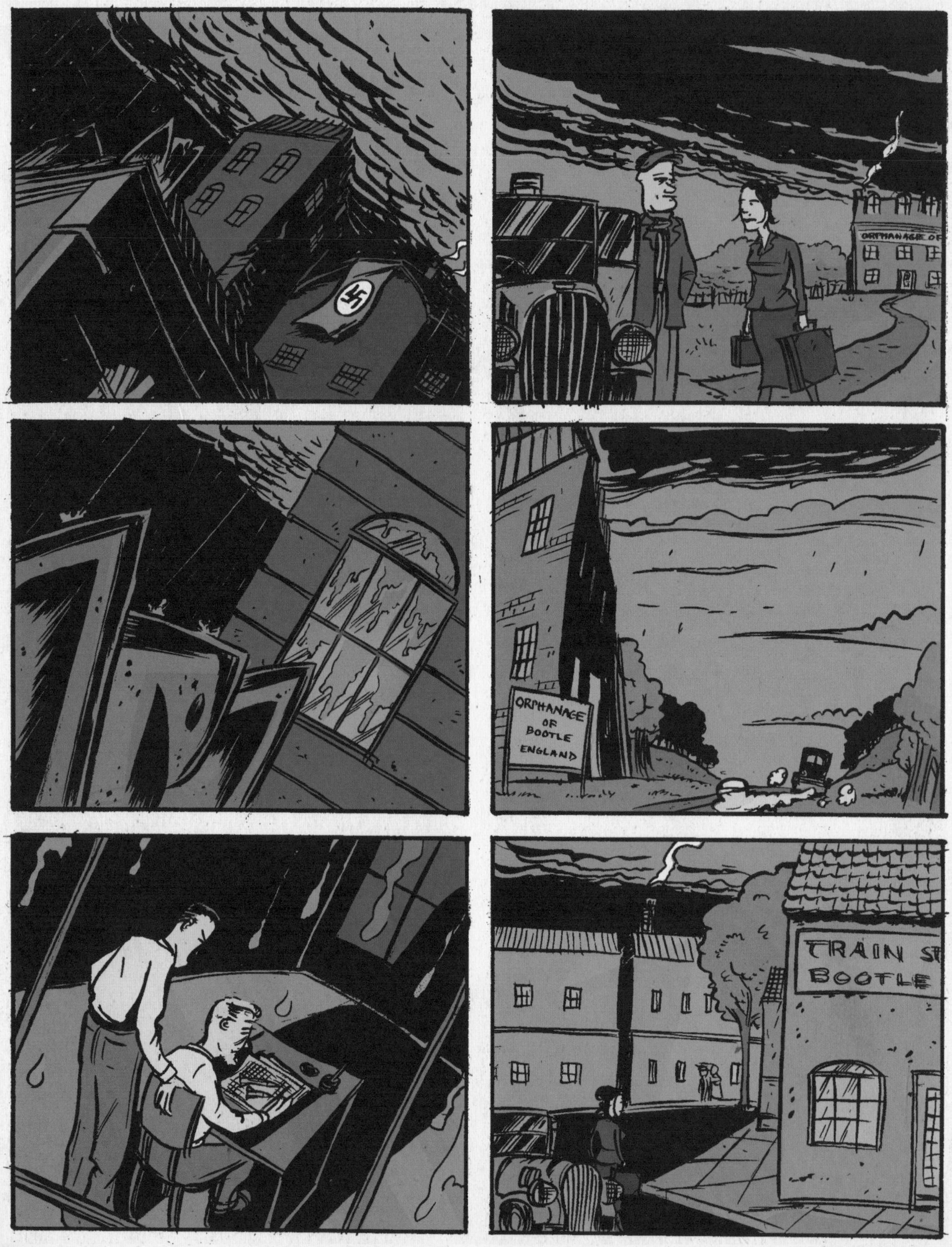

ORPHANAGE OF
ORPHANAGE OF BOOTLE ENGLAND
TRAIN S
BOOTLE

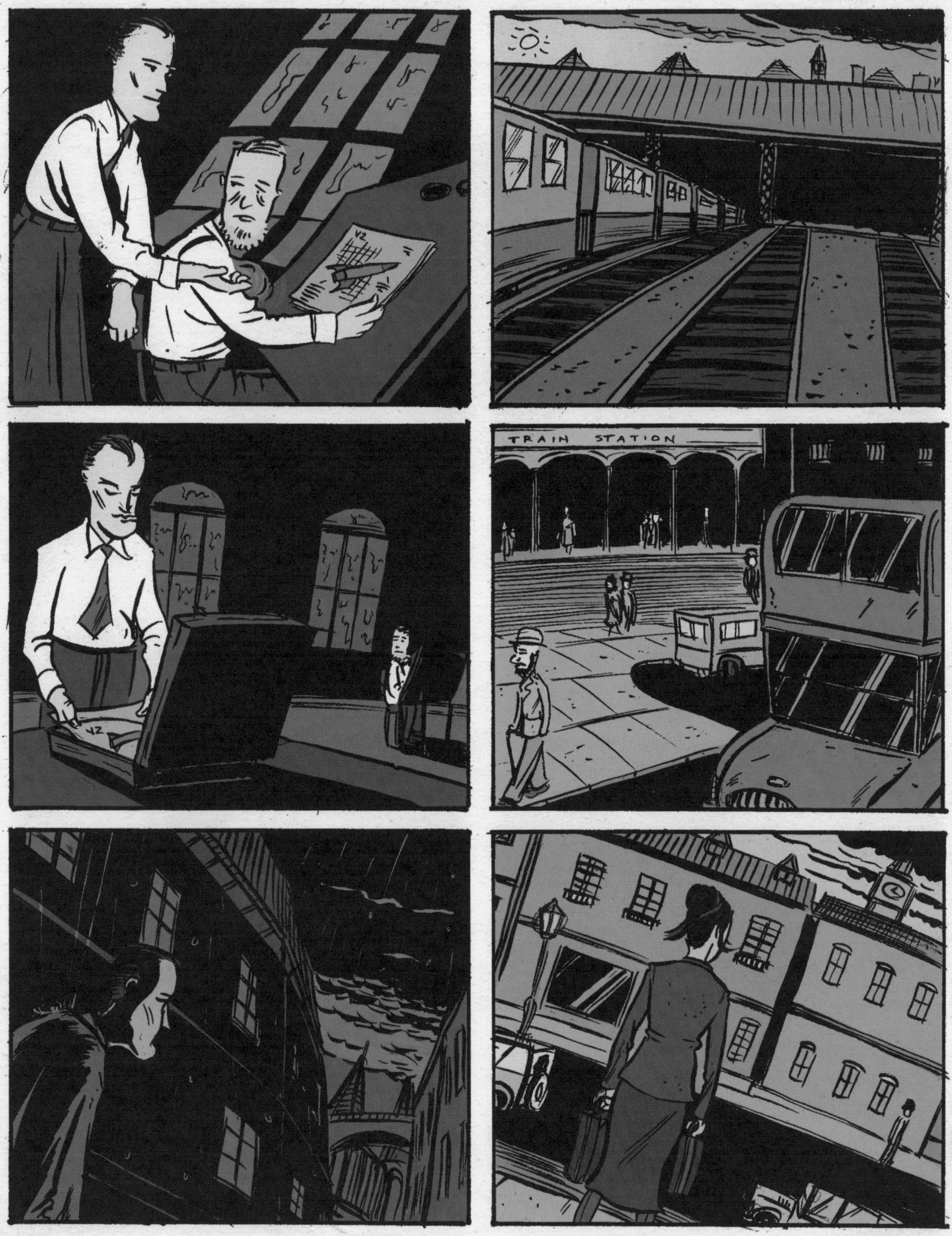
V2
V2
TRAIN STATION

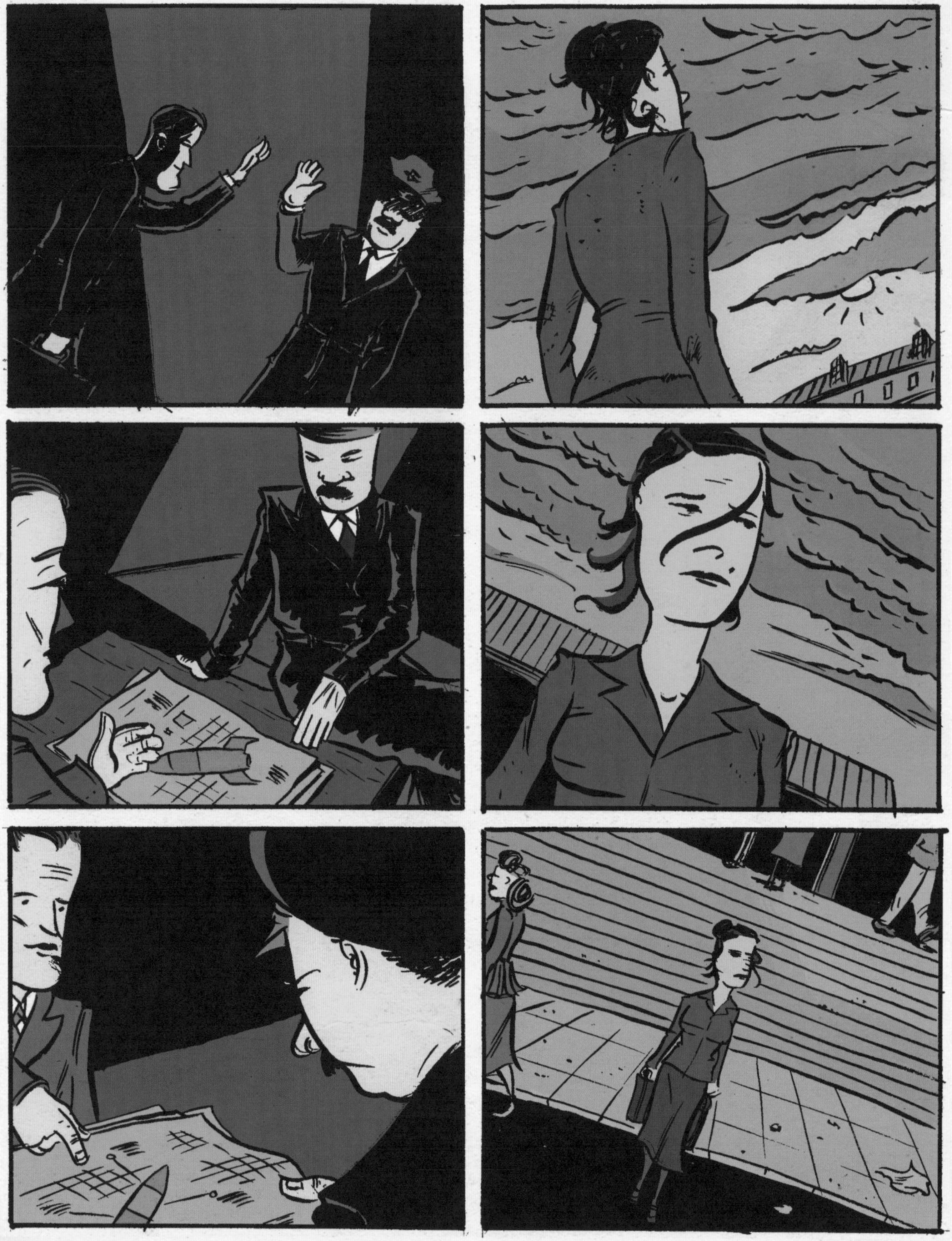

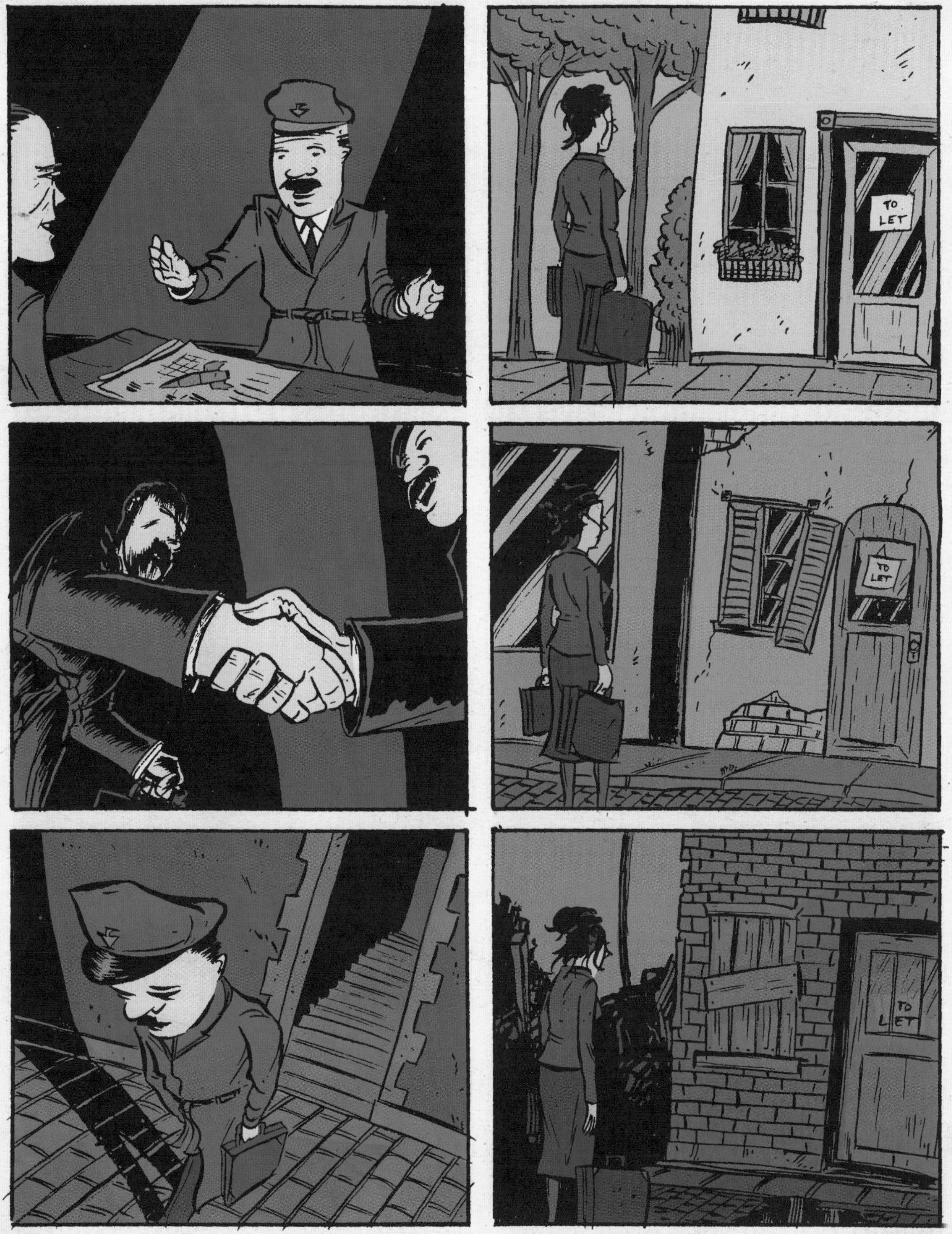
TO LET
TO LET
TO LET

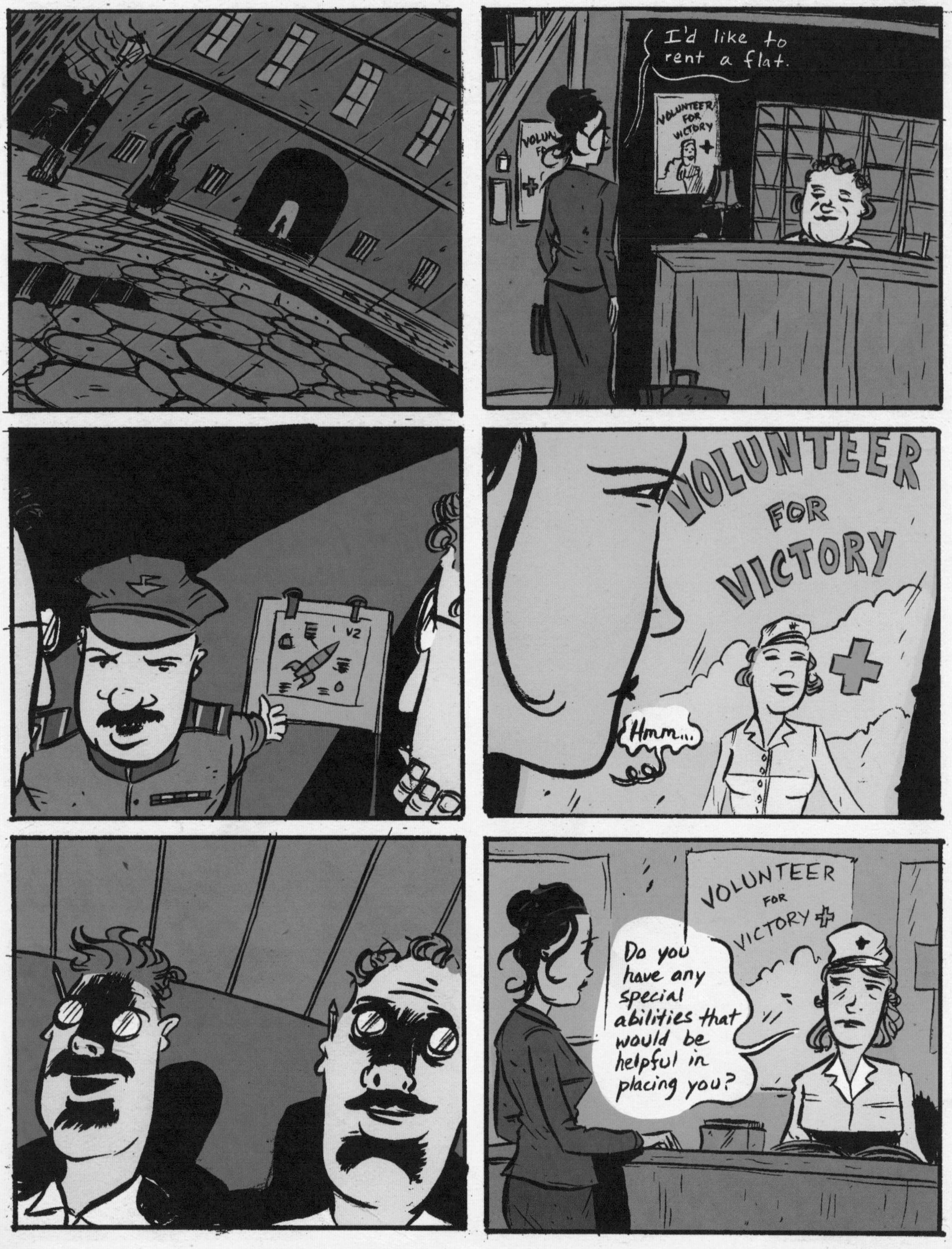
I'd like to rent a flat.
VOLUNTEER FOR VICTORY
V2
VOLUNTEER FOR VICTORY
Hmm...
VOLUNTEER FOR VICTORY
Do you have any special abilities that would be helpful in placing you?

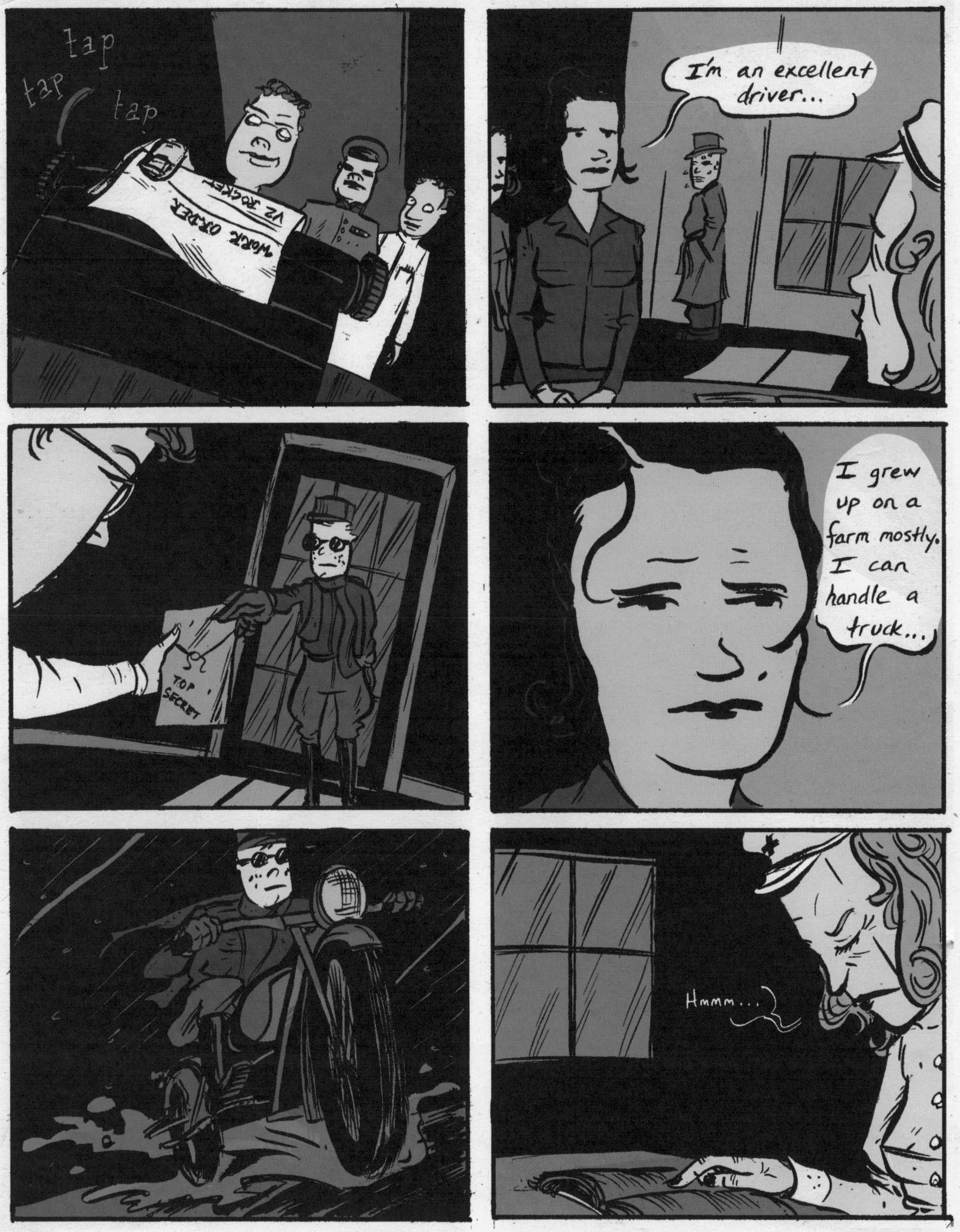
tap
tap
tap
WORK ORDER
V2 ROCKET
I'm an excellent driver...
TOP SECRET
I grew up on a farm mostly. I can handle a truck...
Hmmm...

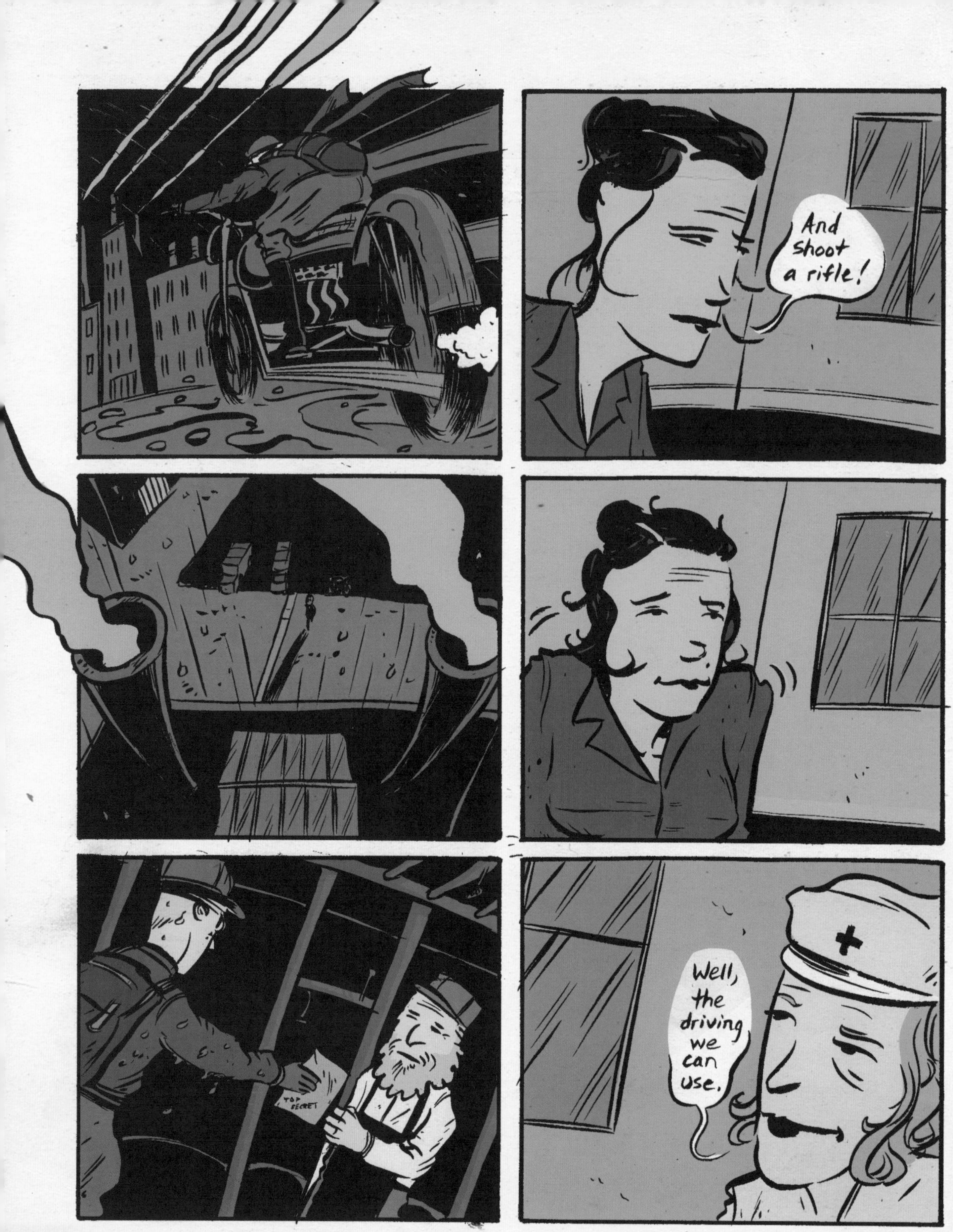
And shoot a rifle!
Well, the driving we can use.

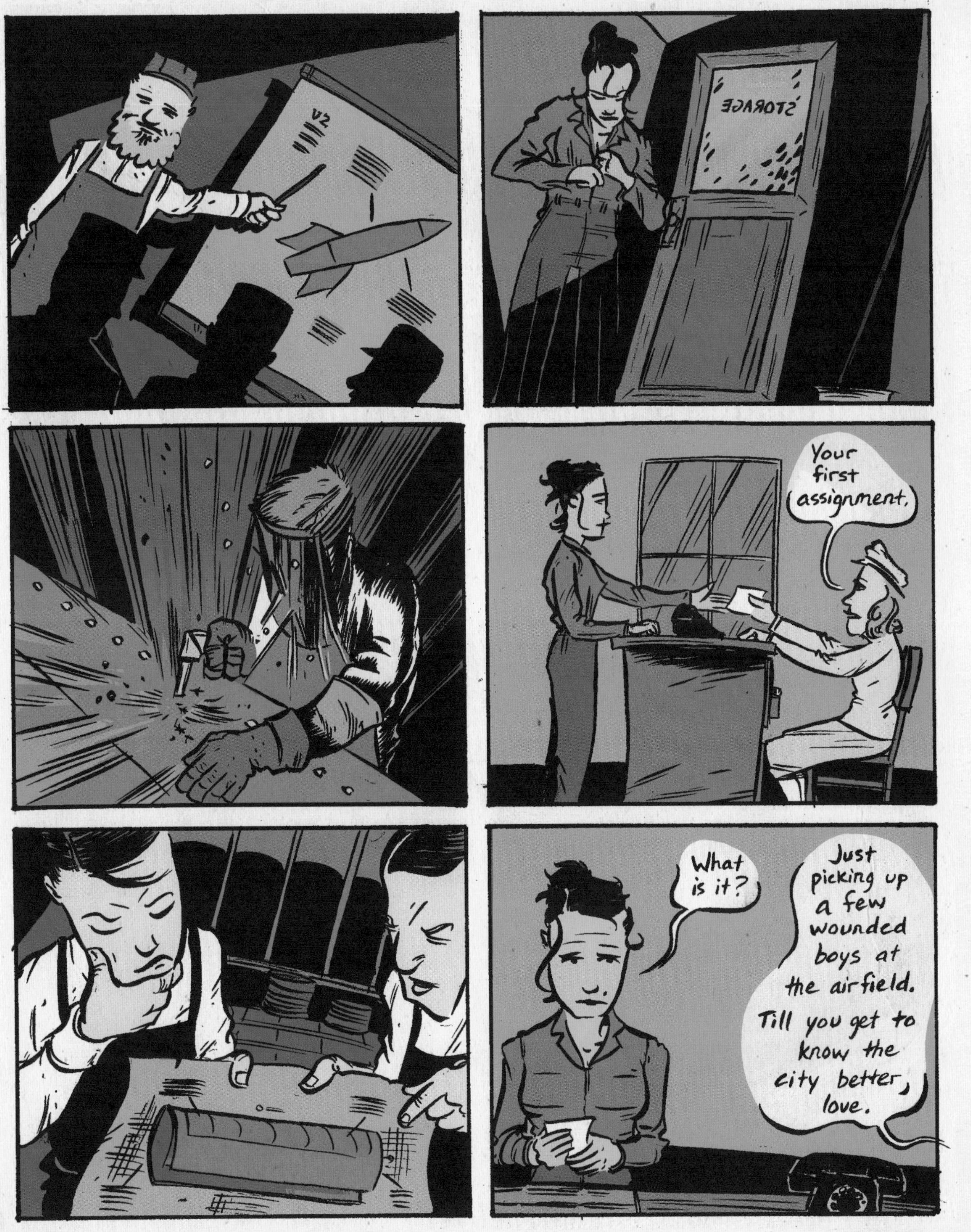
V2
STORAGE
Your first assignment,
What is it?
Just picking up a few wounded boys at the airfield.
Till you get to know the city better, love.

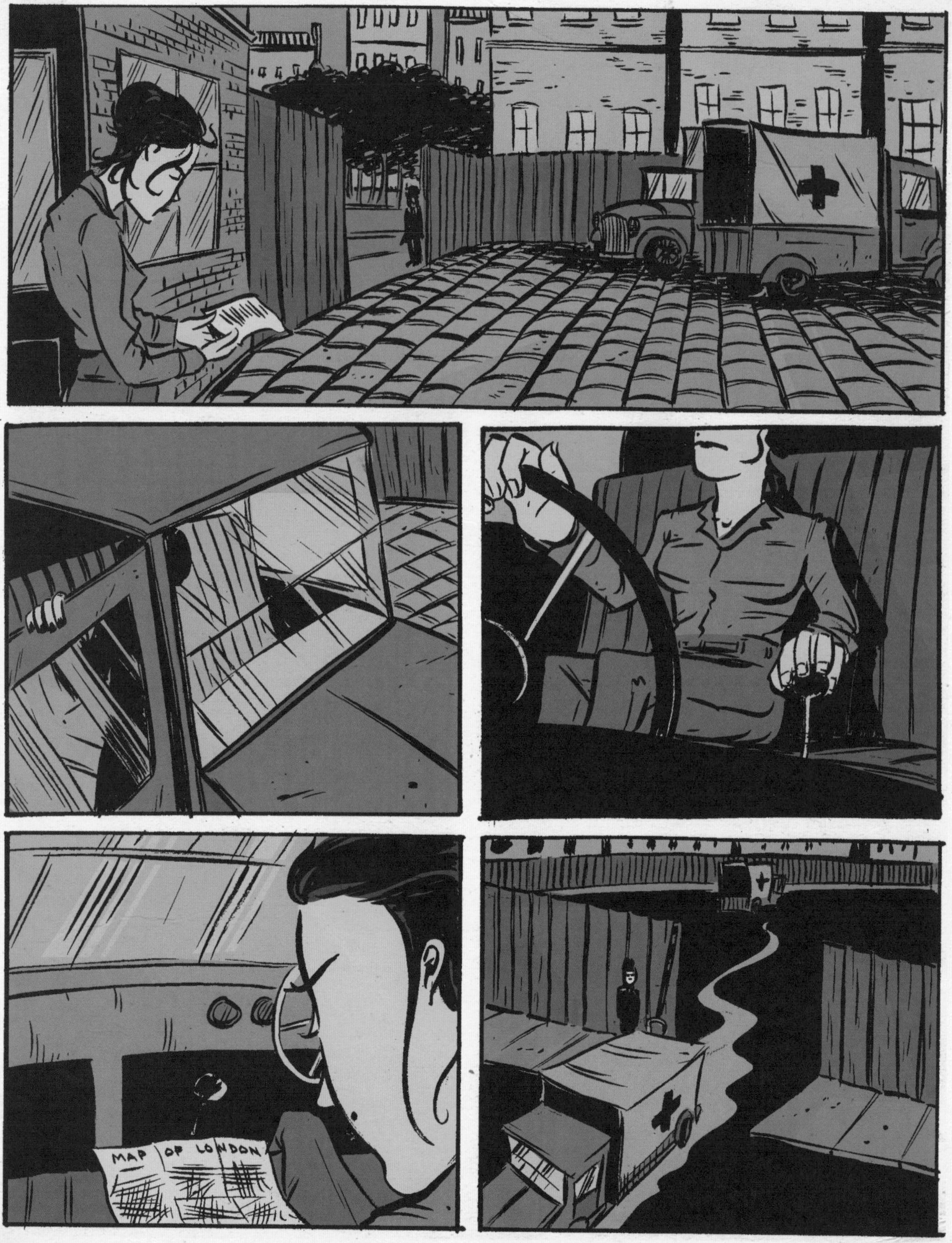
MAP OF LONDON

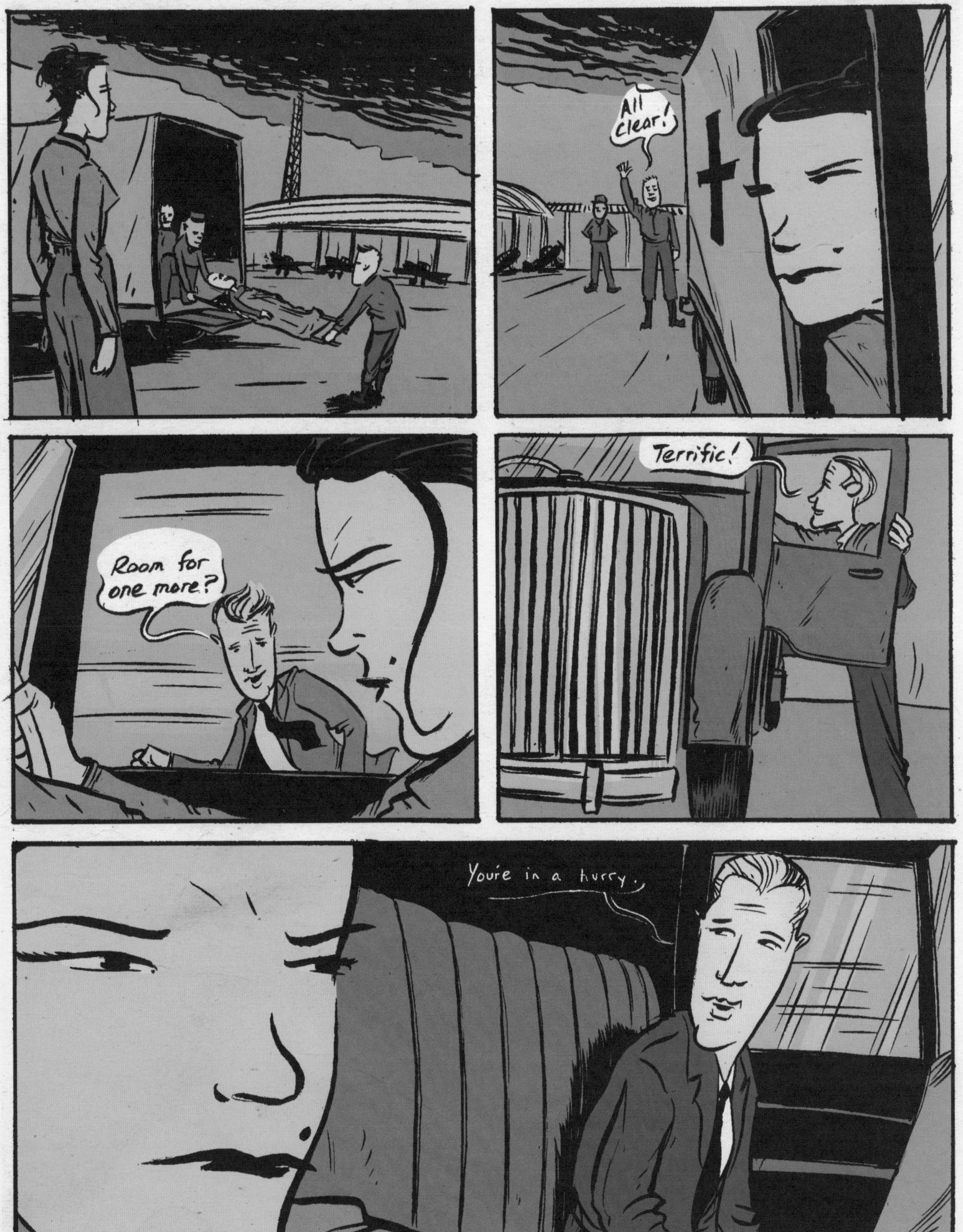
All clear!
Room for one more?
Terrific!
You're in a hurry.

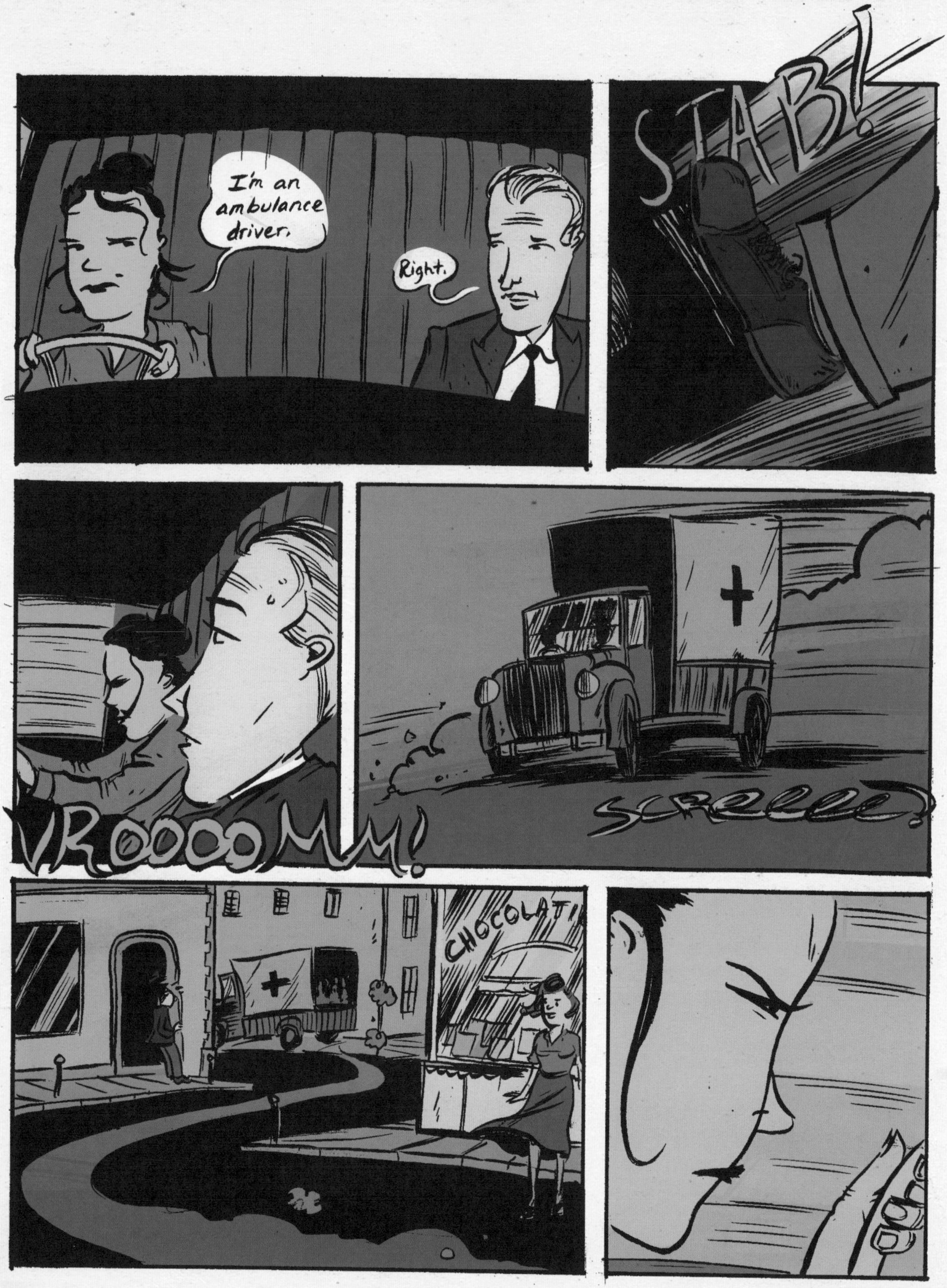
I'm an ambulance driver.
Right.
STAB!
VROOOOMM!
SCREEEE!
CHOCOLATI

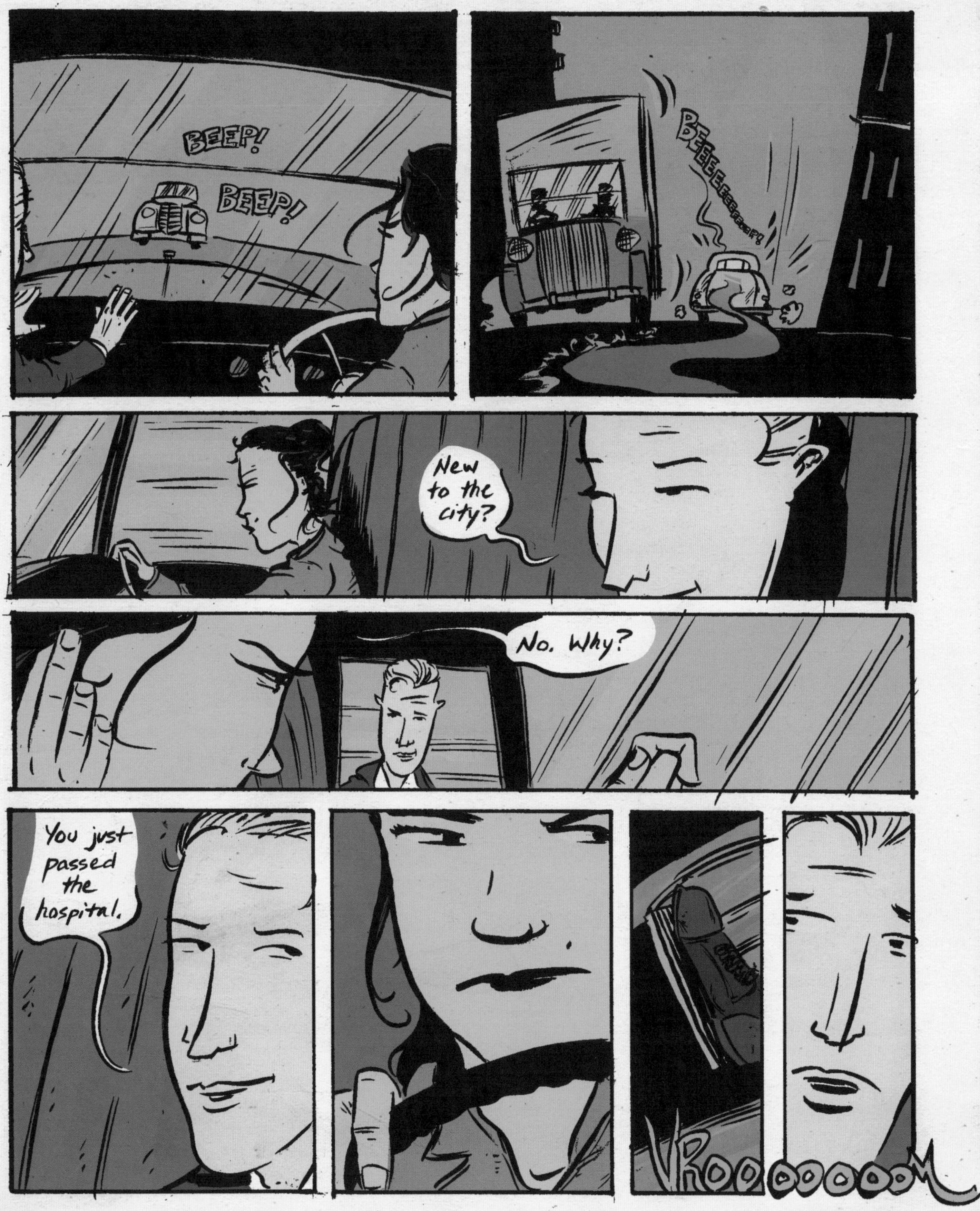
BEEP!
BEEP!
BEEEEEEEEEEEEP!
New to the city?
No. Why?
You just passed the hospital.
VROOOOOOOOM

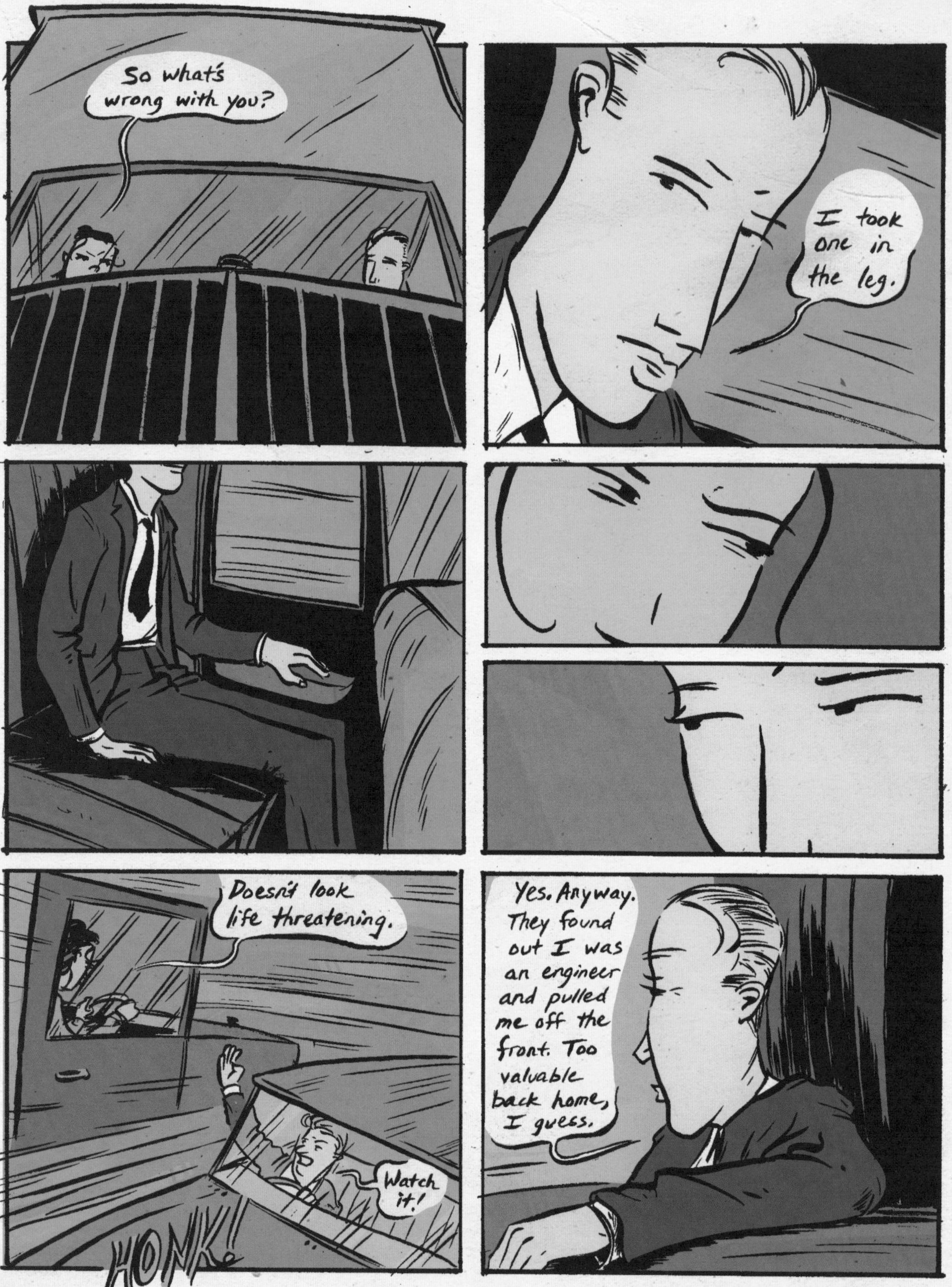
So what's wrong with you?
I took one in the leg.
Doesn't look life threatening.
Watch it!
HONK!
Yes. Anyway. They found out I was an engineer and pulled me off the front. Too valuable back home, I guess.

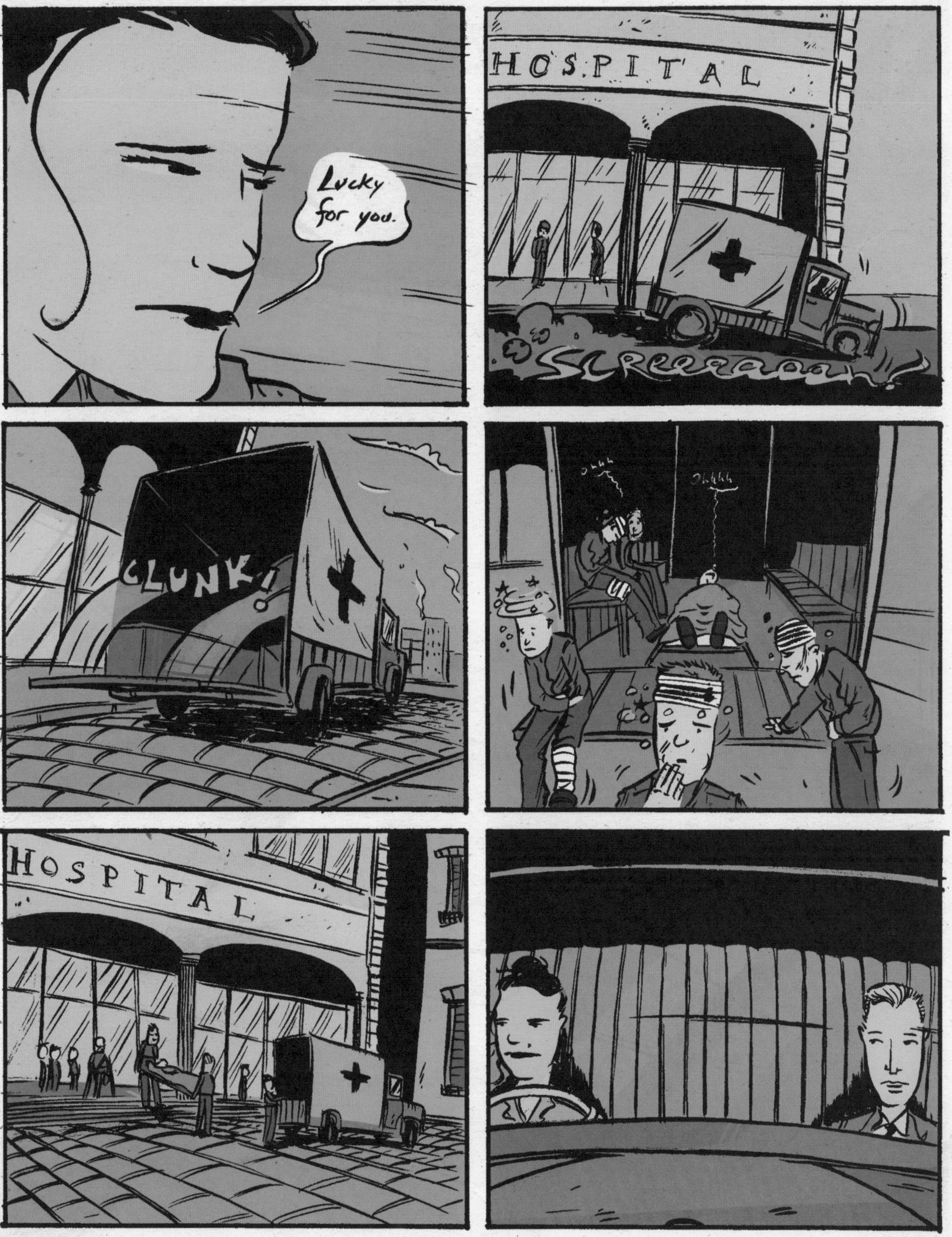
Lucky for you.
HOSPITAL
SCREEEAAAAH!
CLUNK!
Ohhh
Ohhhh
HOSPITAL

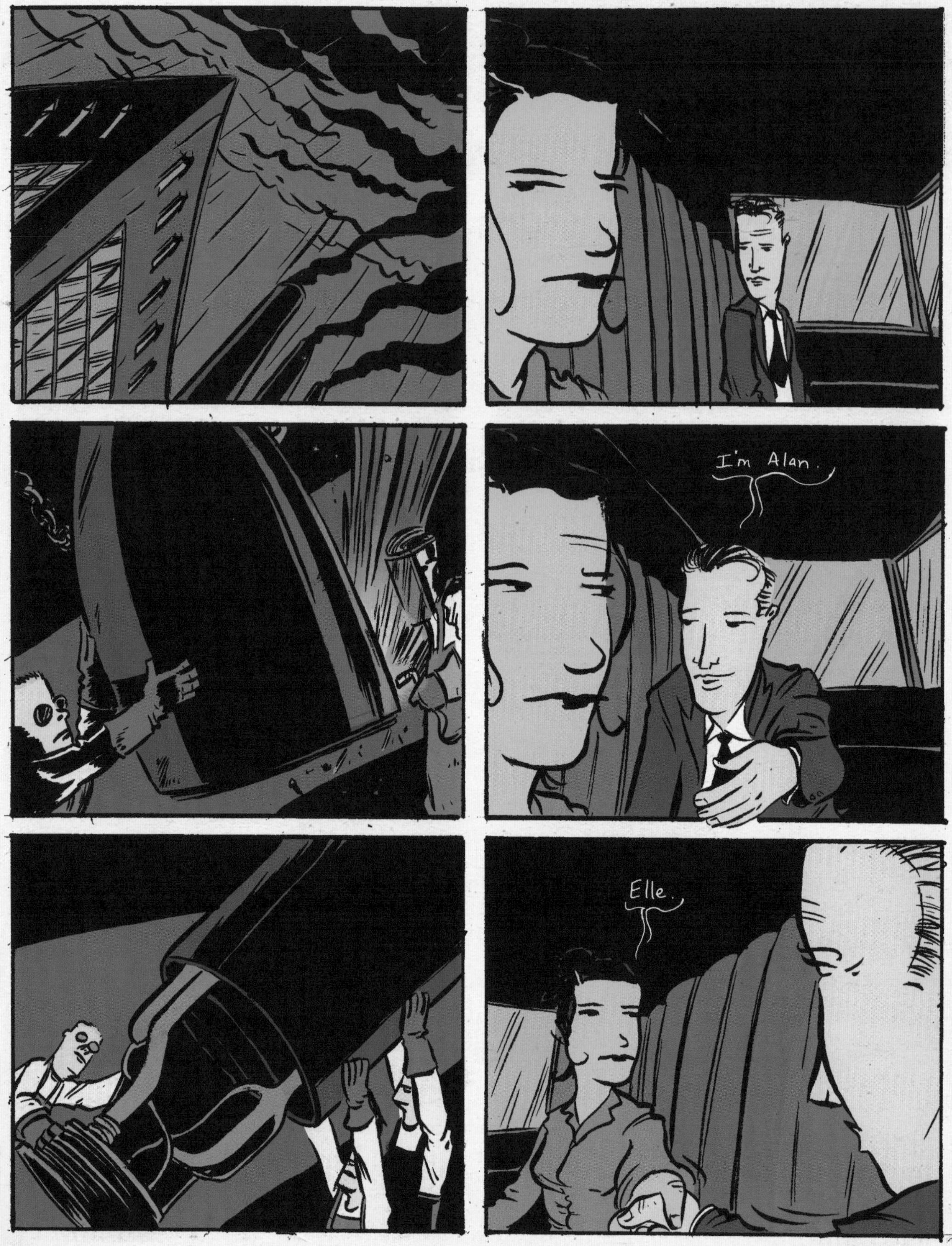
I'm Alan.
Elle.

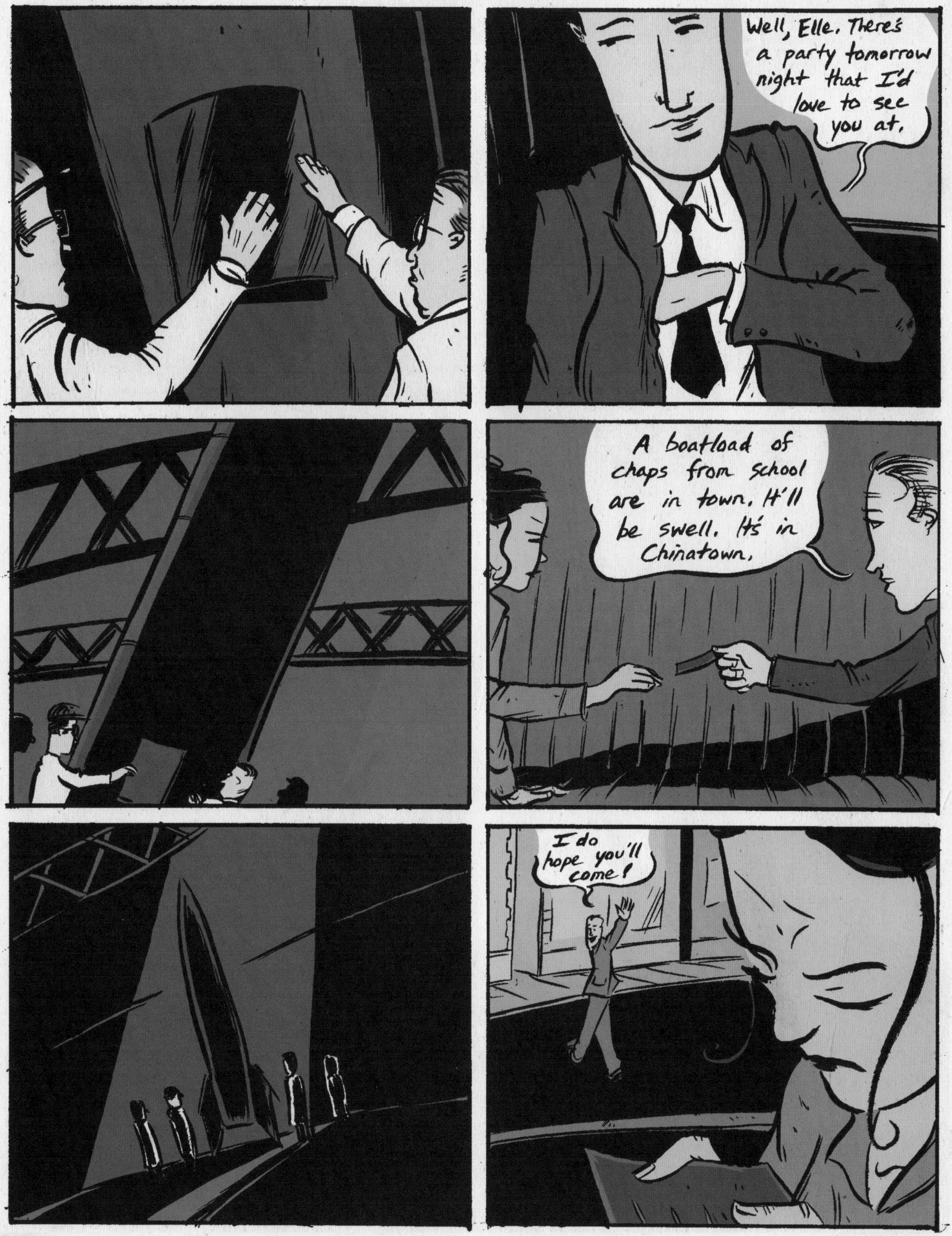
Well, Elle. There's a party tomorrow night that I'd love to see you at.
A boatload of chaps from school are in town. It'll be swell. It's in Chinatown.
I do hope you'll come!

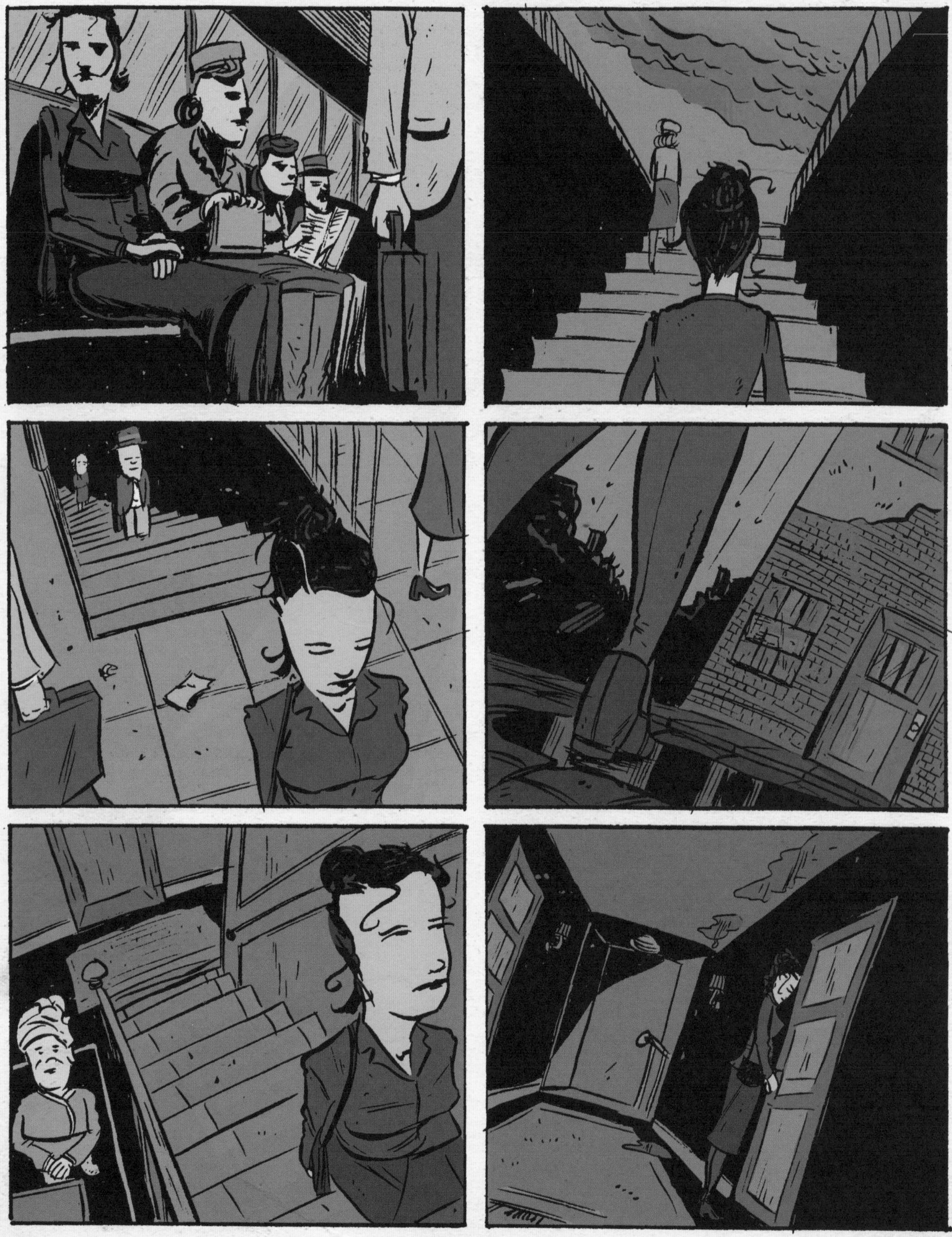

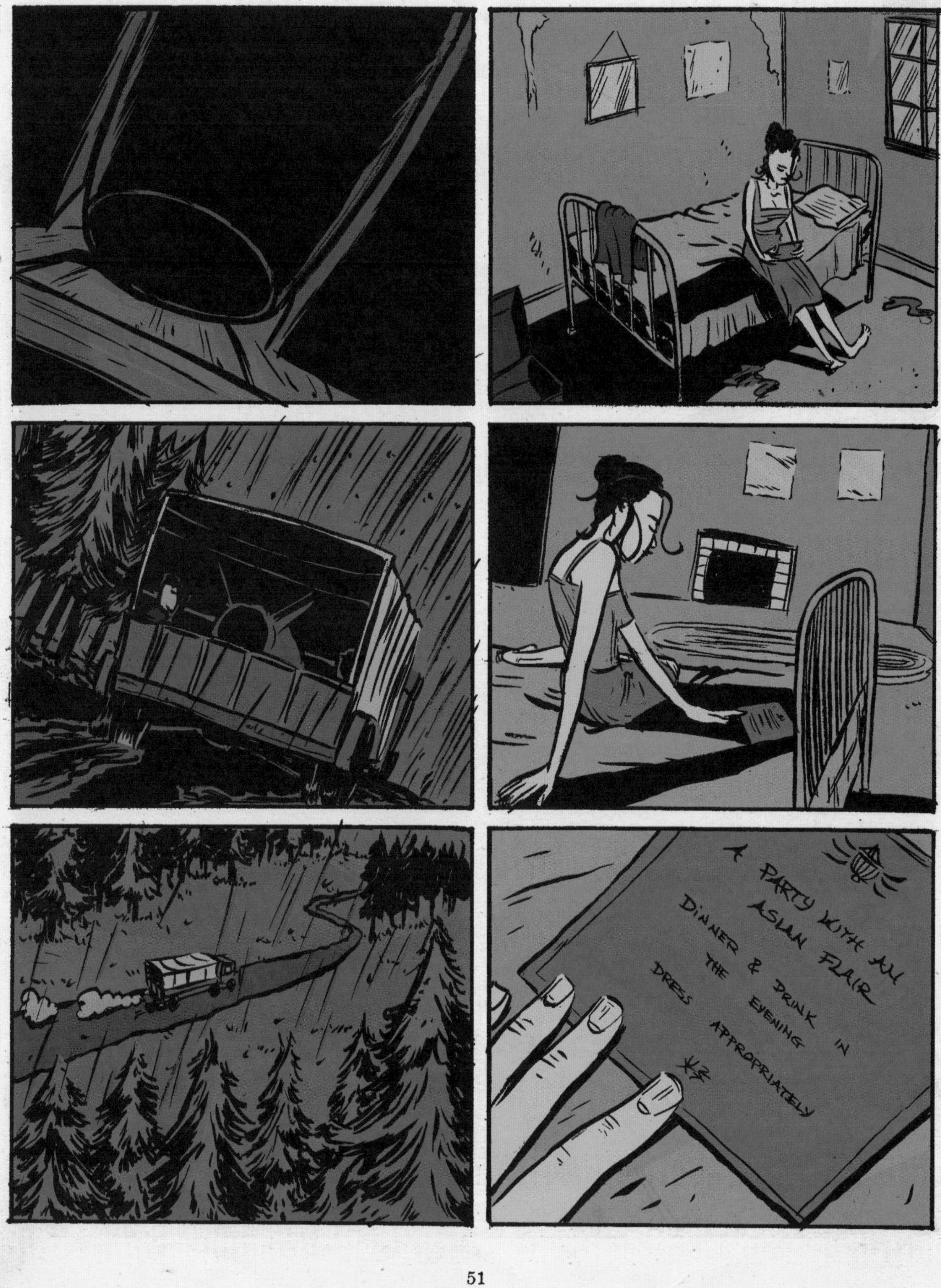
A PARTY WITH AN ASIAN FLAIR
DINNER & DRINK
THE EVENING IN
DRESS APPROPRIATELY

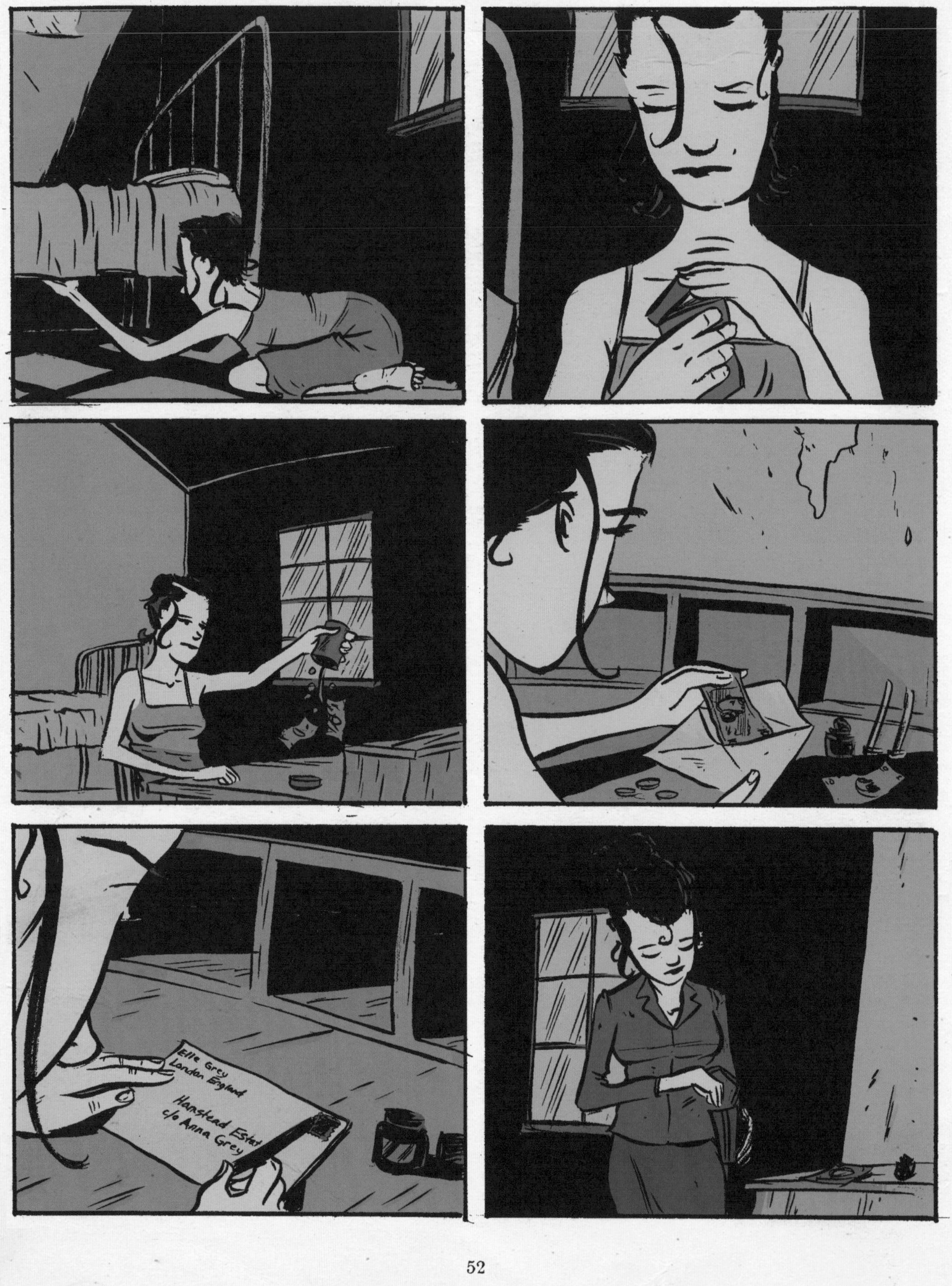
Elle Grey
London England
Hamstead Estat
c/o Anna Grey

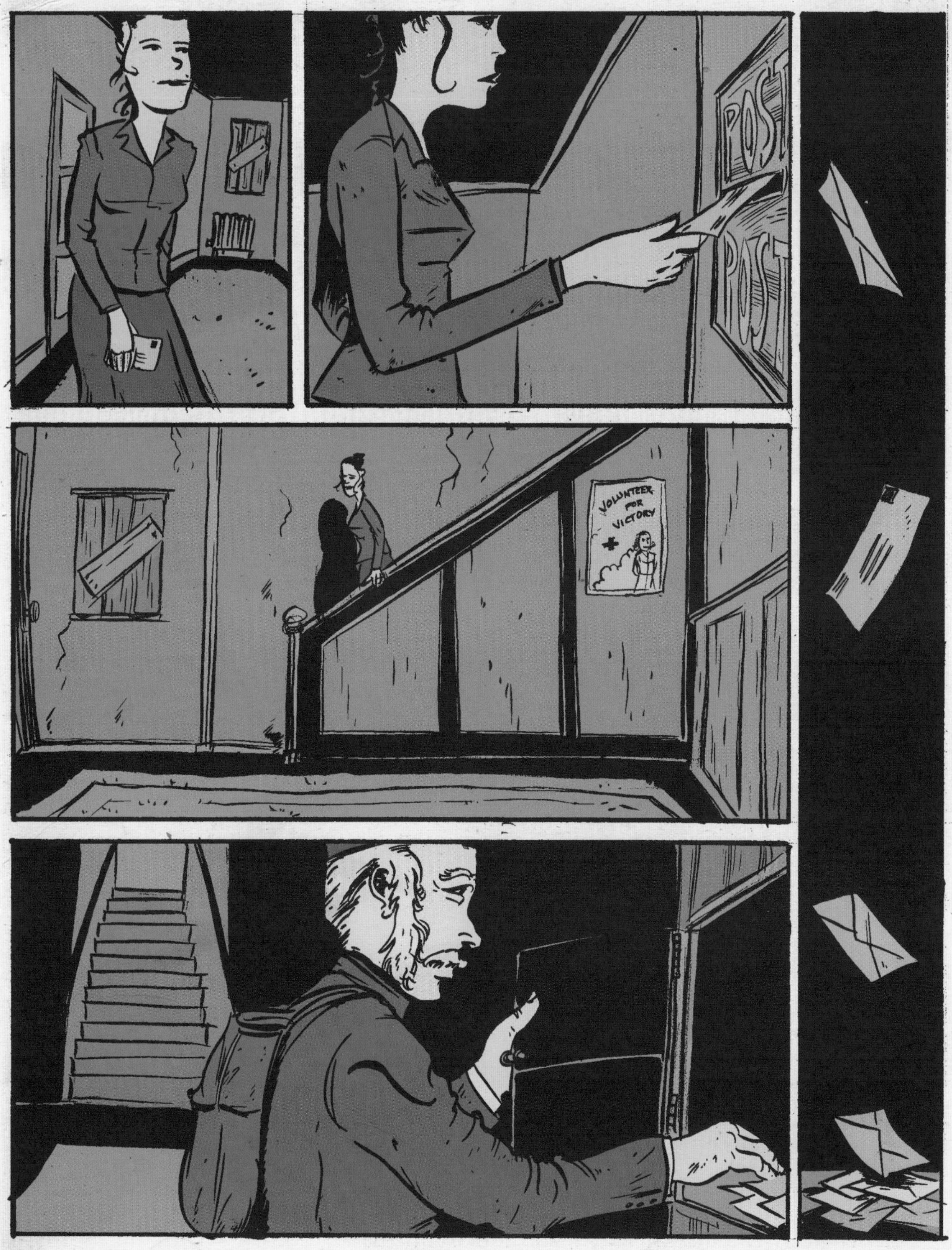
POST
POST
VOLUNTEER FOR VICTORY

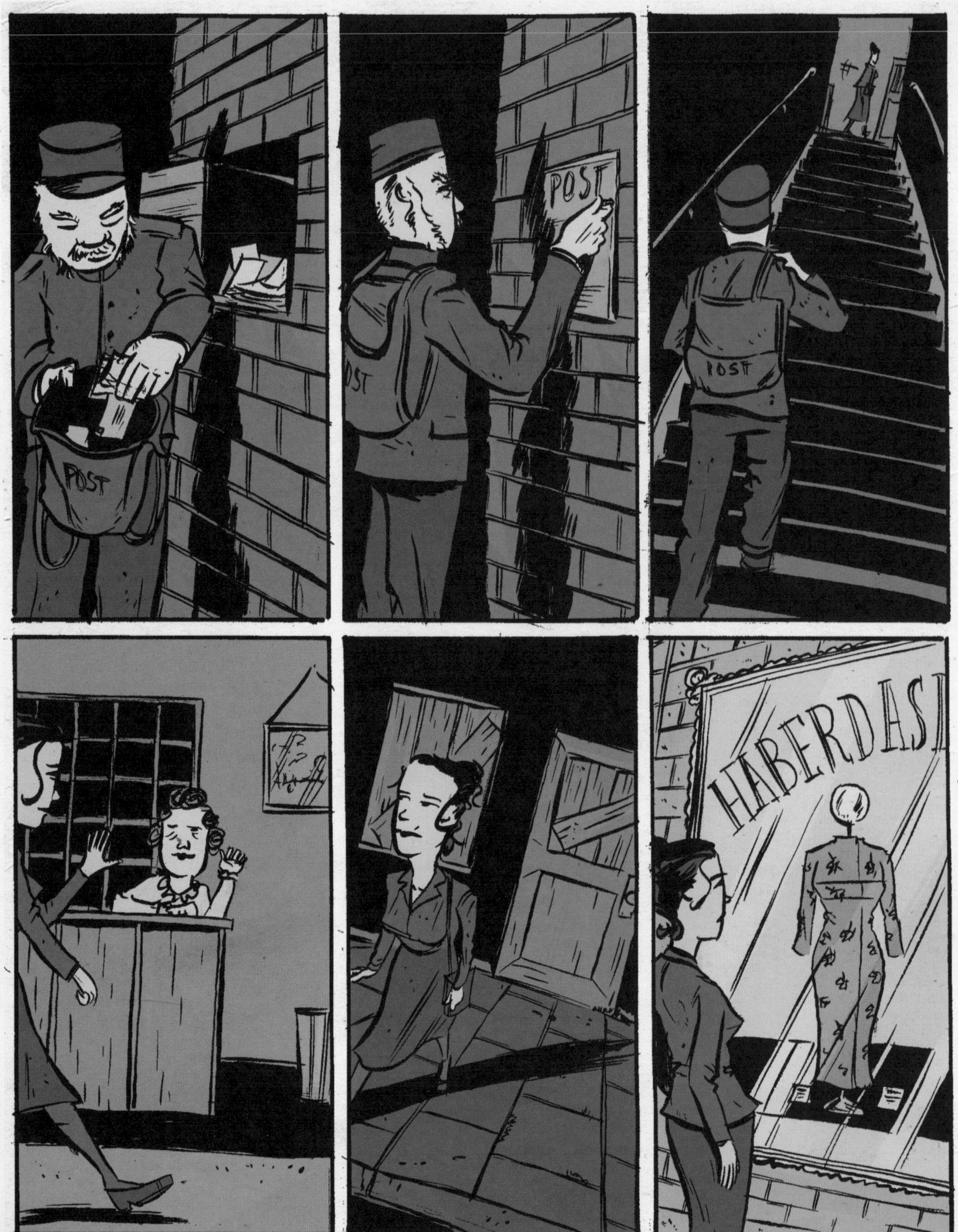
POST
POST
OST
POST
HABERDASI

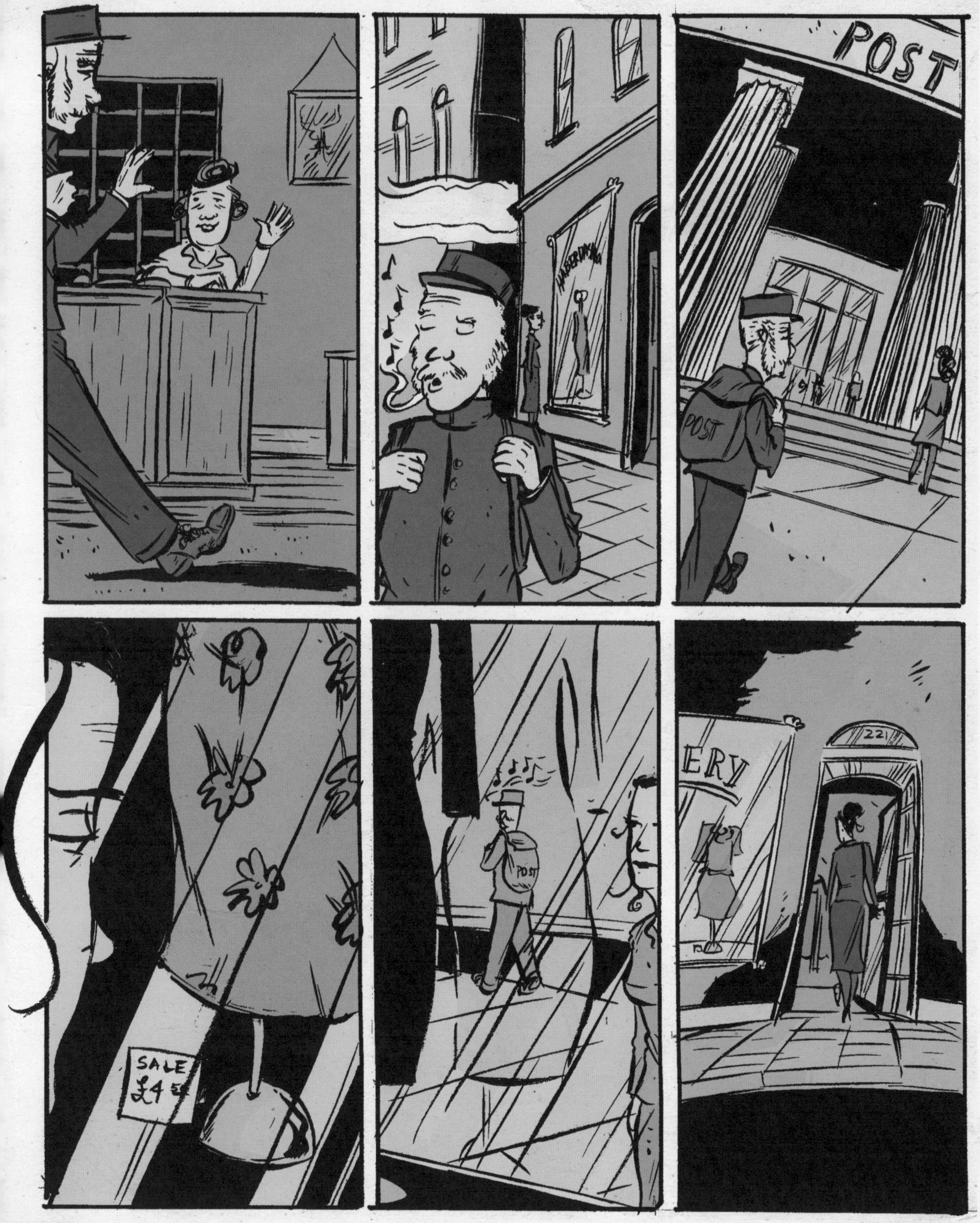
POST
POST
SALE
£4
POST
ERY
221

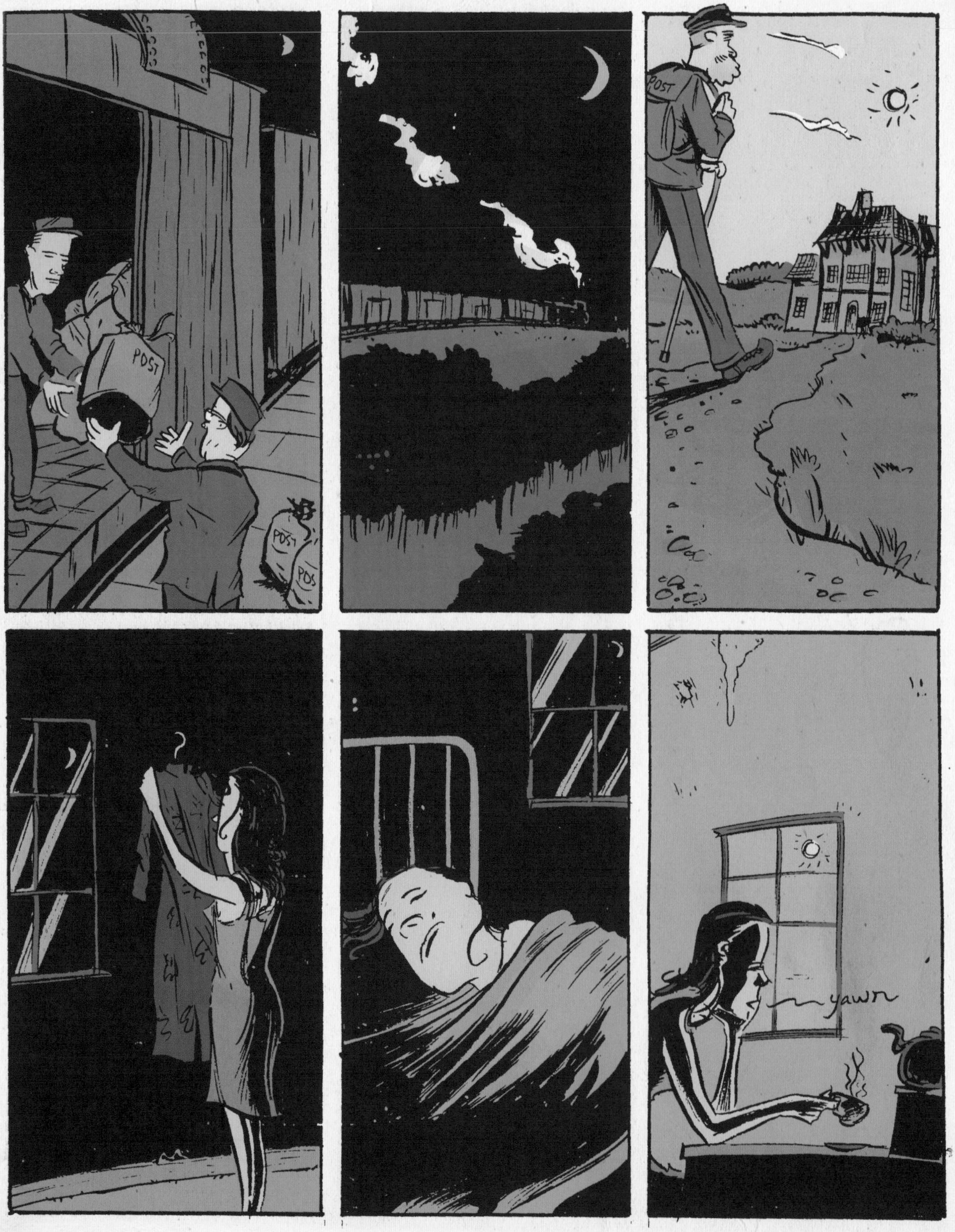
POST
POST
POS
POST
yawn

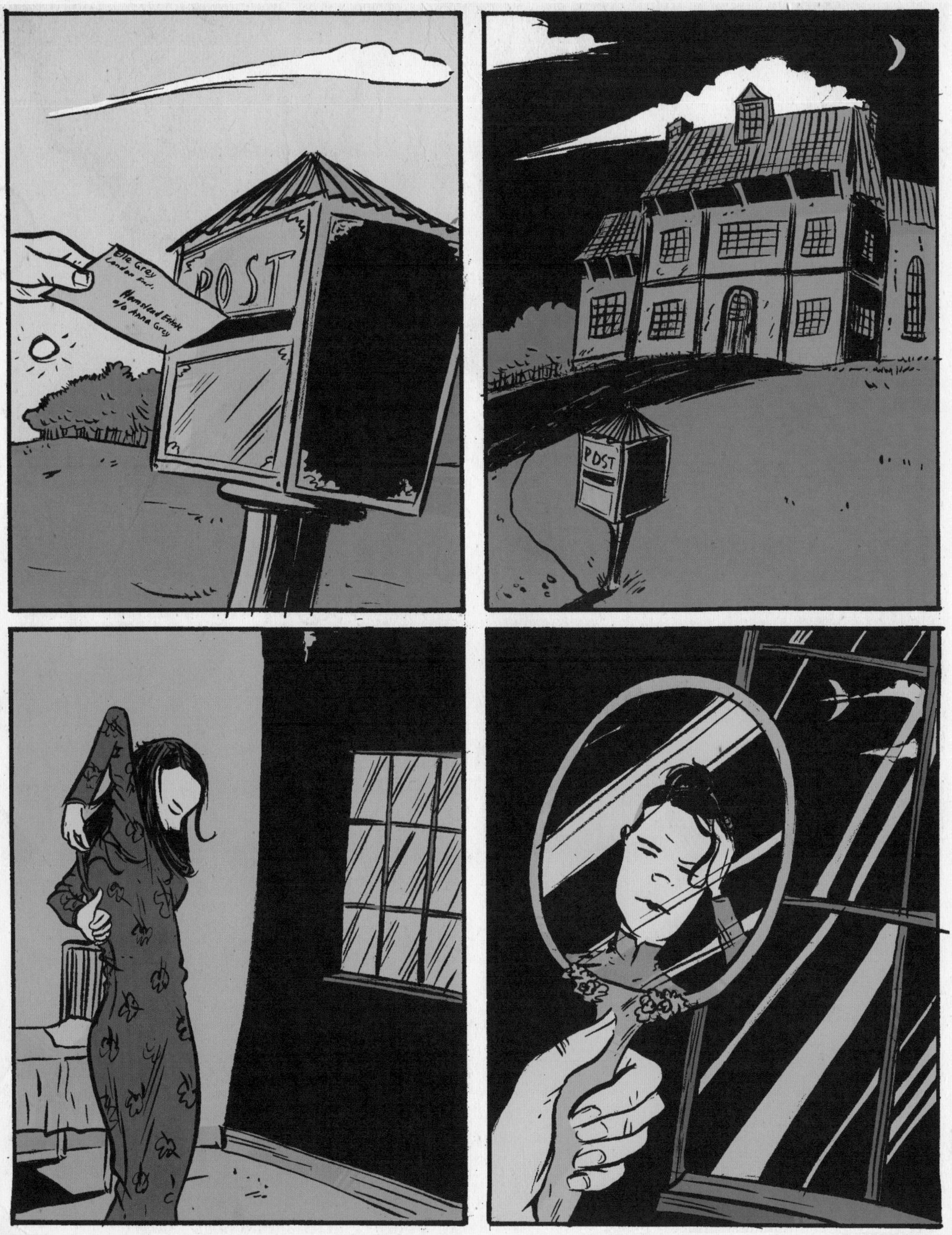
Elle Grey
London Eng.
Hamstead Estate
c/o Anna Grey
POST
POST

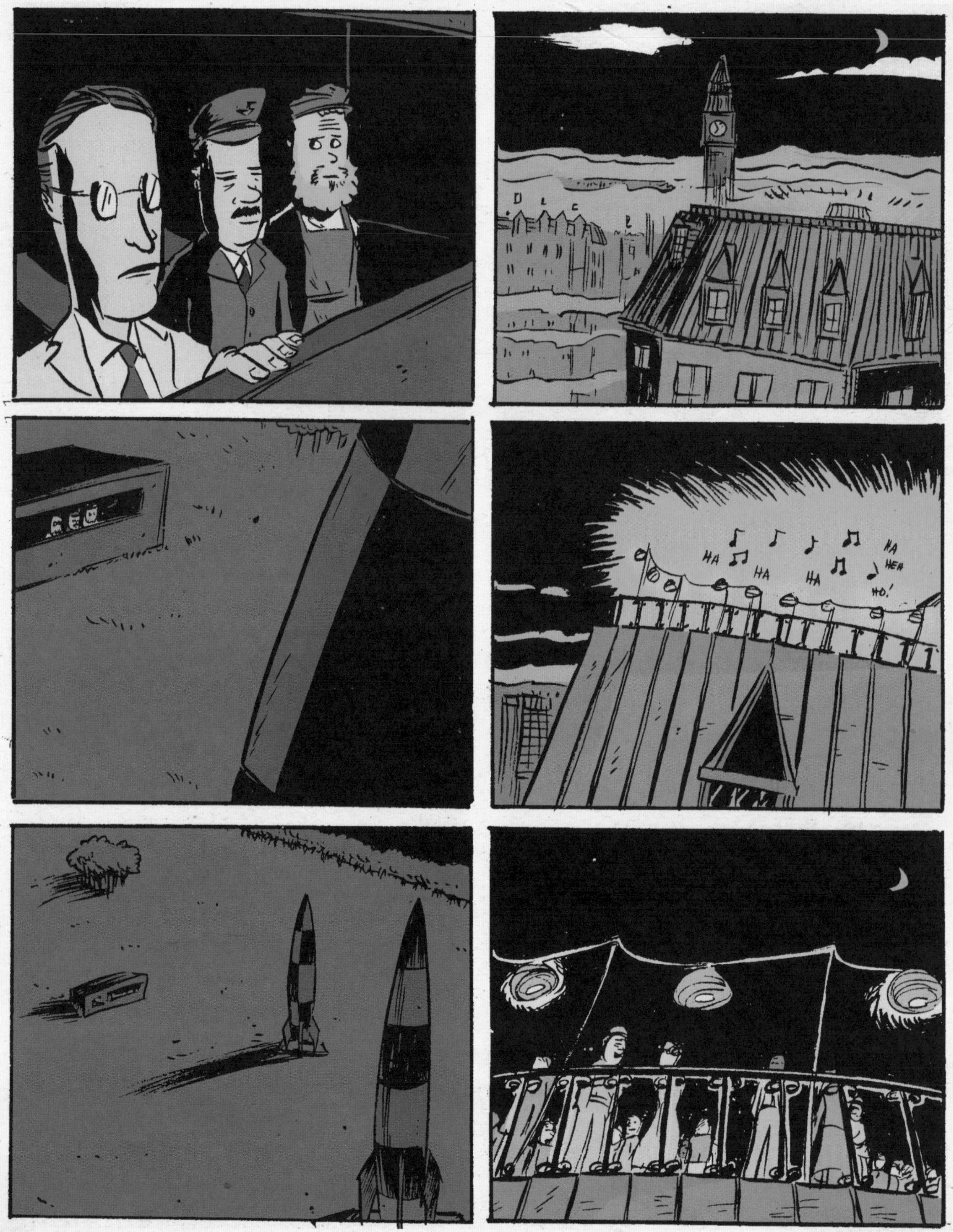
HA HA HA HA HEH HO!

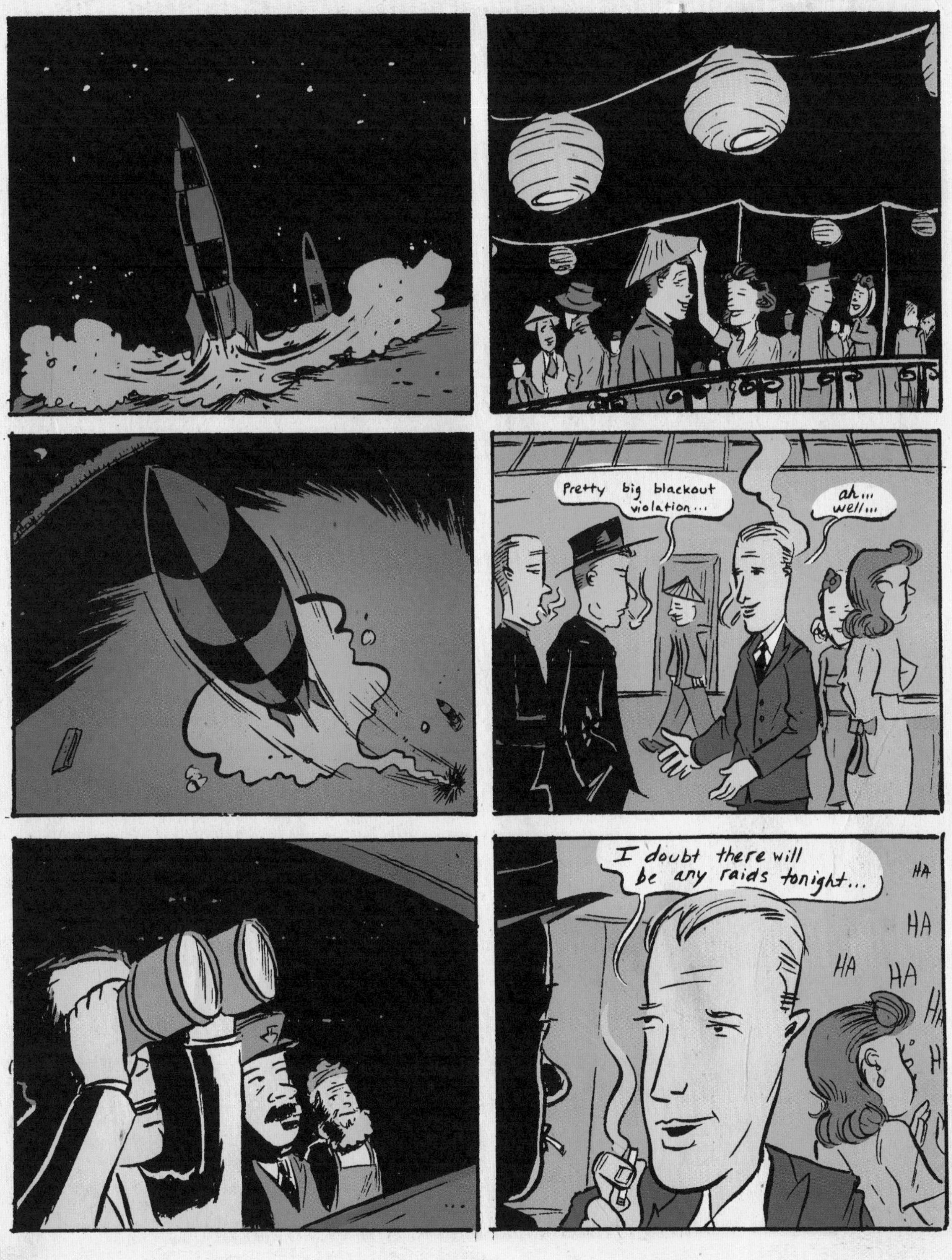

Pretty big blackout violation...
ah... well...
I doubt there will be any raids tonight...
HA
HA
HA
HA

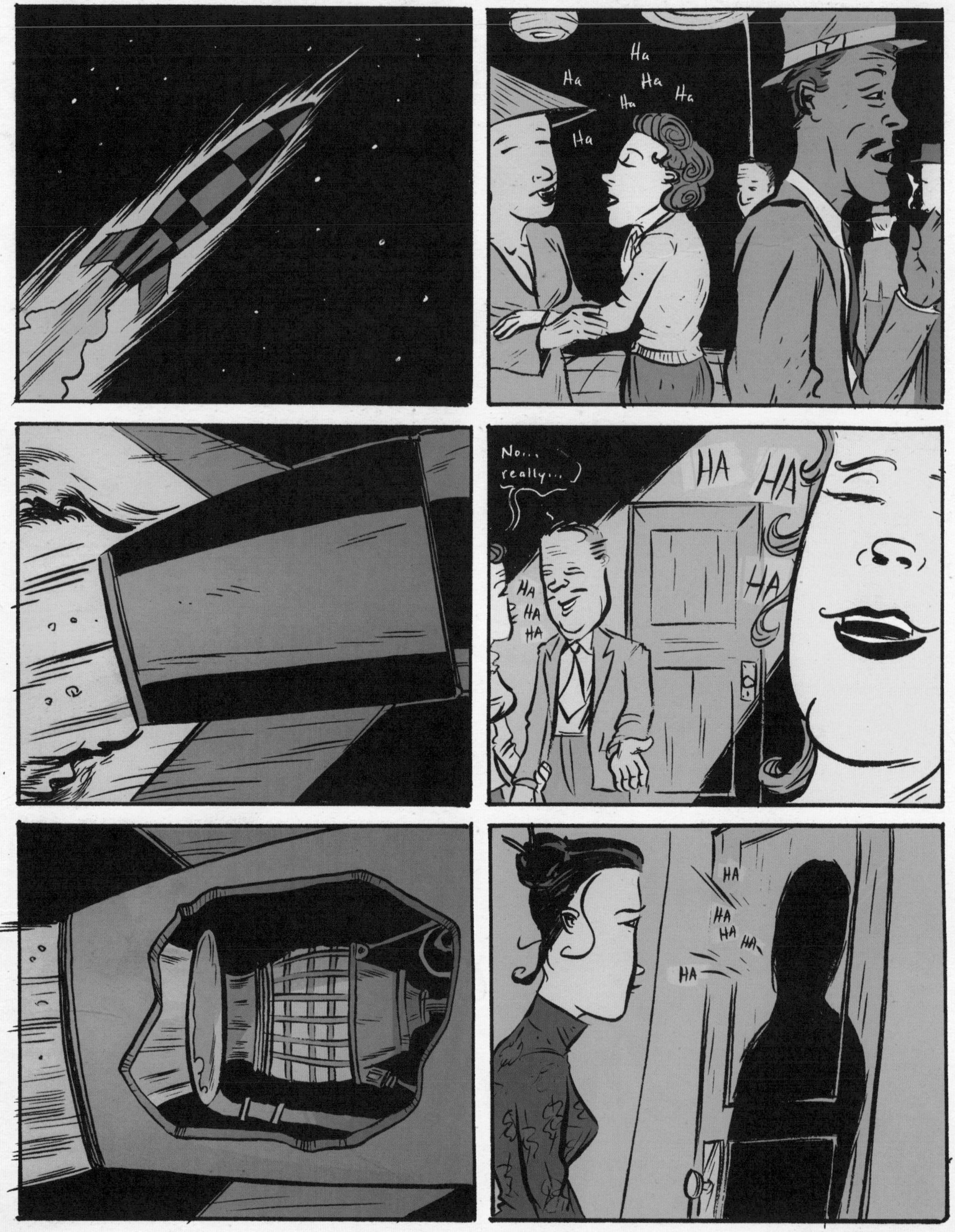
Ha
Ha
Ha
Ha
Ha
Ha
No... really...
HA
HA
HA
HA
HA
HA
HA
HA
HA
HA
HA

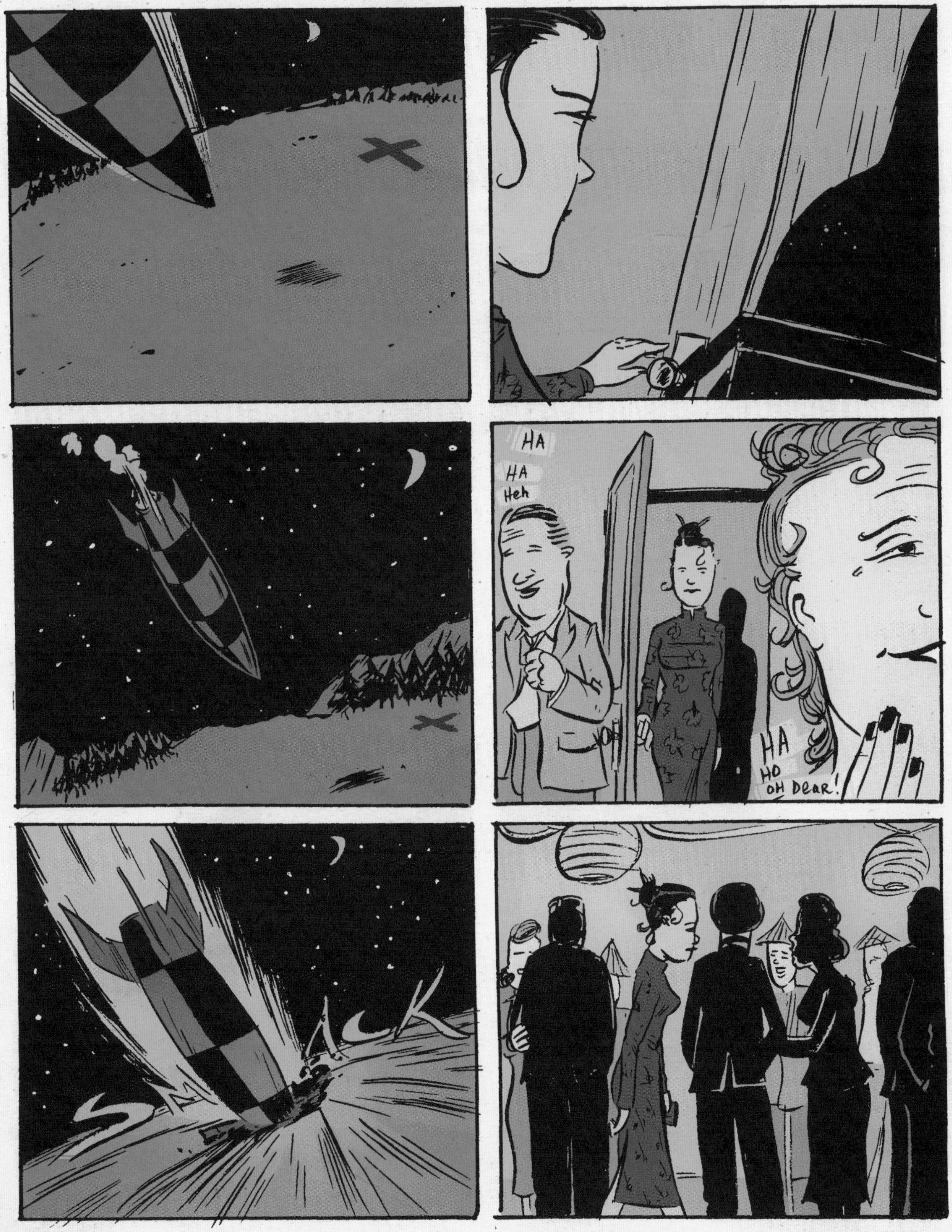
HA
HA
Heh
HA
HO
OH Dear!
SMACK

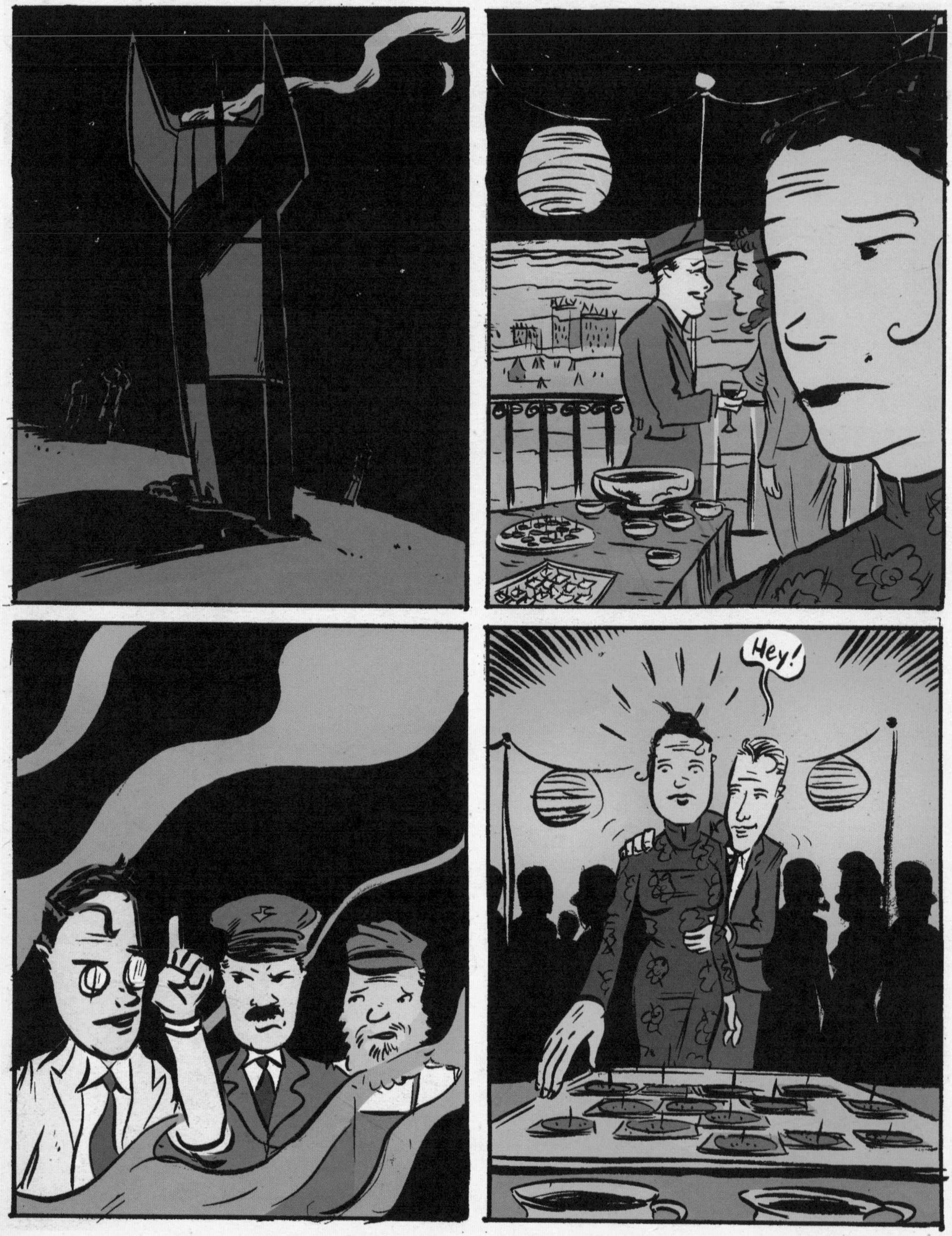
Hey!

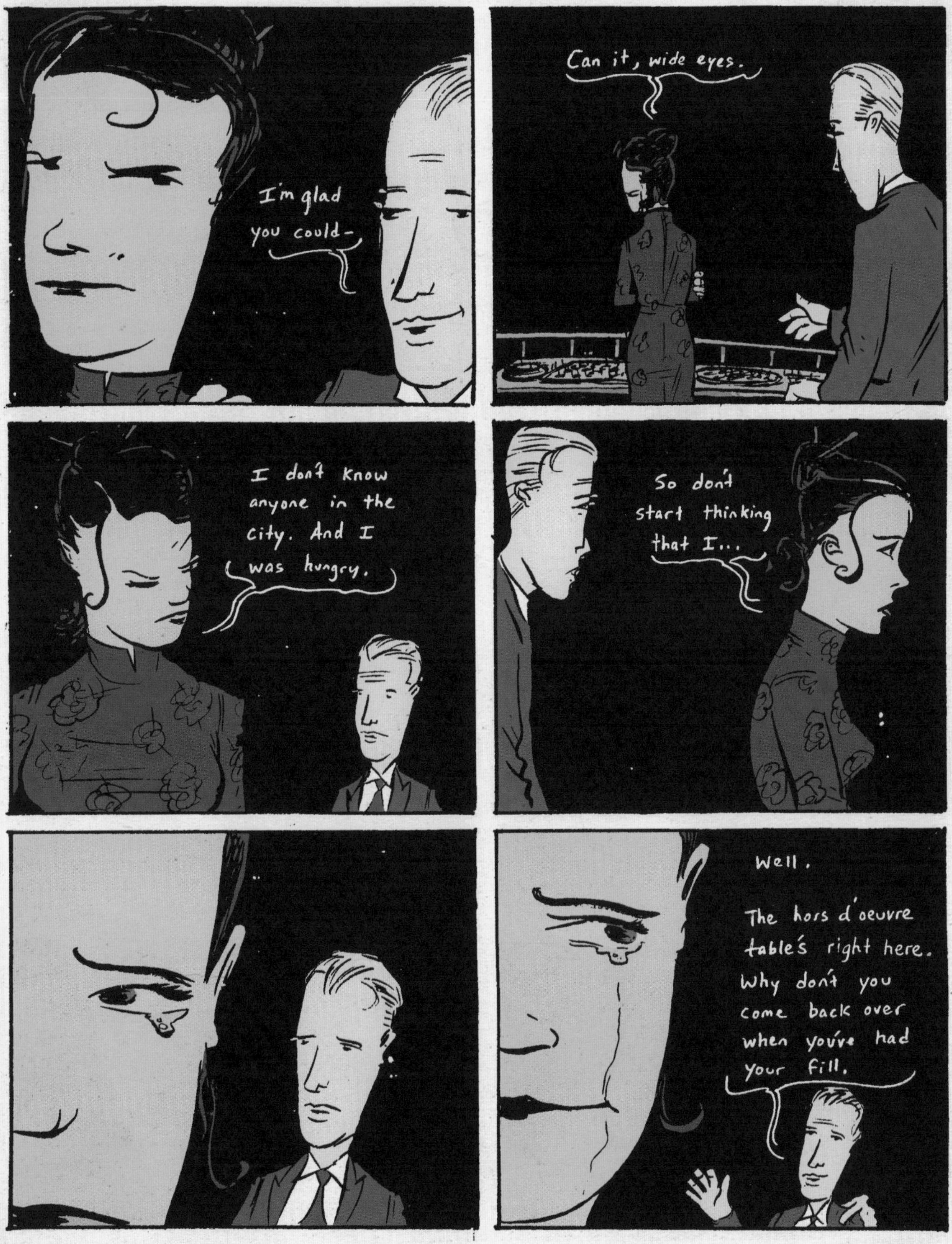

I'm glad you could-
Can it, wide eyes.
I don't know anyone in the city. And I was hungry.
So don't start thinking that I...
Well.
The hors d'oeuvre table's right here. Why don't you come back over when you've had your fill.

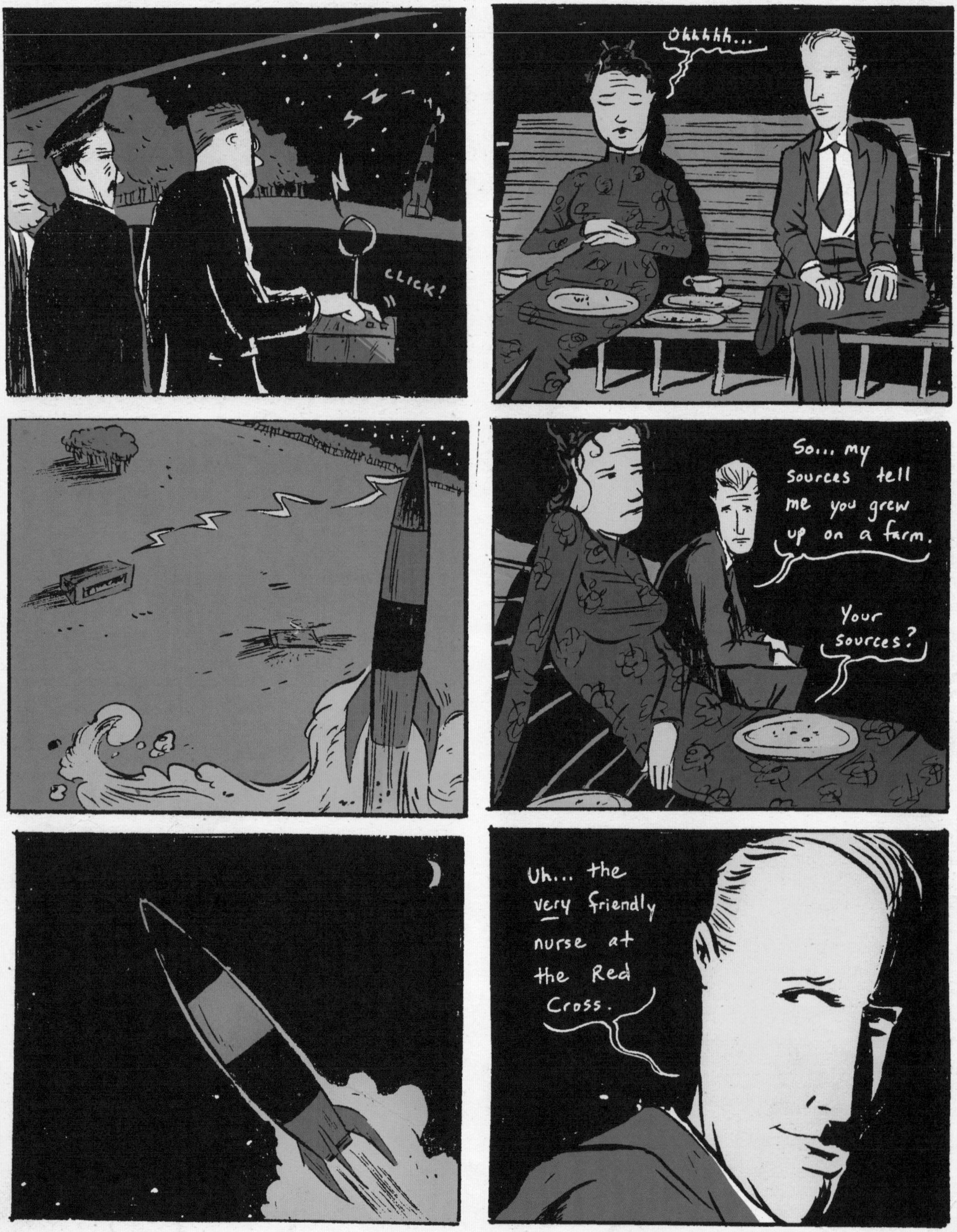
CLICK!
Ohhhhh...
So... my sources tell me you grew up on a farm.
Your sources?
Uh... the very friendly nurse at the Red Cross.

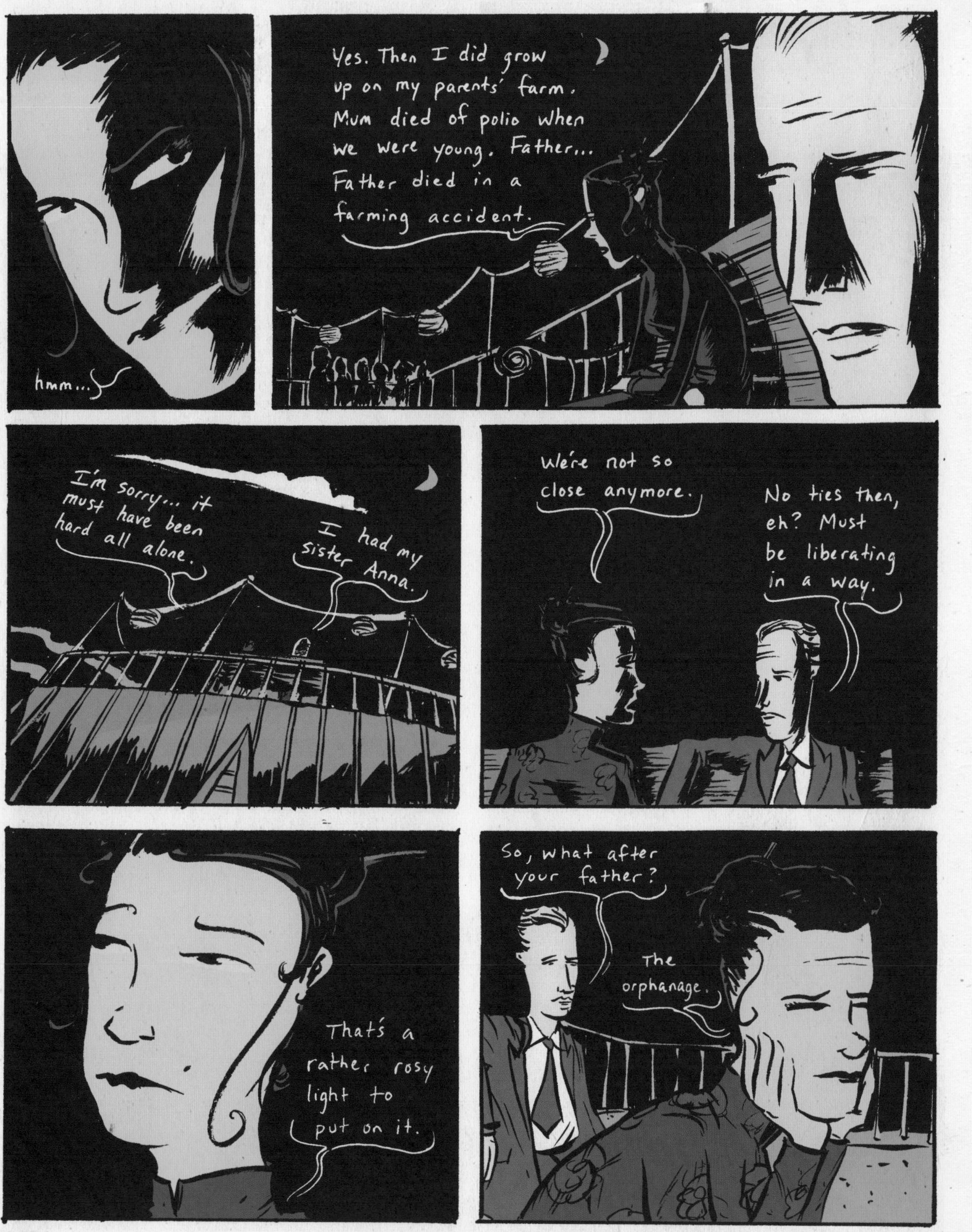

hmm...
Yes. Then I did grow up on my parents' farm. Mum died of polio when we were young. Father... Father died in a farming accident.
I'm sorry... it must have been hard all alone.
I had my sister Anna.
We're not so close anymore.
No ties then, eh? Must be liberating in a way.
That's a rather rosy light to put on it.
So, what after your father?
The orphanage.

No. I'm not too handy cooking or sewing or any of that rubbish. I can drive halfway decently though.

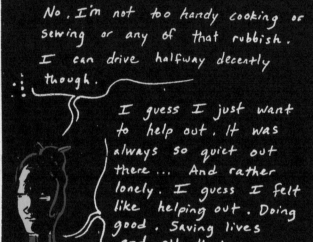

I guess I just want to help out. It was always so quiet out there... And rather lonely. I guess I felt like helping out. Doing good. Saving lives and all that.

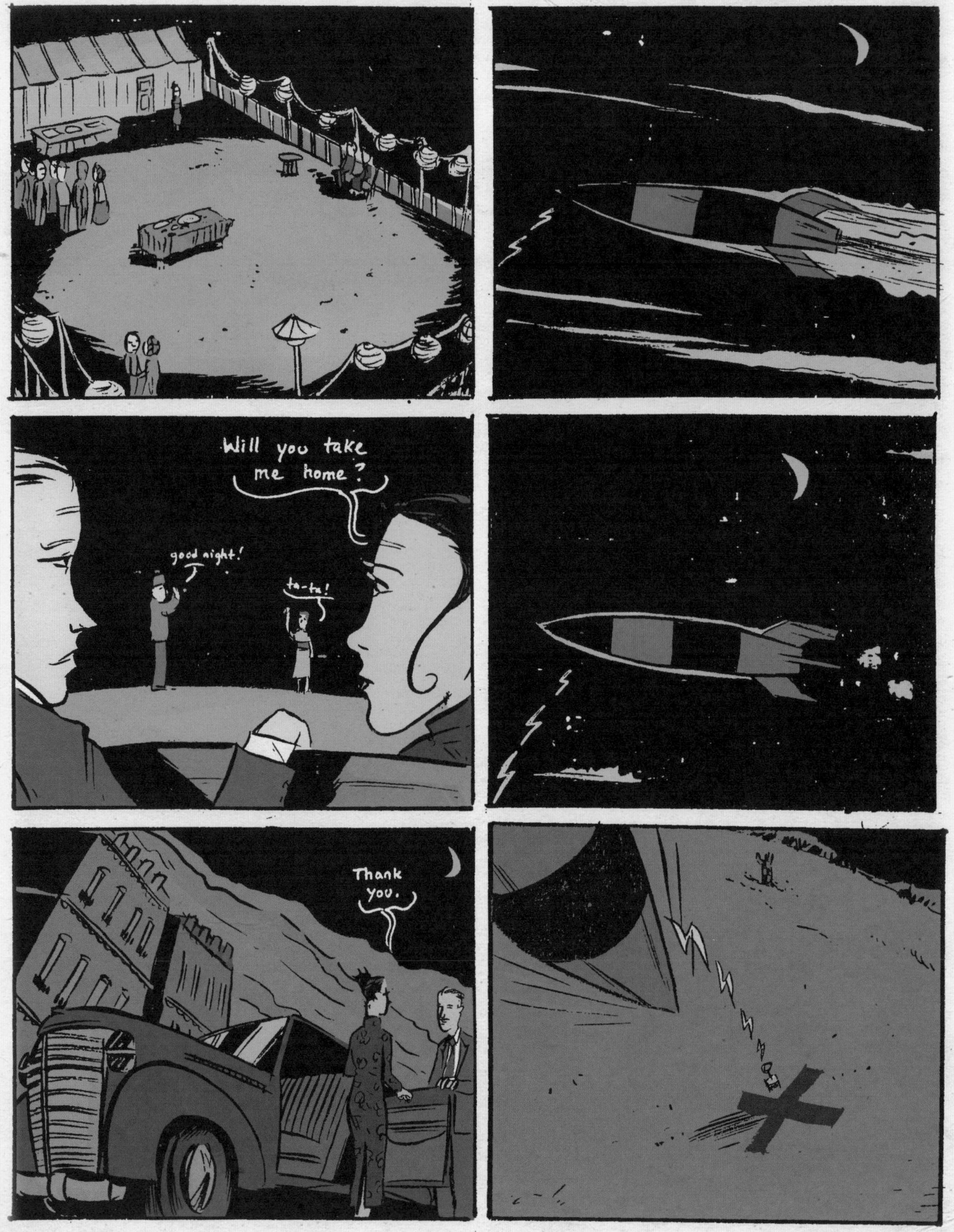
Will you take me home?
good night!
ta-ta!
Thank you.

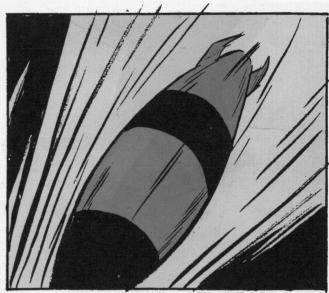

Well, here we are then.

How about lunch next Tuesday?

I... that sounds... I can do that.

CLAP!

CLAP!

SHEW!

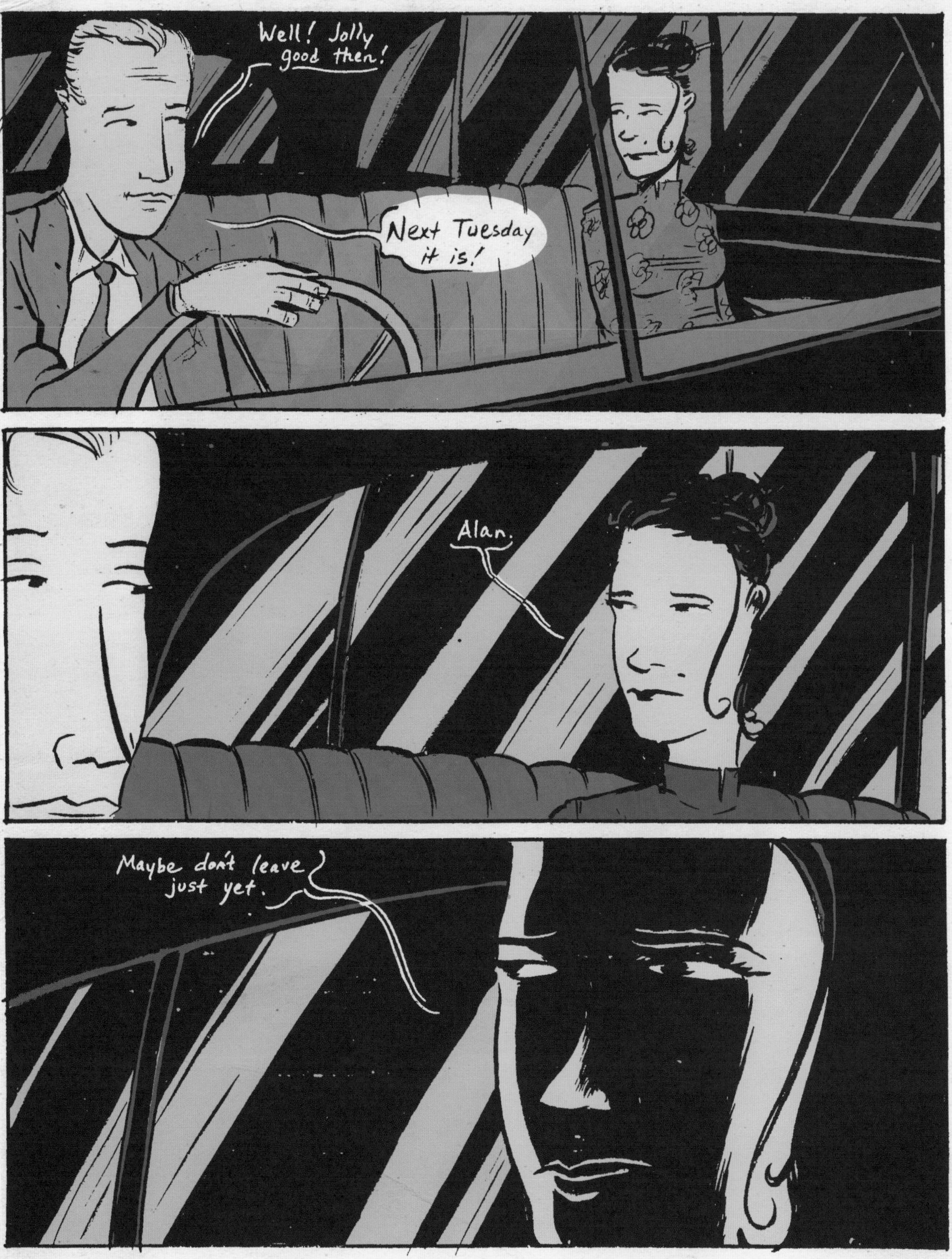
Well! Jolly good then!
Next Tuesday it is!
Alan.
Maybe don't leave just yet.

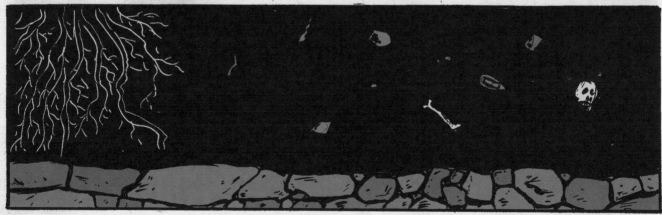

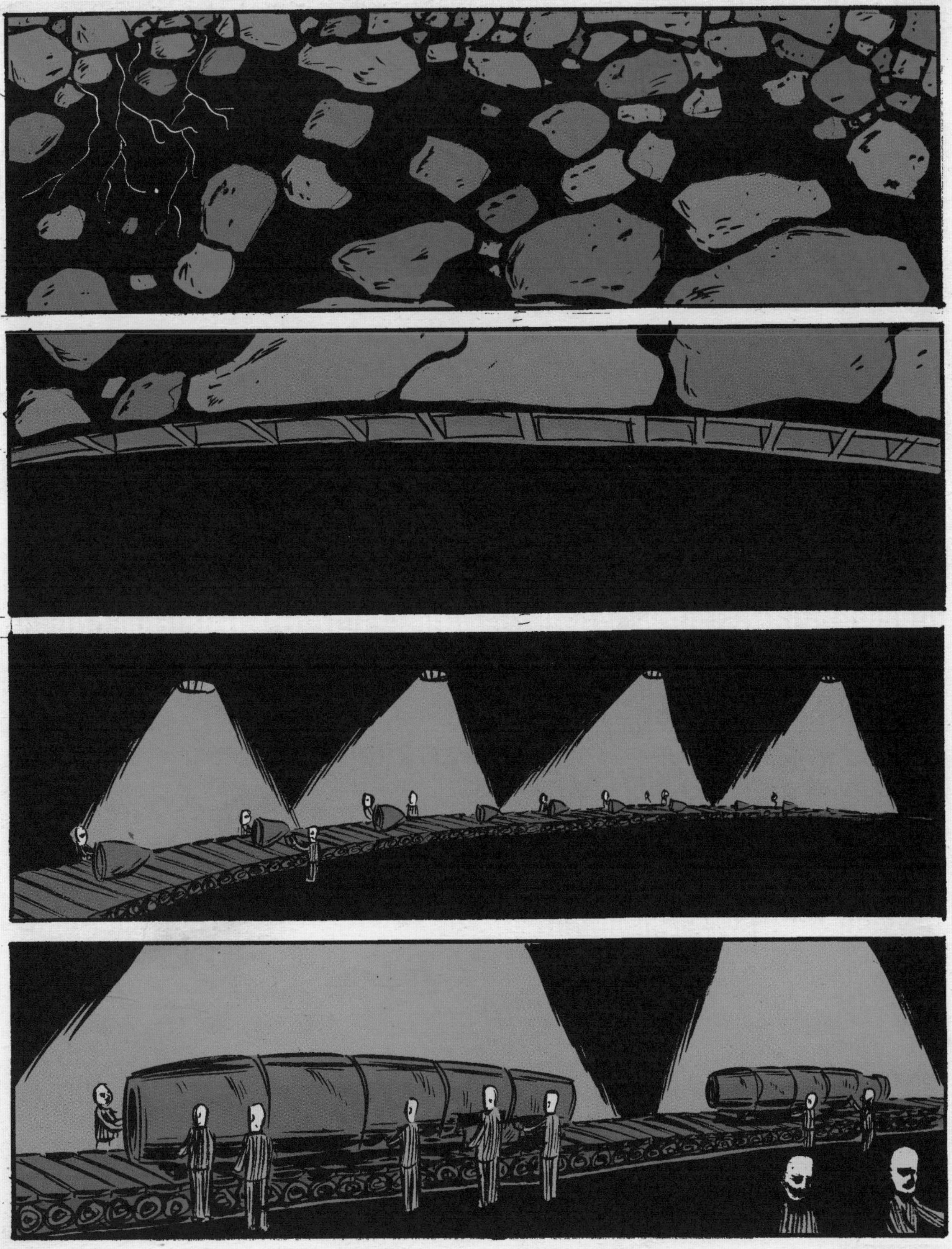

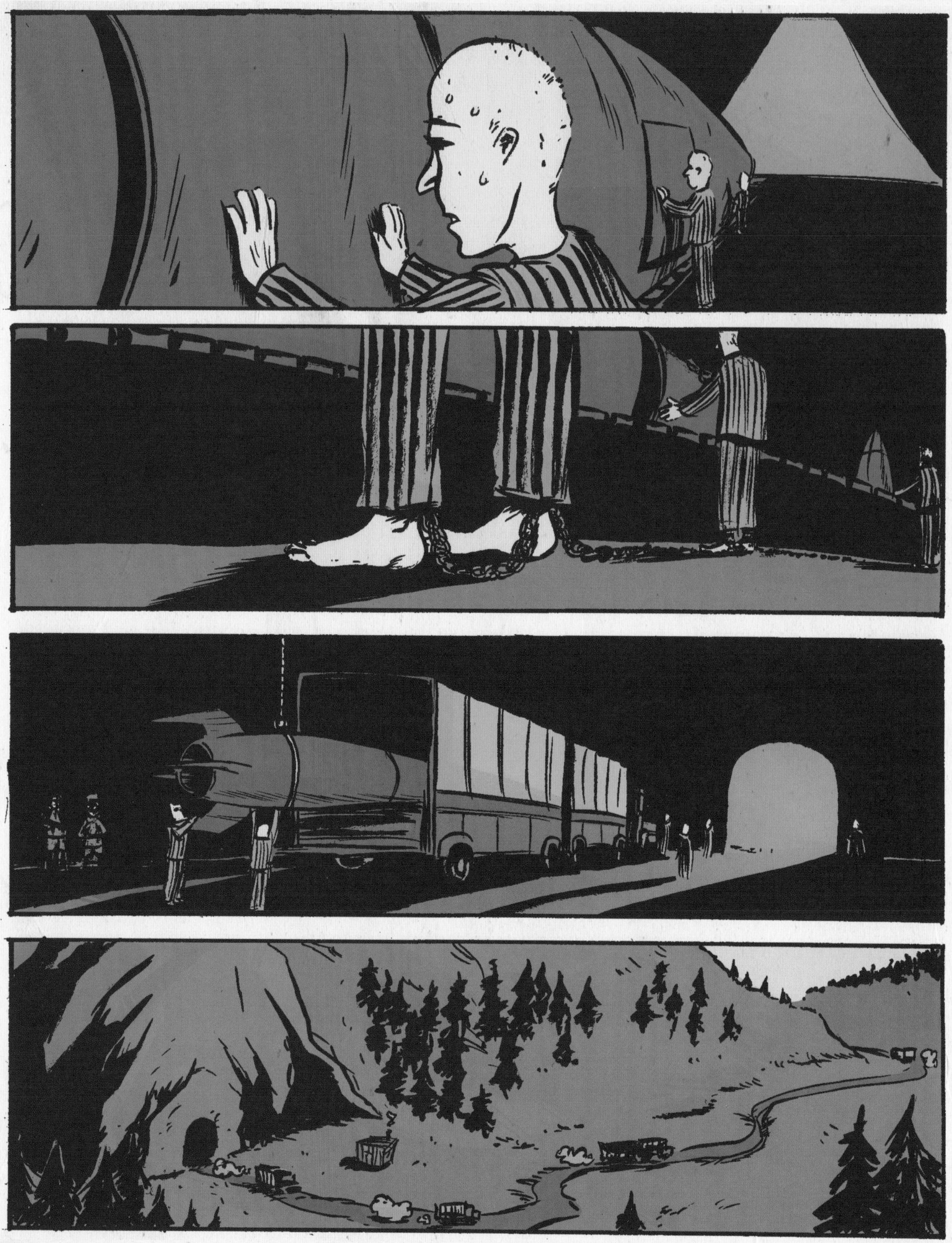

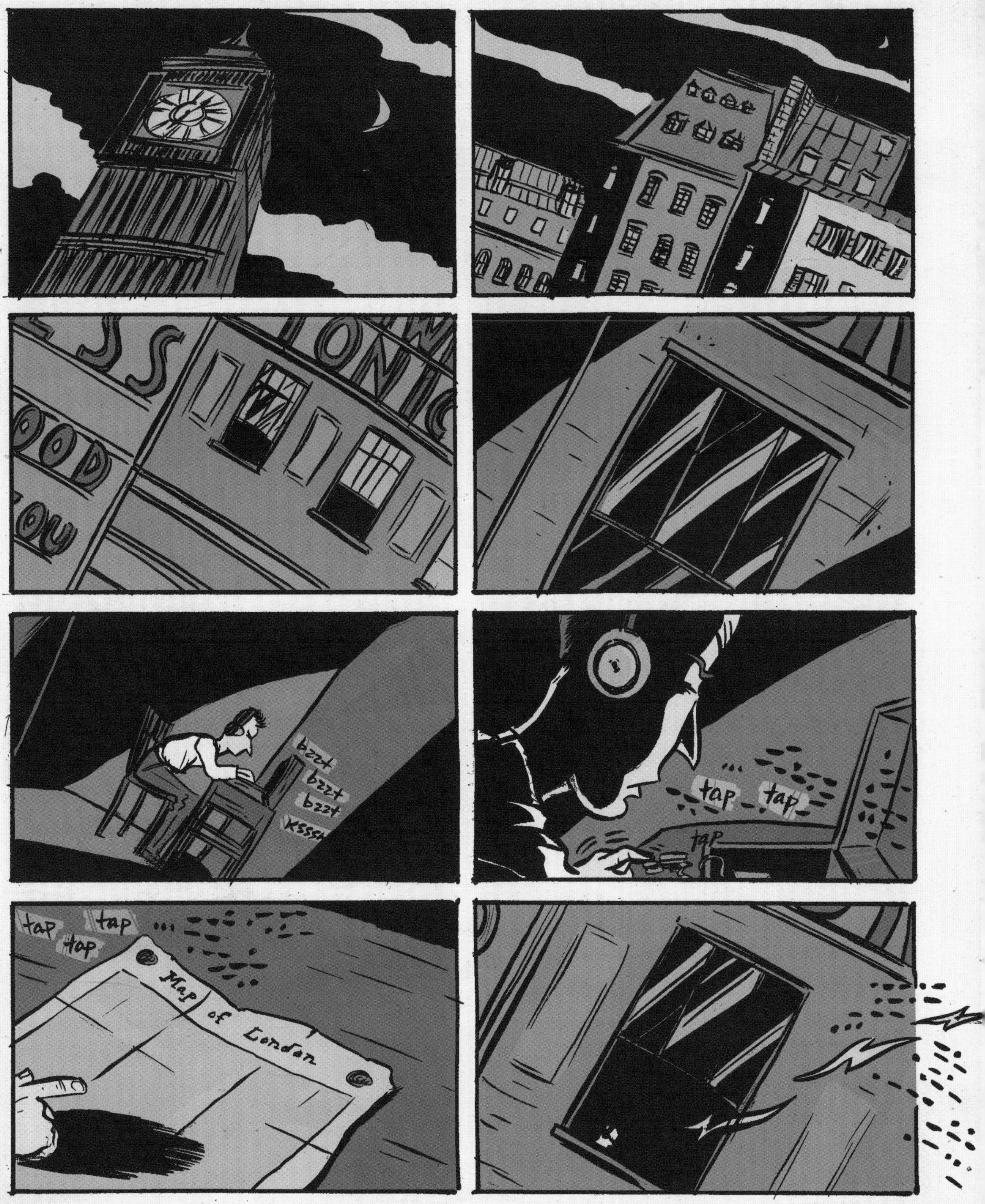
bzzt
bzzt
bzzt
KSSS
tap
tap
tap
tap
tap
tap
Map of London

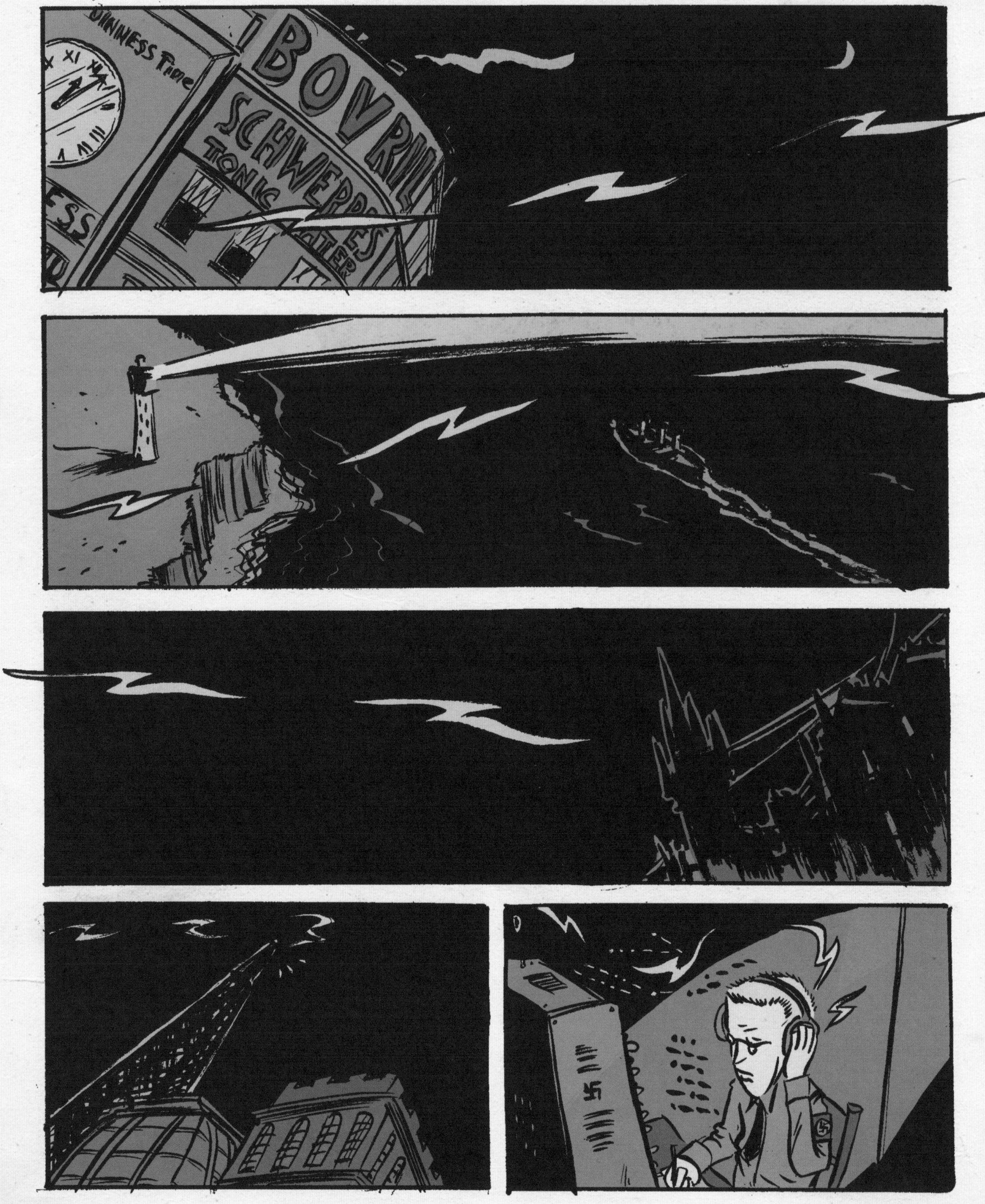
BOVRIL
SCHWEPPES
TONIC

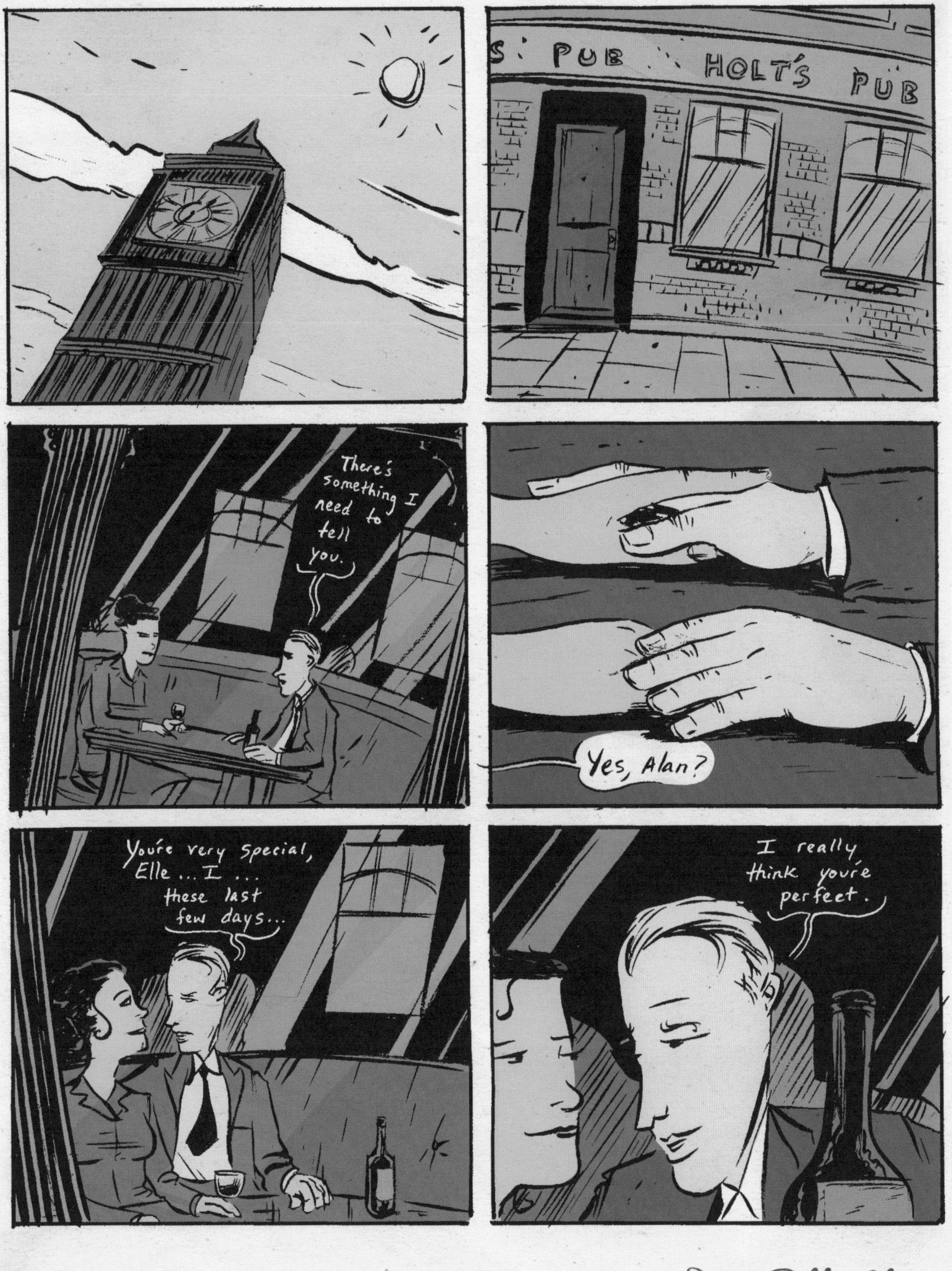
HOLT'S PUB
There's something I need to tell you.
Yes, Alan?
You're very special, Elle ... I ... these last few days...
I really think you're perfect.

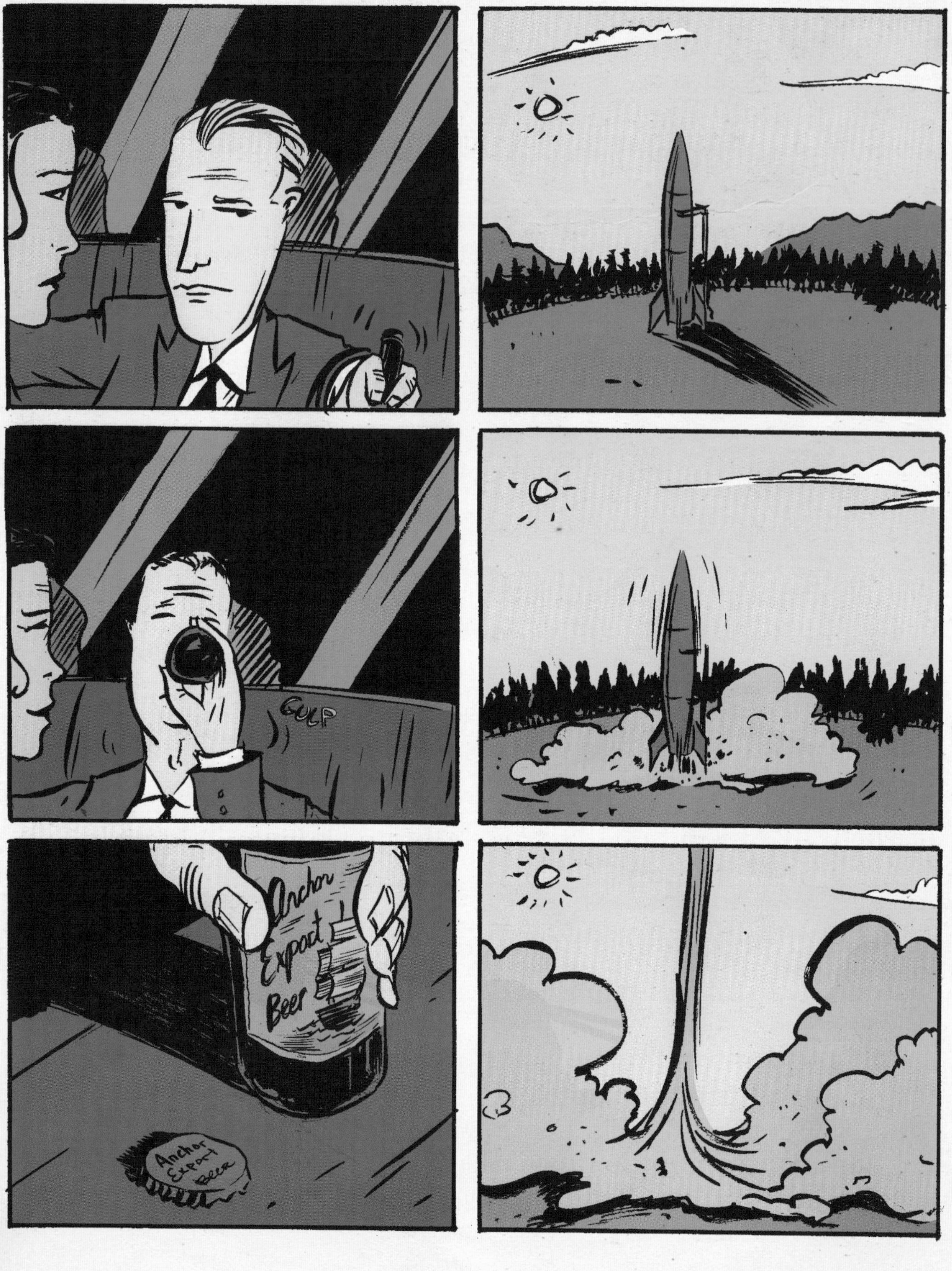
GULP
Anchor Export Beer
Anchor Export Beer

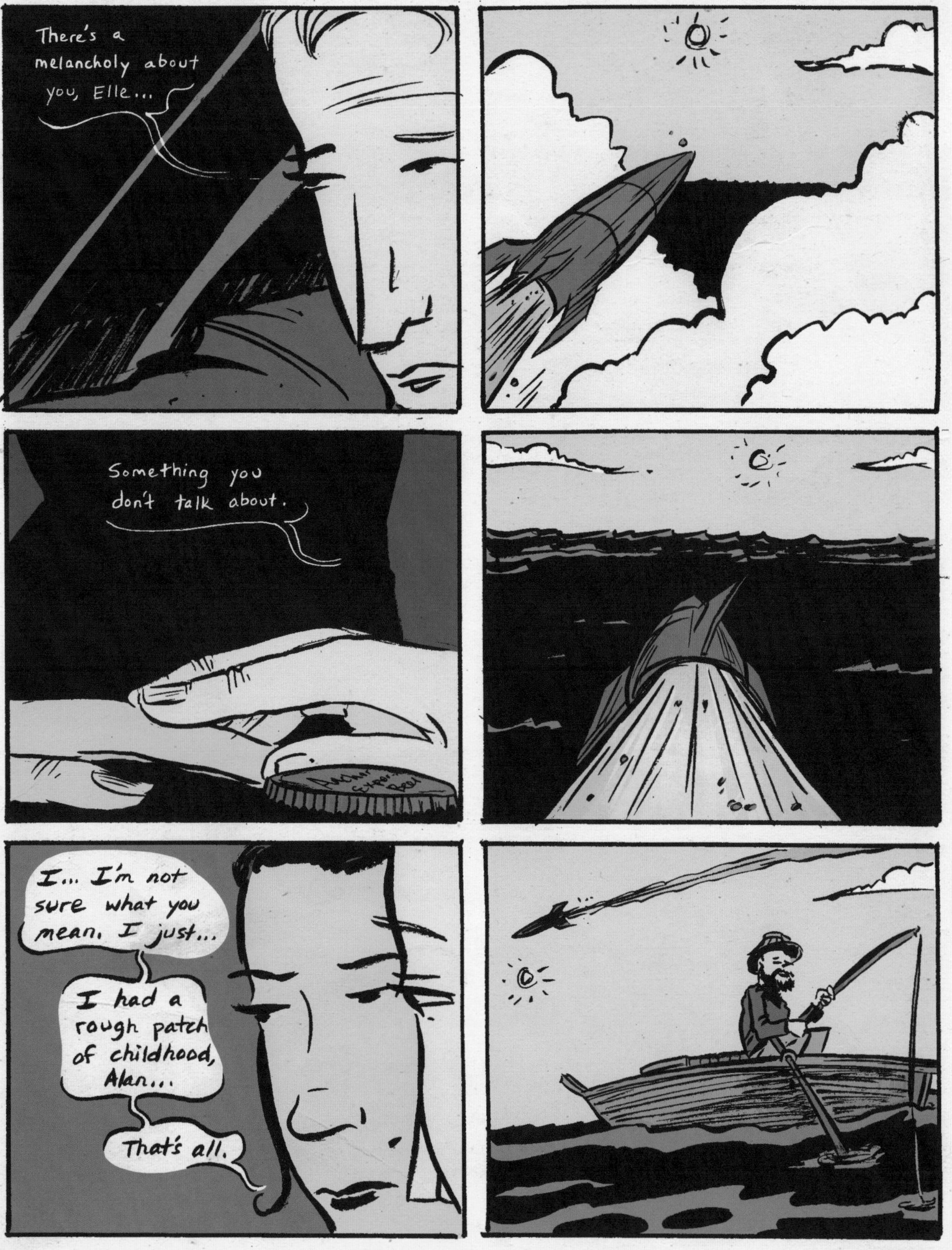
There's a melancholy about you, Elle...
Something you don't talk about.
I... I'm not sure what you mean. I just...
I had a rough patch of childhood, Alan...
That's all.

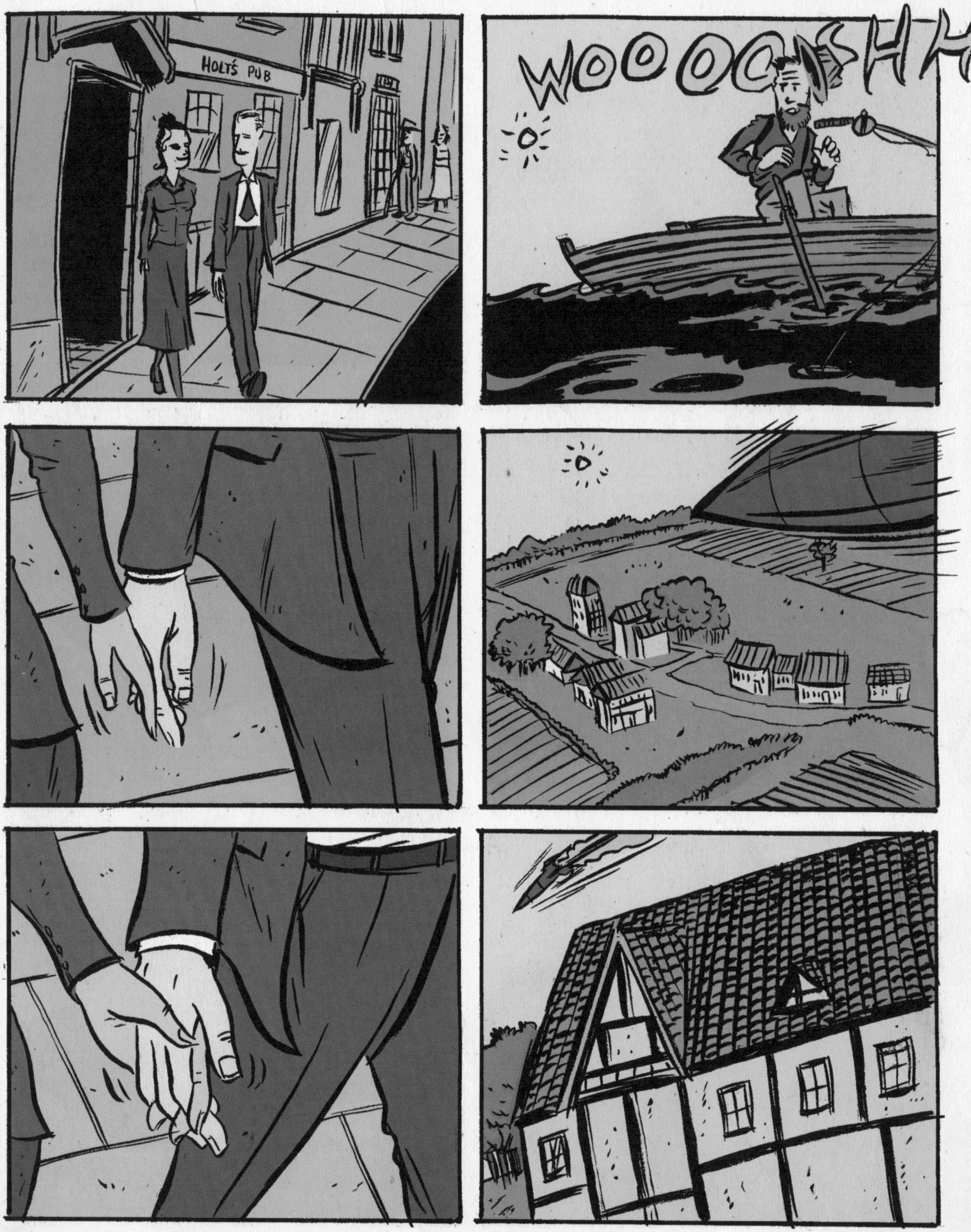
HOLT'S PUB
WOOOOSHH

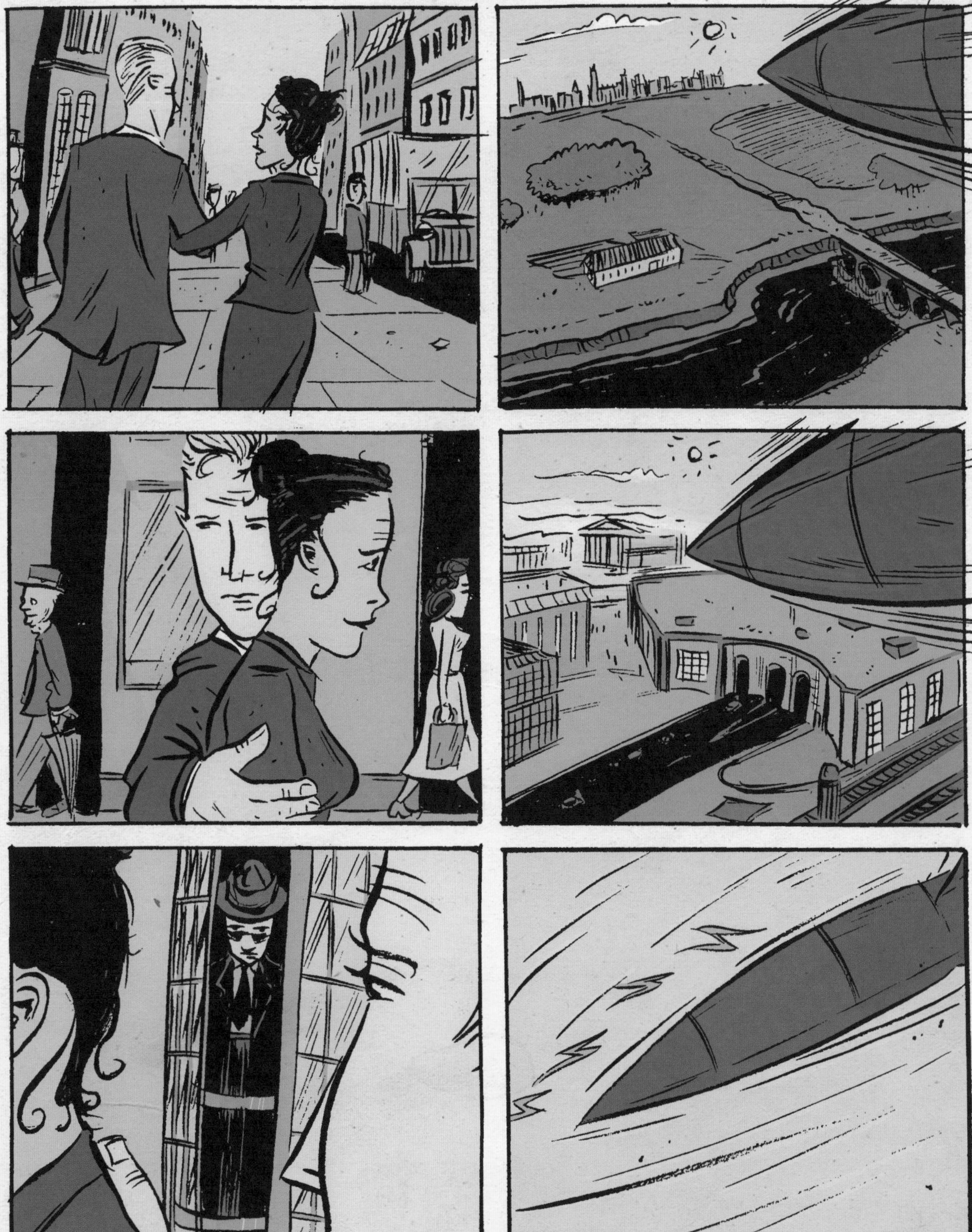

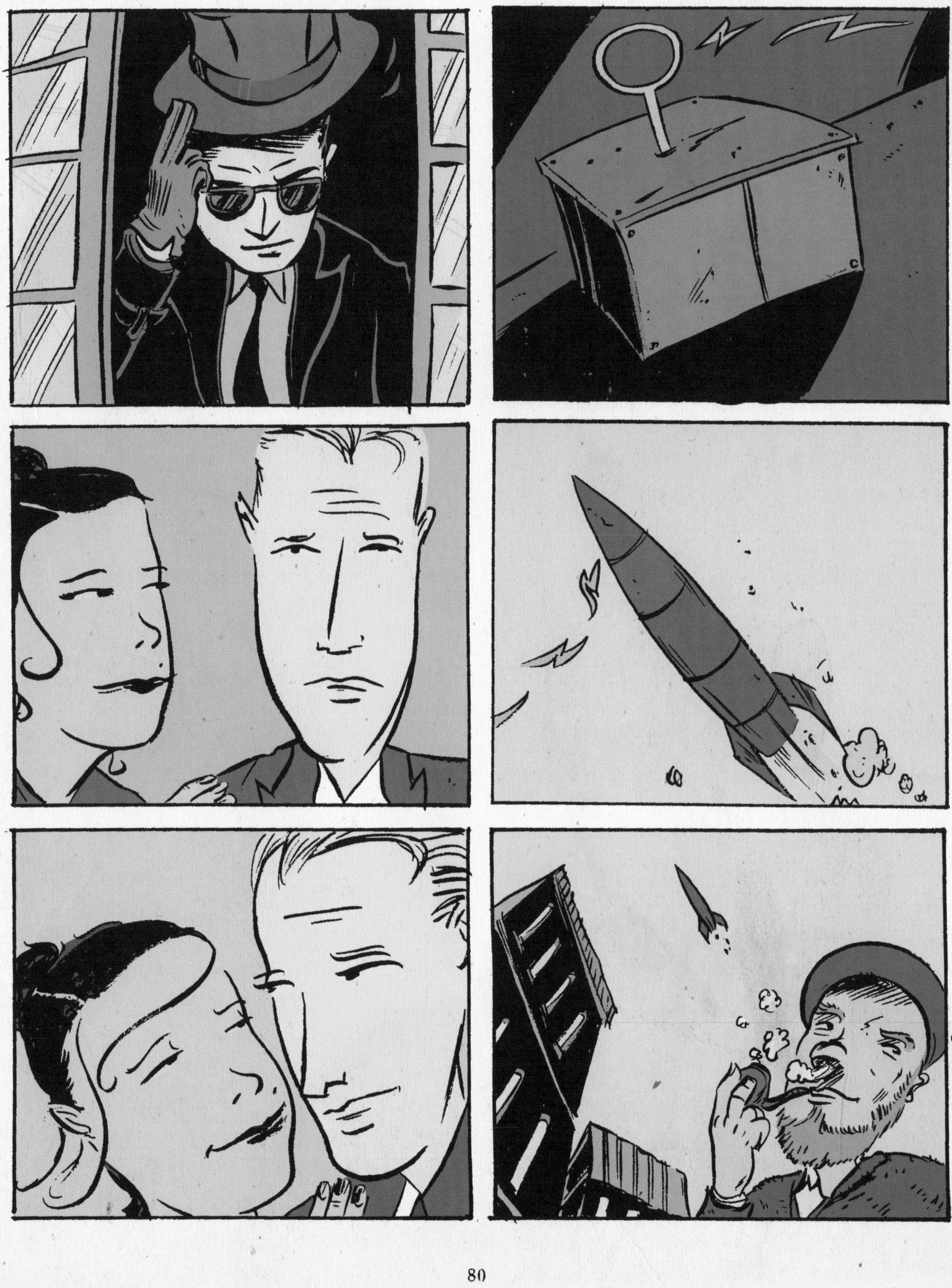

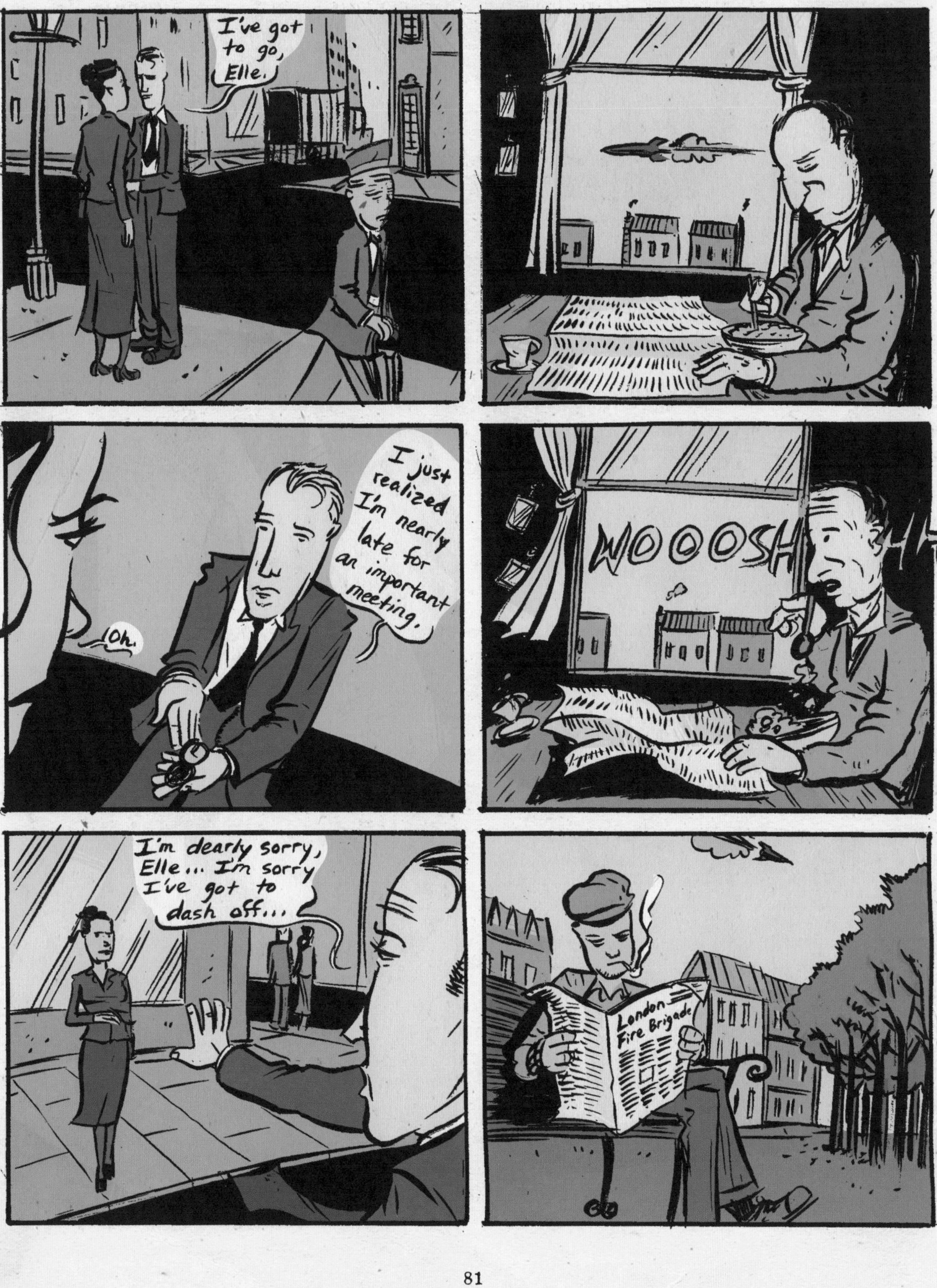
I've got to go, Elle.
I just realized I'm nearly late for an important meeting.
Oh.
WOOOSHHH!
I'm dearly sorry, Elle... I'm sorry I've got to dash off...
London Fire Brigade

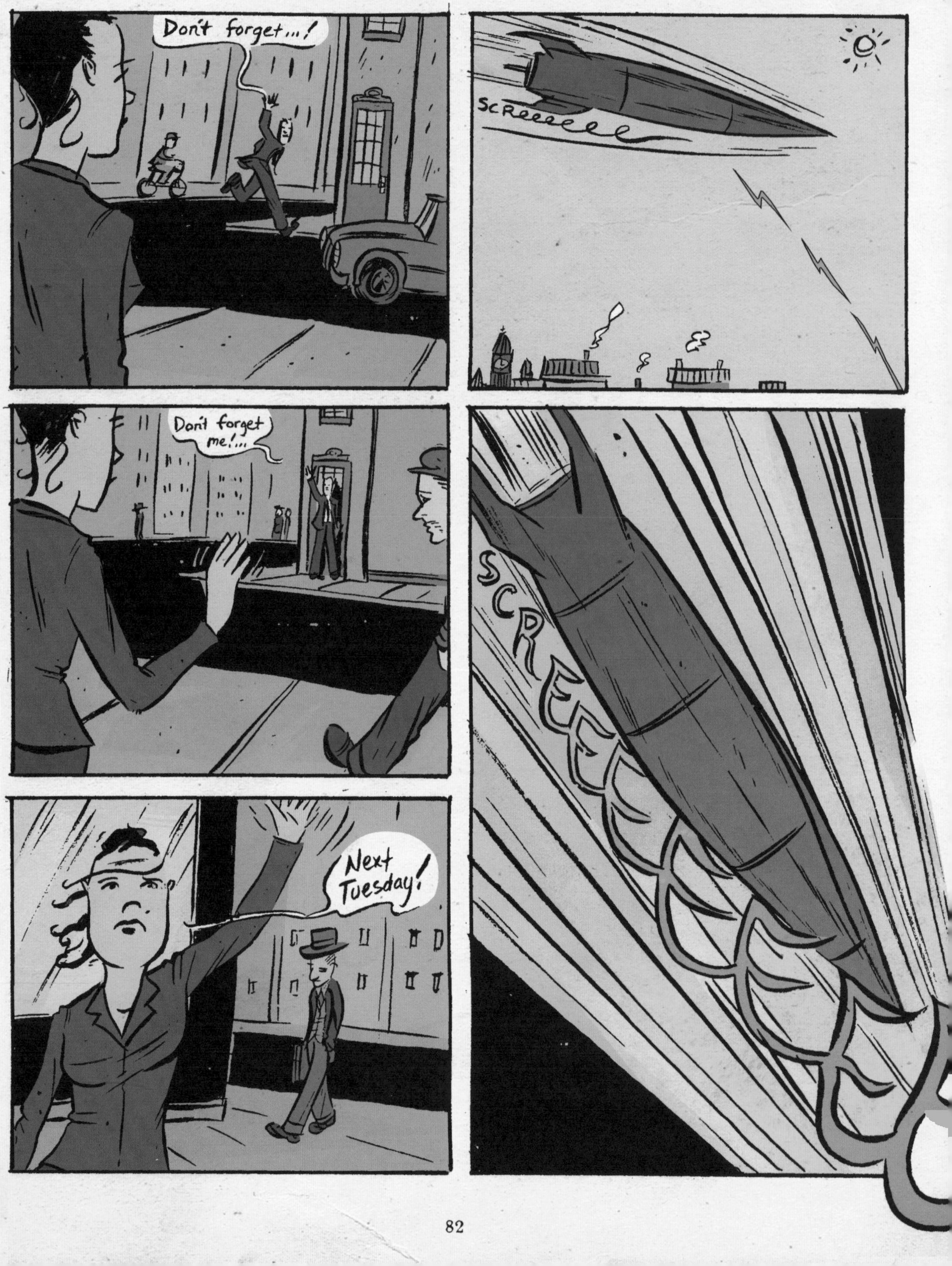
Don't forget...!
SCReeeeeee
Don't forget me!...
SCREEEE
Next Tuesday!

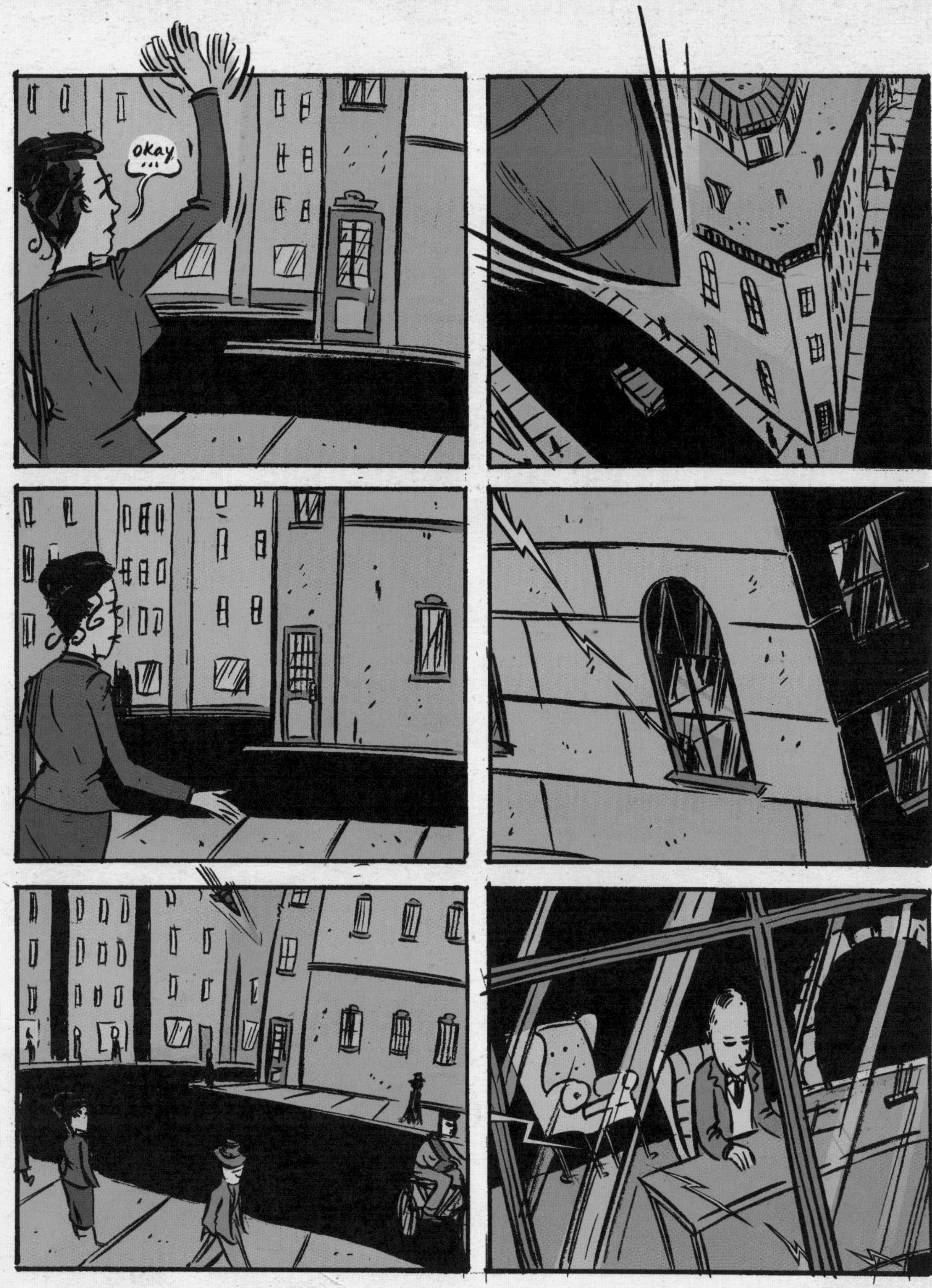
okay...

HISTORY
Let me know when you'll have time for me.
Please... don't leave...!
ART OF WAR
STRATEGY
We're going to need your mind to get through this, Harris.
Thank You ... er... Winston.

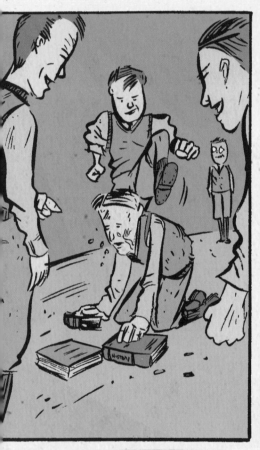

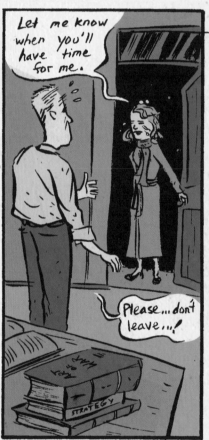

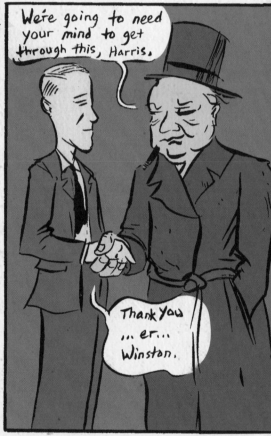

sigh...
YE OLDE
CHESHIRE
CHEESE
PUB
eh?
bollocks...

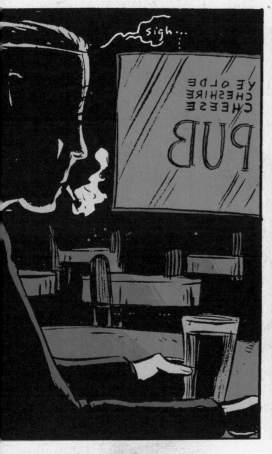

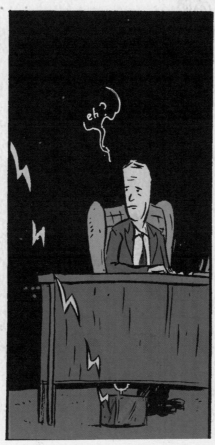

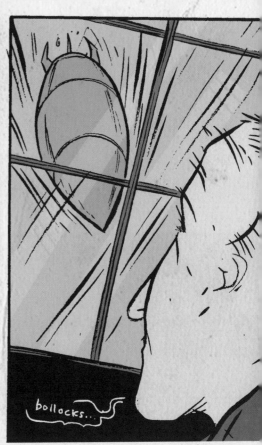

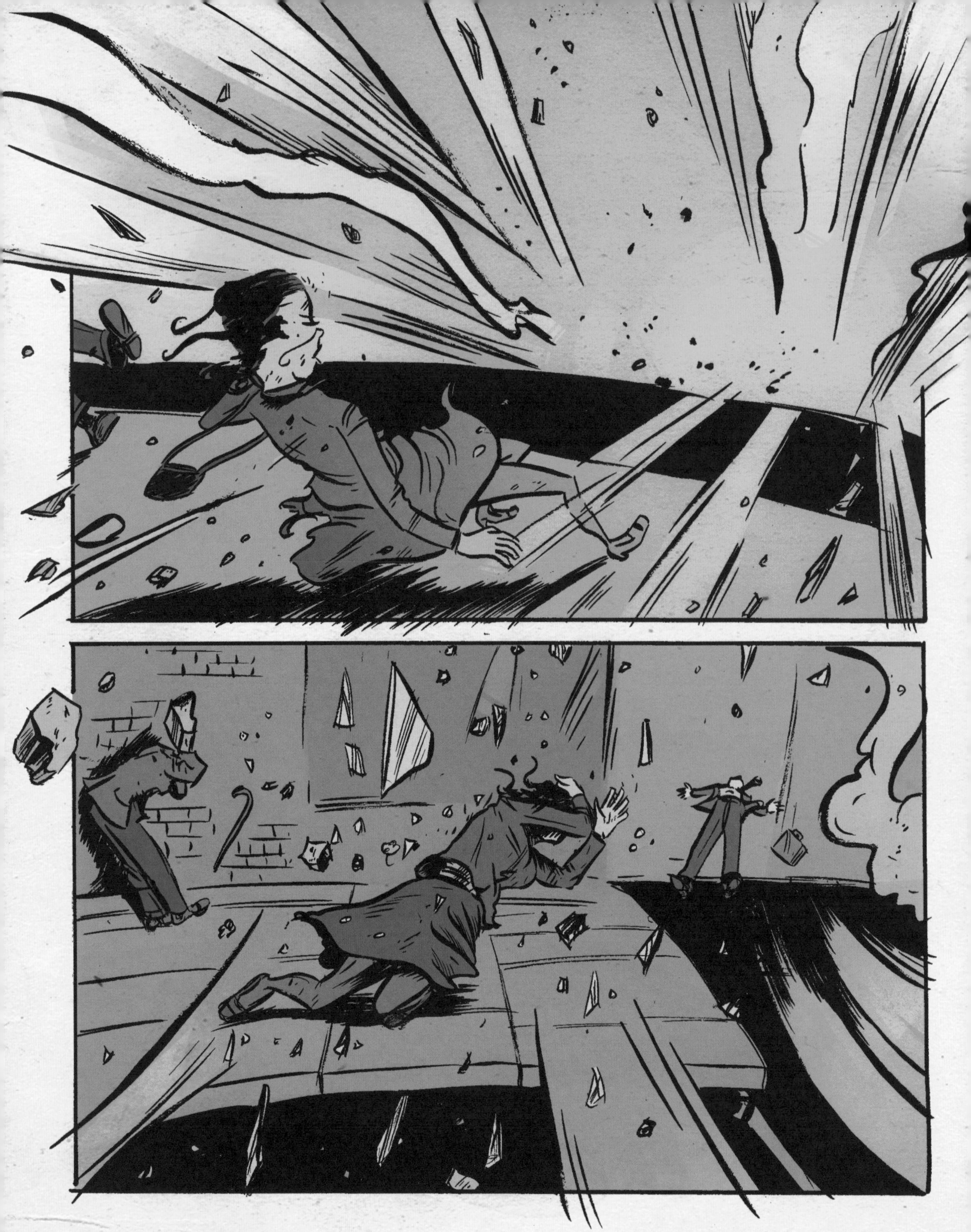

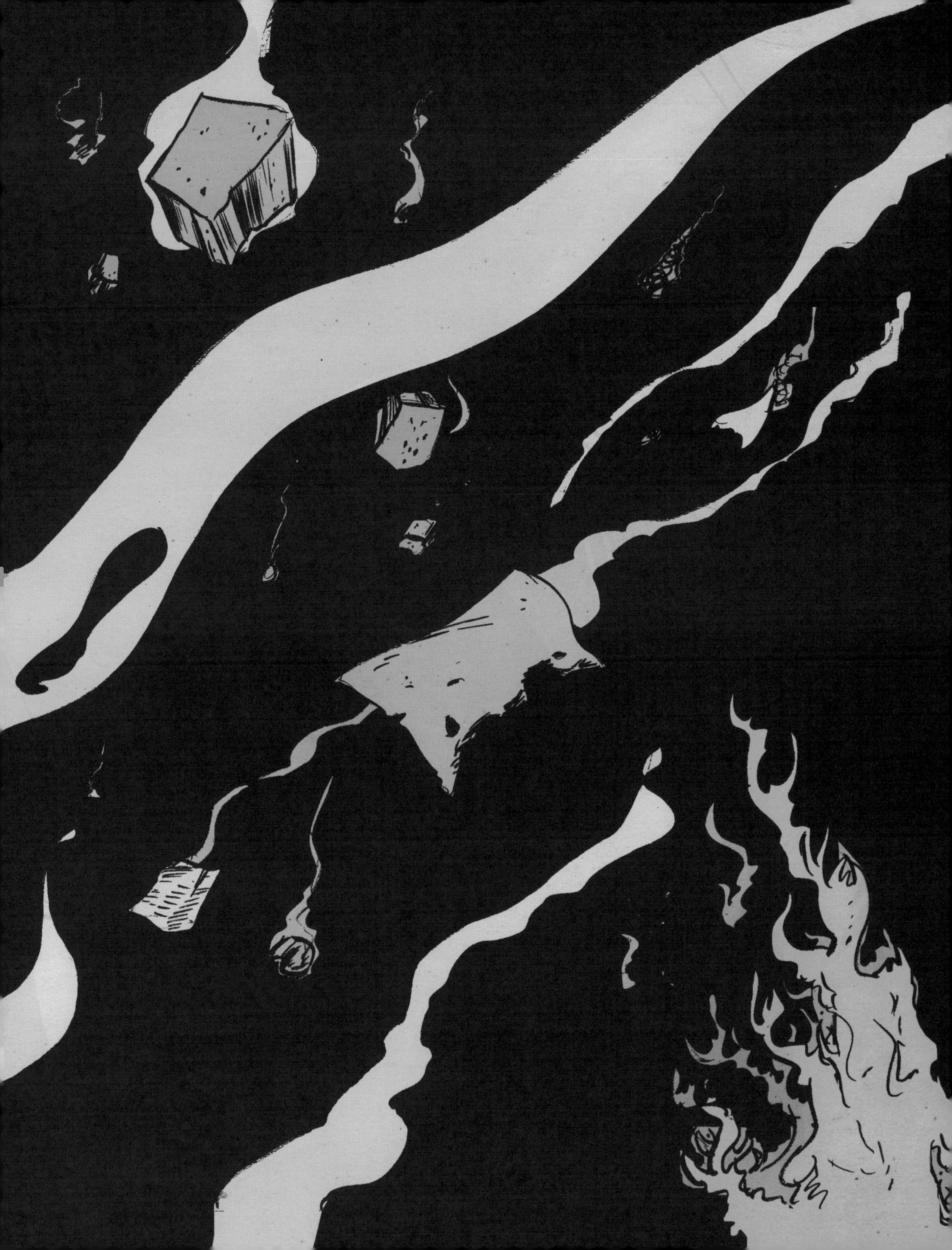

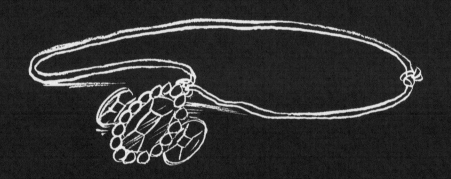

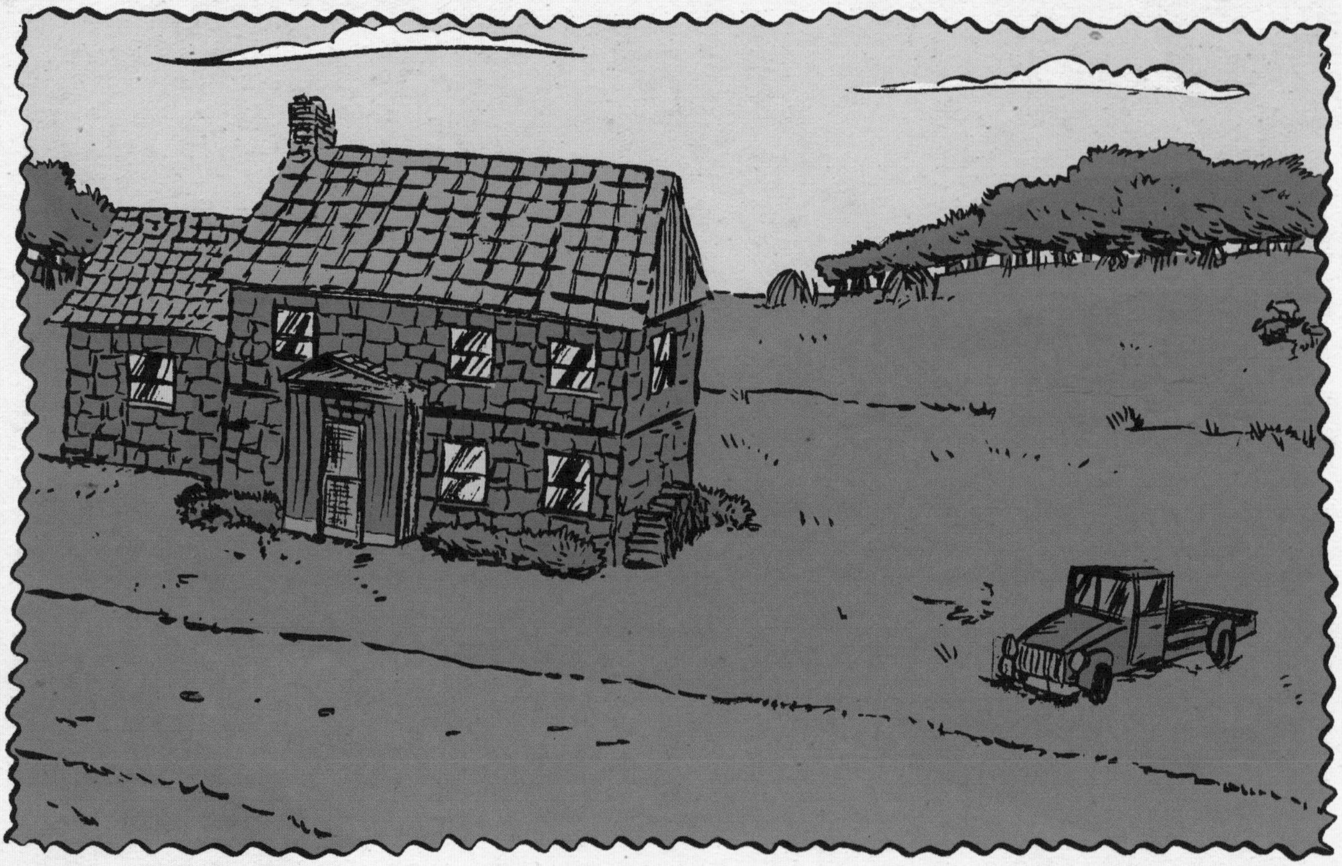

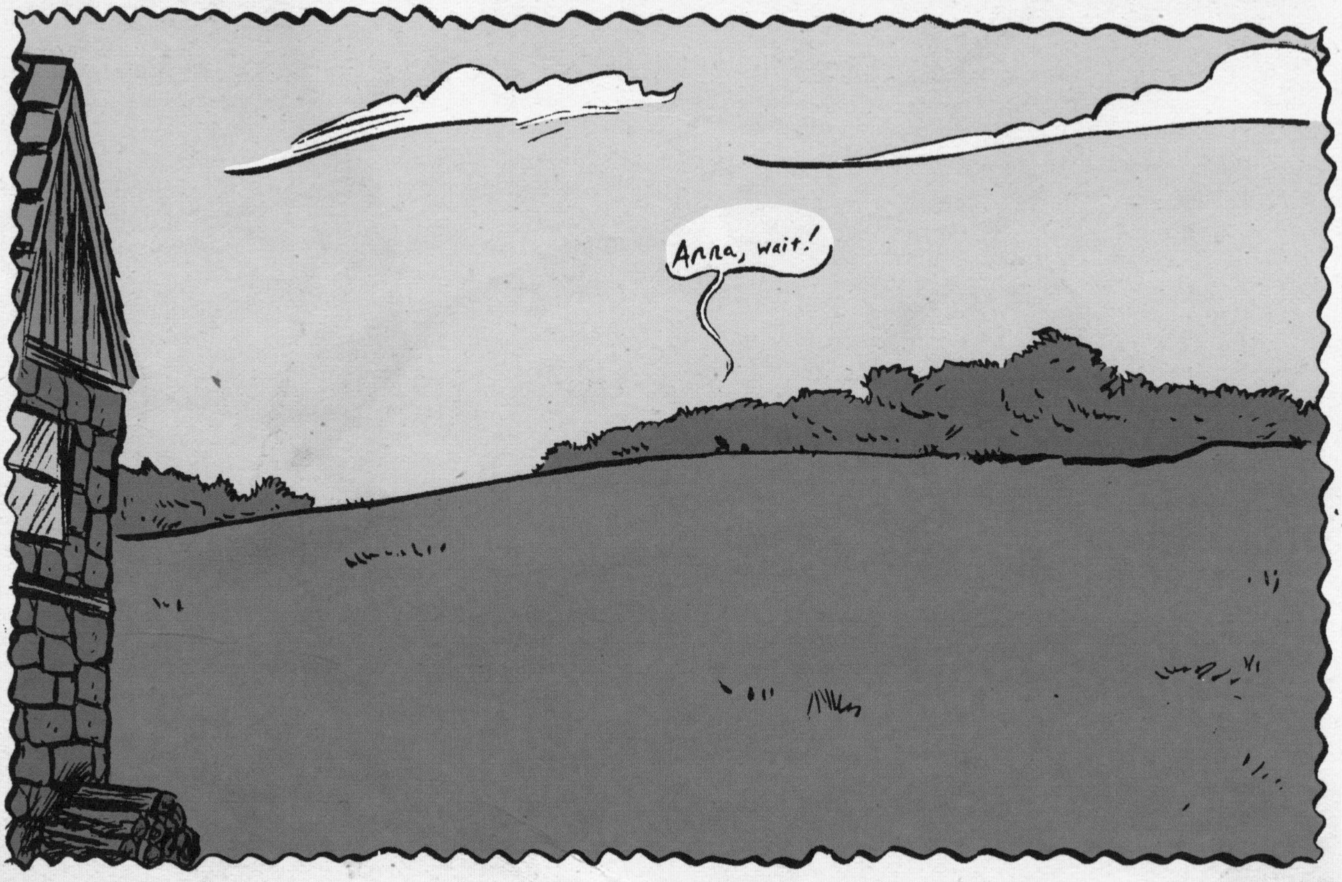
Arra, wait!

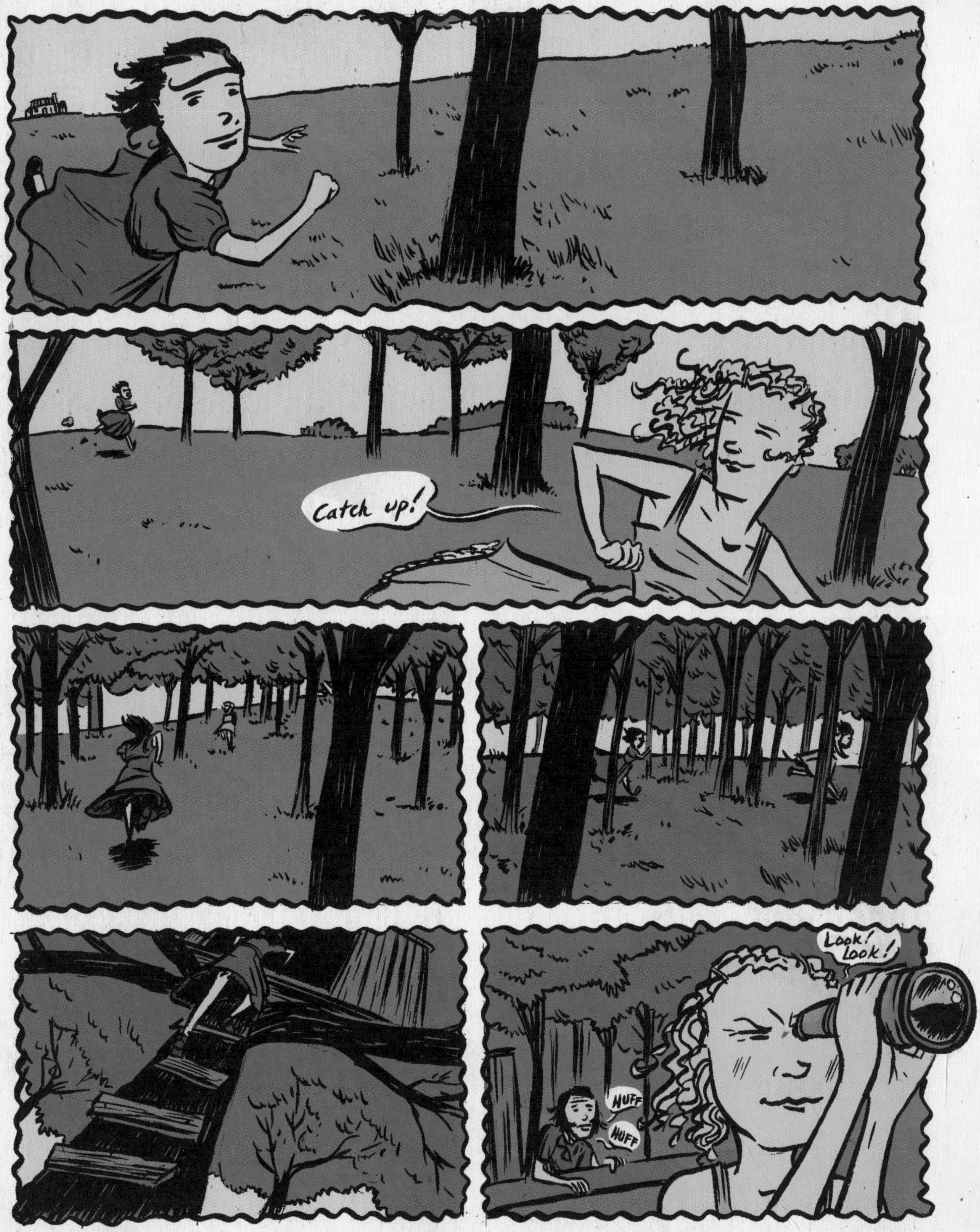
Catch up!
Look! Look!
HUFF
HUFF

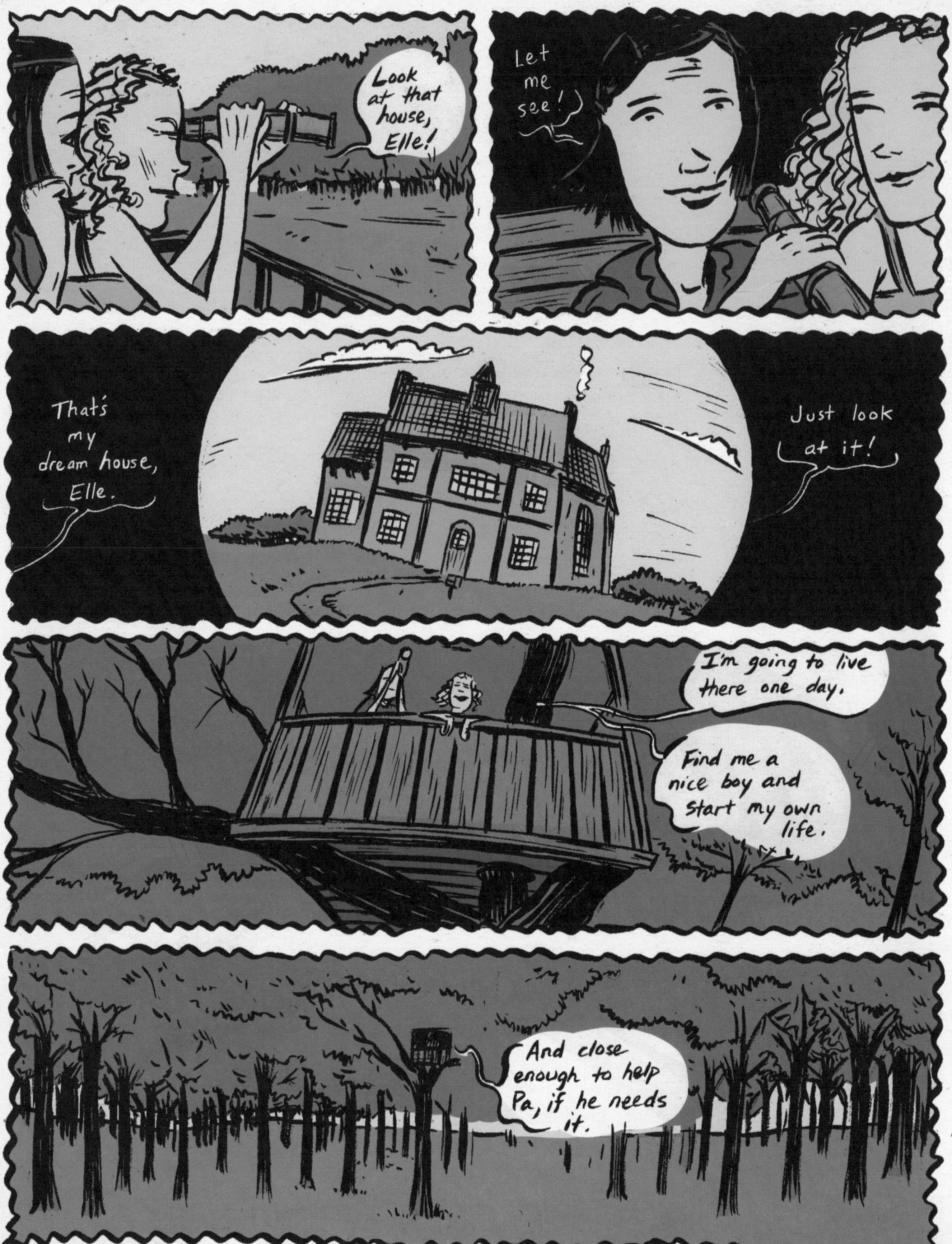
Look at that house, Elle!
Let me see!
That's my dream house, Elle.
Just look at it!
I'm going to live there one day.
Find me a nice boy and start my own life.
And close enough to help Pa, if he needs it.

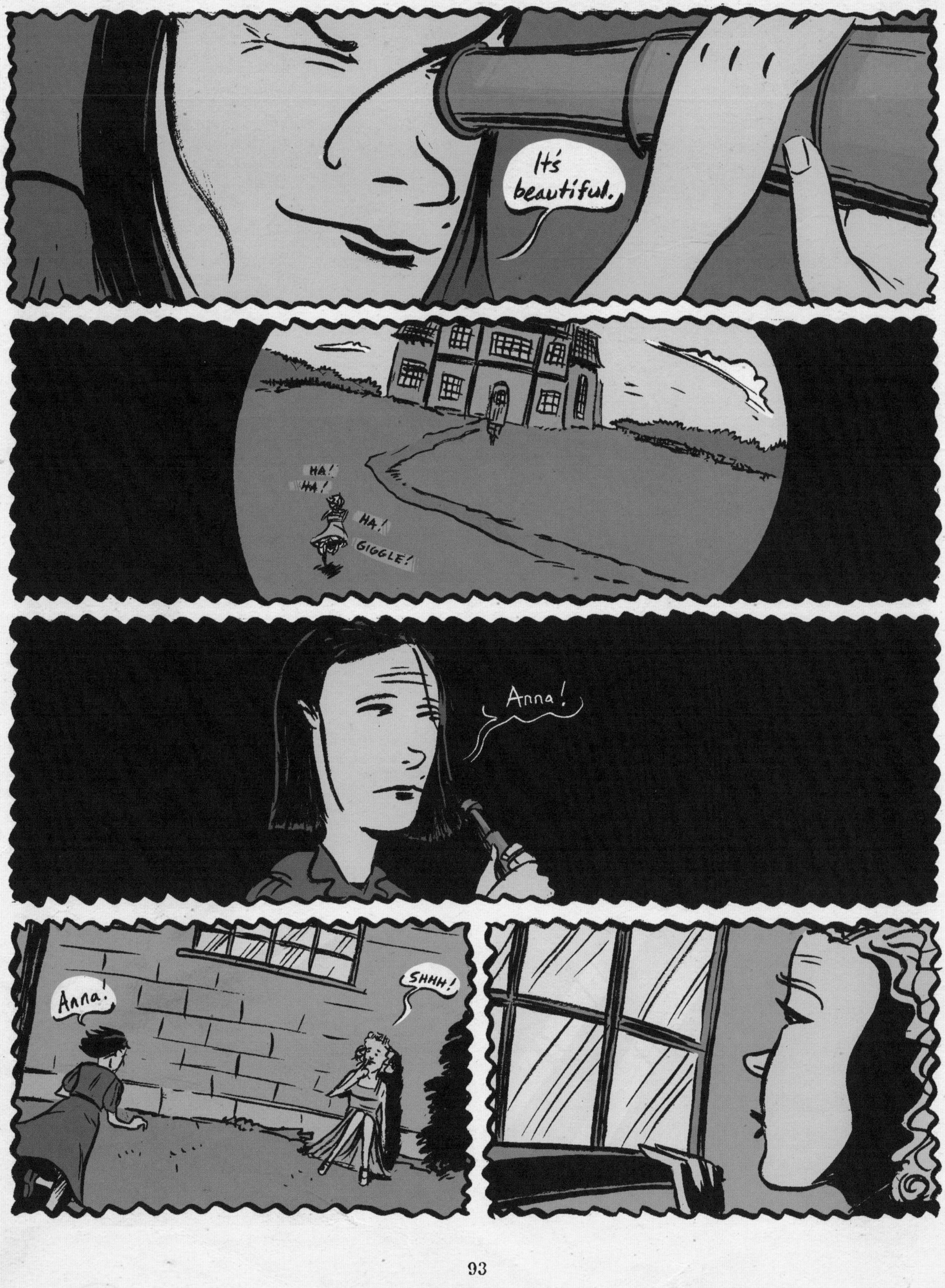
It's beautiful.
HA!
HA!
HA!
GIGGLE!
Anna!
Anna!
SHHH!

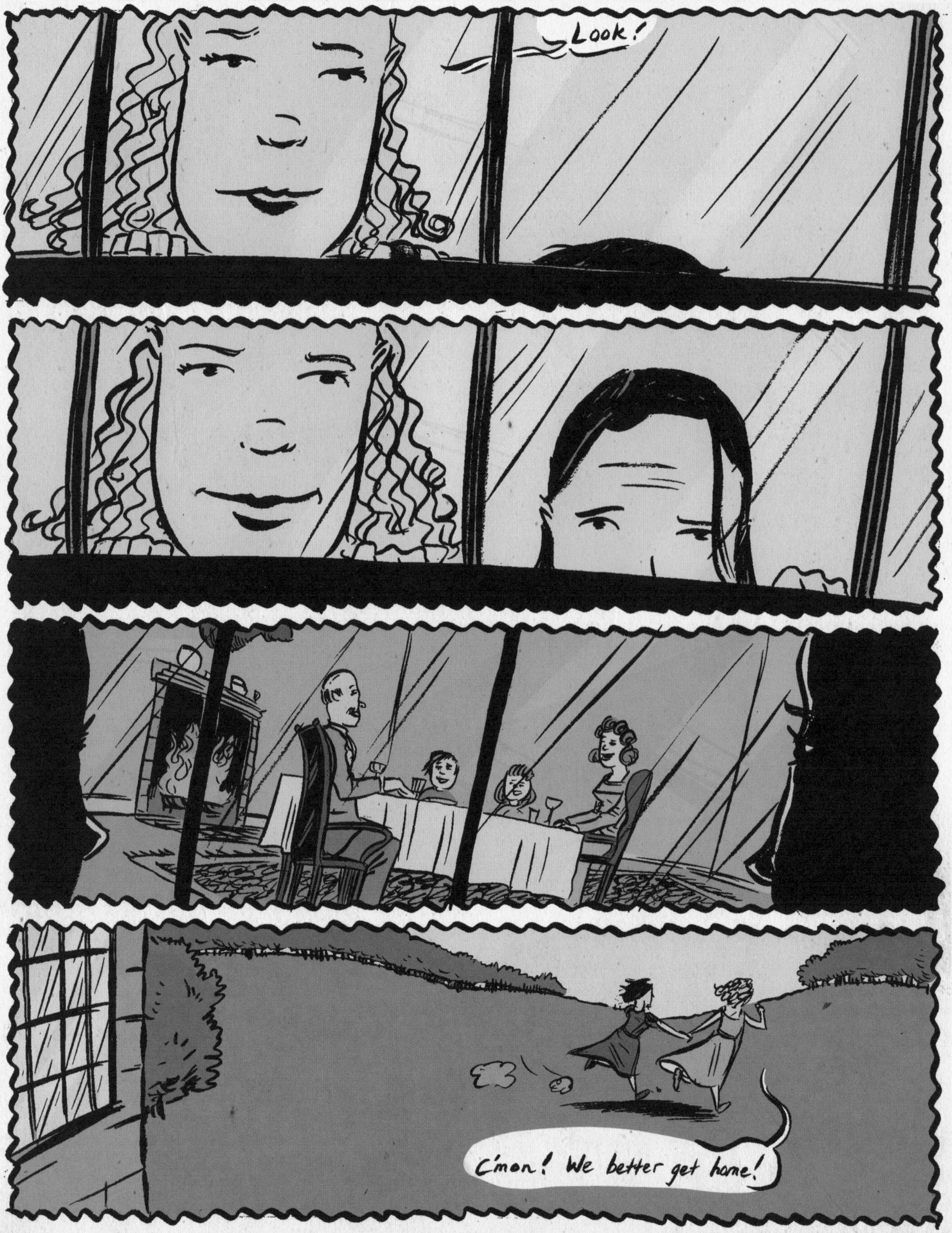
Look!
C'mon! We better get home!

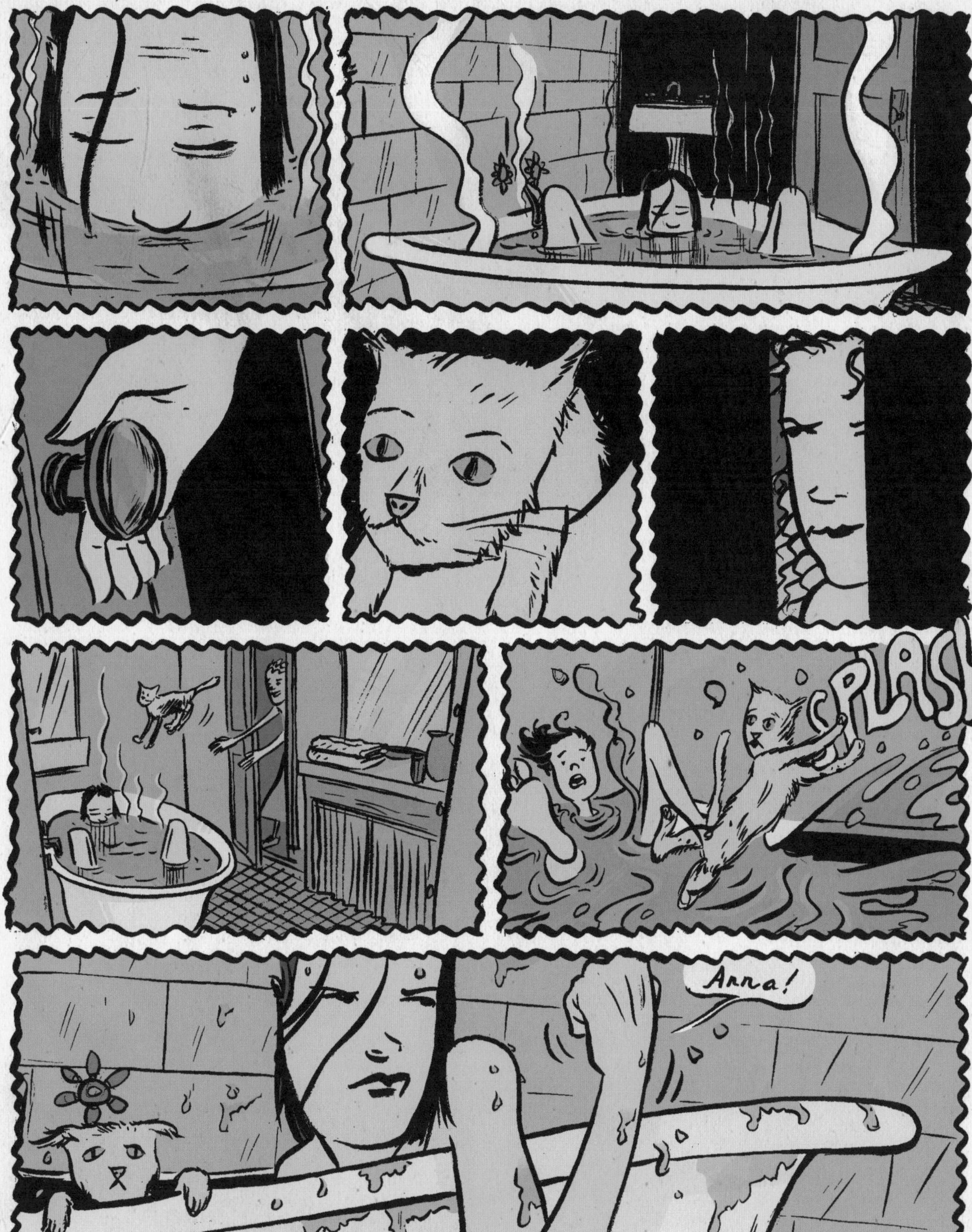
SPLASH!
Anna!

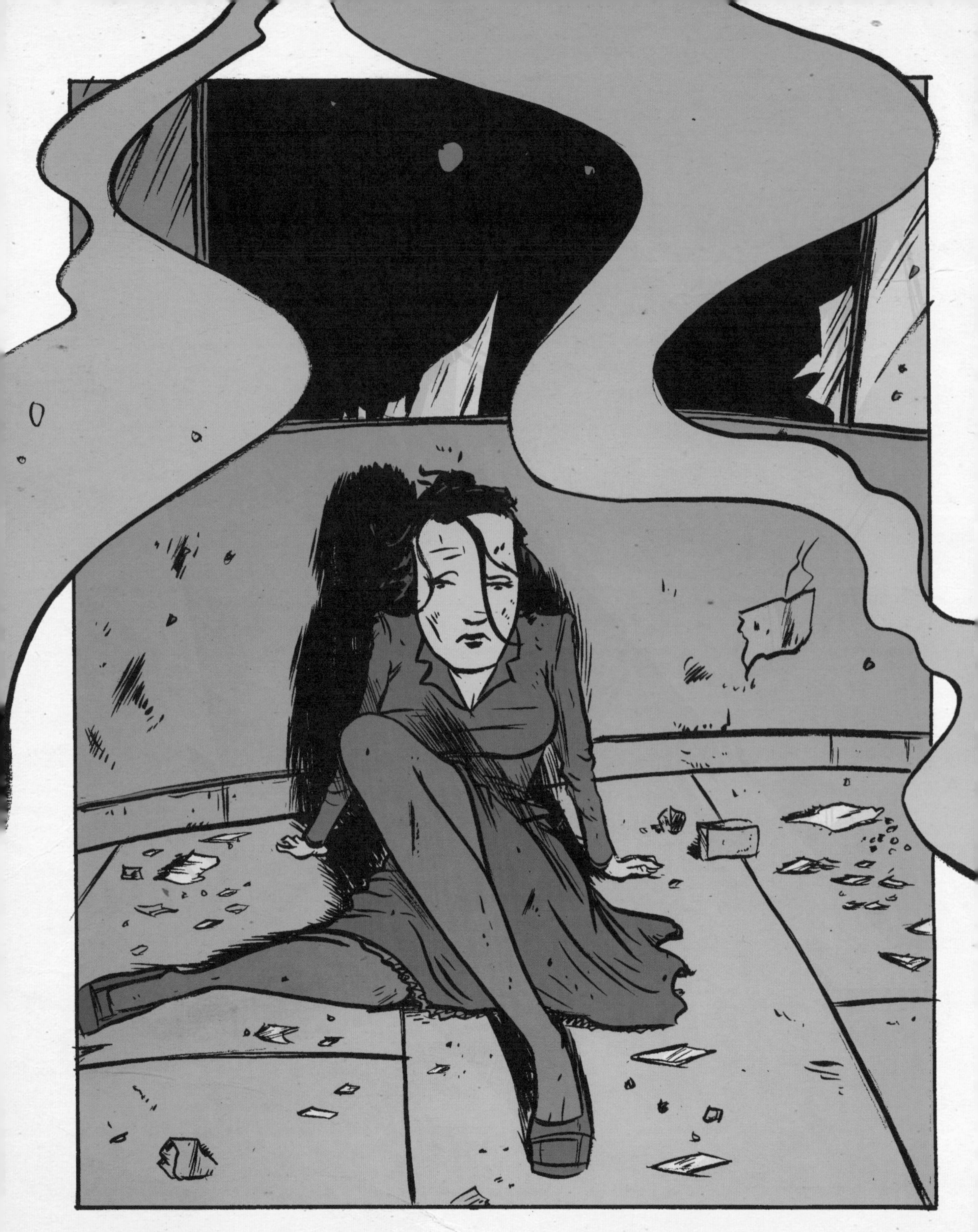

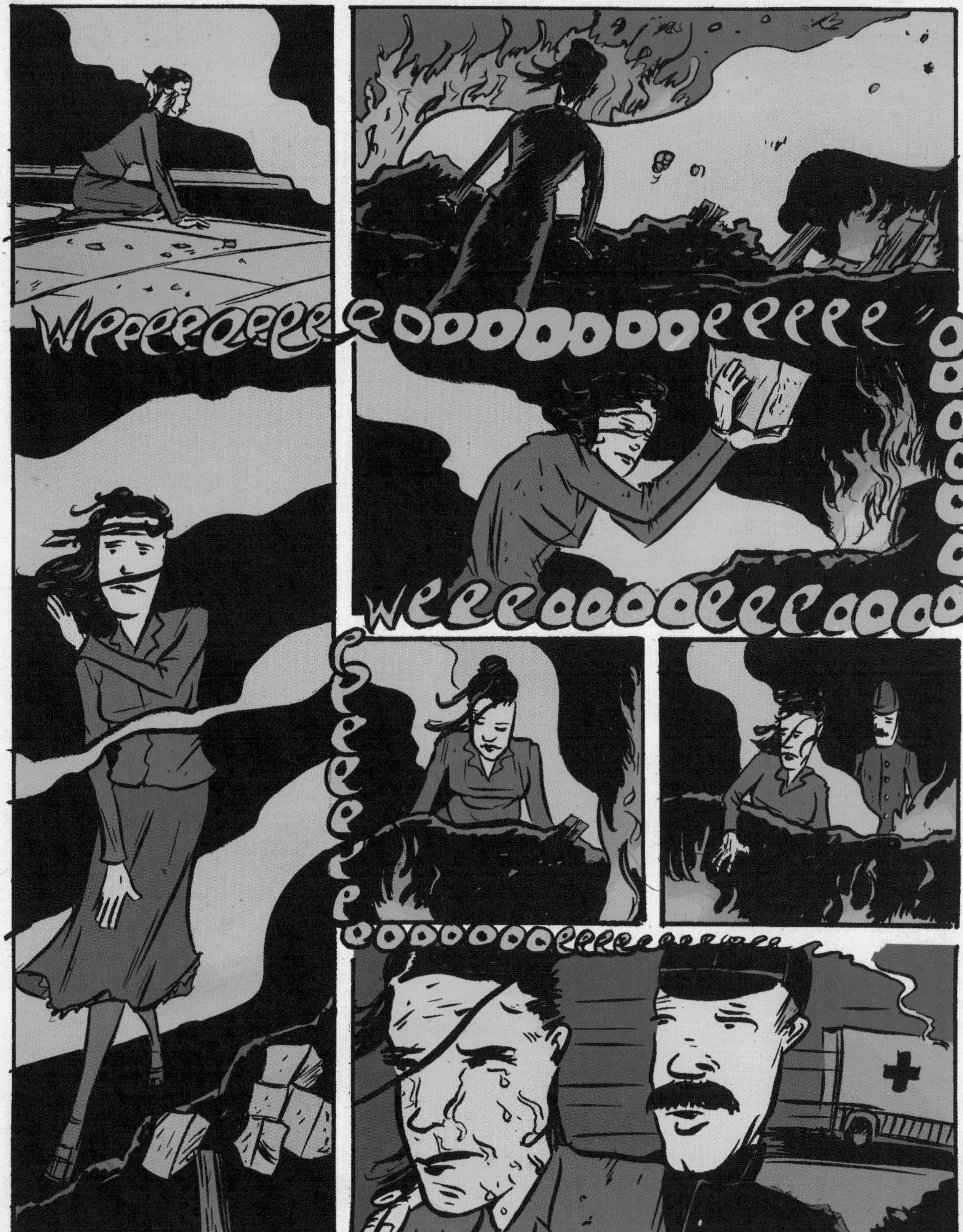

WEEEEEEEEEOOOOOOOOOEEEEEOOOOOOOO
WEEEOOOOOEEEEOOO
EEEEEEEEOOOOOOOOEEEEEEEEEEEEEEEE

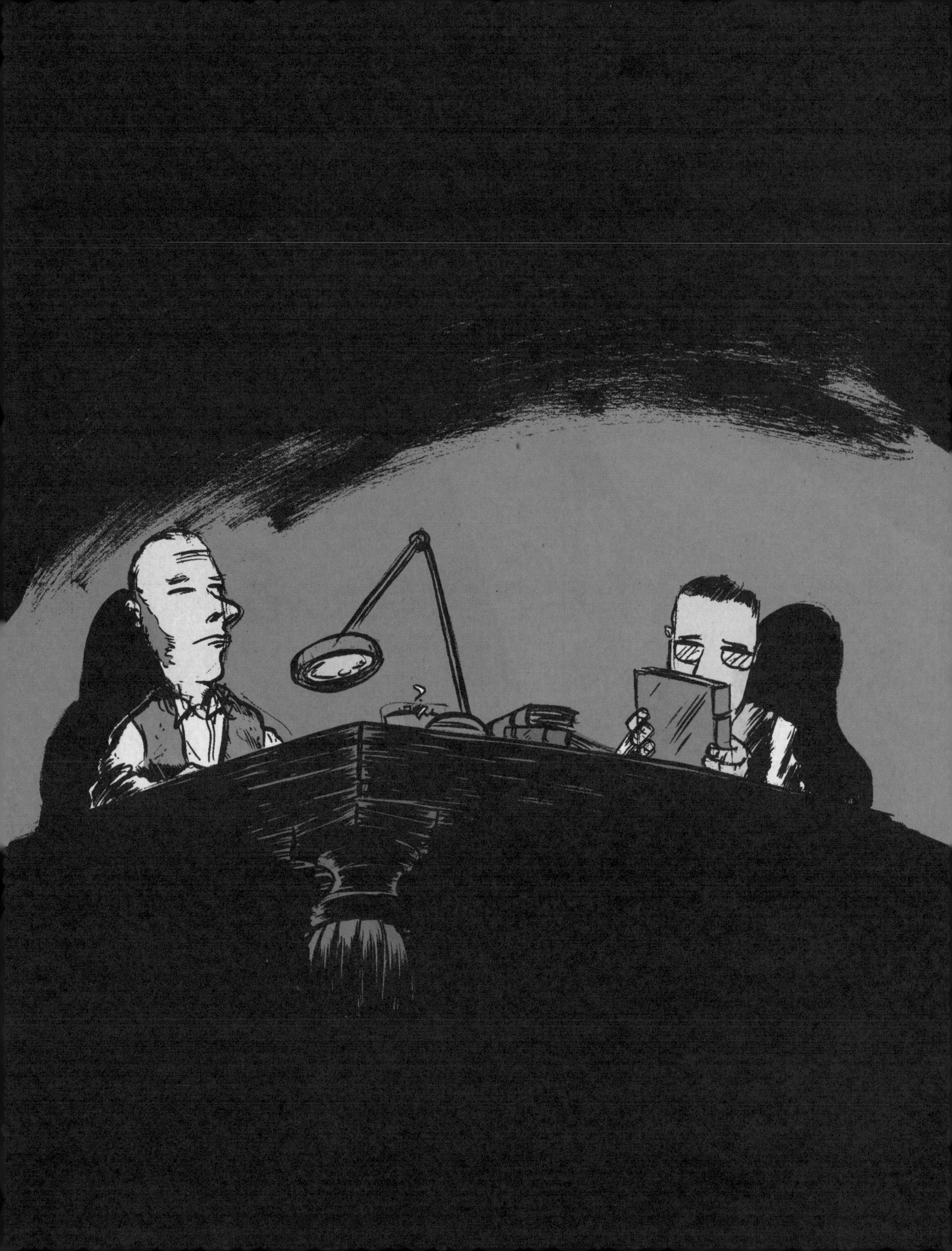

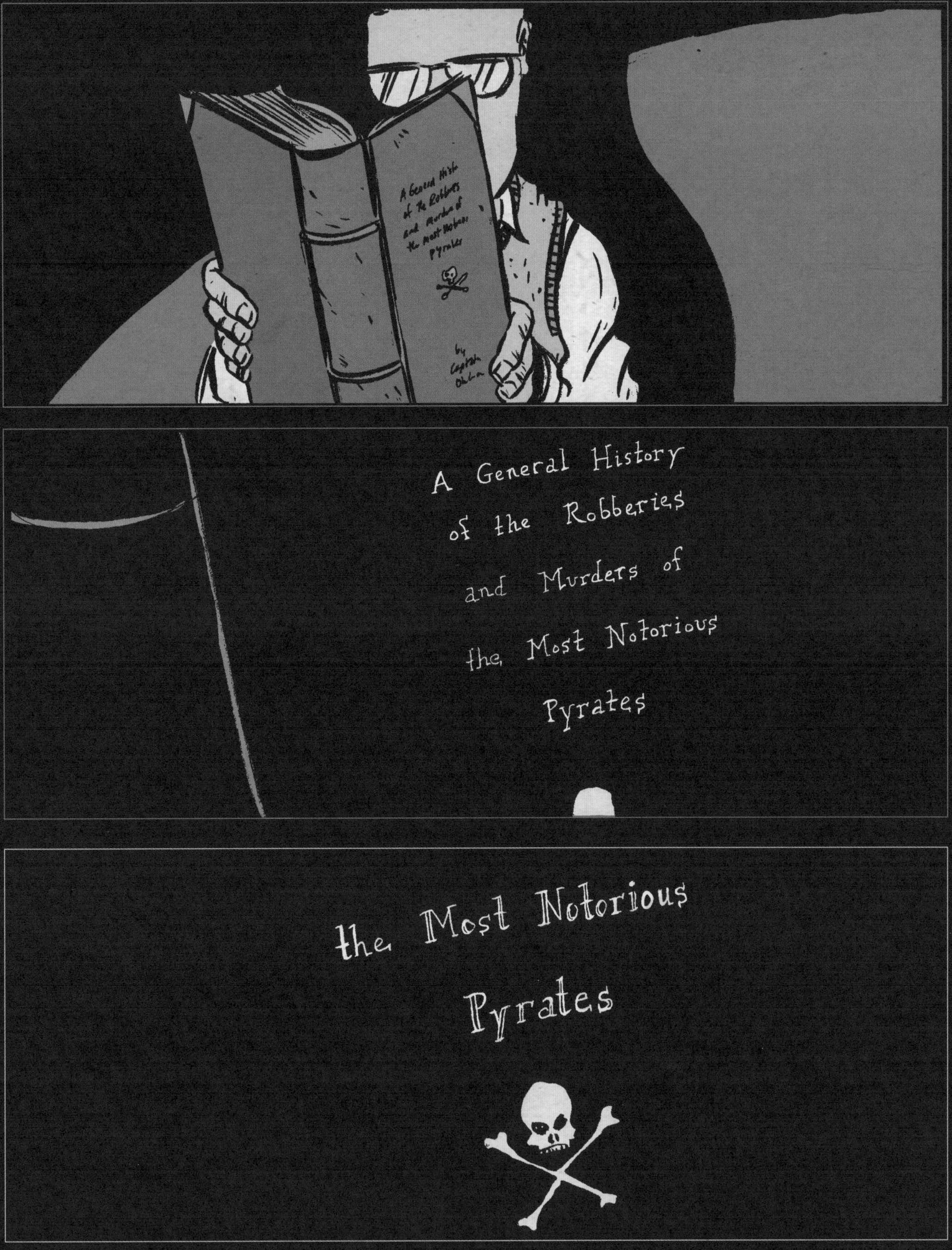
A General History
of the Robberies
and Murders of
the Most Notorious
Pyrates
the Most Notorious
Pyrates

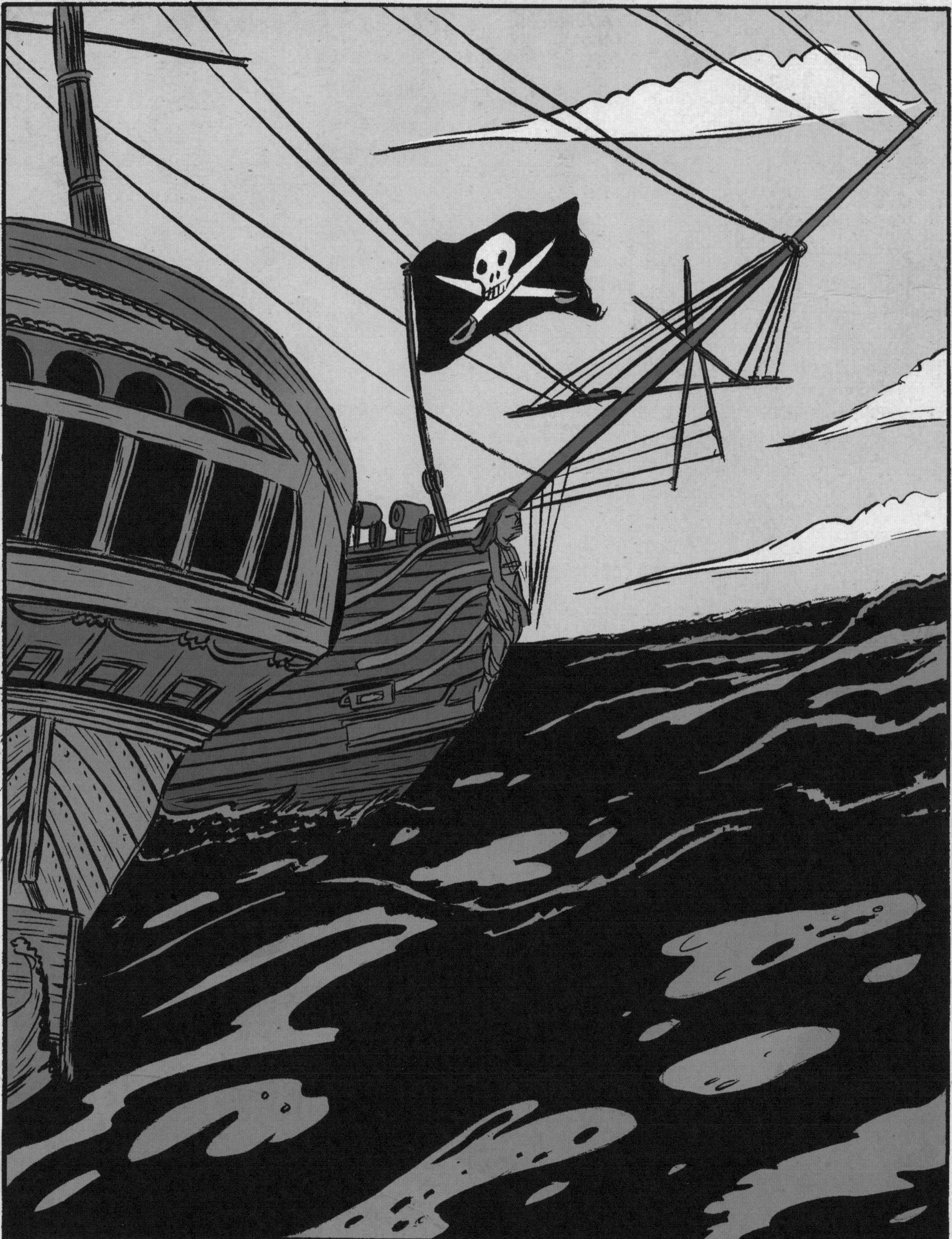

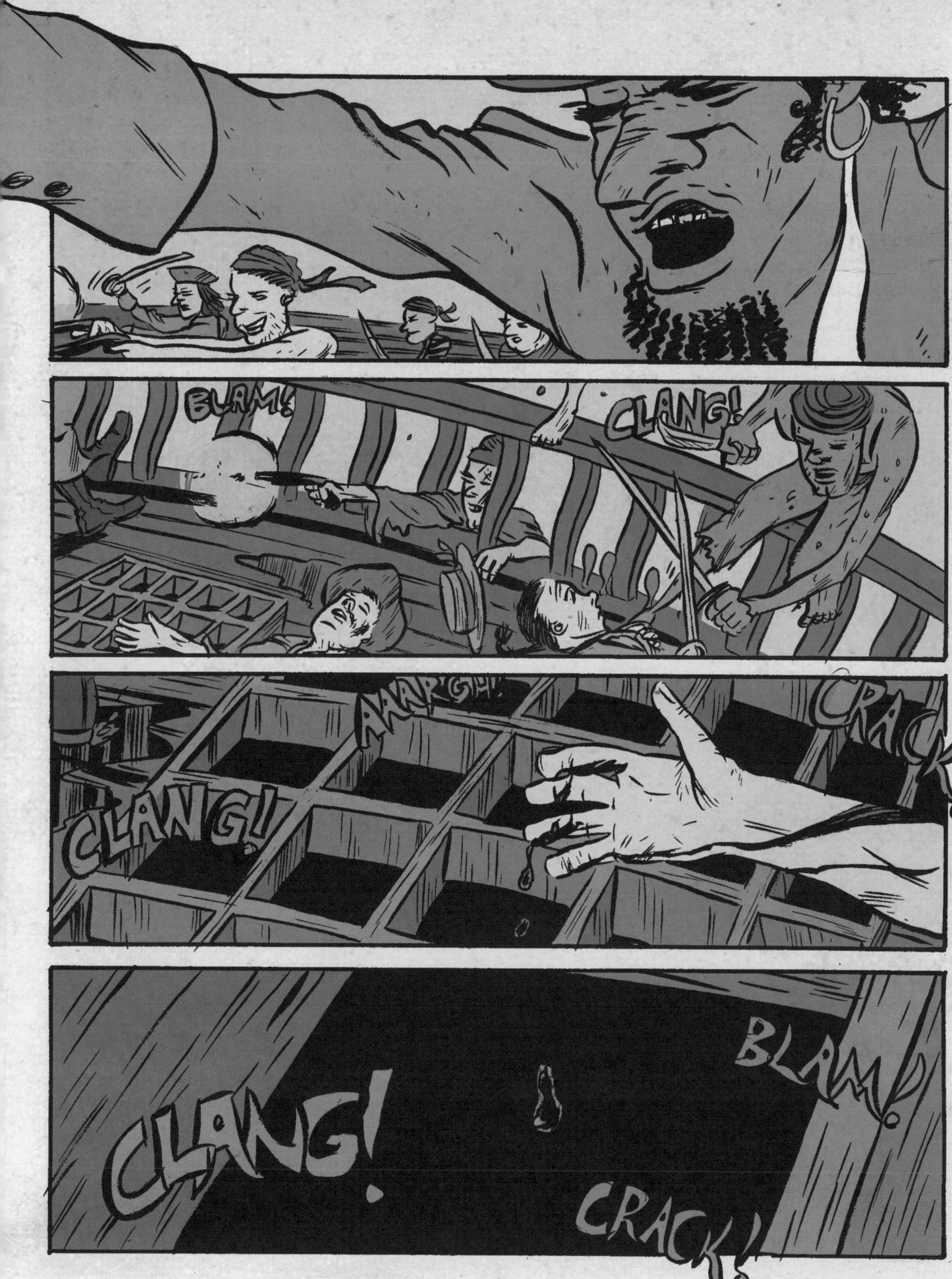
BLAM!
CLANG!
AAARGH!
CRACK!
CLANG!
CLANG!
BLAM!
CRACK!

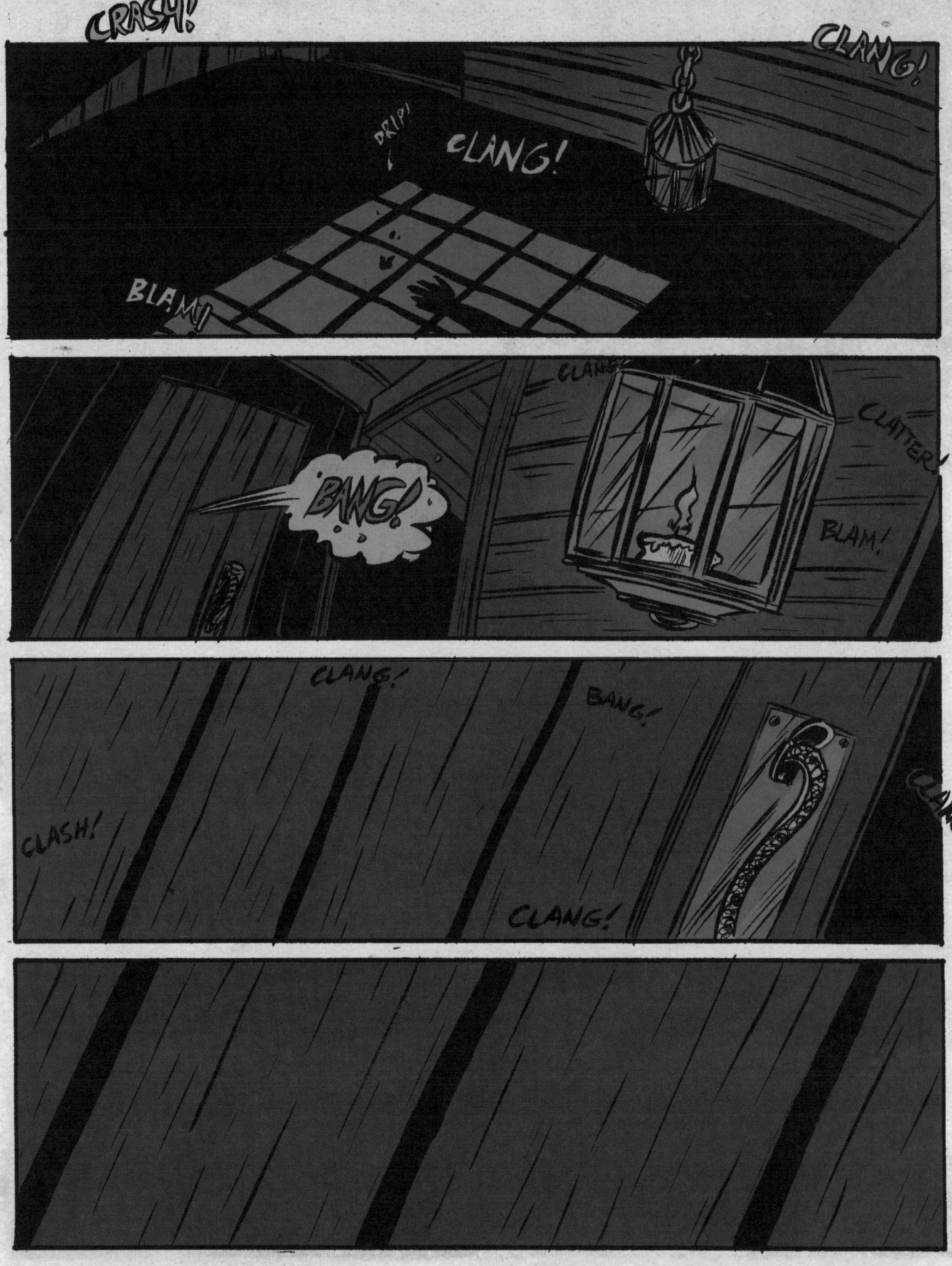
CRASH!
CLANG!
DRIP!
CLANG!
BLAM!
CLANG
BANG!
CLATTER!
BLAM!
CLANG!
BANG!
CLANG!
CLASH!
CLANG!

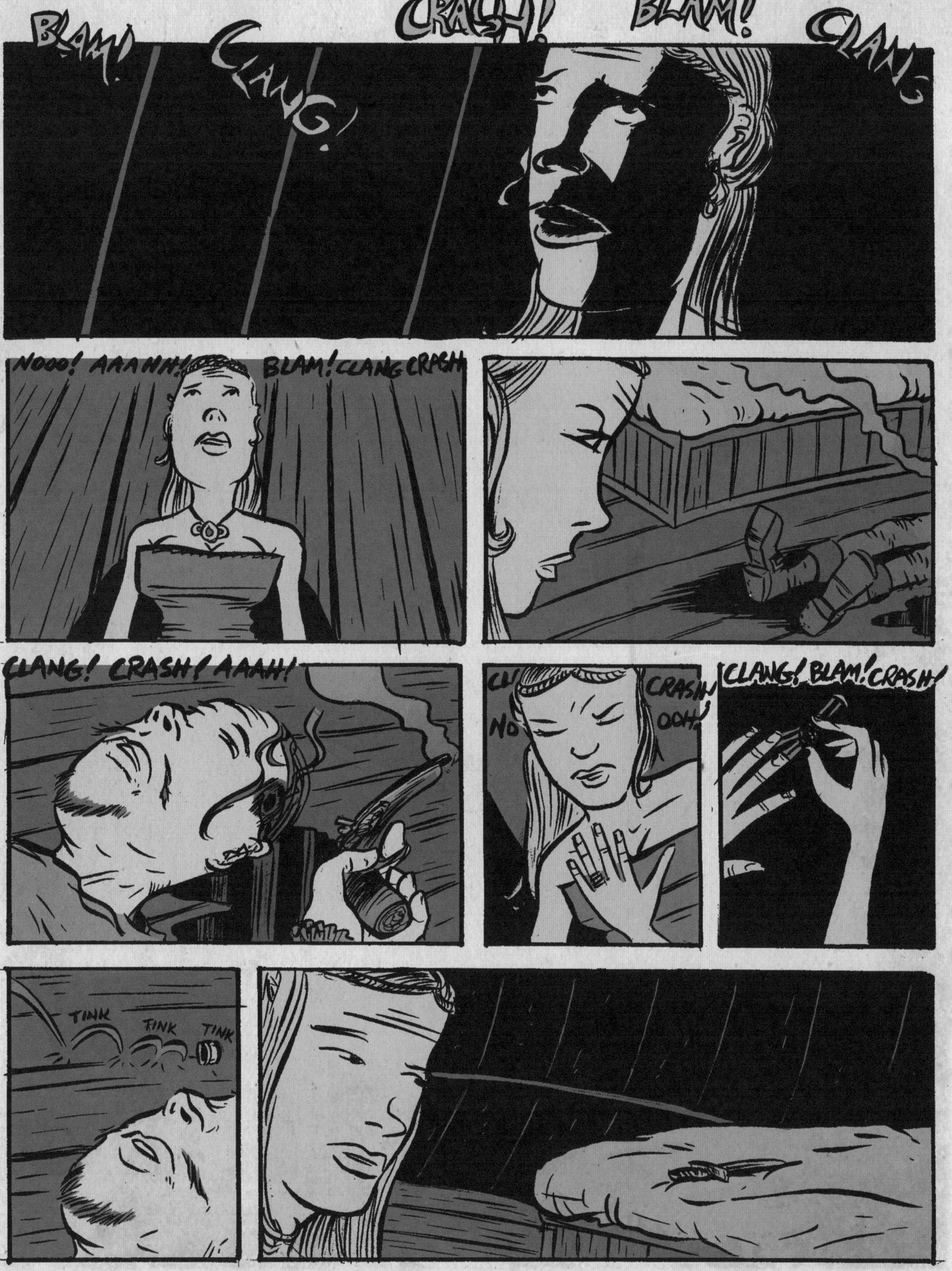
BLAM!
CLANG!
CRASH!
BLAM!
CLANG
NOOO! AAAHH!
BLAM! CLANG CRASH
CLANG! CRASH! AAAH!
CRASH
OOH
CLANG! BLAM! CRASH!
TINK
TINK
TINK

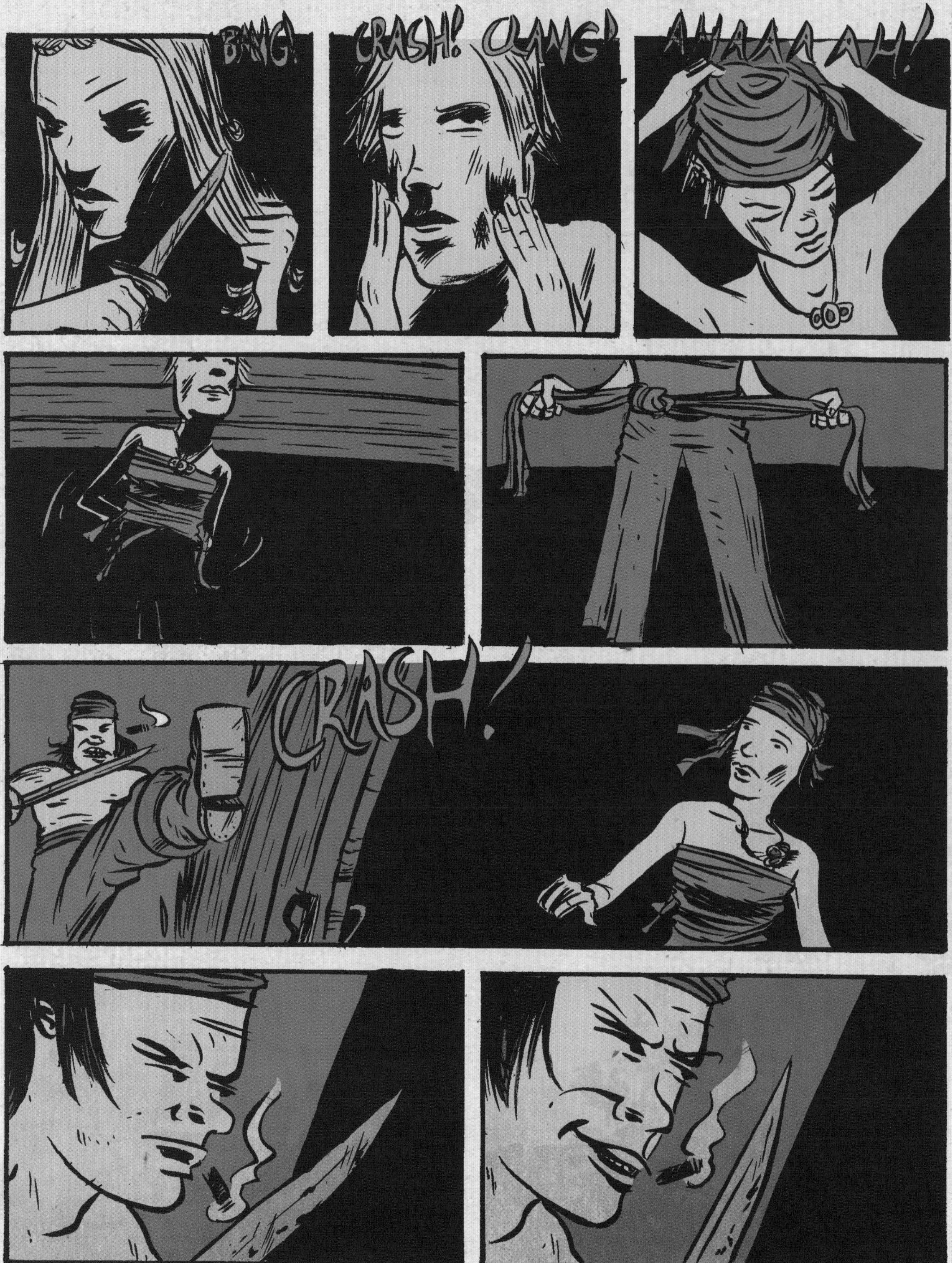
BANG!
CRASH! CLANG!
AHAAAAAH!
CRASH!

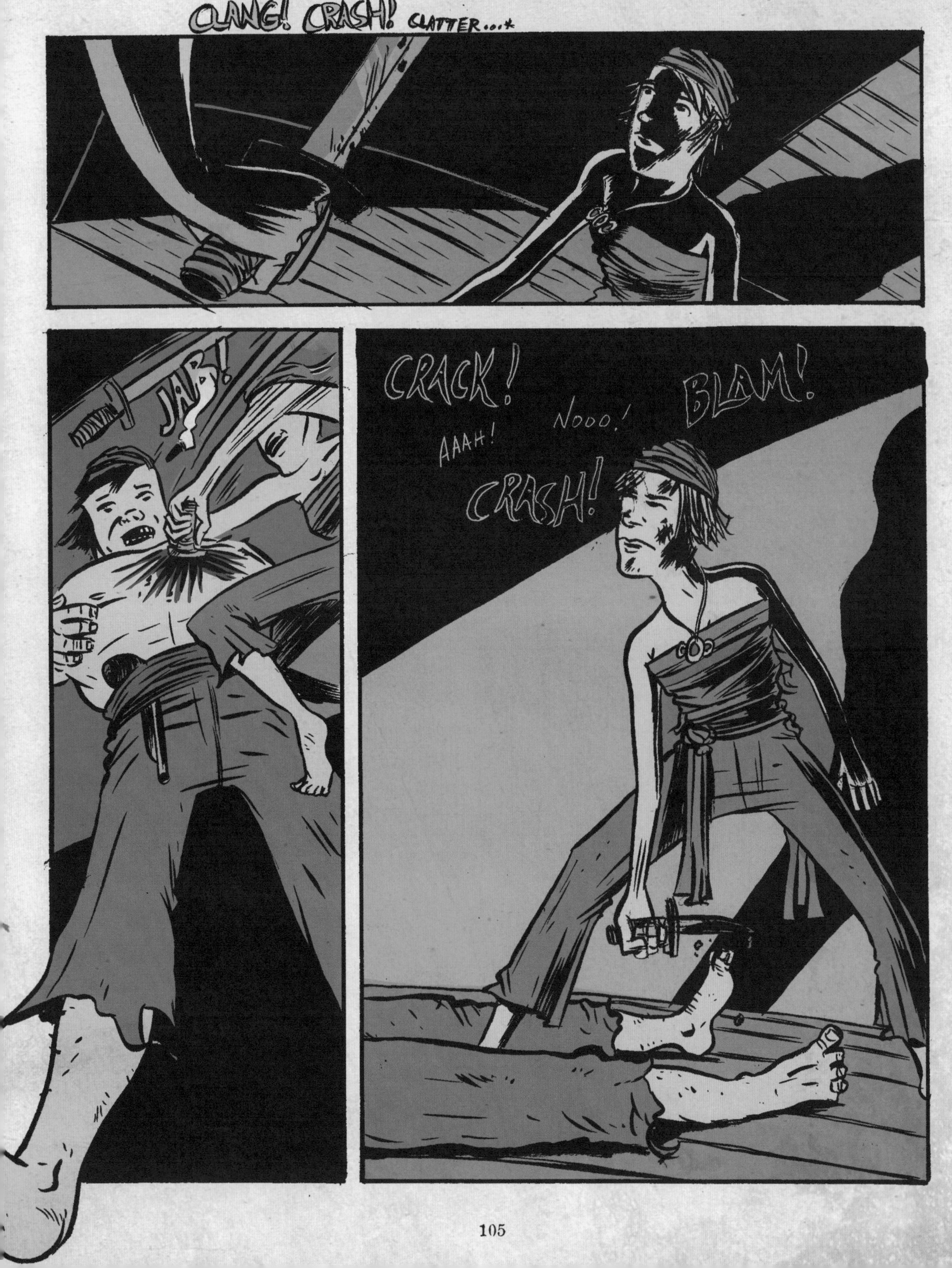
CLANG! CRASH! CLATTER...*
JAB!
CRACK!
AAAH!
NOOO!
BLAM!
CRASH!

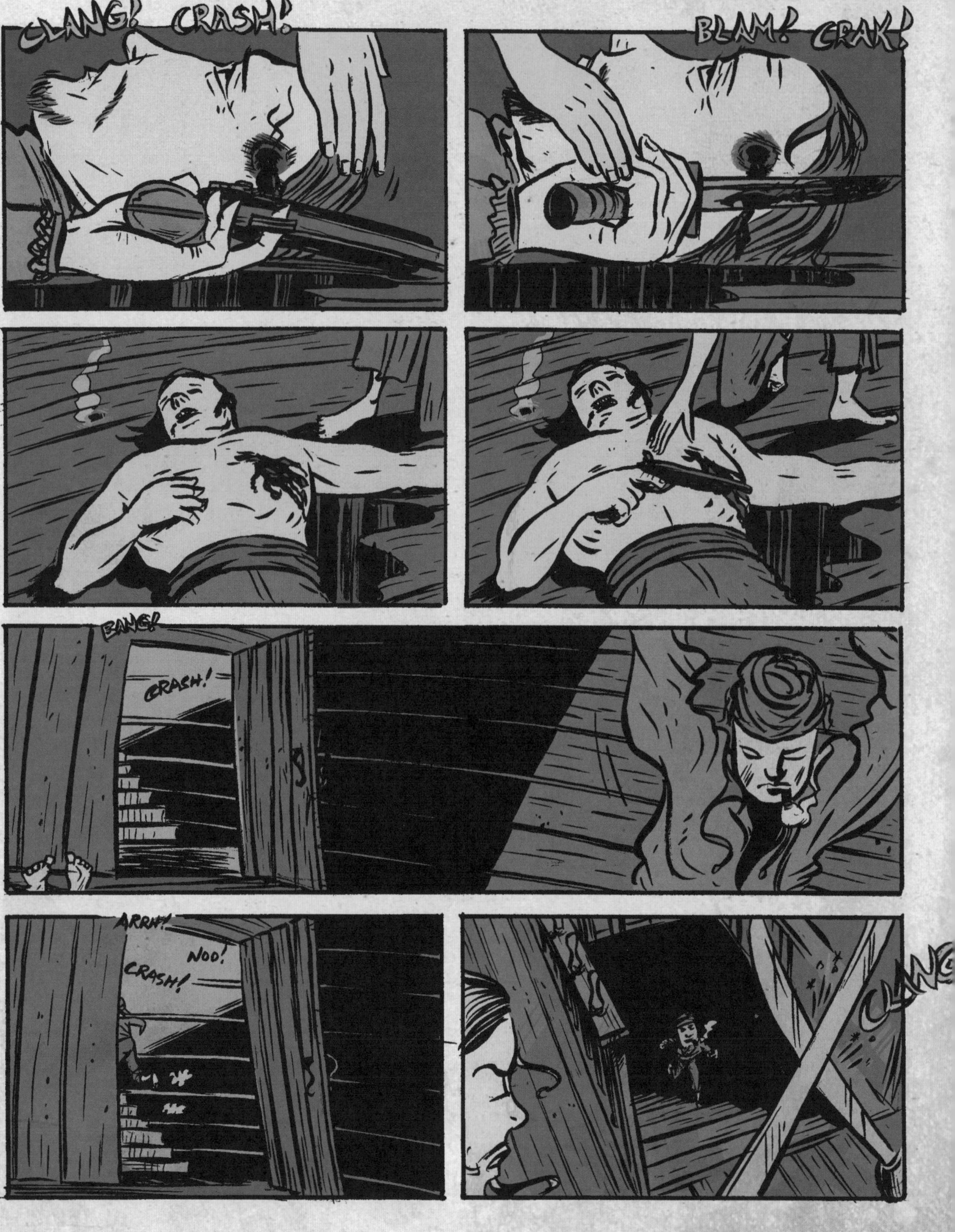
CLANG! CRASH!
BLAM! CRAK!
BANG!
CRASH!
ARRH!
NOO!
CRASH!

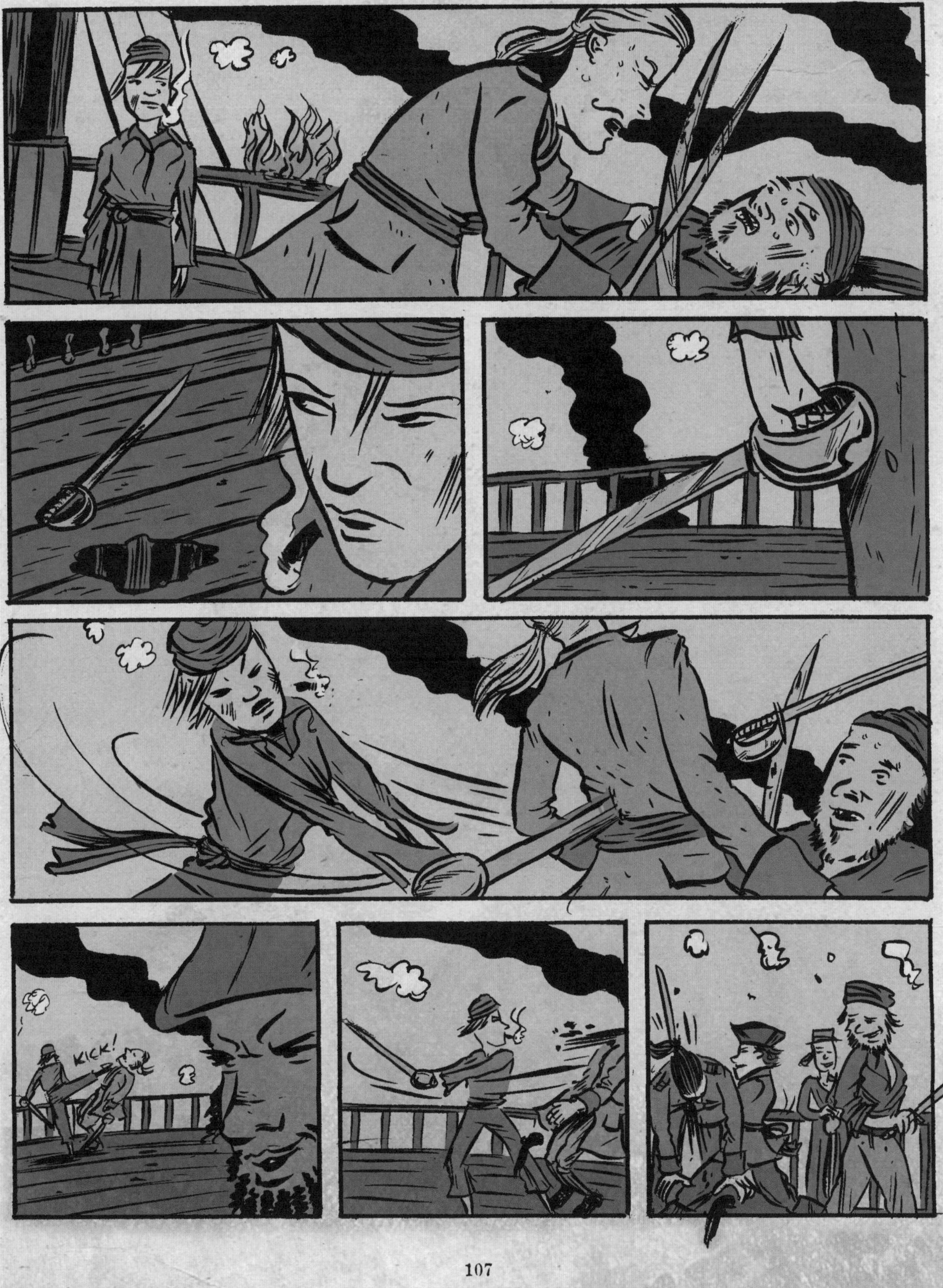
KICK!

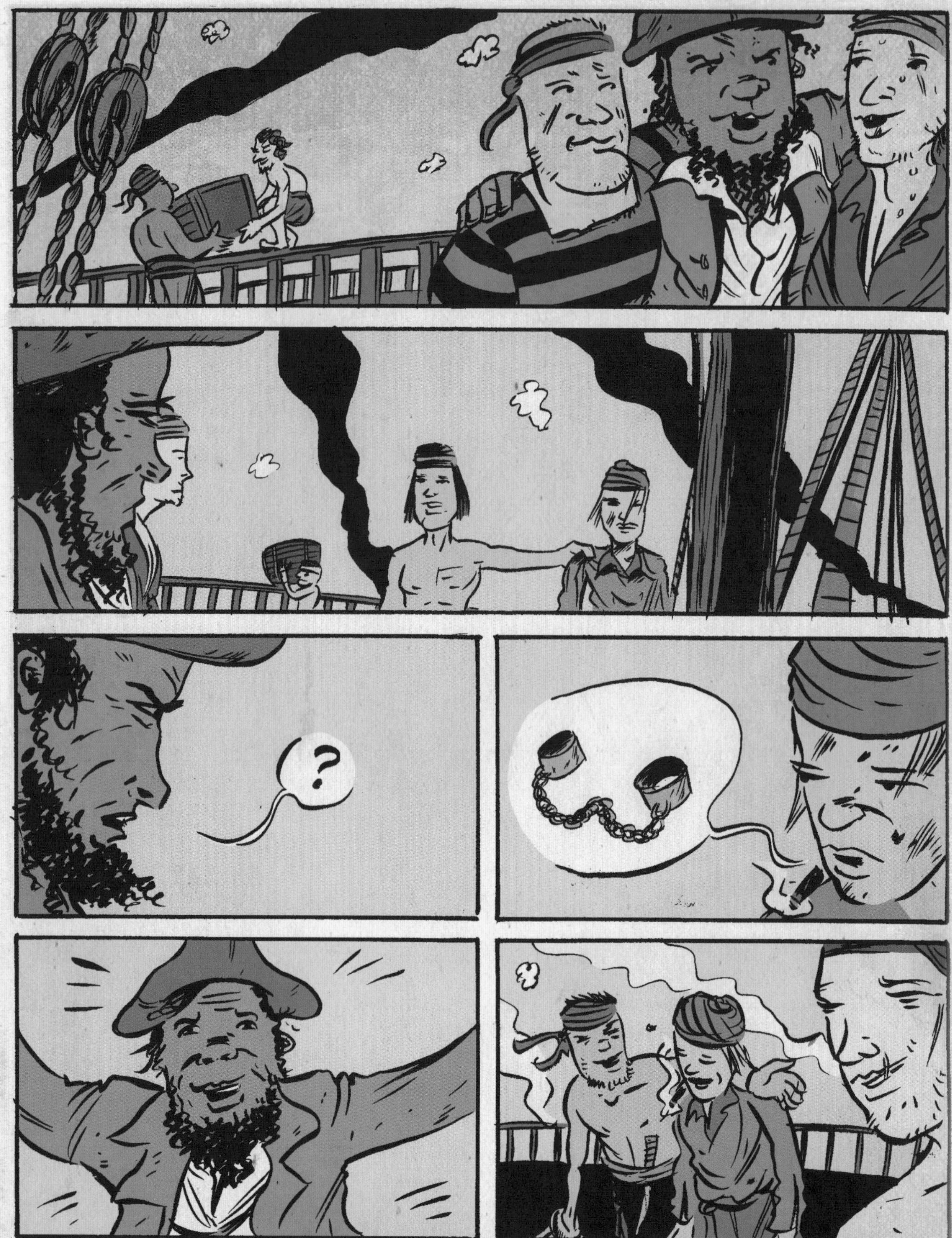
?

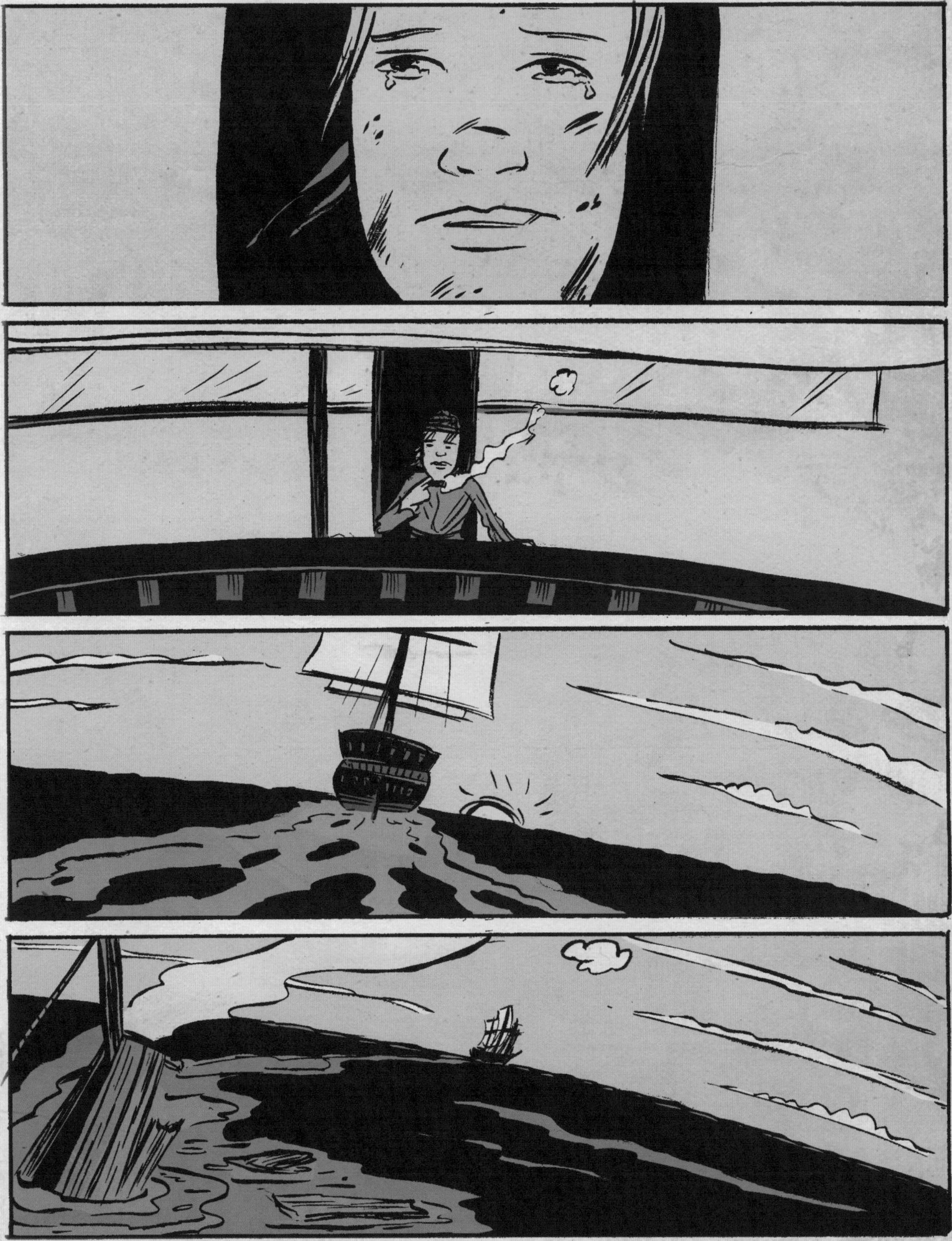

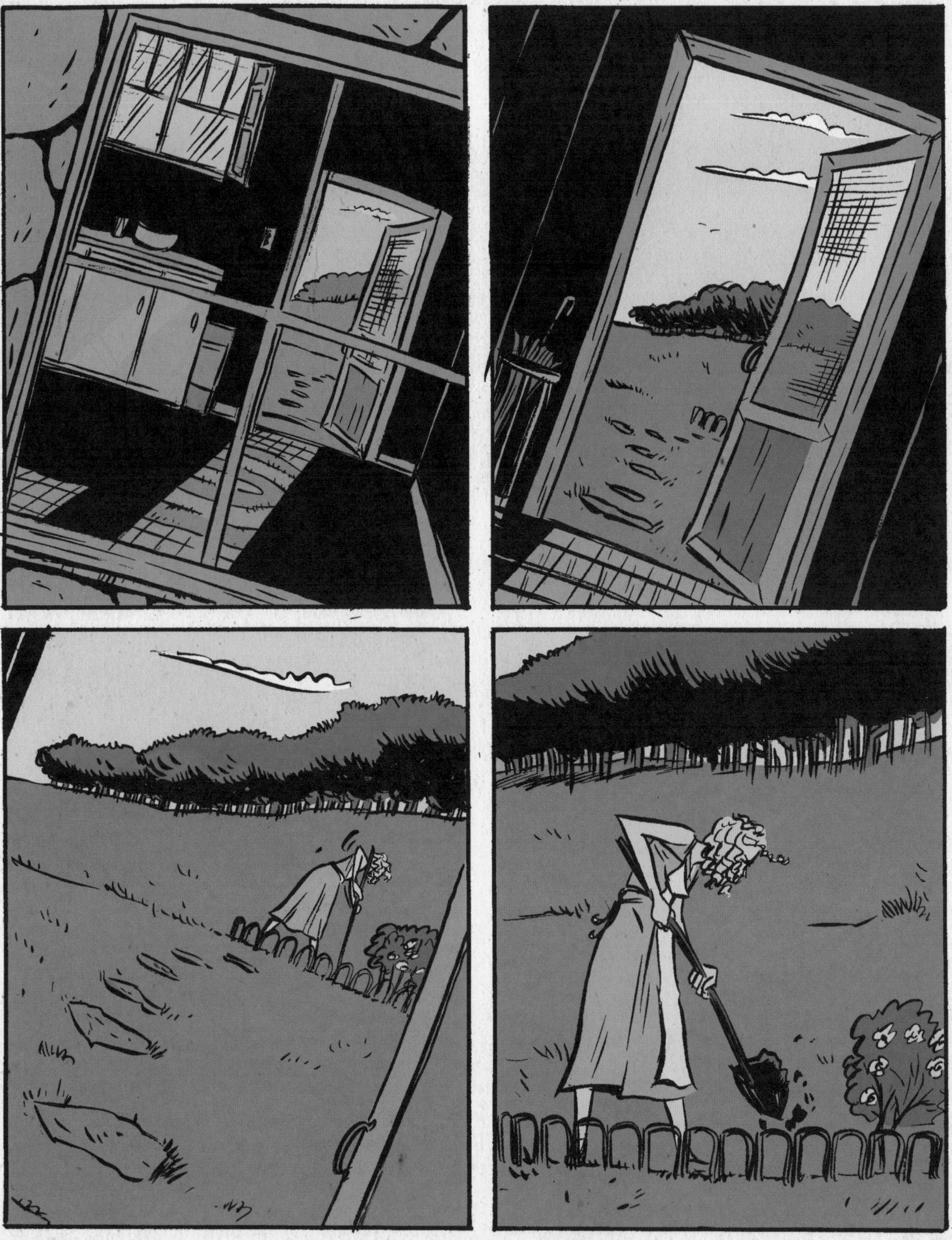

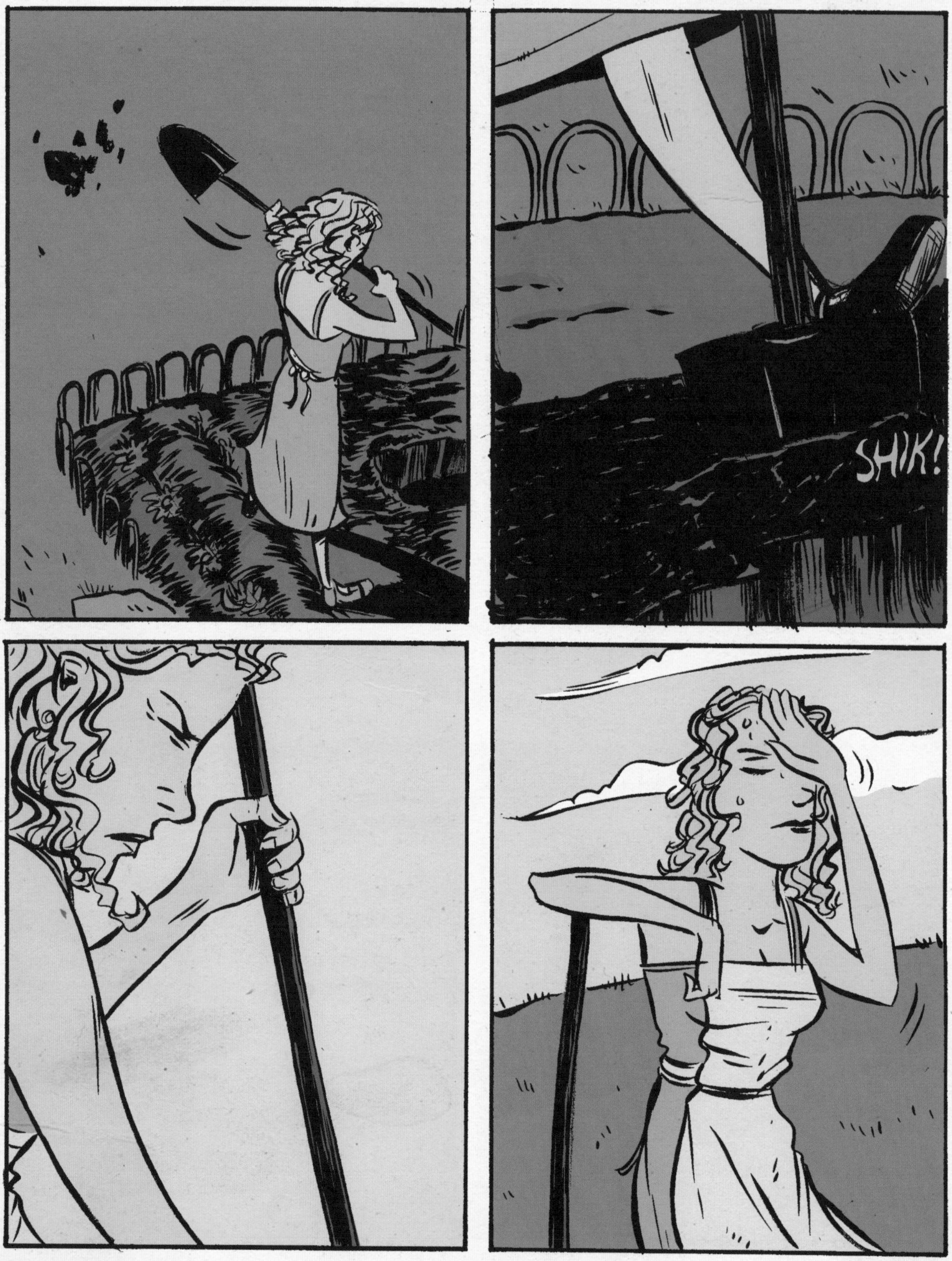
SHIK!

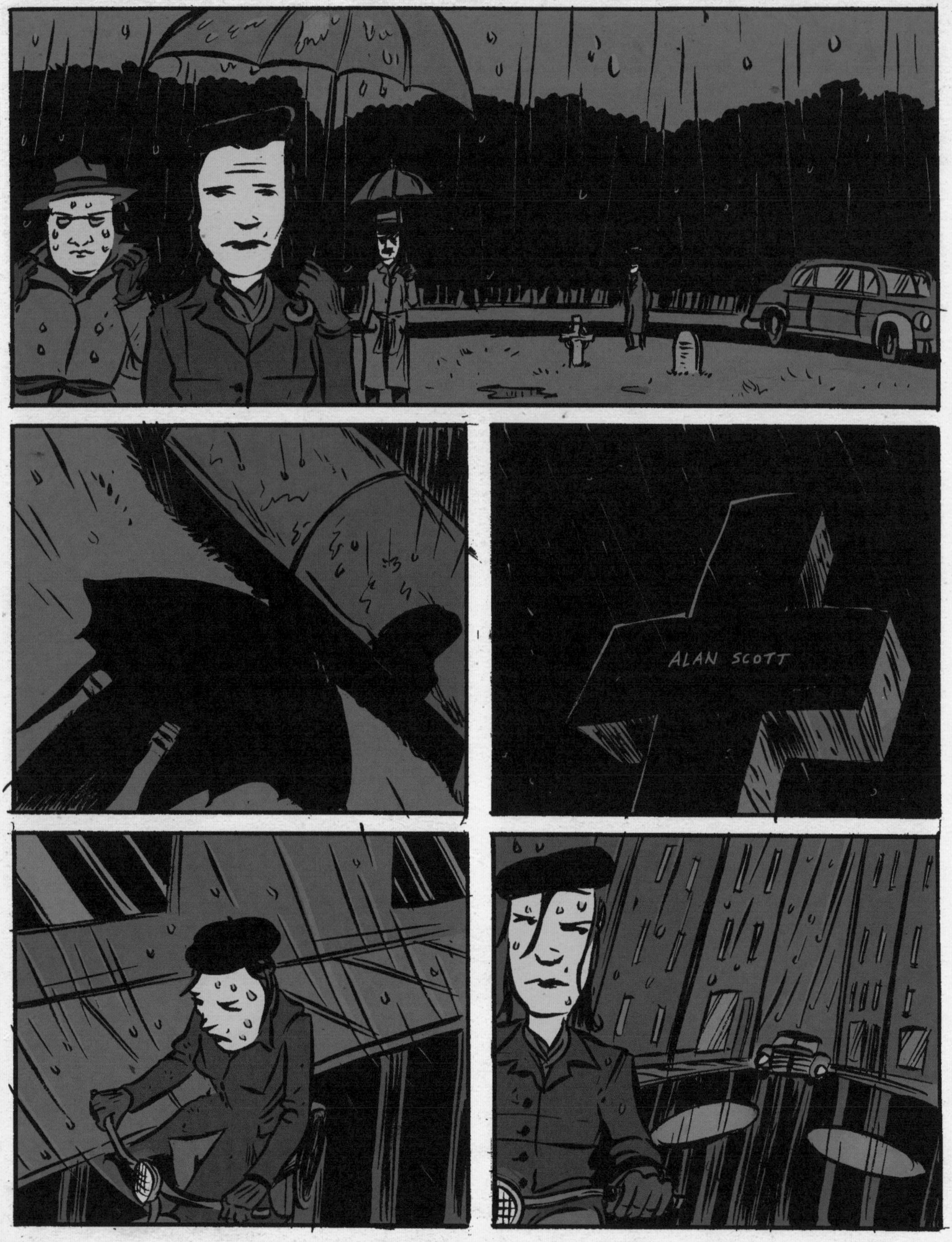
ALAN SCOTT

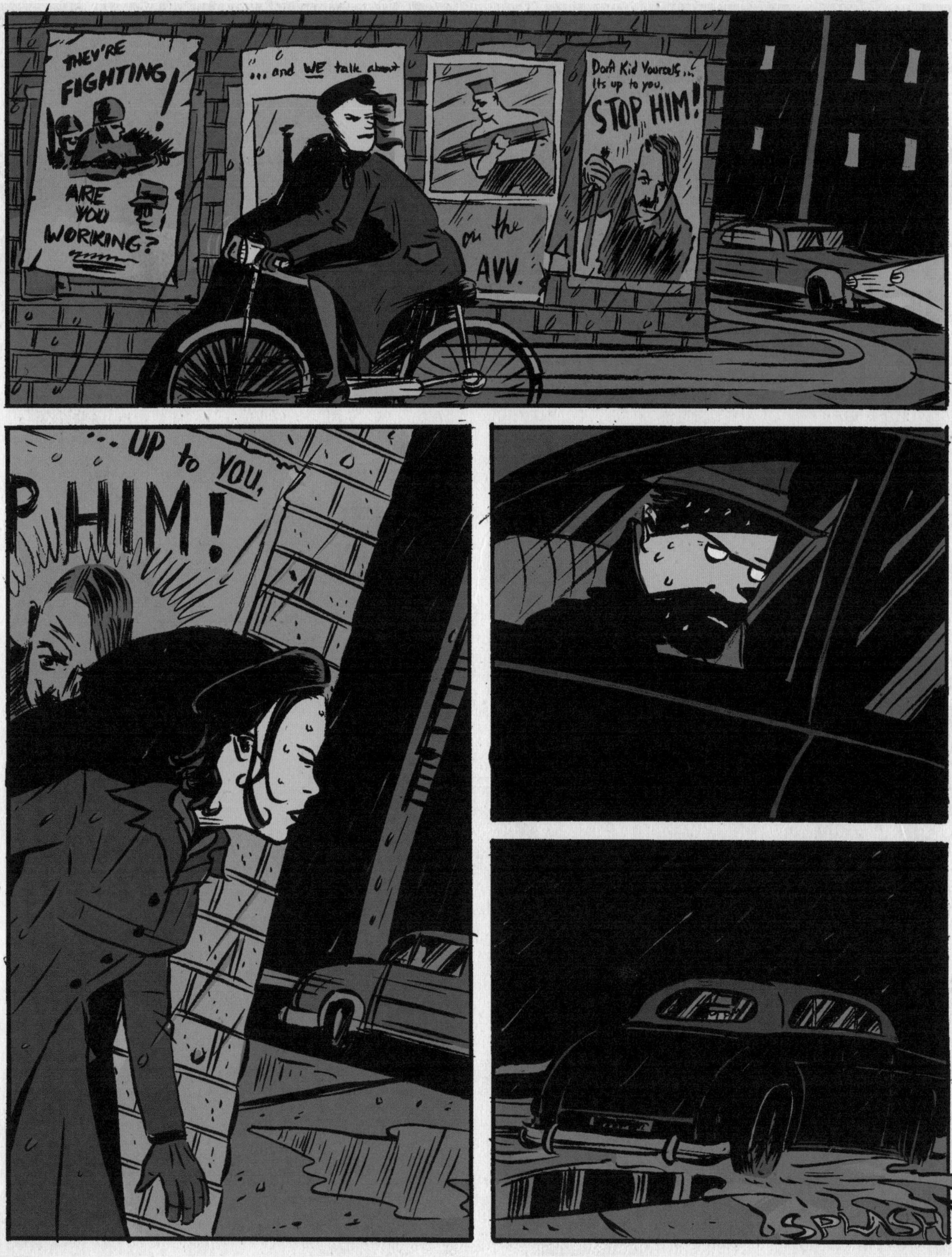
THEY'RE FIGHTING!
ARE YOU WORKING?
... and WE talk about
on the AVV.
Don't Kid Yourself... Its up to you,
STOP HIM!
... UP to YOU,
P HIM!
SPLASH

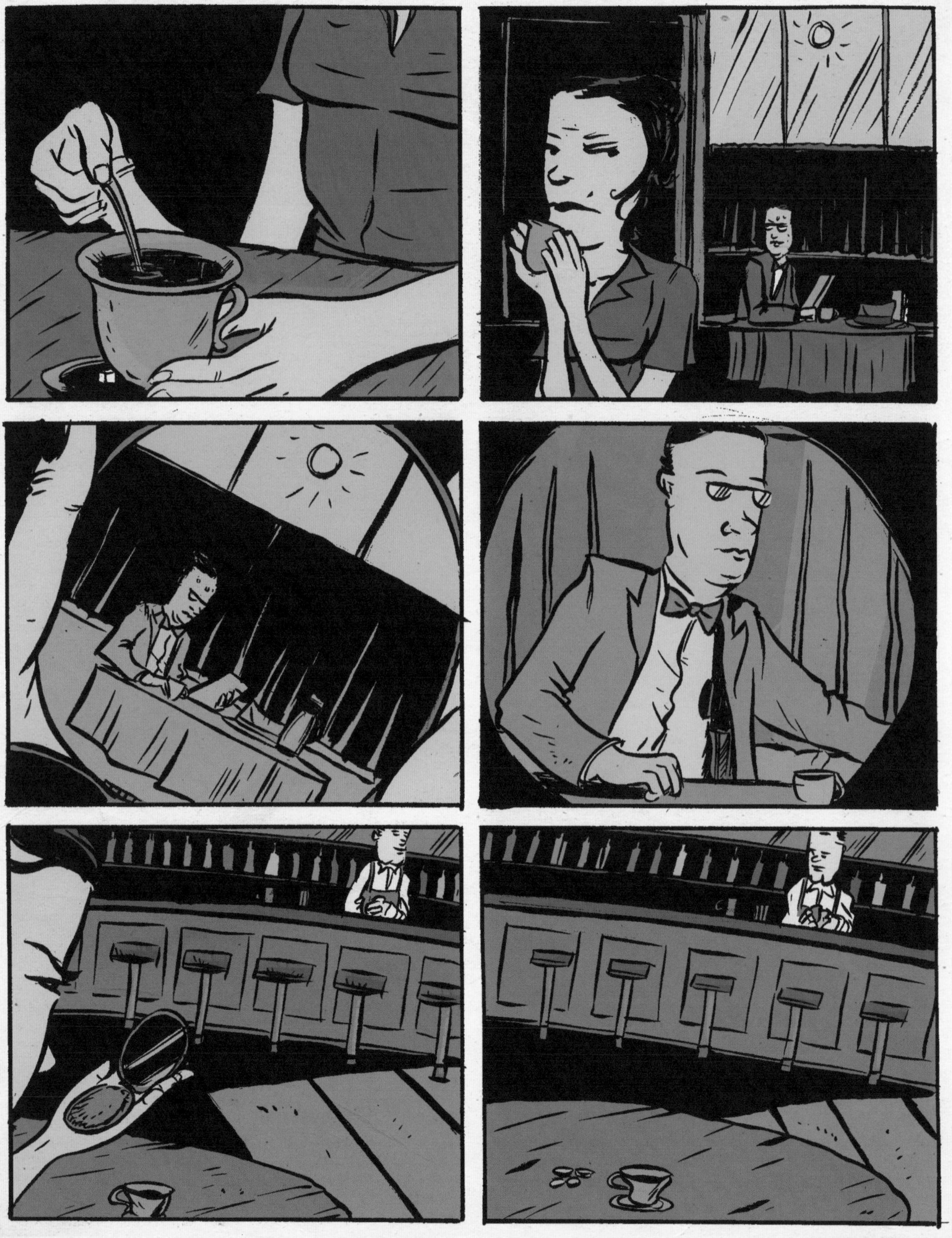

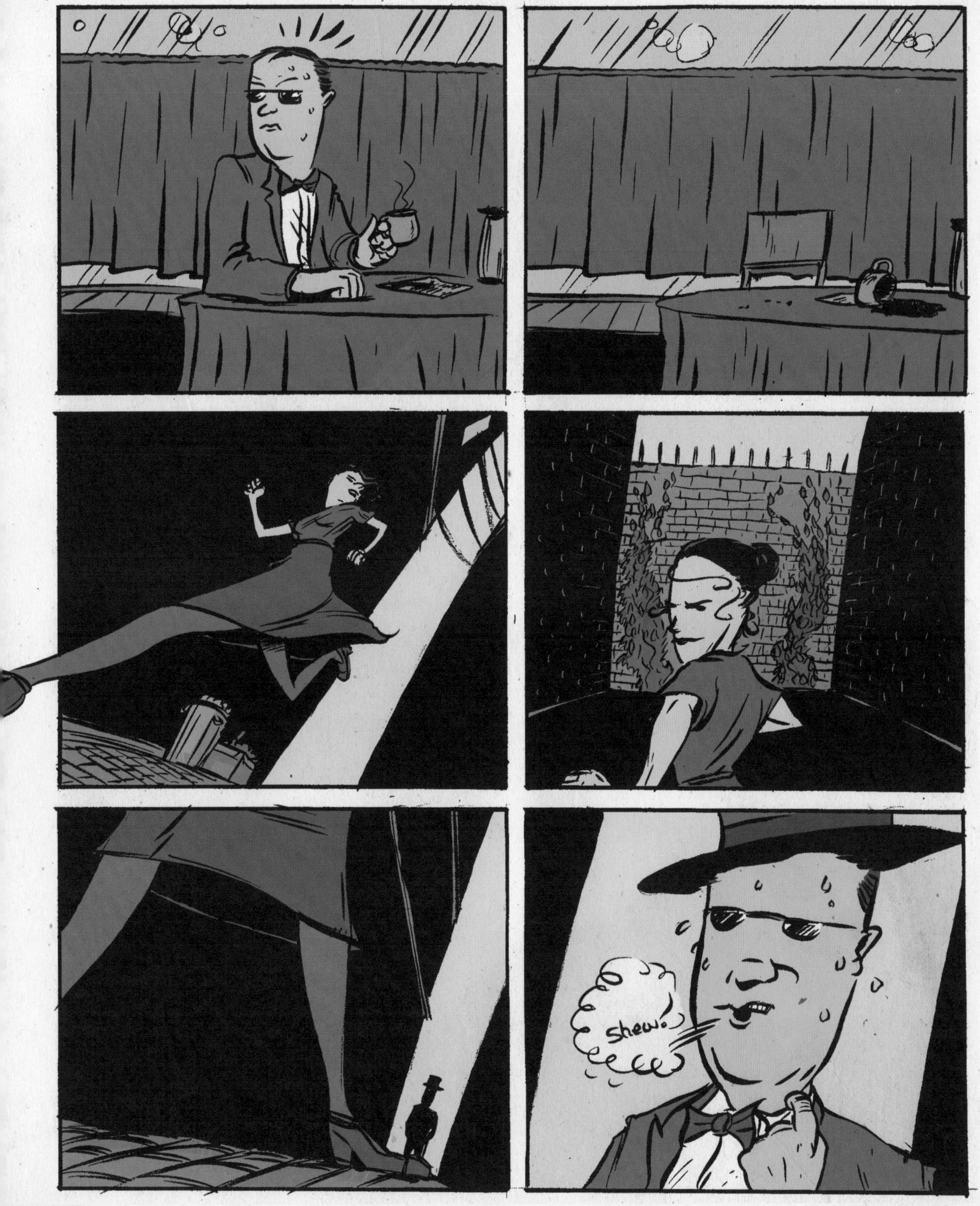
shew.

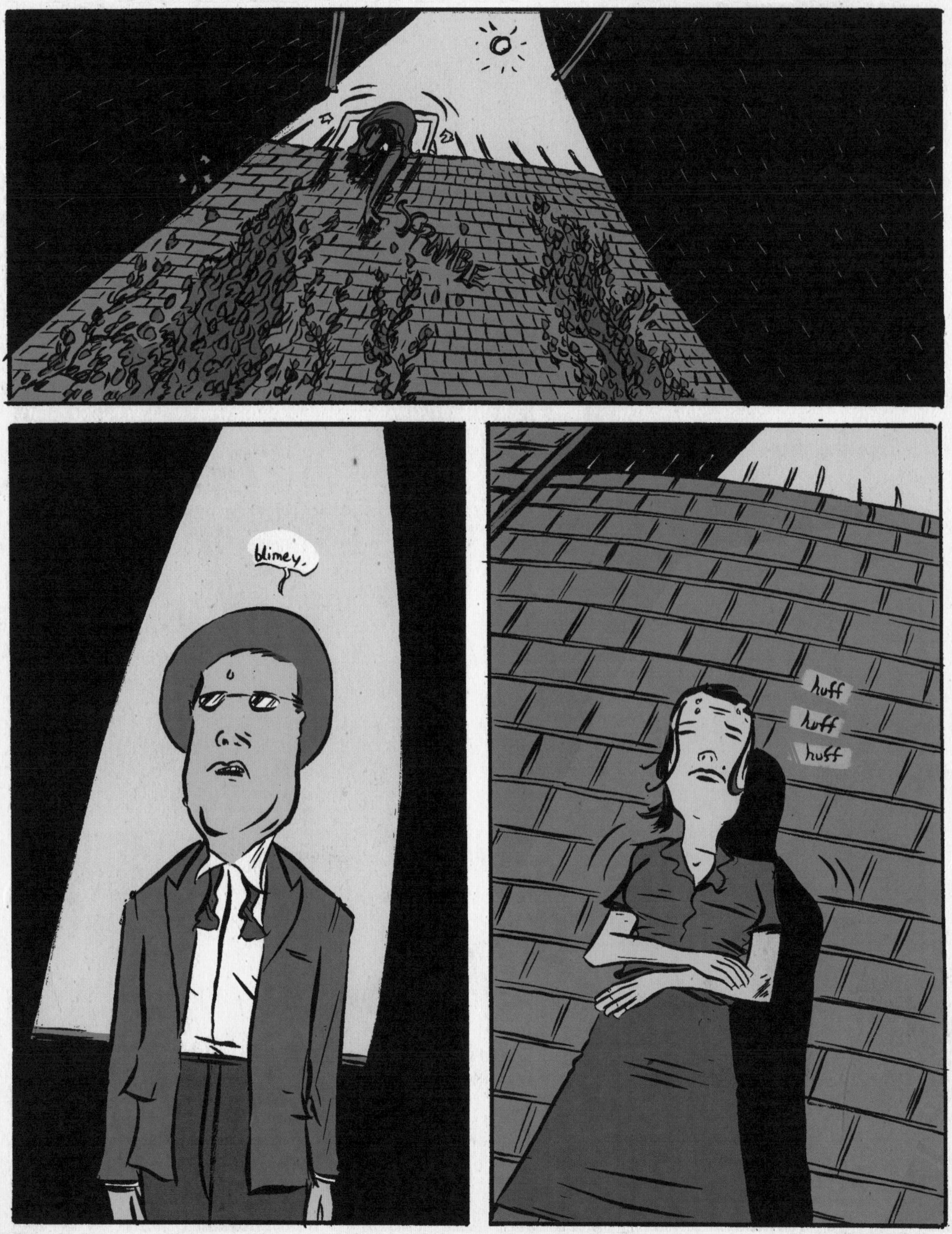
SCRAMBLE
blimey.
huff
huff
huff

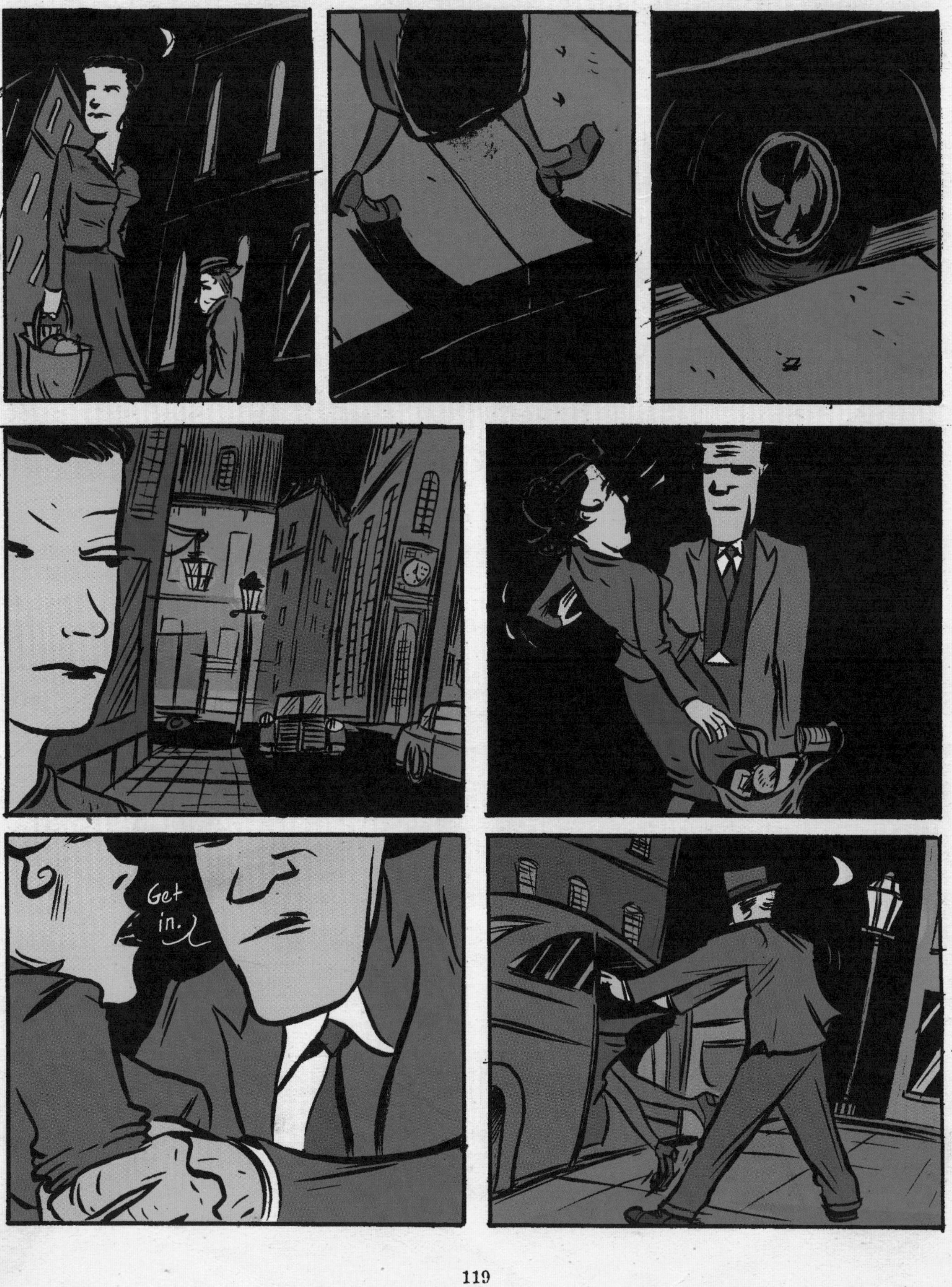
Get in.

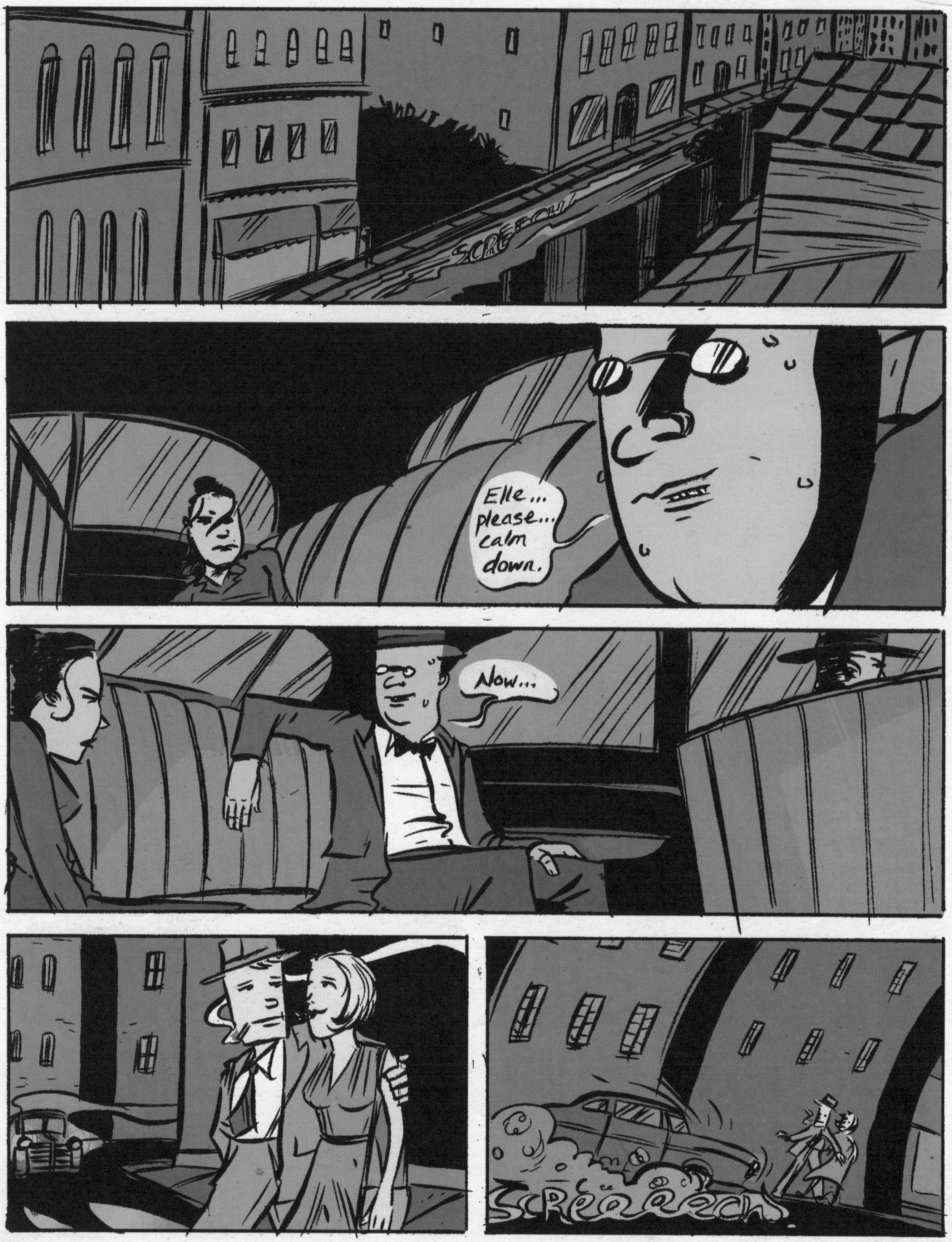
SCREECH!
Elle... please... calm down.
Now...
SCREEEECH

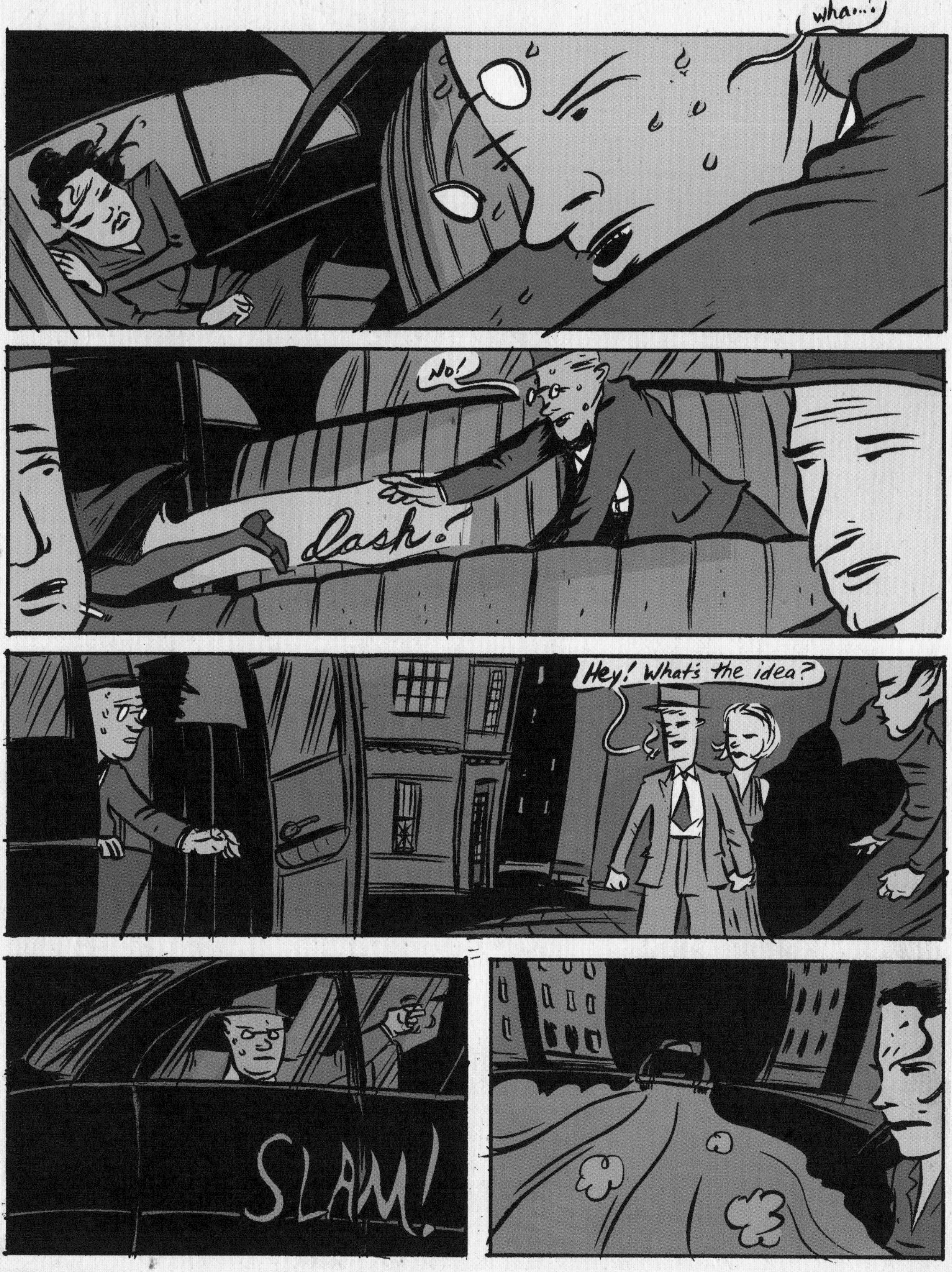
wha...?
No!
dash.
Hey! What's the idea?
SLAM!

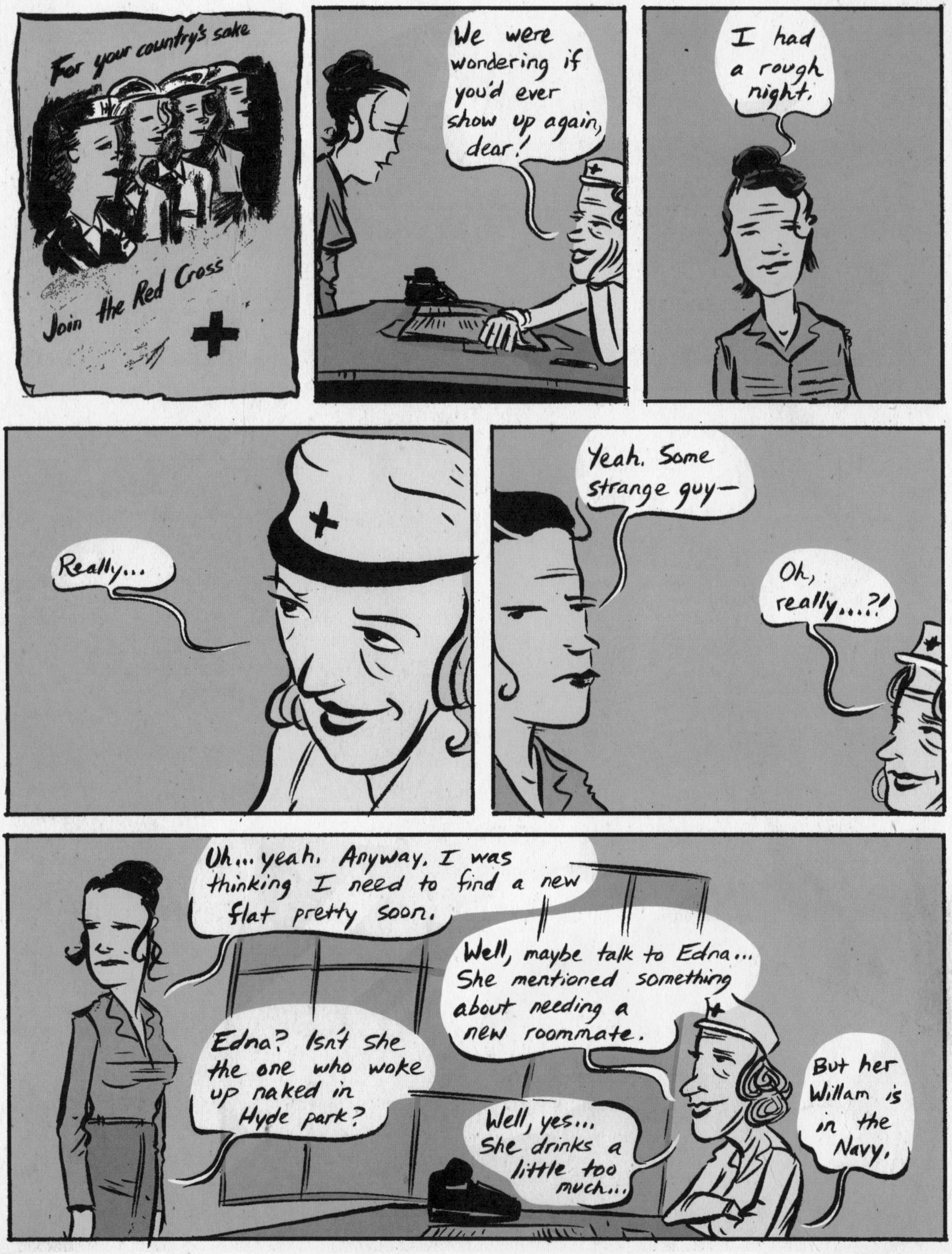
For your country's sake
Join the Red Cross
We were wondering if you'd ever show up again, dear!
I had a rough night.
Really...
Yeah. Some strange guy—
Oh, really...?!
Oh... yeah. Anyway. I was thinking I need to find a new flat pretty soon.
Well, maybe talk to Edna... She mentioned something about needing a new roommate.
Edna? Isn't she the one who woke up naked in Hyde park?
Well, yes... She drinks a little too much...
But her Willam is in the Navy.

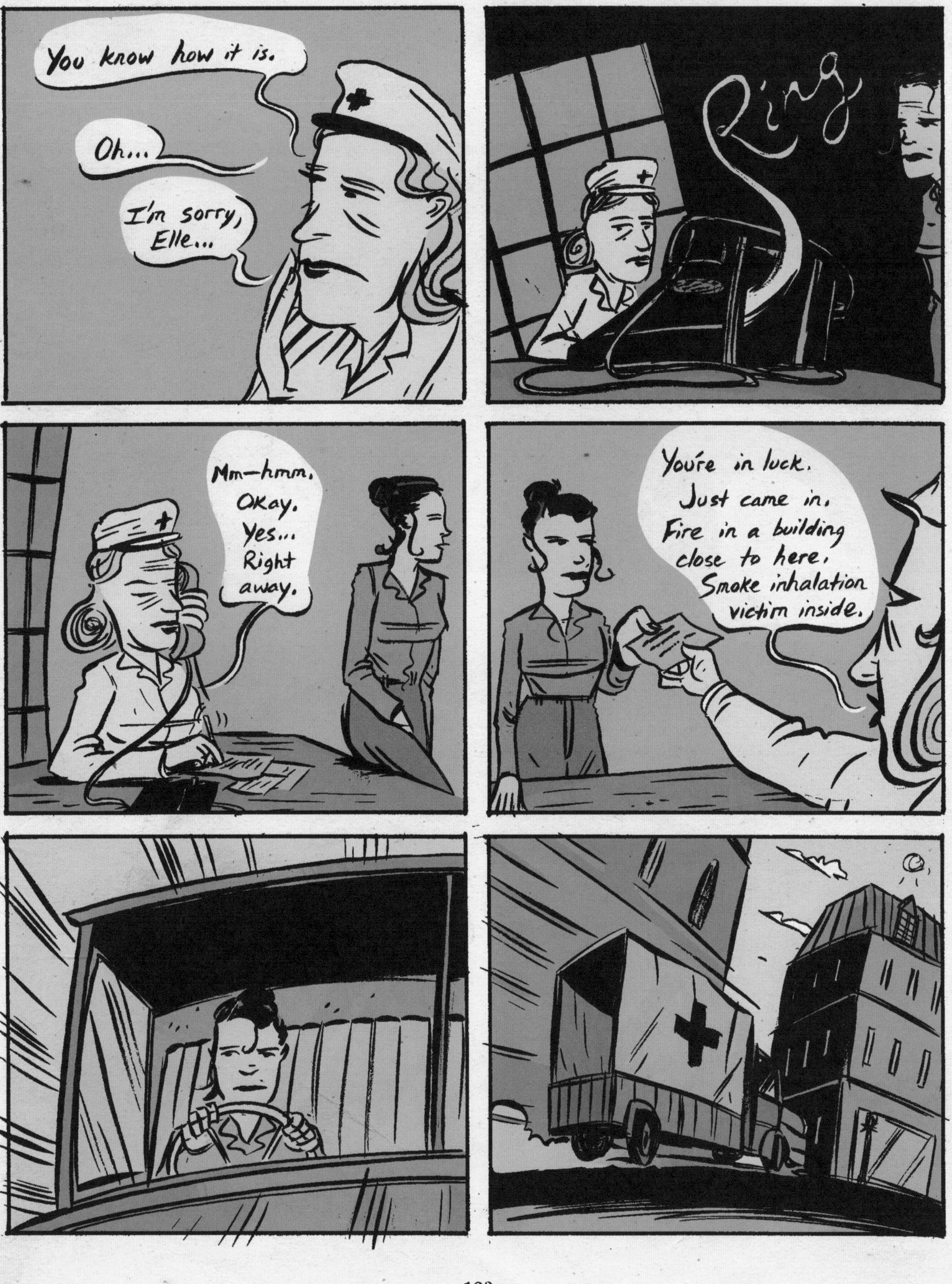
You know how it is.
Oh...
I'm sorry, Elle...
Ring
Mm-hmm. Okay. Yes... Right away.
You're in luck. Just came in. Fire in a building close to here. Smoke inhalation victim inside.

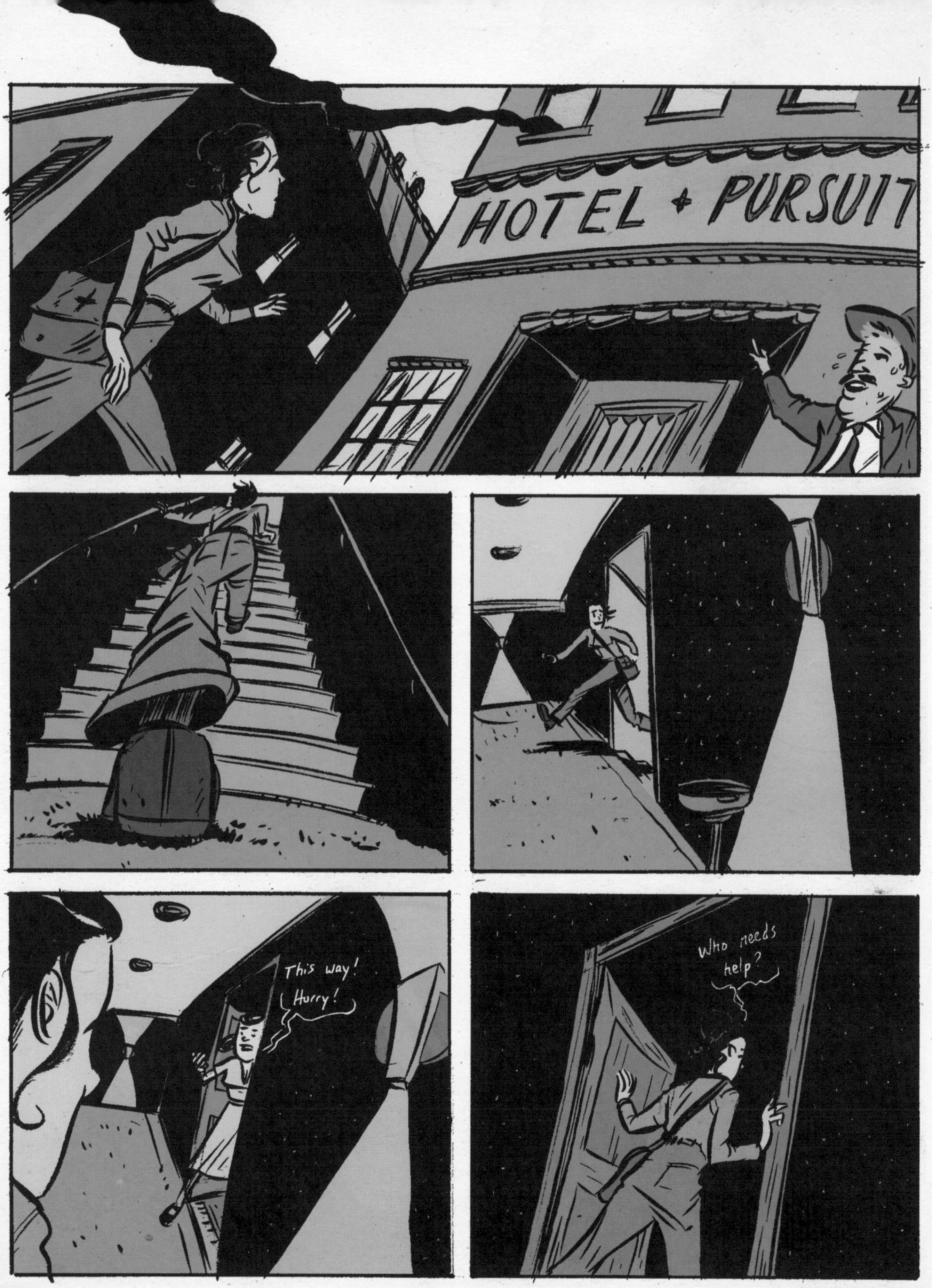
HOTEL + PURSUIT
This way! Hurry!
Who needs help?

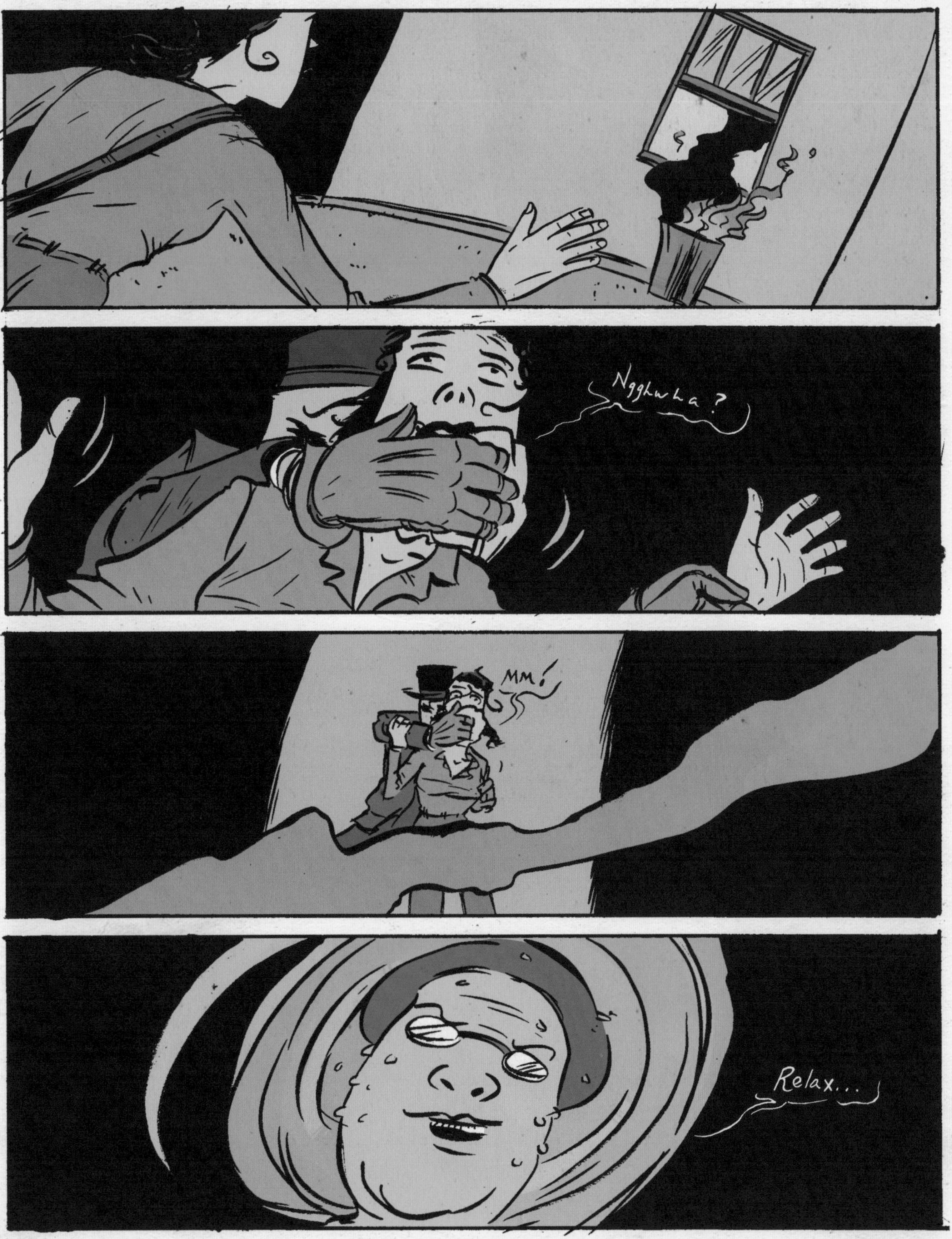
Ngghwha?
MM!
Relax...

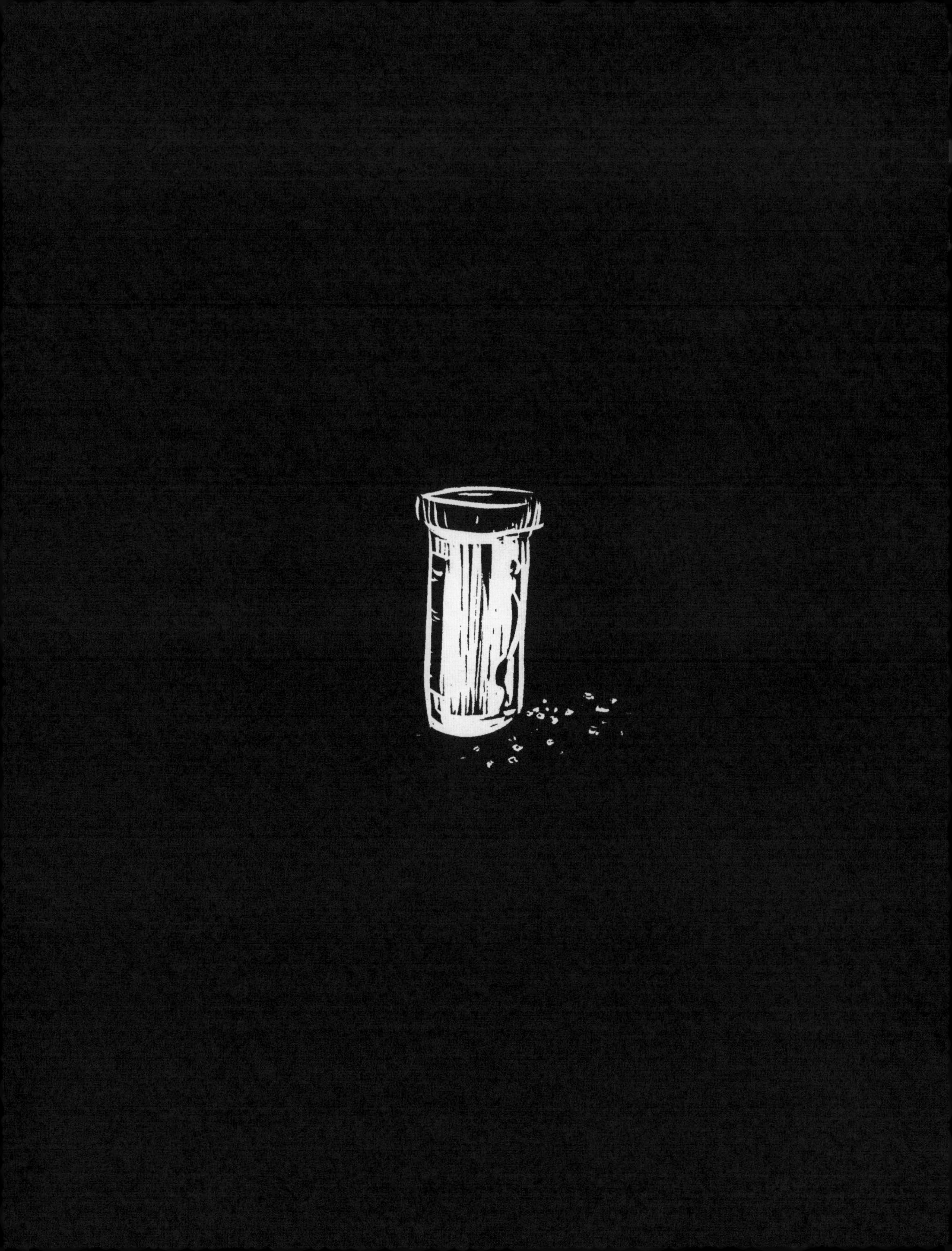

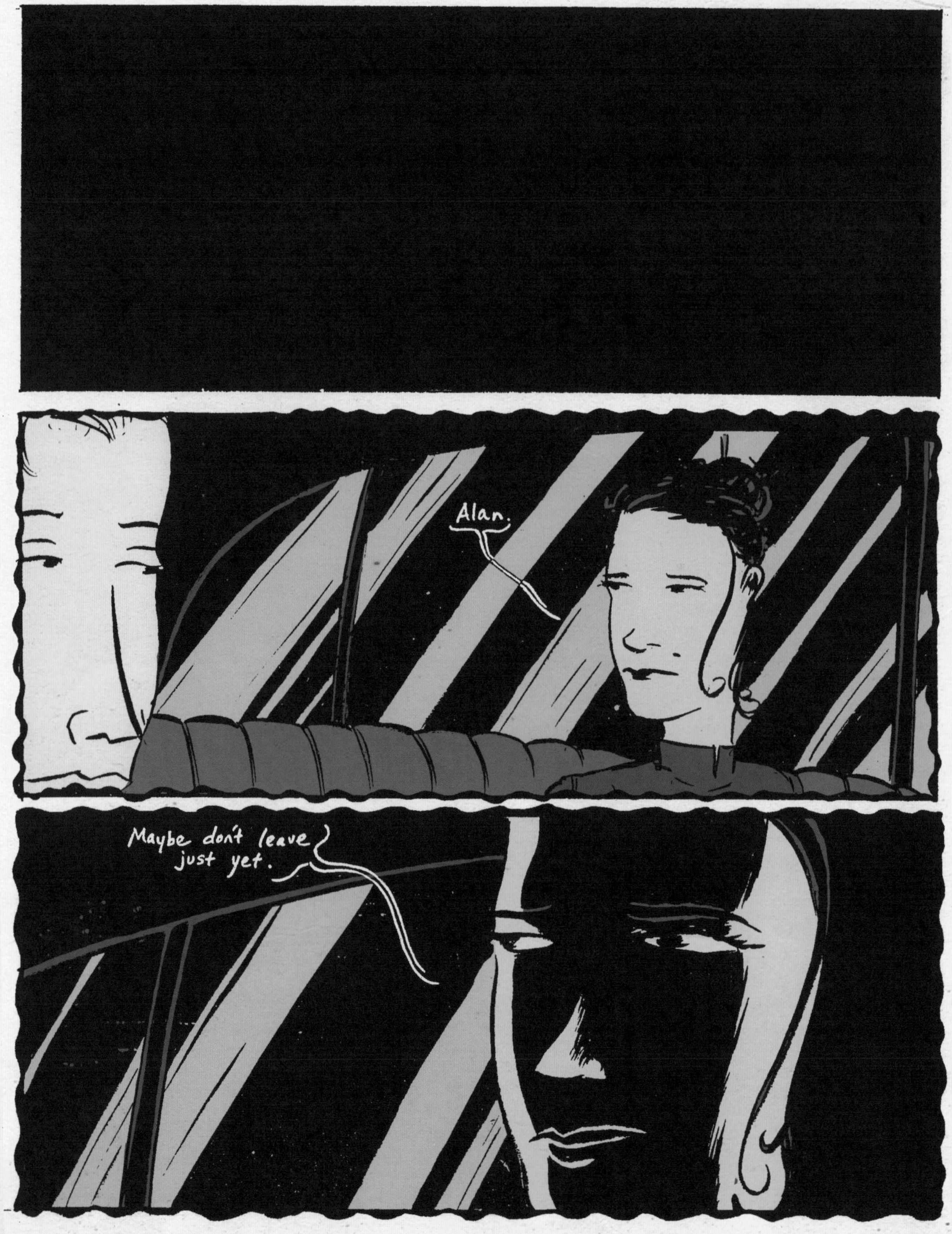
Alan.
Maybe don't leave just yet.

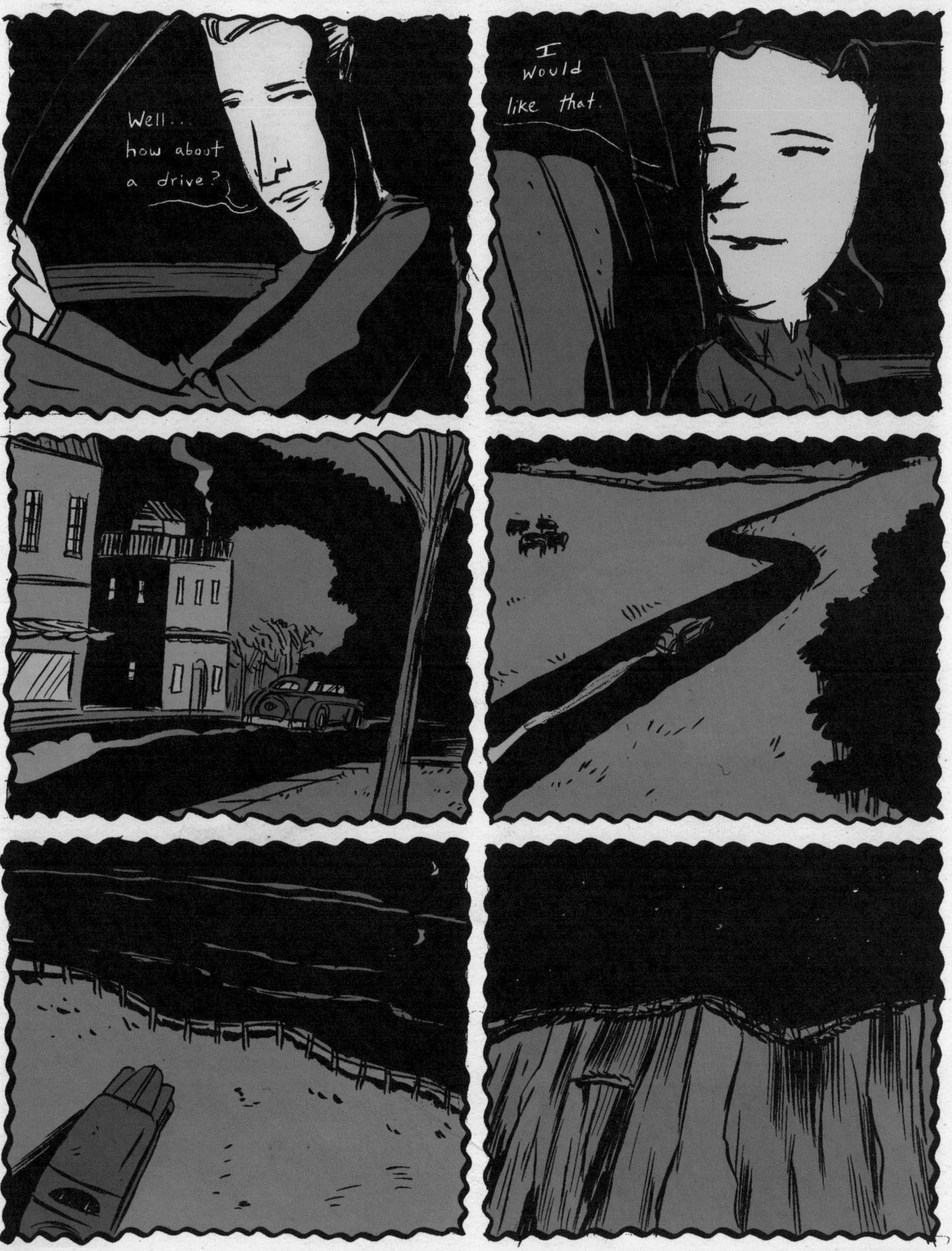
Well...
how about
a drive?
I
would
like that.

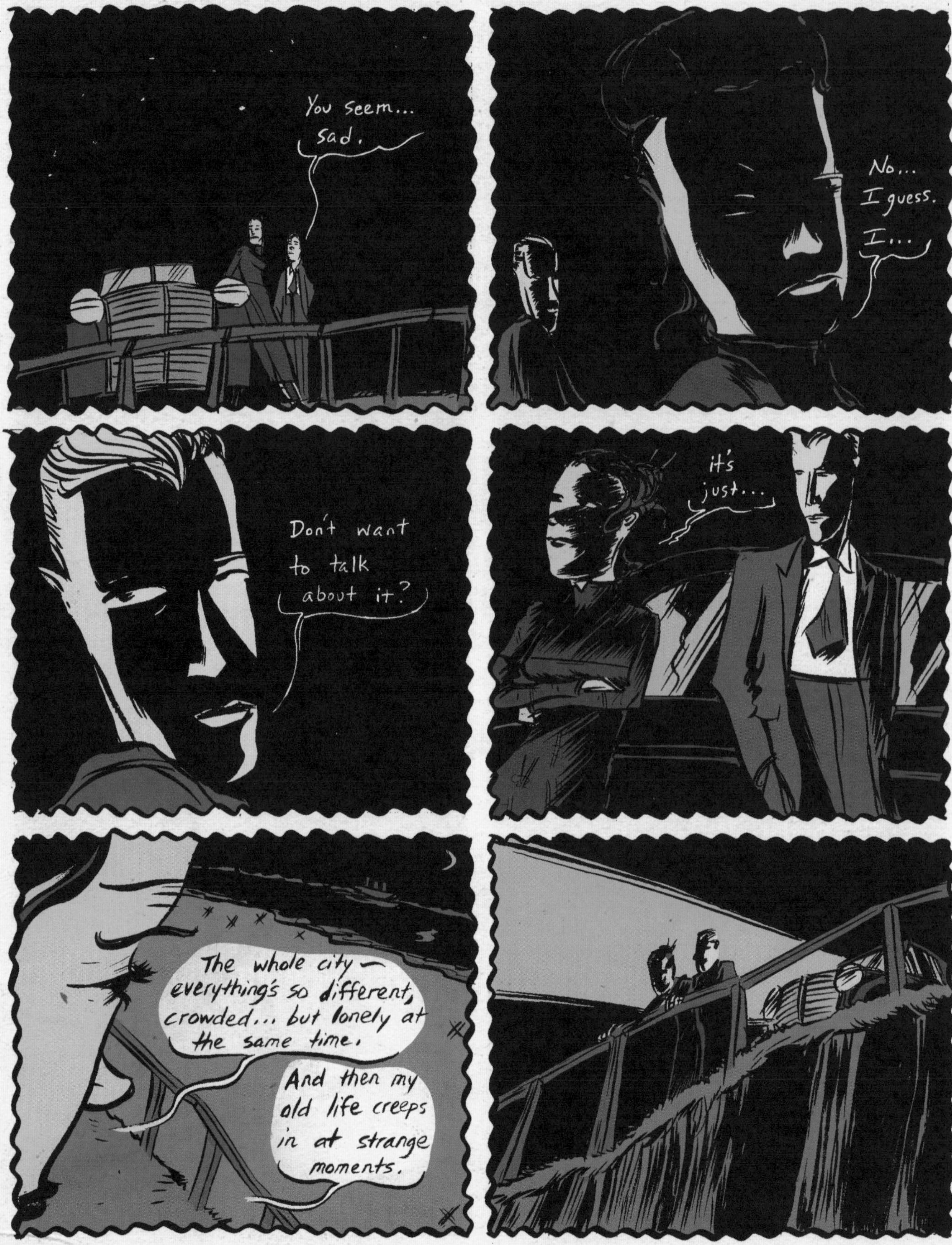

You seem... sad.
No... I guess. I...
Don't want to talk about it?
it's just...
The whole city— everything's so different, crowded... but lonely at the same time.
And then my old life creeps in at strange moments.

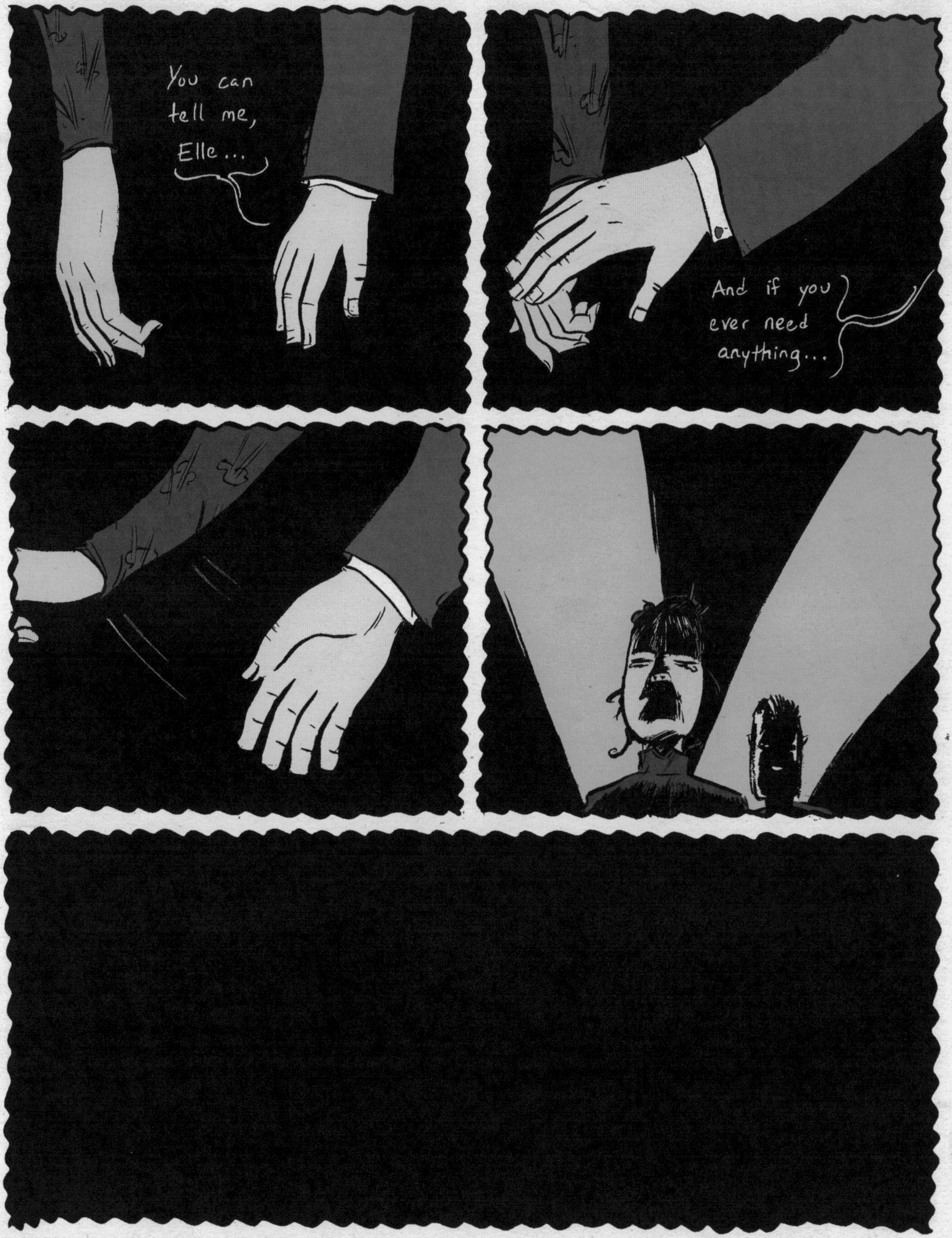
You can tell me, Elle...
And if you ever need anything...

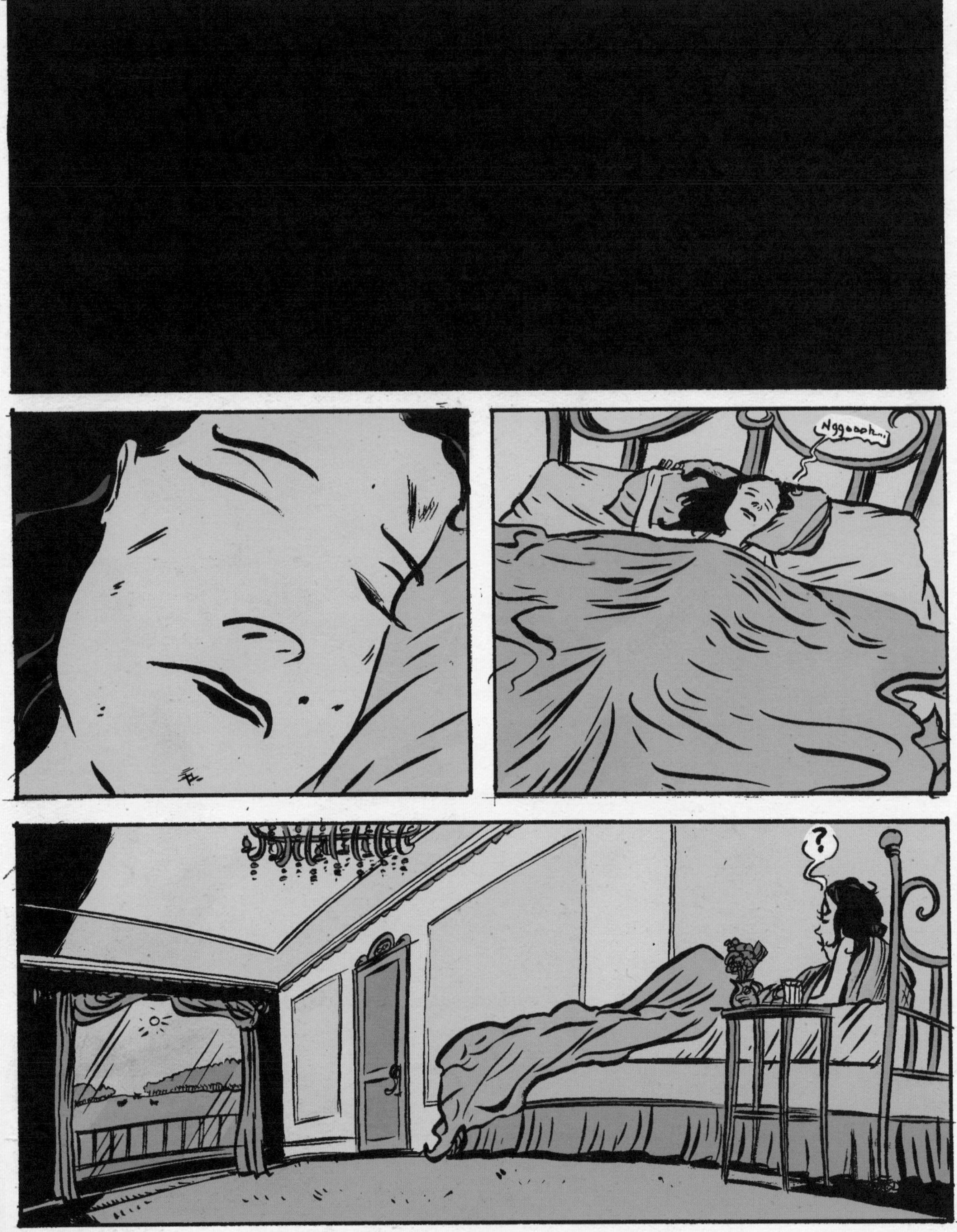
Nggoooh...
?

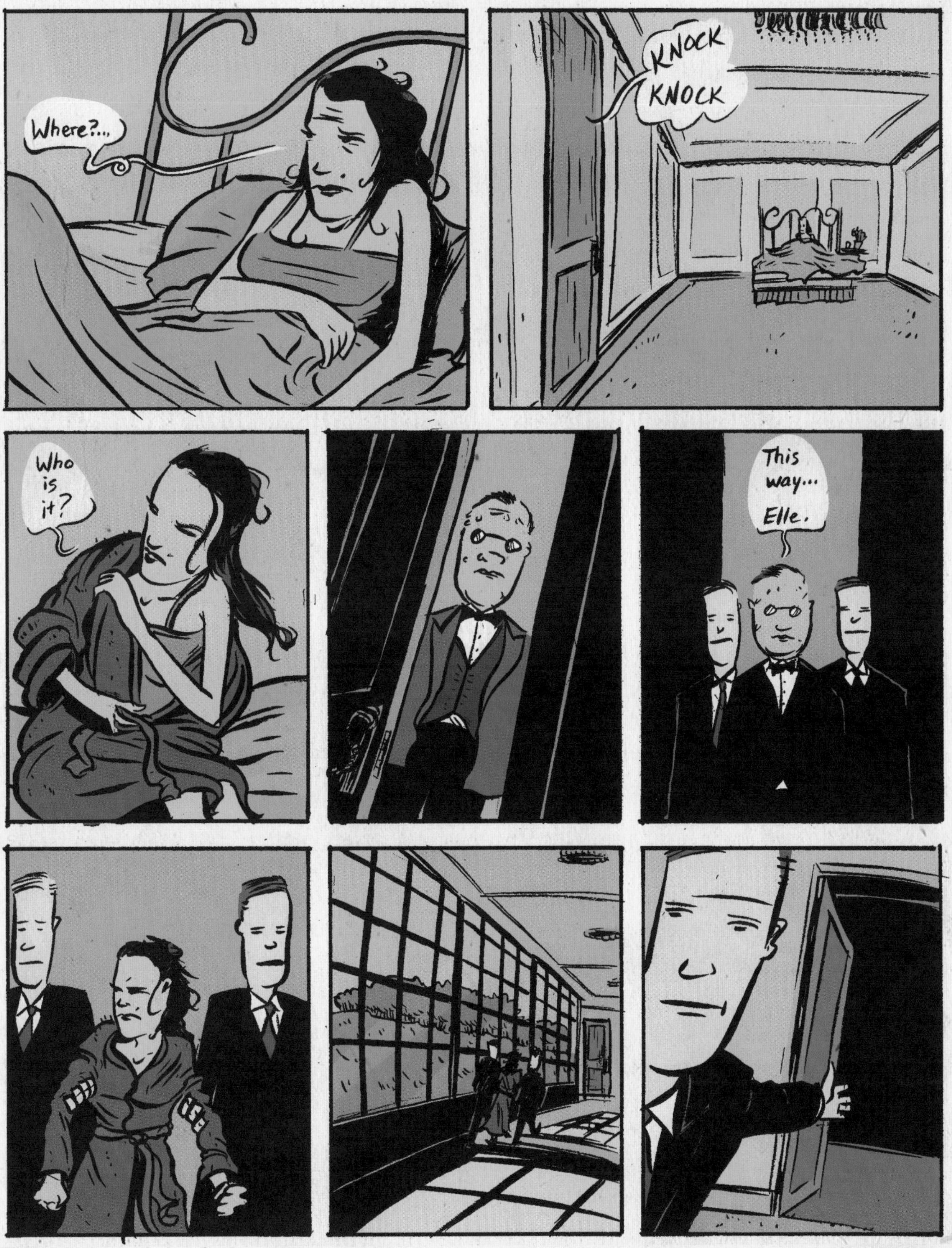
Where?...
KNOCK KNOCK
Who is it?
This way... Elle.

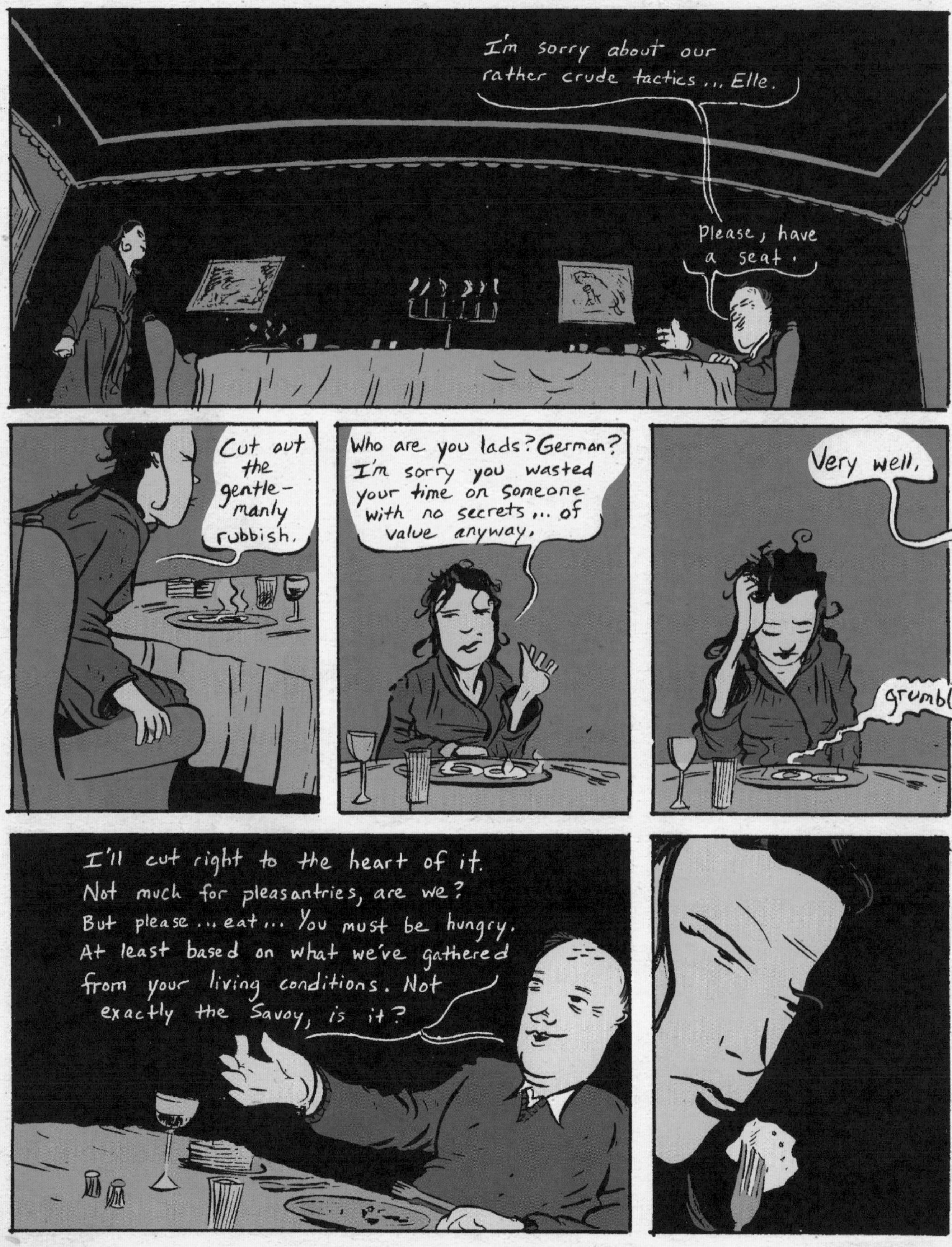
I'm sorry about our rather crude tactics... Elle.
Please, have a seat.
Cut out the gentle-manly rubbish.
Who are you lads? German? I'm sorry you wasted your time on someone with no secrets... of value anyway.
Very well.
grumble
I'll cut right to the heart of it. Not much for pleasantries, are we? But please... eat... You must be hungry. At least based on what we've gathered from your living conditions. Not exactly the Savoy, is it?

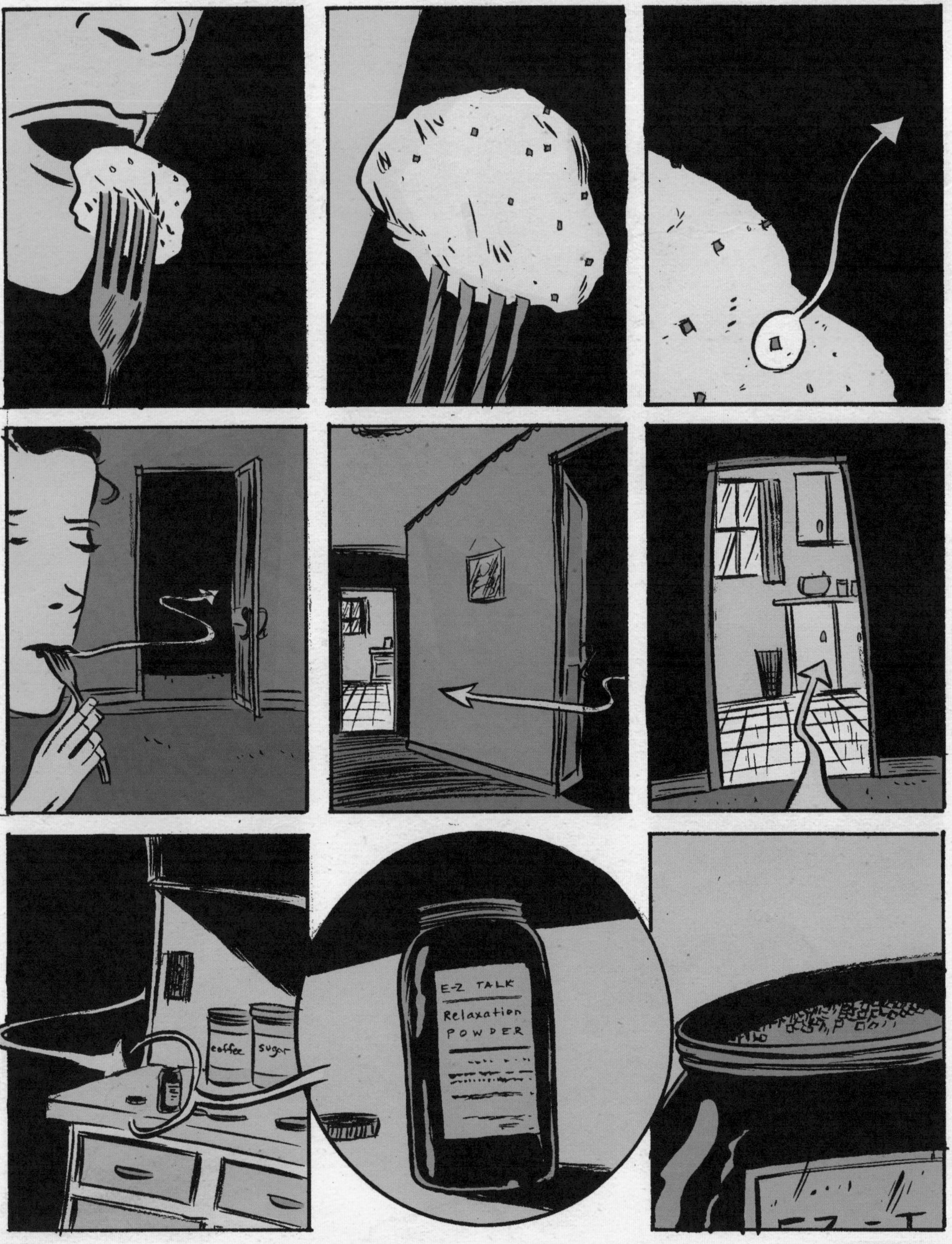
coffee
sugar
E-Z TALK
Relaxation
POWDER

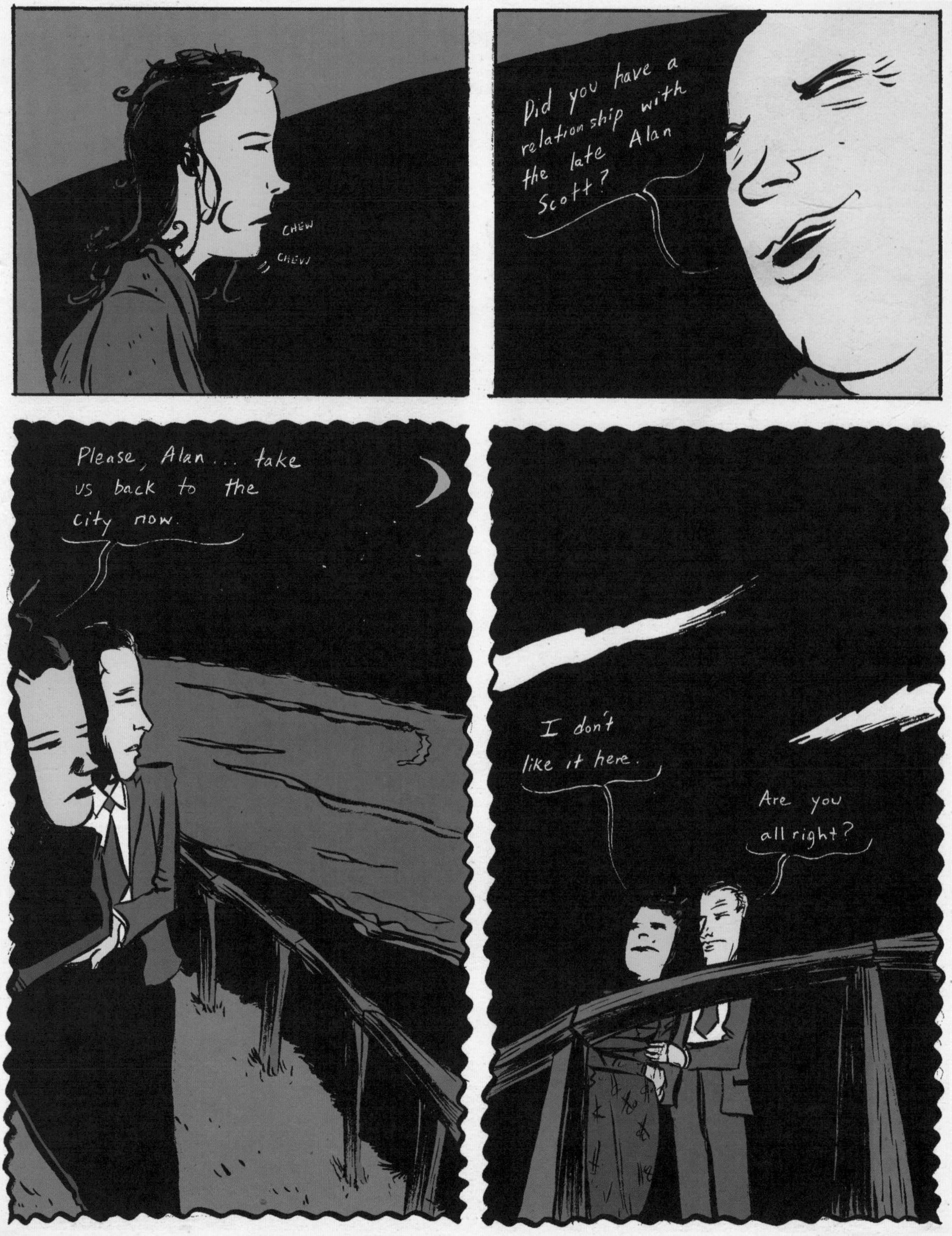
CHEW
CHEW
Did you have a relationship with the late Alan Scott?
Please, Alan... take us back to the city now.
I don't like it here.
Are you all right?

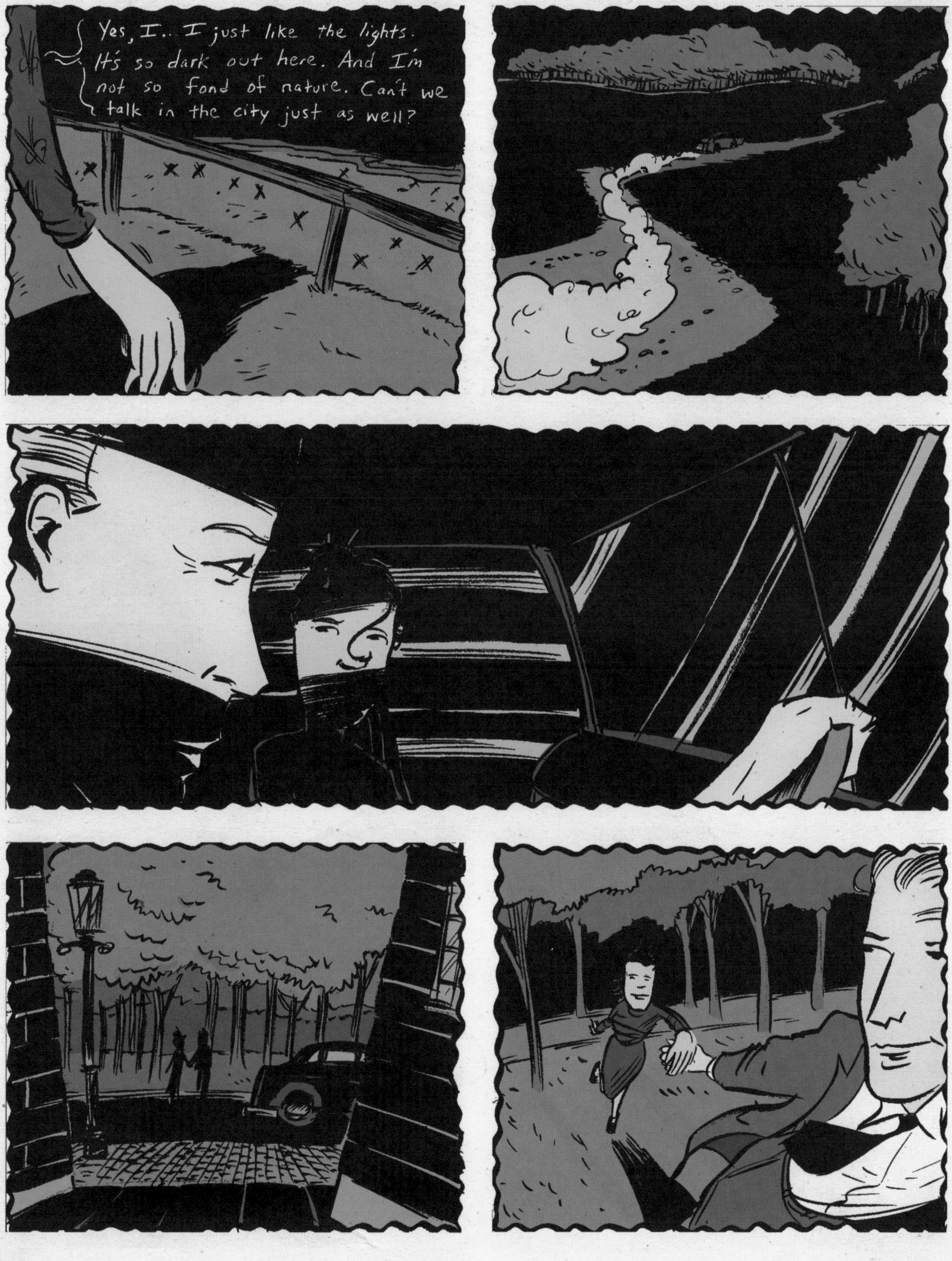
Yes, I... I just like the lights. It's so dark out here. And I'm not so fond of nature. Can't we talk in the city just as well?

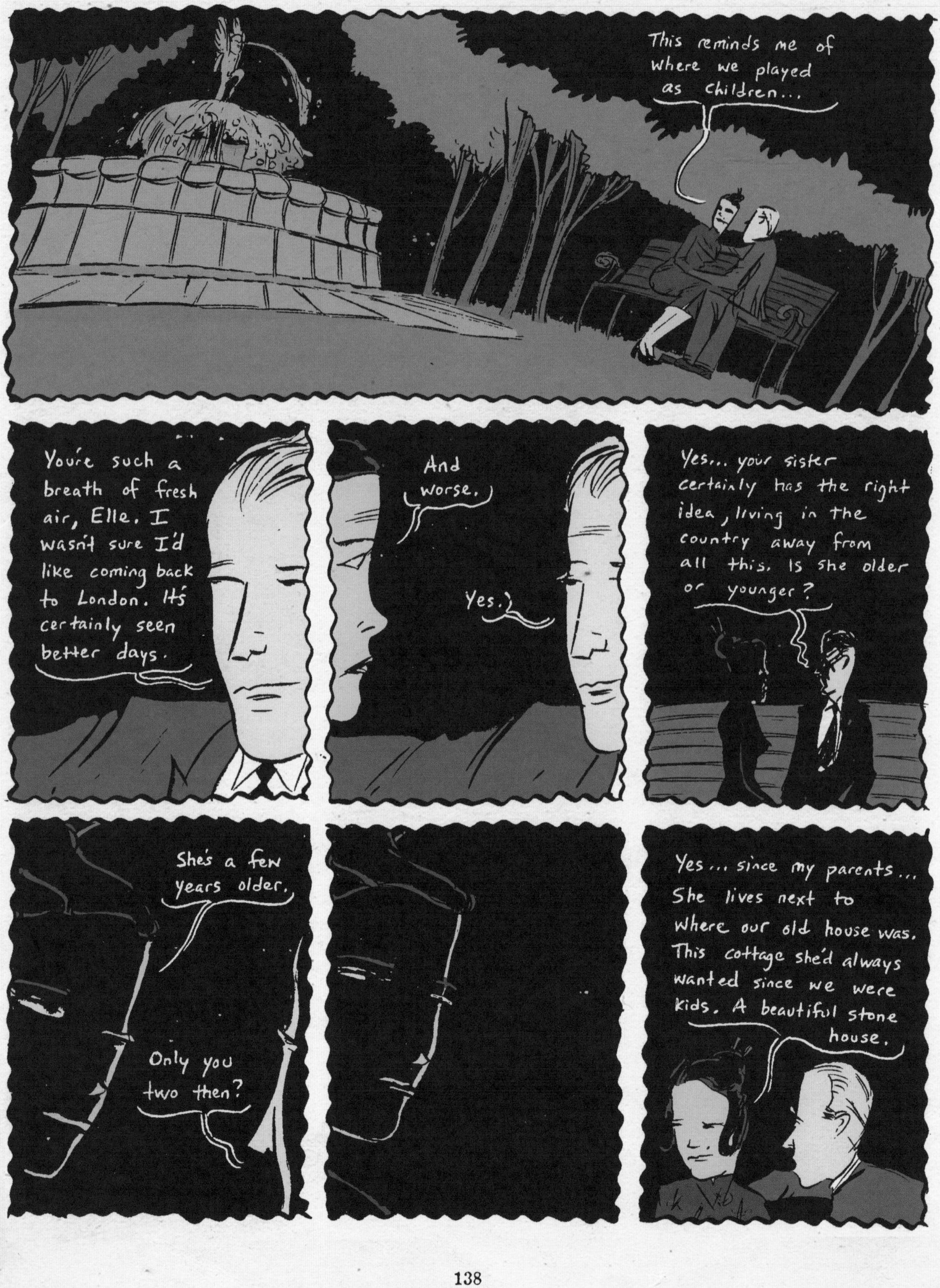
This reminds me of where we played as children...
You're such a breath of fresh air, Elle. I wasn't sure I'd like coming back to London. It's certainly seen better days.
And worse.
Yes.
Yes... your sister certainly has the right idea, living in the country away from all this. Is she older or younger?
She's a few years older.
Only you two then?
Yes... since my parents... She lives next to where our old house was. This cottage she'd always wanted since we were kids. A beautiful stone house.

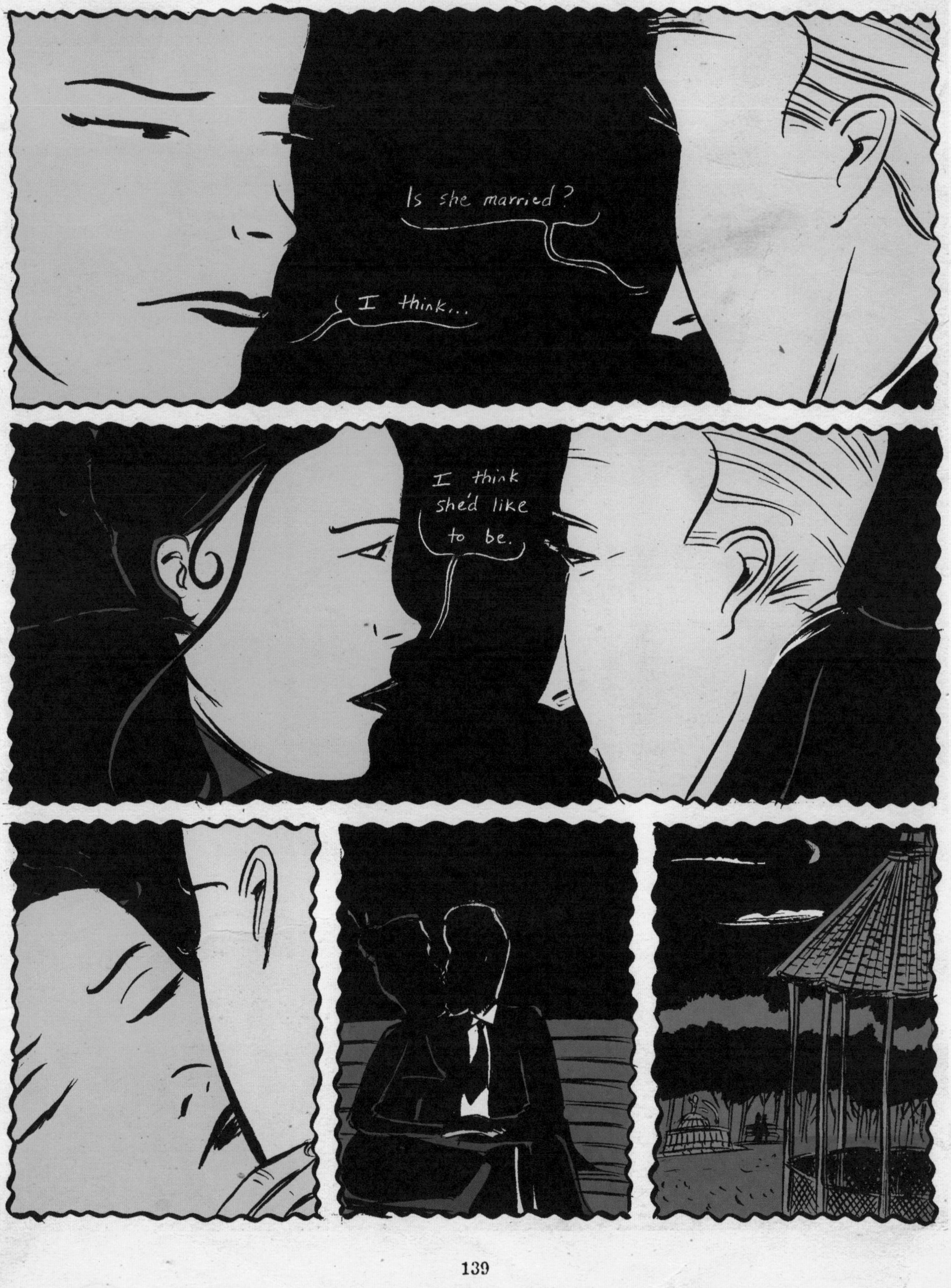
Is she married?
I think...
I think she'd like to be.

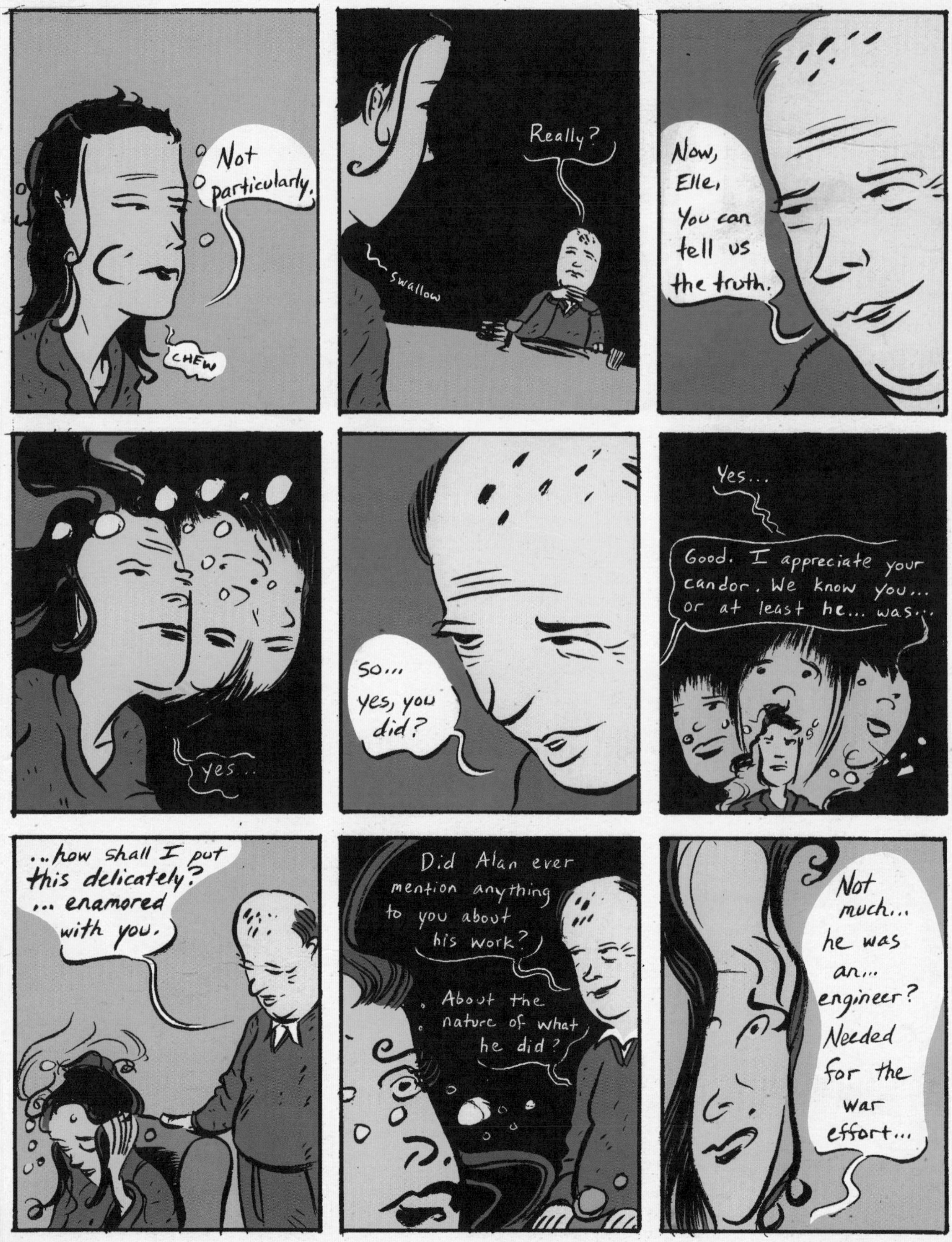
Not particularly.
CHEW
Really?
swallow
Now, Elle, You can tell us the truth.
yes...
So... yes, you did?
Yes...
Good. I appreciate your candor. We know you... or at least he... was...
...how shall I put this delicately? ... enamored with you.
Did Alan ever mention anything to you about his work?
About the nature of what he did?
Not much... he was an... engineer? Needed for the war effort...

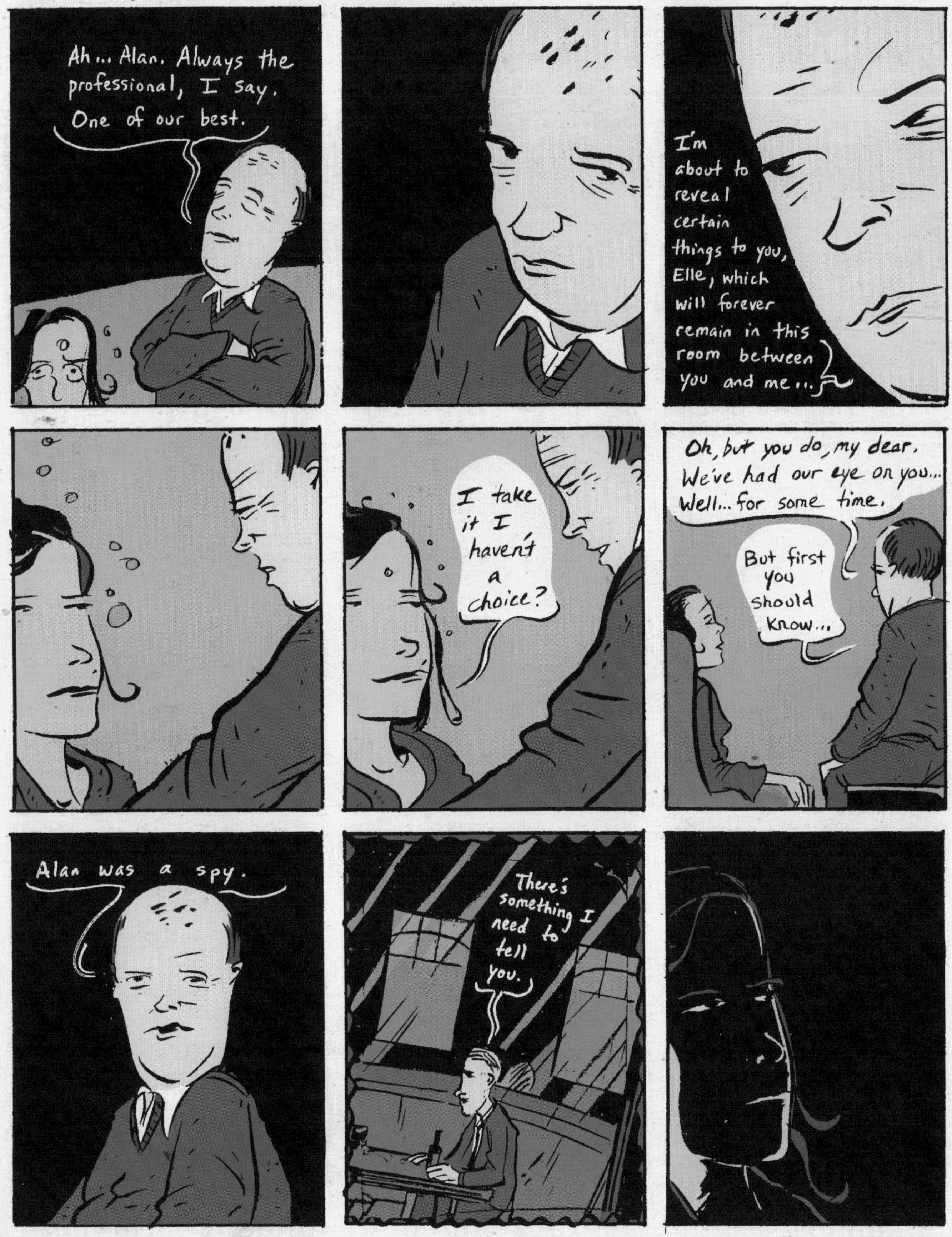

Ah... Alan. Always the professional, I say. One of our best.
I'm about to reveal certain things to you, Elle, which will forever remain in this room between you and me...
I take it I haven't a choice?
Oh, but you do, my dear. We've had our eye on you... Well... for some time.
But first you should know...
Alan was a spy.
There's something I need to tell you.

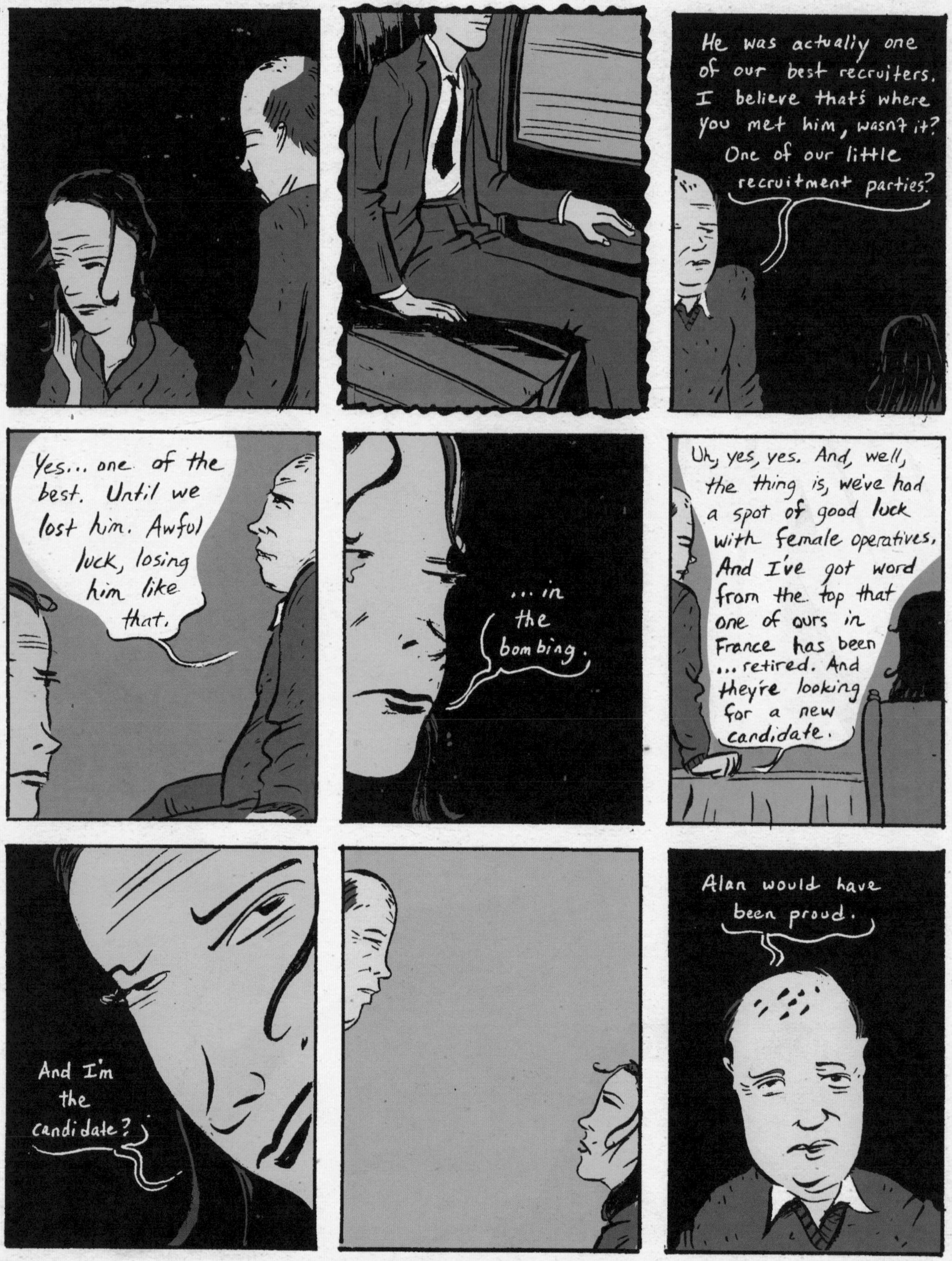
He was actually one of our best recruiters. I believe that's where you met him, wasn't it? One of our little recruitment parties?
Yes... one of the best. Until we lost him. Awful luck, losing him like that.
...in the bombing.
Uh, yes, yes. And, well, the thing is, we've had a spot of good luck with female operatives. And I've got word from the top that one of ours in France has been ...retired. And they're looking for a new candidate.
And I'm the candidate?
Alan would have been proud.

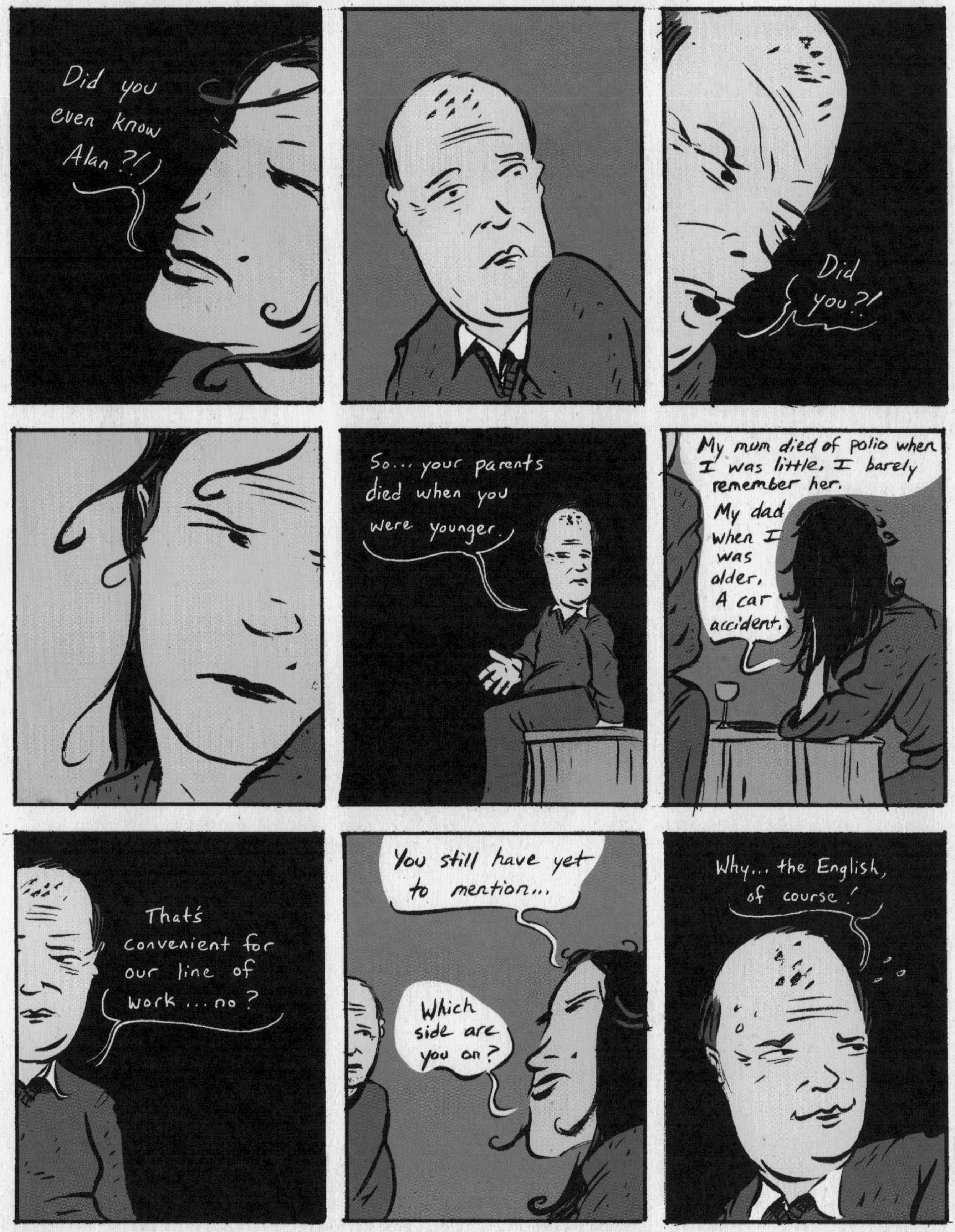

Did you even know Alan?!
Did you?!
So... your parents died when you were younger.
My mum died of polio when I was little. I barely remember her.
My dad when I was older. A car accident.
That's convenient for our line of work... no?
You still have yet to mention...
Which side are you on?
Why... the English, of course!

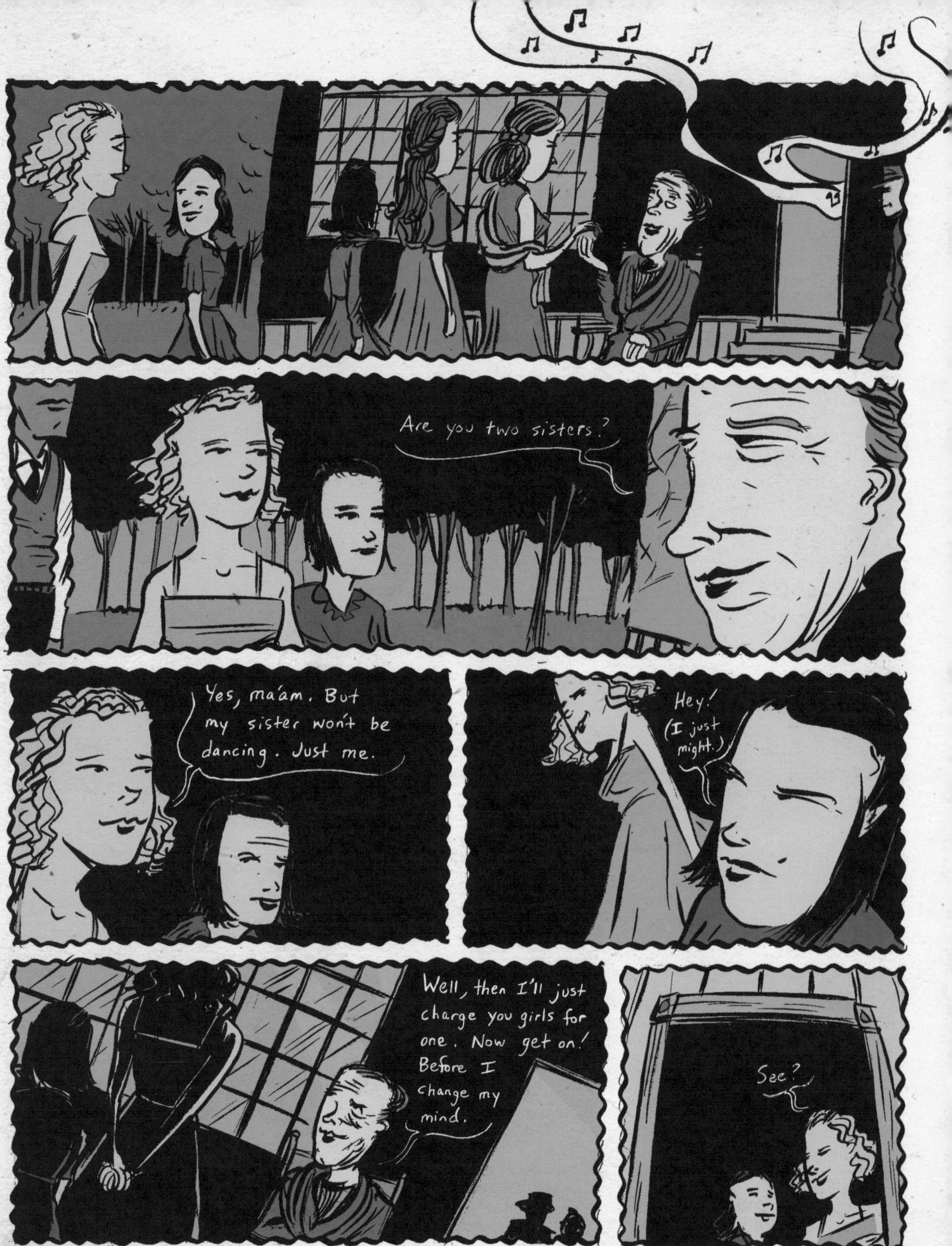

Are you two sisters?
Yes, ma'am. But my sister won't be dancing. Just me.
Hey! (I just might.)
Well, then I'll just charge you girls for one. Now get on! Before I change my mind.
See?

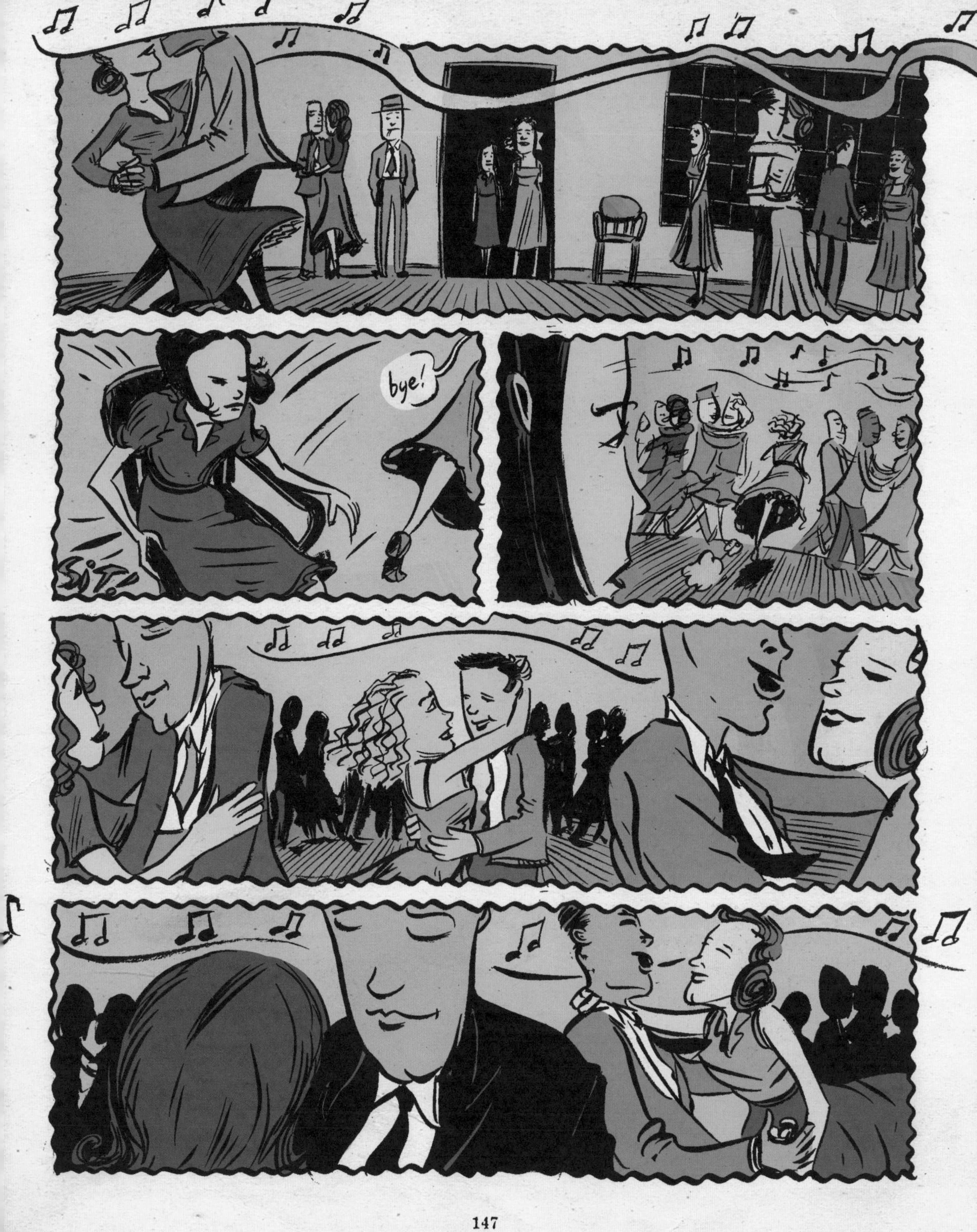
bye!
SIT!

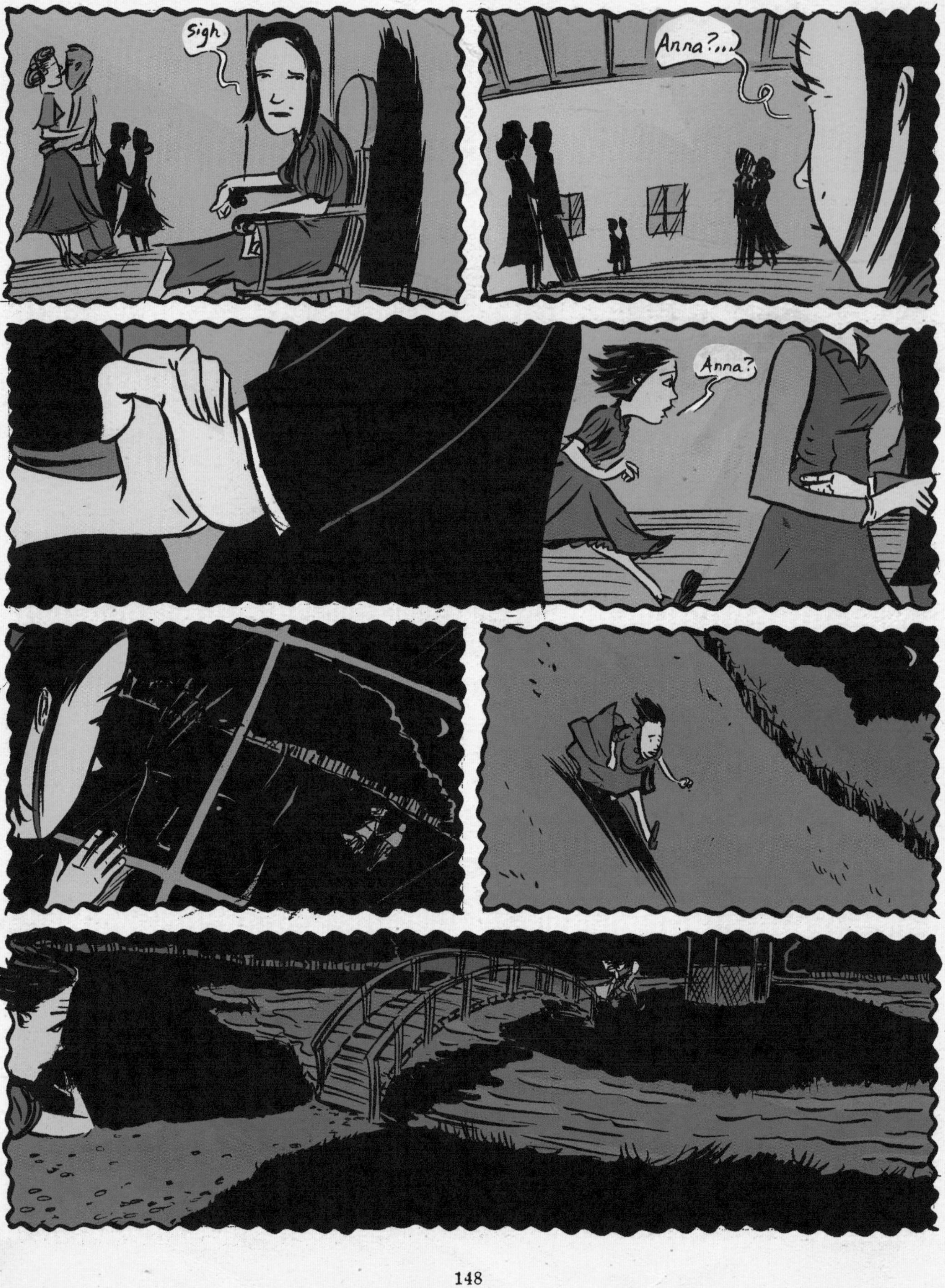
Sigh
Anna?...
Anna?

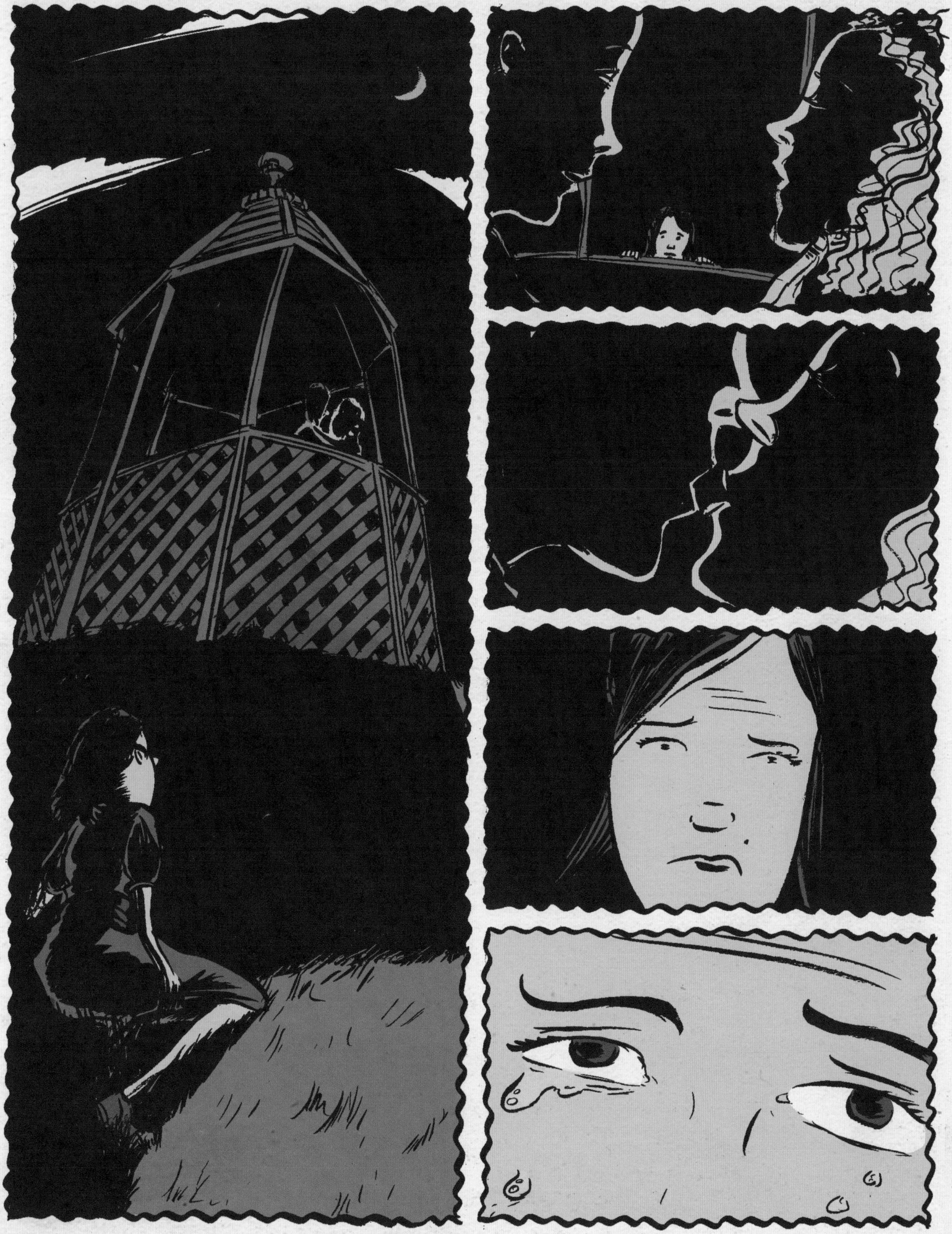

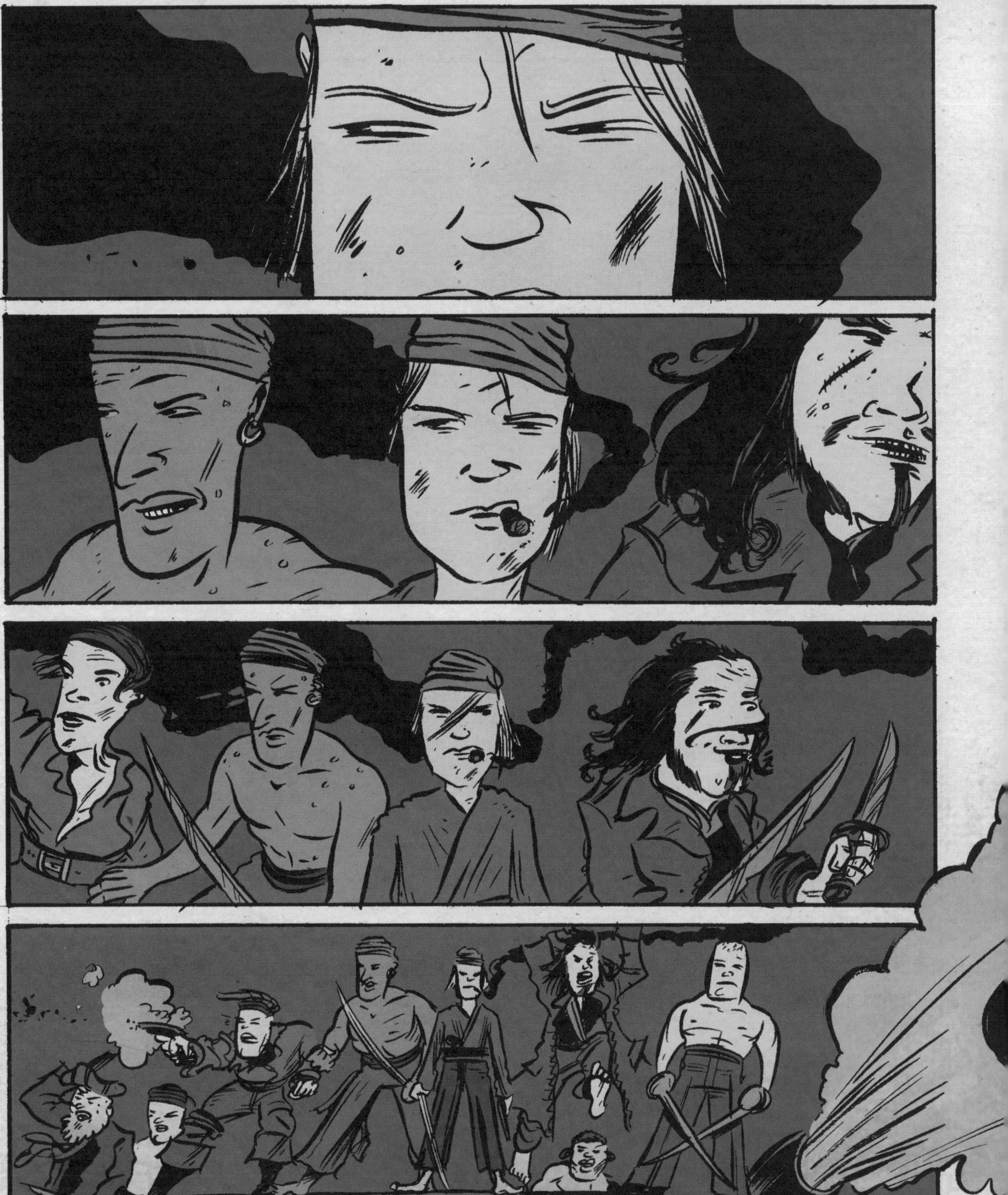

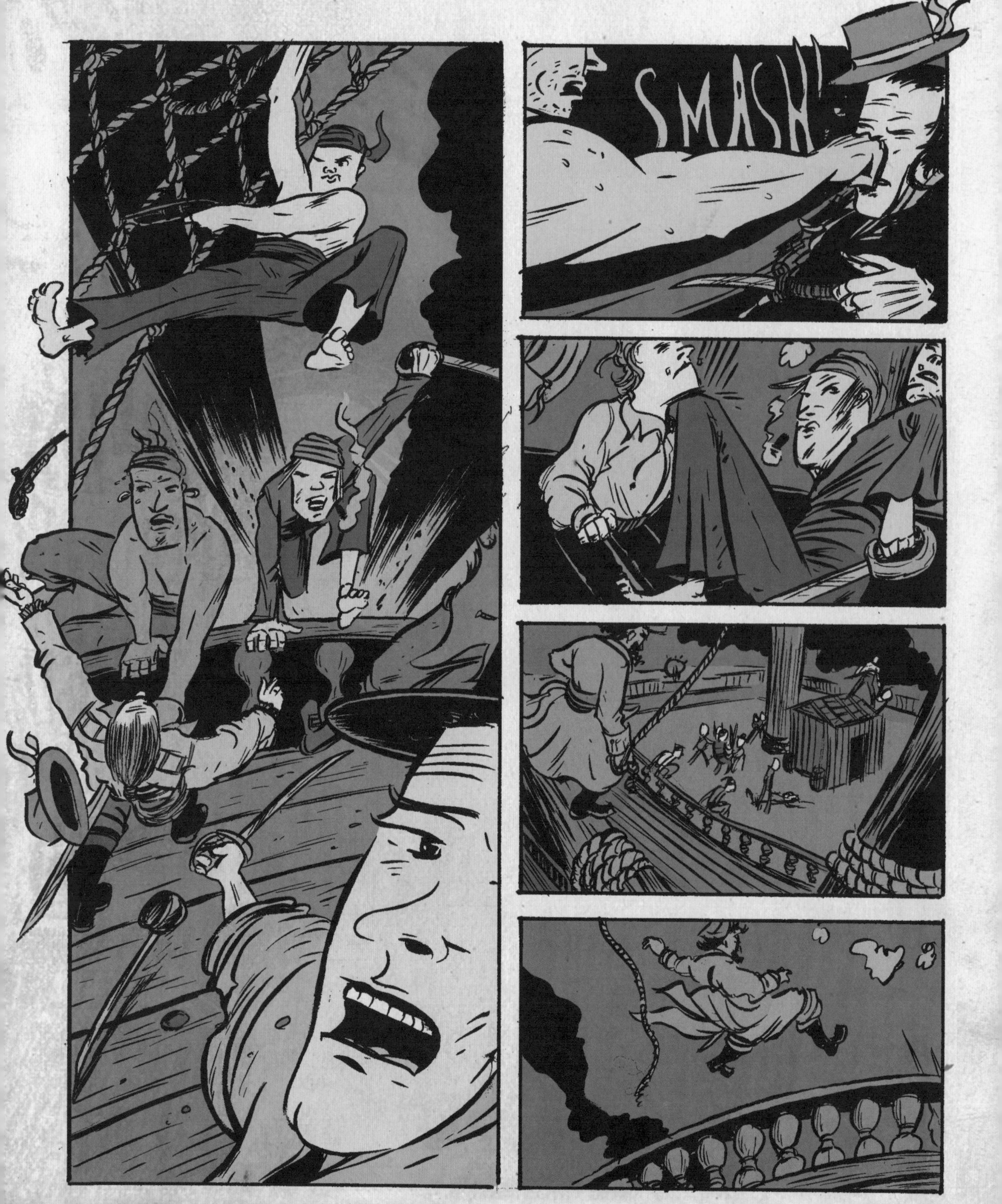
SMASH!

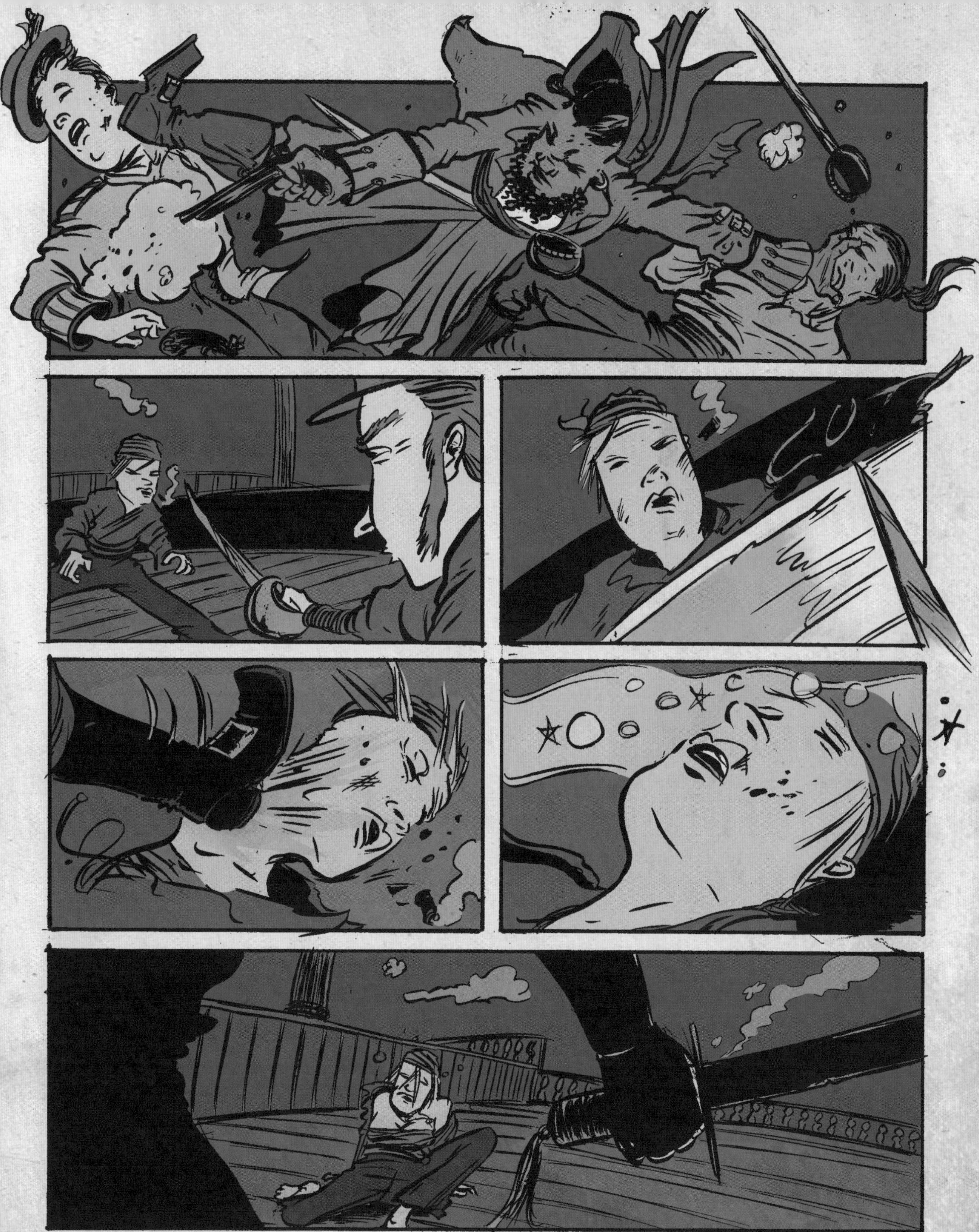

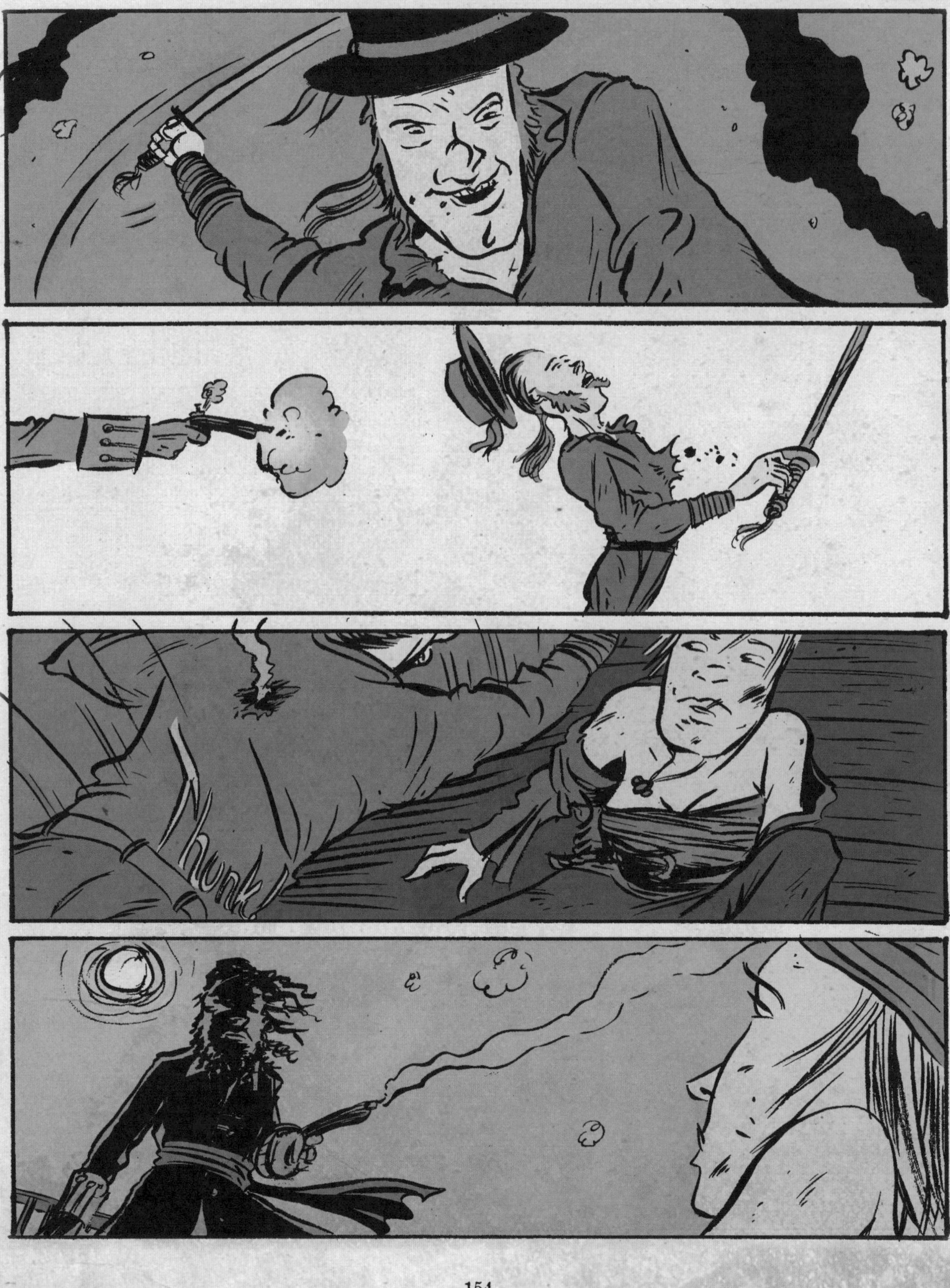
thunk!

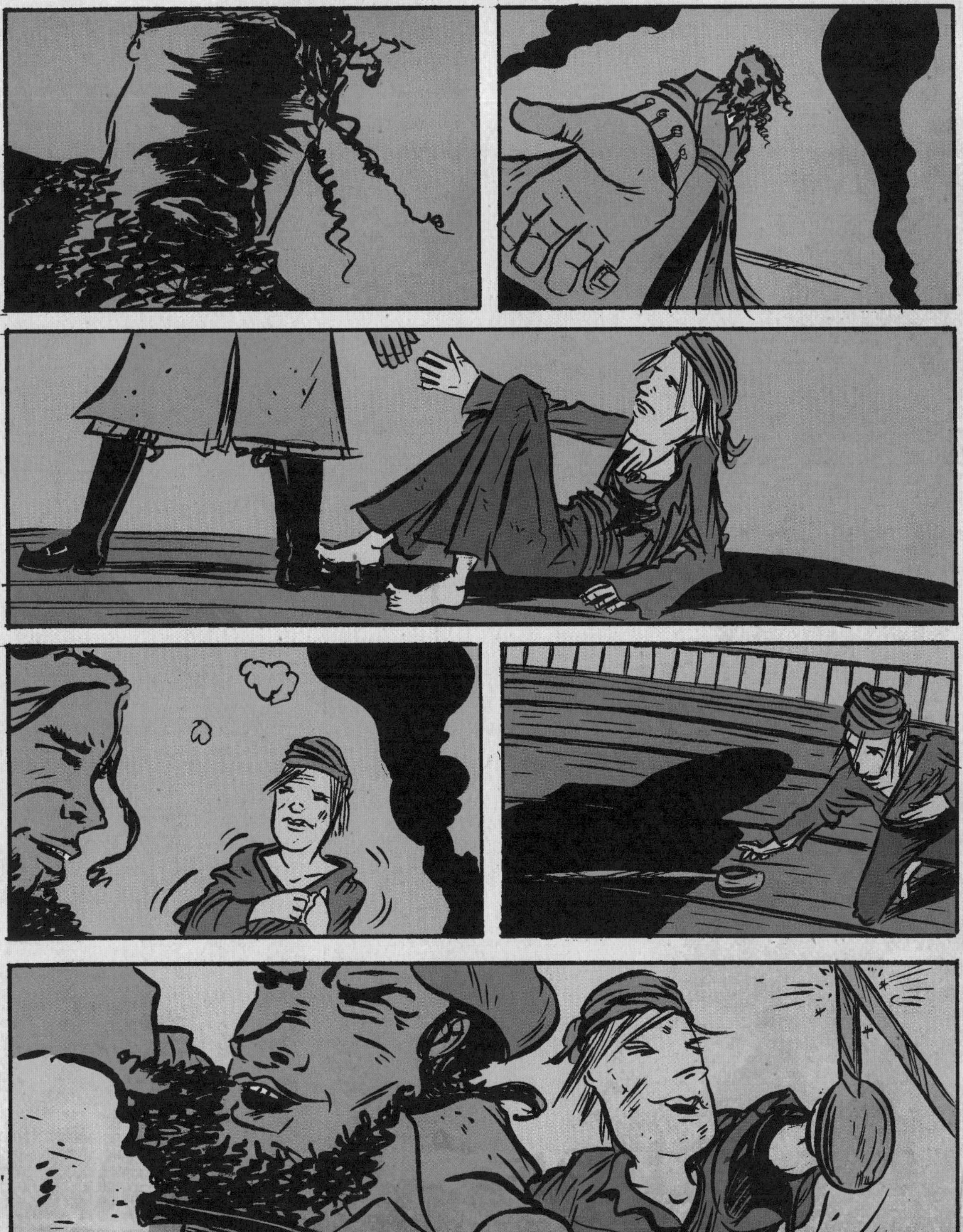

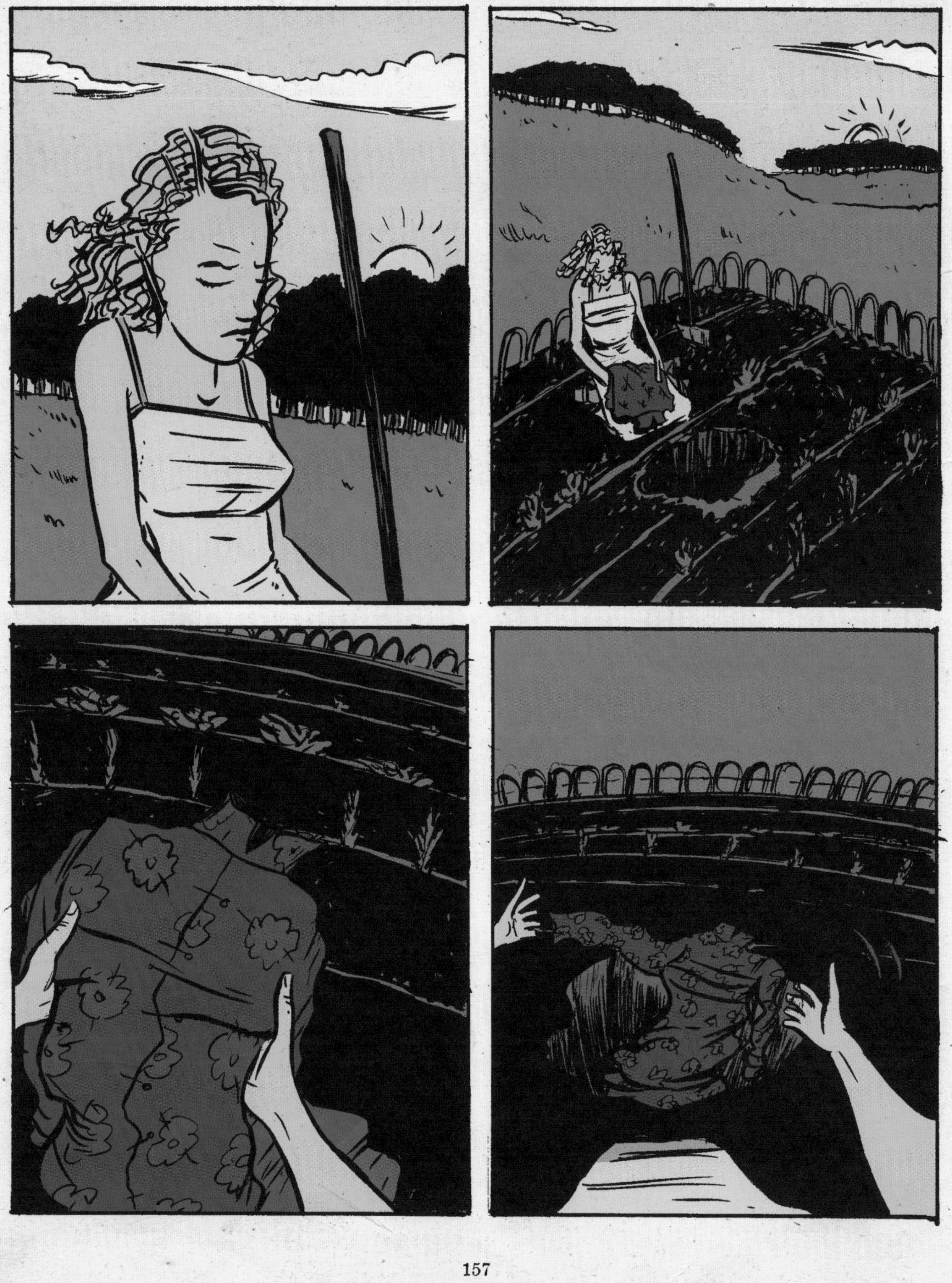

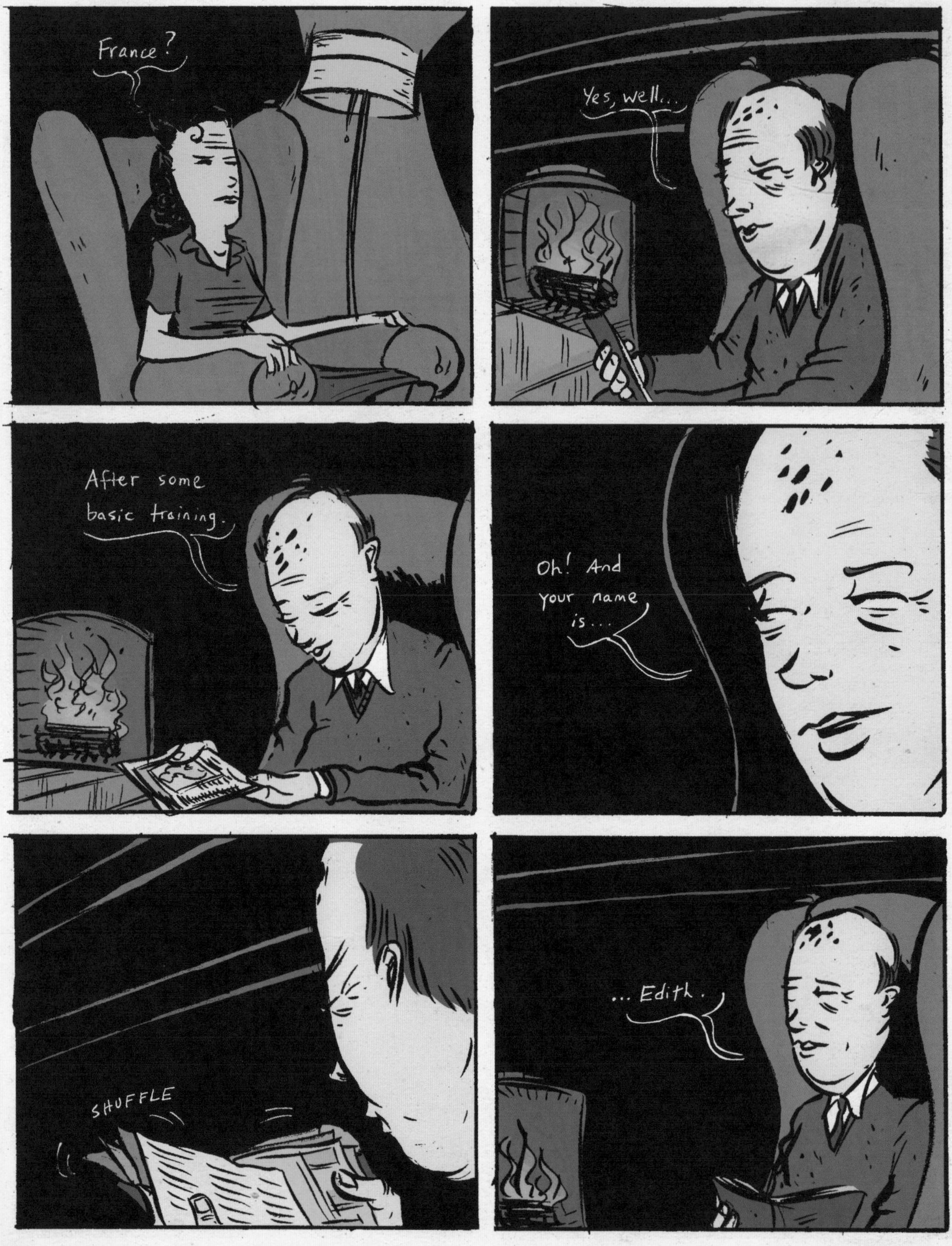
France?
Yes, well...
After some basic training.
Oh! And your name is...
SHUFFLE
...Edith.

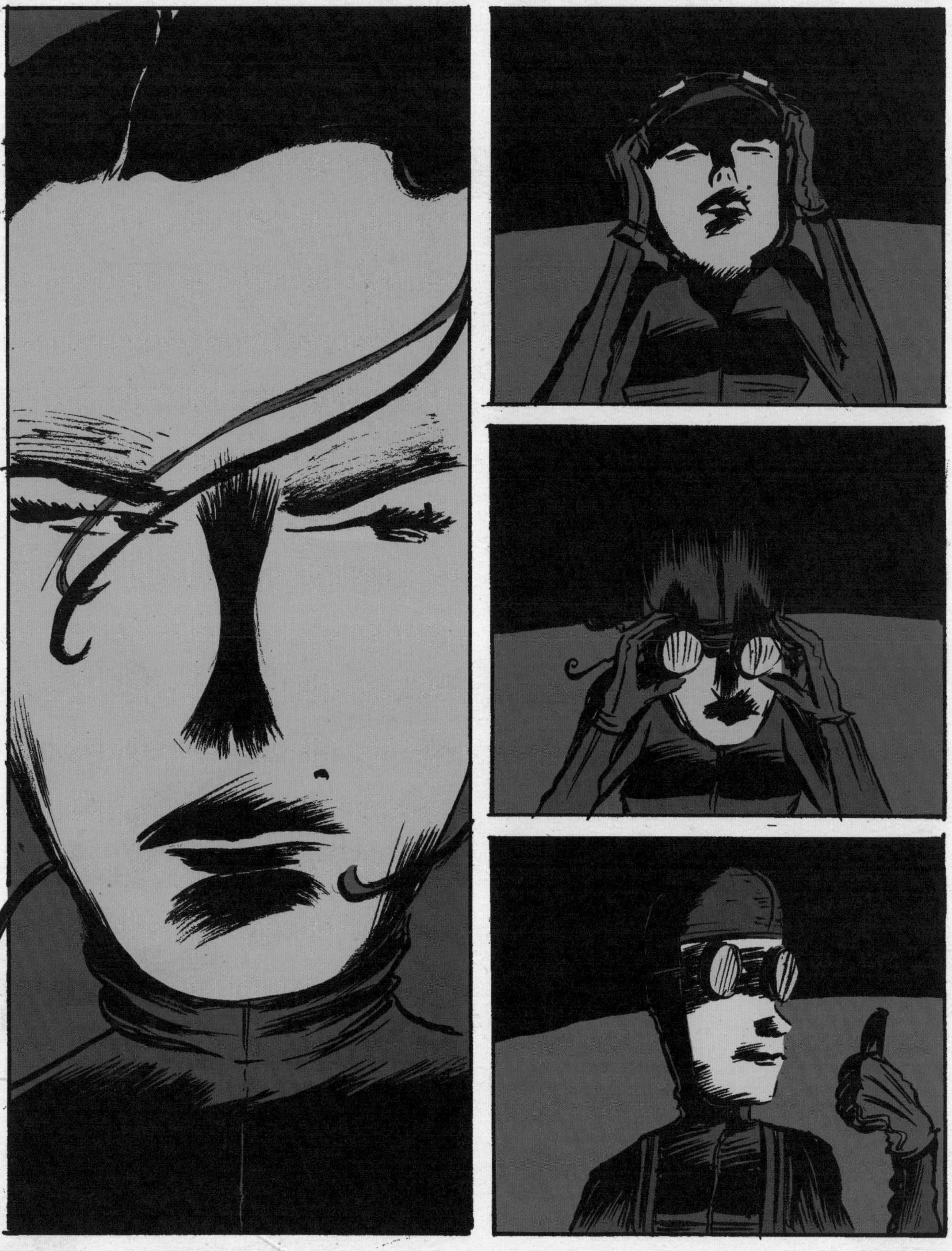

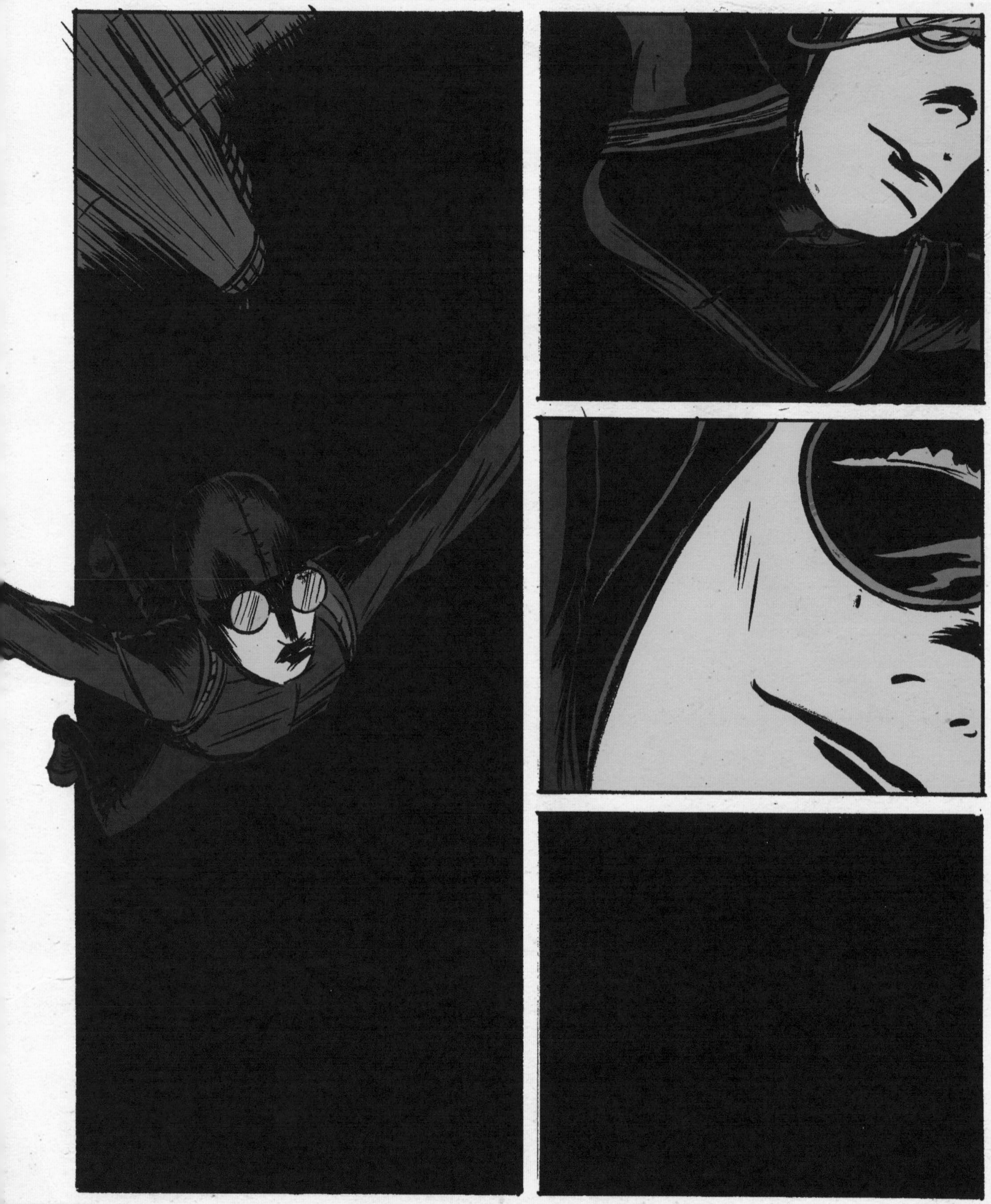

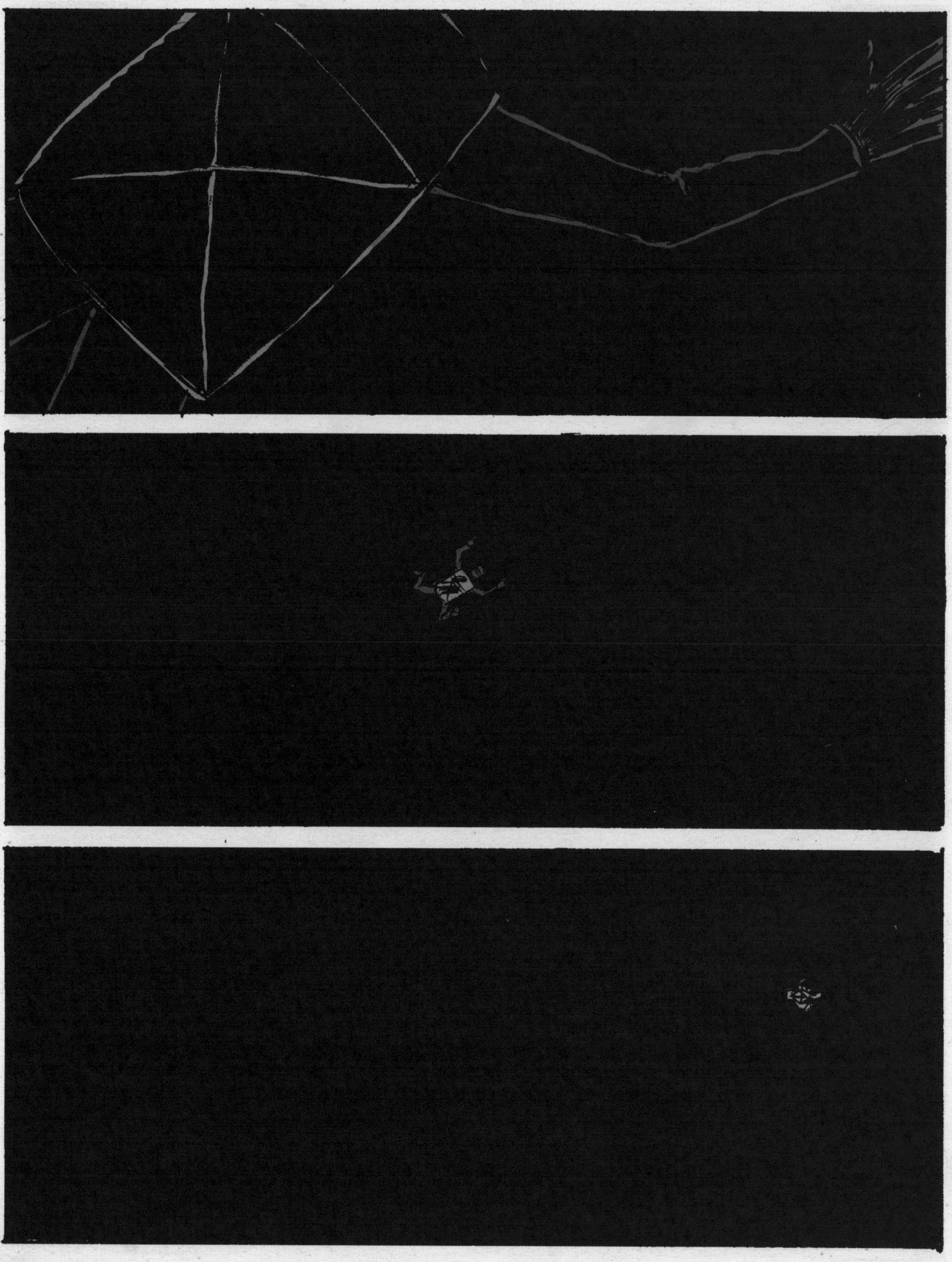

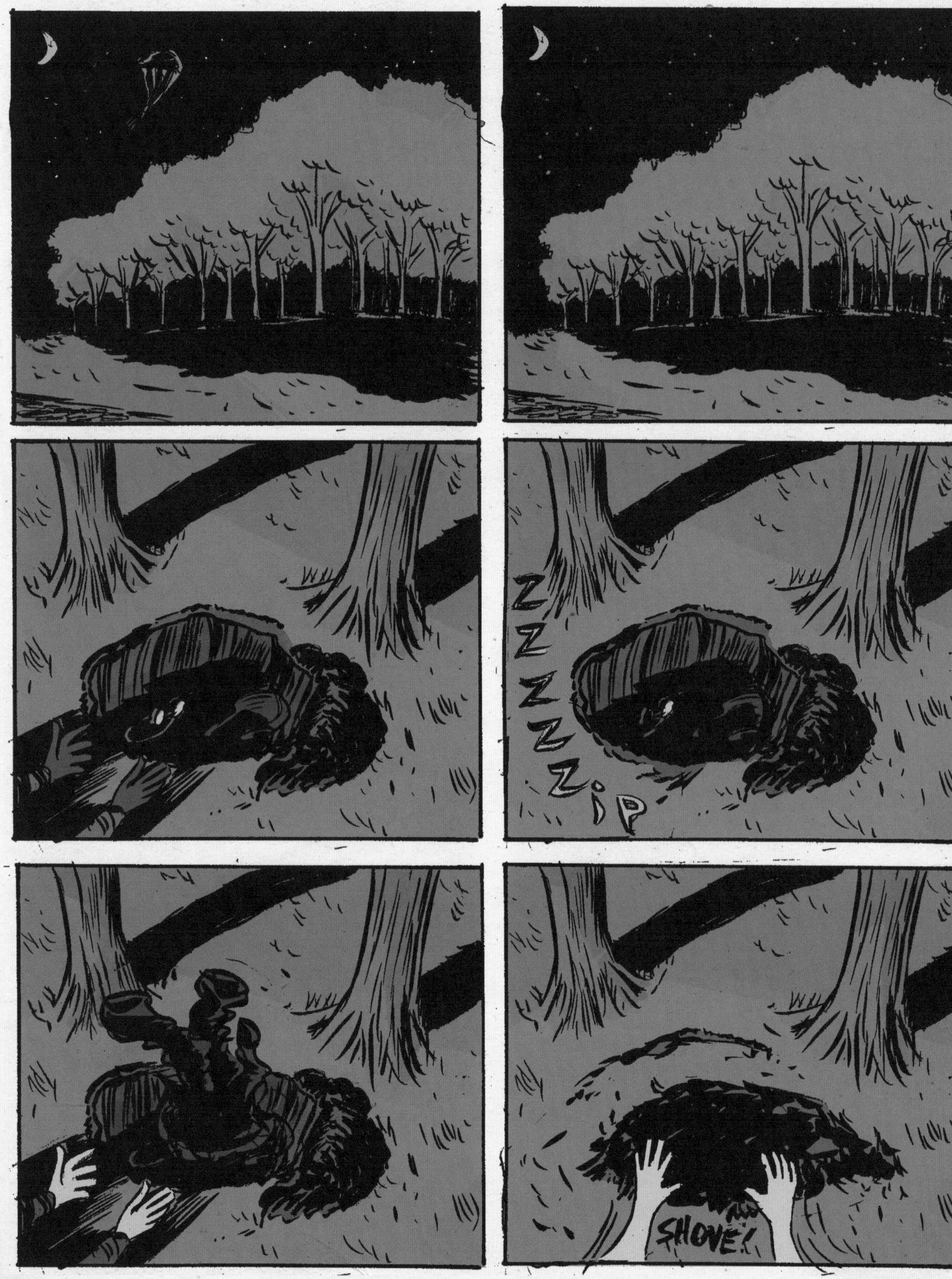
ZZZZZZip
SHOVE!

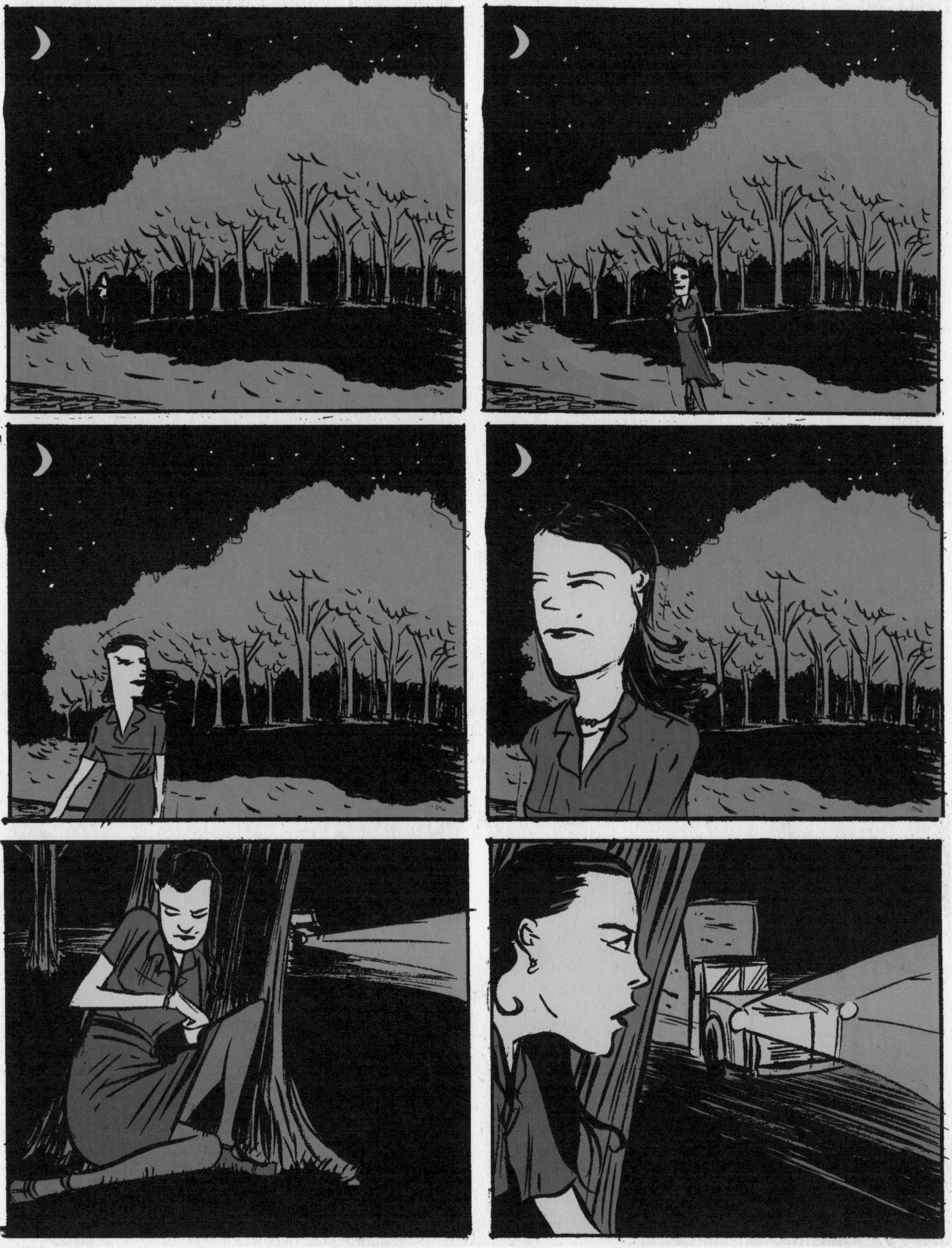

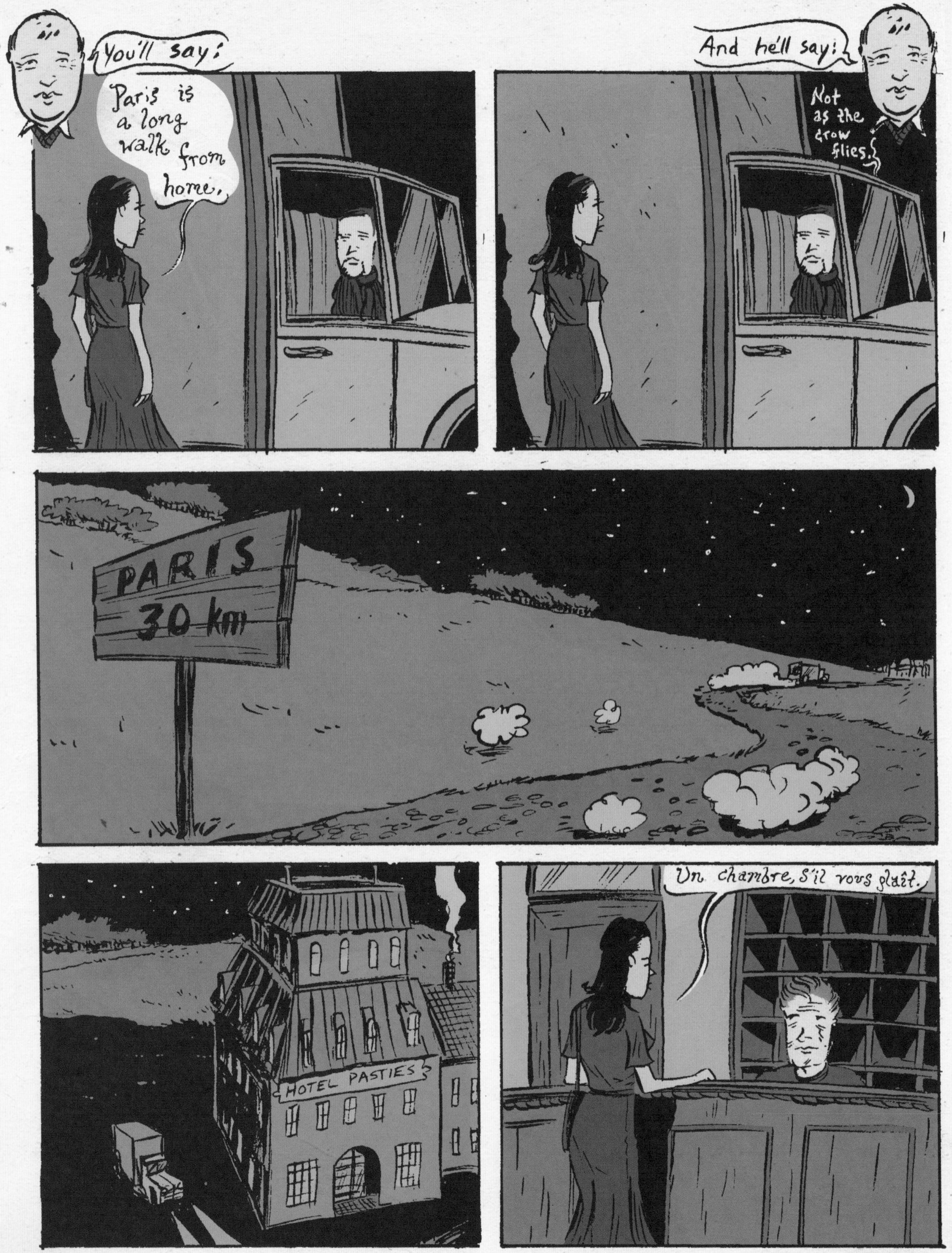
You'll say:
Paris is a long walk from home.
And he'll say:
Not as the crow flies.
PARIS 30 km
HOTEL PASTIES
Un chambre, s'il vous plaît.

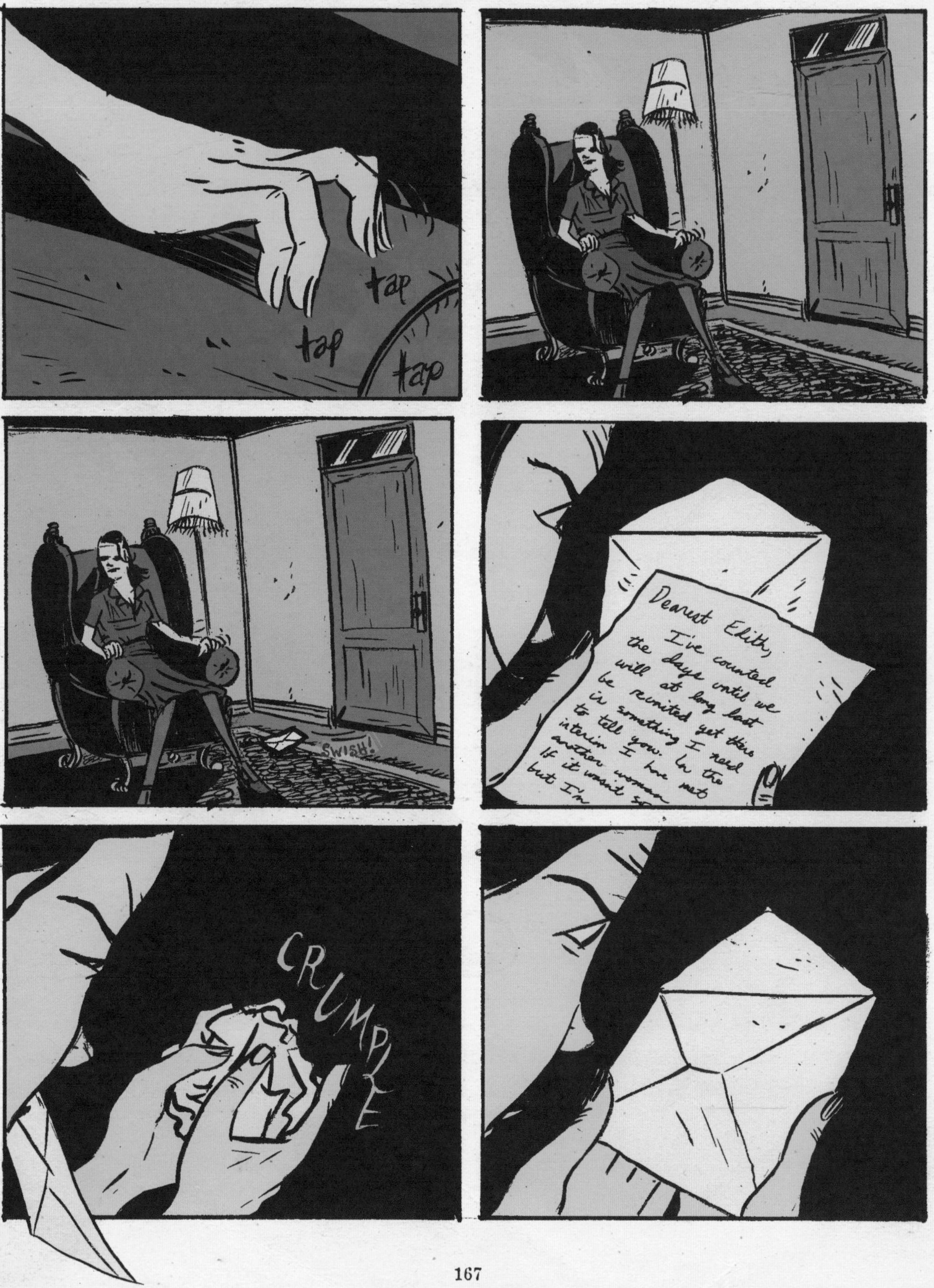
tap
tap
tap
SWISH!
Dearest Edith,
I've counted
the days until we
will at long last
be reunited yet there
is something I need
to tell you. In the
interim I have met
another woman
If it wasn't so
but I'm
CRUMPLE

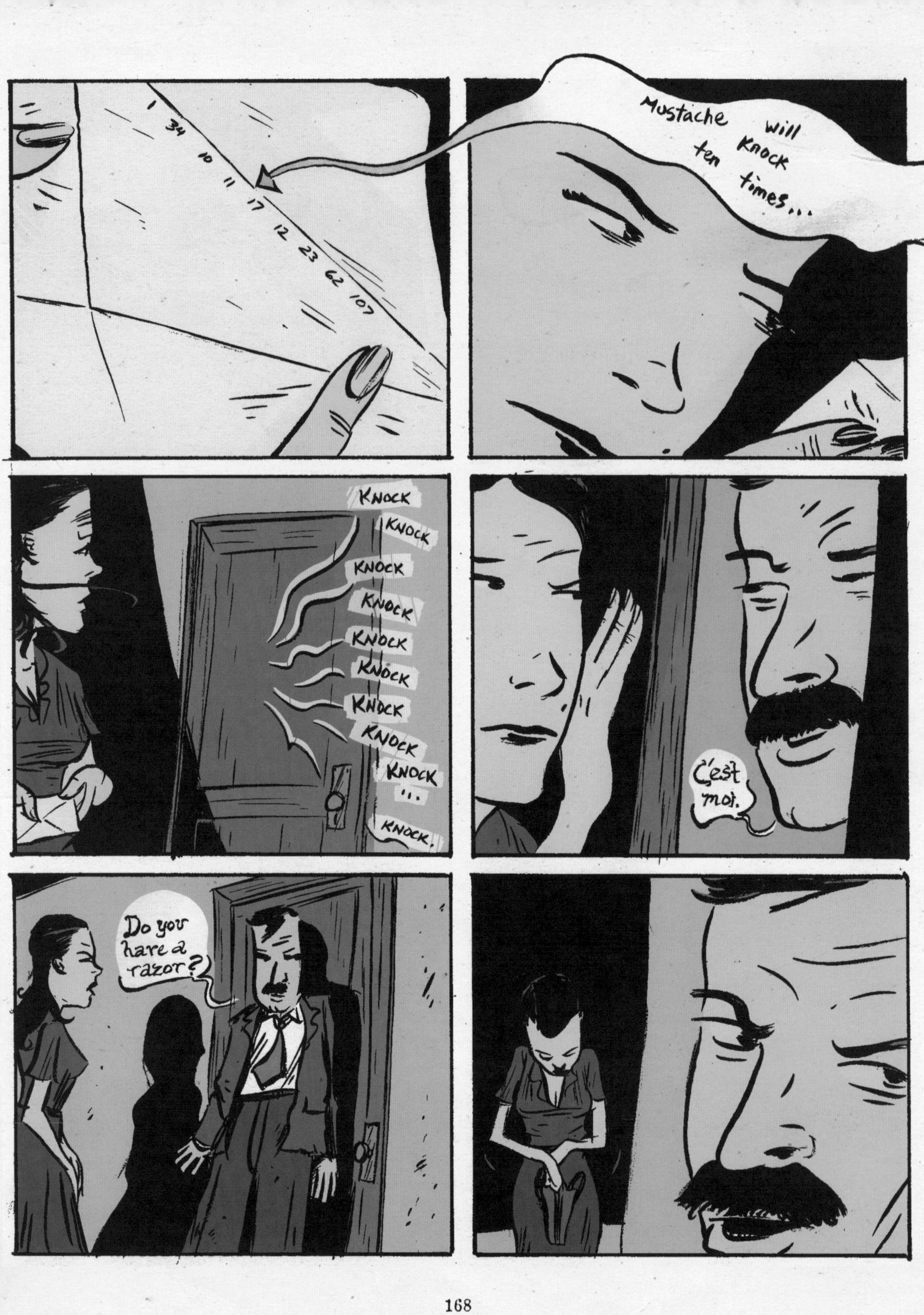
1
34
10
11
17
12
23
62
107
Mustache will knock ten times...
KNOCK
KNOCK
KNOCK
KNOCK
KNOCK
KNOCK
KNOCK
KNOCK
KNOCK
..
KNOCK.
C'est moi.
Do you have a razor?

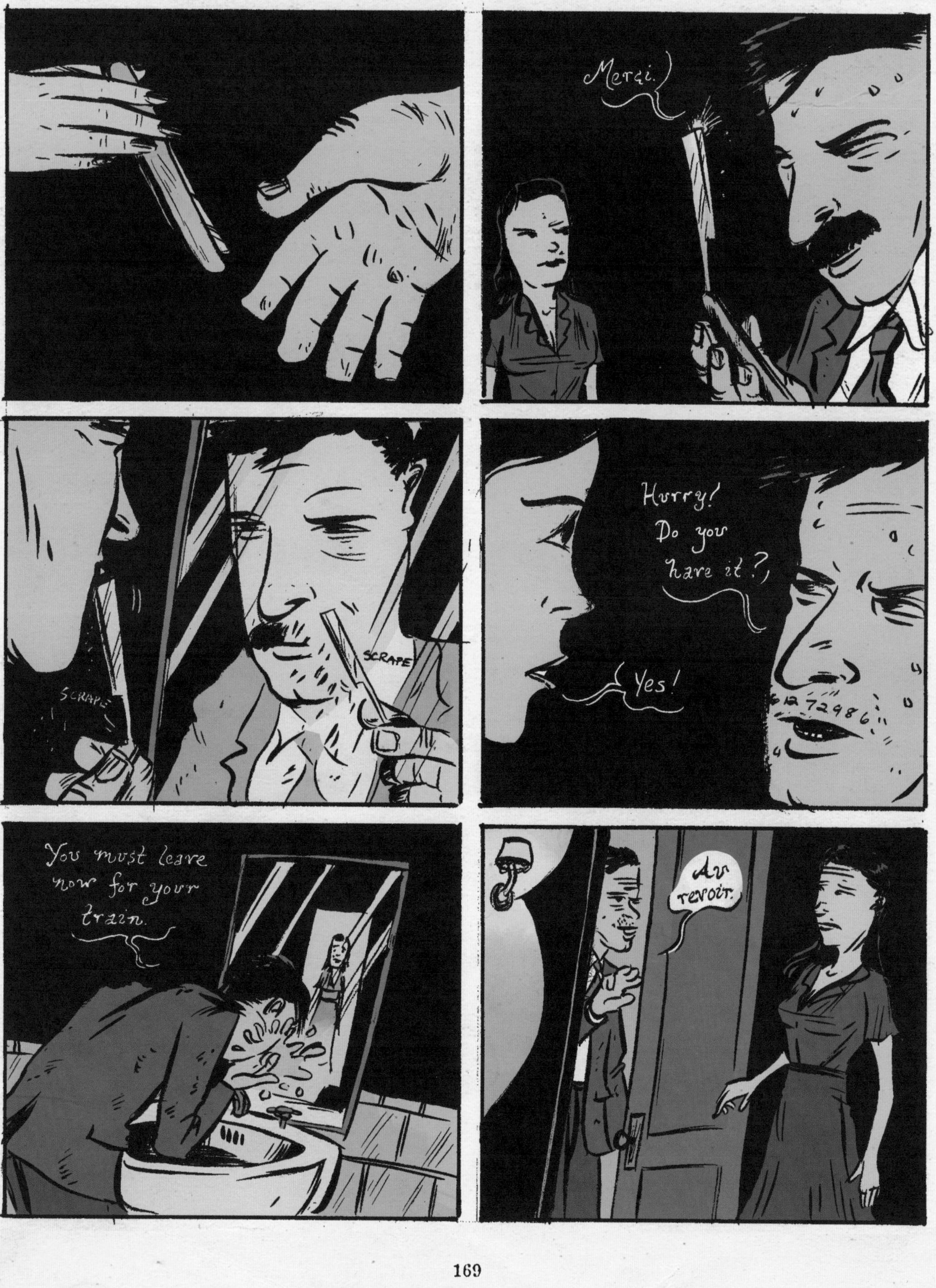
Merci.
SCRAPE
SCRAPE
Hurry! Do your have it?
Yes!
You must leave now for your train.
Au revoir.

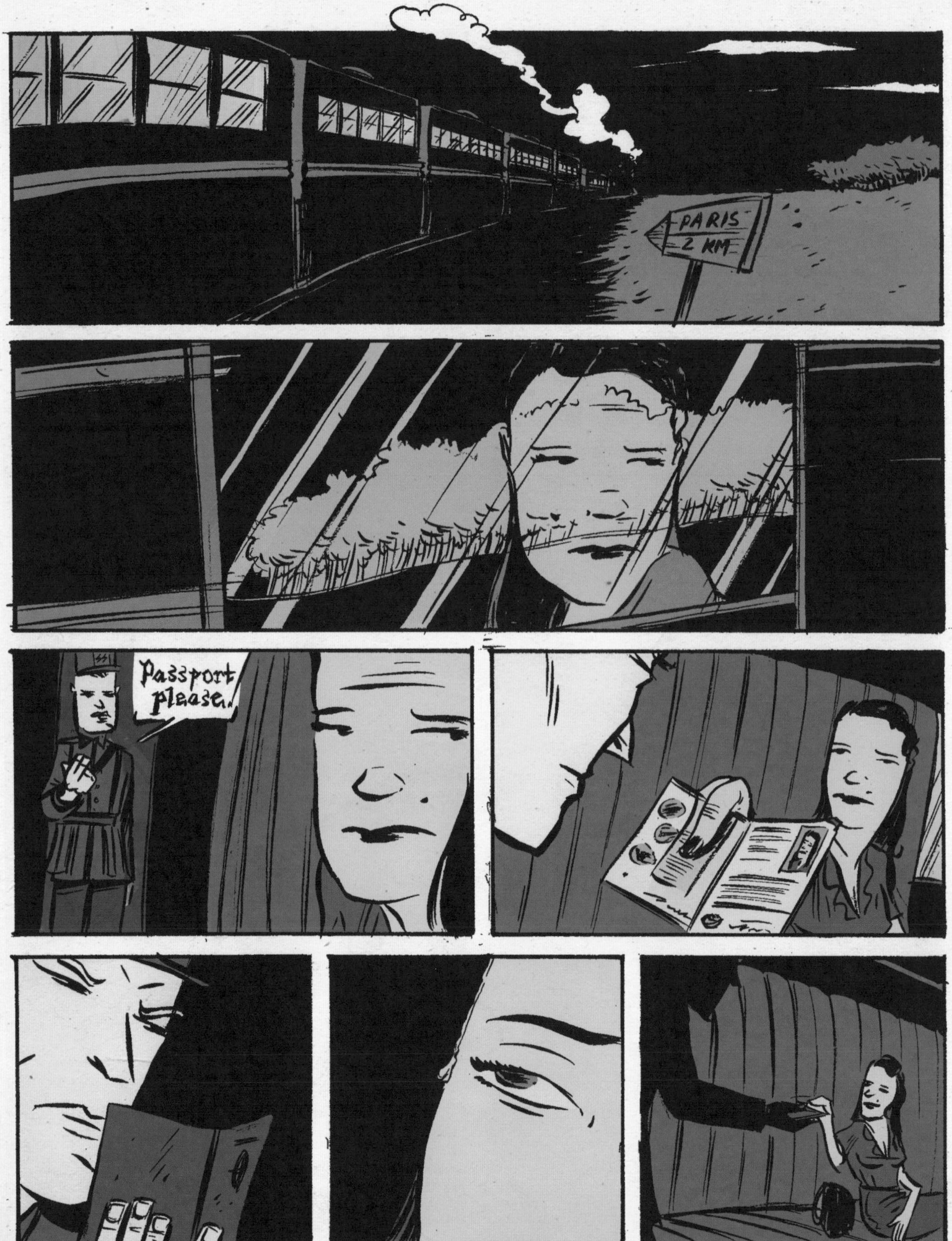
PARIS
2 KM
Passport please.

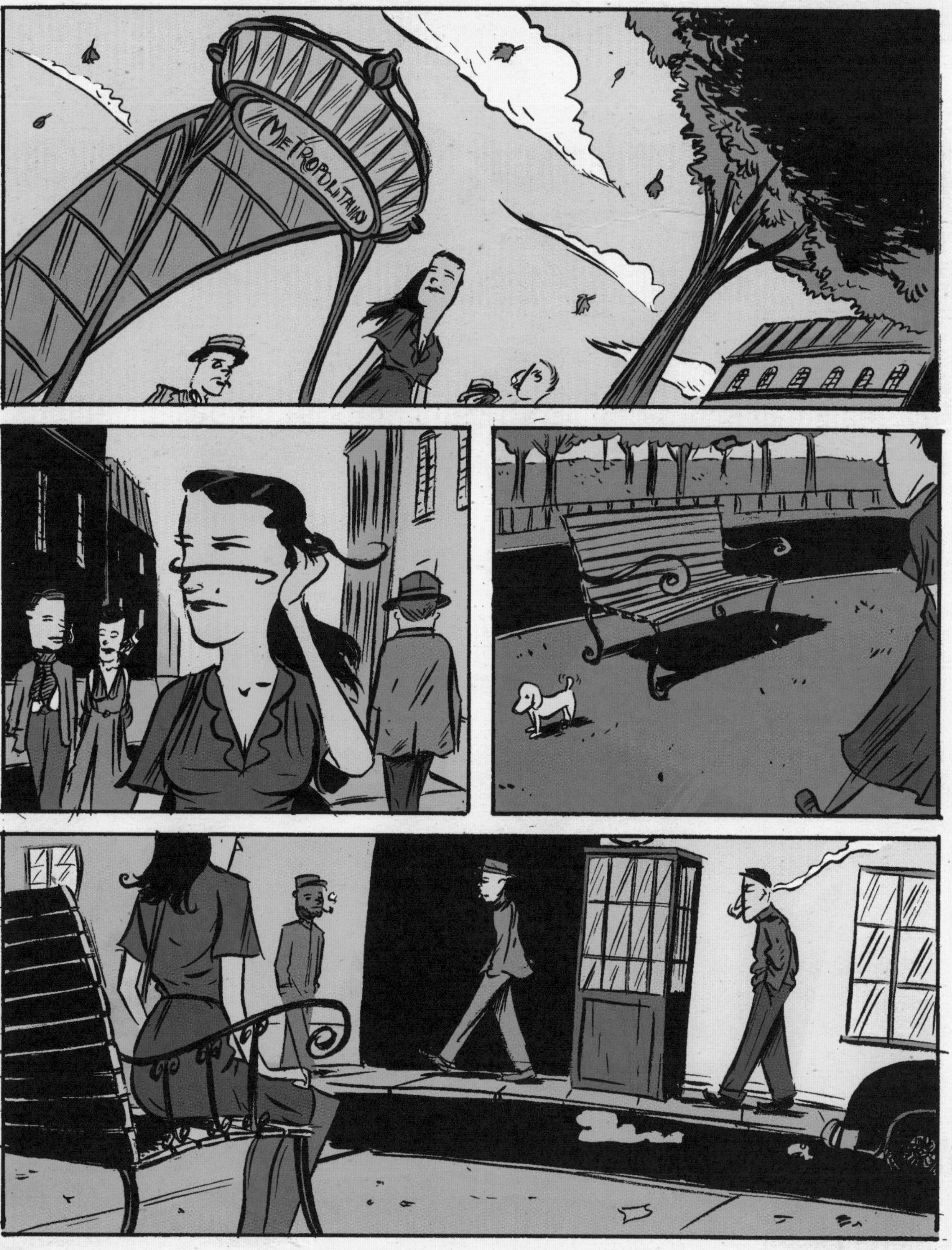
METROPOLITAIN

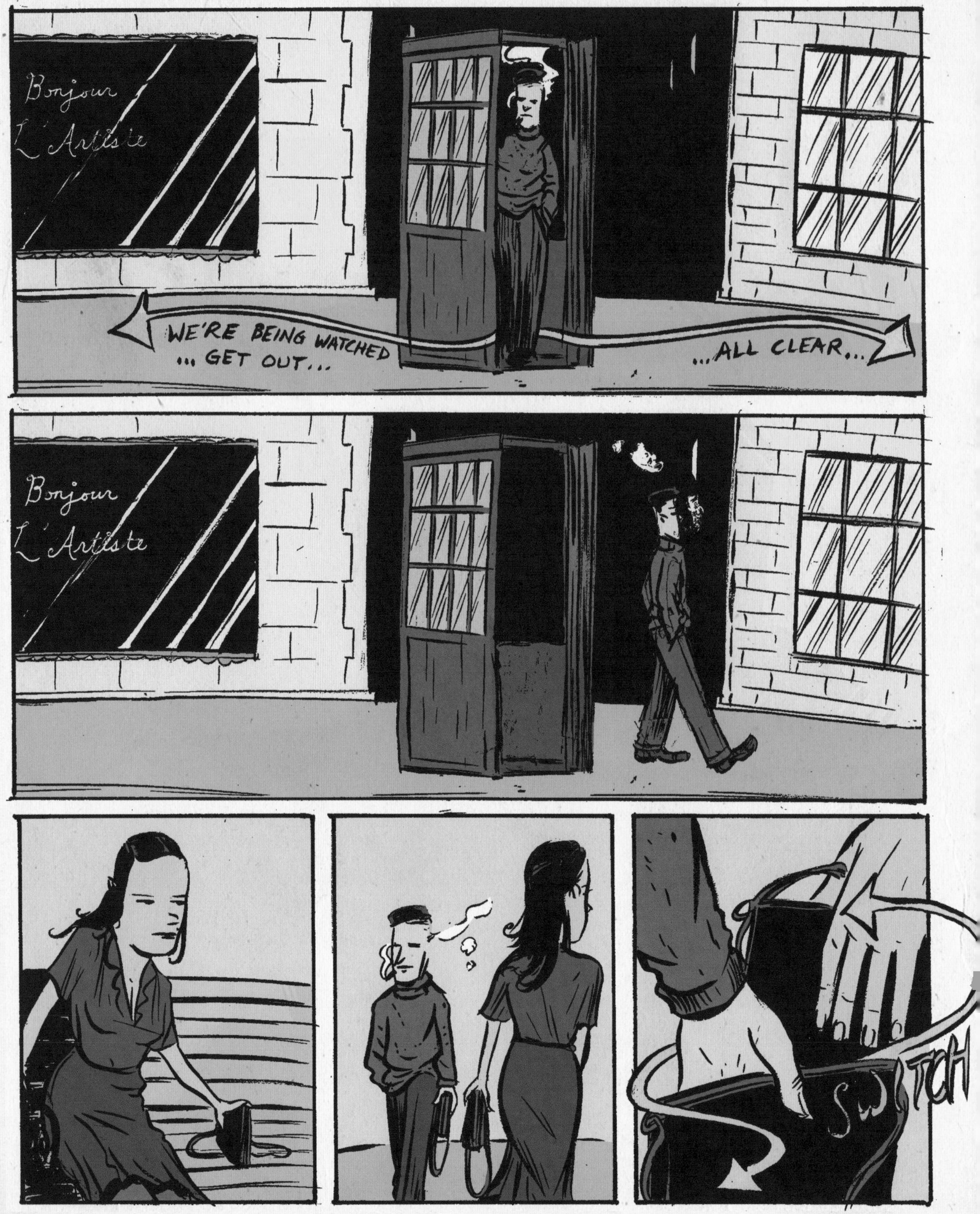
Bonjour L'Artiste
WE'RE BEING WATCHED ... GET OUT...
...ALL CLEAR...
Bonjour L'Artiste
SWITCH

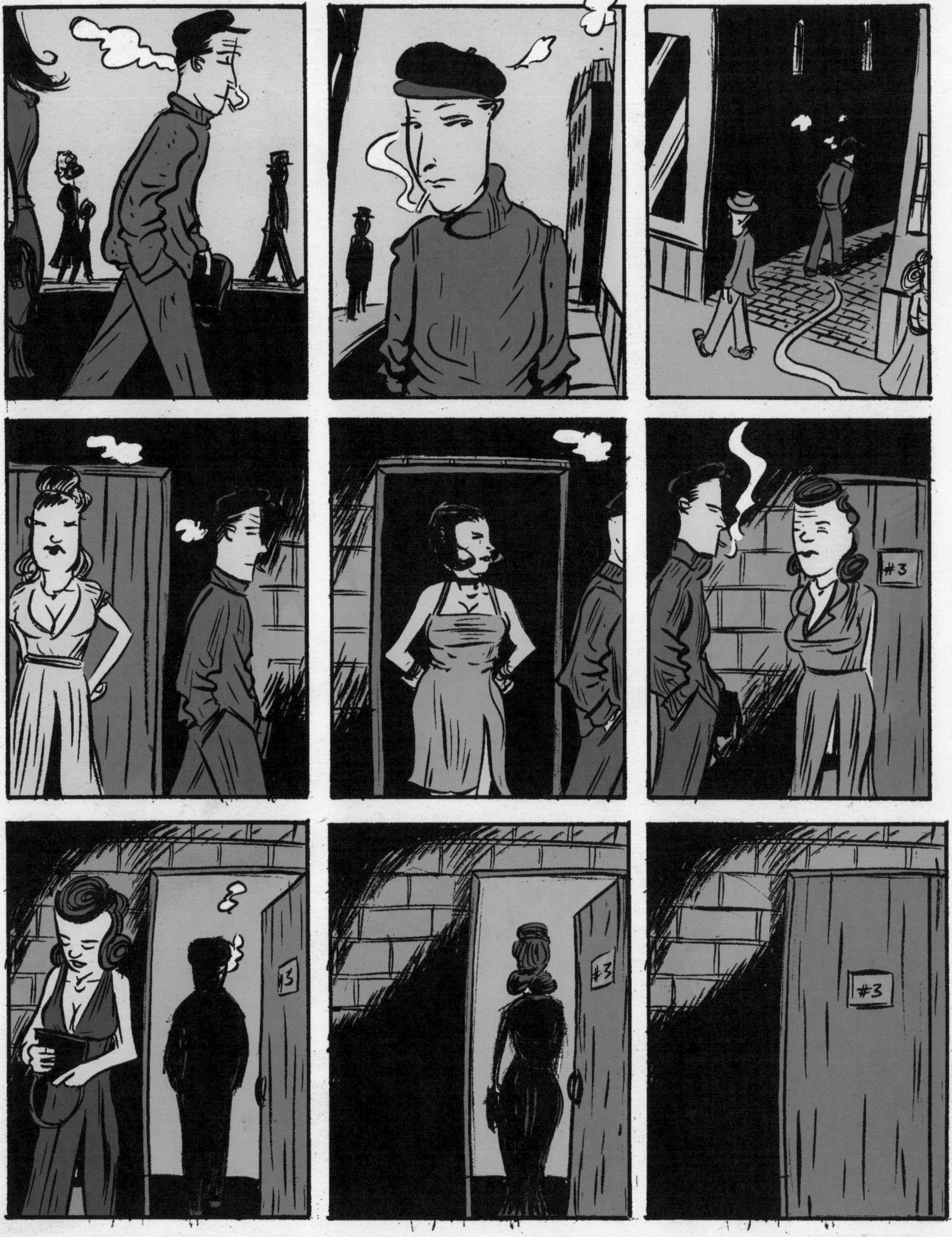
#3
#3
#3
#3

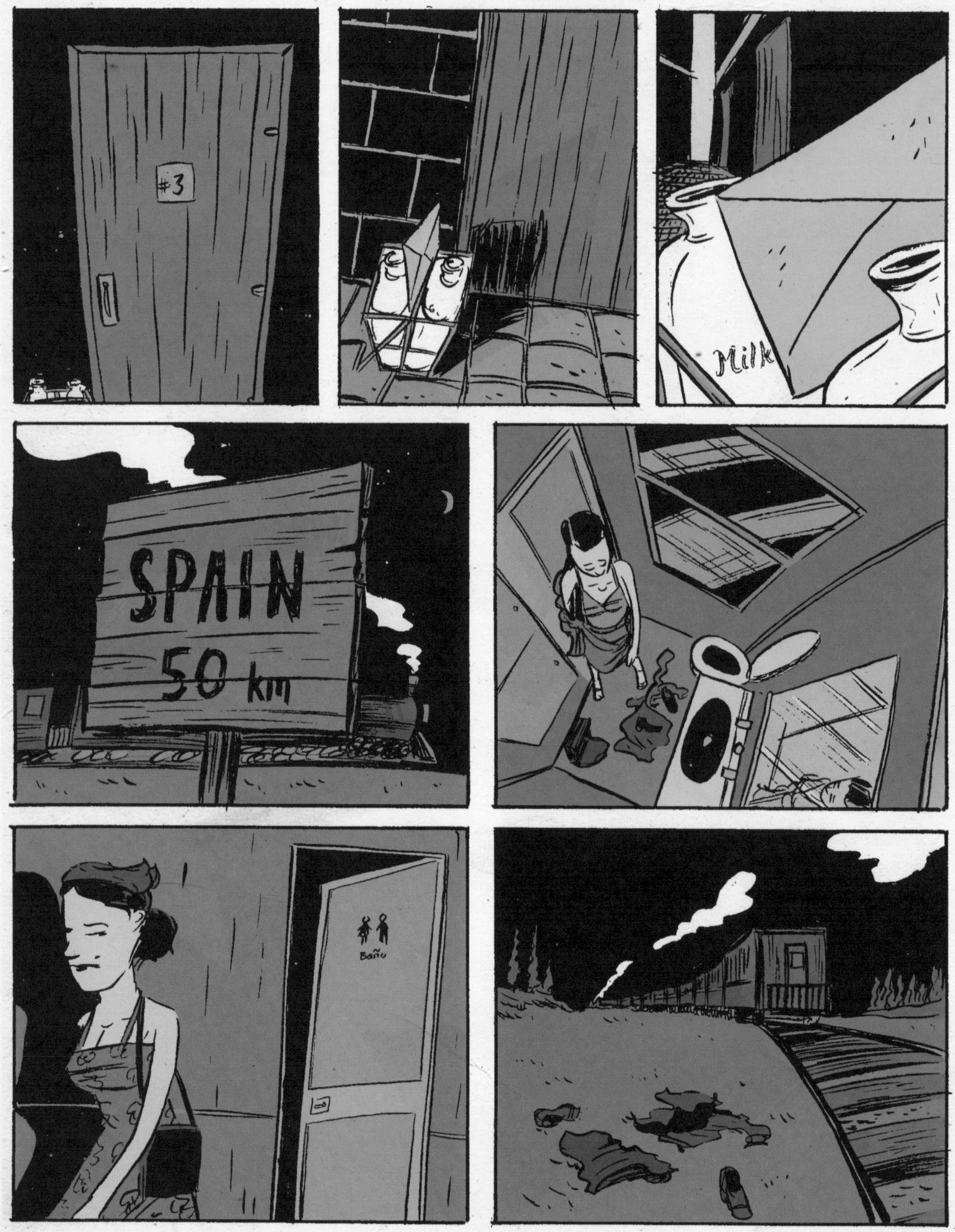
#3
Milk
SPAIN
50 km
Baño

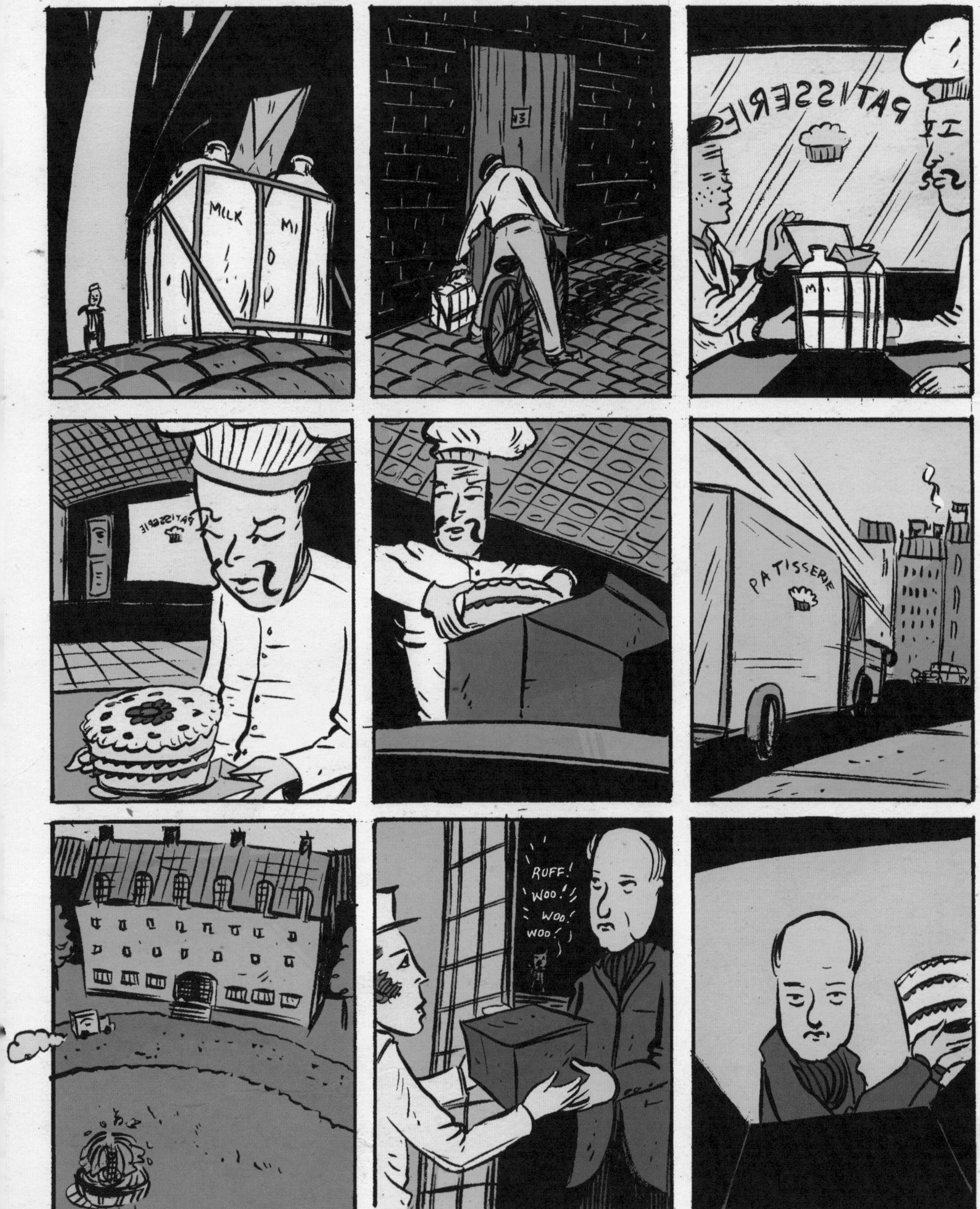
MILK
MI
PATISSERIE
PATISSERIE
PATISSERIE
RUFF!
WOO!
WOO!
WOO!

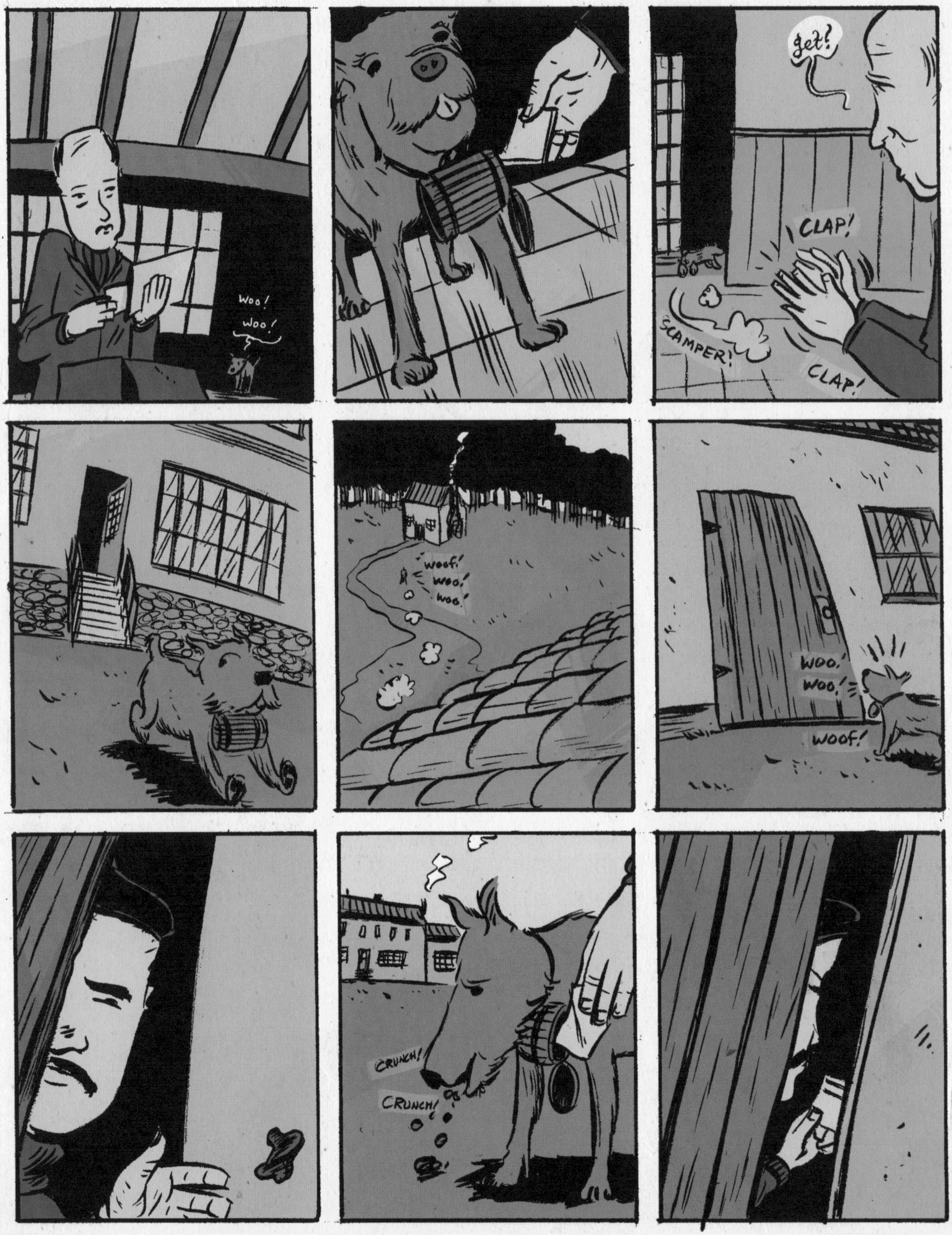
Woo!
Woo!
get?
CLAP!
SCAMPER!
CLAP!
woof!
woo!
woo!
WOO!
WOO!
WOOF!
CRUNCH!
CRUNCH!

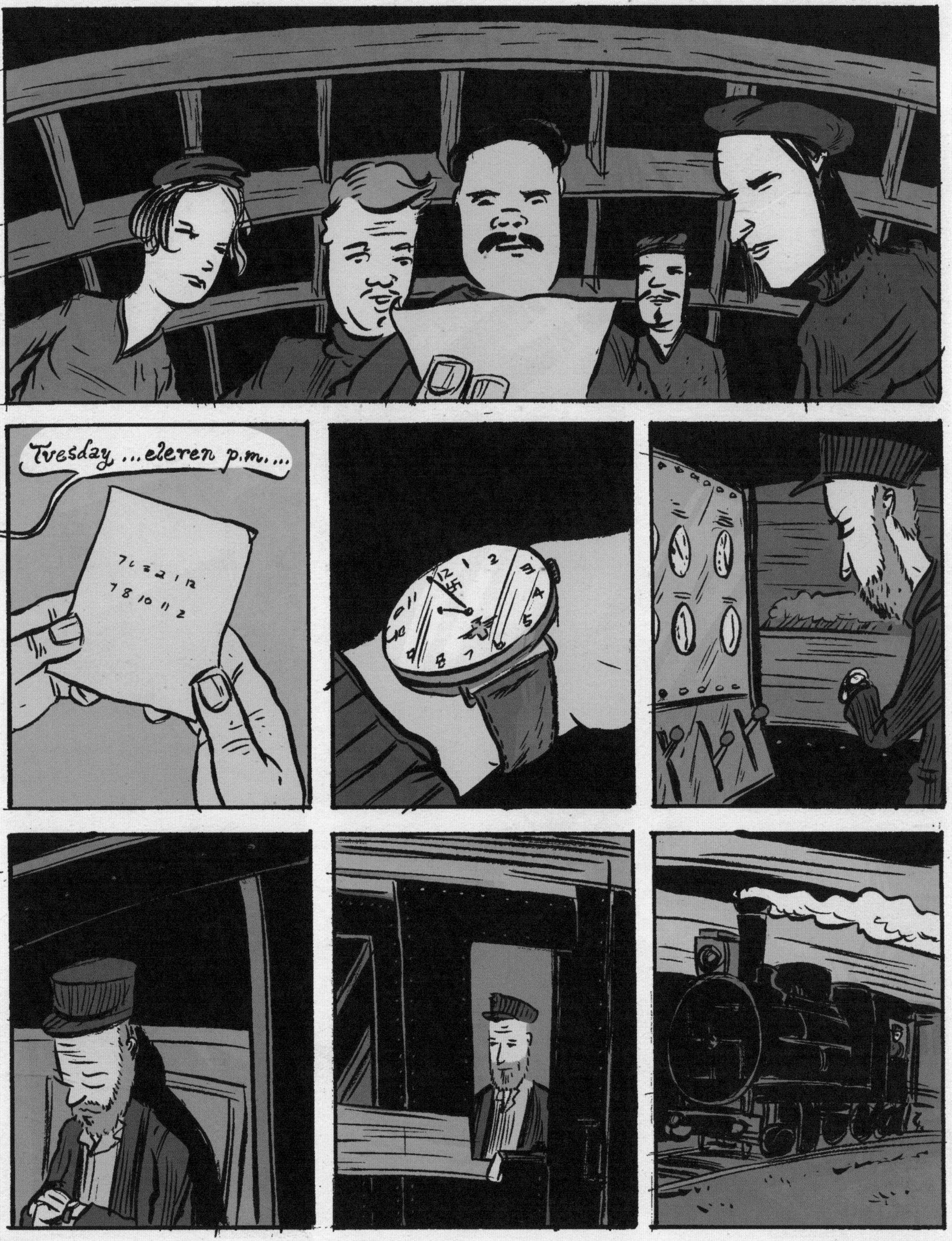
Tuesday ... eleven p.m. ...

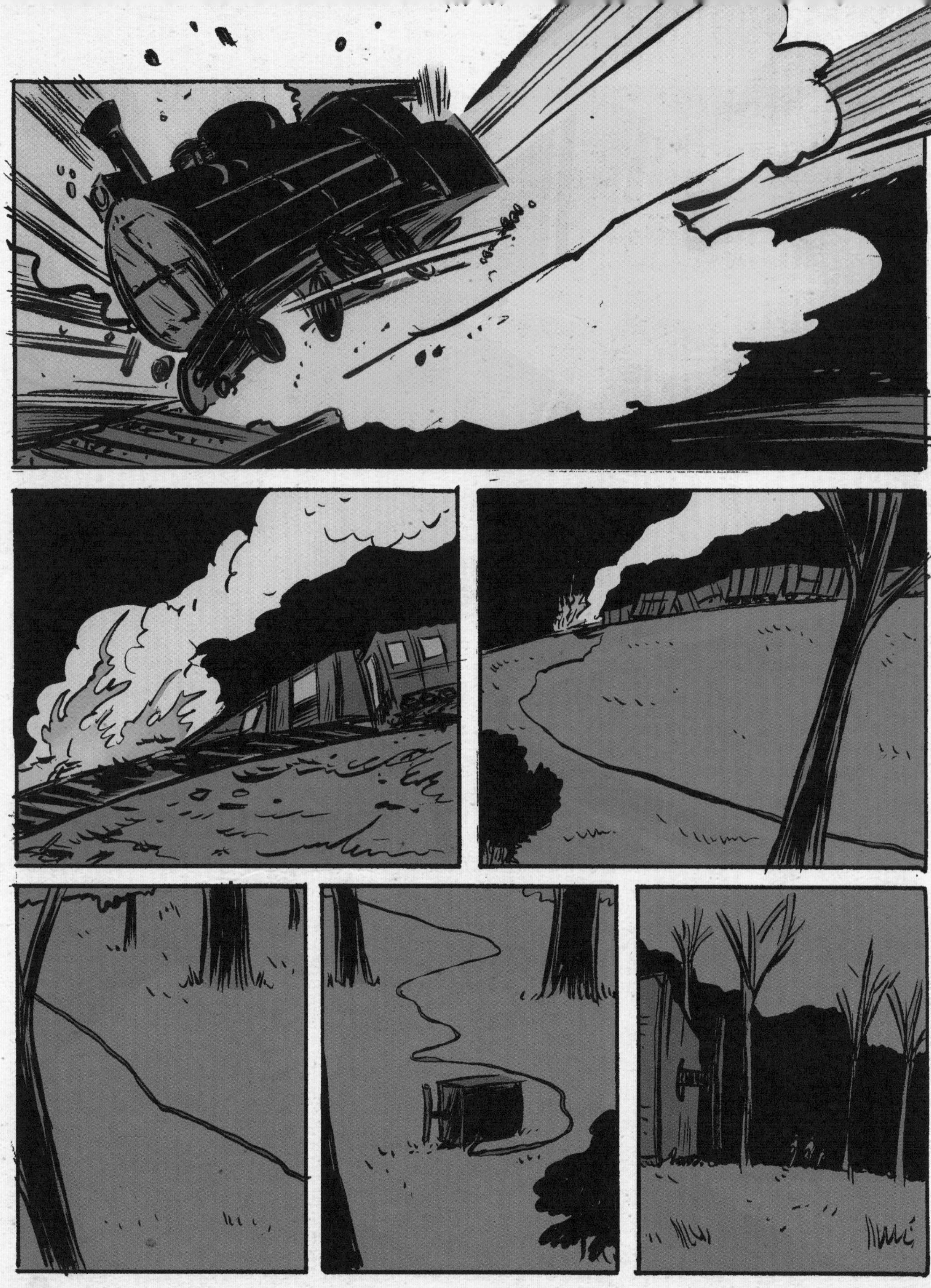

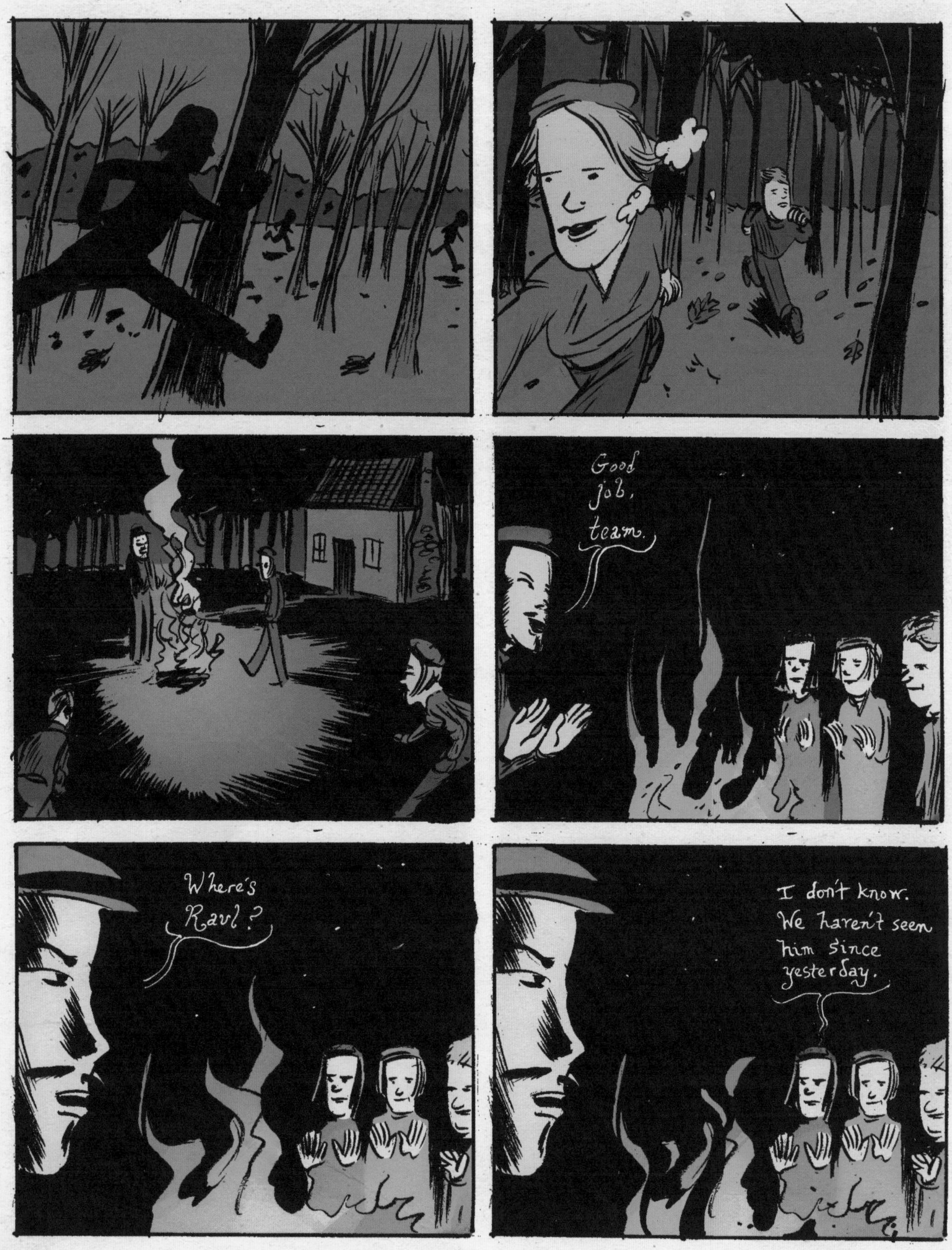
Good job, team.
Where's Raul?
I don't know. We haven't seen him since yesterday.

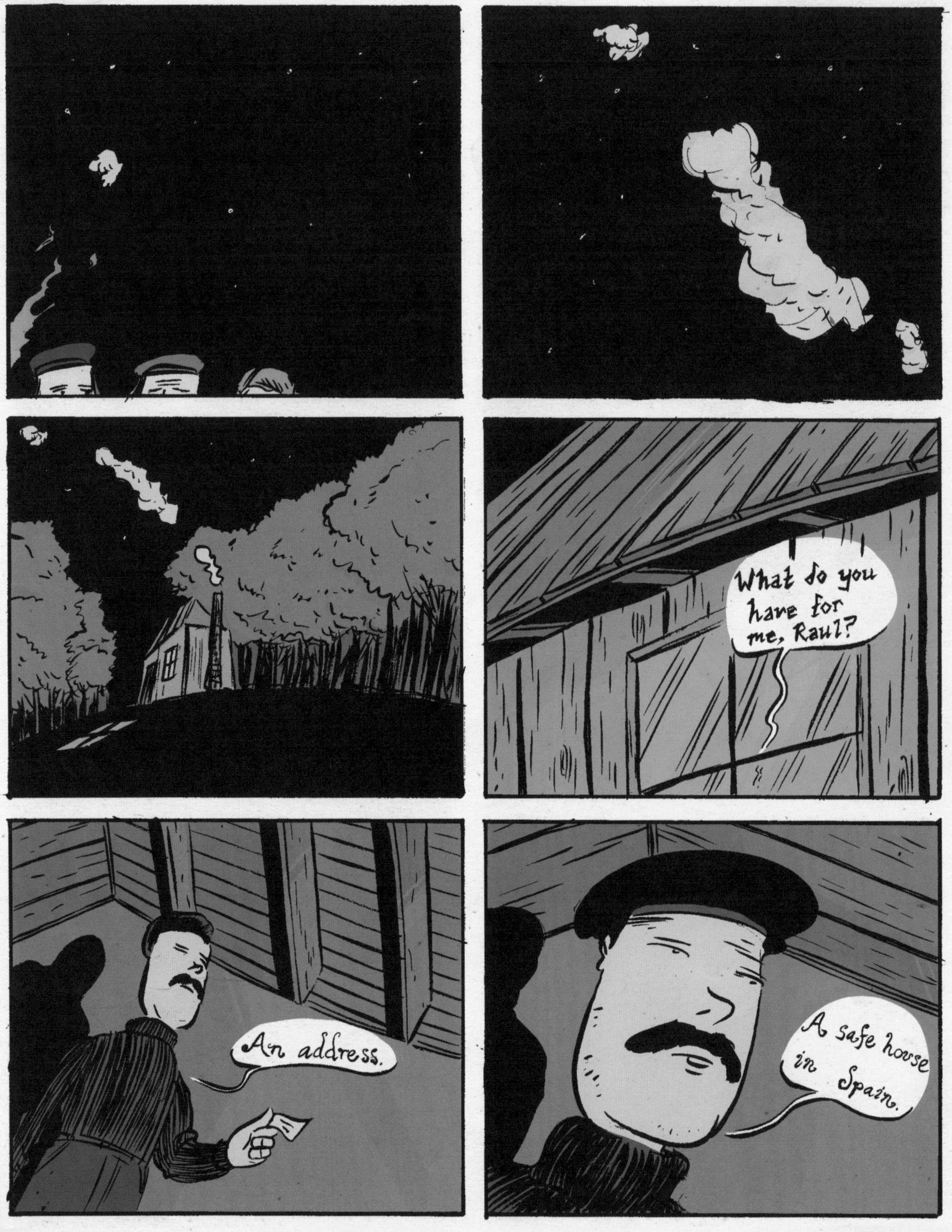
What do you have for me, Raul?
An address.
A safe house in Spain.

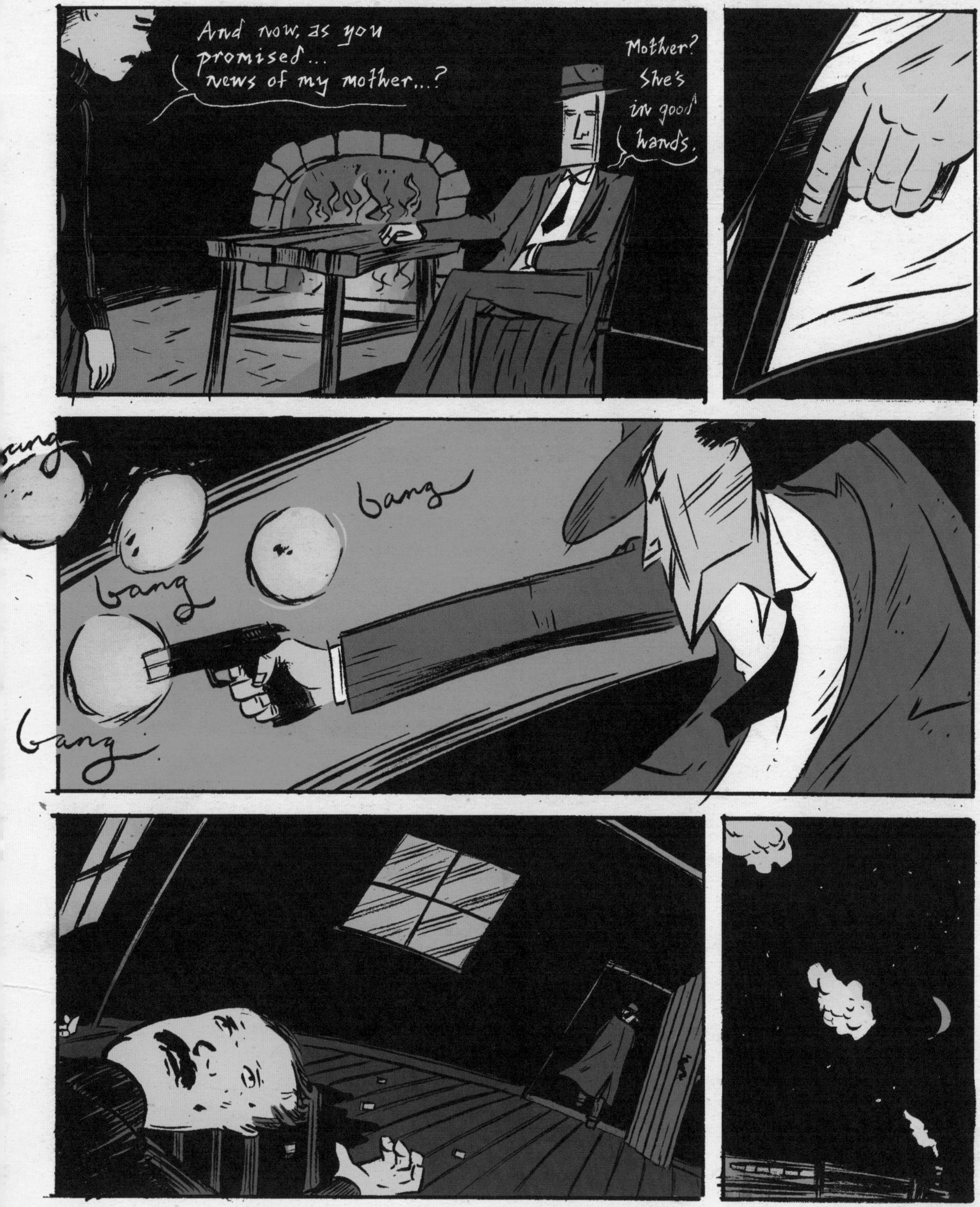
And now, as you promised... news of my mother...?
Mother? She's in good hands.
bang
bang
bang
bang

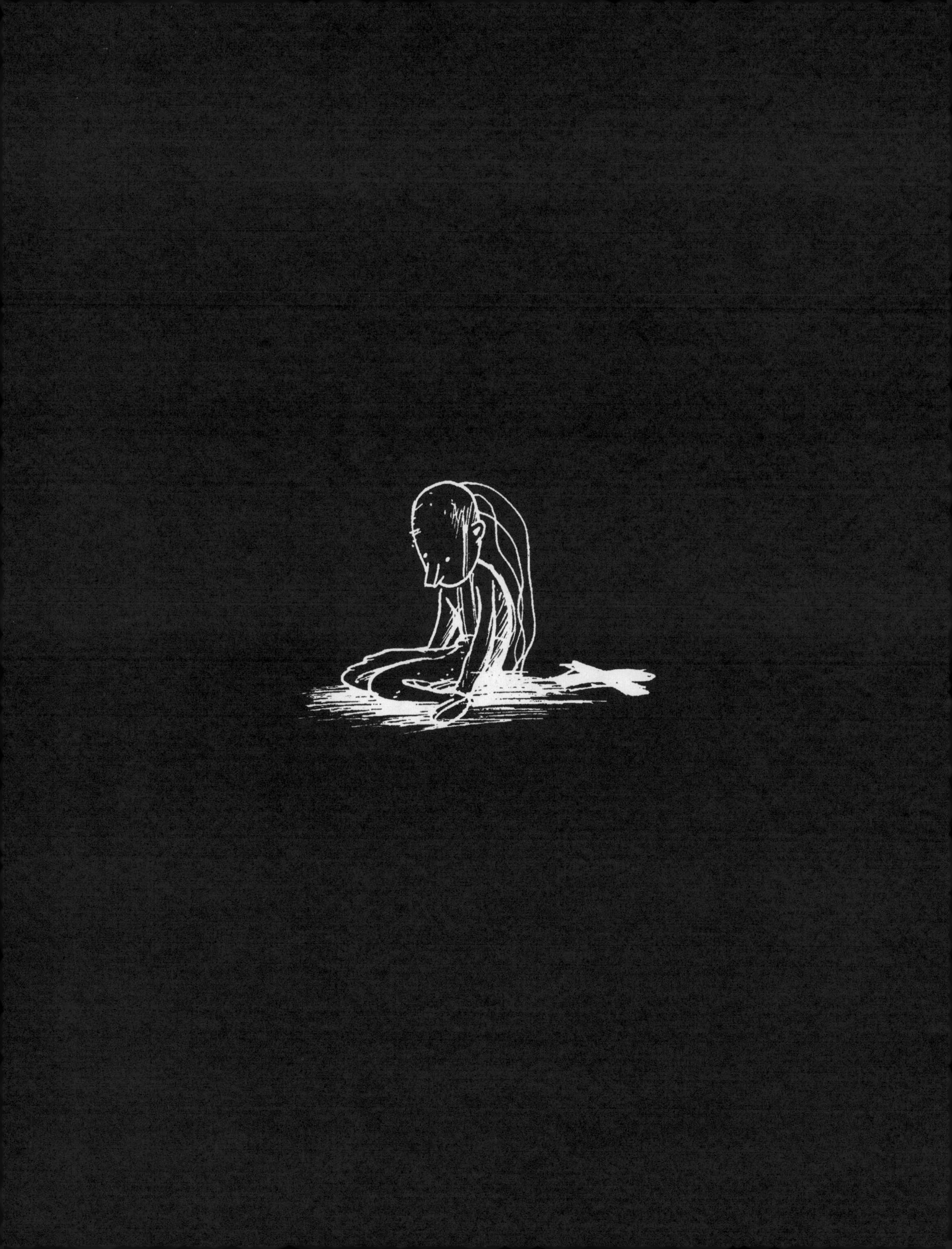

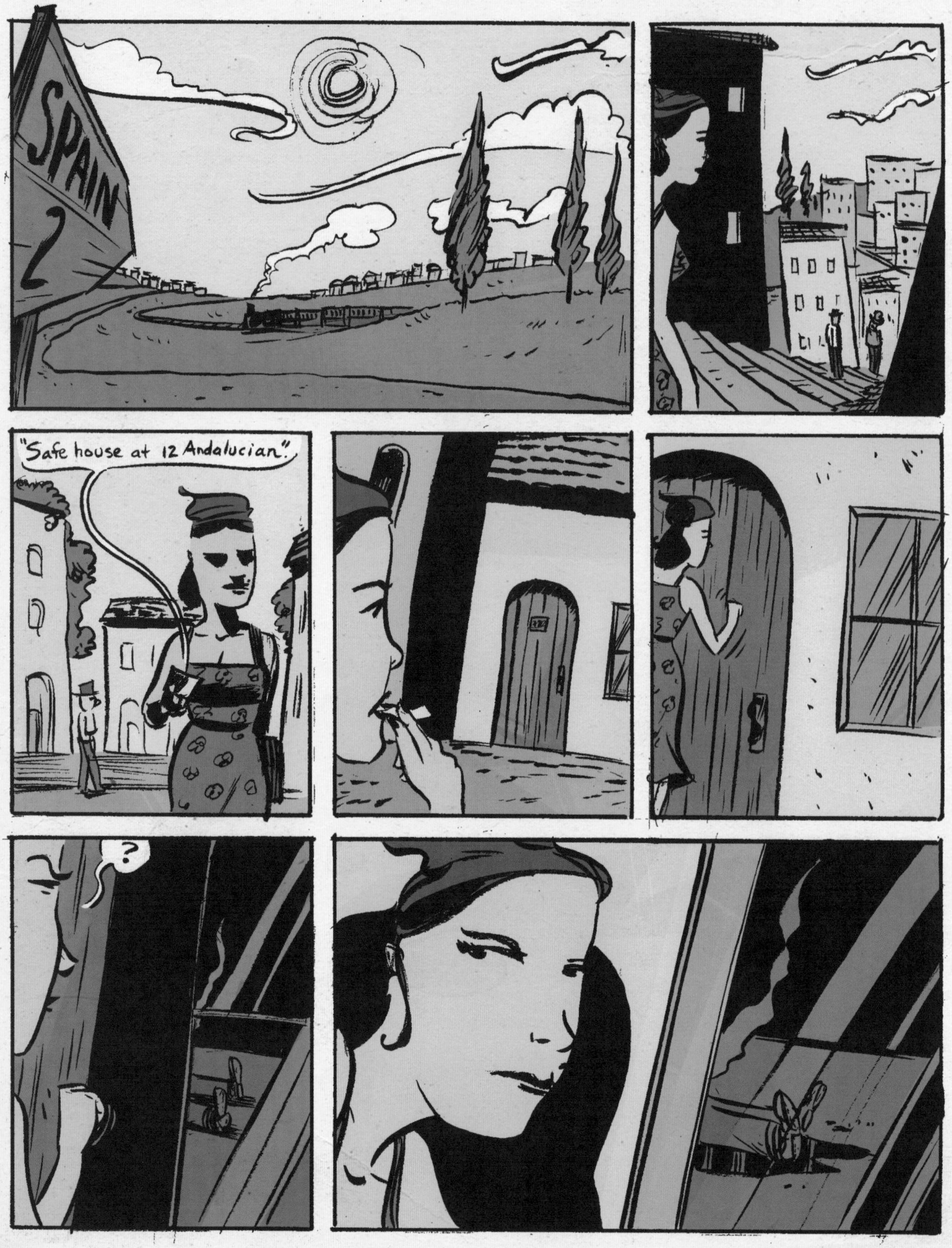
SPAIN
2
"Safe house at 12 Andalucian".
?

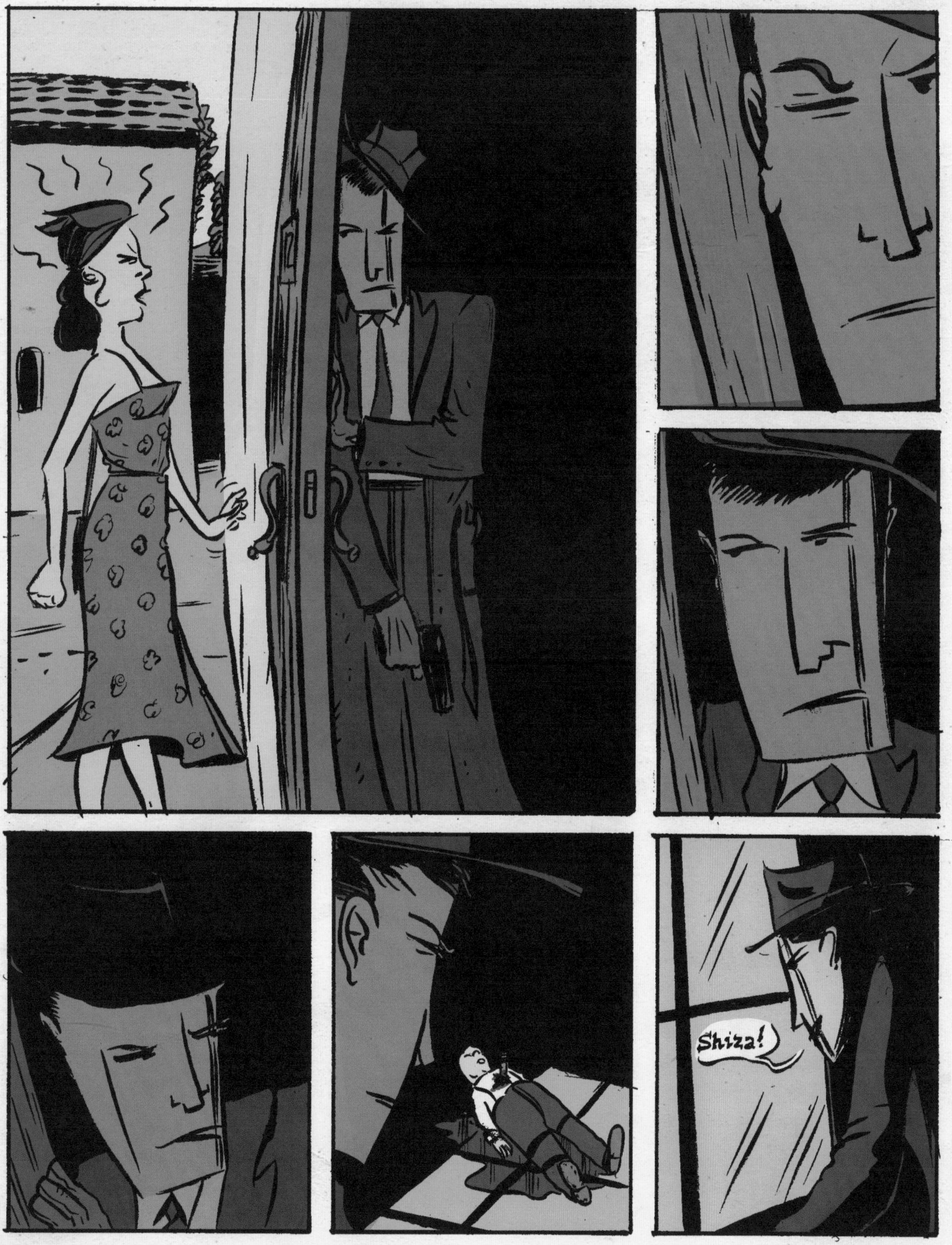
Shiza!

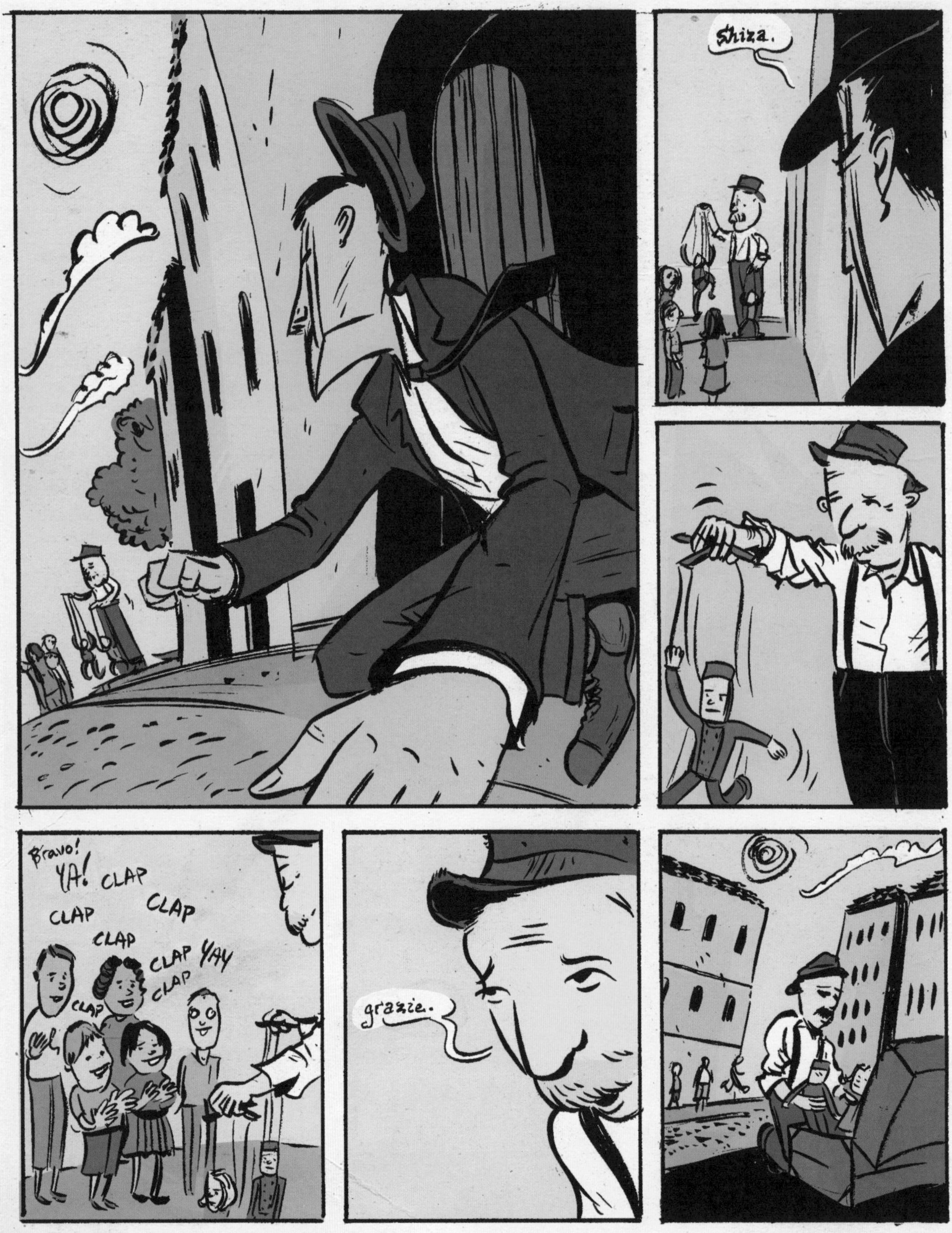
Shiza.
Bravo!
YA!
CLAP
CLAP
CLAP
CLAP
CLAP
CLAP
YAY
CLAP
grazie.

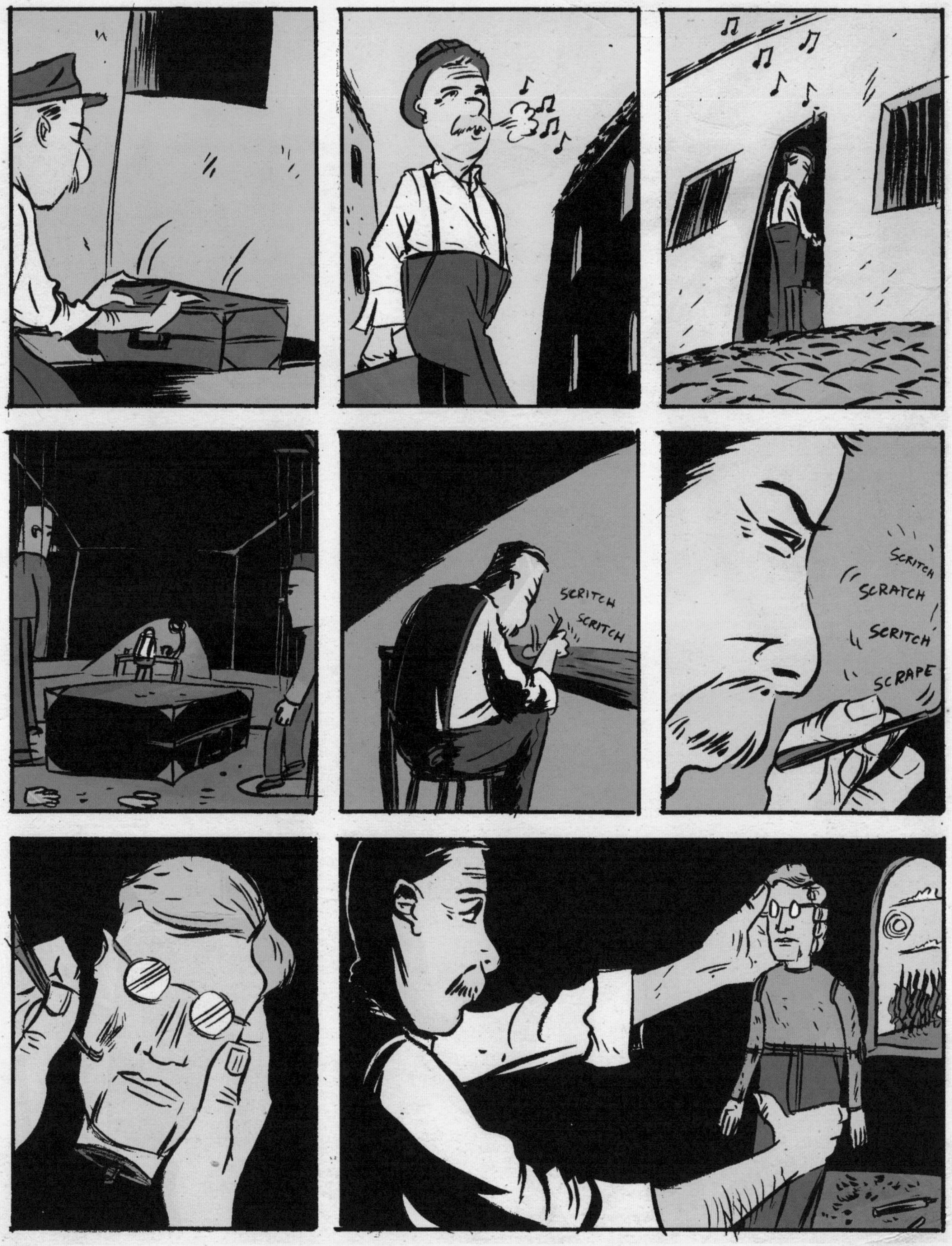
SCRITCH
SCRITCH
SCRITCH
SCRATCH
SCRITCH
SCRAPE

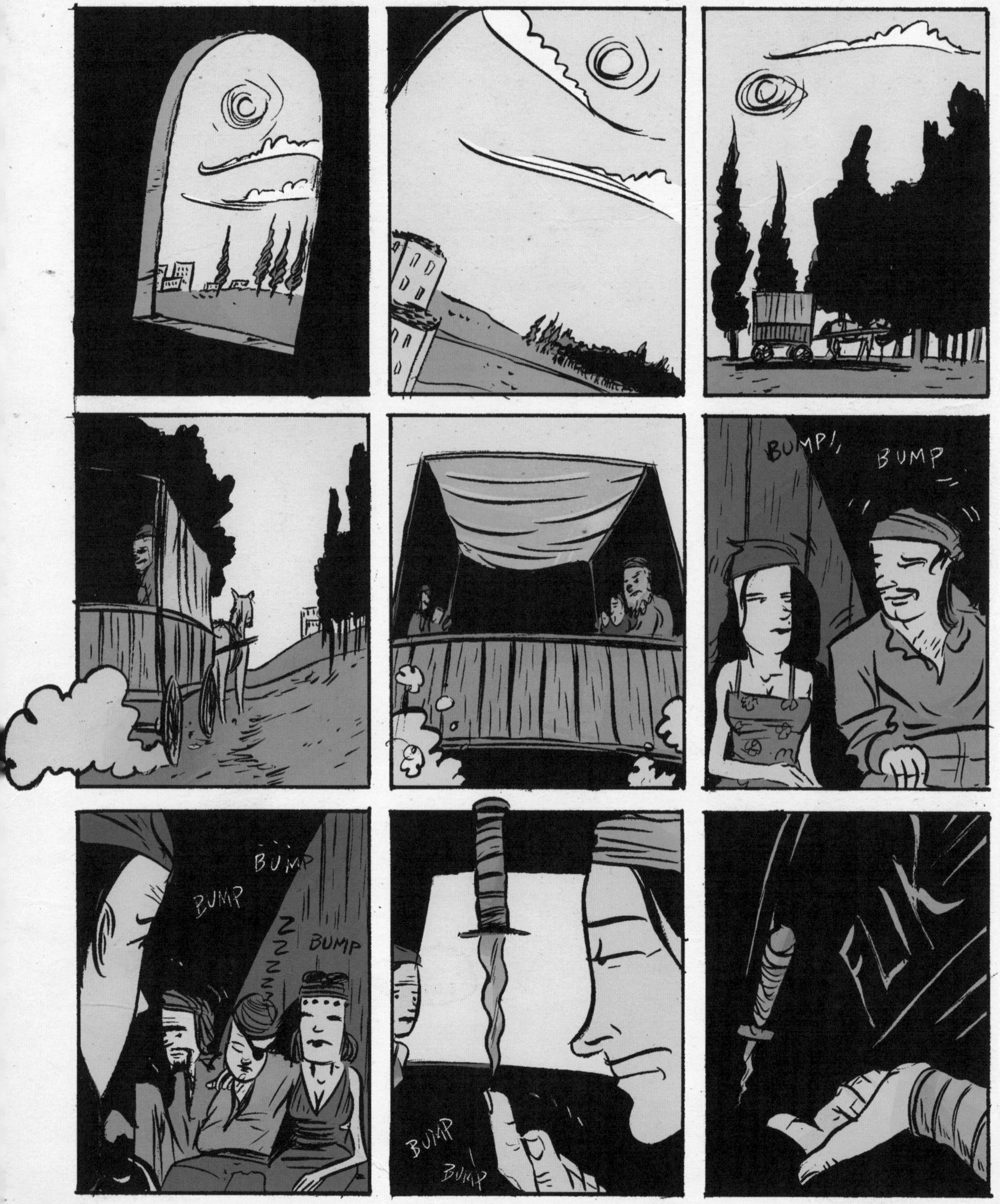
BUMP!
BUMP
BUMP
BUMP
ZZZZ
BUMP
BUMP
BUMP
FLIK

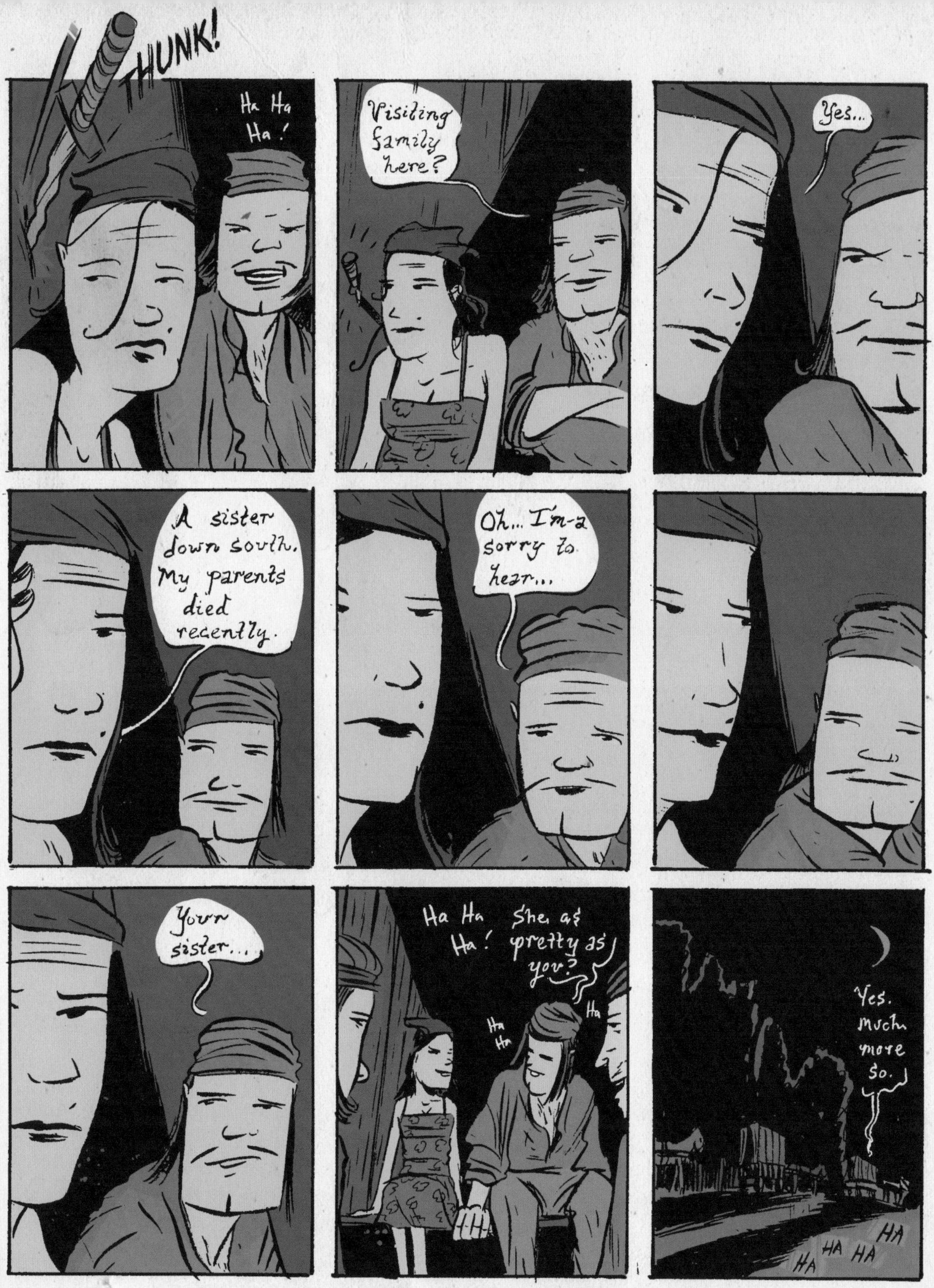
THUNK!
Ha Ha Ha!
Visiting family here?
Yes...
A sister down south. My parents died recently.
Oh... I'm-a sorry to hear...
Your sister...
Ha Ha Ha!
She as pretty as you?
Ha Ha
Ha
Yes. Much more so.
HA HA HA HA

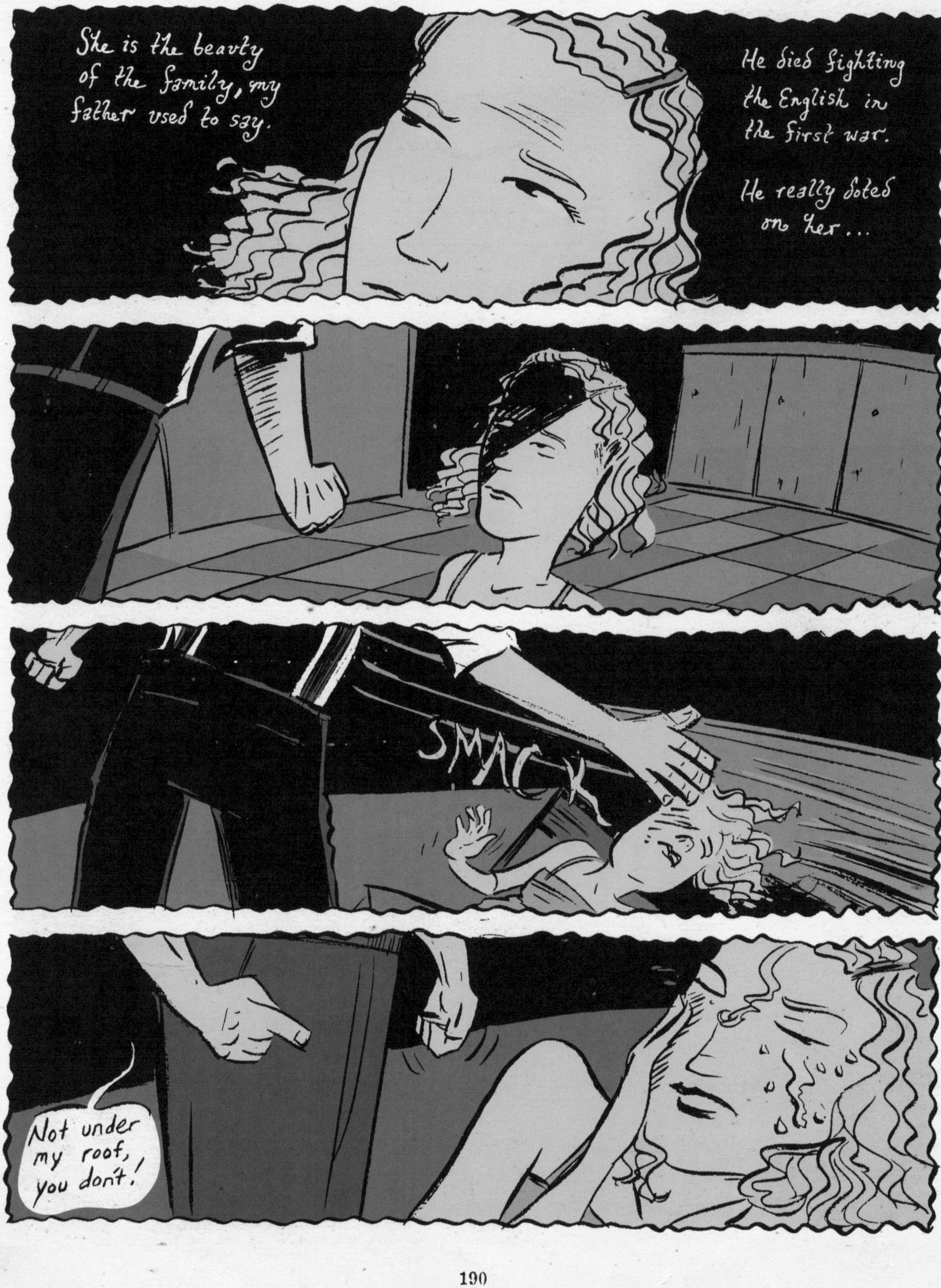
She is the beauty of the family, my father used to say.
He died fighting the English in the first war.
He really doted on her...
SMACK
Not under my roof, you don't!

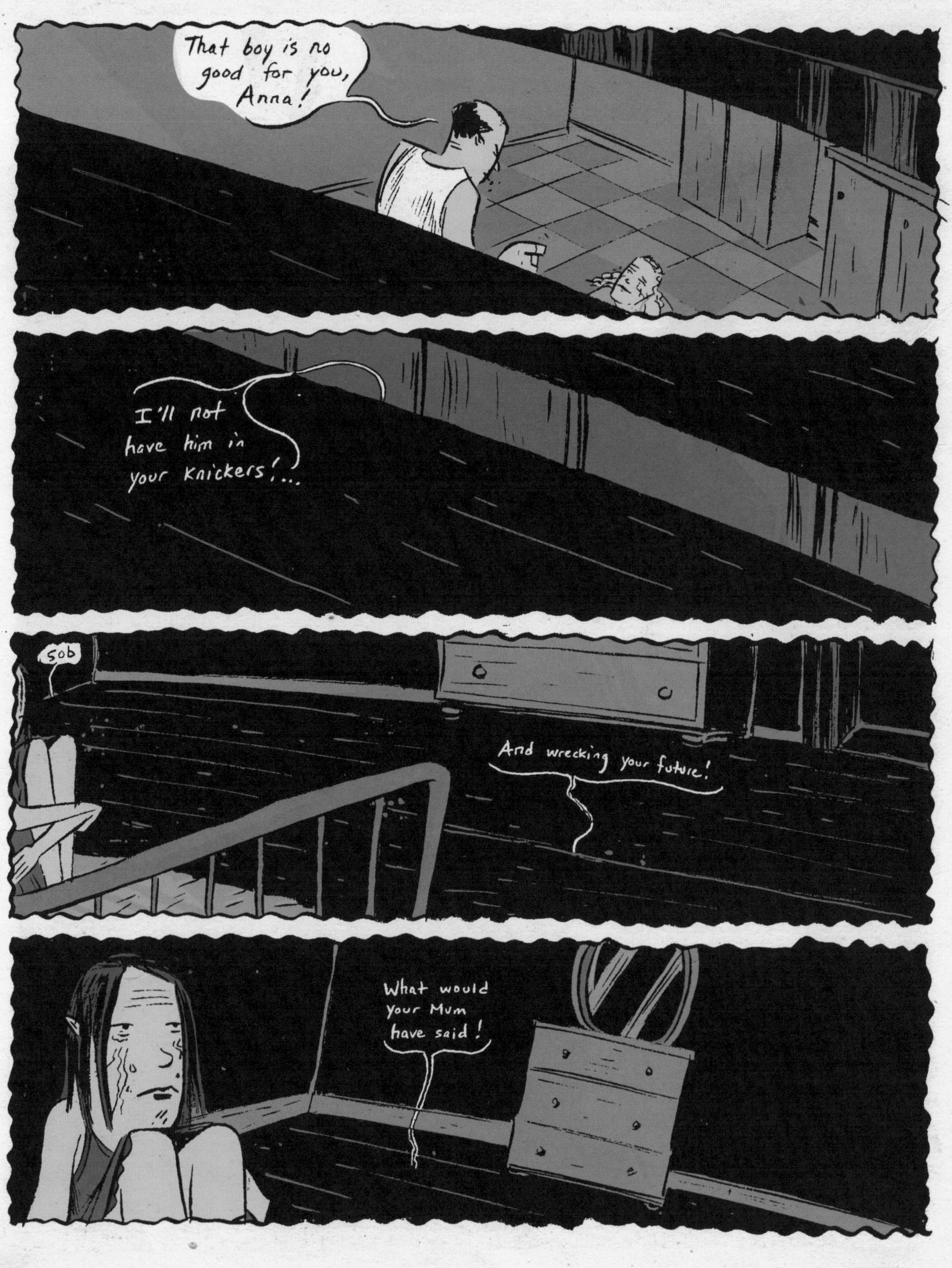
That boy is no good for you, Anna!
I'll not have him in your knickers!...
sob
And wrecking your future!
What would your Mum have said!

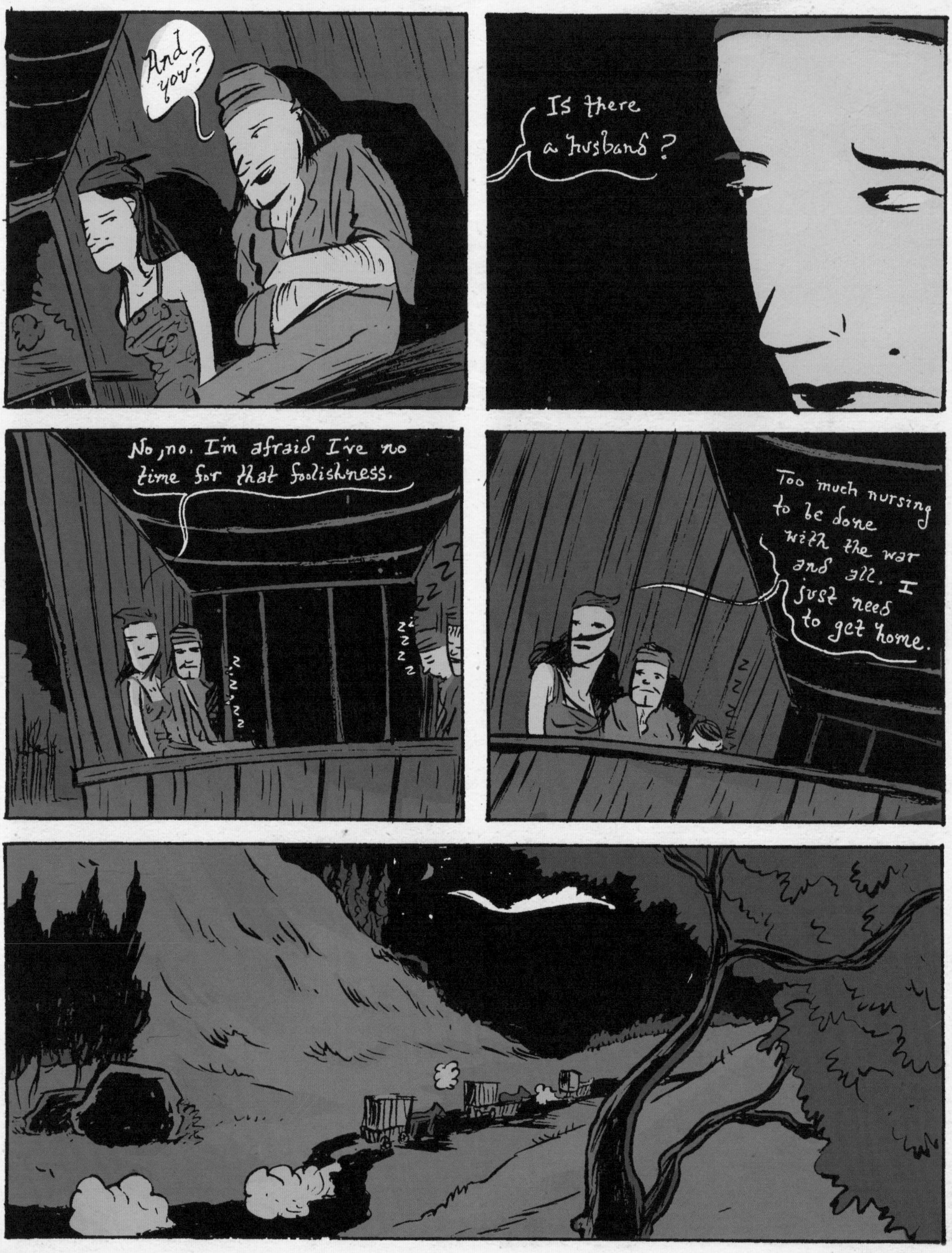
And you?
Is there a husband?
No, no. I'm afraid I've no time for that foolishness.
Too much nursing to be done with the war and all. I just need to get home.

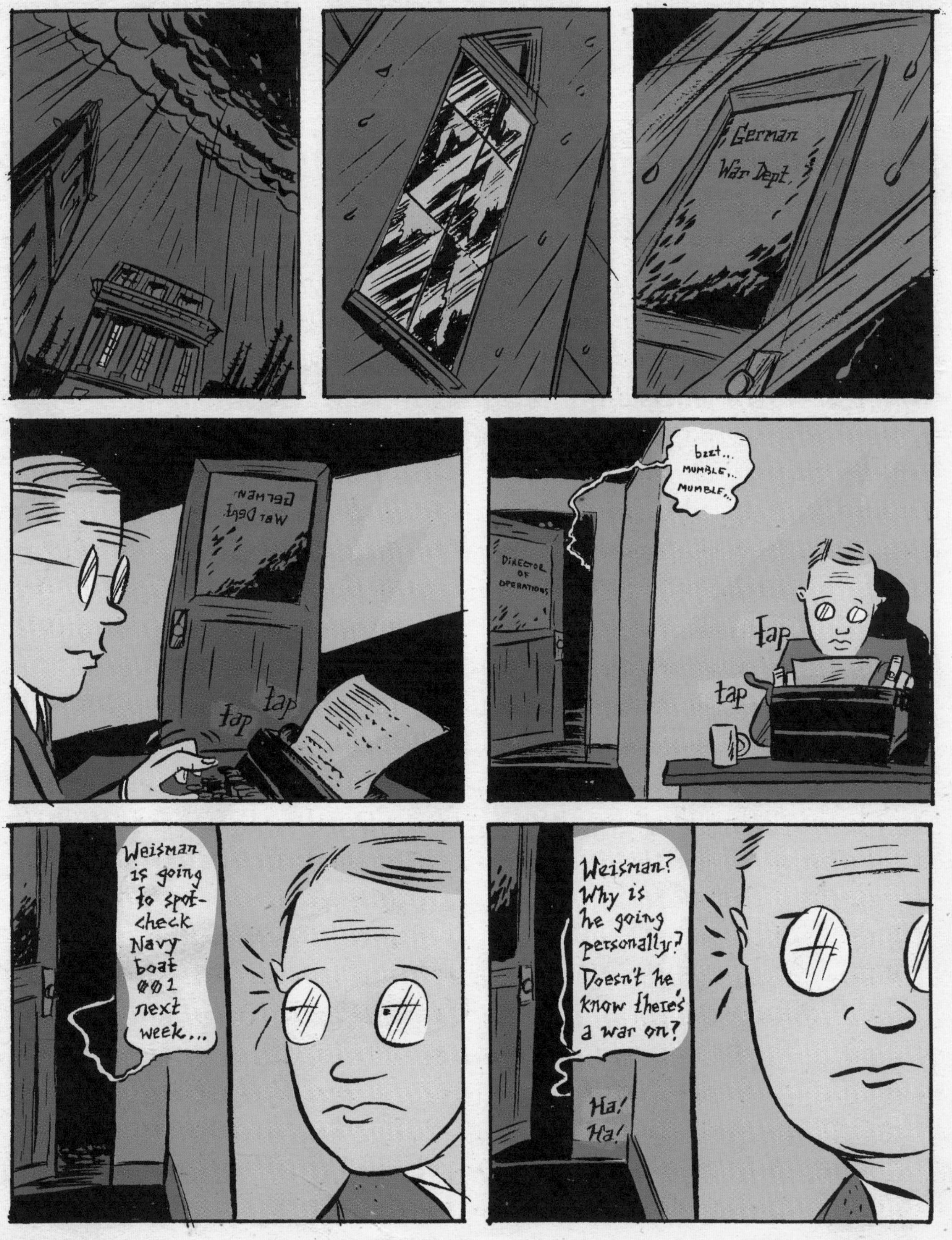
German
War Dept.
German
War Dept.
tap
tap
bzzt... MUMBLE... MUMBLE...
DIRECTOR OF OPERATIONS
tap
tap
Weisman is going to spot-check Navy boat 001 next week...
Weisman? Why is he going personally? Doesn't he know there's a war on?
Ha! Ha!

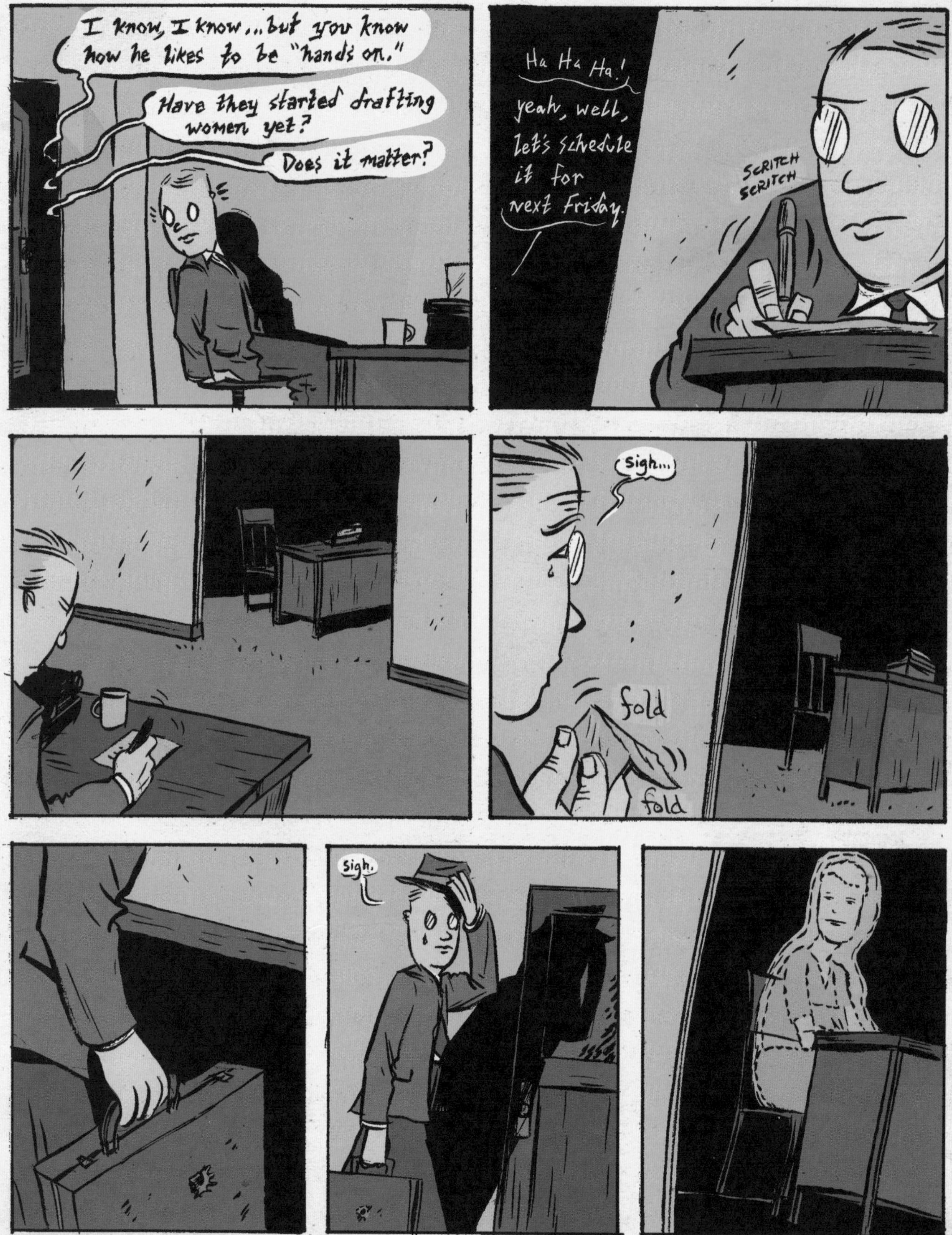
I know, I know... but you know how he likes to be "hands on."
Have they started drafting women yet?
Does it matter?
Ha Ha Ha!
yeah, well, let's schedule it for next Friday.
SCRITCH SCRITCH
sigh...
fold
fold
sigh.

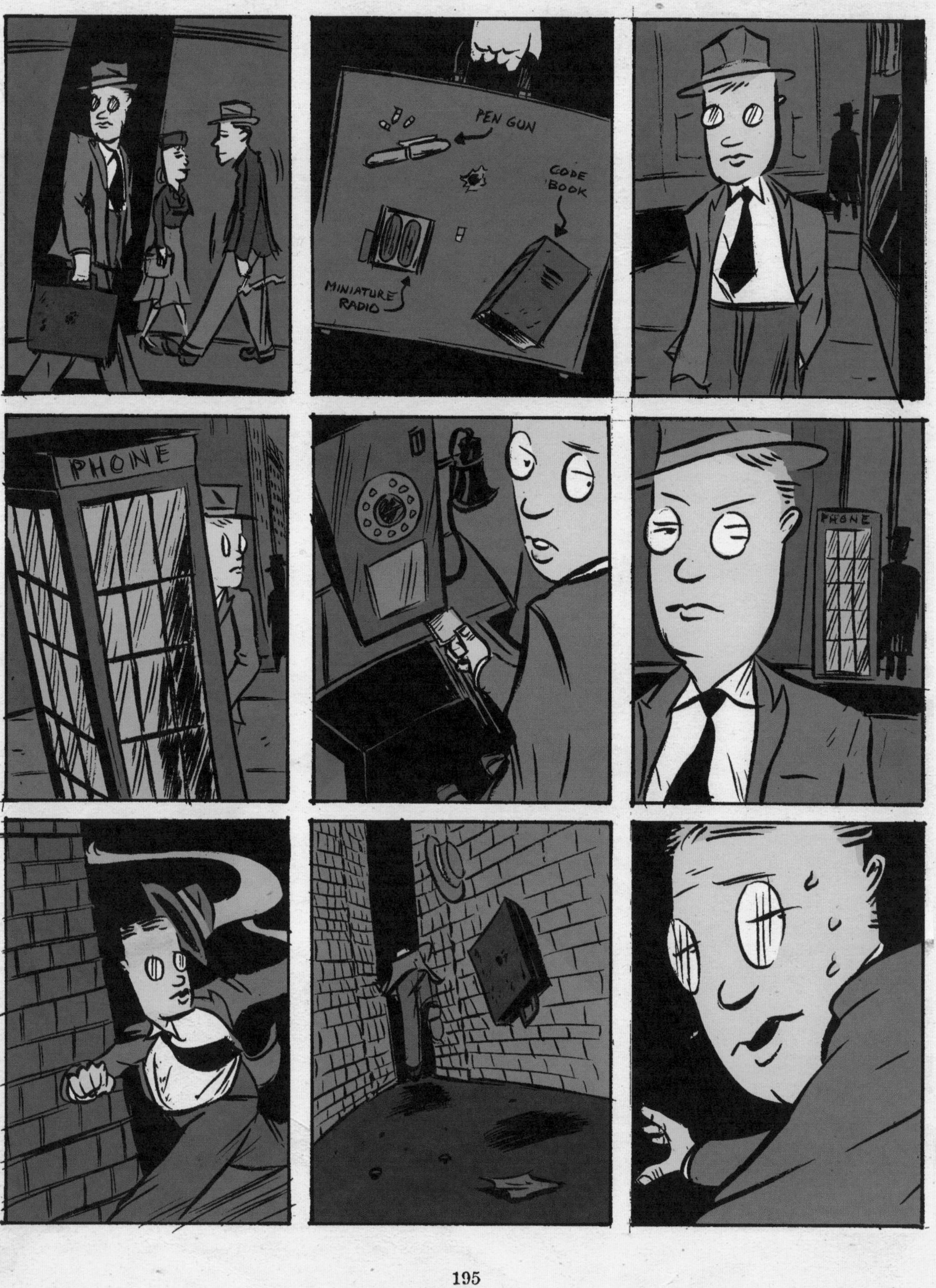
PEN GUN
CODE BOOK
MINIATURE RADIO
PHONE
PHONE

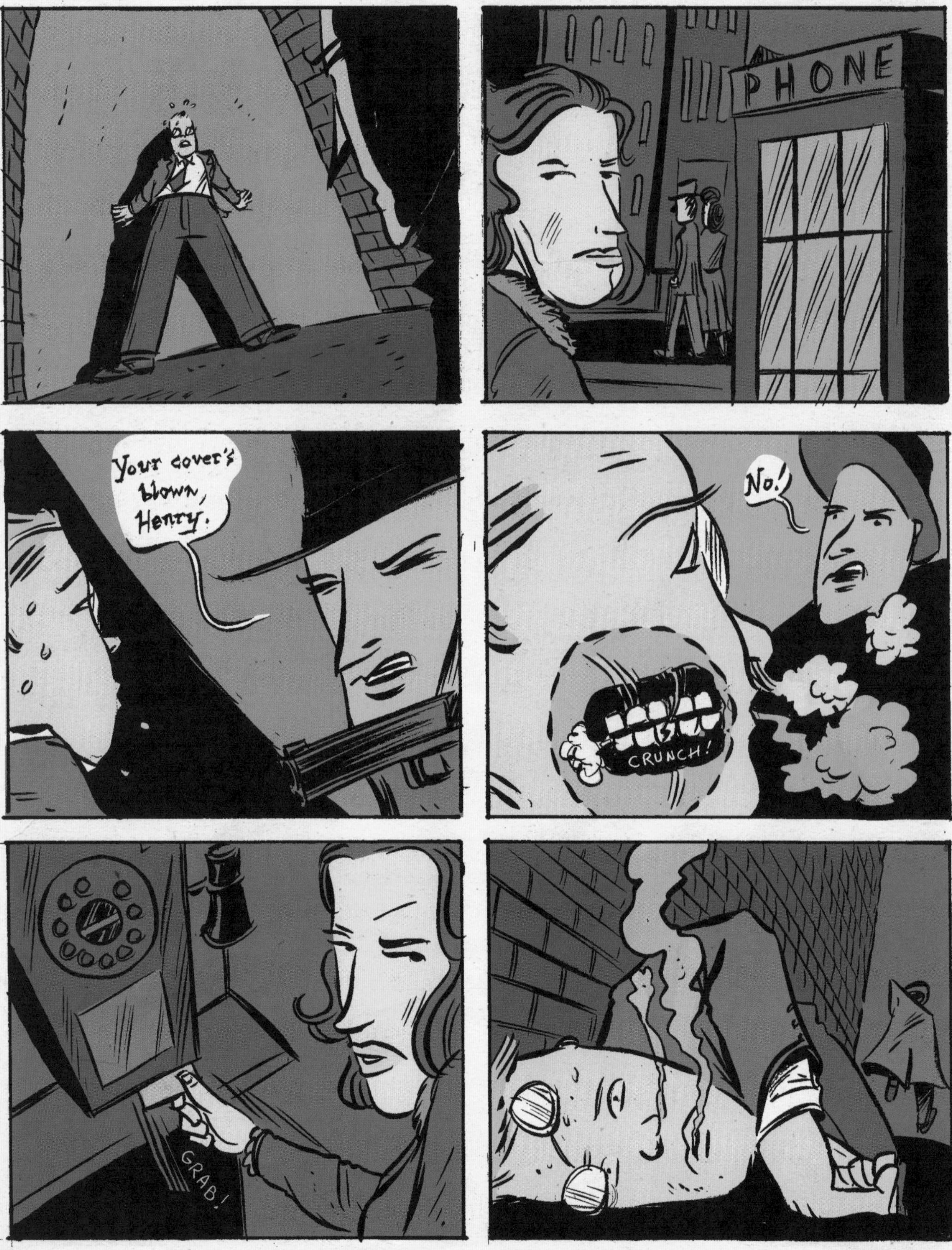
PHONE
Your cover's blown, Henry.
No!
CRUNCH!
GRAB!

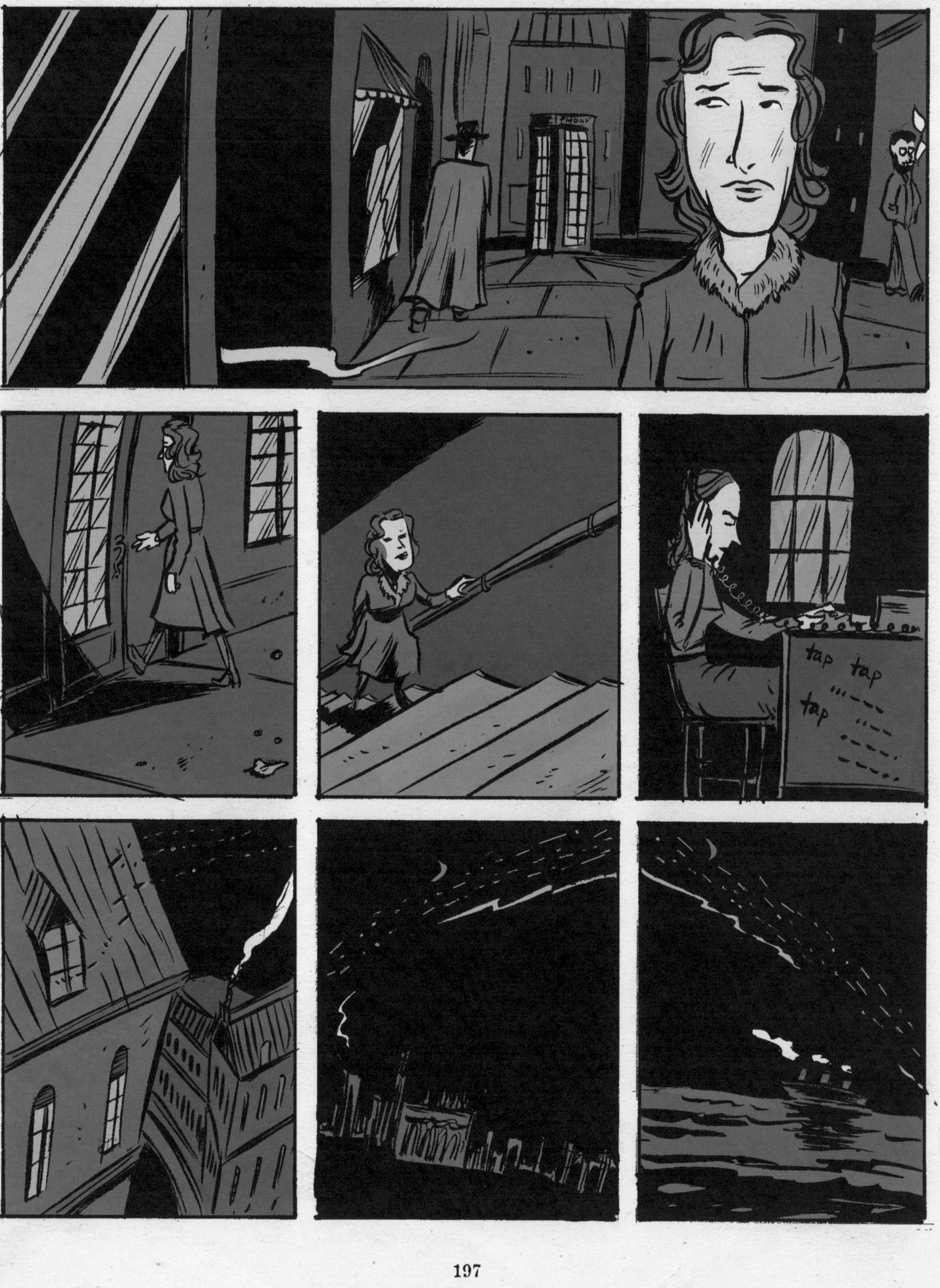
tap tap
tap

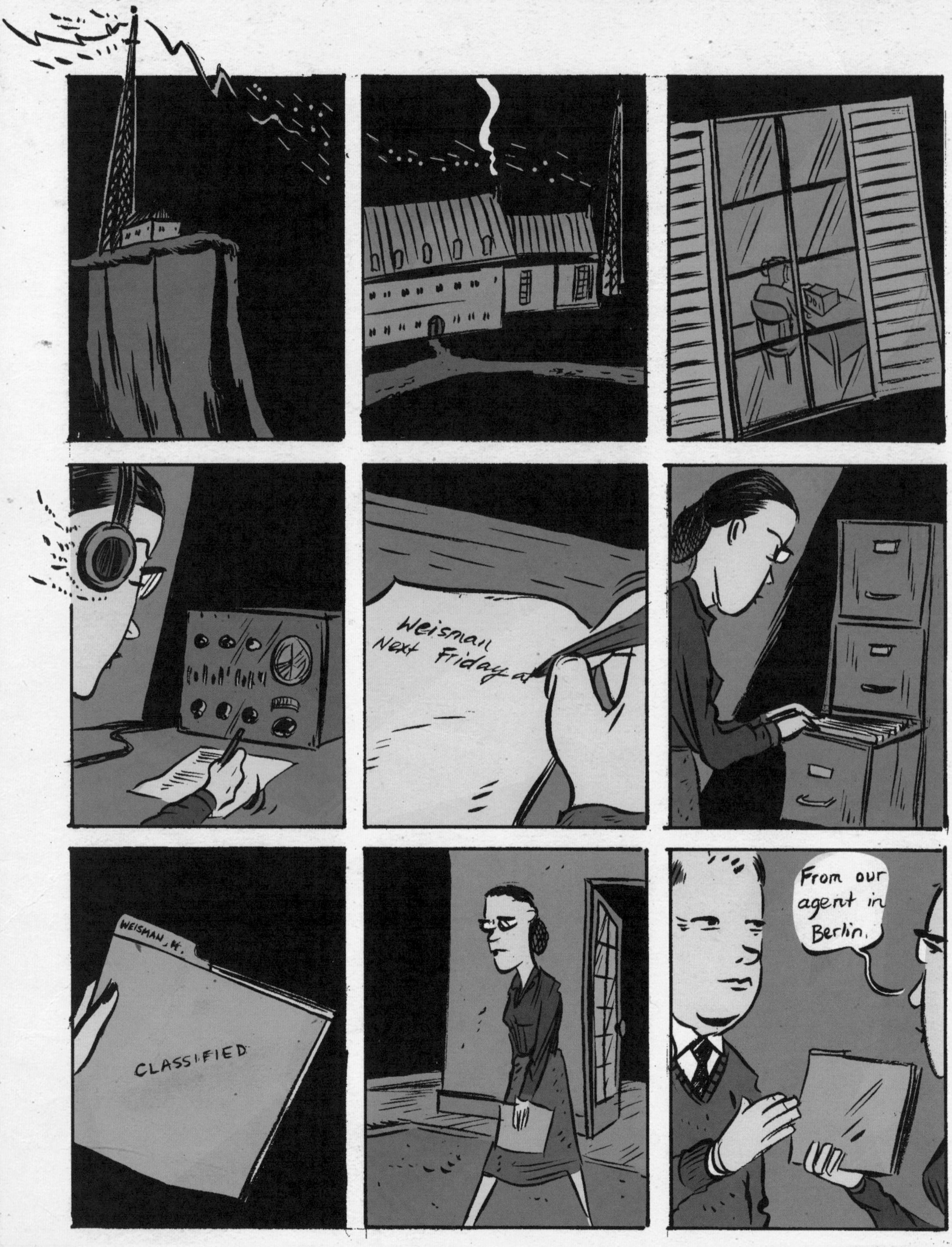
Weisman
Next Friday at
WEISMAN, H.
CLASSIFIED
From our agent in Berlin.

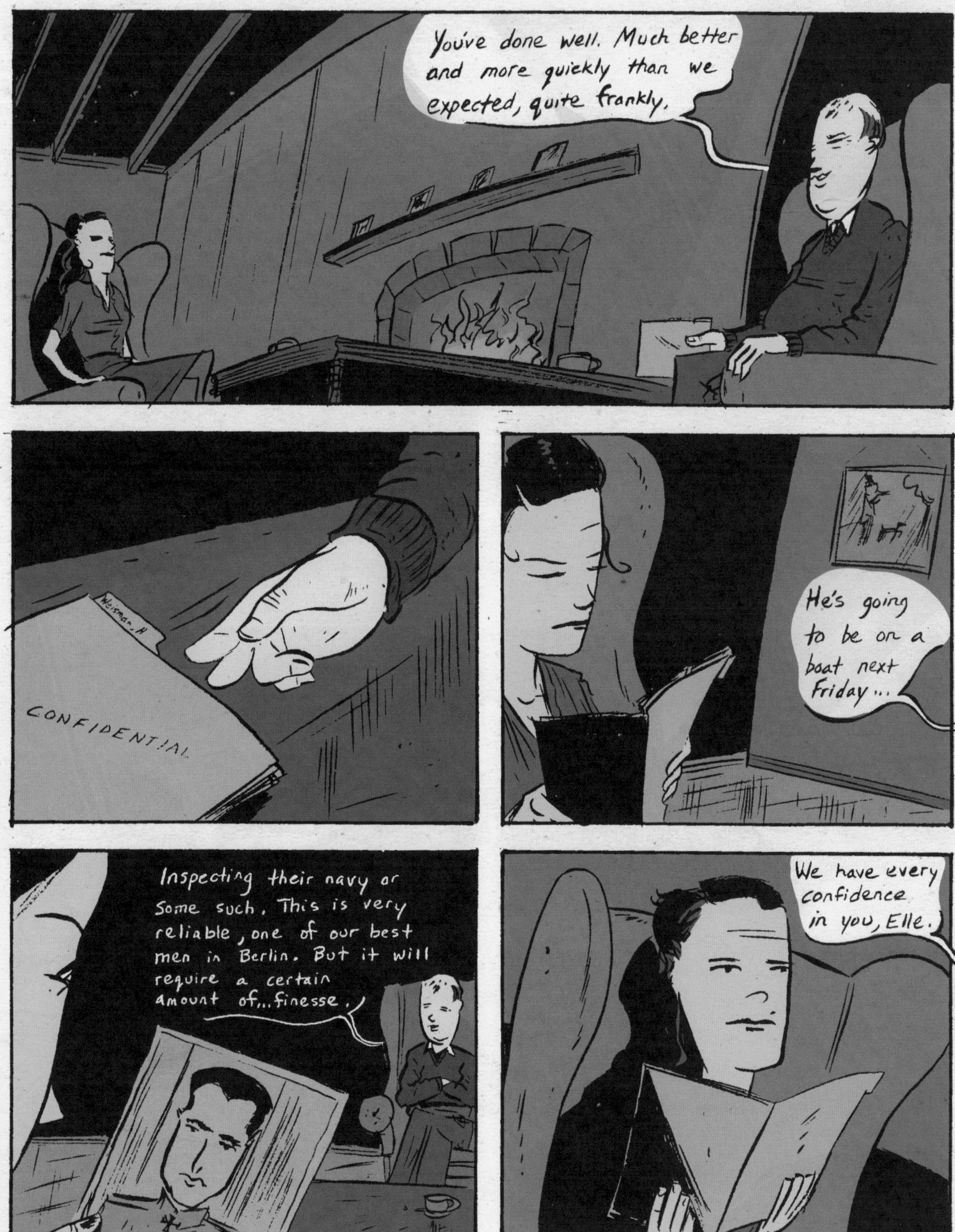
You've done well. Much better and more quickly than we expected, quite frankly.
Weisman, H
CONFIDENTIAL
He's going to be on a boat next Friday...
Inspecting their navy or some such. This is very reliable, one of our best men in Berlin. But it will require a certain amount of... finesse.
We have every confidence in you, Elle.

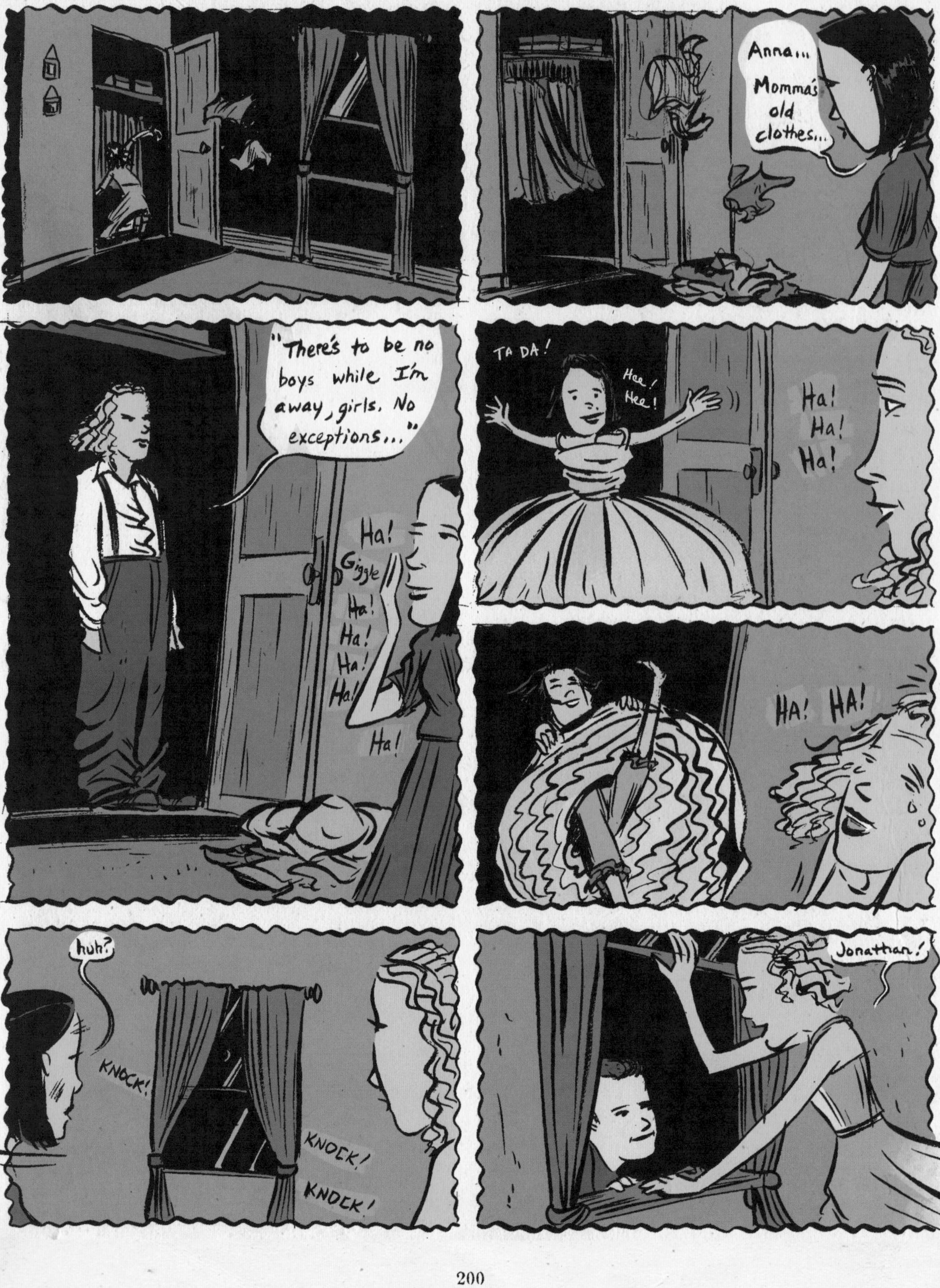
Anna...
Momma's old clothes...
"There's to be no boys while I'm away, girls. No exceptions..."
Ha!
Giggle
Ha!
Ha!
Ha!
Ha!
Ha!
TA DA!
Hee! Hee!
Ha! Ha! Ha!
HA! HA!
huh?
KNOCK!
KNOCK!
KNOCK!
Jonathan!

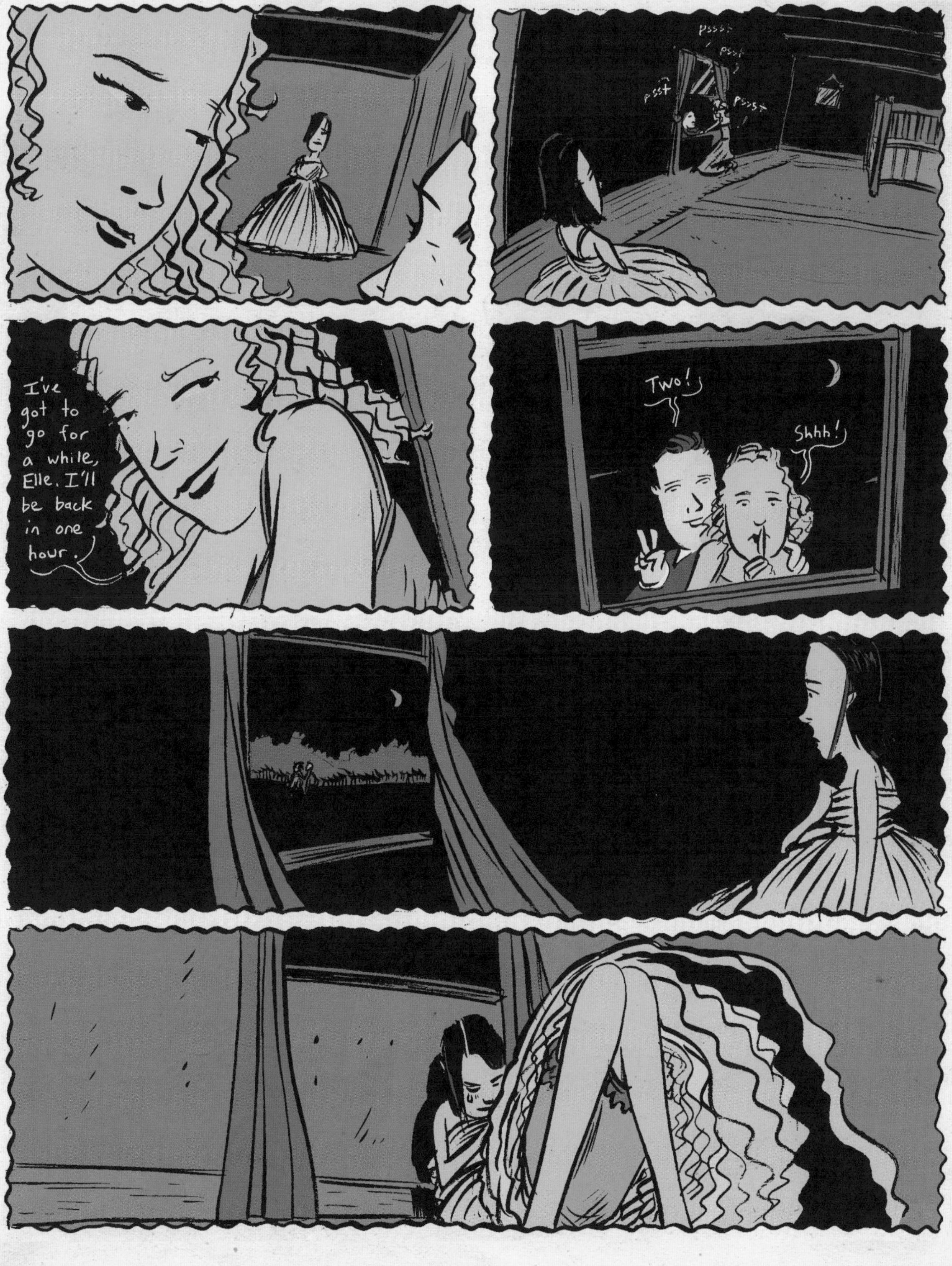
psssst
psst
psst
psssst
I've got to go for a while, Elle. I'll be back in one hour.
Two!
Shhh!

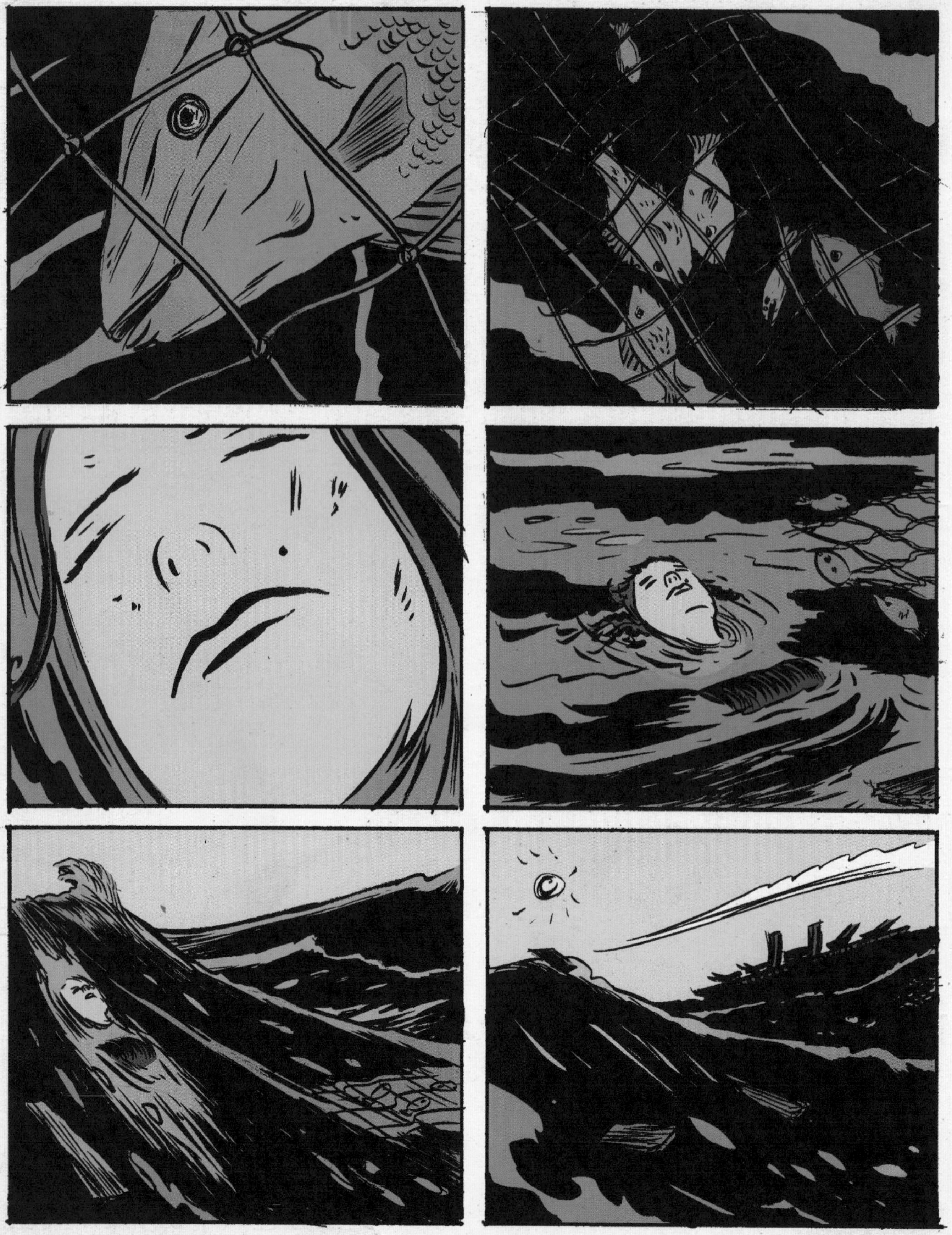

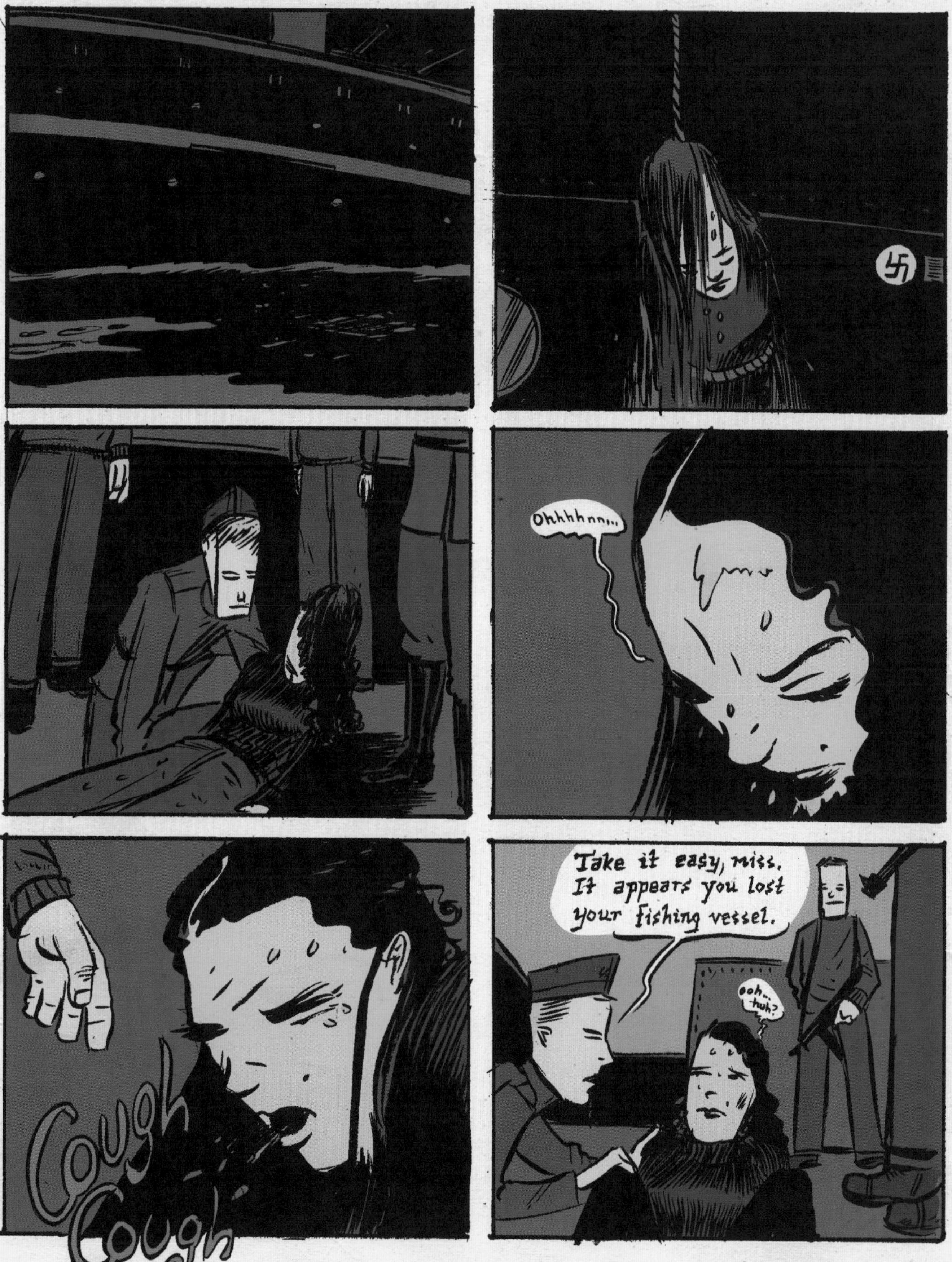
Ohhhhnnn...
Cough
Cough
Take it easy, miss. It appears you lost your fishing vessel.
ooh... huh?

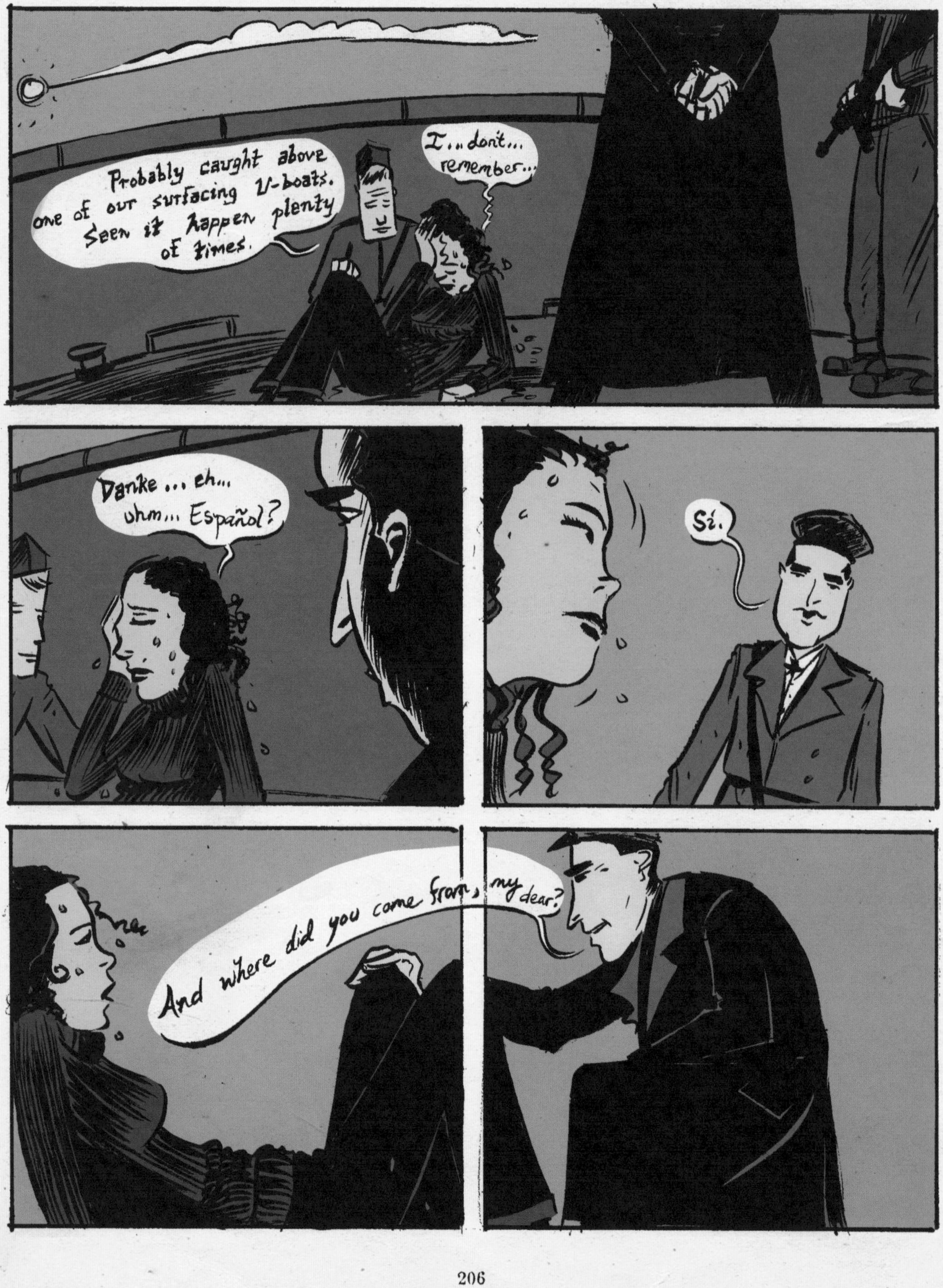
Probably caught above one of our surfacing U-boats. Seen it happen plenty of times.
I... don't... remember...
Danke... eh... uhm... Español?
Sí.
And where did you come from, my dear?

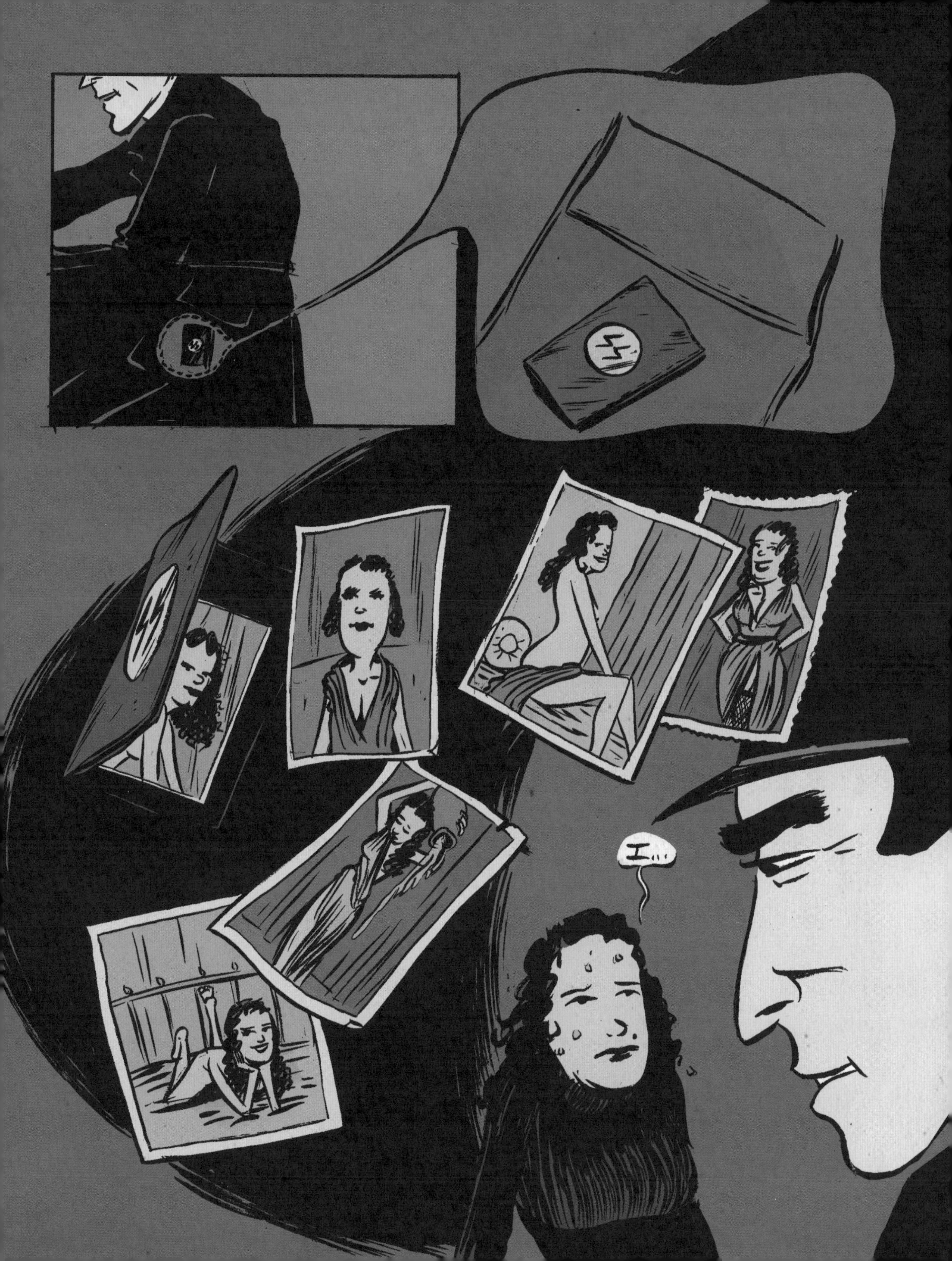
I...

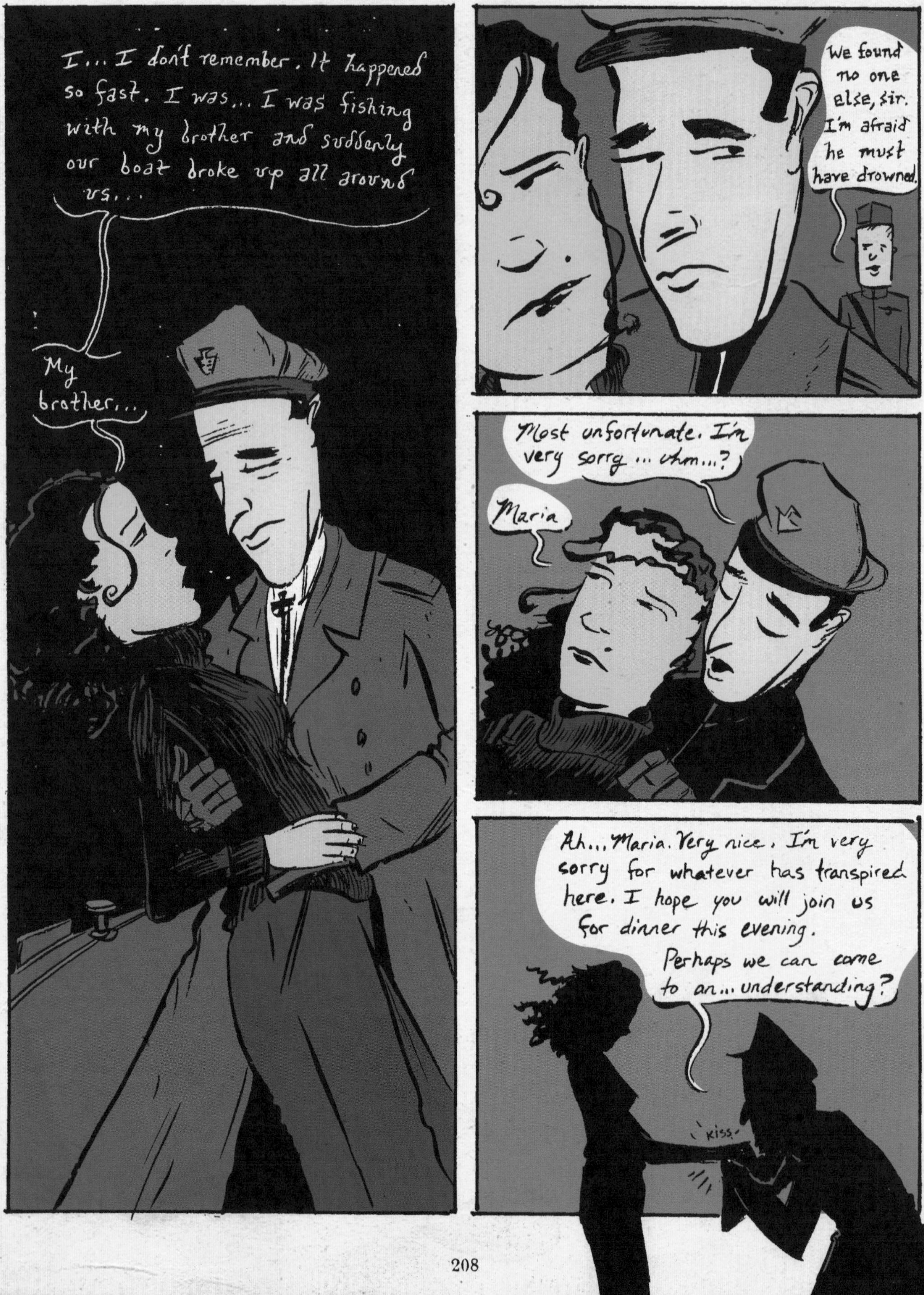
I... I don't remember. It happened so fast. I was... I was fishing with my brother and suddenly our boat broke up all around us...
My brother...
We found no one else, sir. I'm afraid he must have drowned.
Most unfortunate. I'm very sorry ... uhm...?
Maria
Ah... Maria. Very nice. I'm very sorry for whatever has transpired here. I hope you will join us for dinner this evening.
Perhaps we can come to an... understanding?
KISS

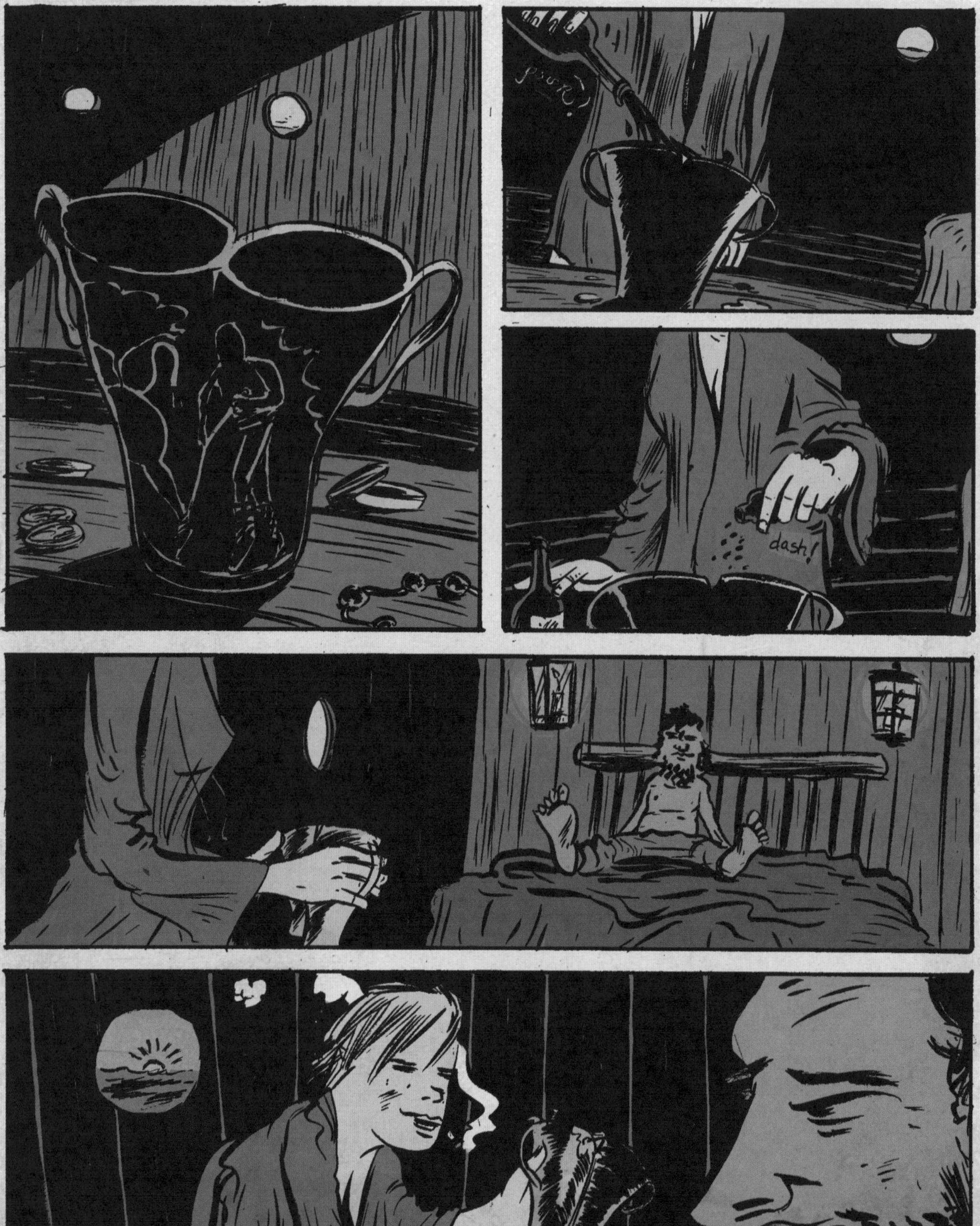
pour!
dash!

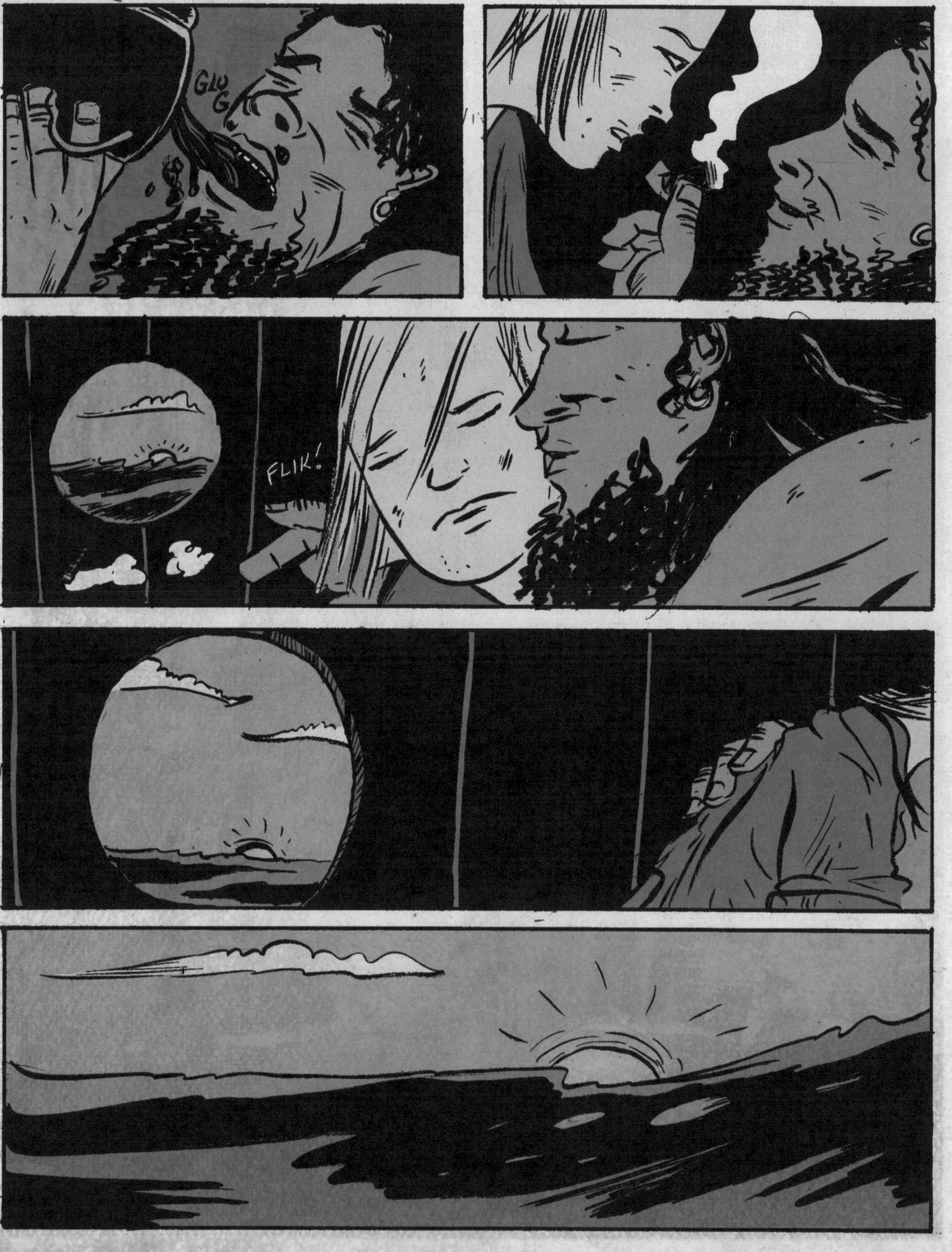
GLUG
FLIK!

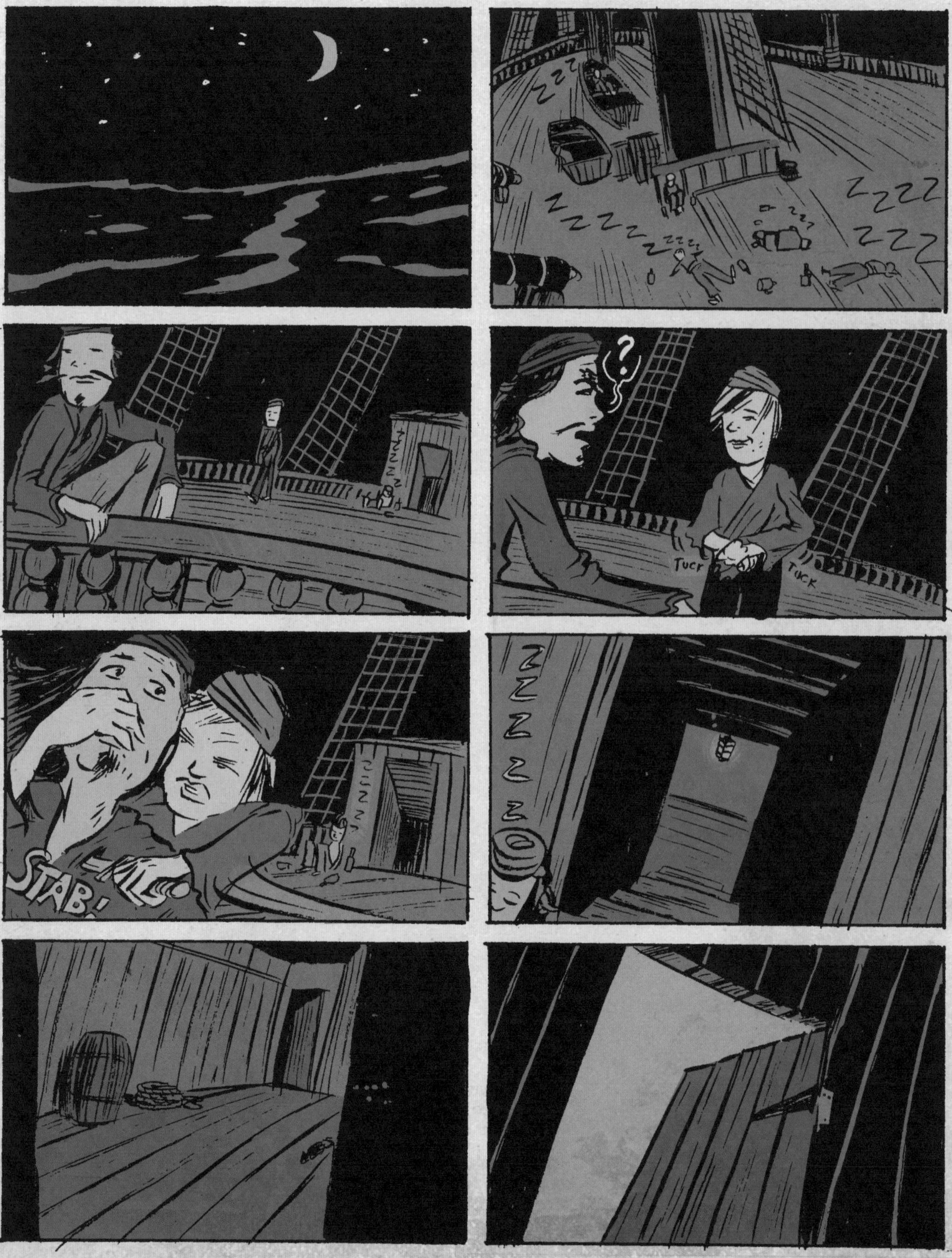

TUCK
TUCK
STAB!

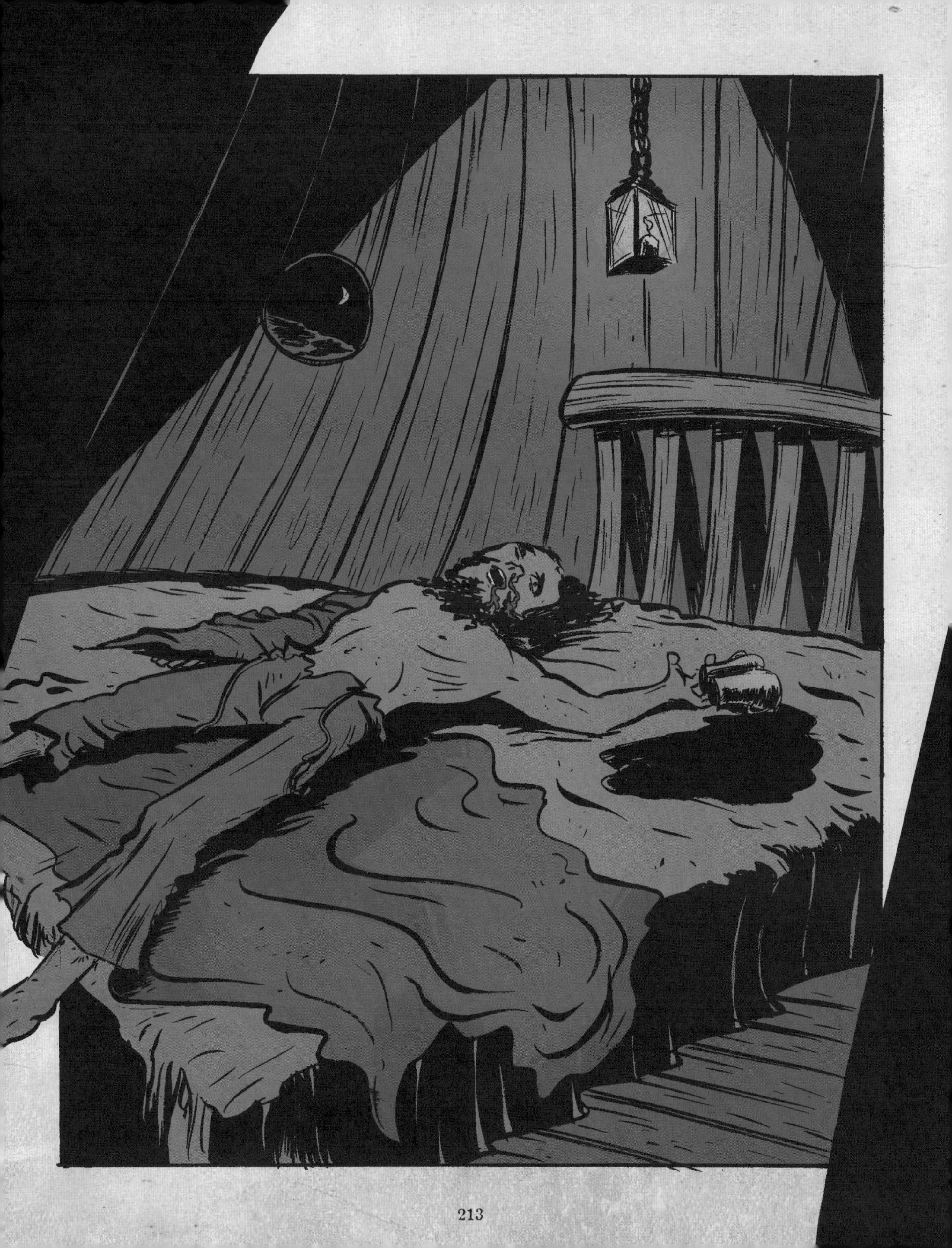

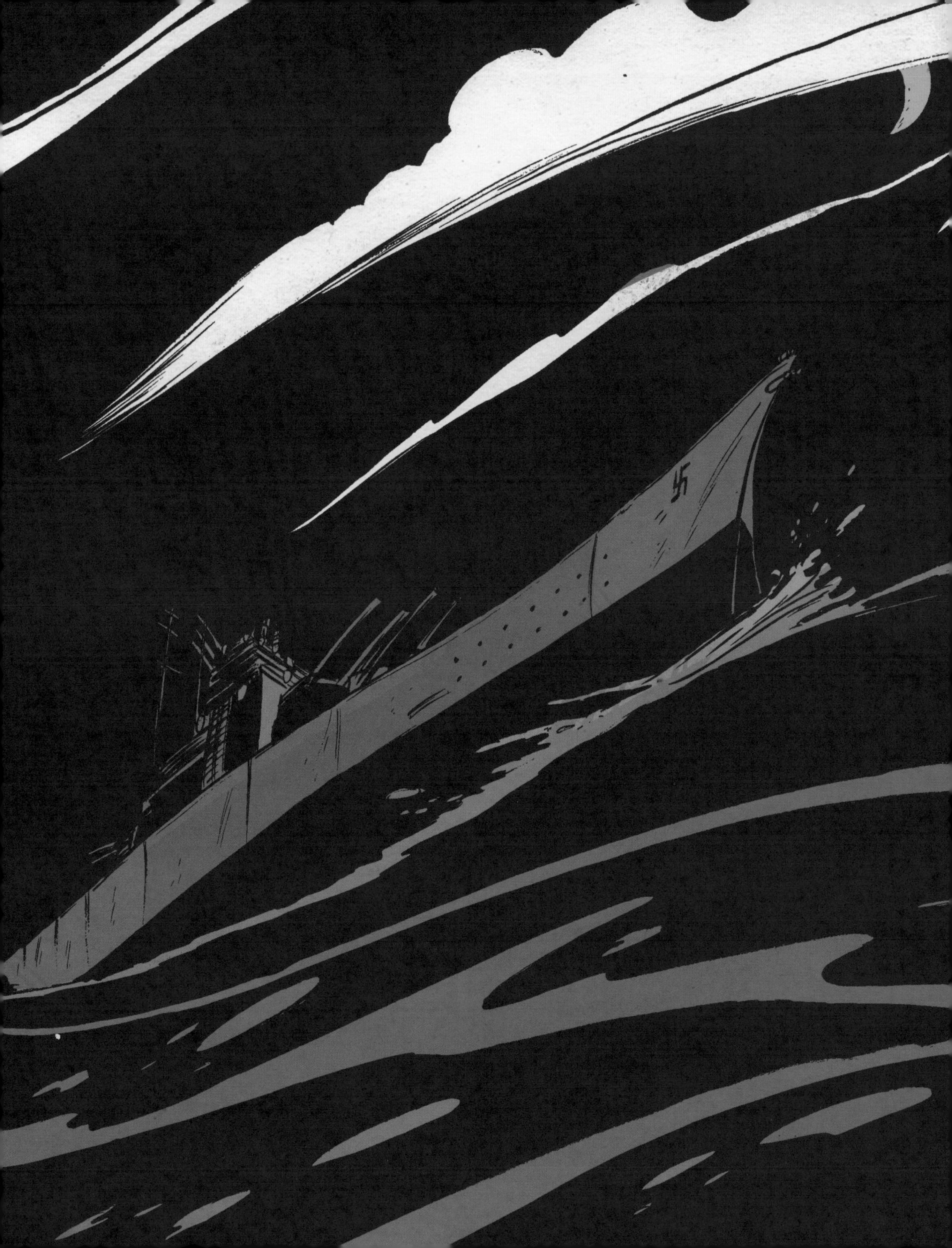

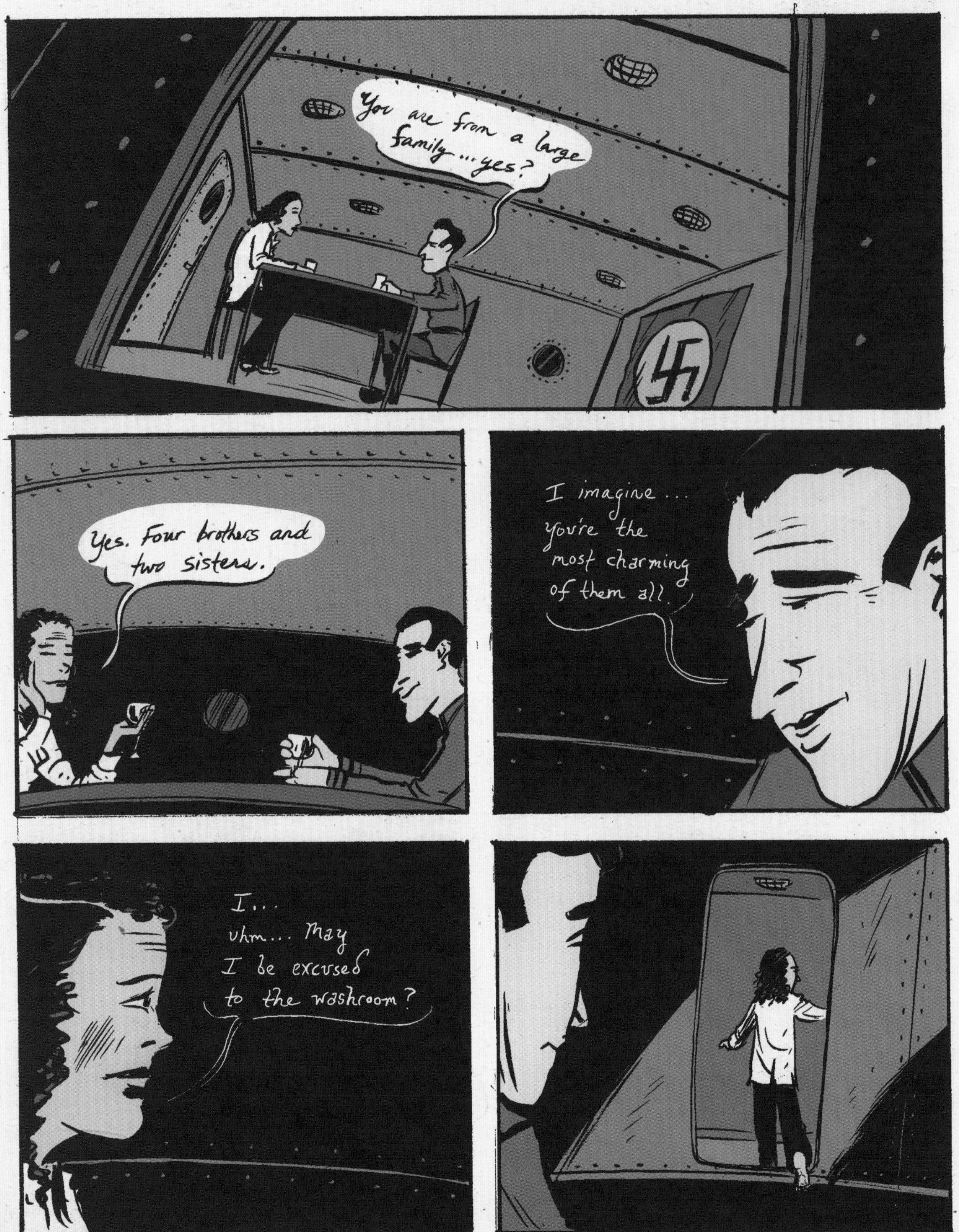
You are from a large family...yes?
Yes. Four brothers and two sisters.
I imagine... you're the most charming of them all.
I... uhm... May I be excused to the washroom?

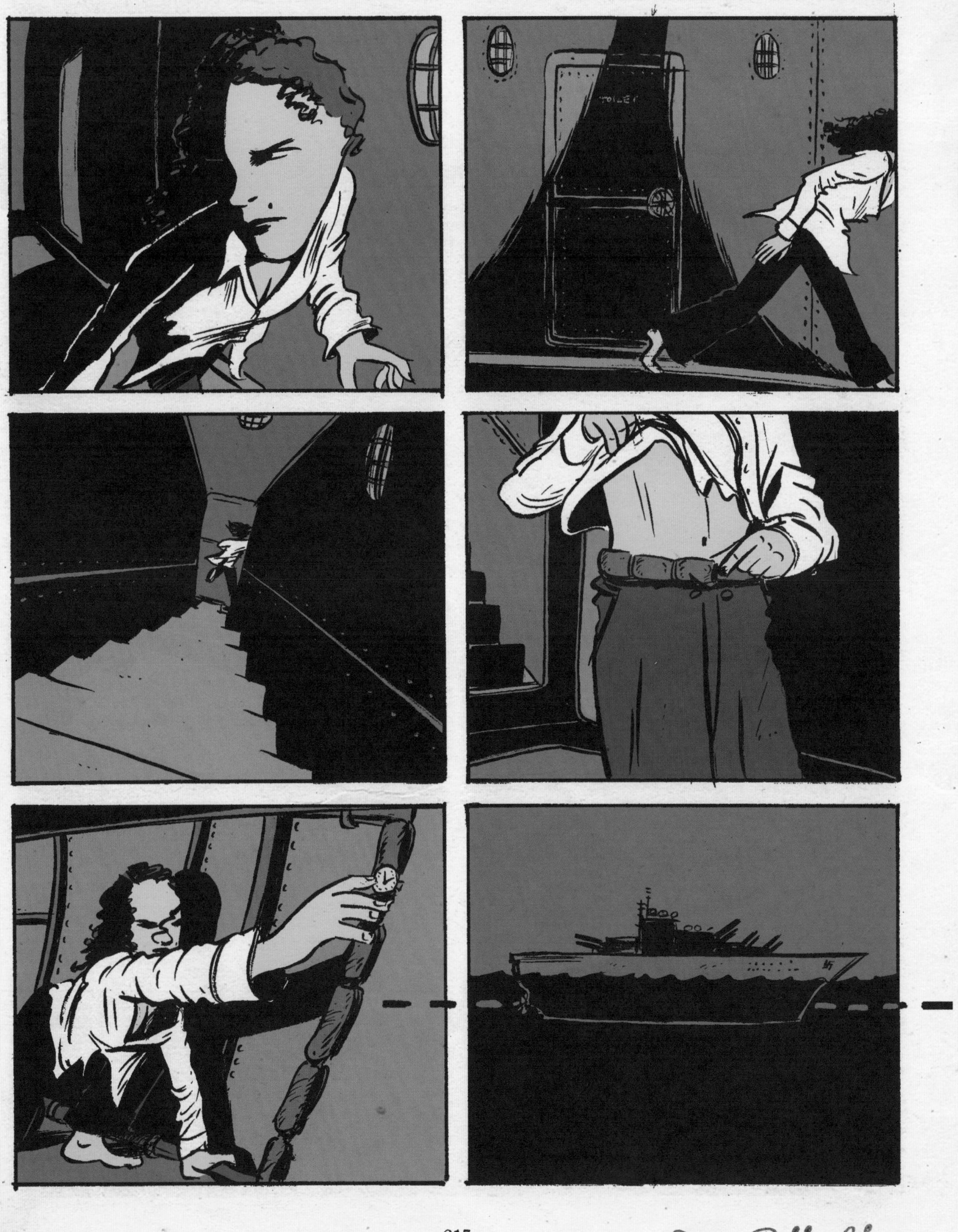
TOILET

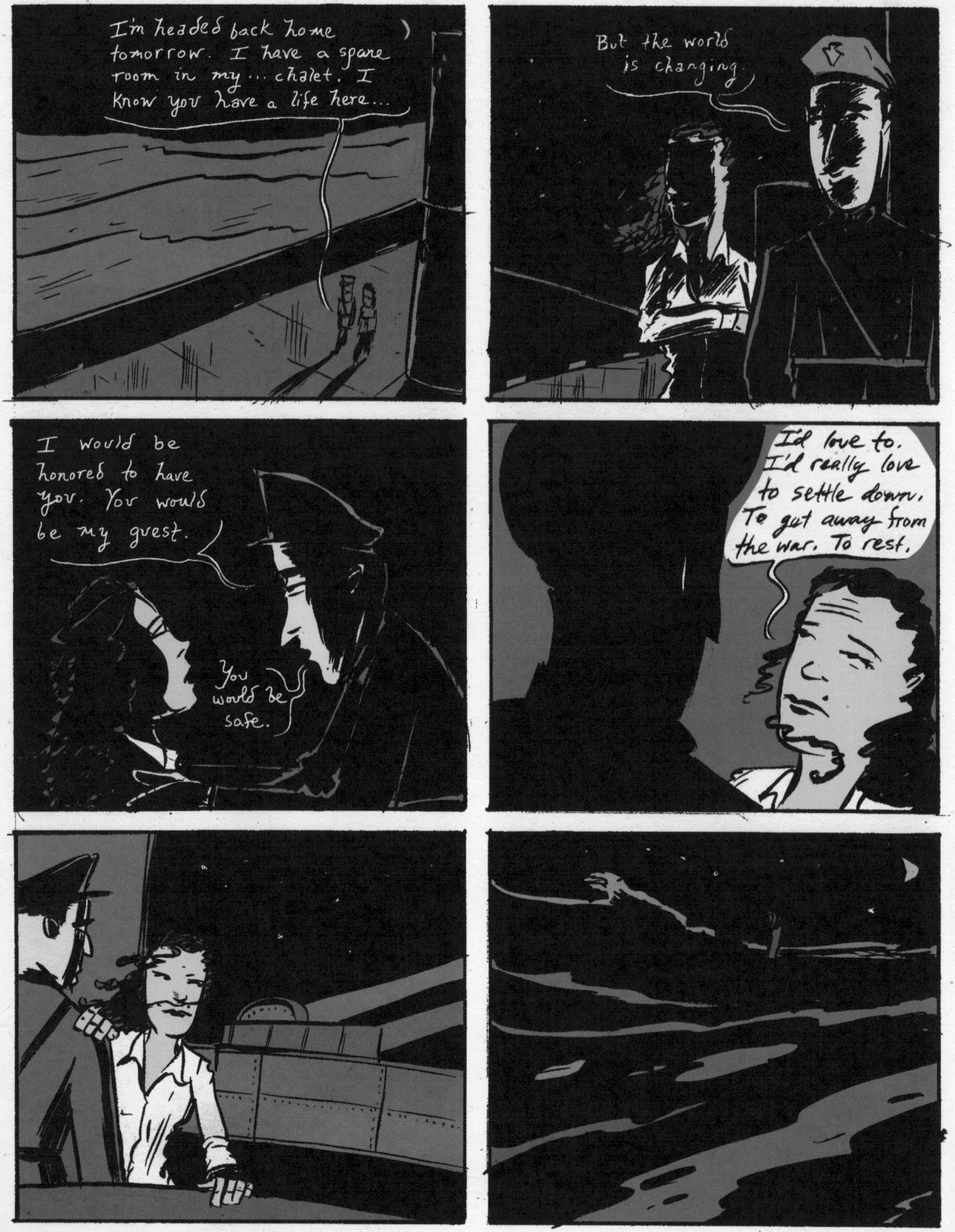
I'm headed back home tomorrow. I have a spare room in my... chalet. I know you have a life here...
But the world is changing.
I would be honored to have you. You would be my guest.
You would be safe.
I'd love to. I'd really love to settle down. To get away from the war. To rest.

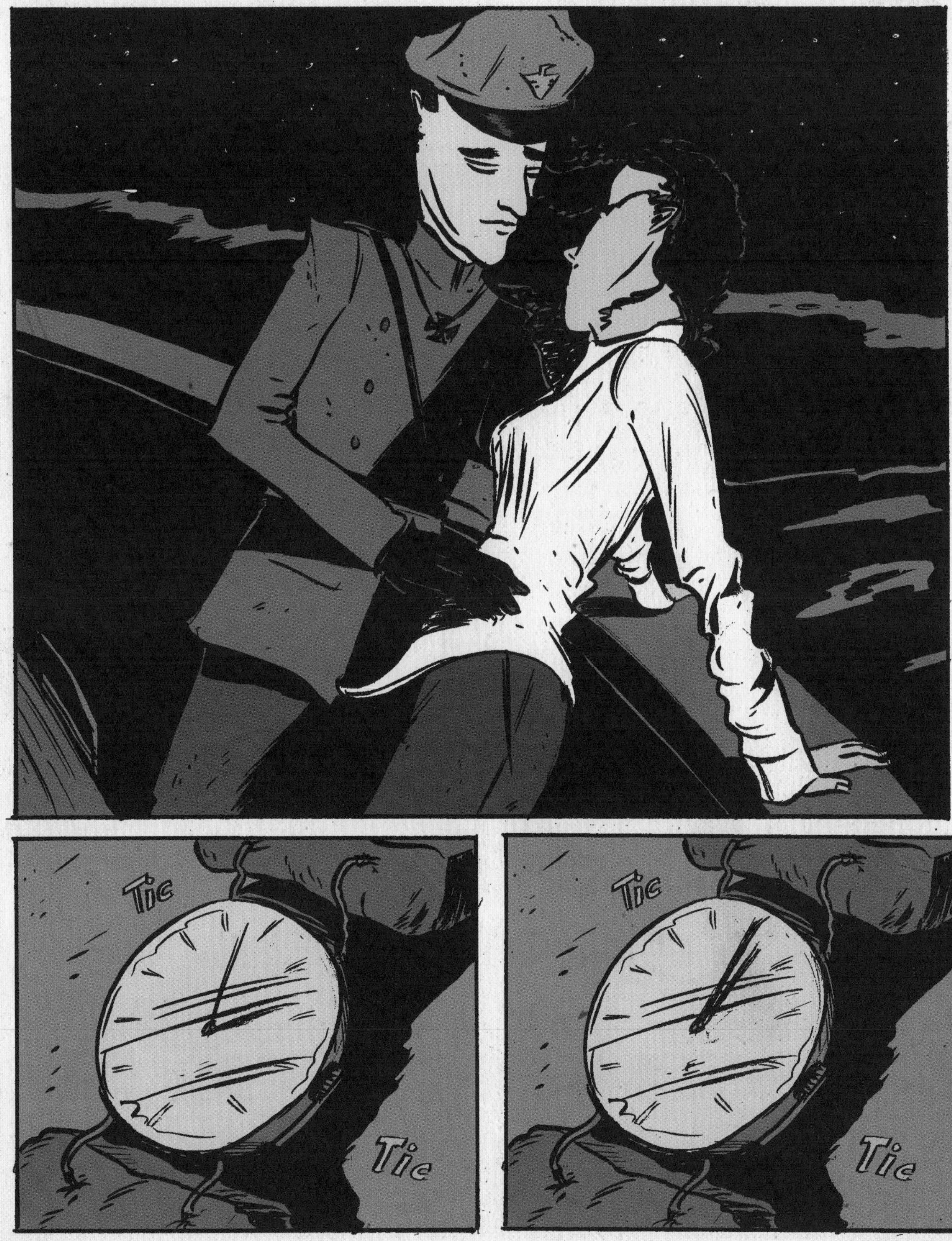
Tic
Tic
Tic
Tic

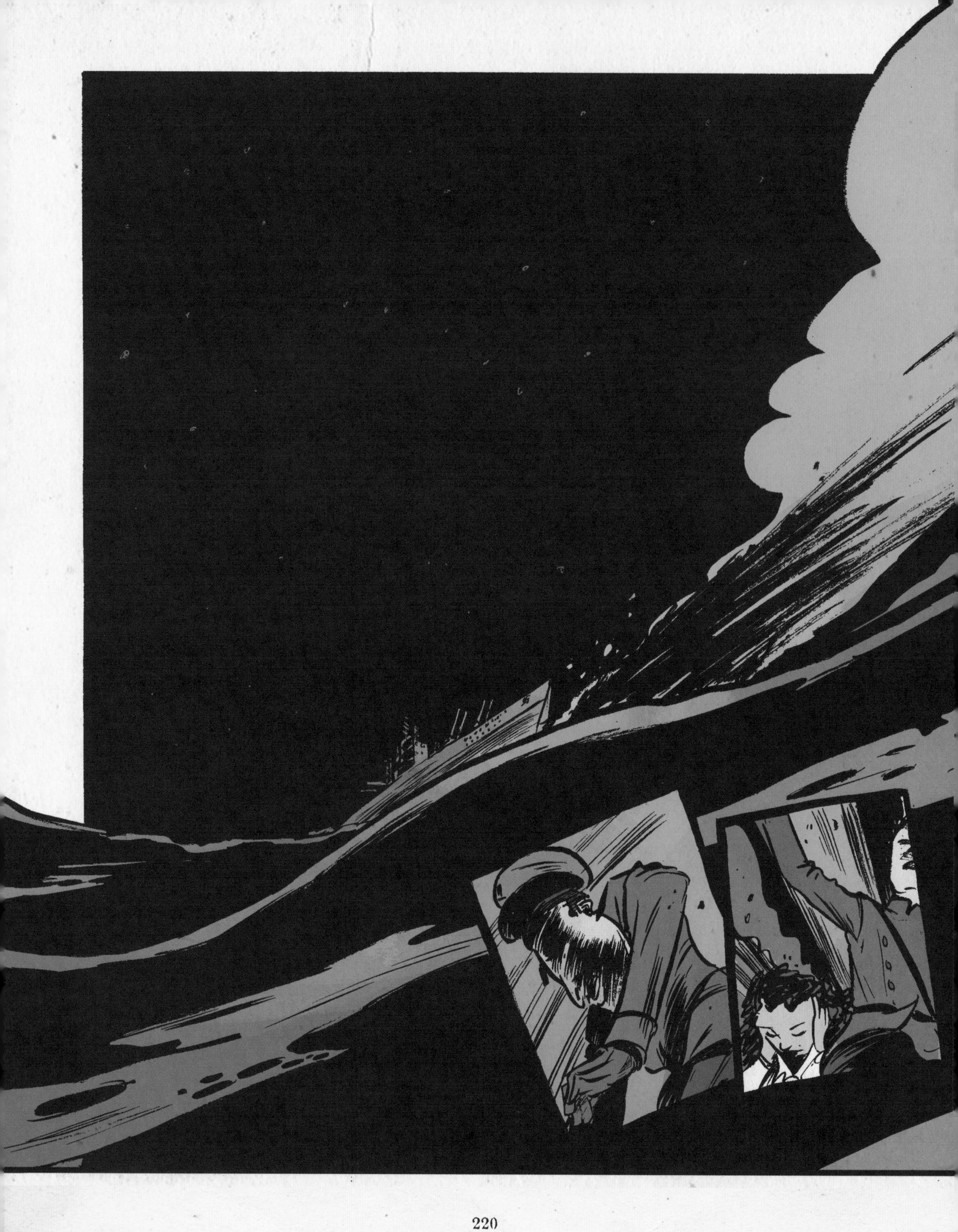

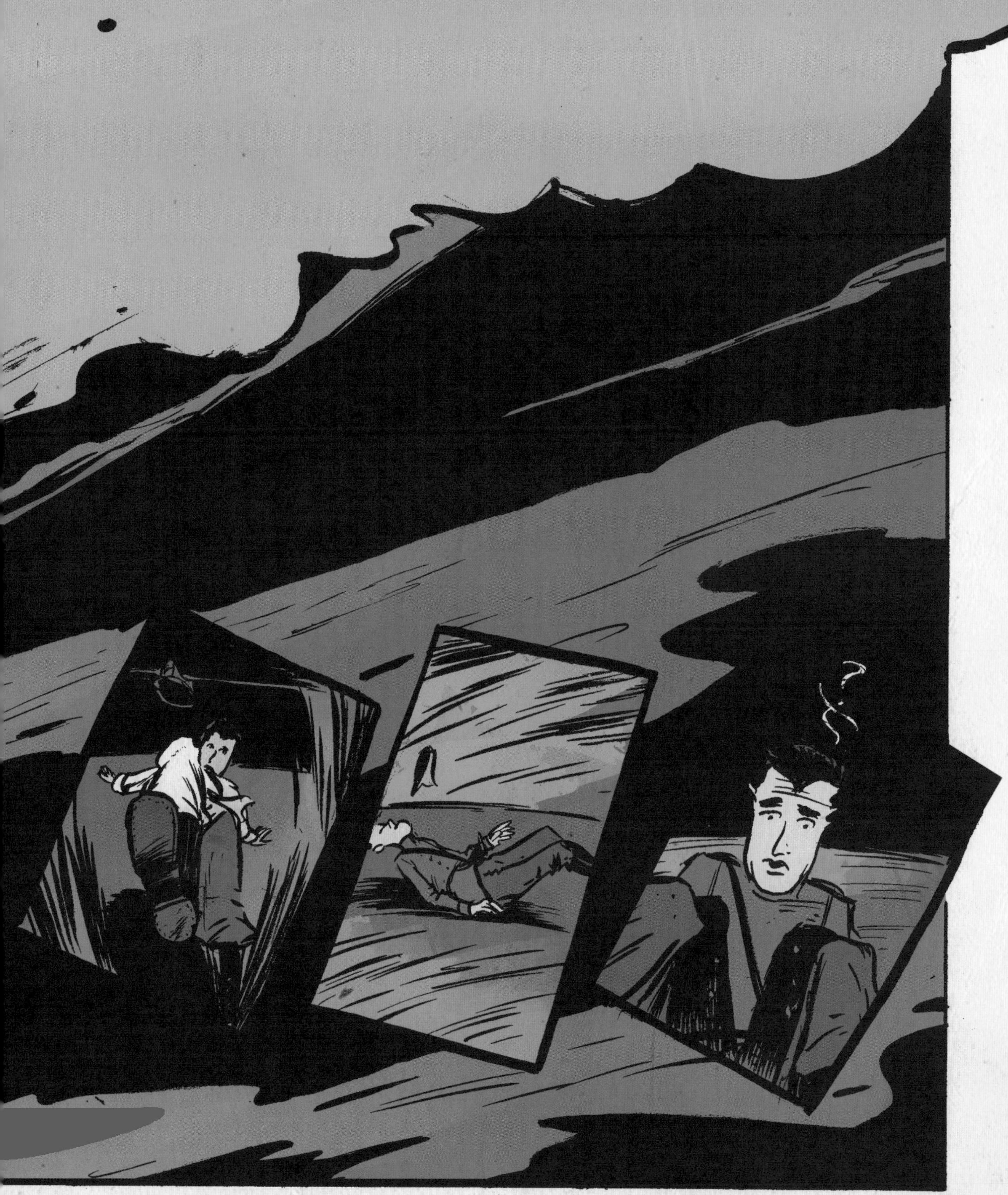

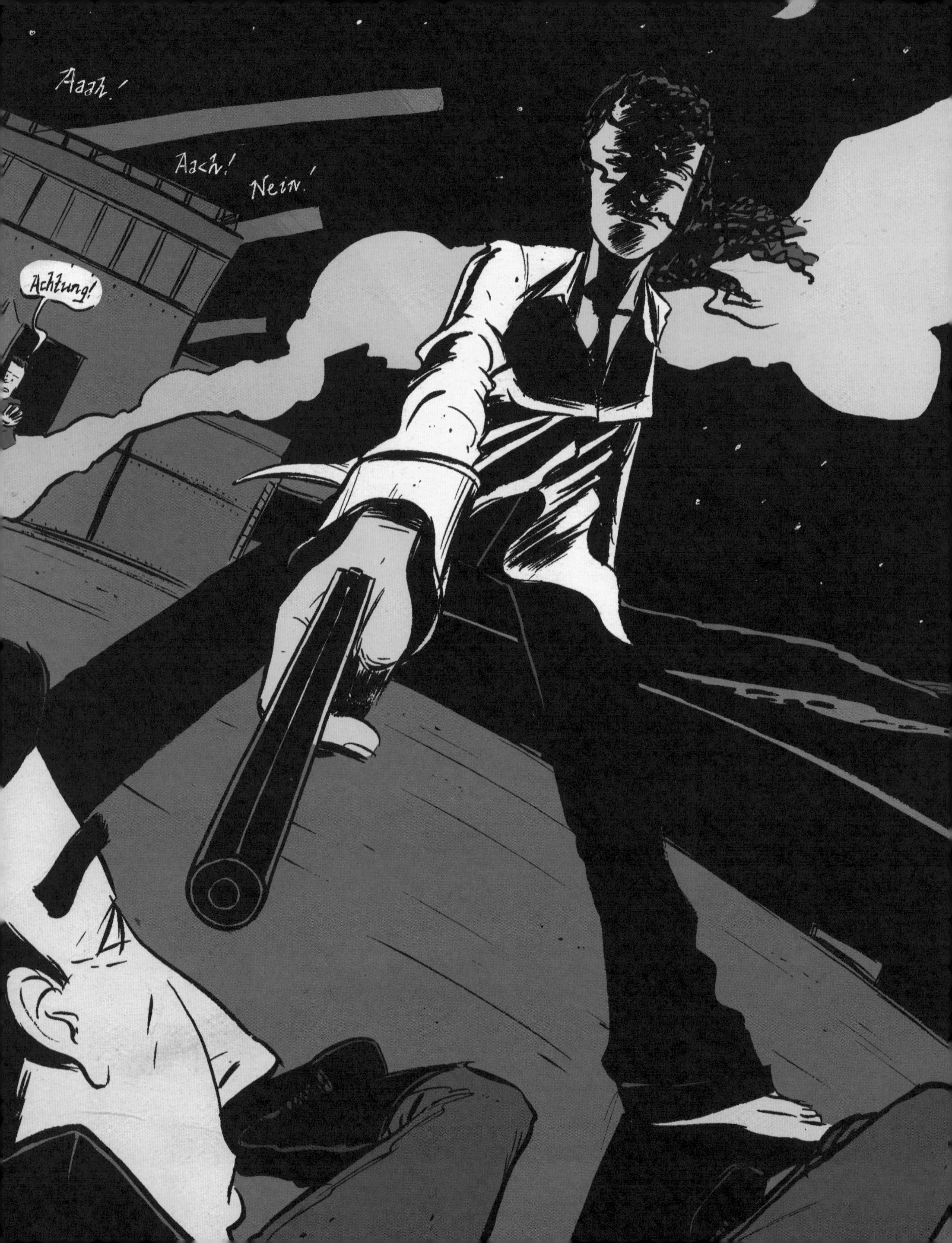
Aaah!
Aach!
Nein!
Achtung!

Hold it like this or you'll never catch anything.

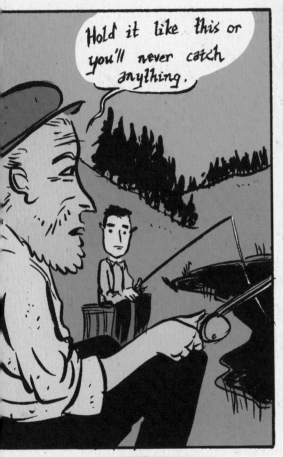

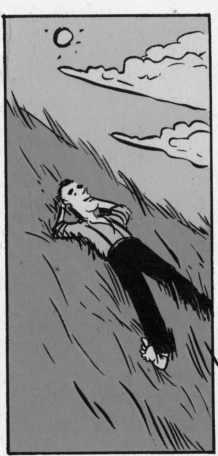

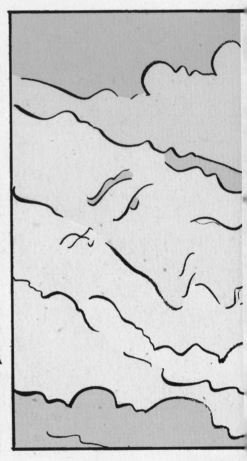

No, Weisman!
SMAK!
ACHTUNG!
For valor...

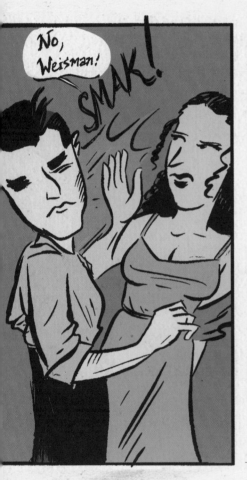

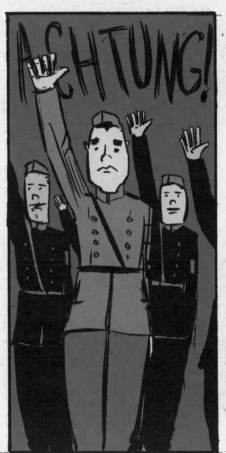

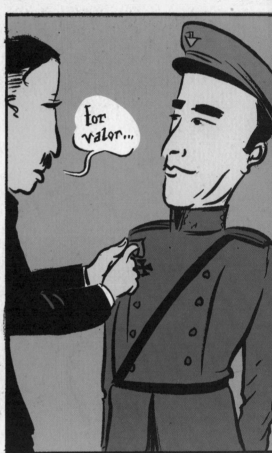

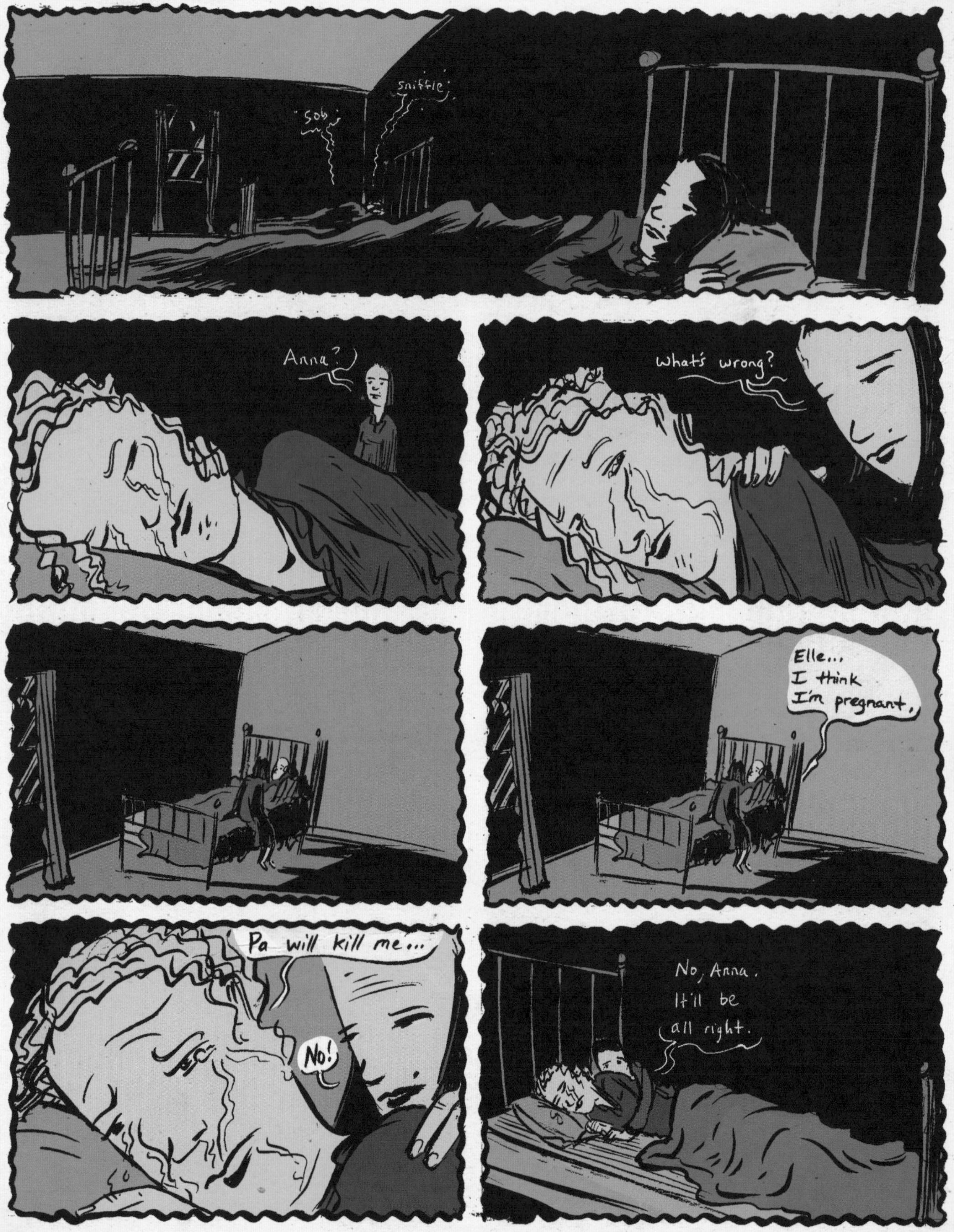
sob
sniffle
Anna?
What's wrong?
Elle... I think I'm pregnant.
Pa will kill me...
No!
No, Anna. It'll be all right.

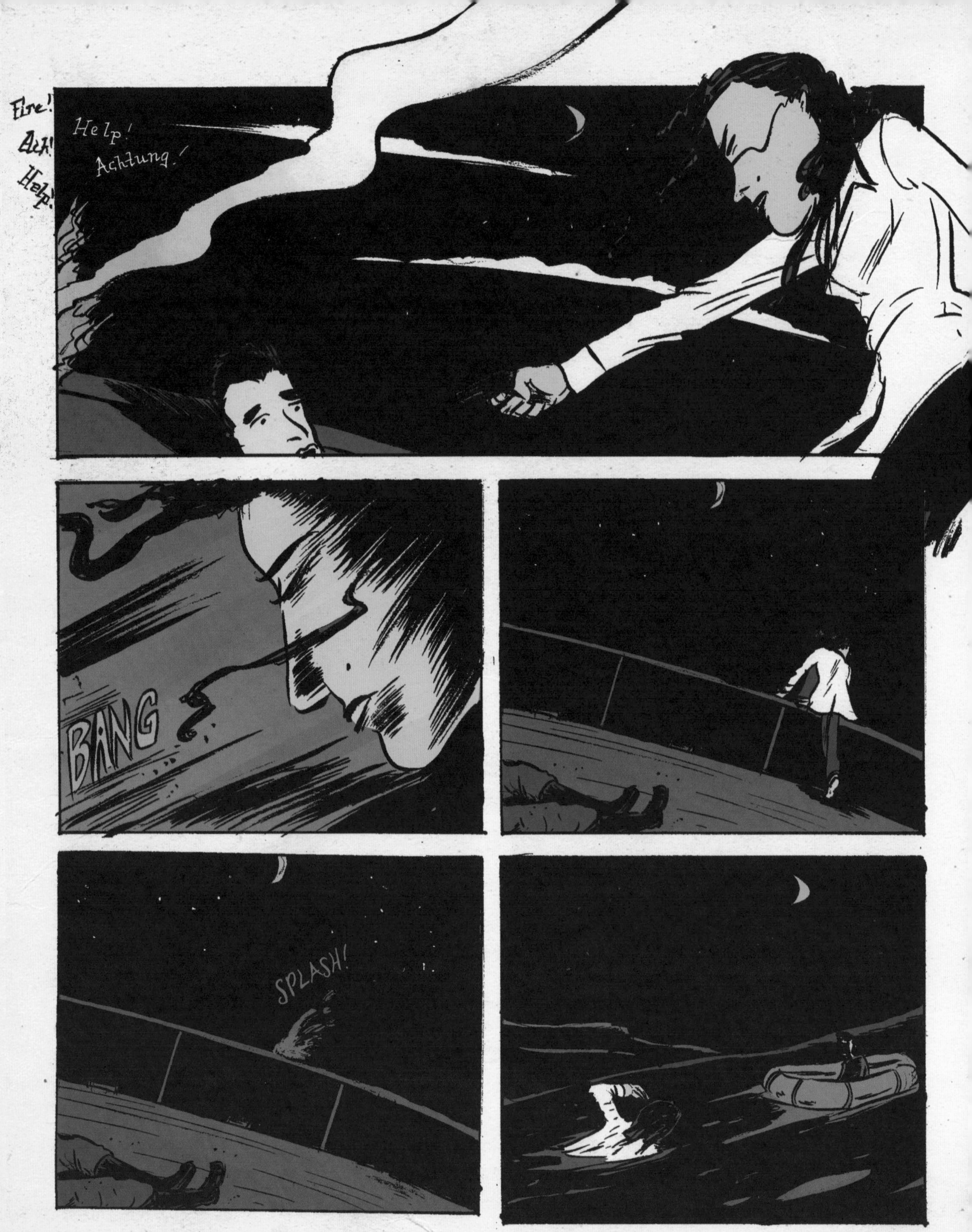
Fire!
Ach!
Help!
Help!
Achtung!
BANG
SPLASH!

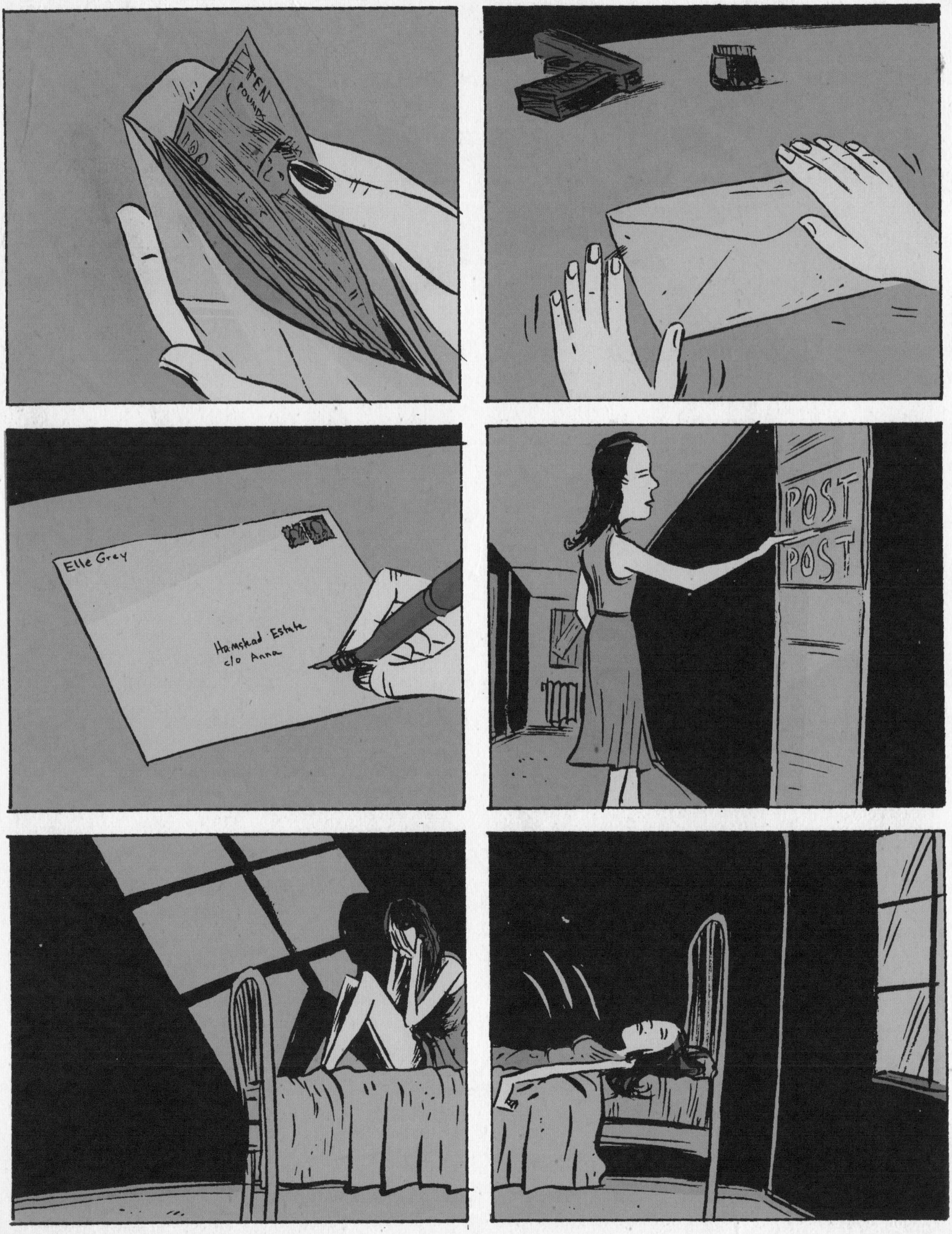

TEN
POUNDS
Elle Grey
Hamstead Estate
c/o Anna
POST
POST

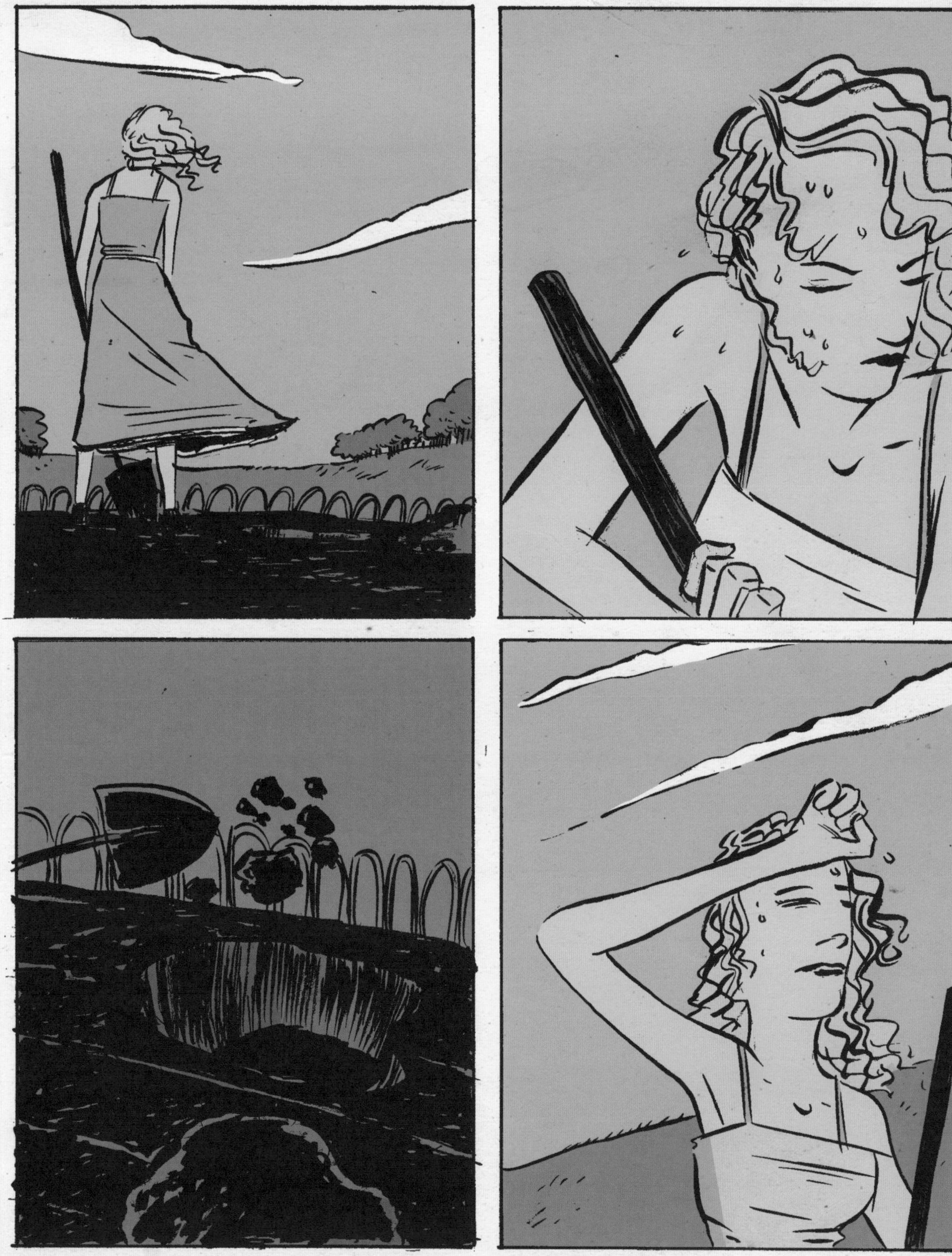

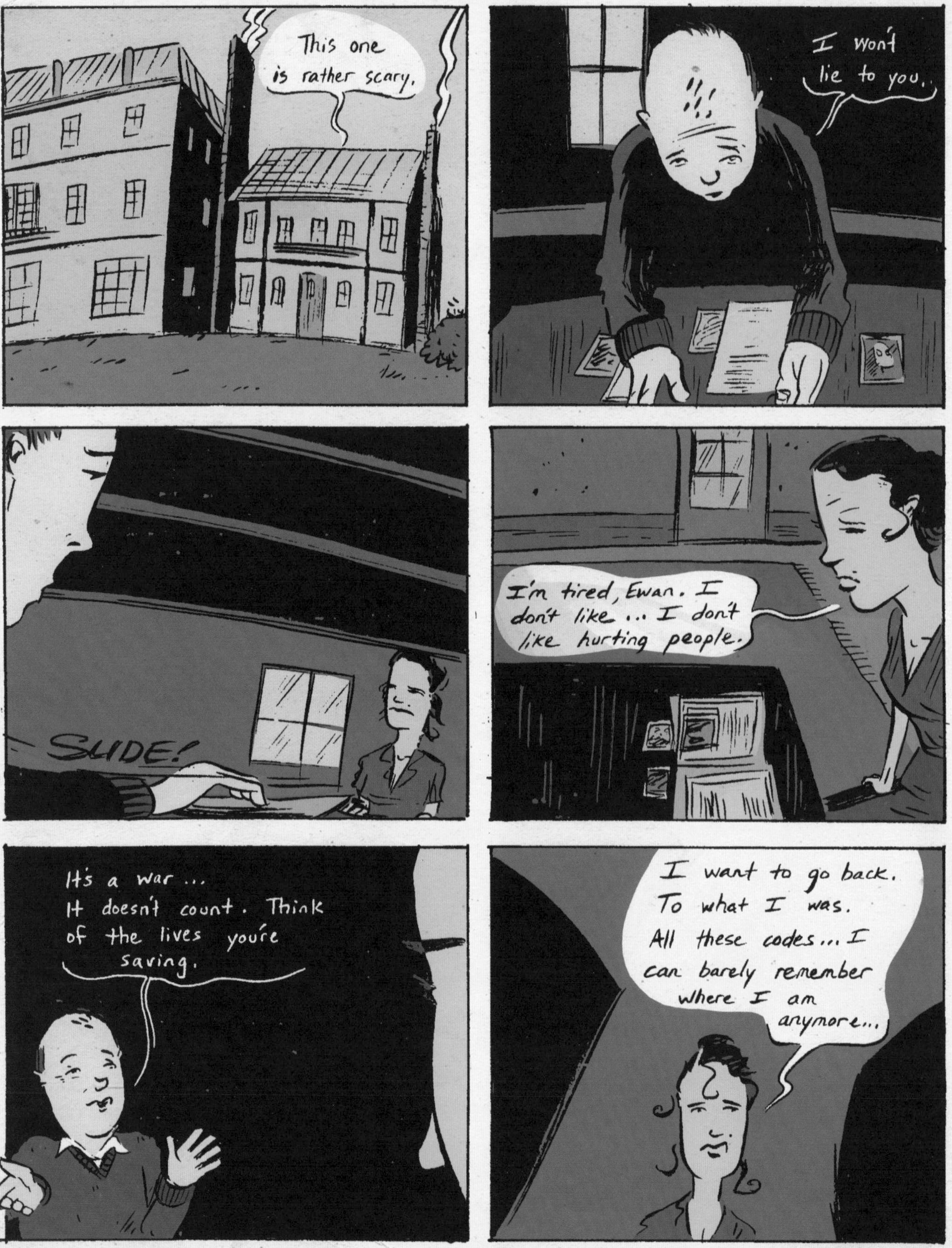
This one is rather scary.
I won't lie to you.
SLIDE!
I'm tired, Ewan. I don't like... I don't like hurting people.
It's a war... It doesn't count. Think of the lives you're saving.
I want to go back. To what I was. All these codes... I can barely remember where I am anymore...

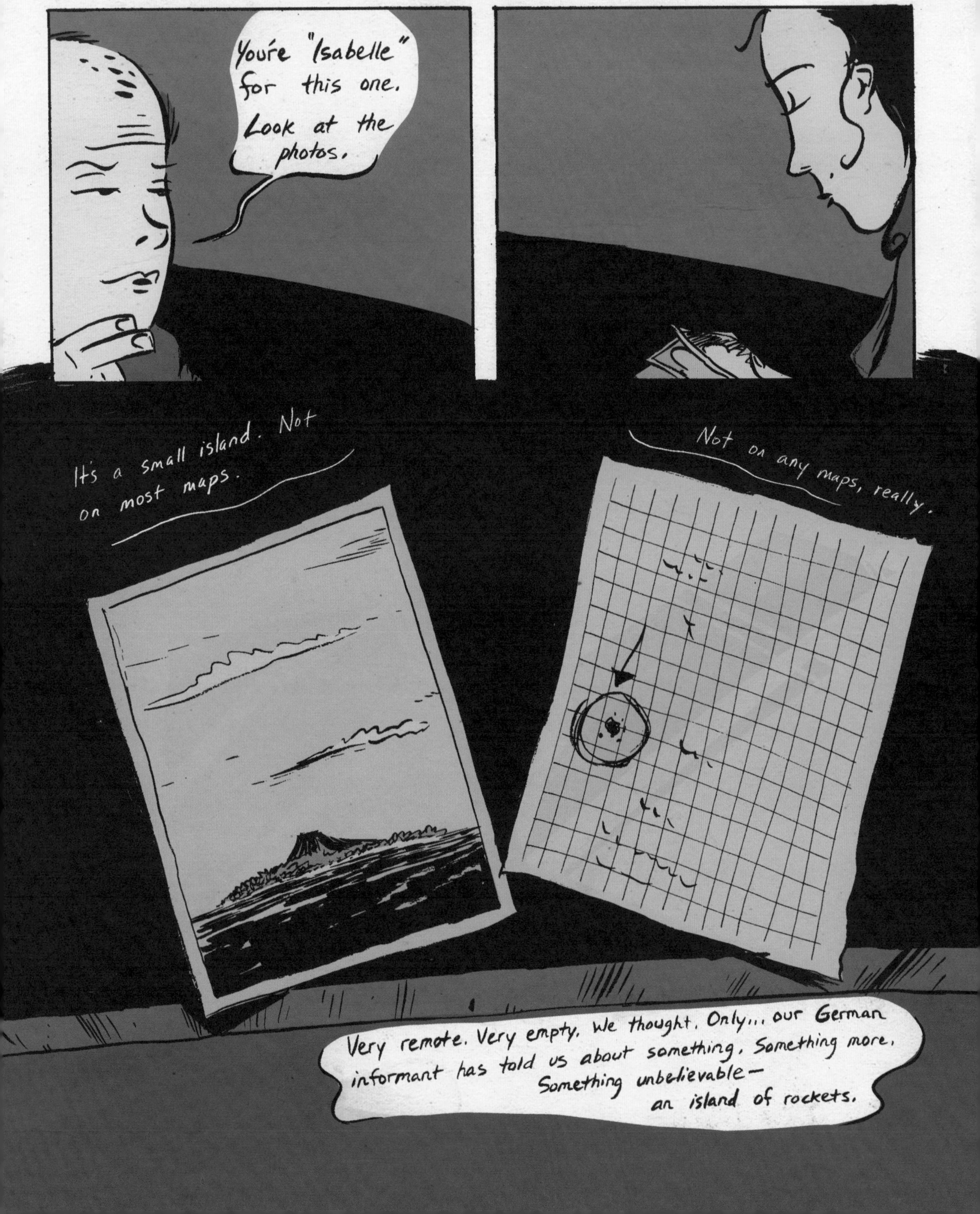

You're "Isabelle" for this one. Look at the photos.
It's a small island. Not on most maps.
Not on any maps, really.
Very remote. Very empty. We thought. Only... our German informant has told us about something. Something more. Something unbelievable— an island of rockets.

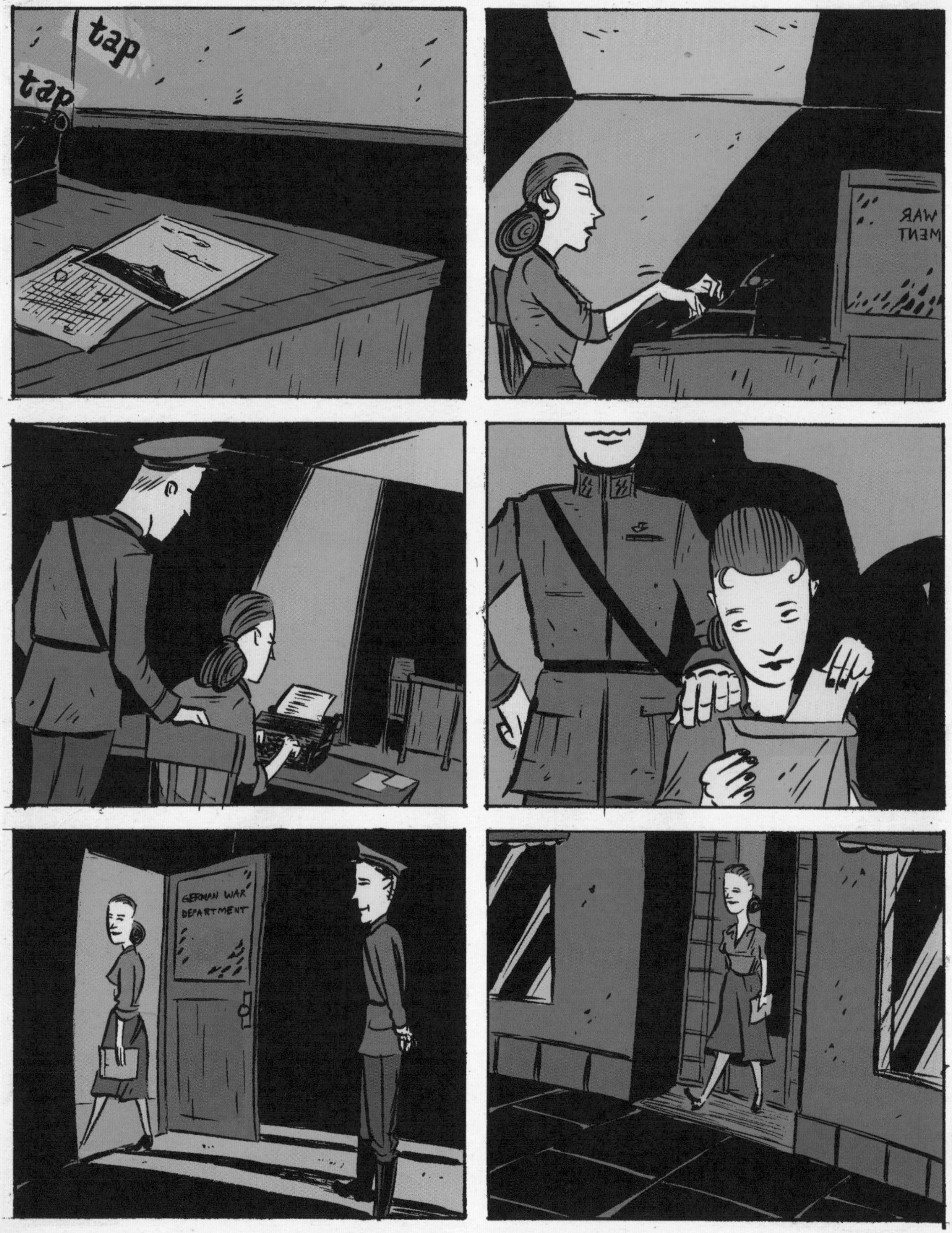
tap
tap
WAR
MENT
GERMAN WAR
DEPARTMENT

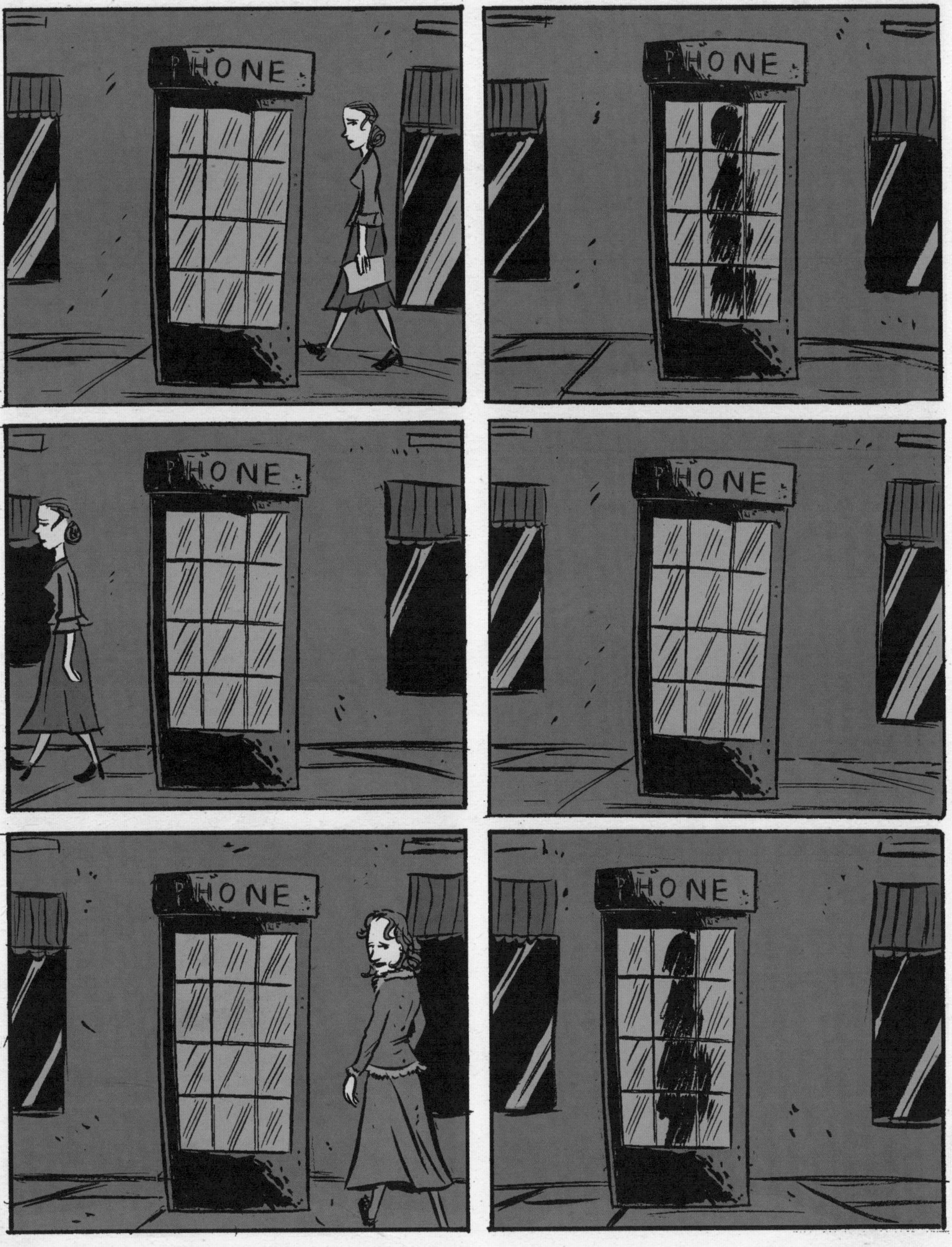
PHONE
PHONE
PHONE
PHONE
PHONE
PHONE

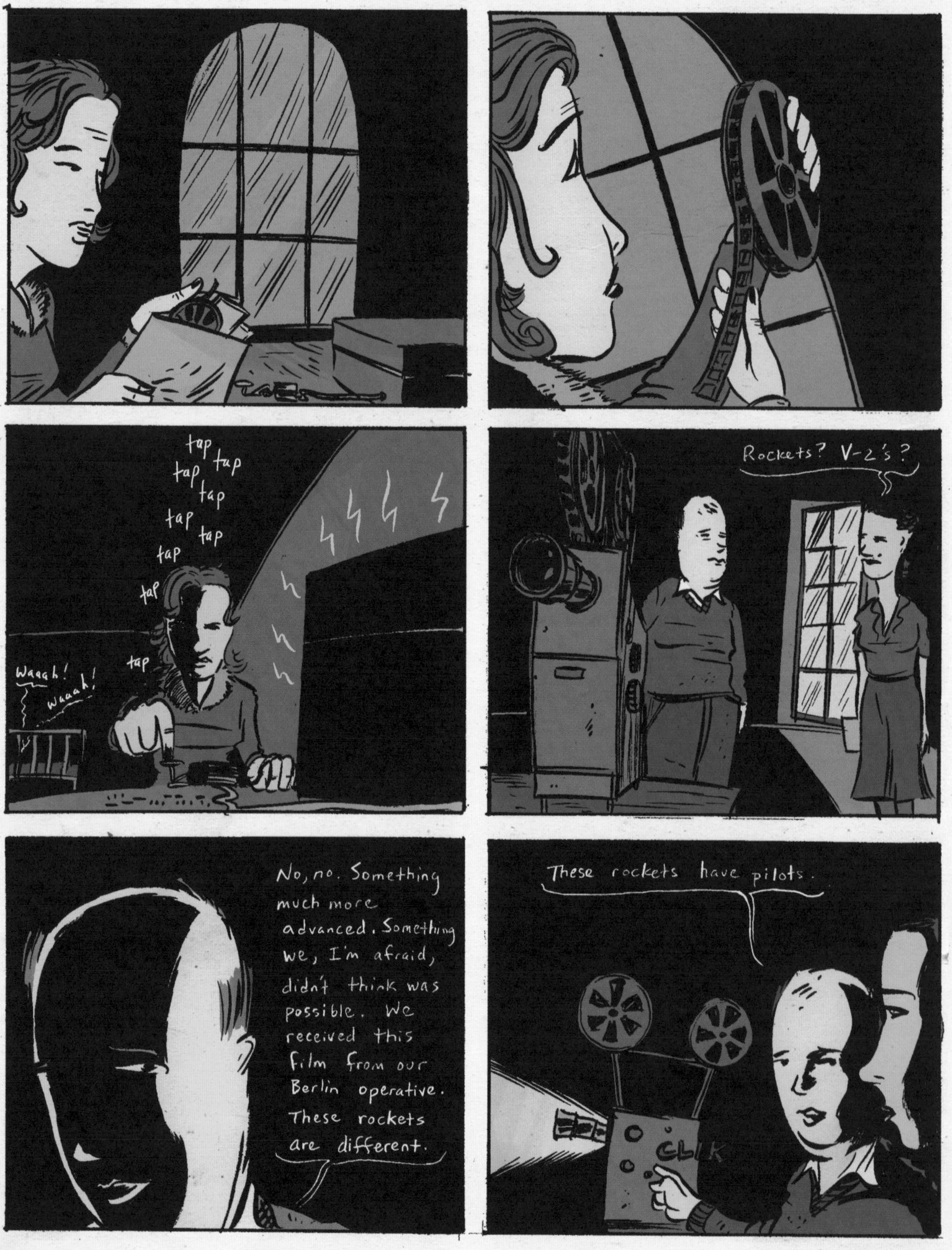
tap tap tap tap tap tap tap tap tap
Waaah! Waaah!
Rockets? V-2's?
No, no. Something much more advanced. Something we, I'm afraid, didn't think was possible. We received this film from our Berlin operative. These rockets are different.
These rockets have pilots.
CLIK

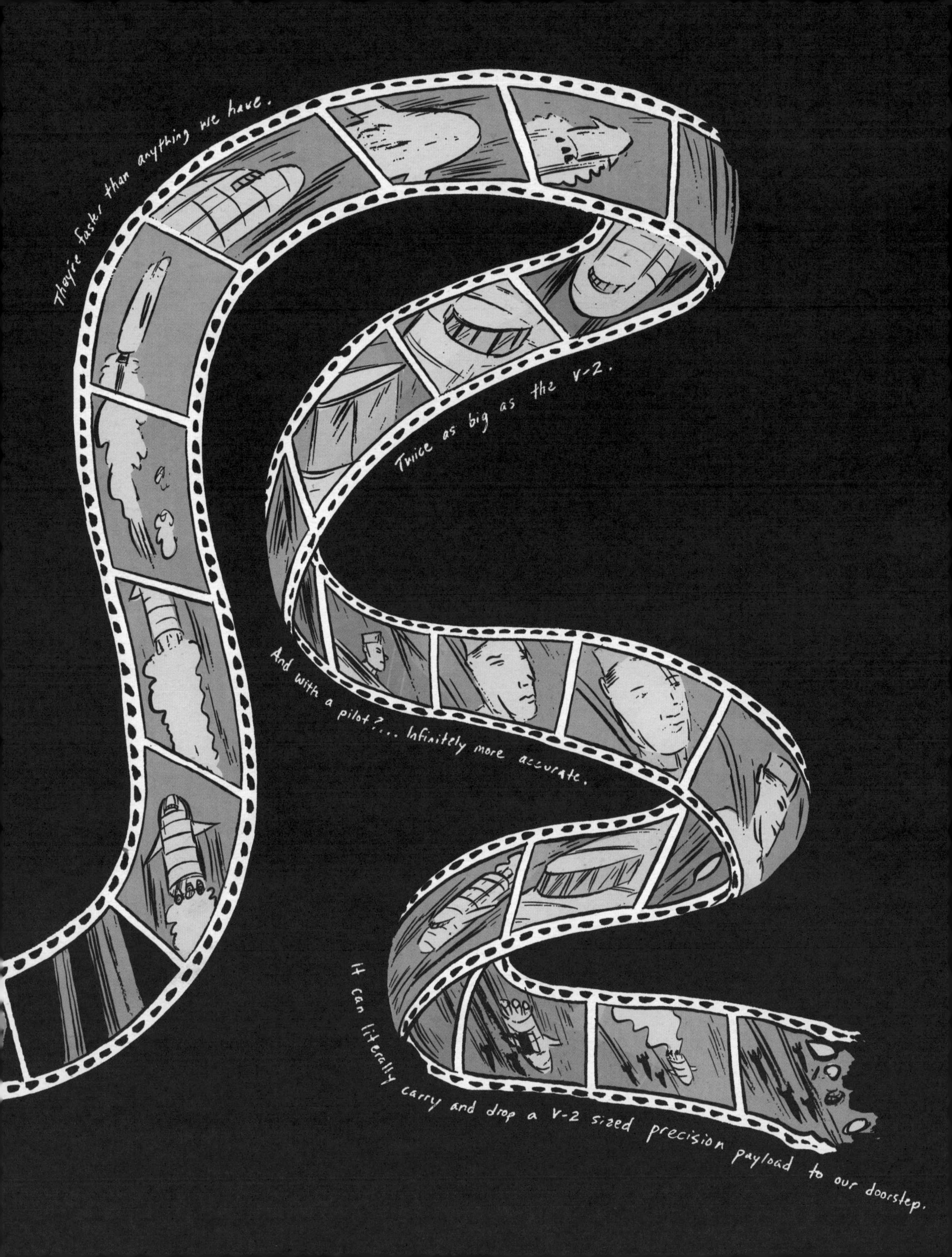

They're faster than anything we have.
Twice as big as the V-2.
And with a pilot?... Infinitely more accurate.
It can literally carry and drop a V-2 sized precision payload to our doorstep.

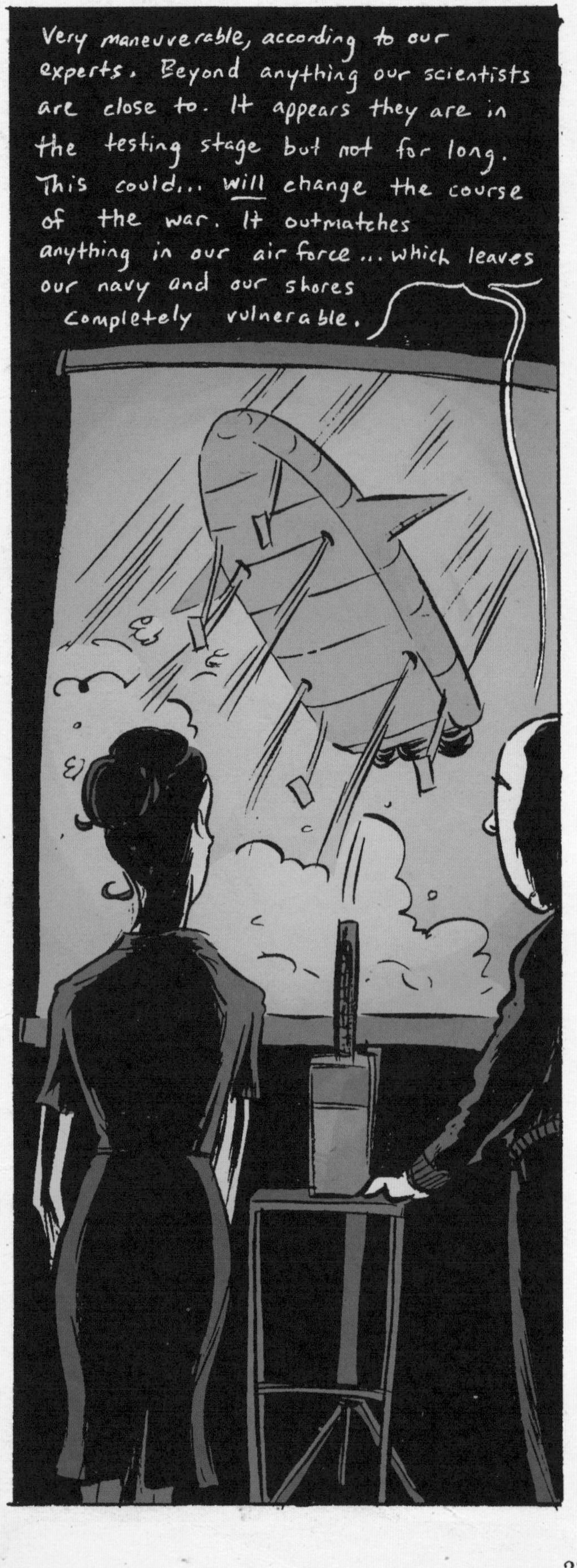
Very maneuverable, according to our experts. Beyond anything our scientists are close to. It appears they are in the testing stage but not for long. This could... will change the course of the war. It outmatches anything in our air force... which leaves our navy and our shores completely vulnerable.

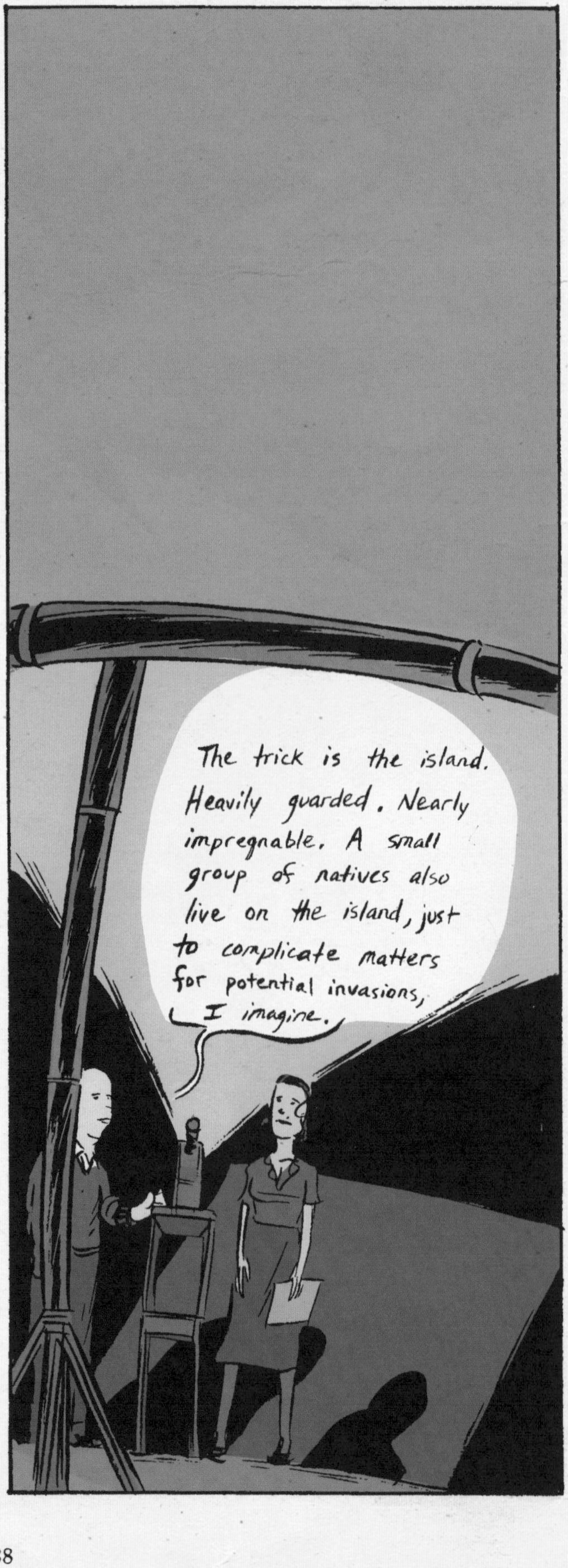
The trick is the island. Heavily guarded. Nearly impregnable. A small group of natives also live on the island, just to complicate matters for potential invasions, I imagine.

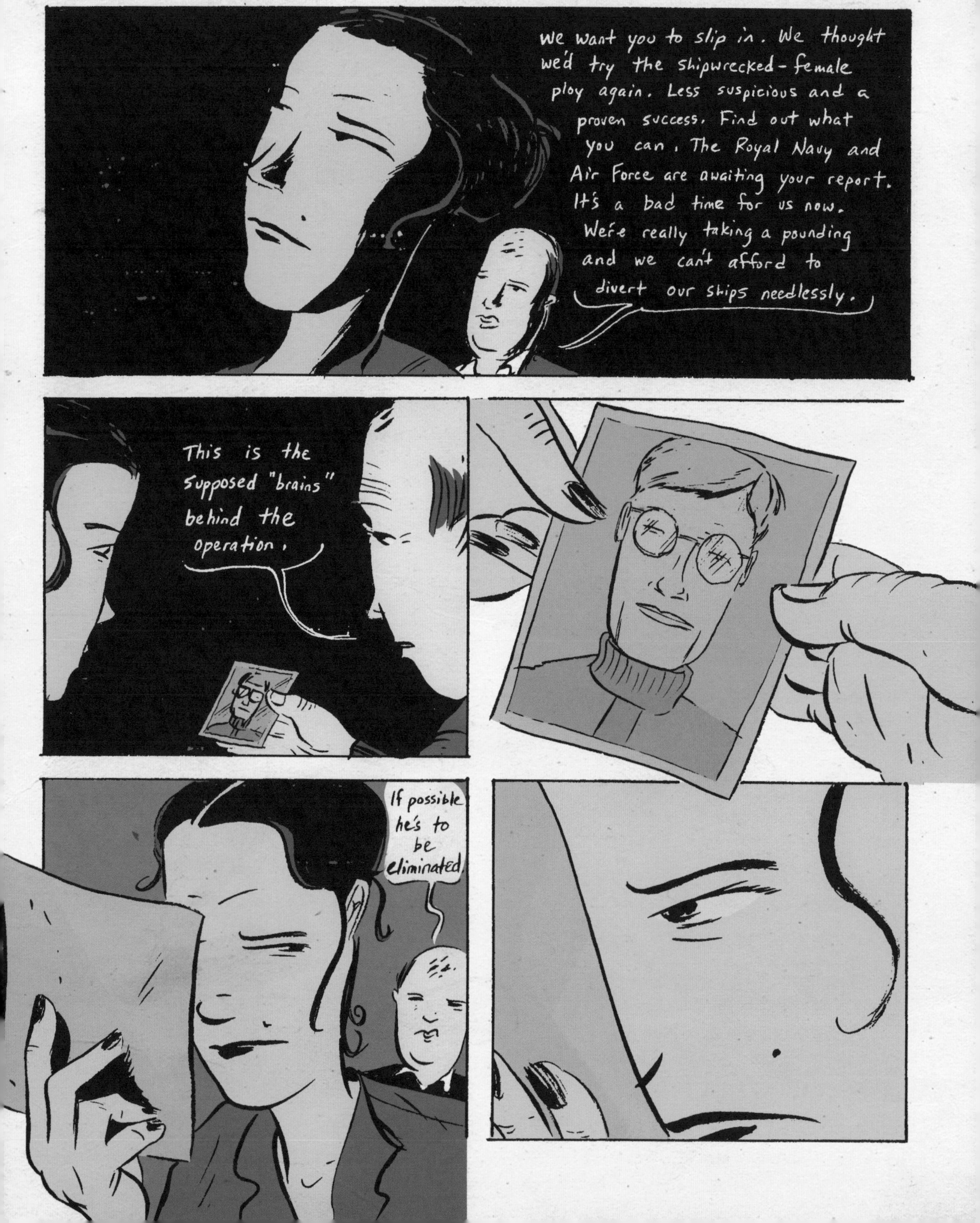
We want you to slip in. We thought we'd try the shipwrecked-female ploy again. Less suspicious and a proven success. Find out what you can. The Royal Navy and Air Force are awaiting your report. It's a bad time for us now. We're really taking a pounding and we can't afford to divert our ships needlessly.
This is the supposed "brains" behind the operation.
If possible he's to be eliminated.

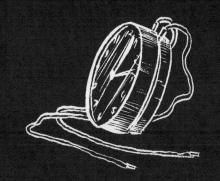

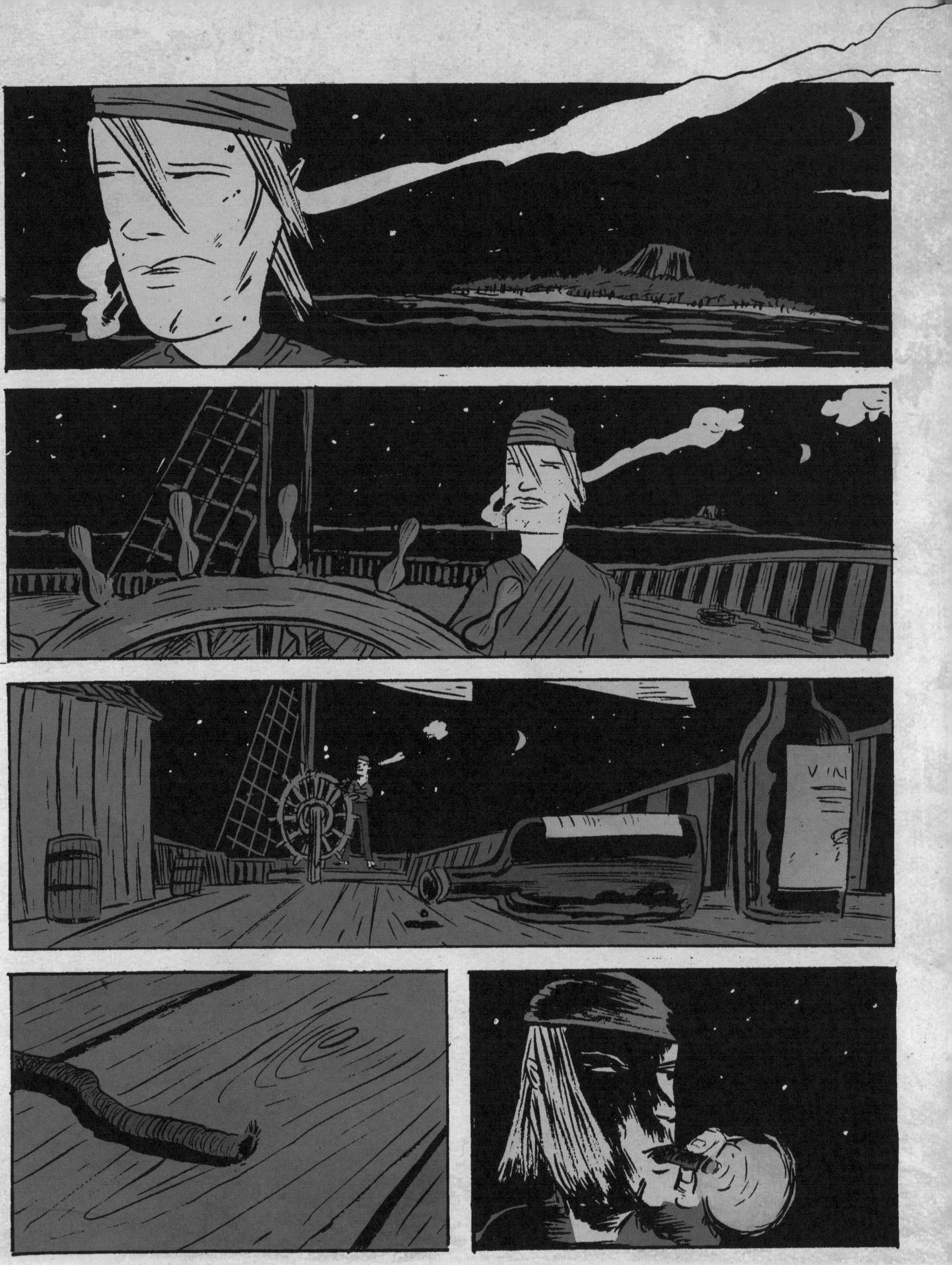
VIN

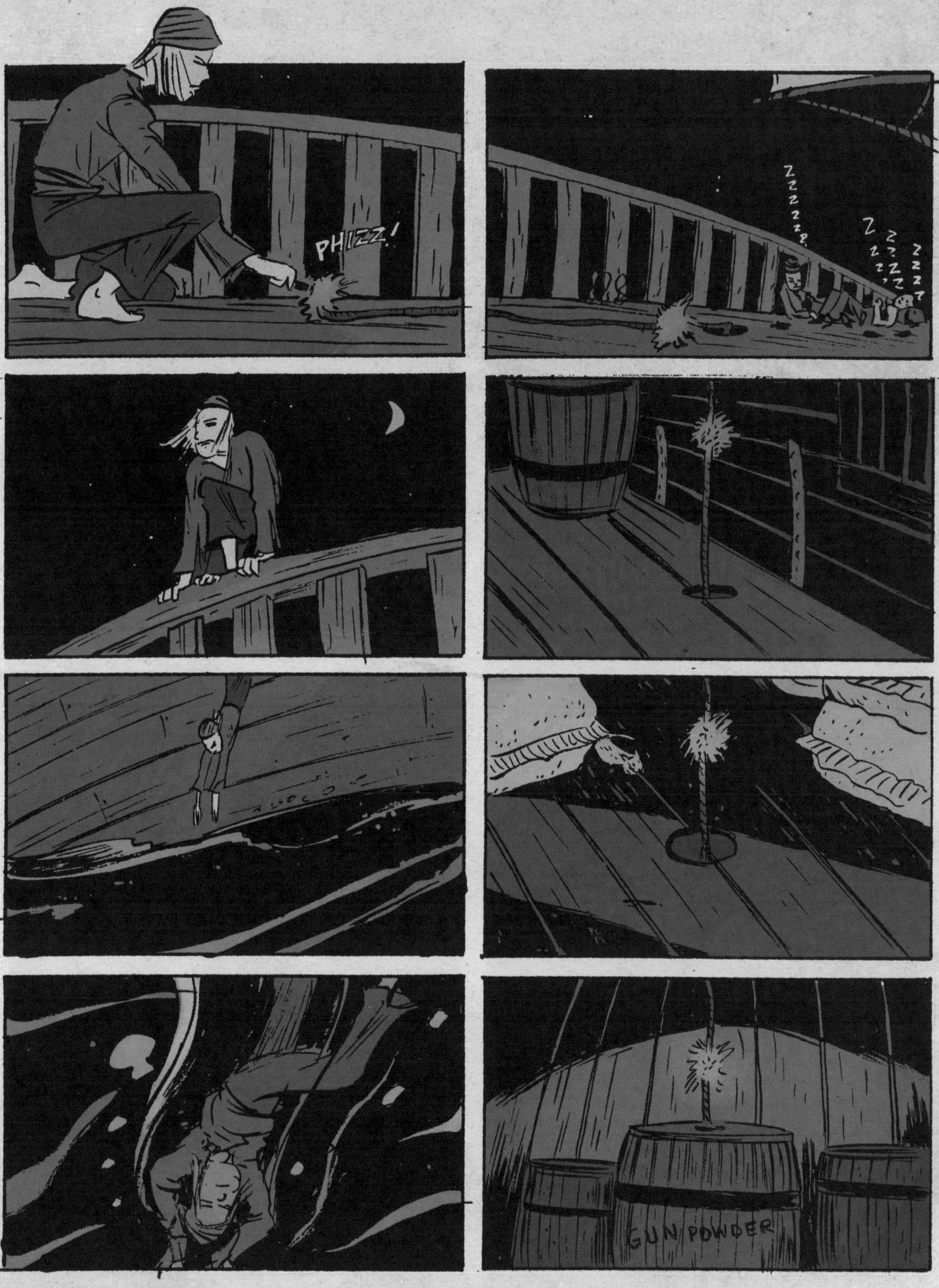
PHIZZ!
ZZZZZ
ZZZZ
GUN POWDER

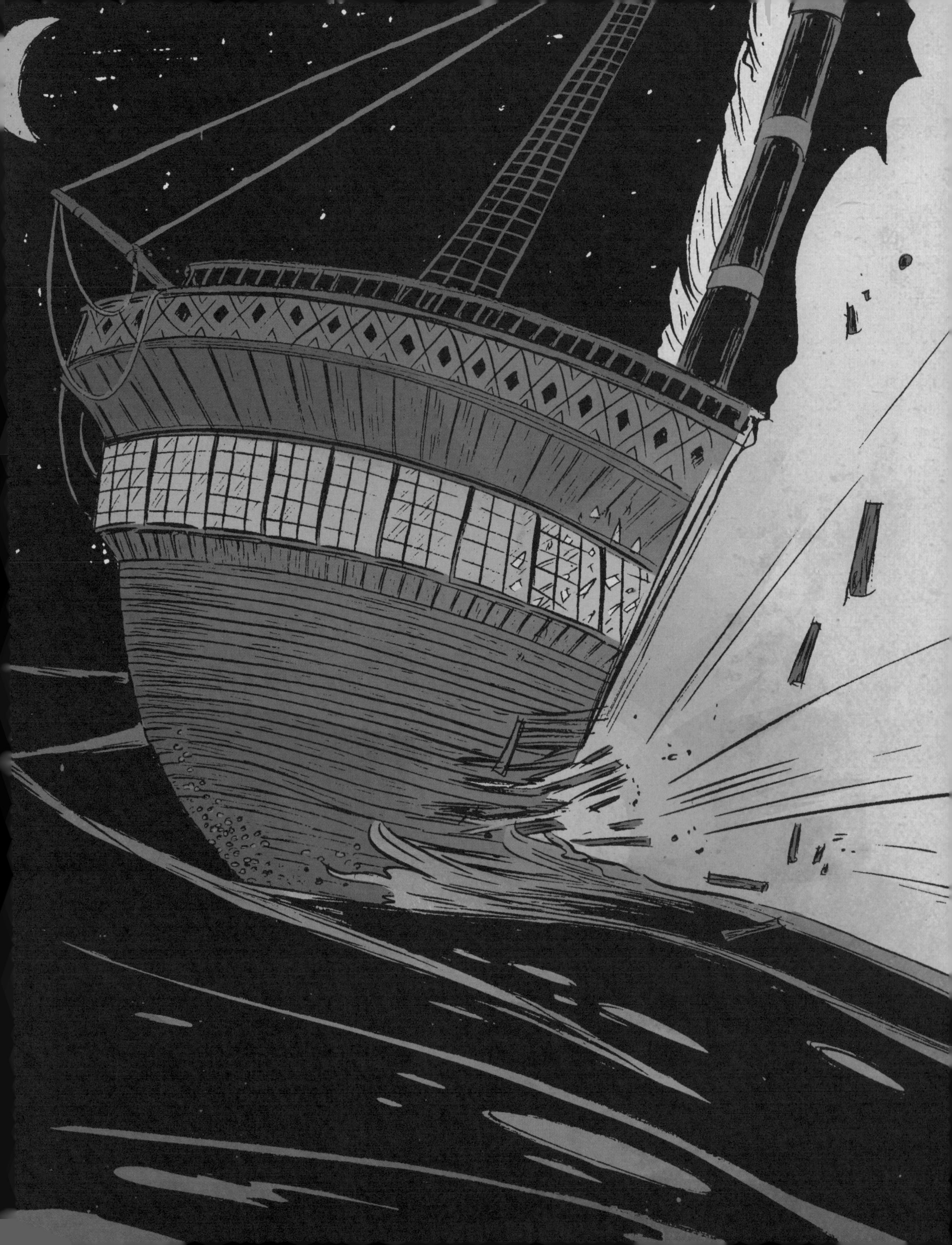

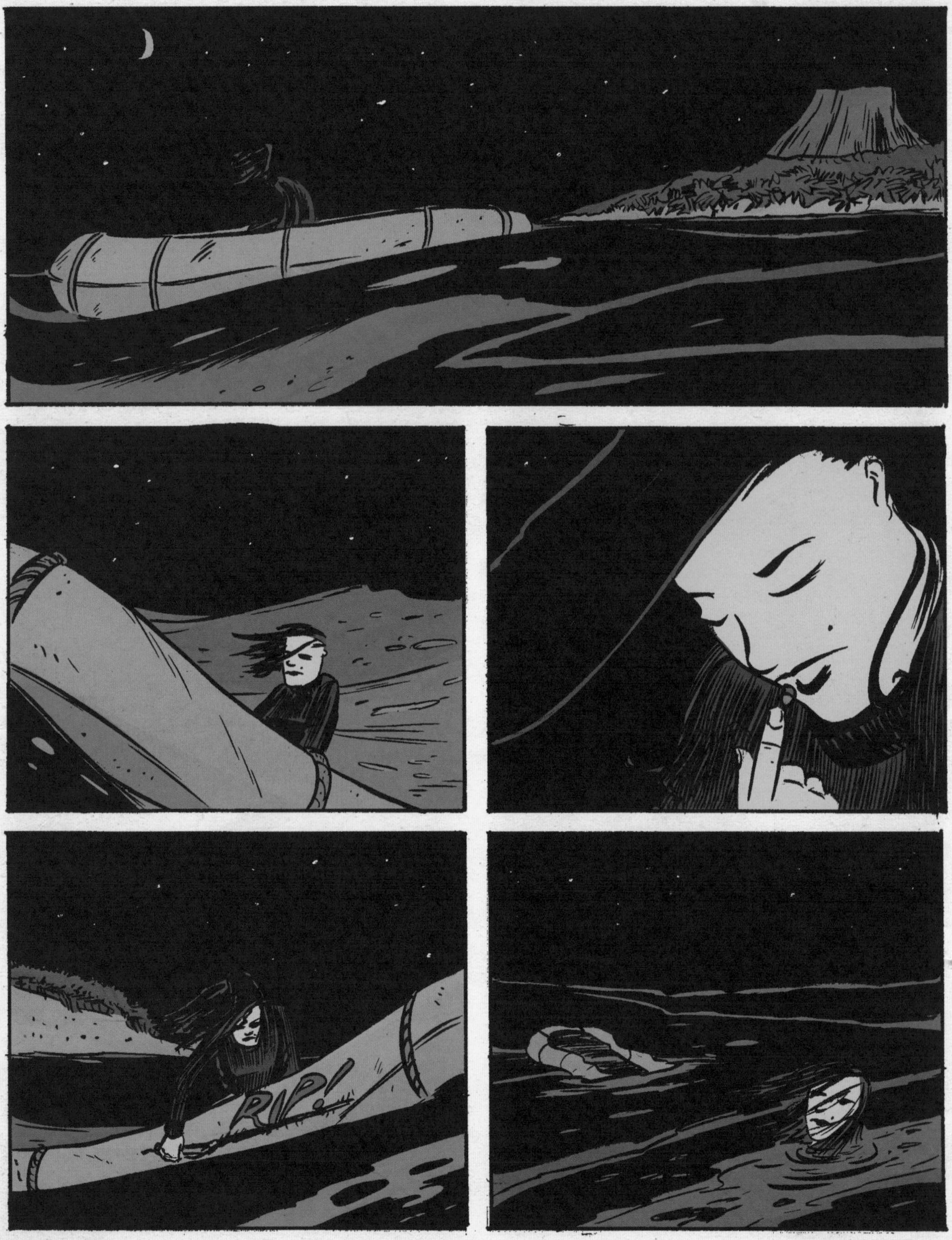
RIP!

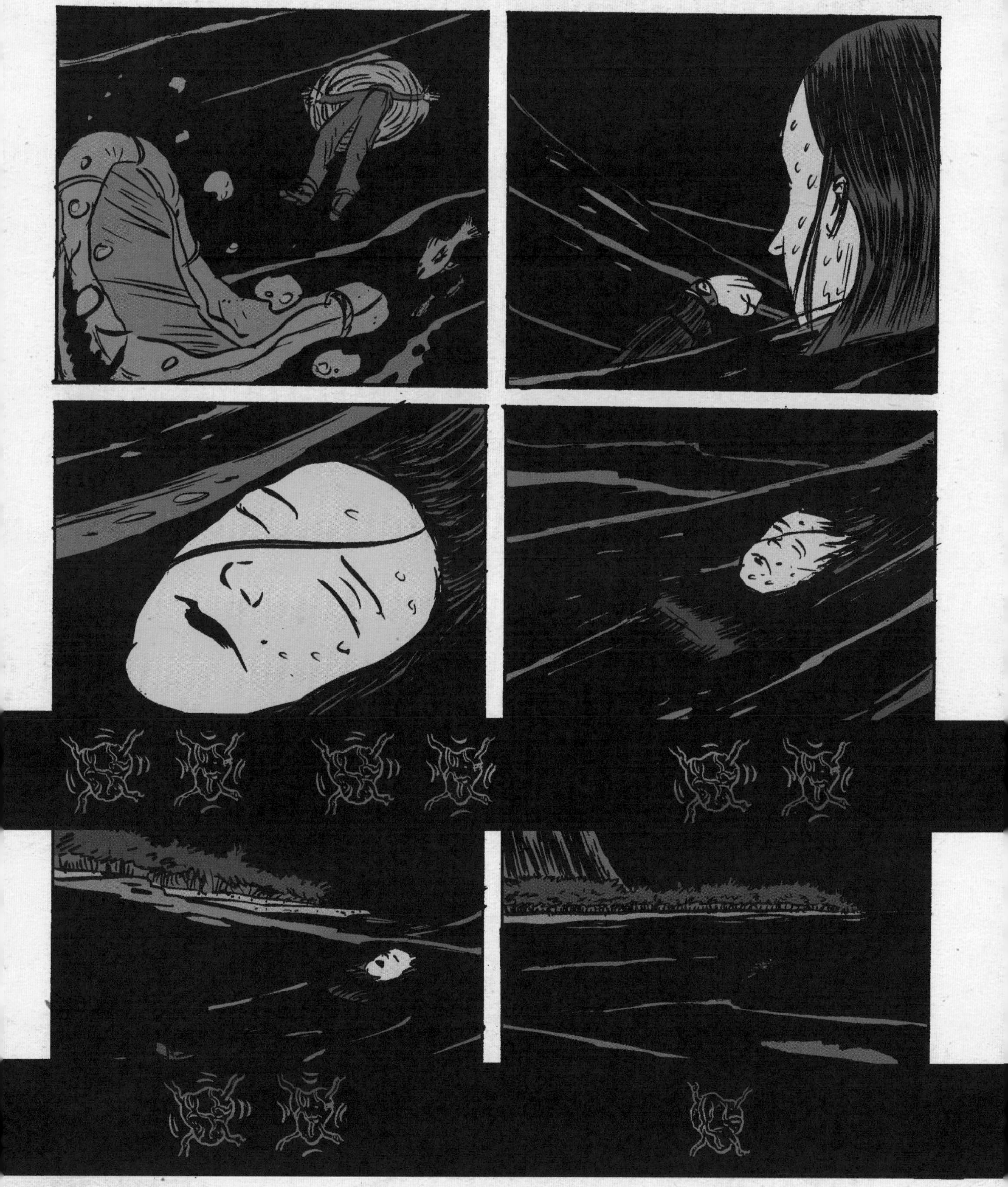

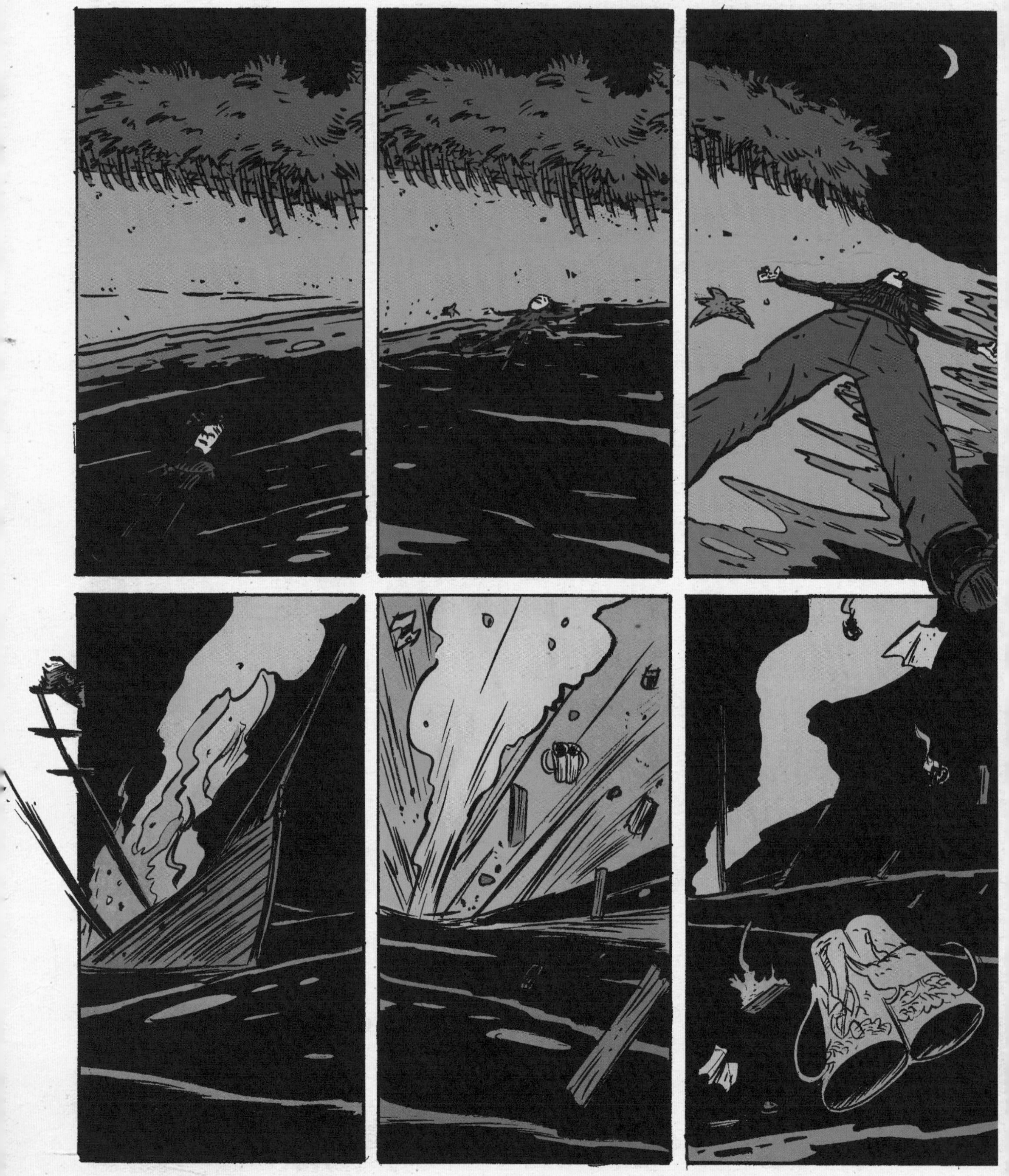

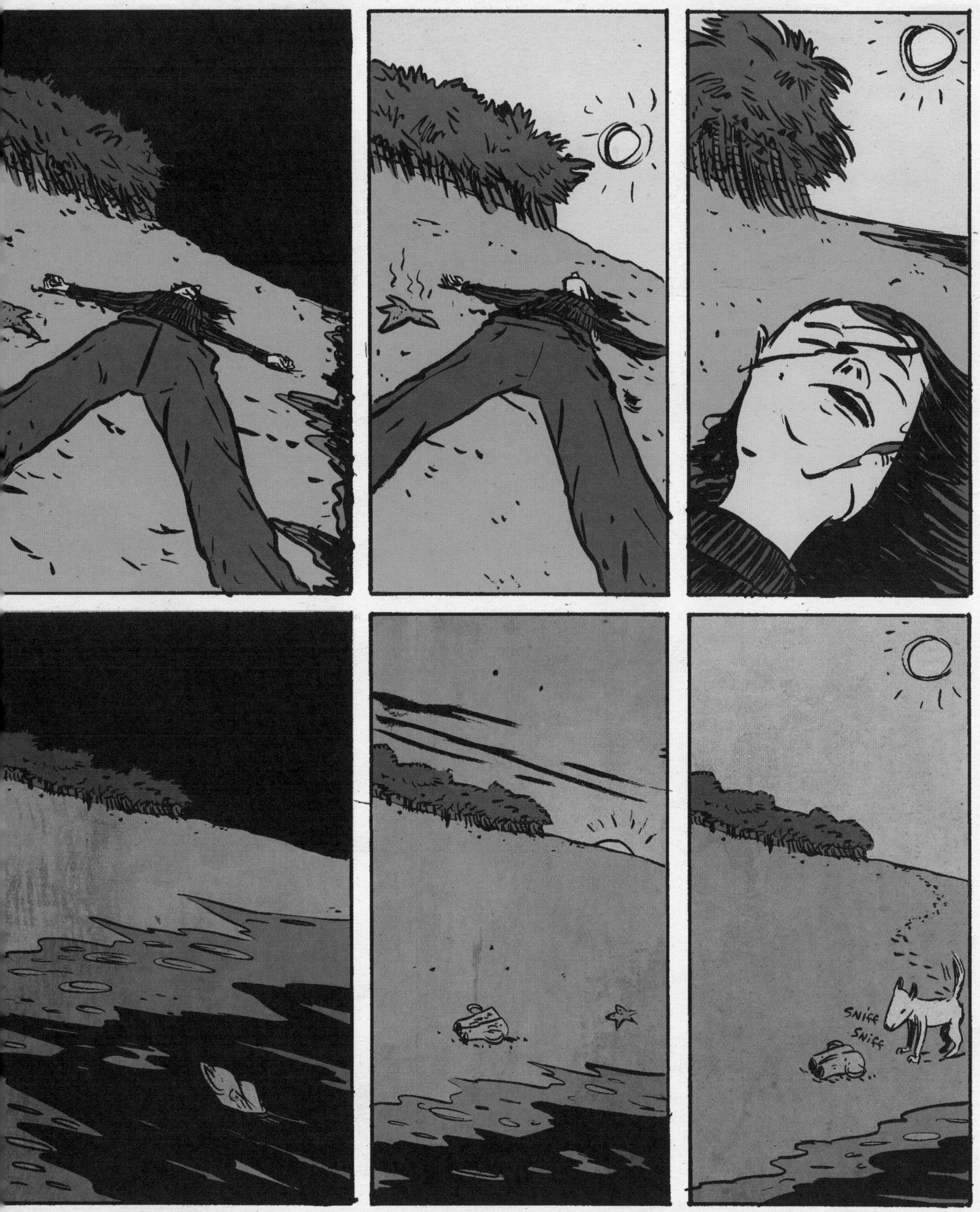
SNIFF
SNIFF

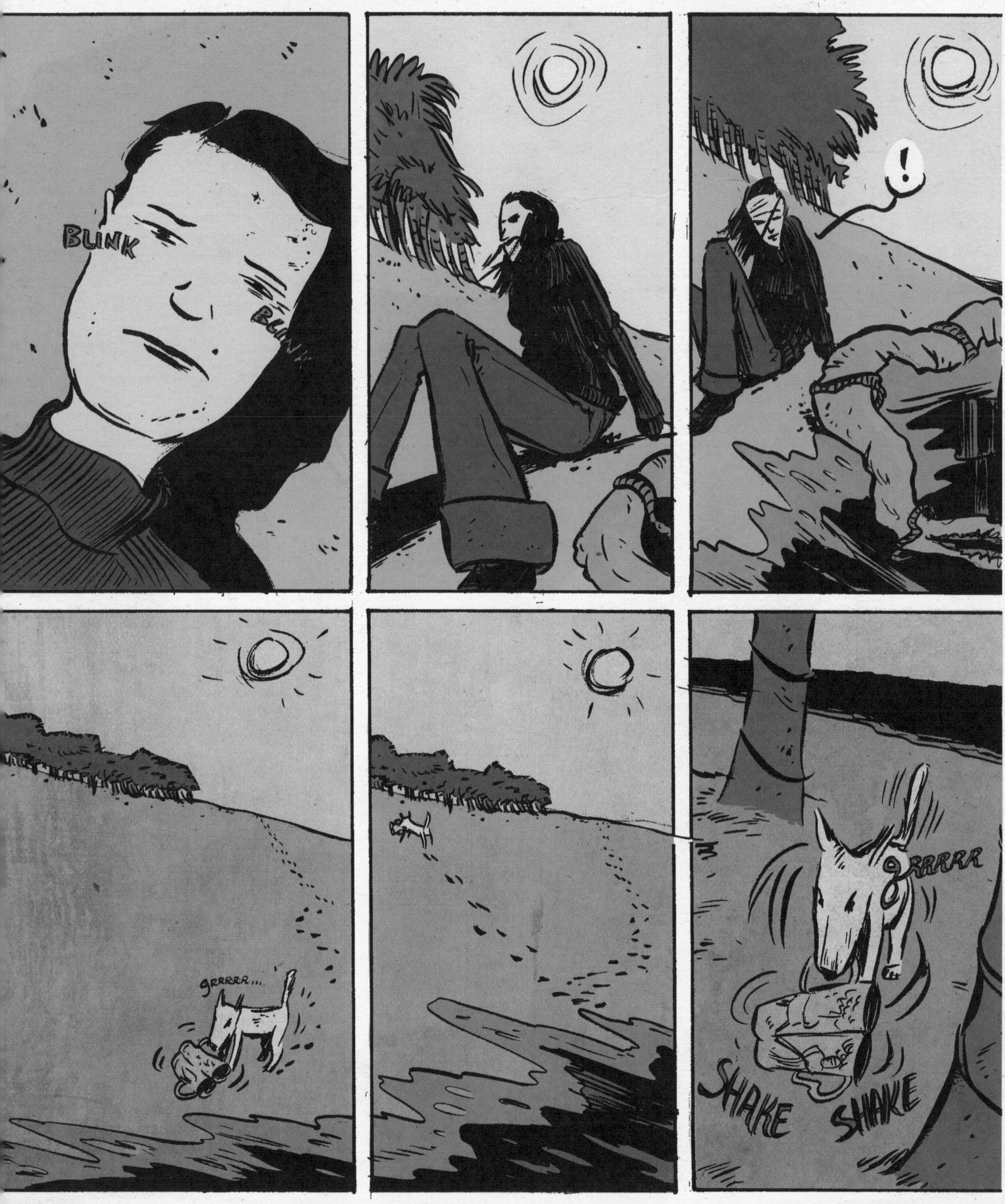
BLINK
BLINK
!
GRRRRR...
GRRRRR
SHAKE
SHAKE

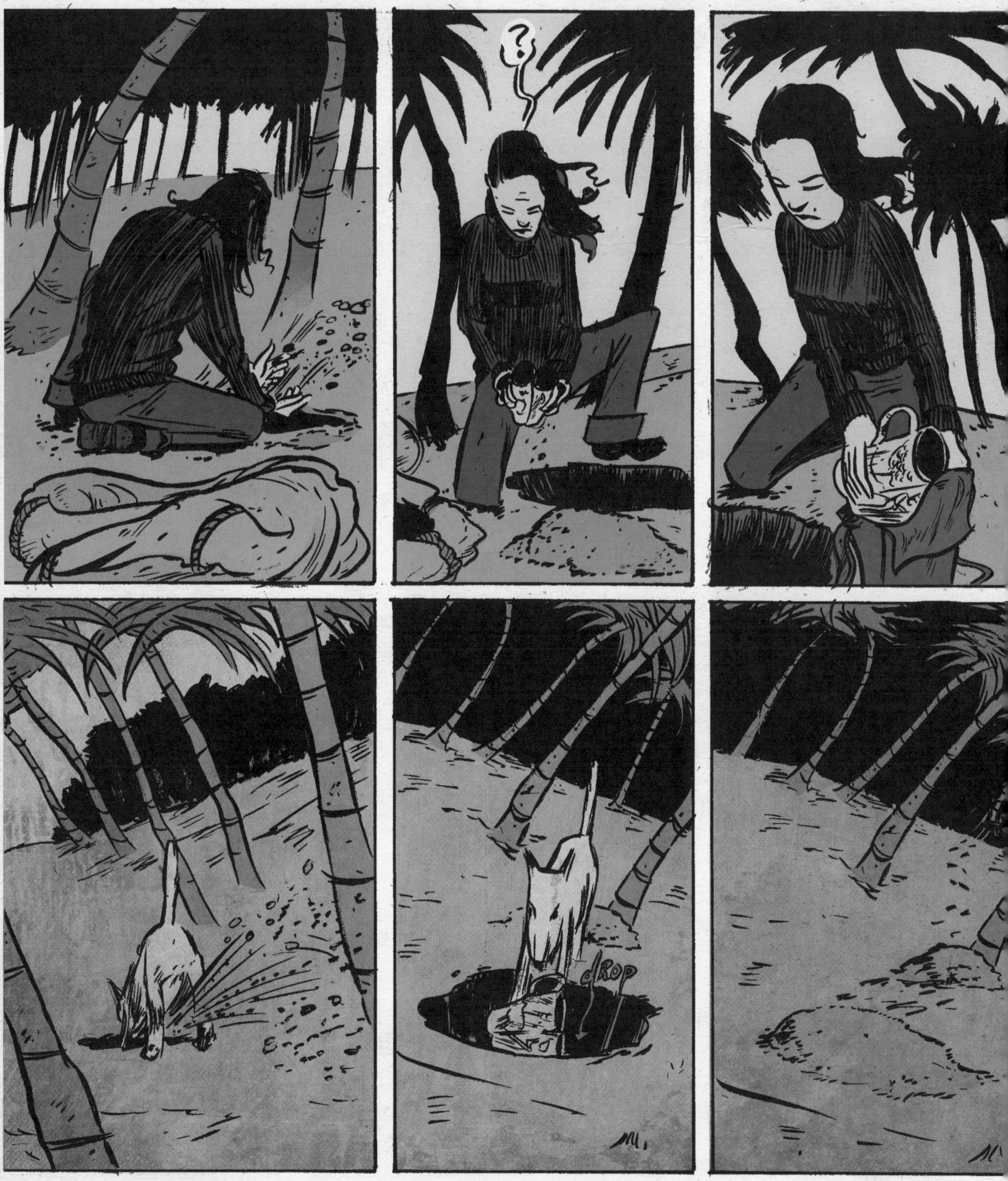
?
DROP

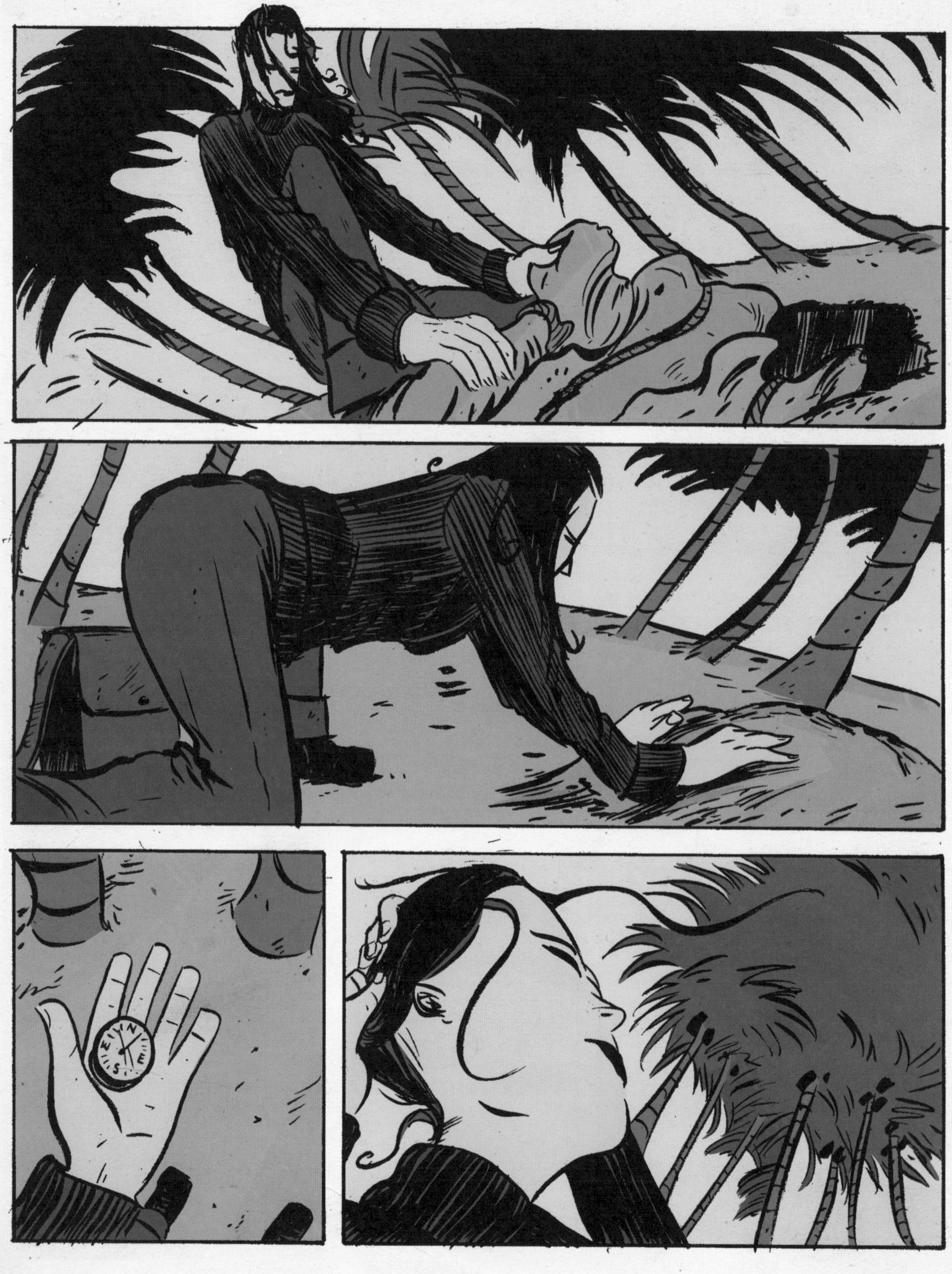

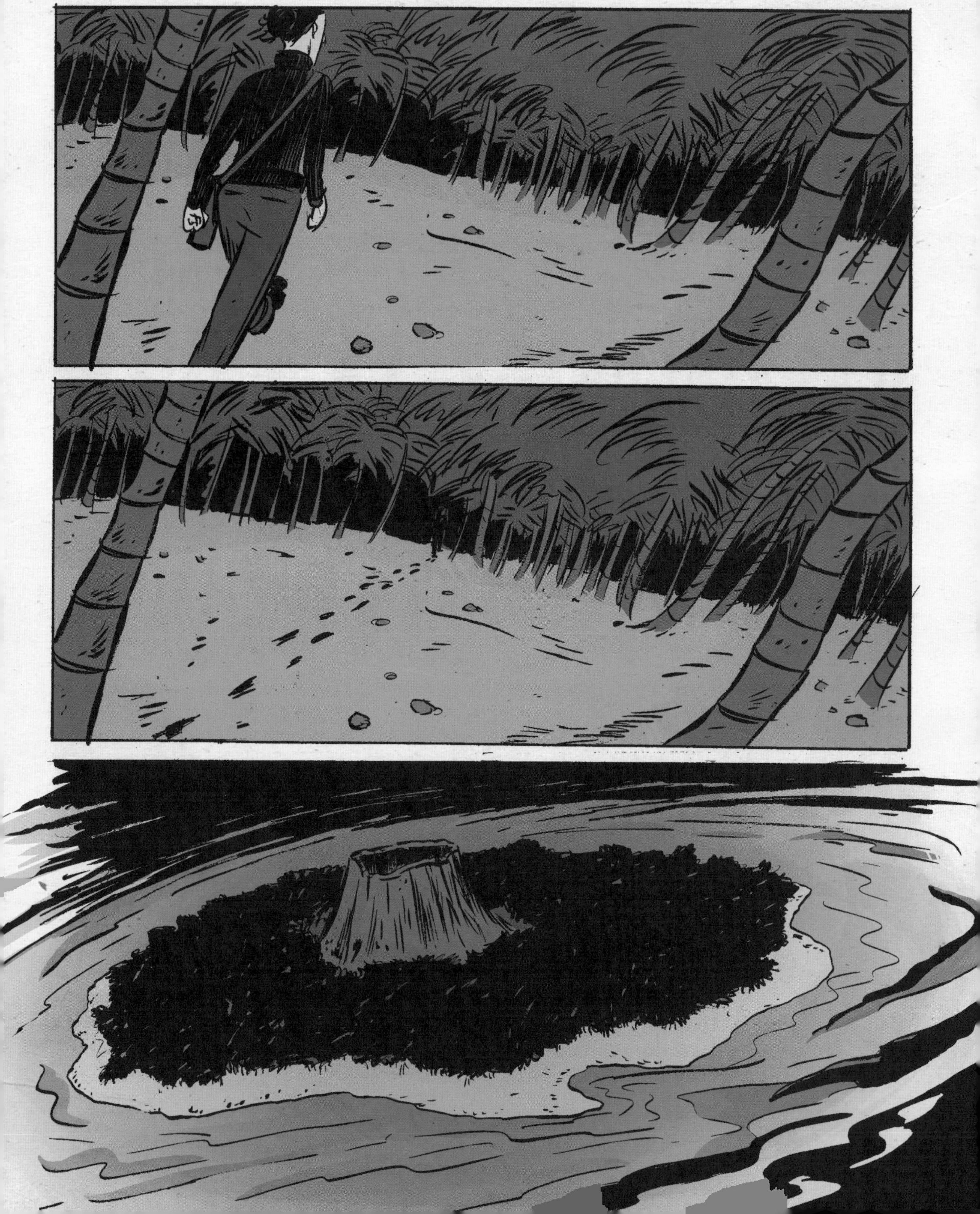

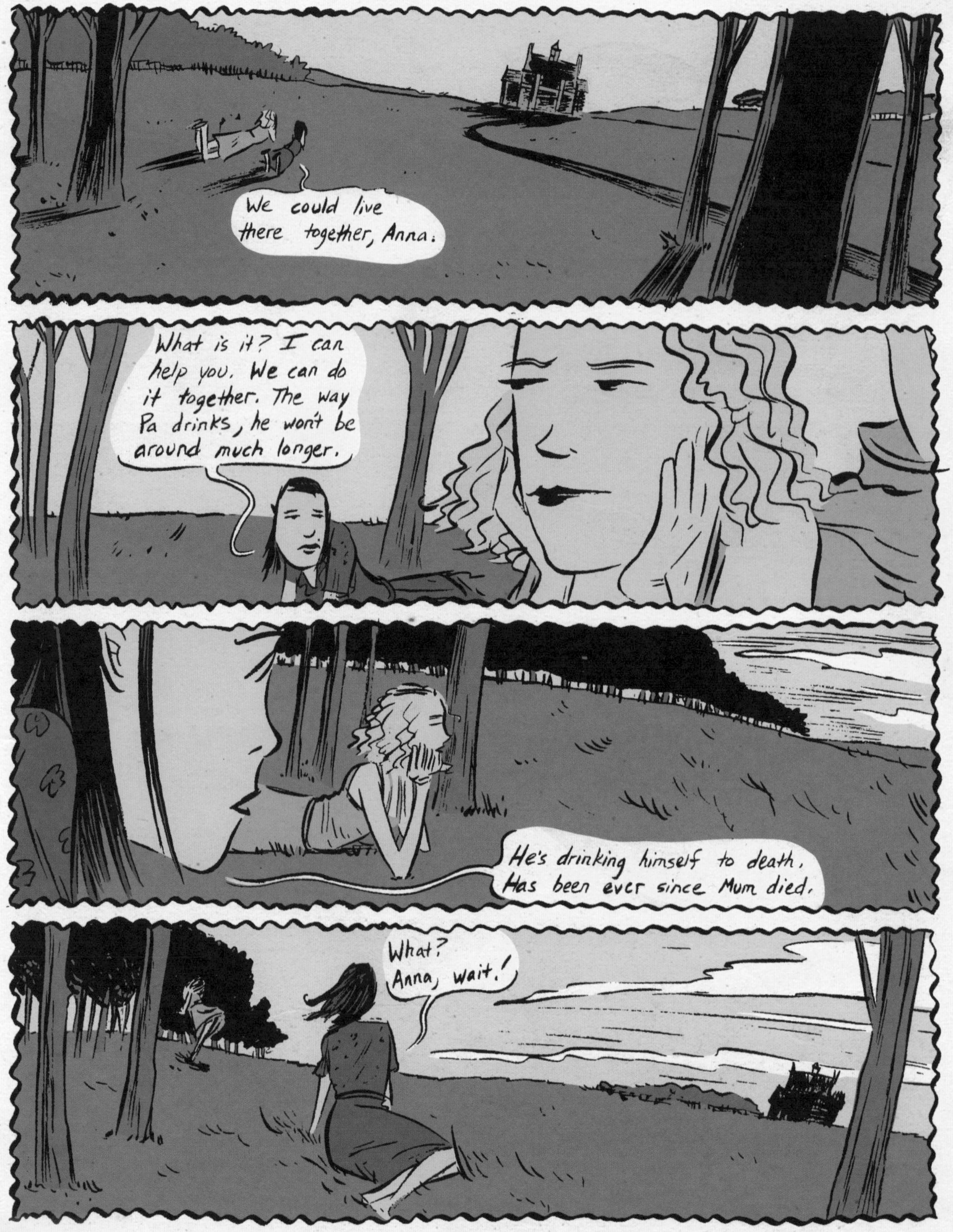
We could live there together, Anna.
What is it? I can help you. We can do it together. The way Pa drinks, he won't be around much longer.
He's drinking himself to death. Has been ever since Mum died.
What? Anna, wait!

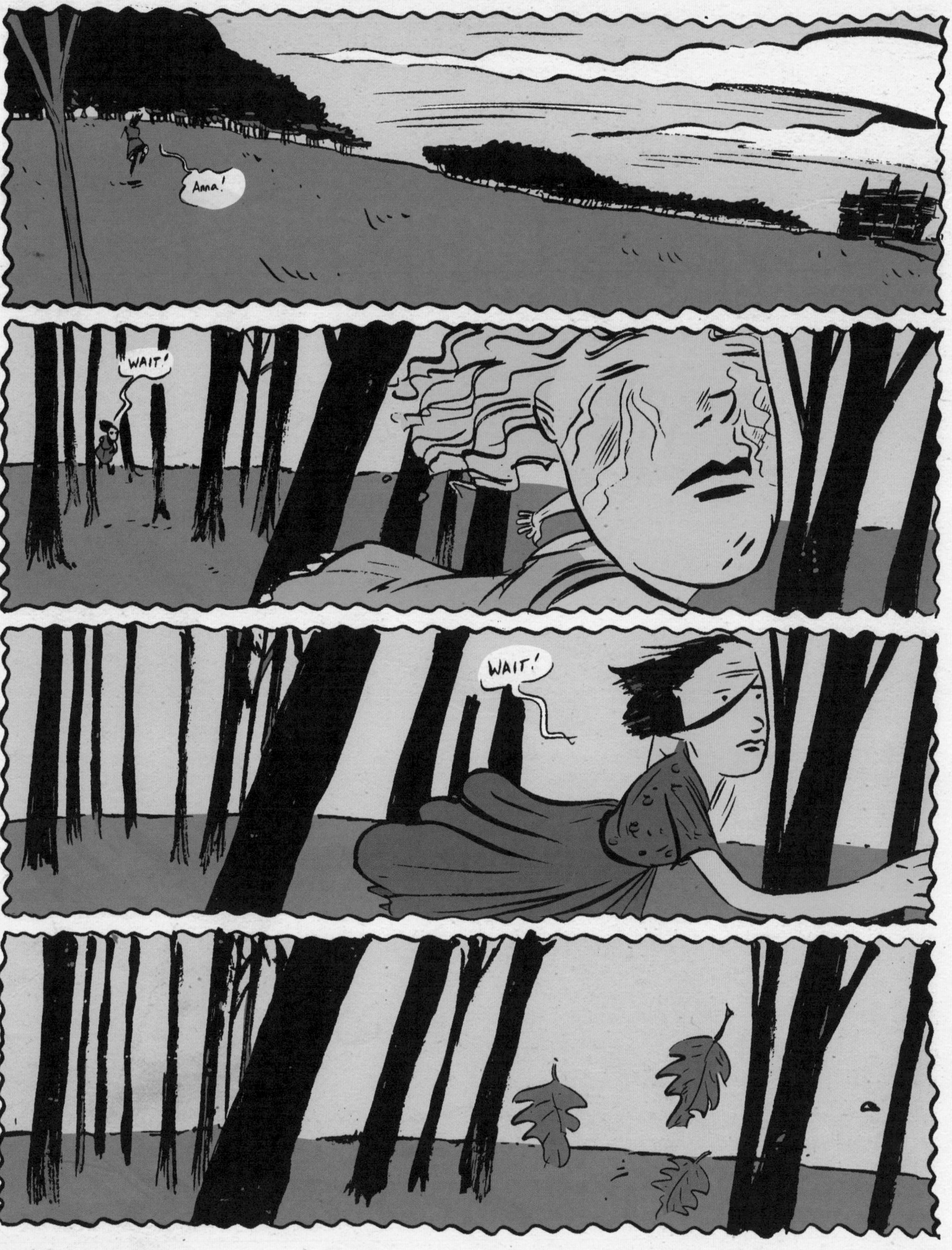
Anna!
WAIT!
WAIT!

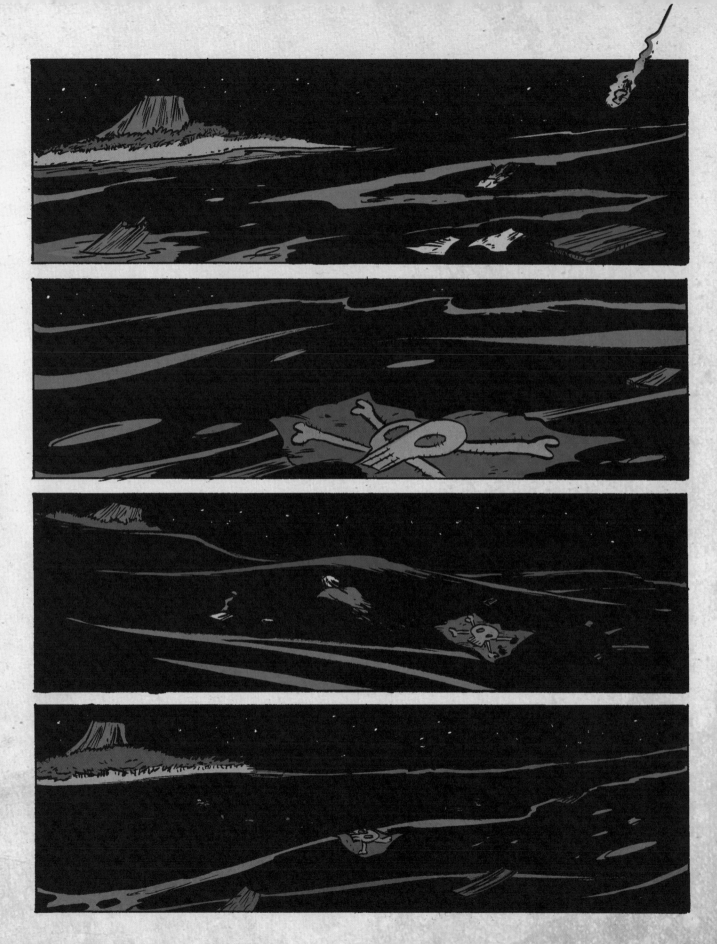

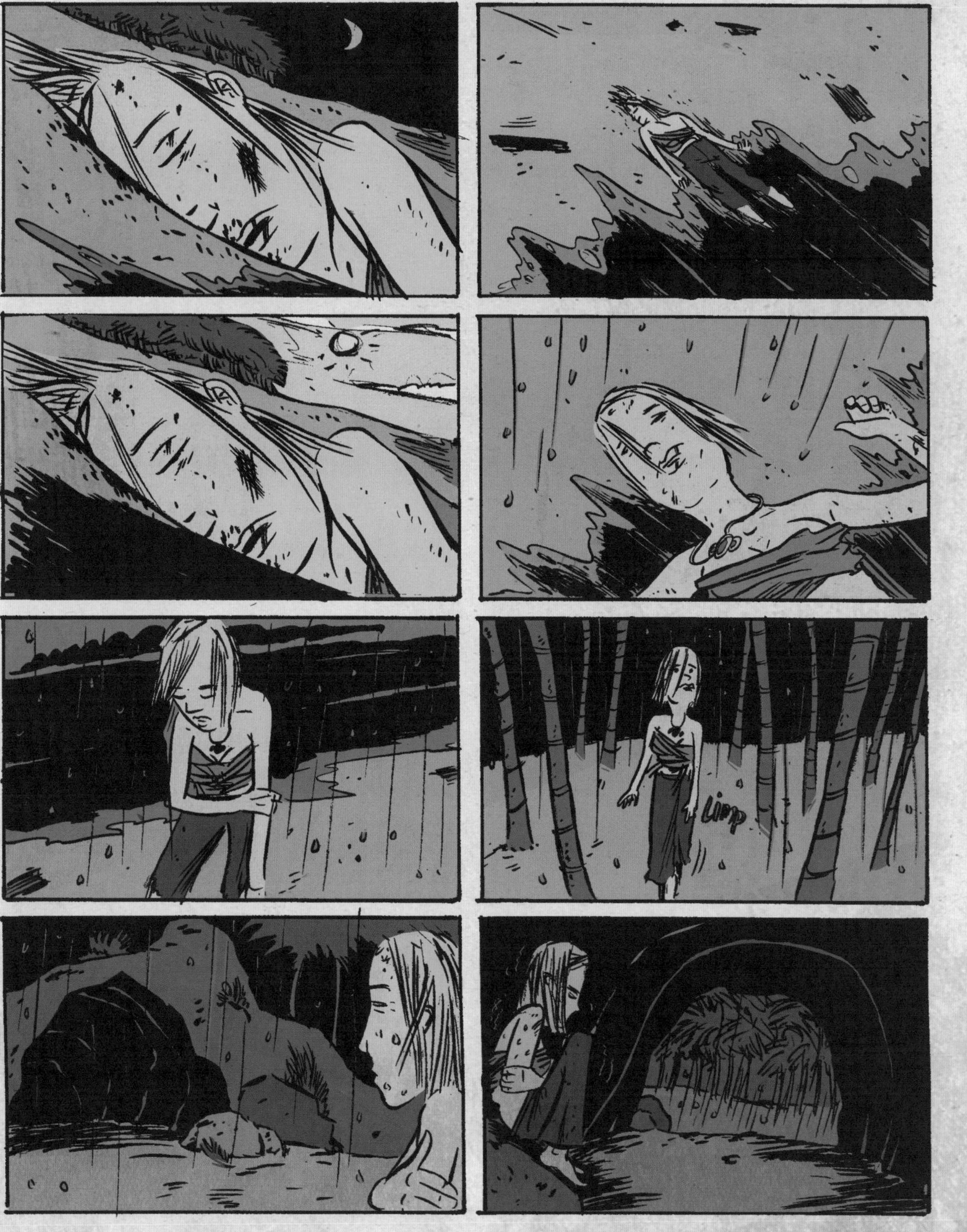
Limp

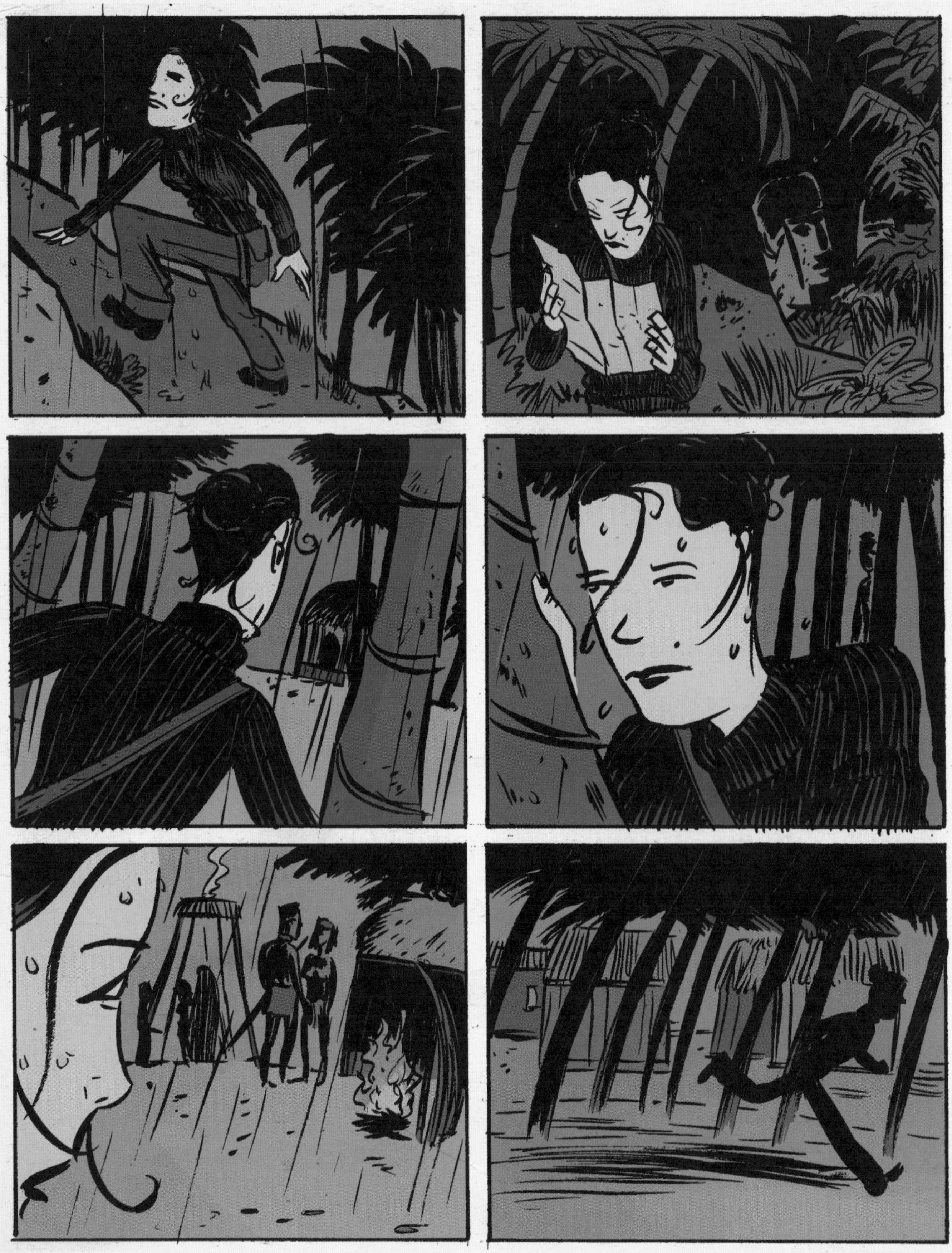

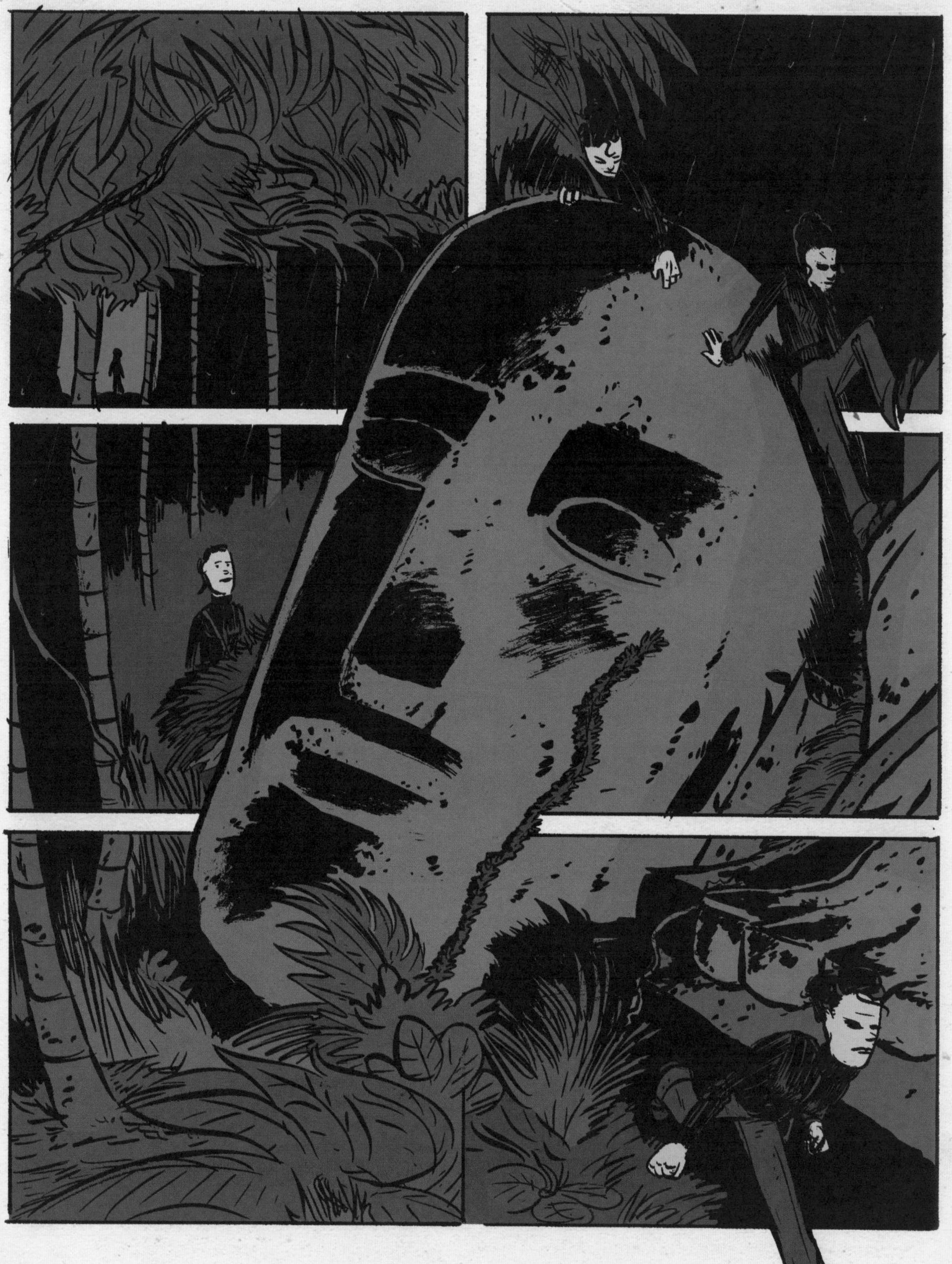

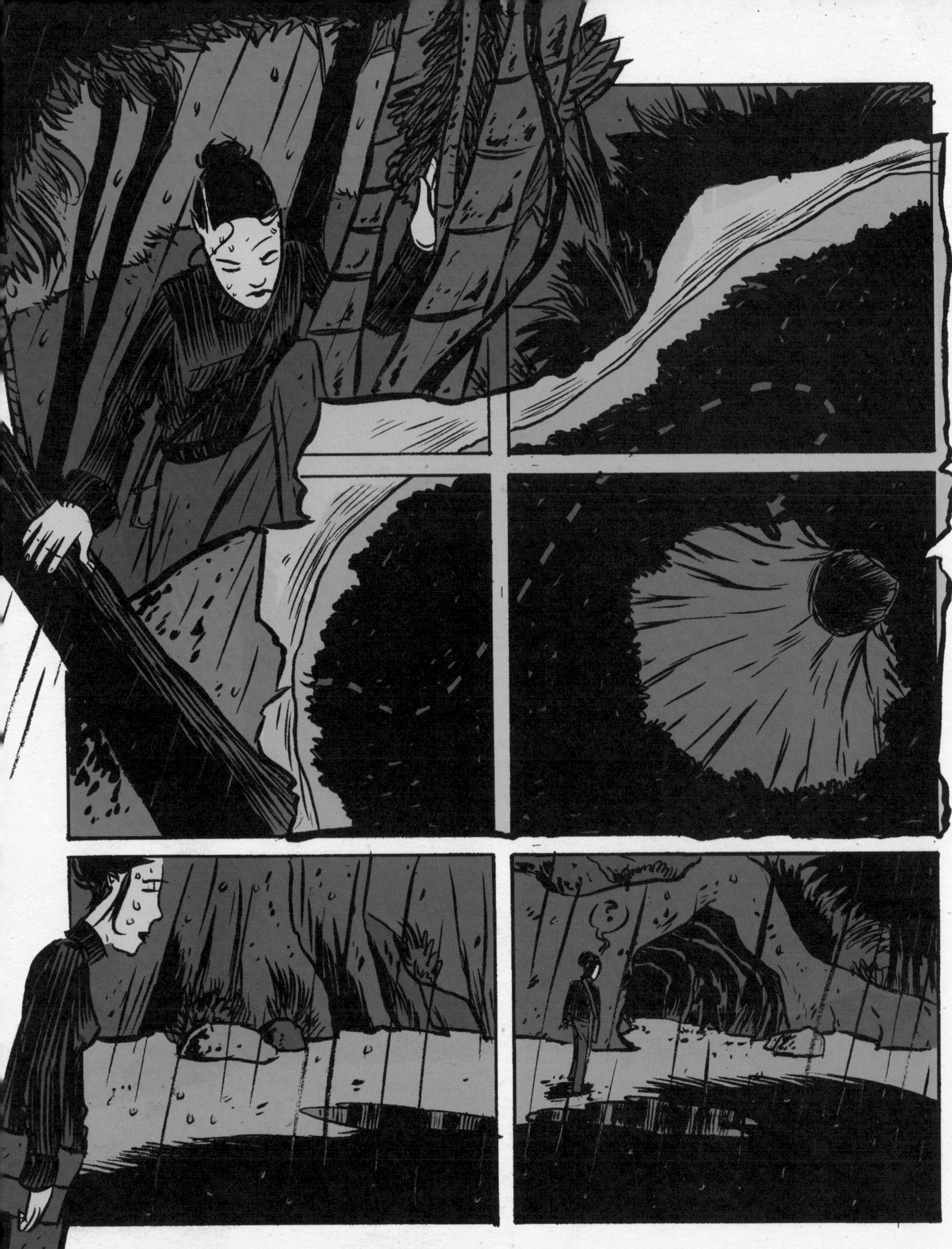
?

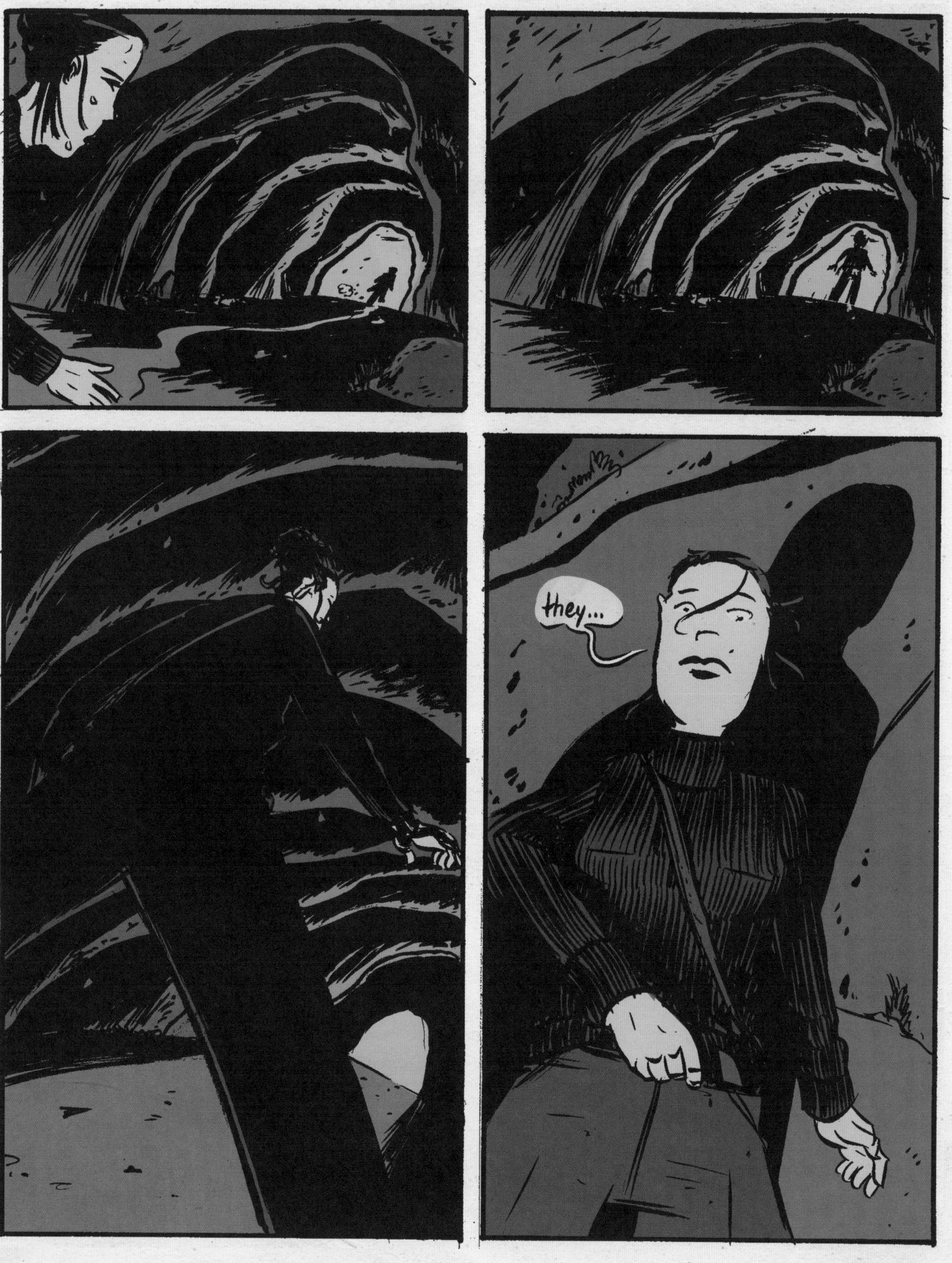
they...

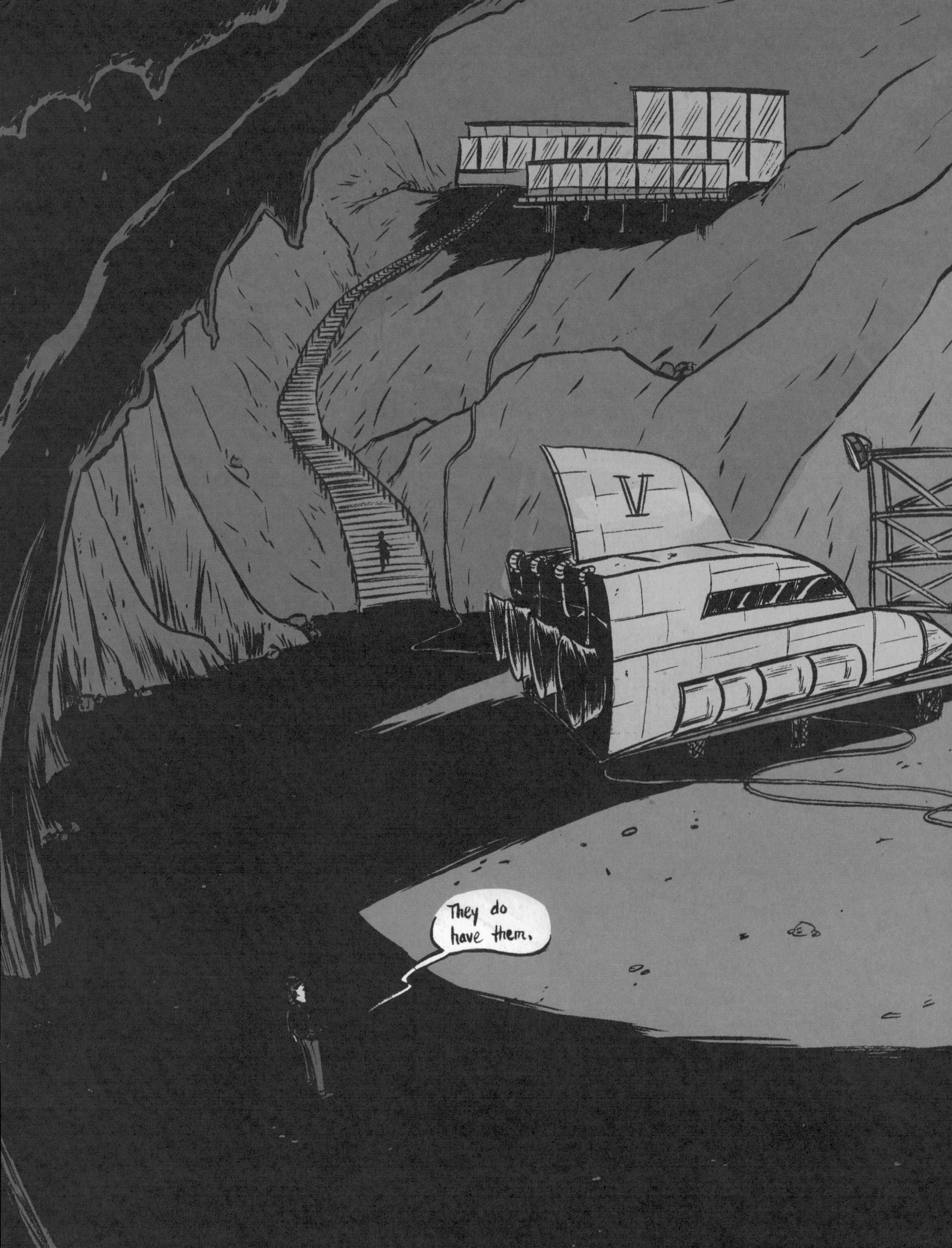
V
They do have them.

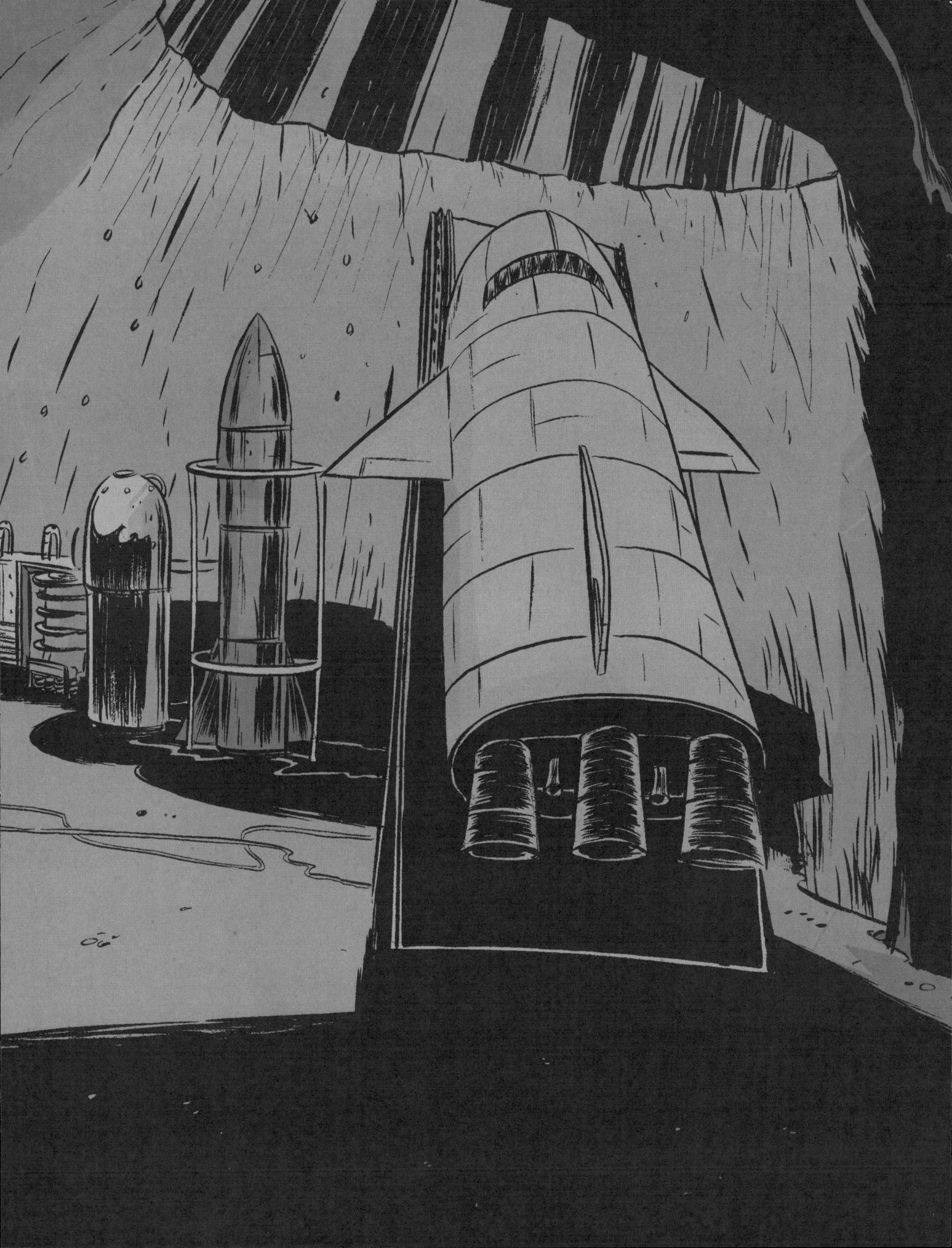

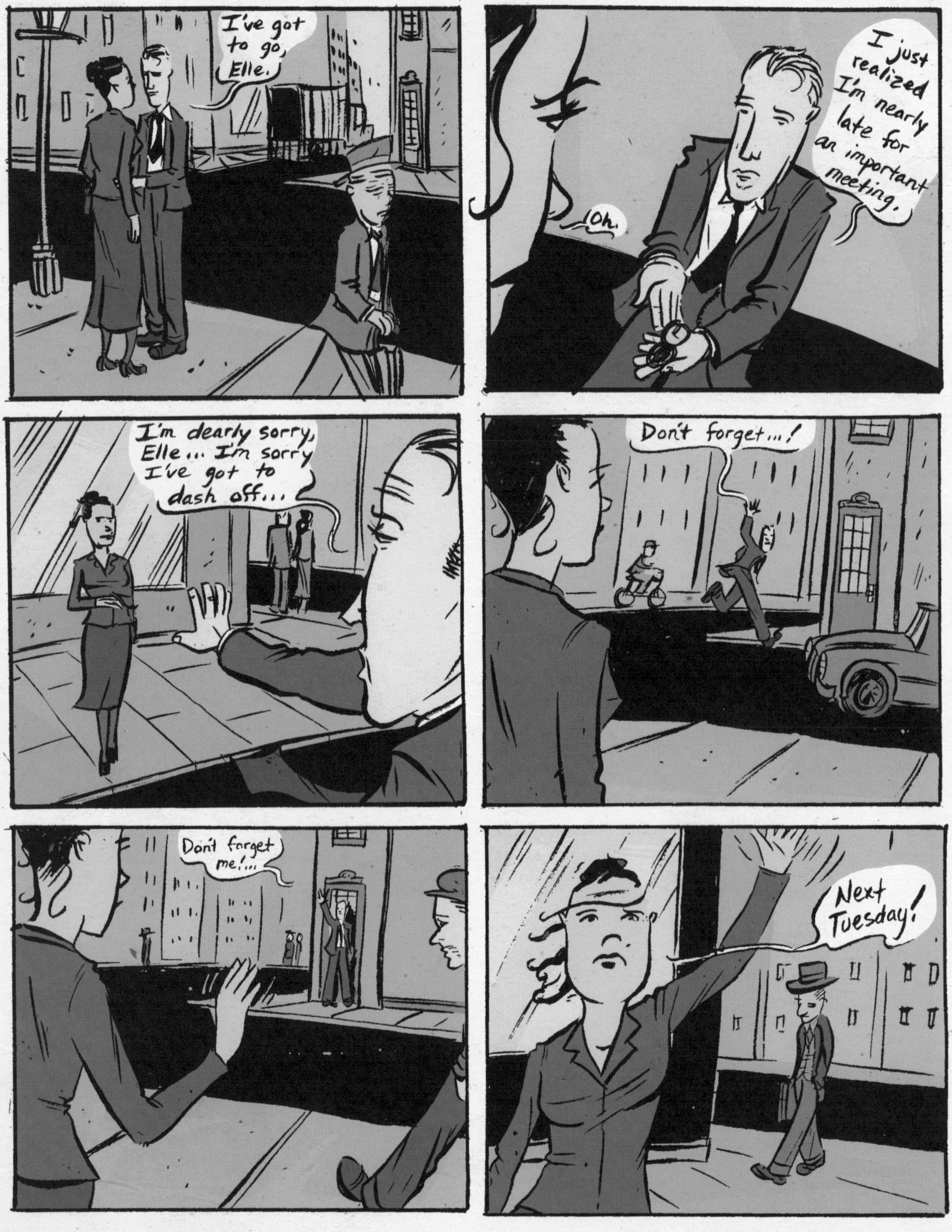
I've got to go, Elle.
I just realized I'm nearly late for an important meeting.
Oh.
I'm dearly sorry, Elle... I'm sorry I've got to dash off...
Don't forget...!
Don't forget me!...
Next Tuesday!

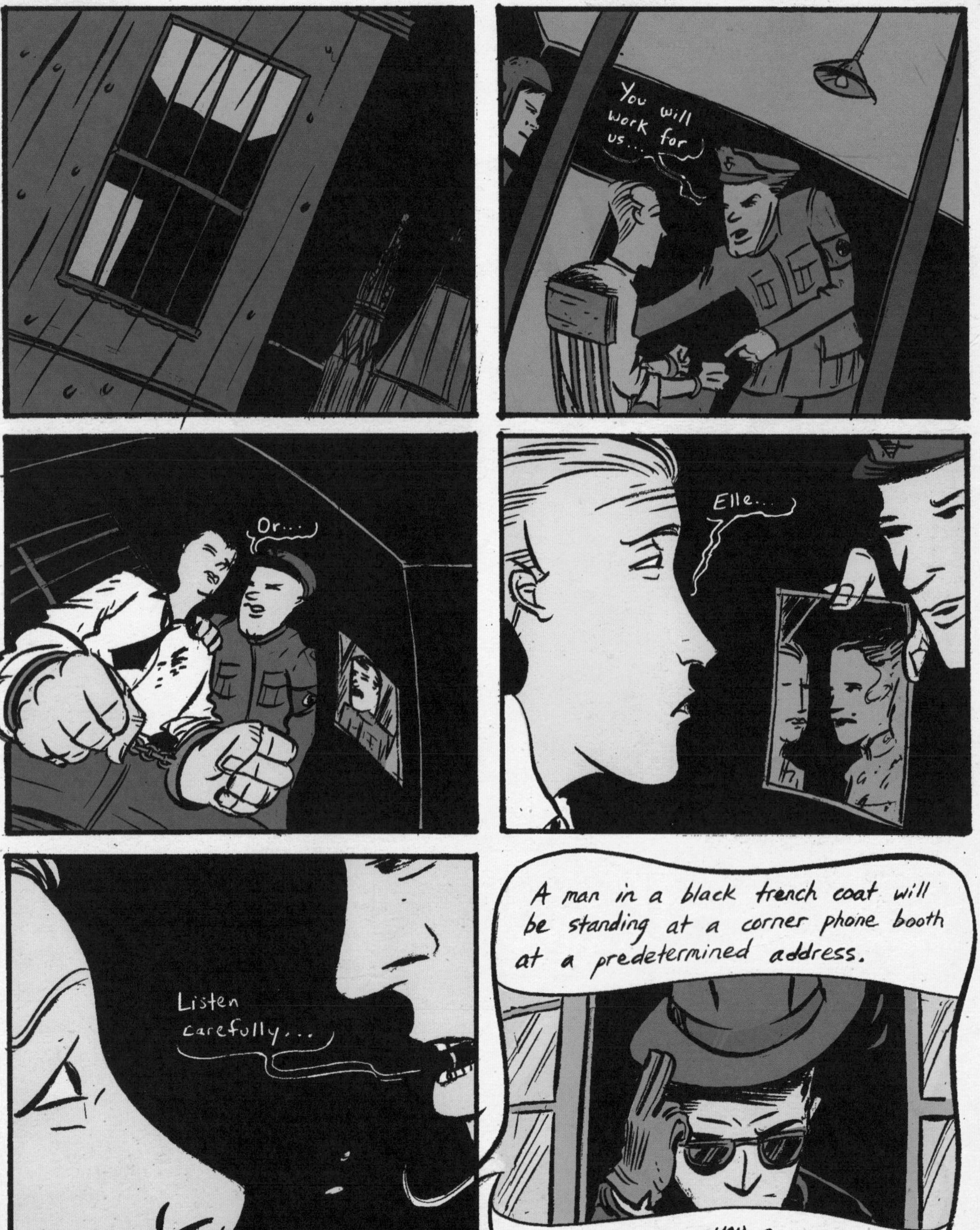
You will work for us...
Or...
Elle...
Listen carefully...
A man in a black trench coat will be standing at a corner phone booth at a predetermined address.
He will give you a signal.

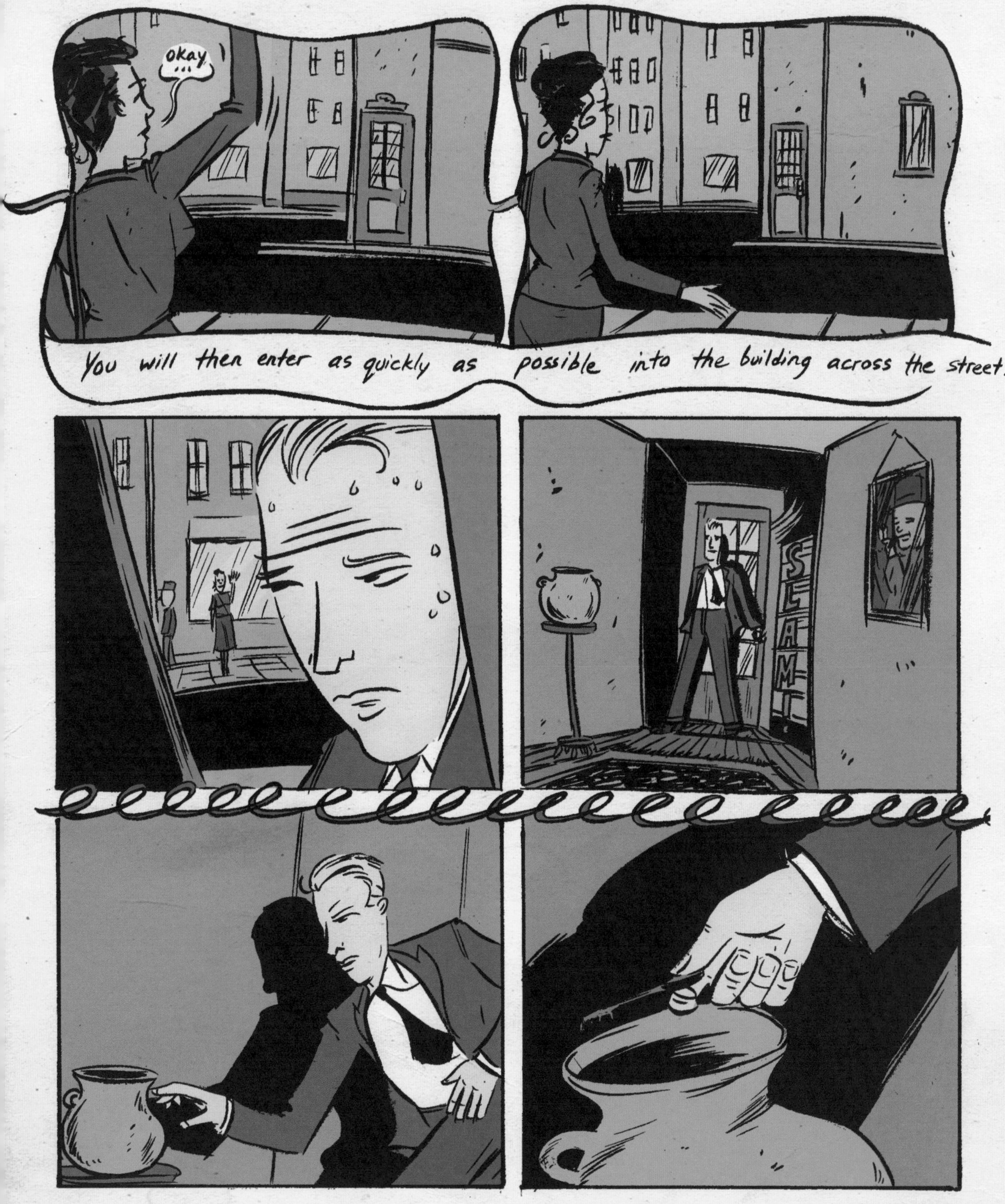
Okay...
You will then enter as quickly as possible into the building across the street.
SLAM!

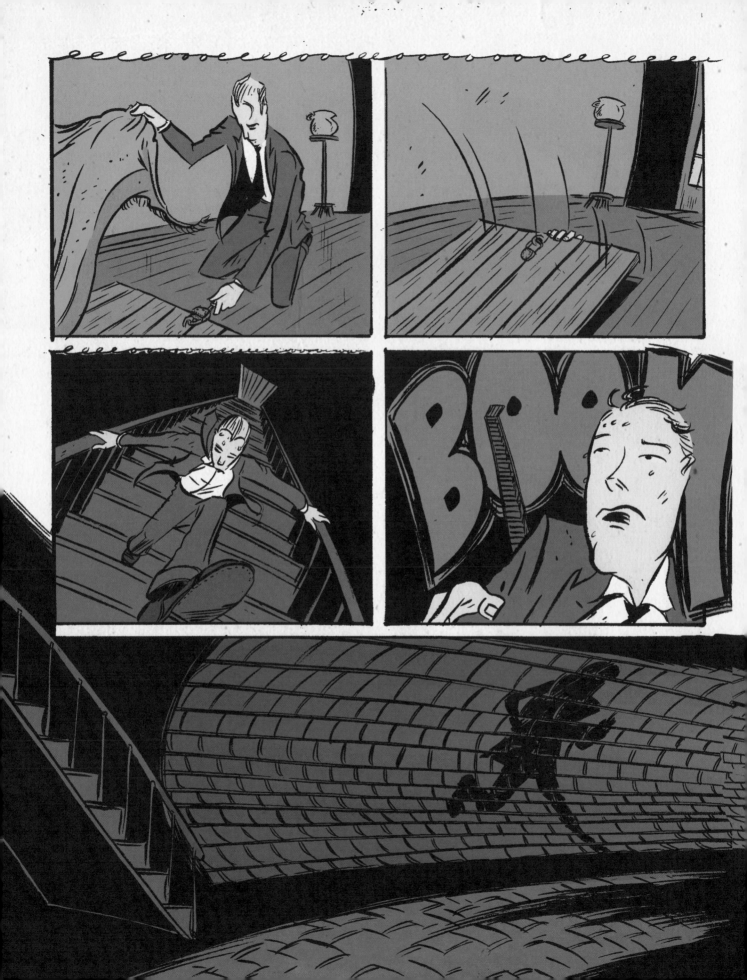

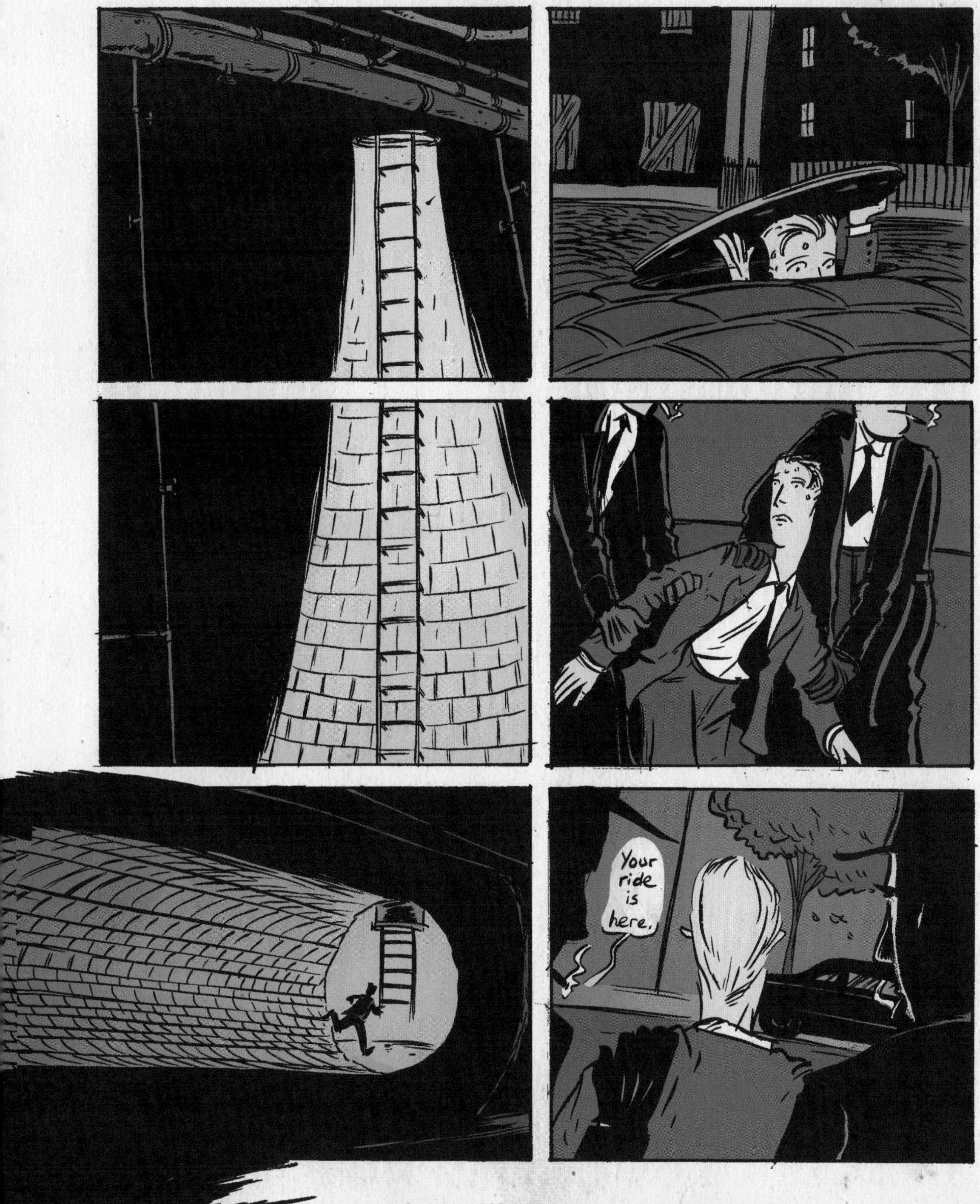
Your ride is here.

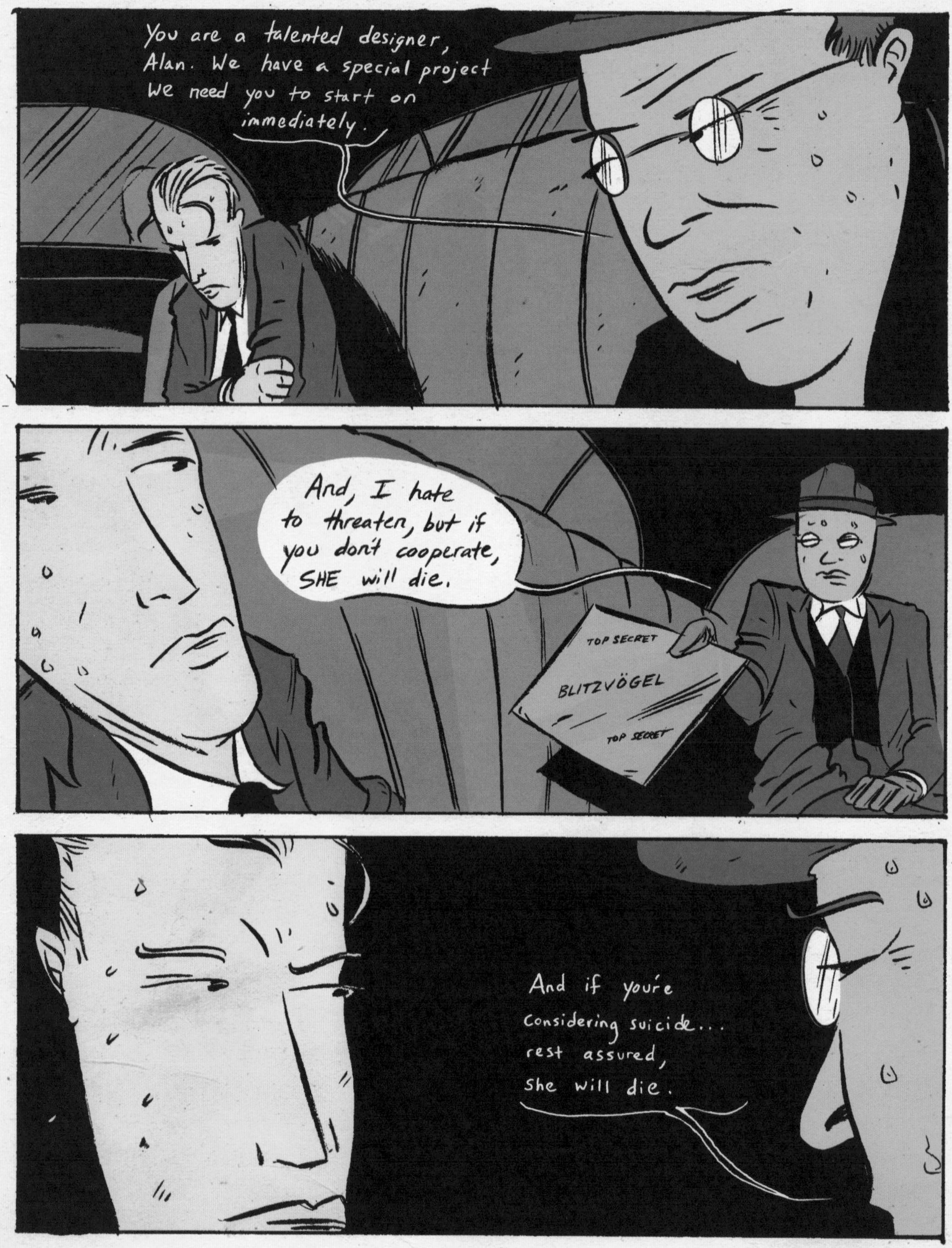
You are a talented designer, Alan. We have a special project we need you to start on immediately.
And, I hate to threaten, but if you don't cooperate, SHE will die.
TOP SECRET
BLITZVÖGEL
TOP SECRET
And if you're considering suicide... rest assured, she will die.

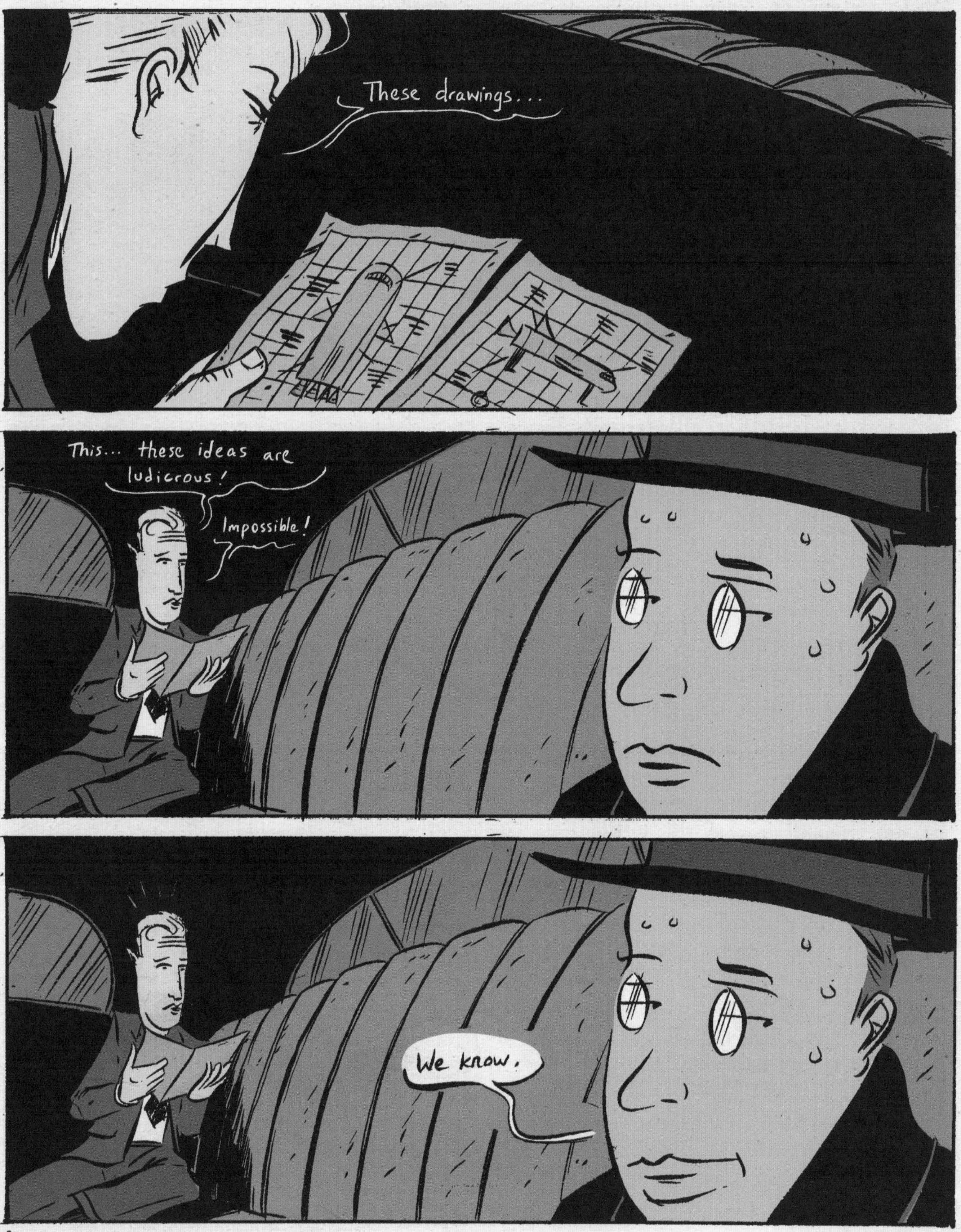
These drawings...
This... these ideas are ludicrous!
Impossible!
We know.

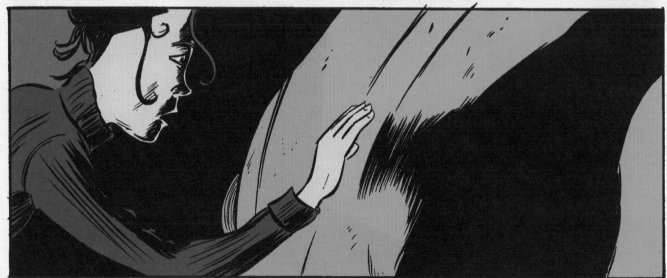

SCUFFLE

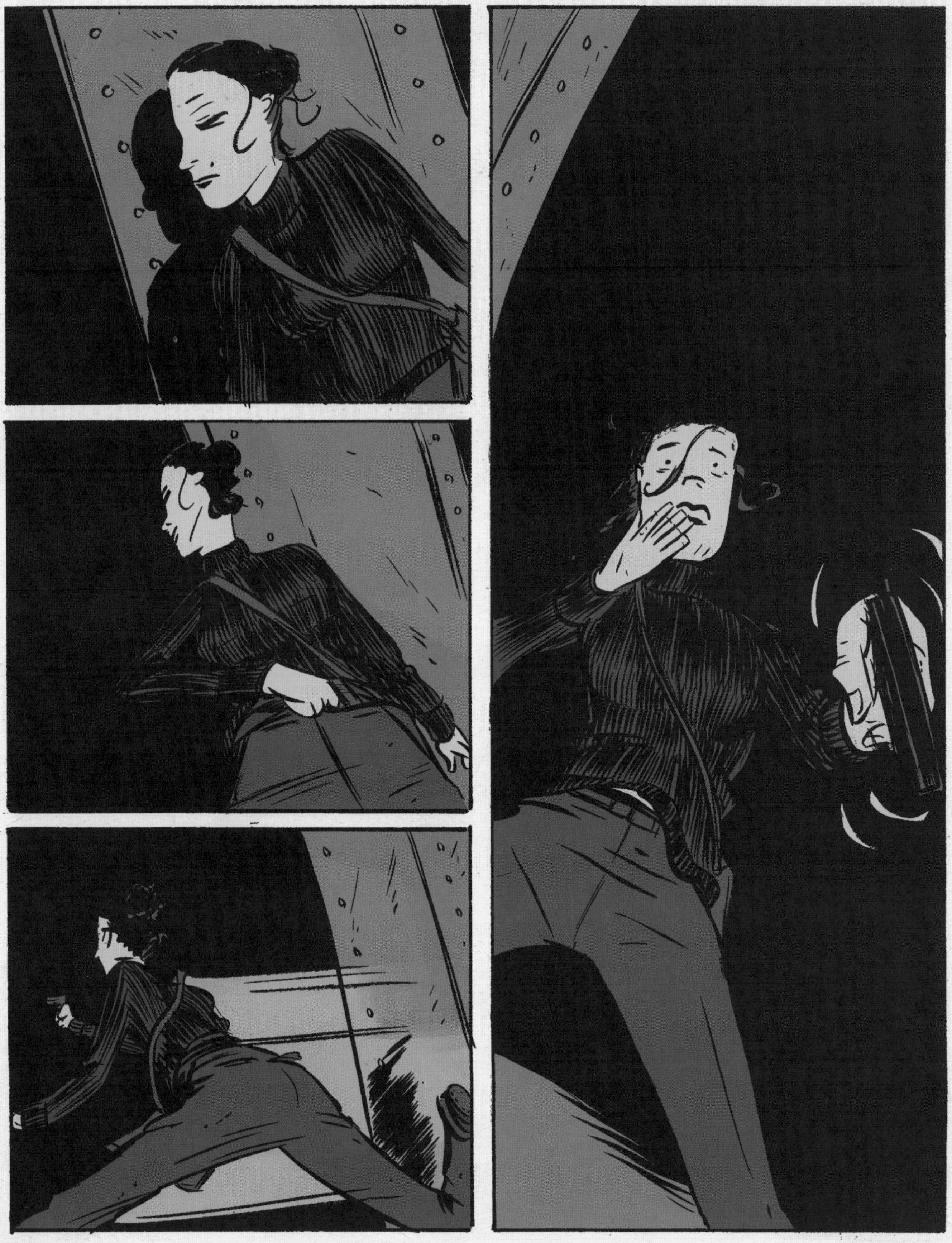

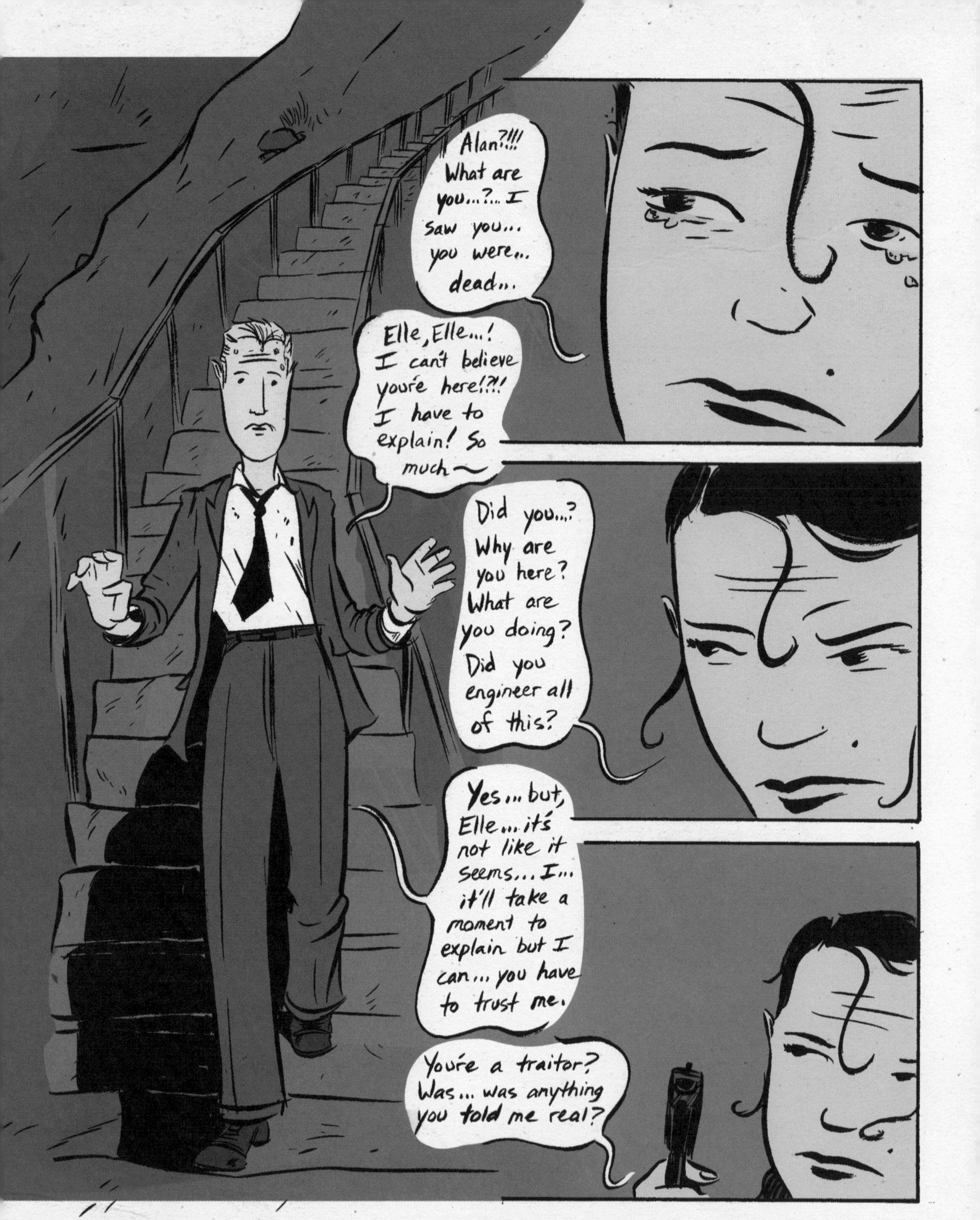
Alan?!!! What are you...?... I saw you... you were... dead...
Elle, Elle...! I can't believe you're here!?!! I have to explain! So much~
Did you...? Why are you here? What are you doing? Did you engineer all of this?
Yes... but, Elle... it's not like it seems... I... it'll take a moment to explain but I can... you have to trust me.
You're a traitor? Was... was anything you told me real?

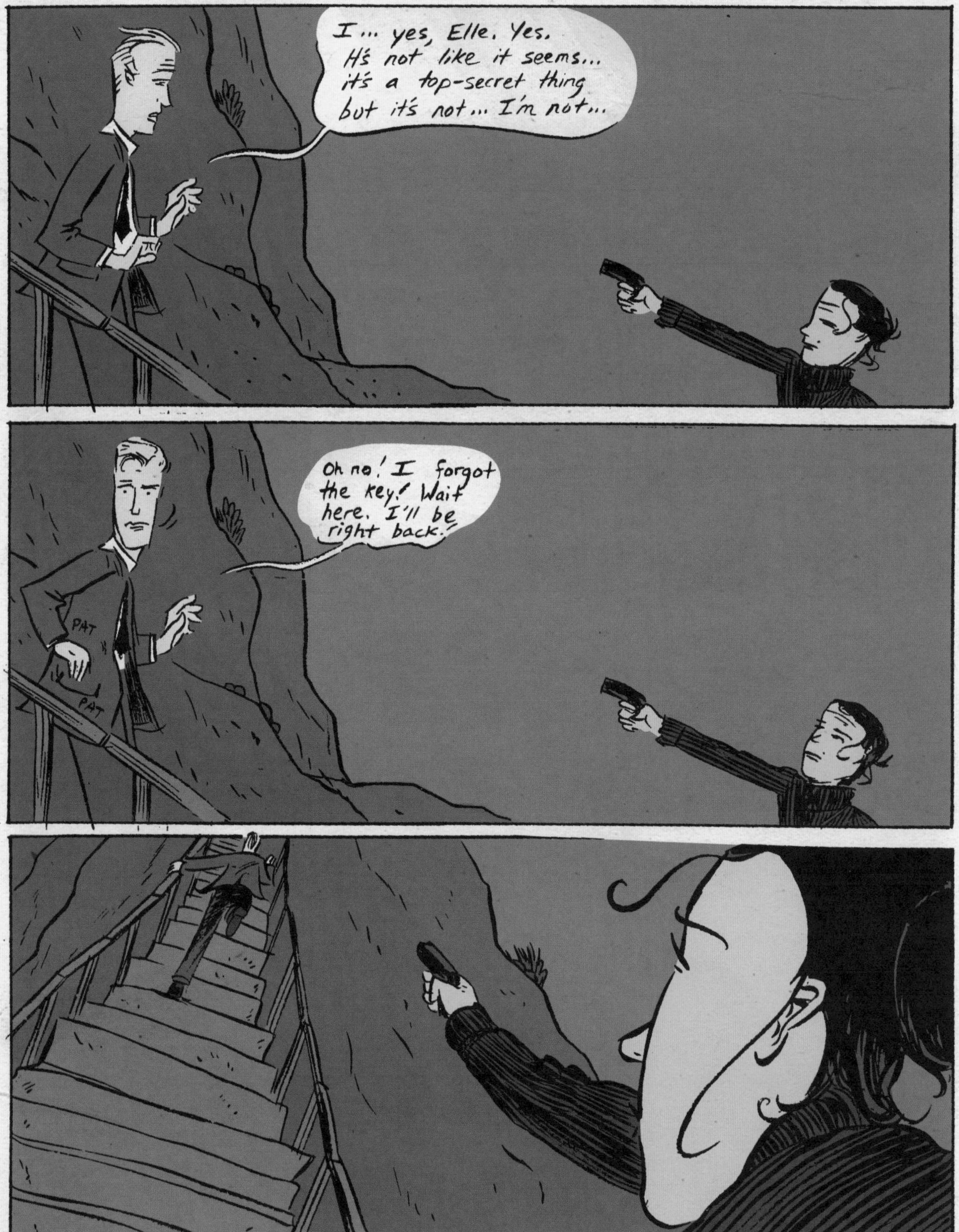
I... yes, Elle. Yes. It's not like it seems... it's a top-secret thing but it's not... I'm not...
Oh no! I forgot the key! Wait here. I'll be right back.
PAT
PAT

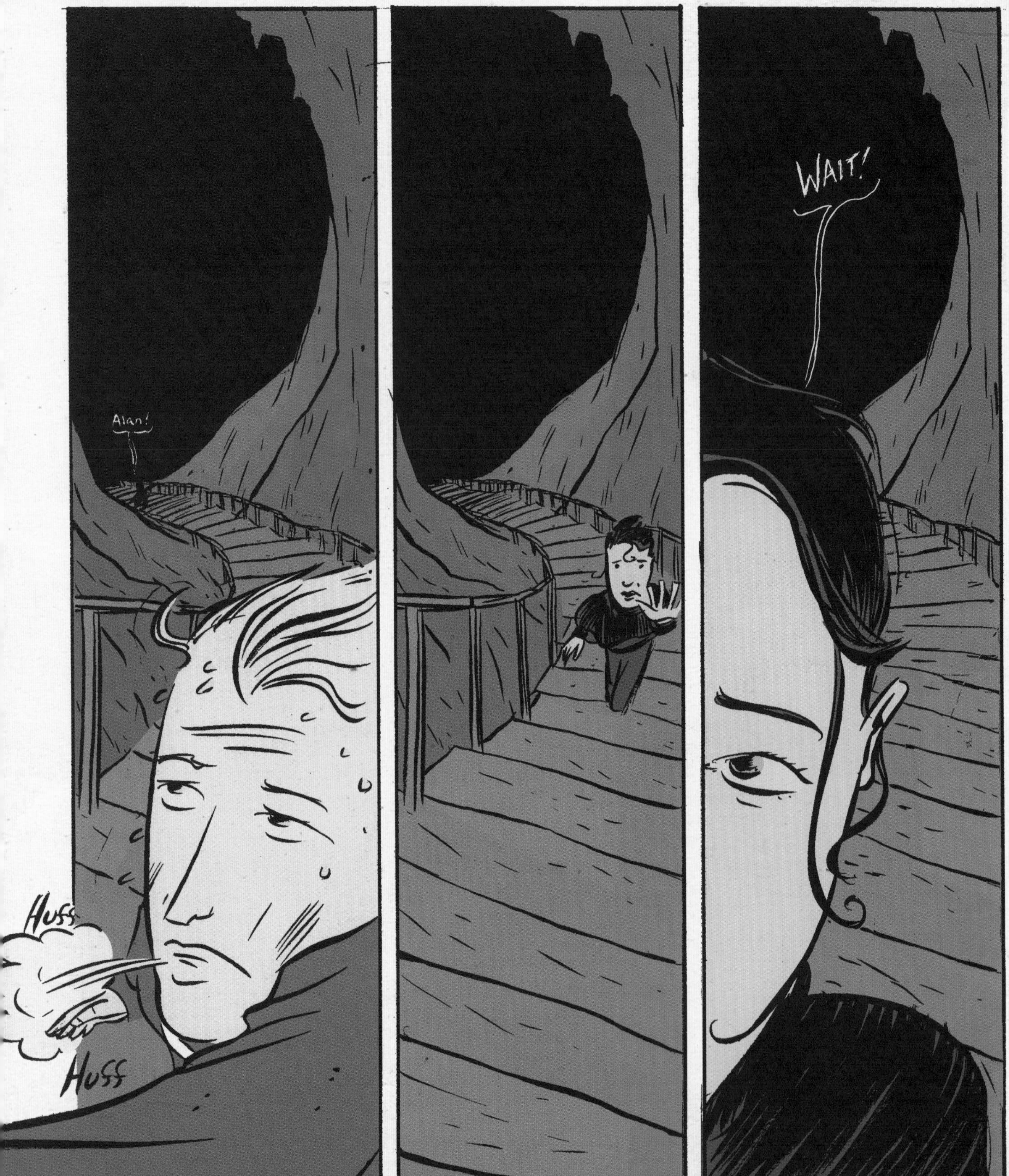
Alan!
HUFF
HUFF
WAIT!

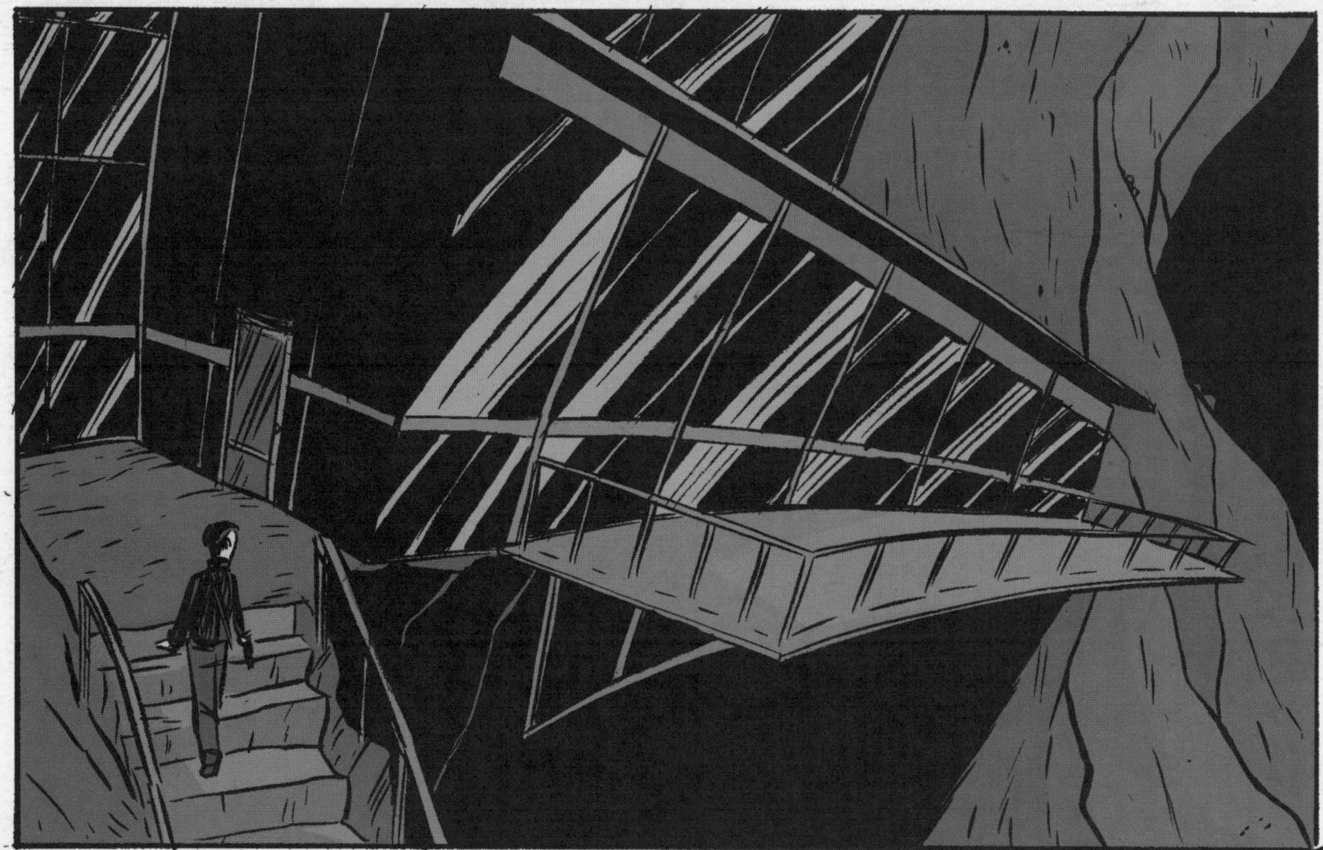

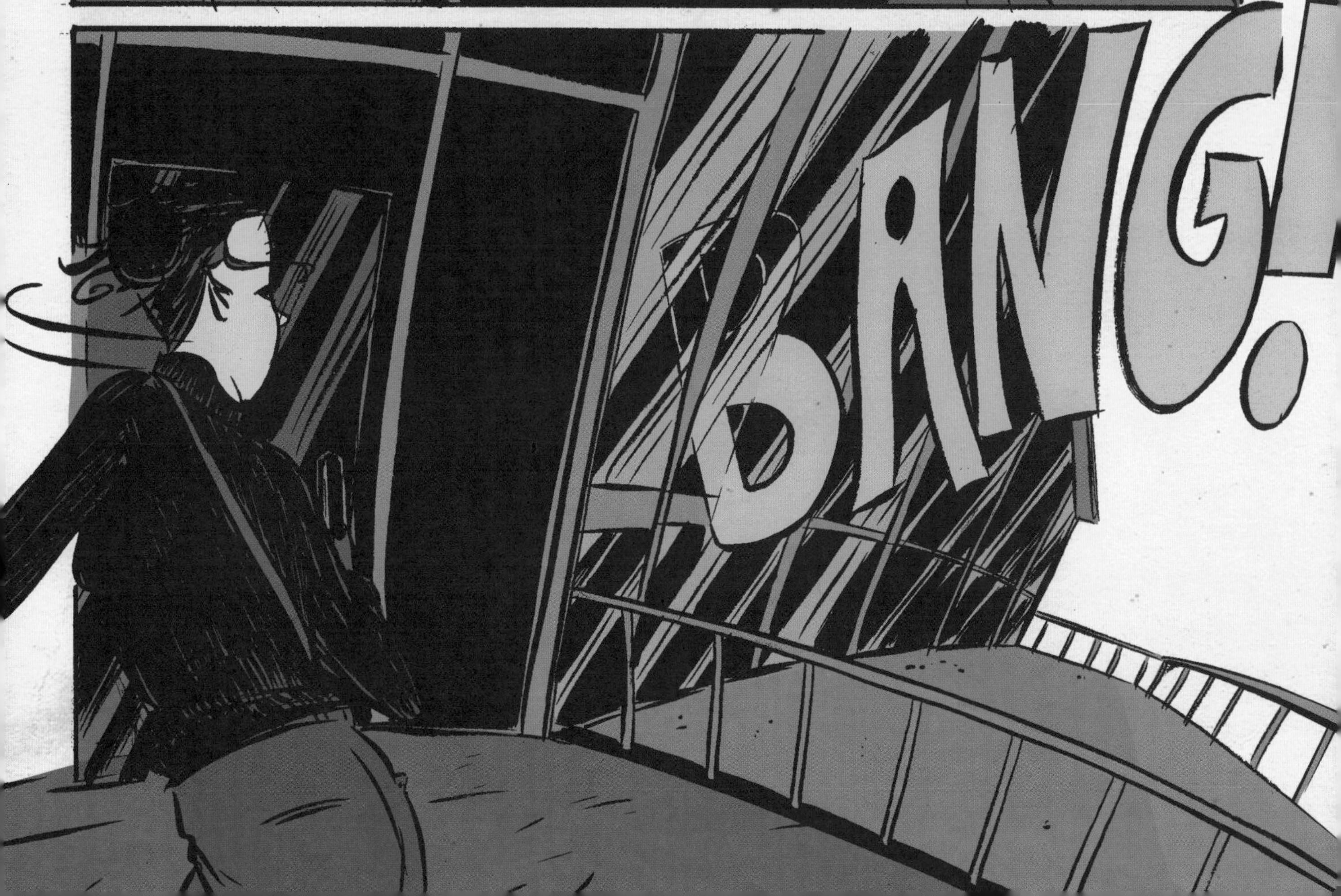
BANG!

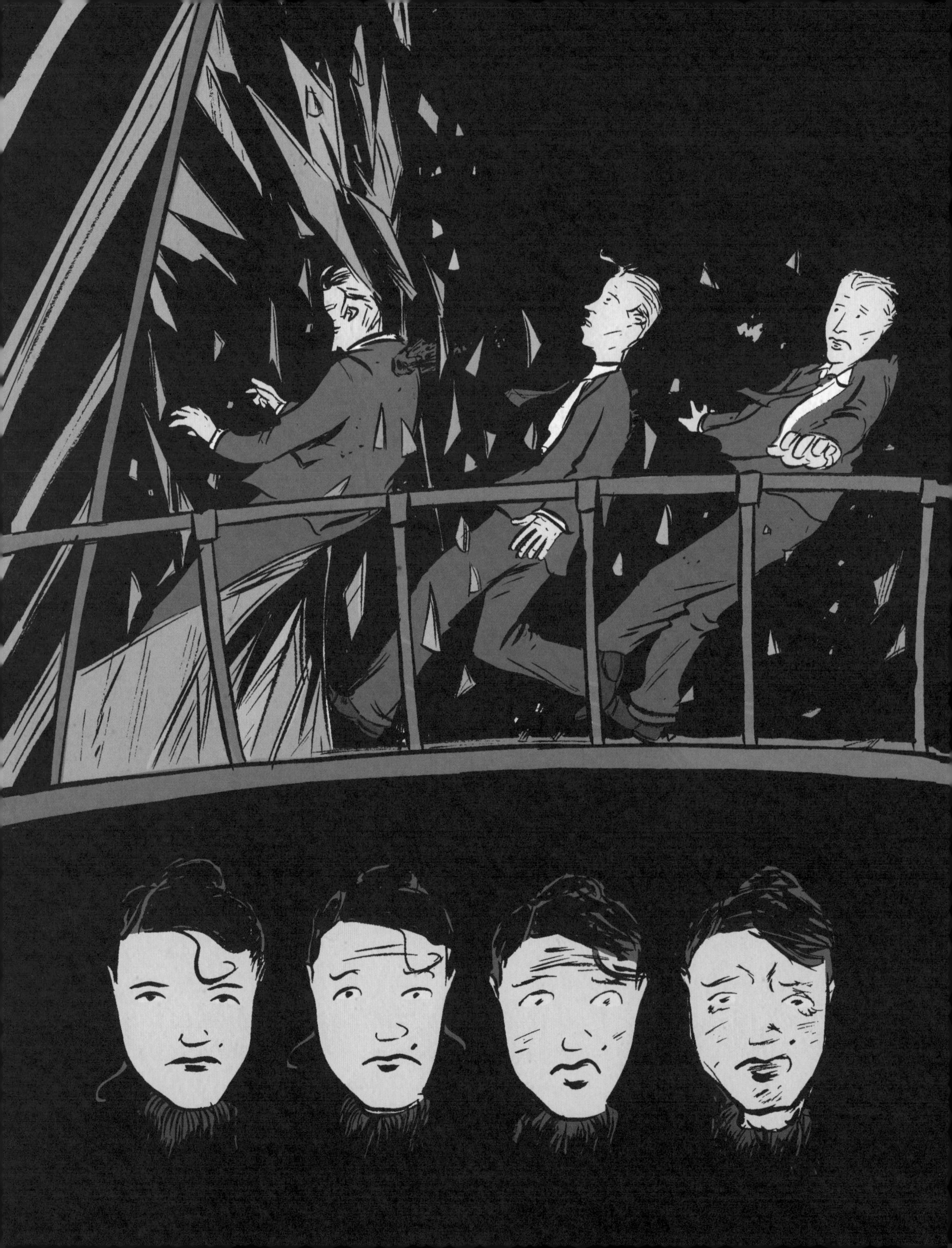

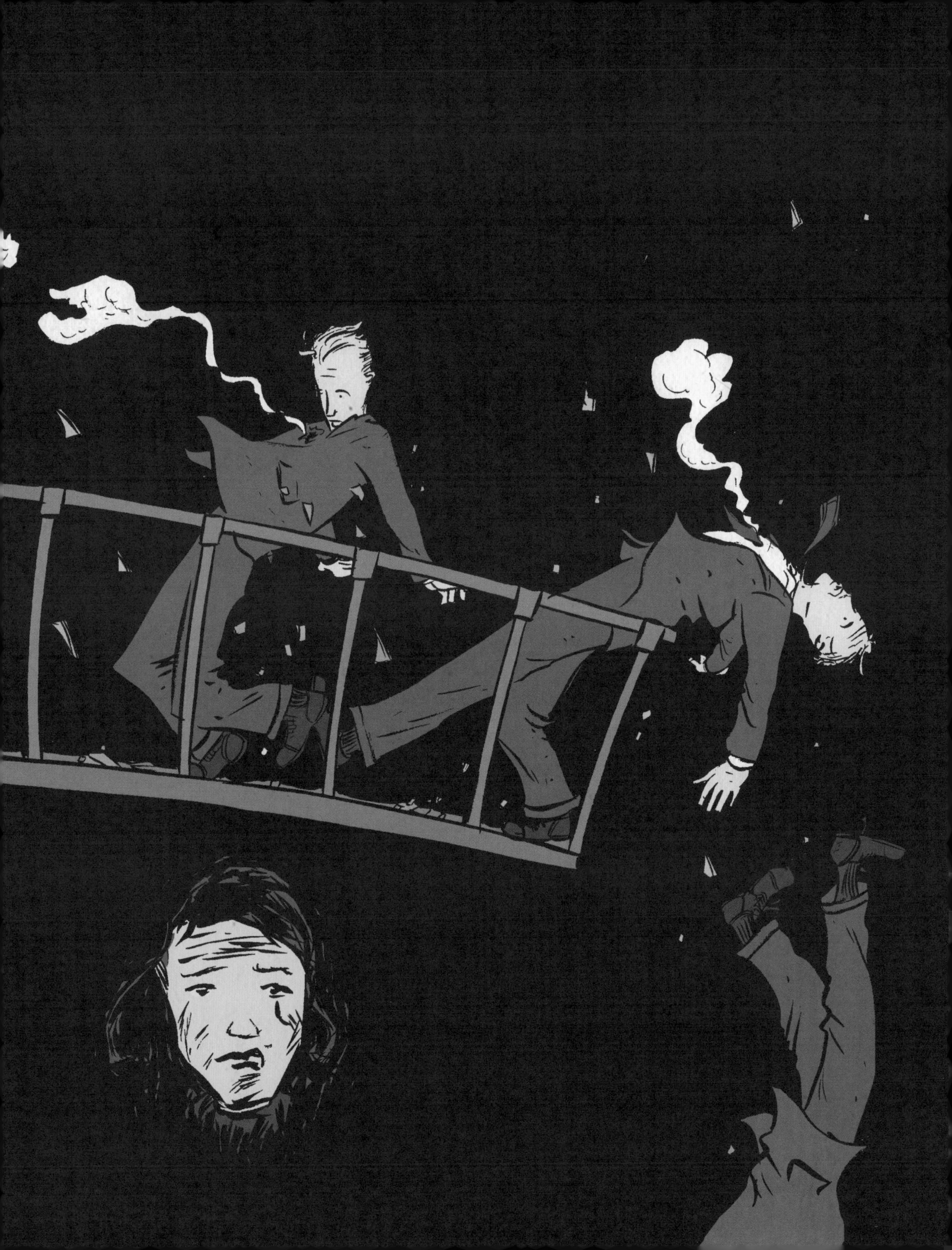

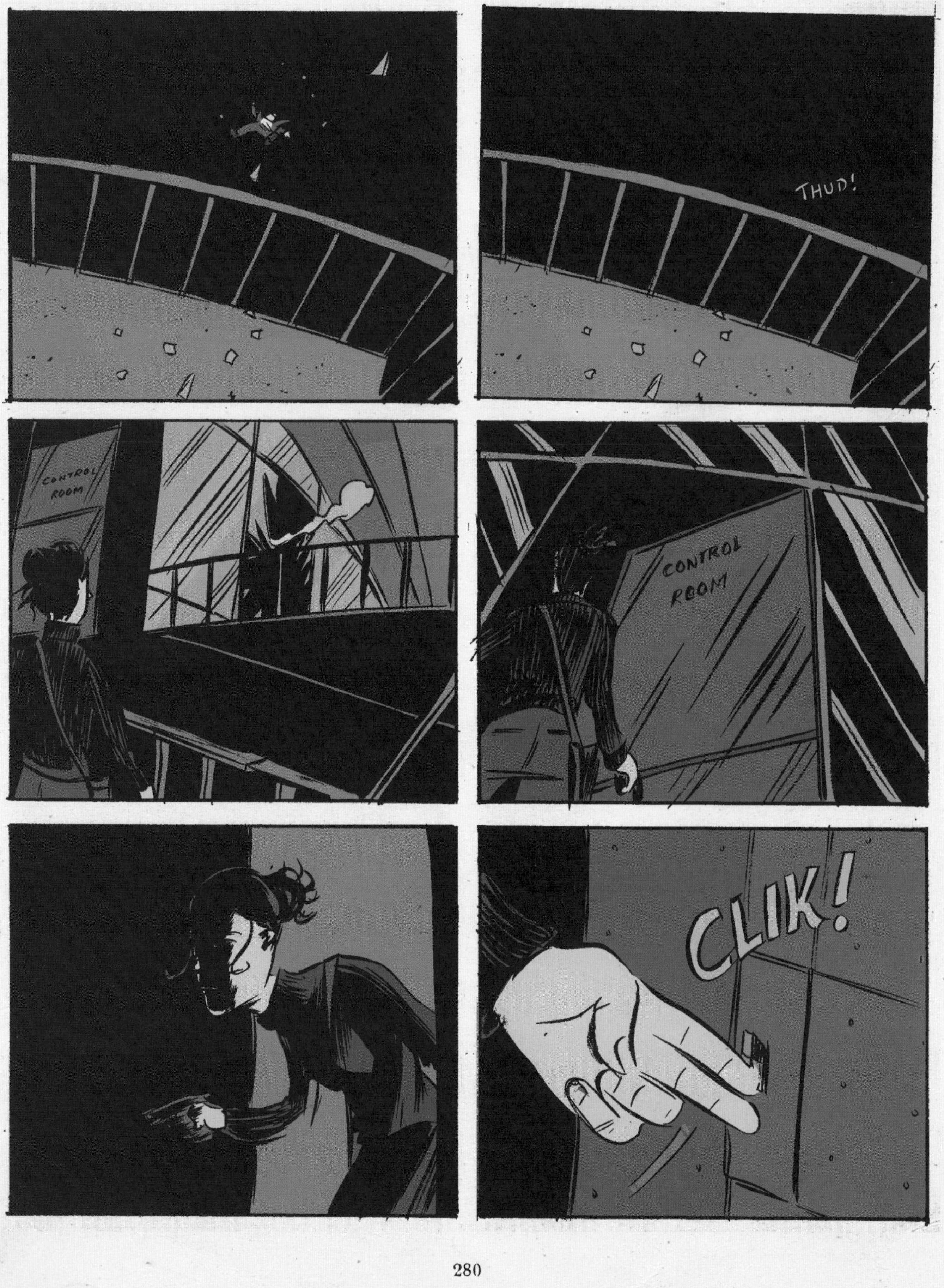
THUD!
CONTROL ROOM
CONTROL ROOM
CLIK!

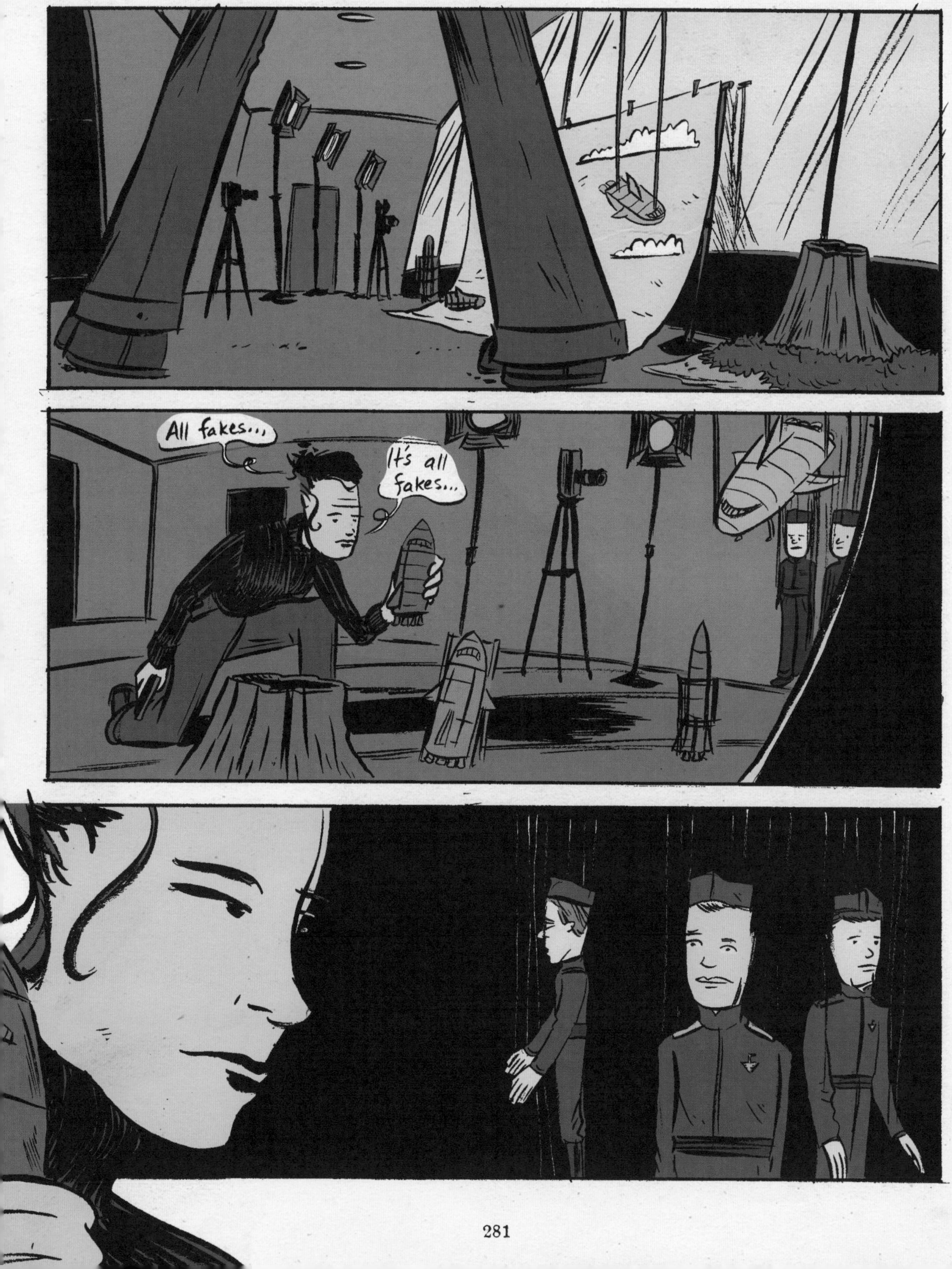
All fakes...
It's all fakes...

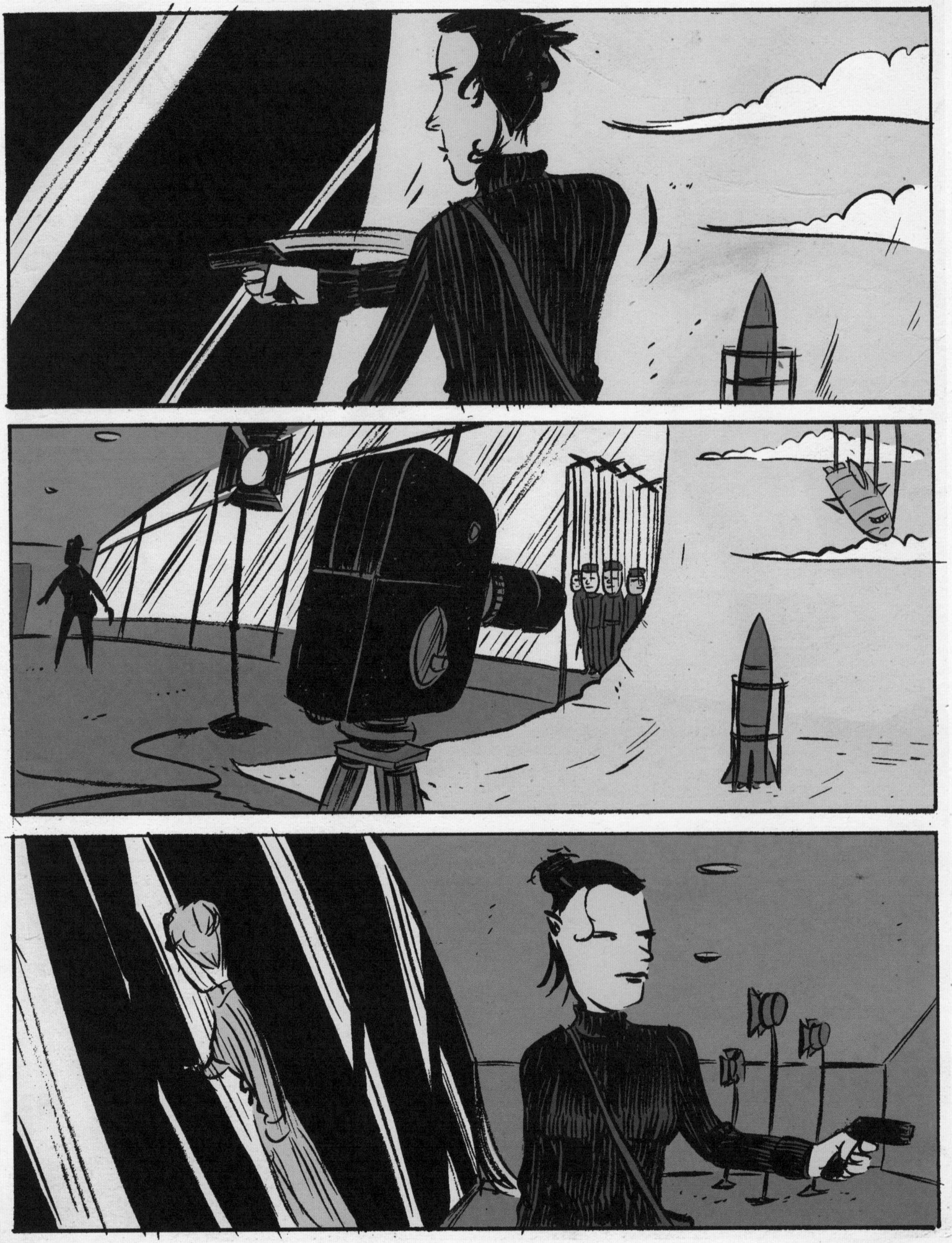

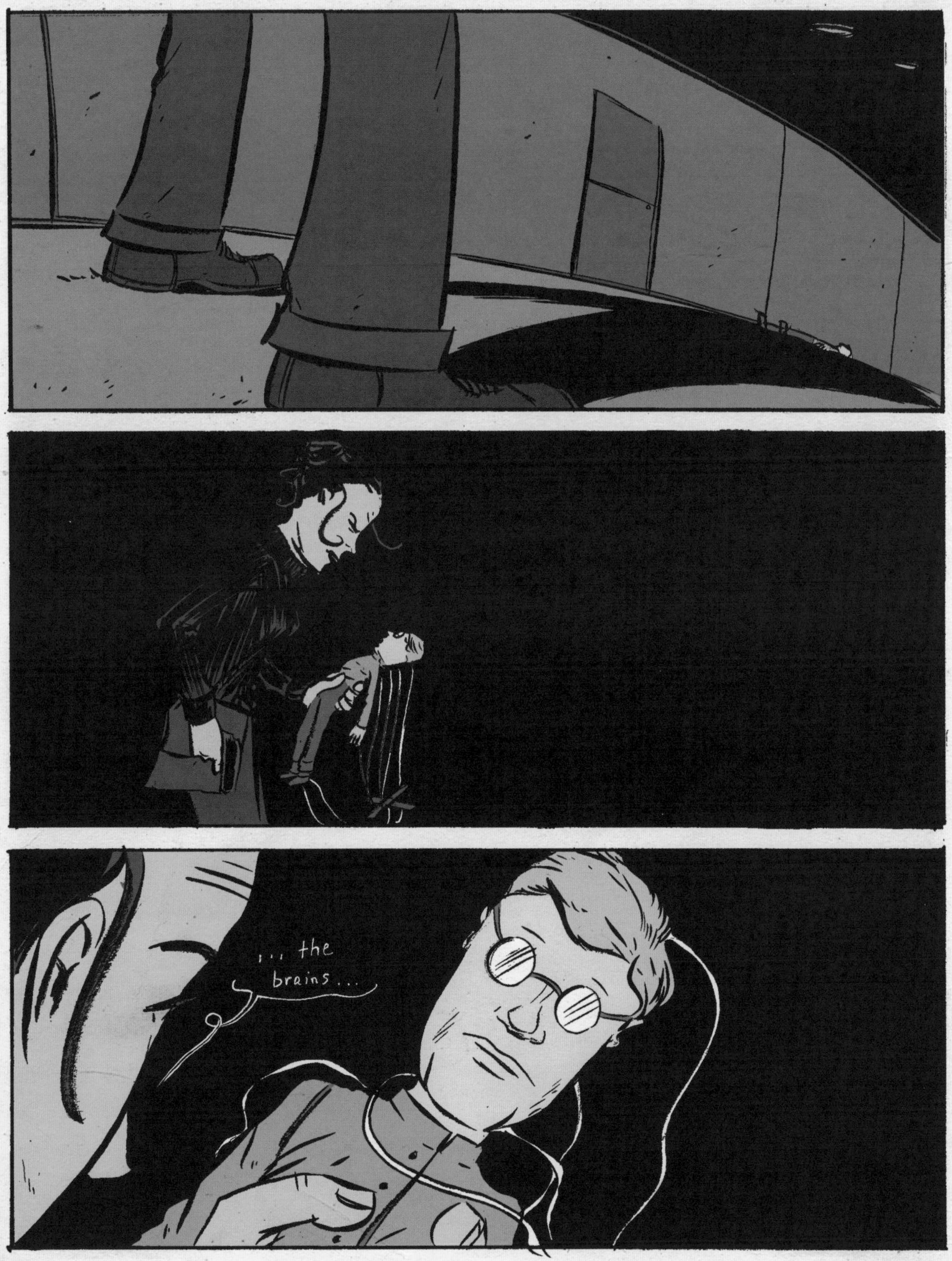
... the brains...

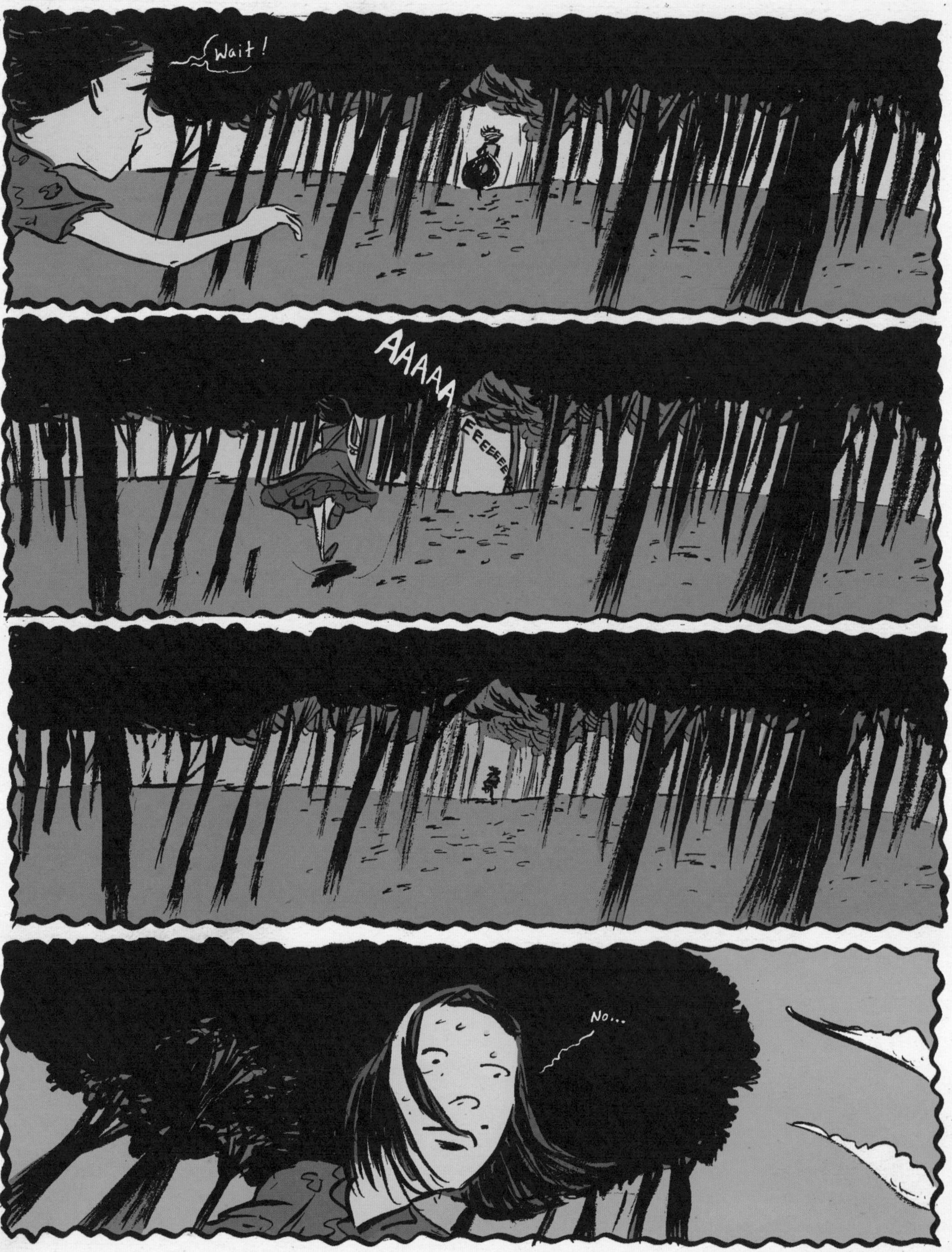
Wait!
AAAAAEEEEEE
No...

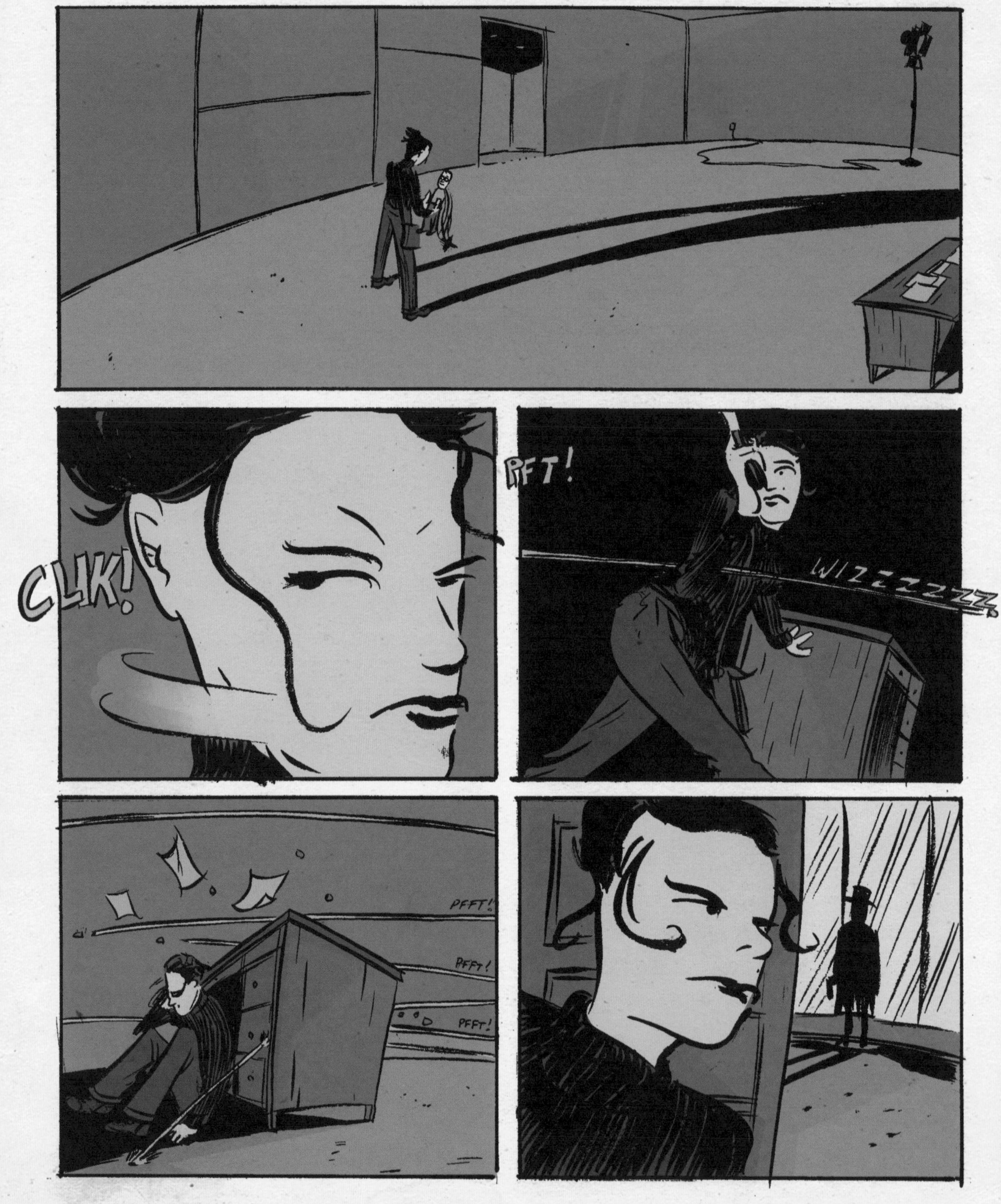
CLIK!
PFT!
WIZZZZZZZZ
PFFT!
PFFT!
PFFT!

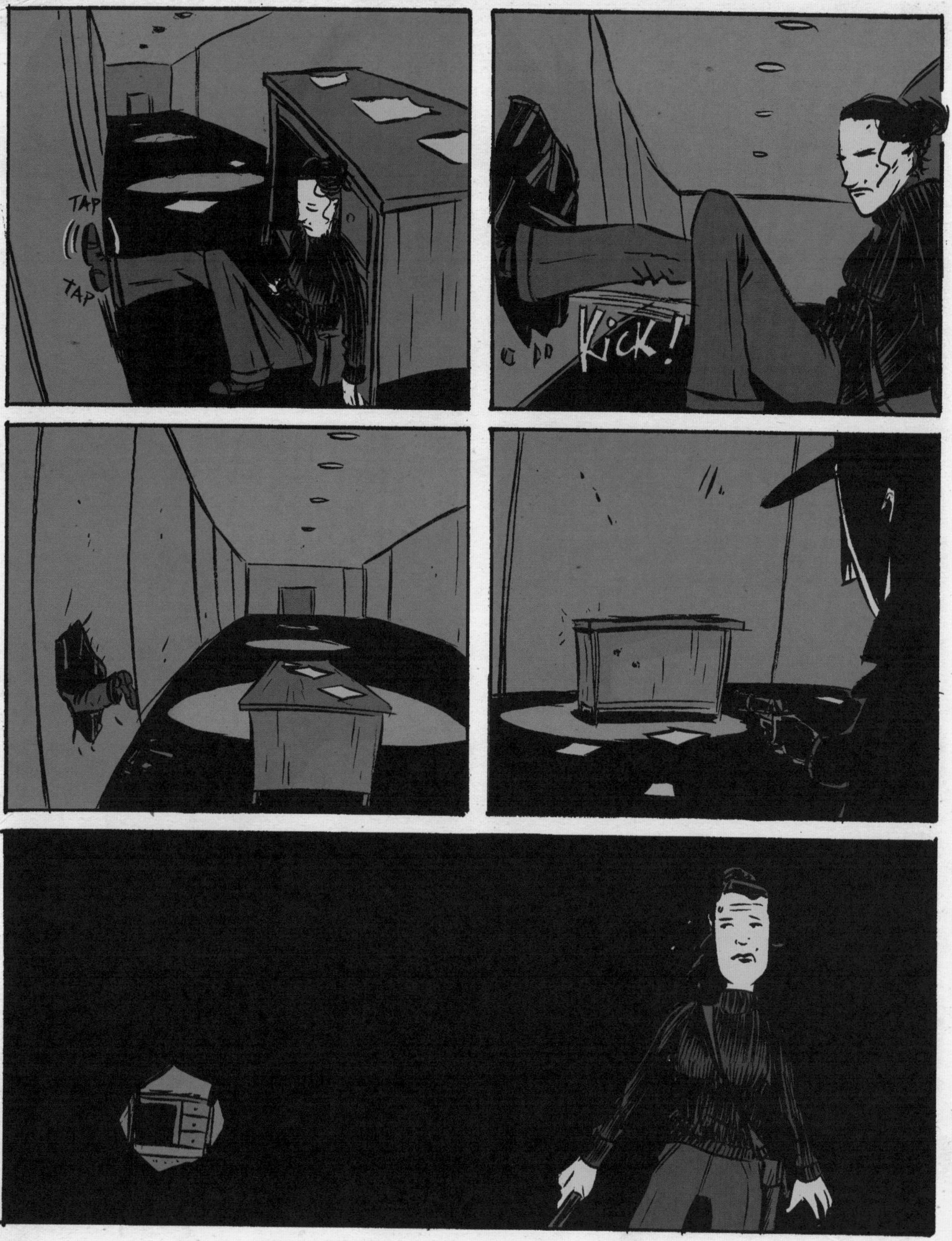
TAP
TAP
KICK!

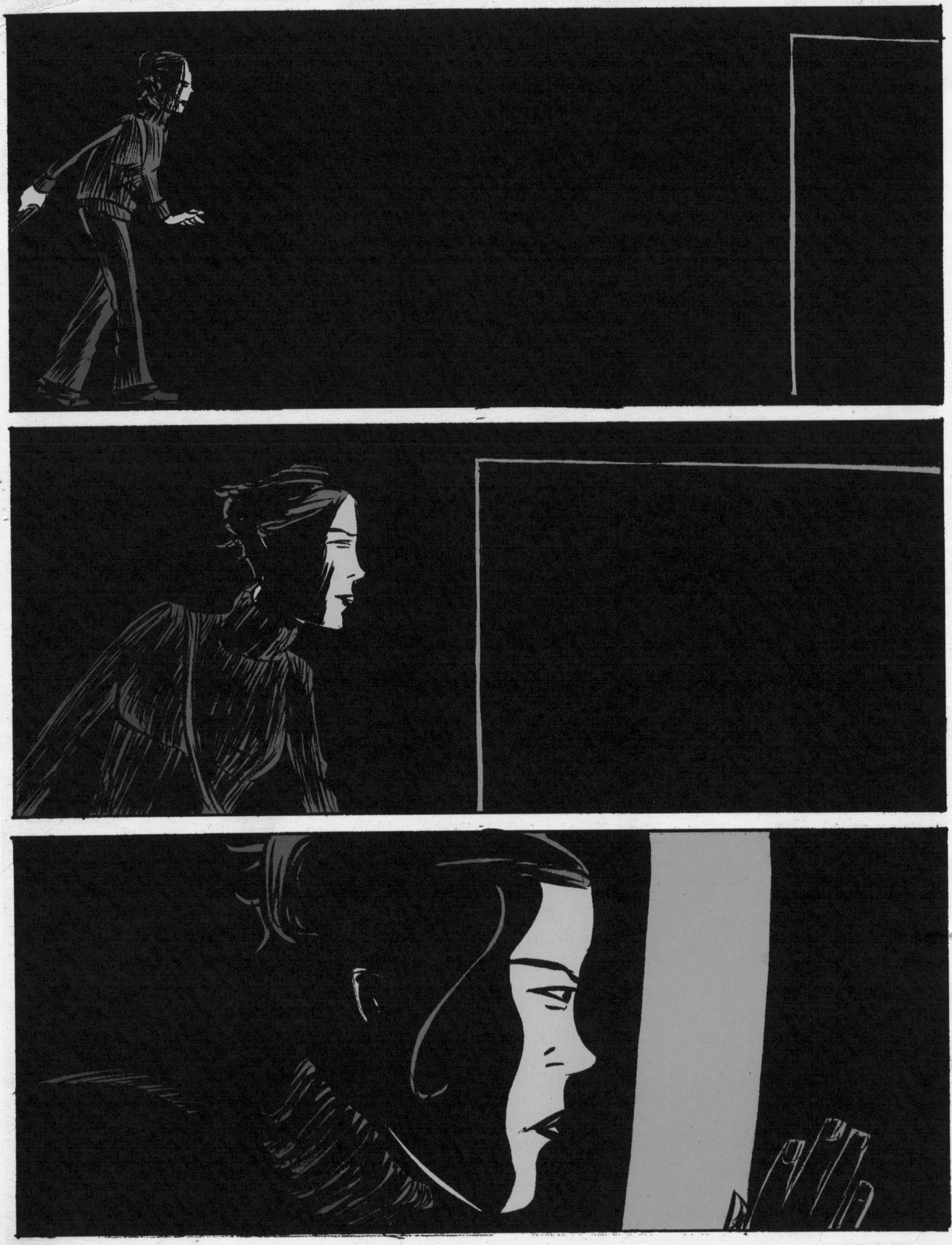

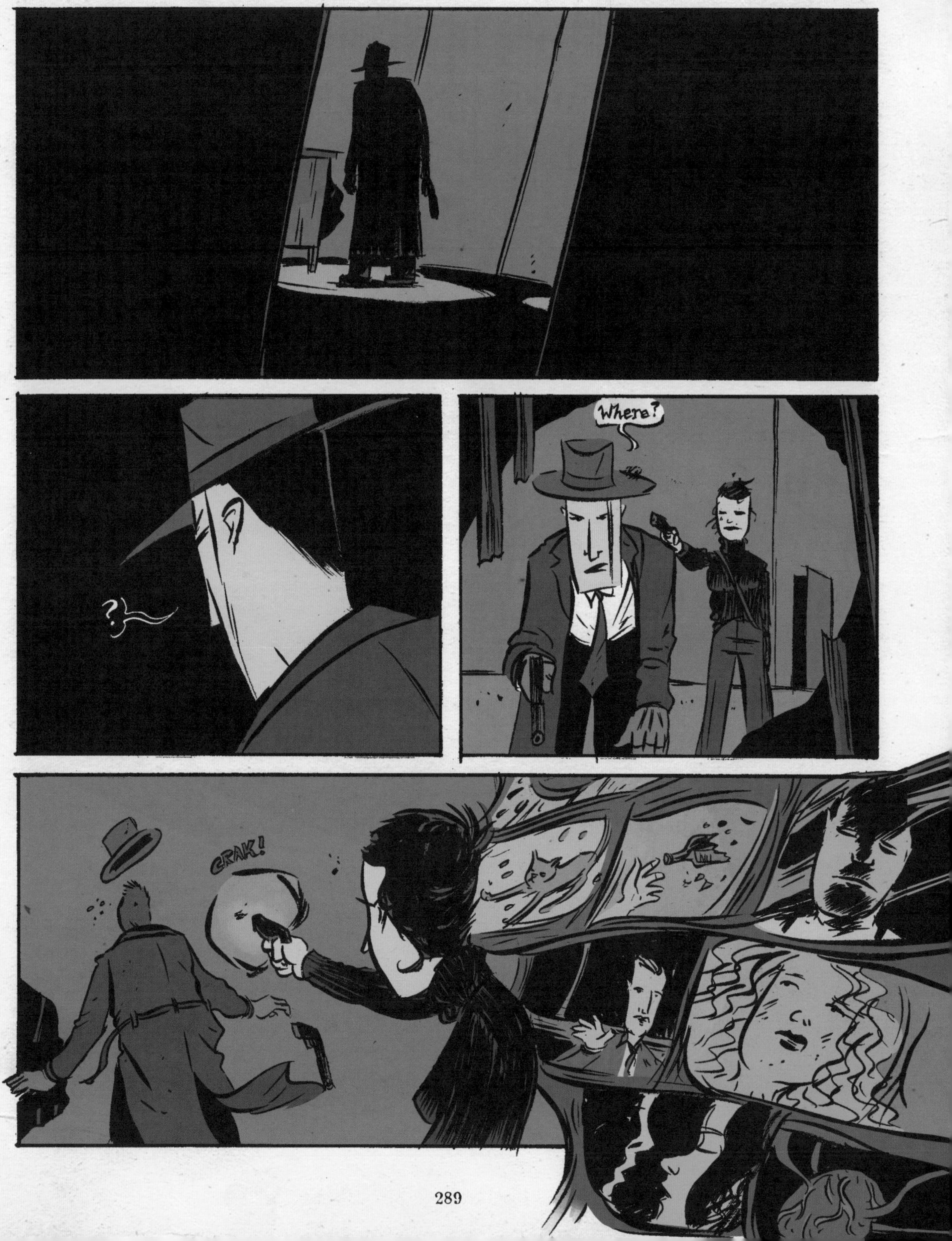
?
Where?
CRAK!

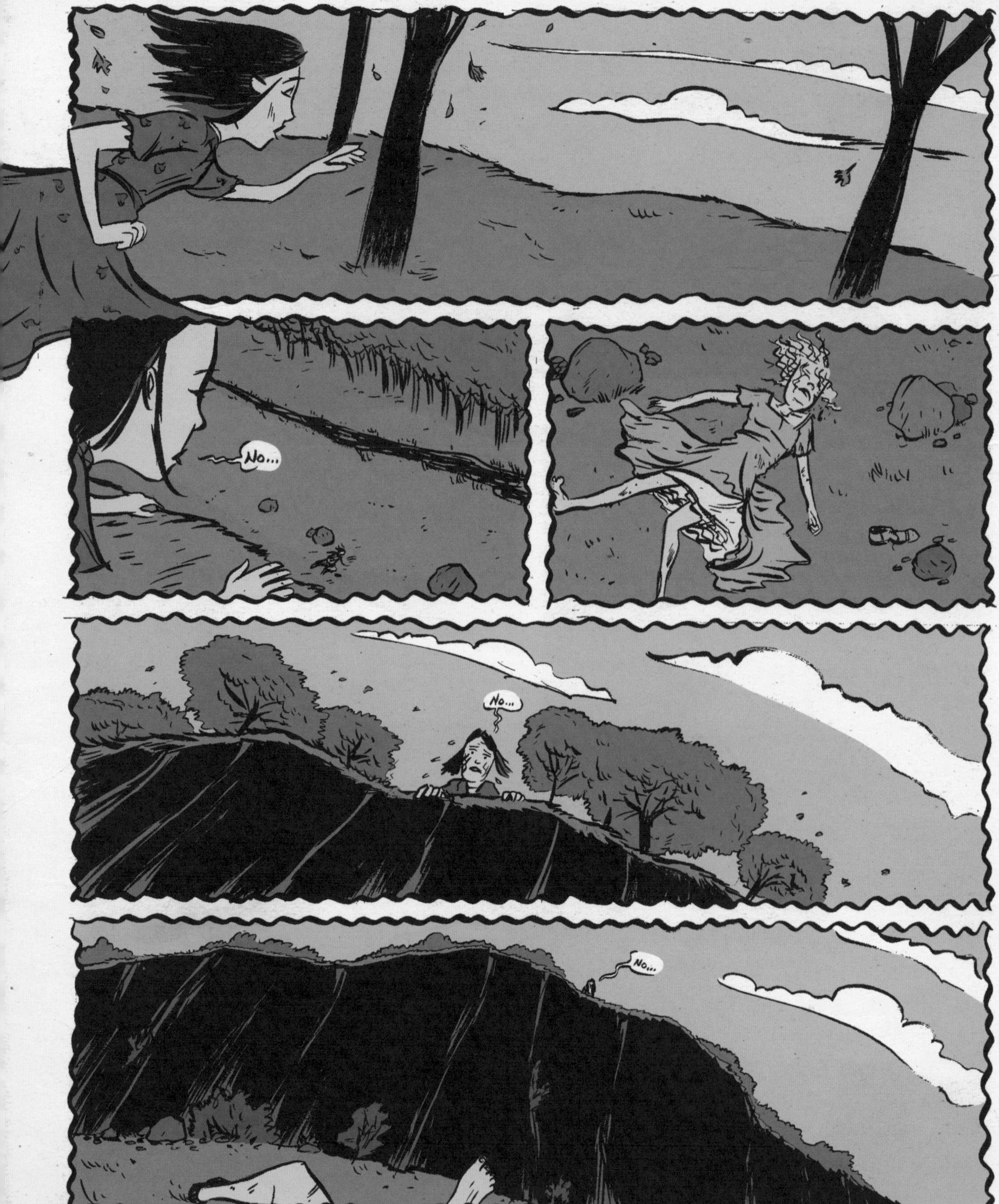
No...
No...
No...

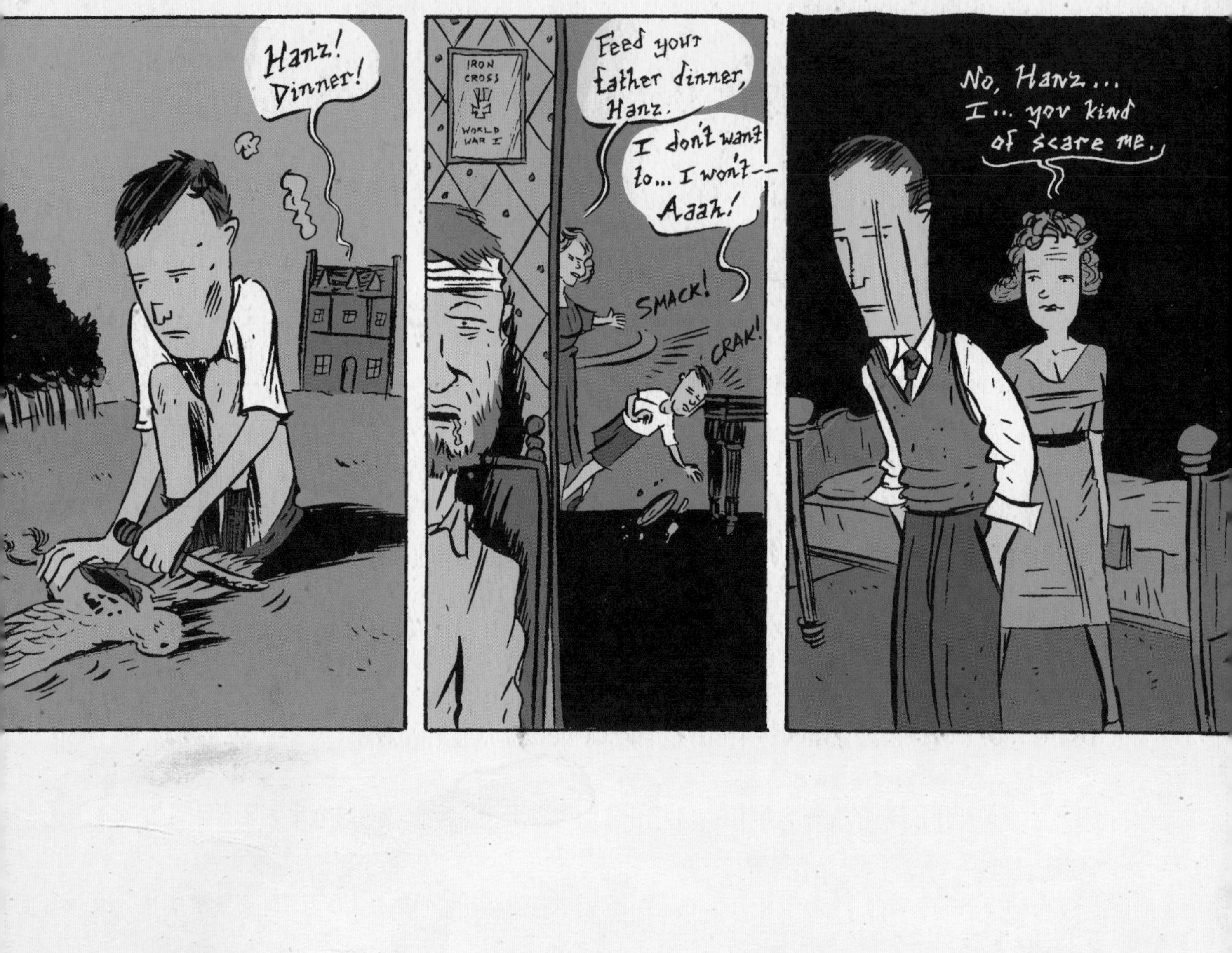
Hanz! Dinner!
IRON CROSS
WORLD WAR I
Feed your father dinner, Hanz.
I don't want to... I won't-- Aaah!
SMACK!
CRAK!
No, Hanz... I... you kind of scare me.

JOIN NOW!
HITLER'S SPECIAL SERVICES AND GESTAPO IS LOOKING FOR THE NATION'S INTELLIGENT YOUTH INQUIRE AT THE LOCAL SS OFFICE
GIRL FOUND MURDERED
Excellent work, Hanz.
This... these ideas are ludicrous!
Impossible!
WE know.

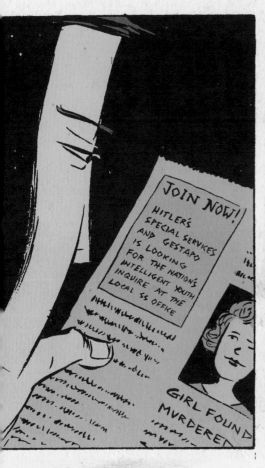

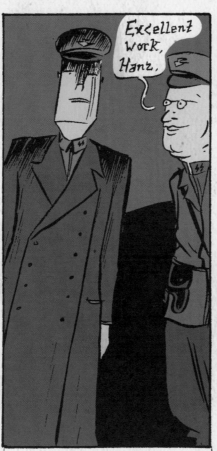

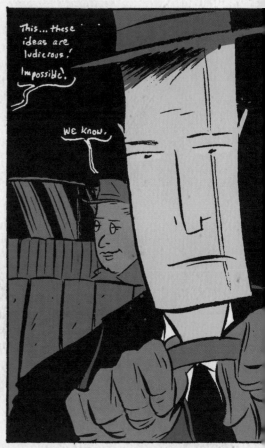

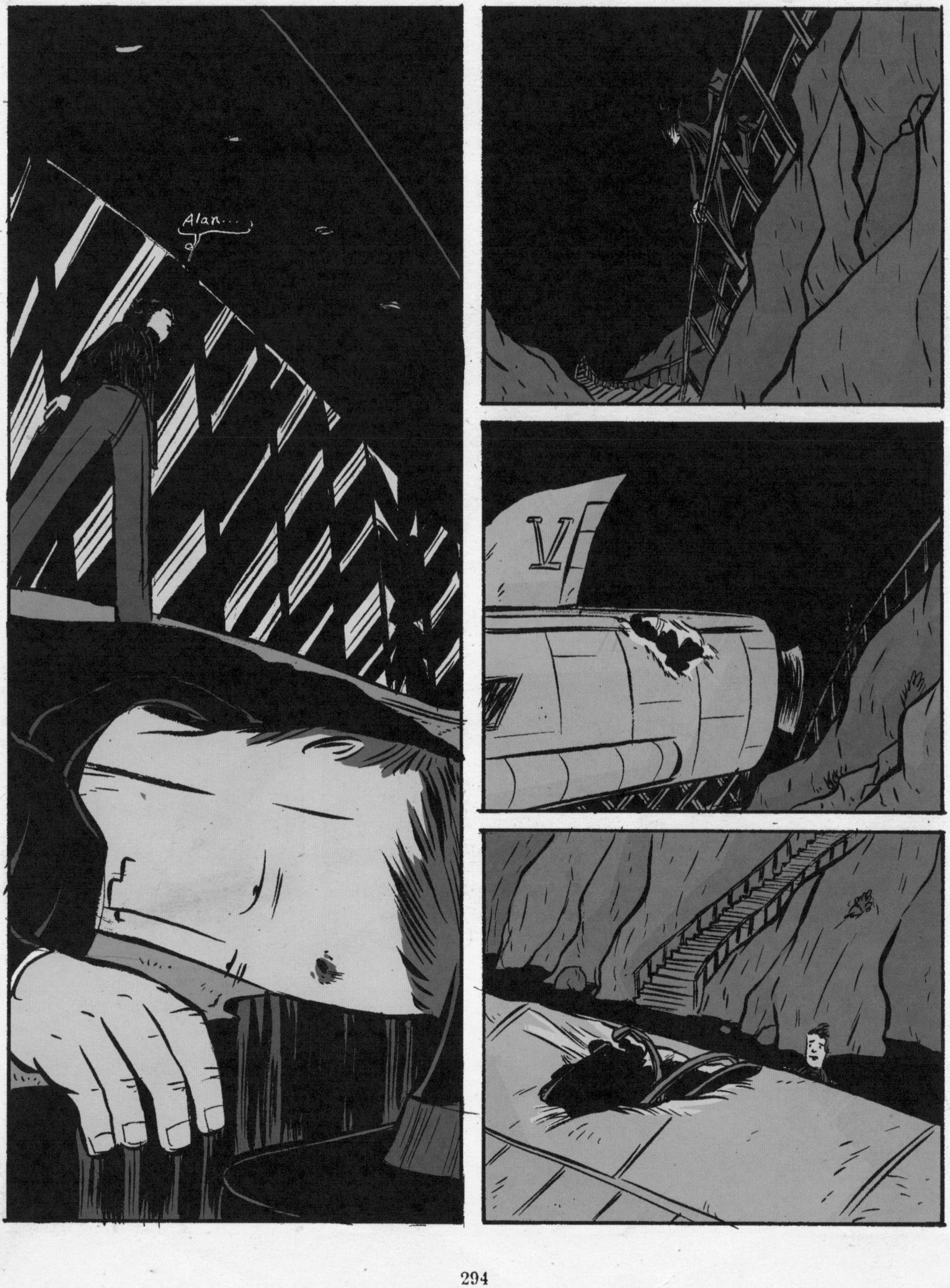
Alan...

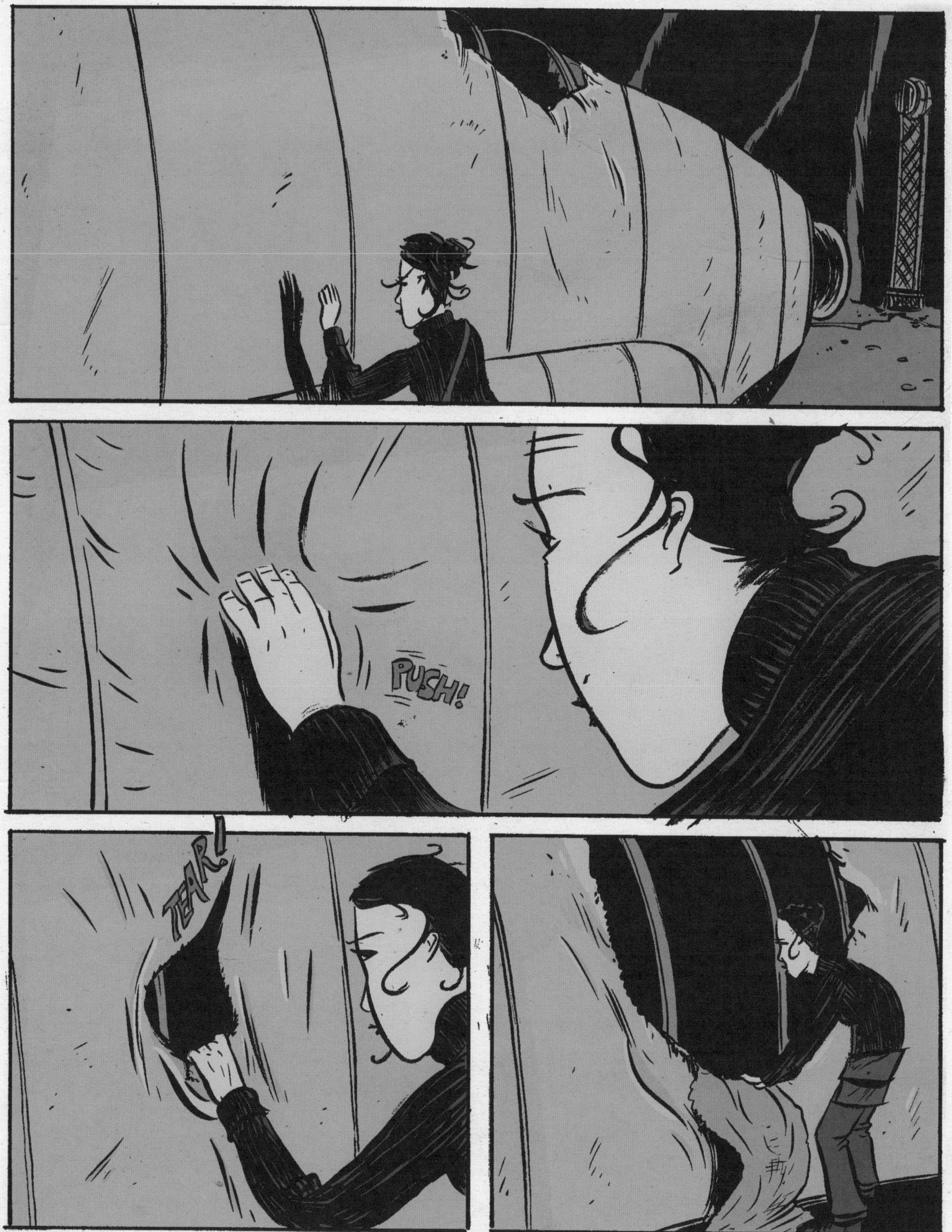
PUSH!
TEAR!

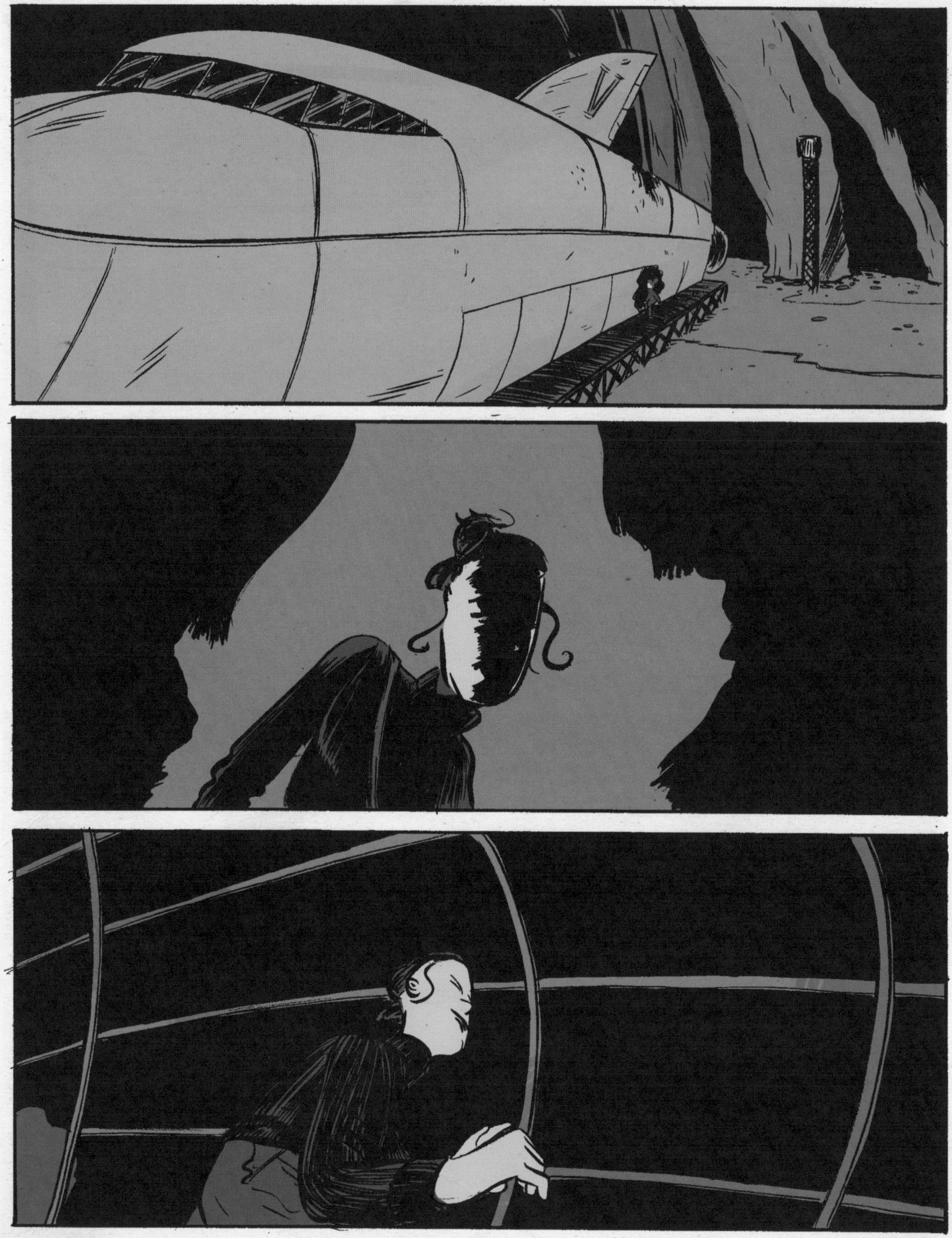

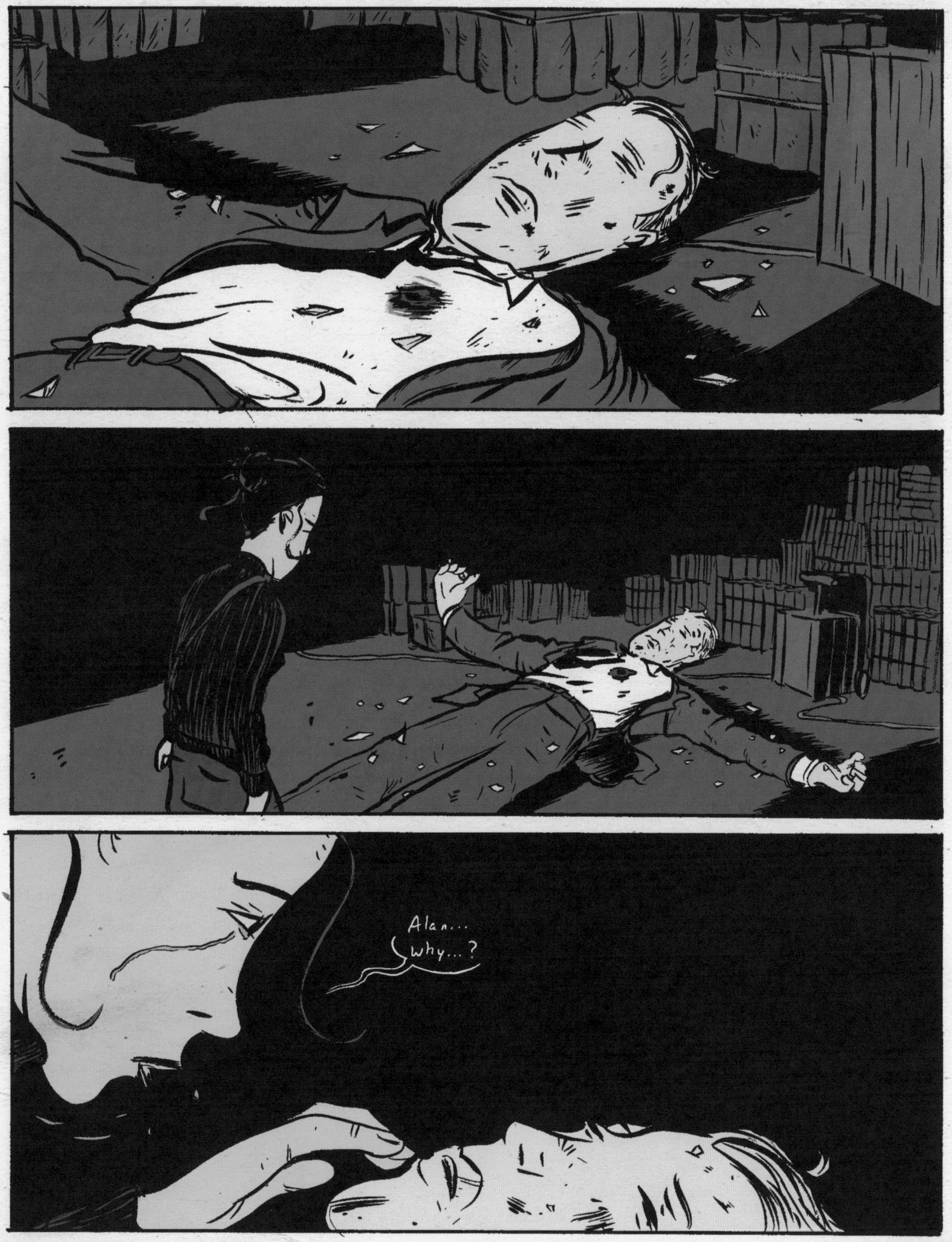
Alan... why...?

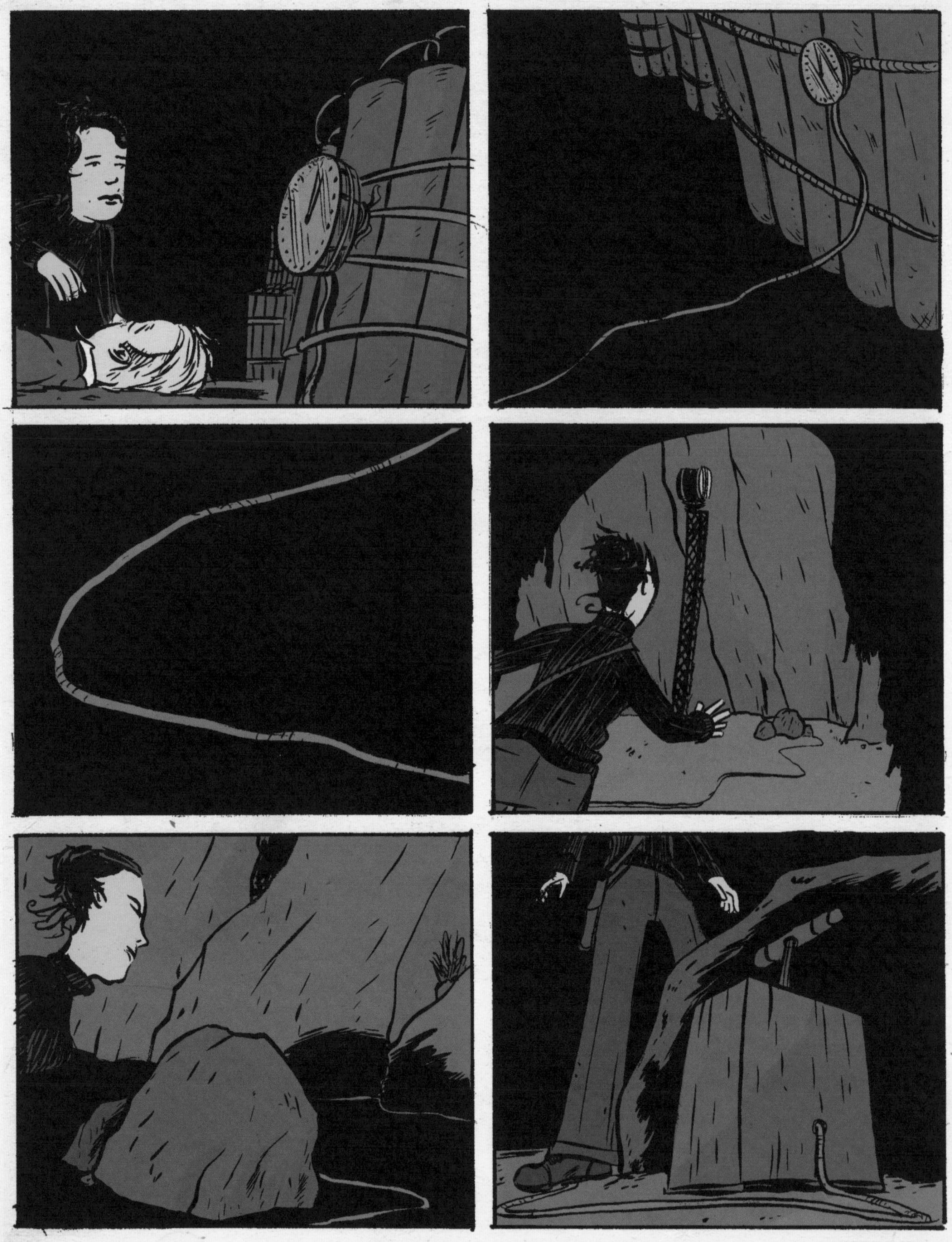

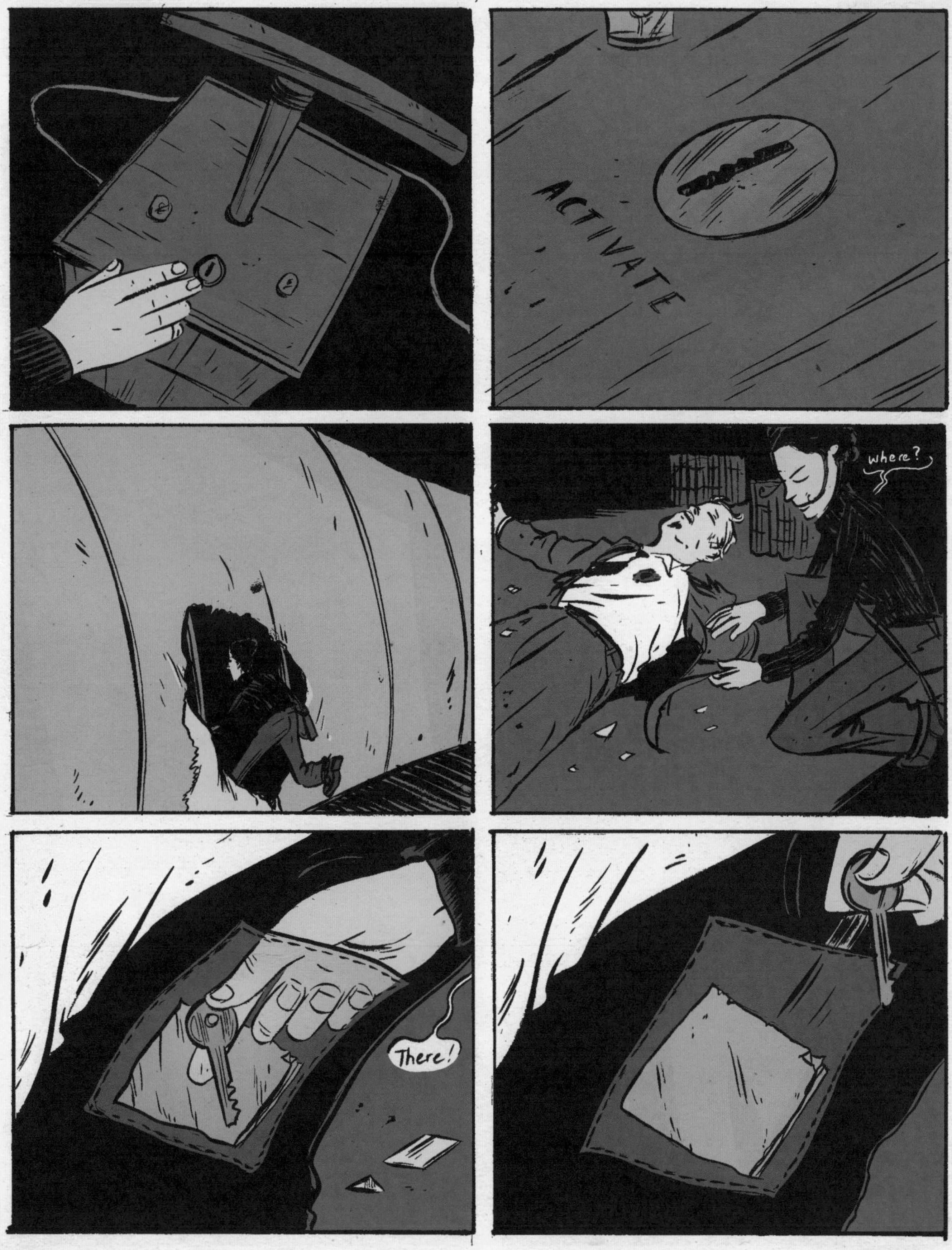
ACTIVATE
where?
There!

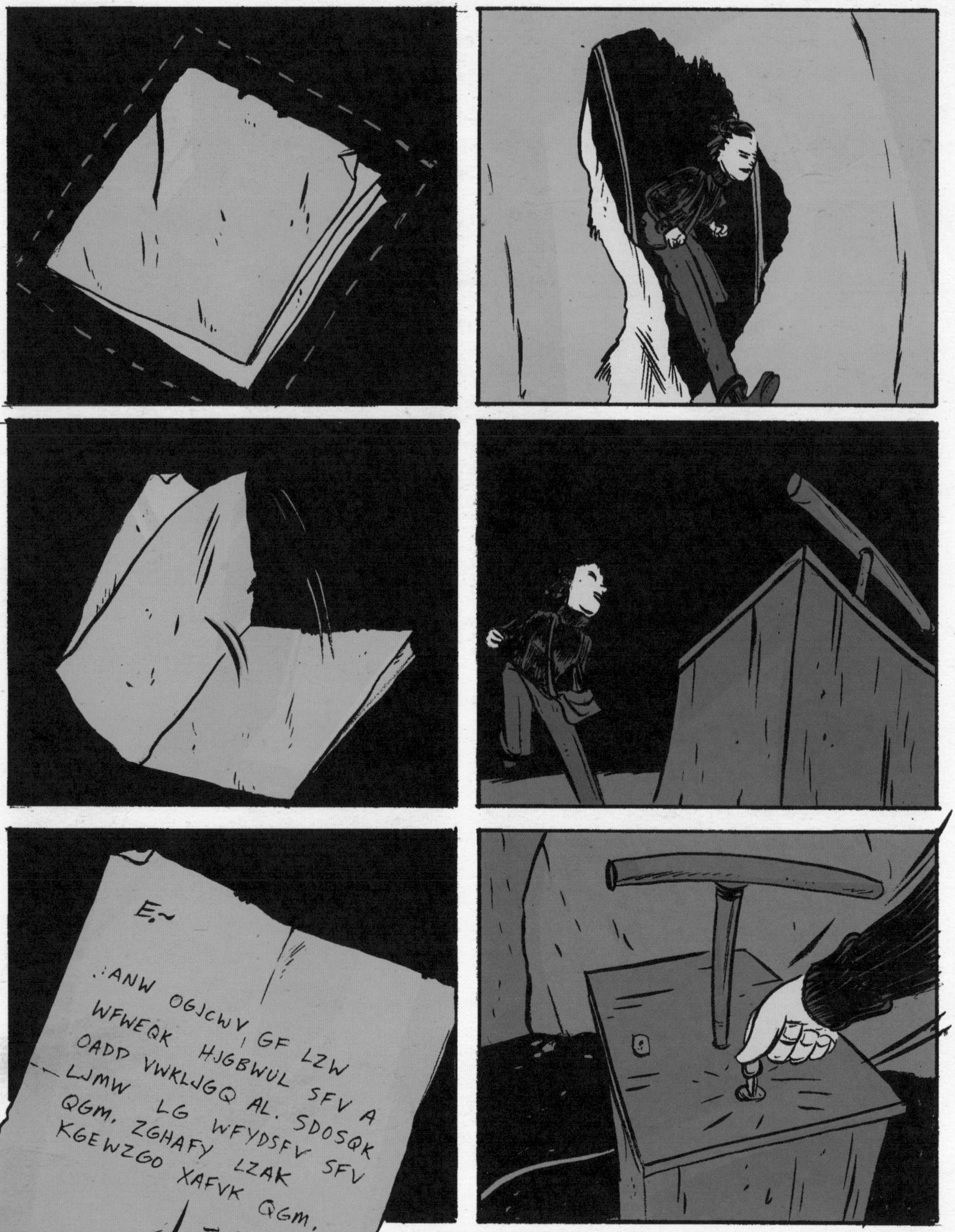
E.~
ANW OGJCWV, GF LZW
WFWEQK HJGBWUL SFV A
OADD VWKLJGQ AL. SDOSQK
LJMW LG WFYDSFV SFV
QGM. ZGHAFY LZAK
KGEWZGO XAFVK QGM.
—A.

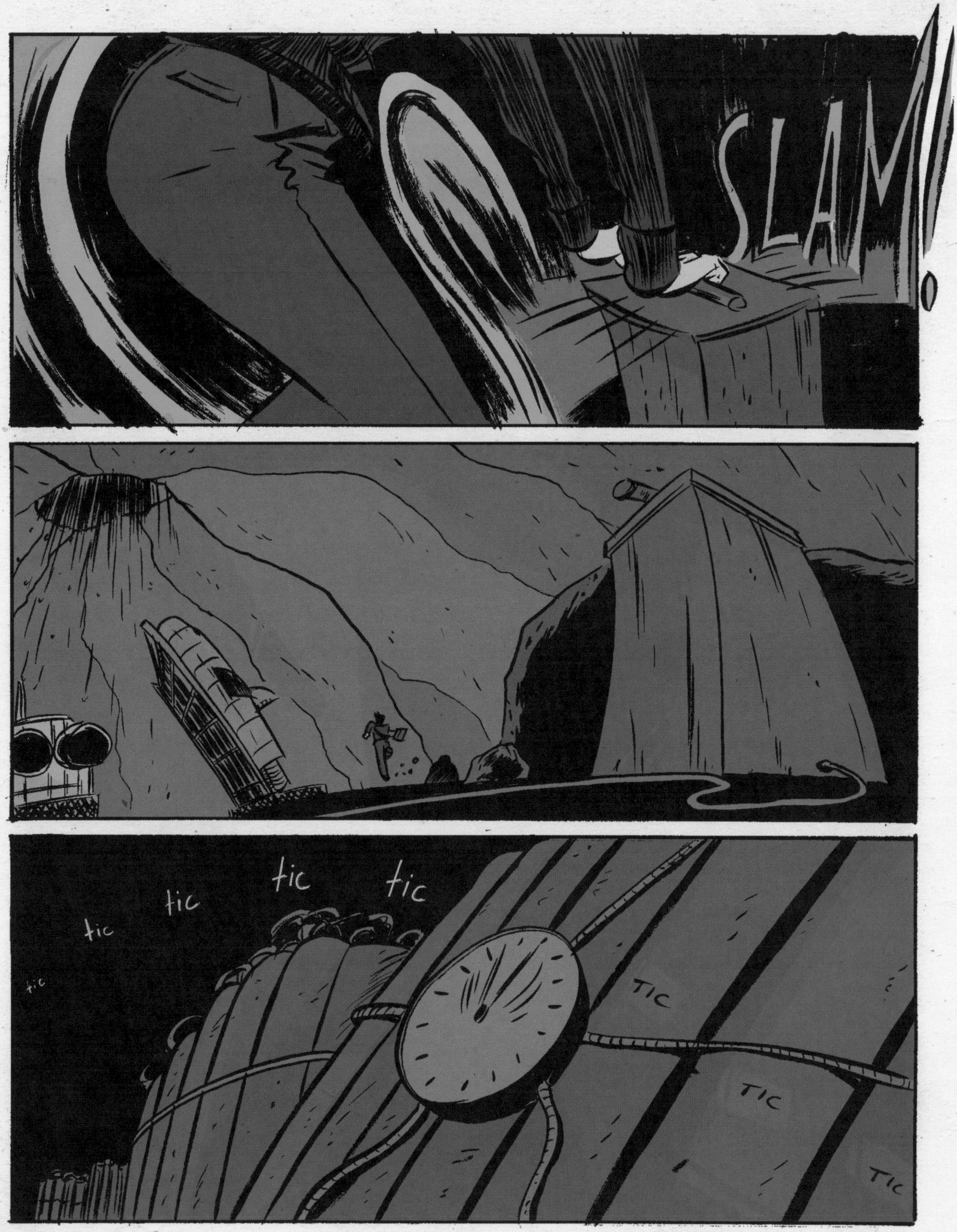
SLAM!
tic
tic
tic
tic
tic
TIC
TIC
TIC

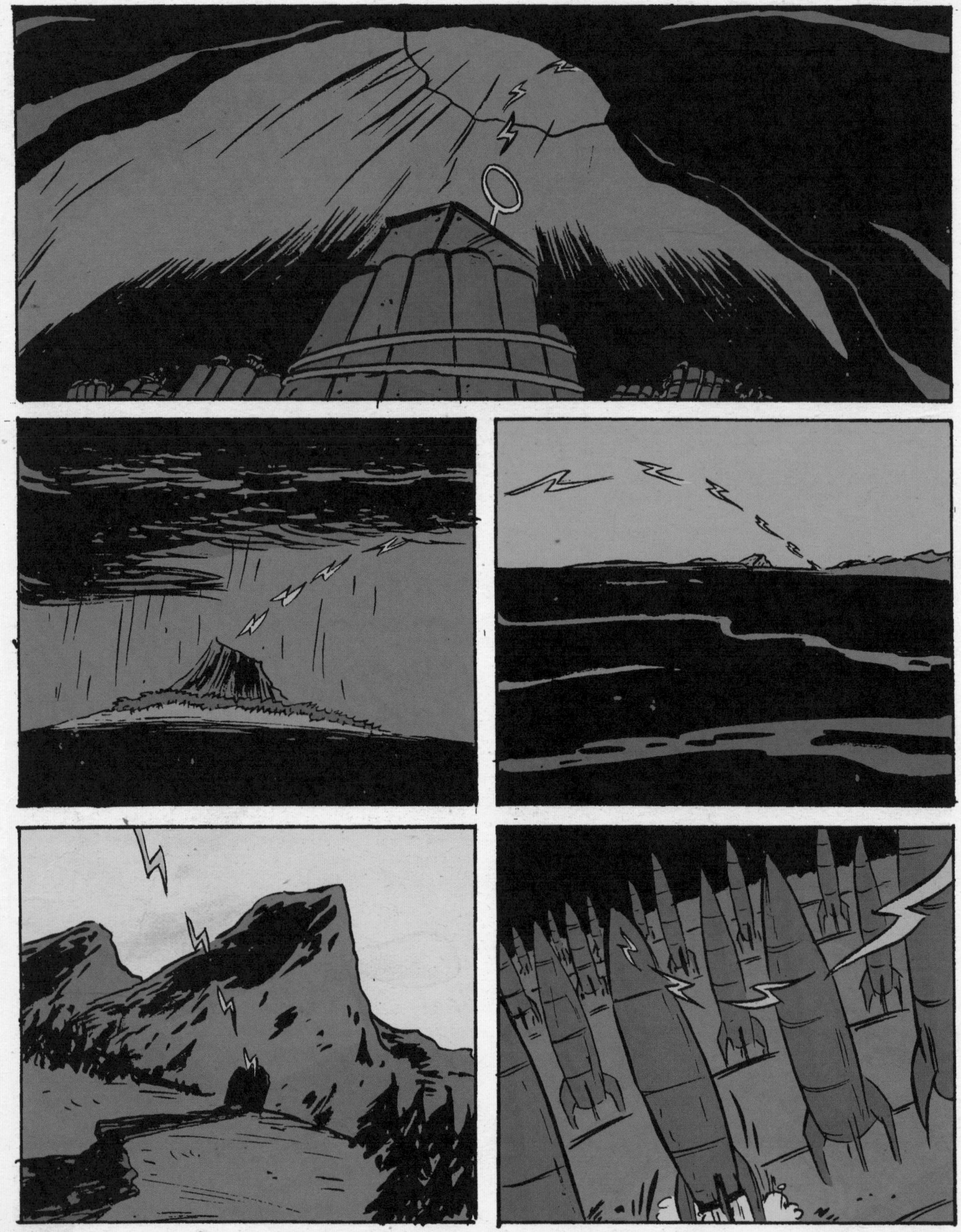

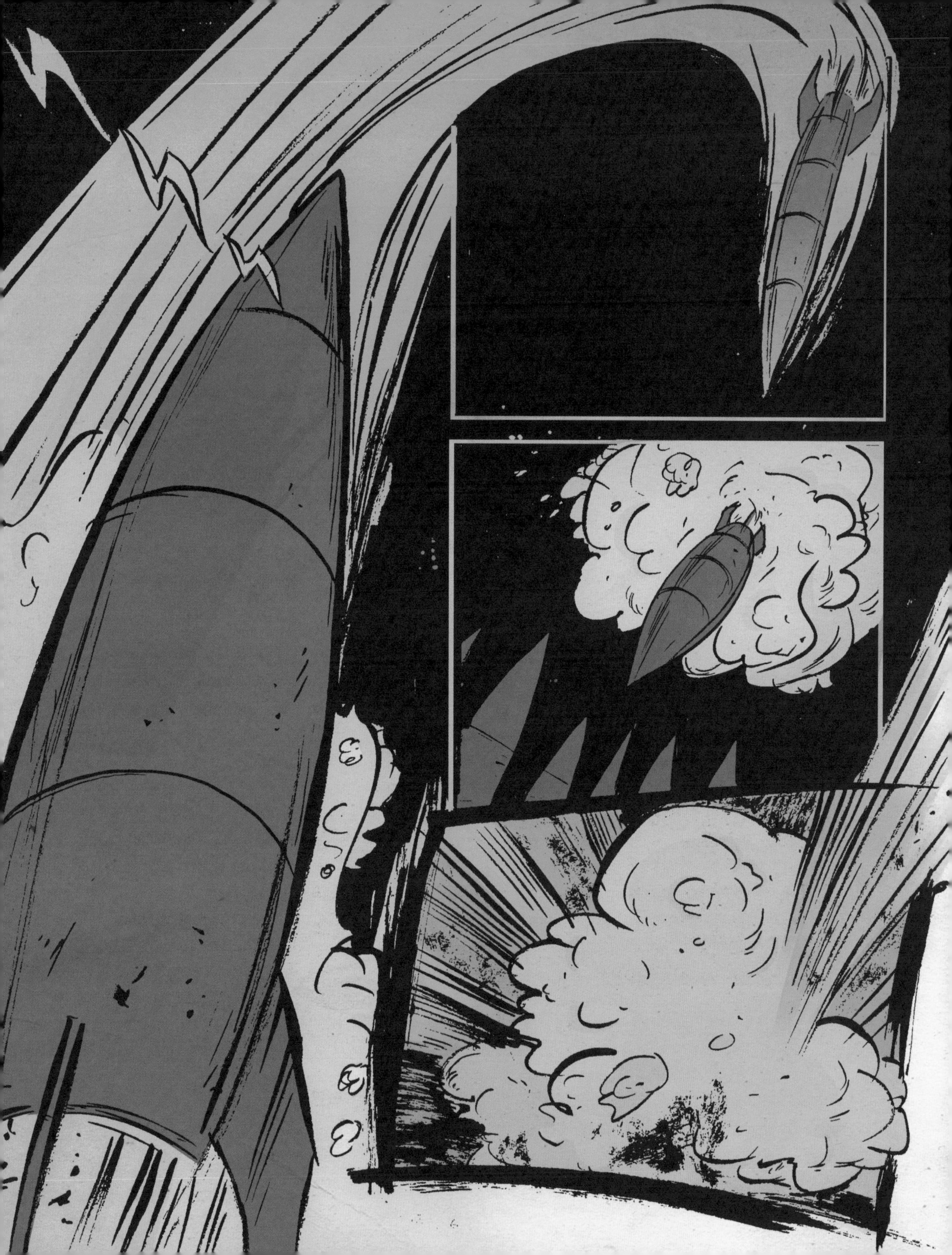

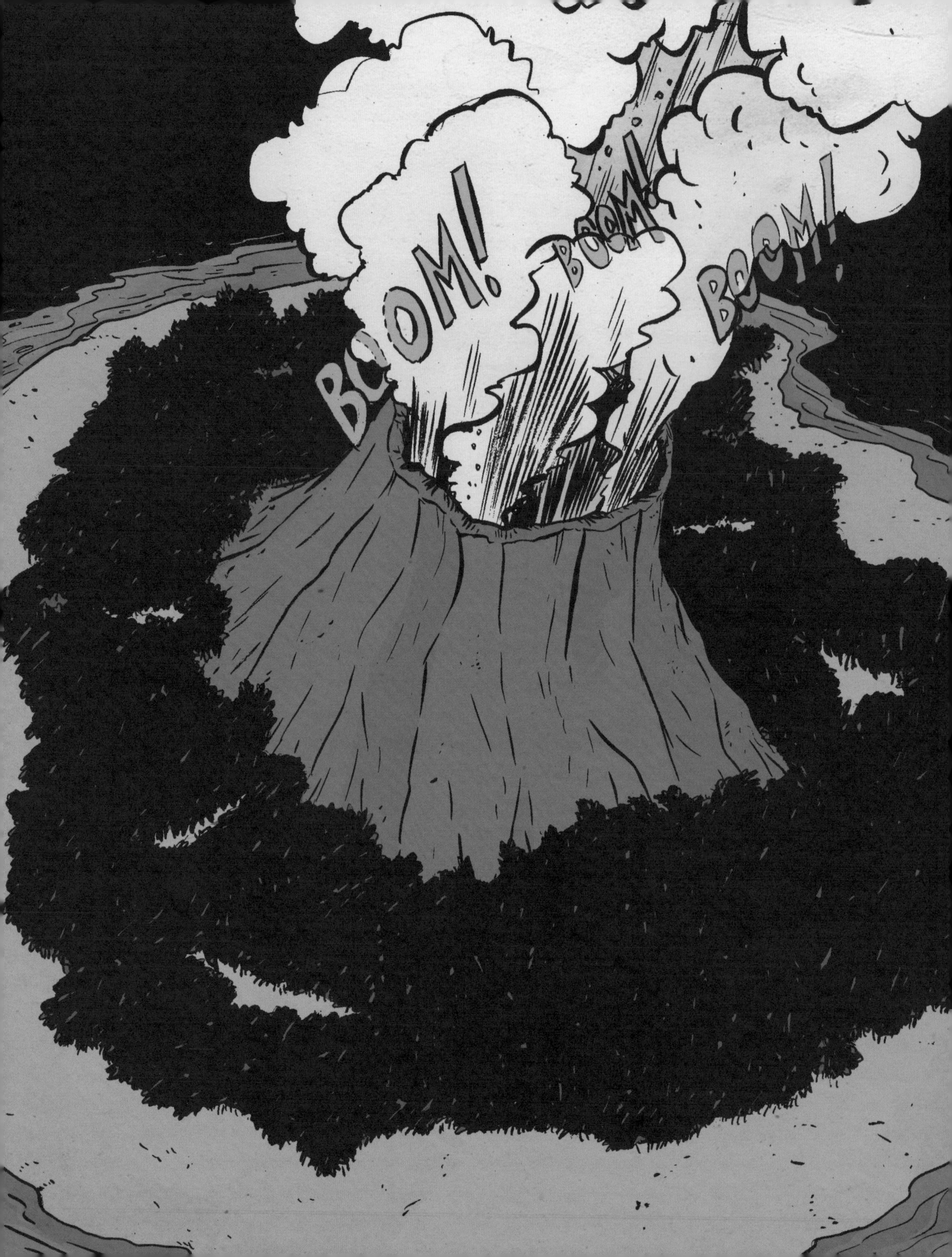
BOOM!
BOOM!
BOOM!

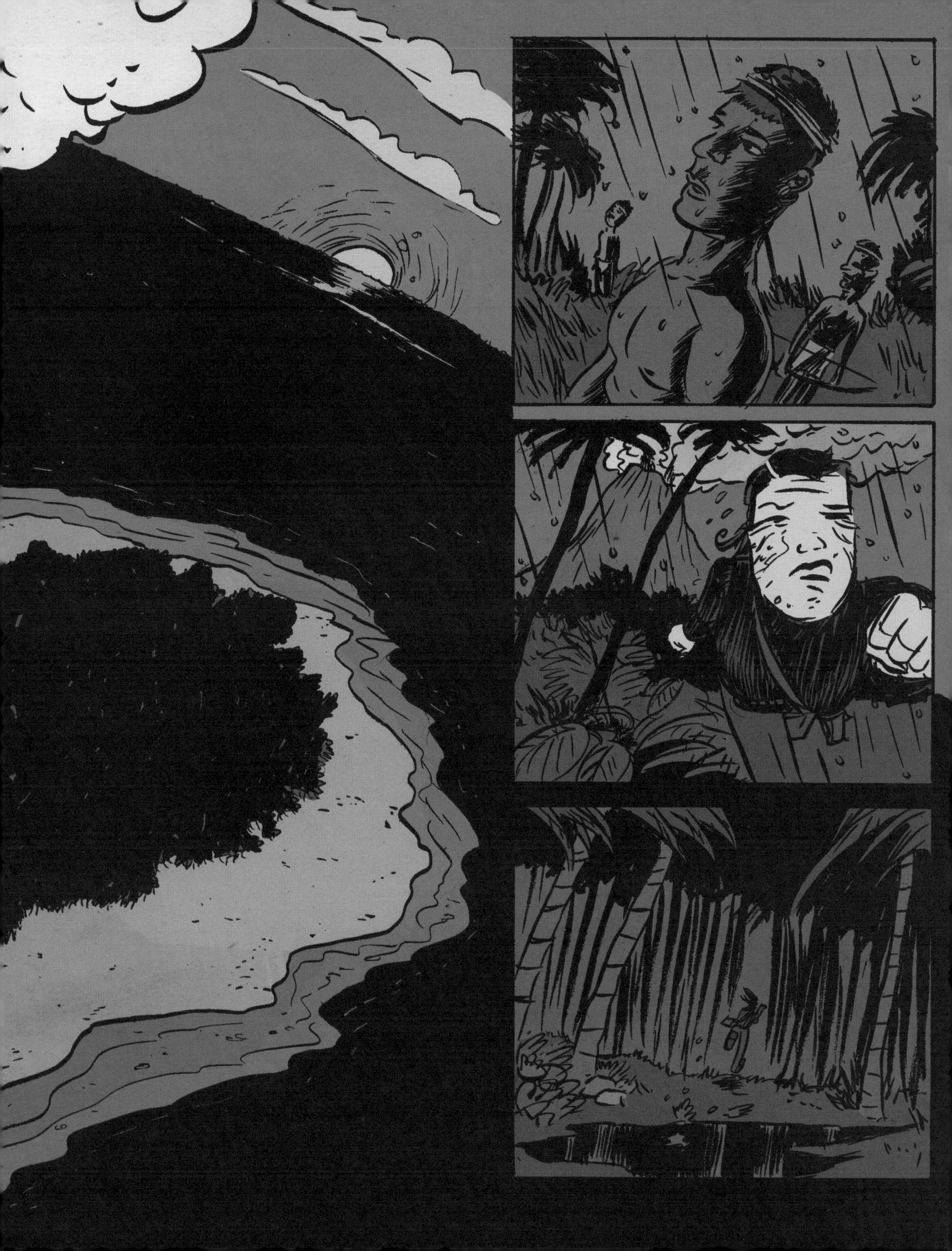

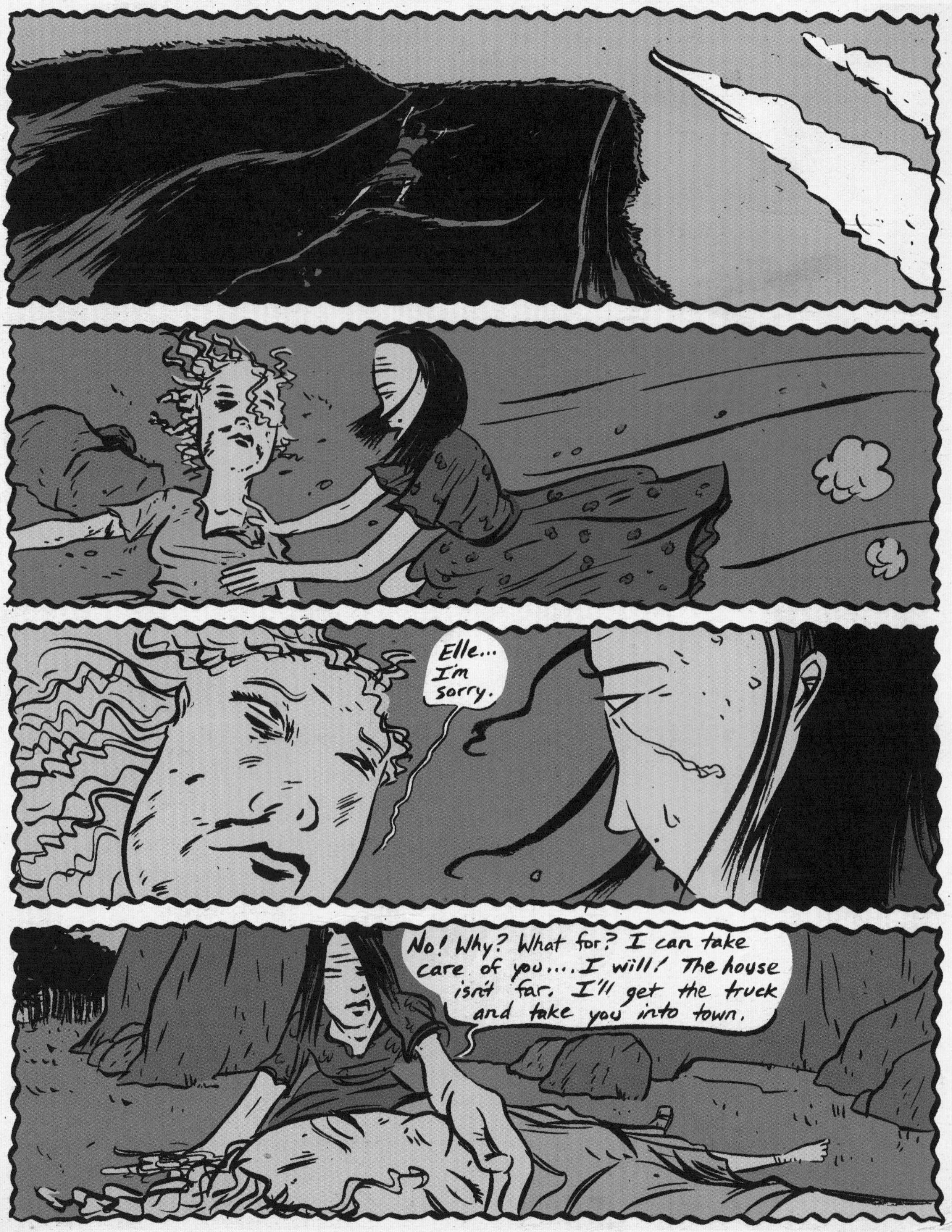
Elle... I'm sorry.
No! Why? What for? I can take care of you.... I will! The house isn't far. I'll get the truck and take you into town.

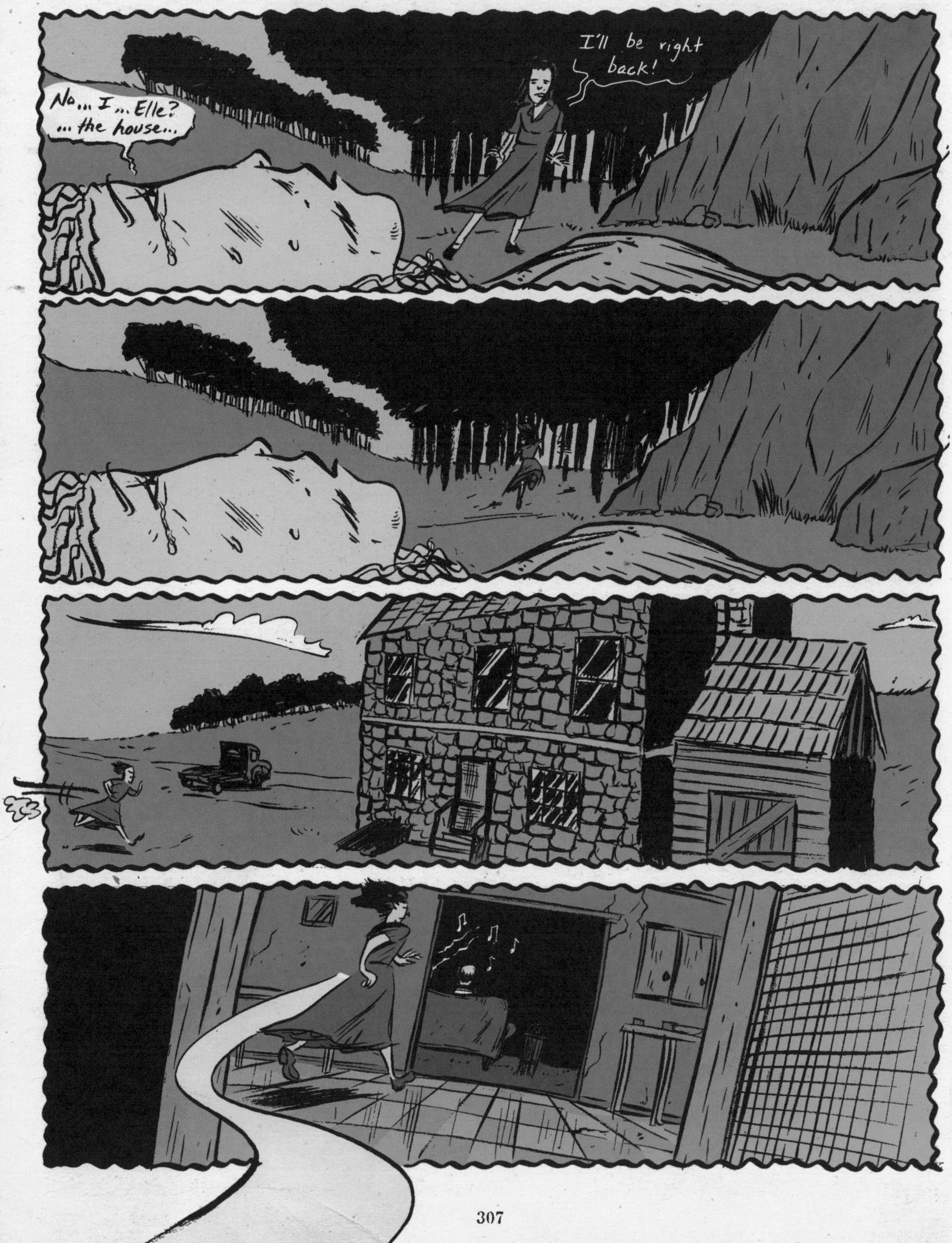
No... I... Elle? ... the house...
I'll be right back!

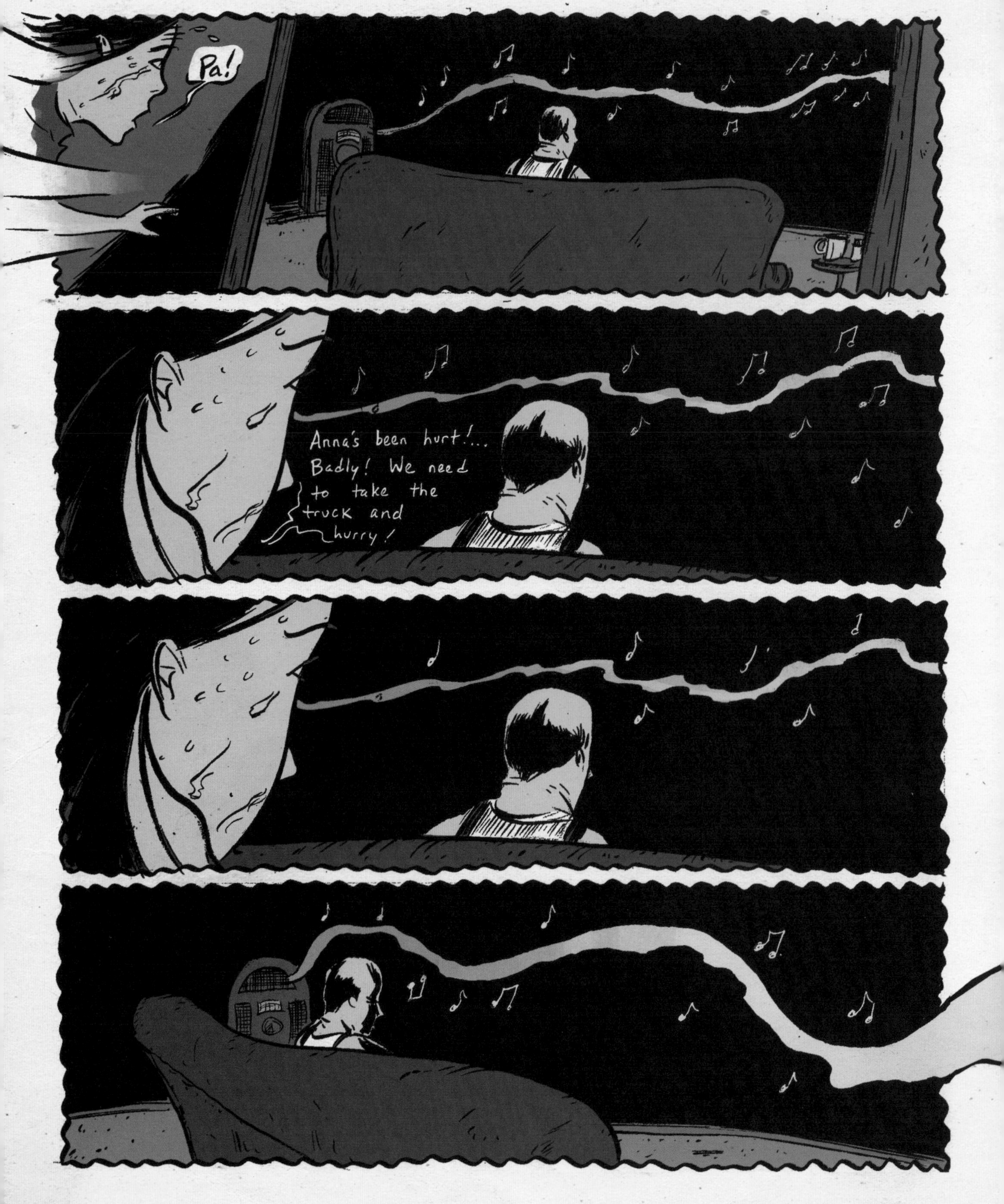
Pa!
Anna's been hurt!... Badly! We need to take the truck and hurry!

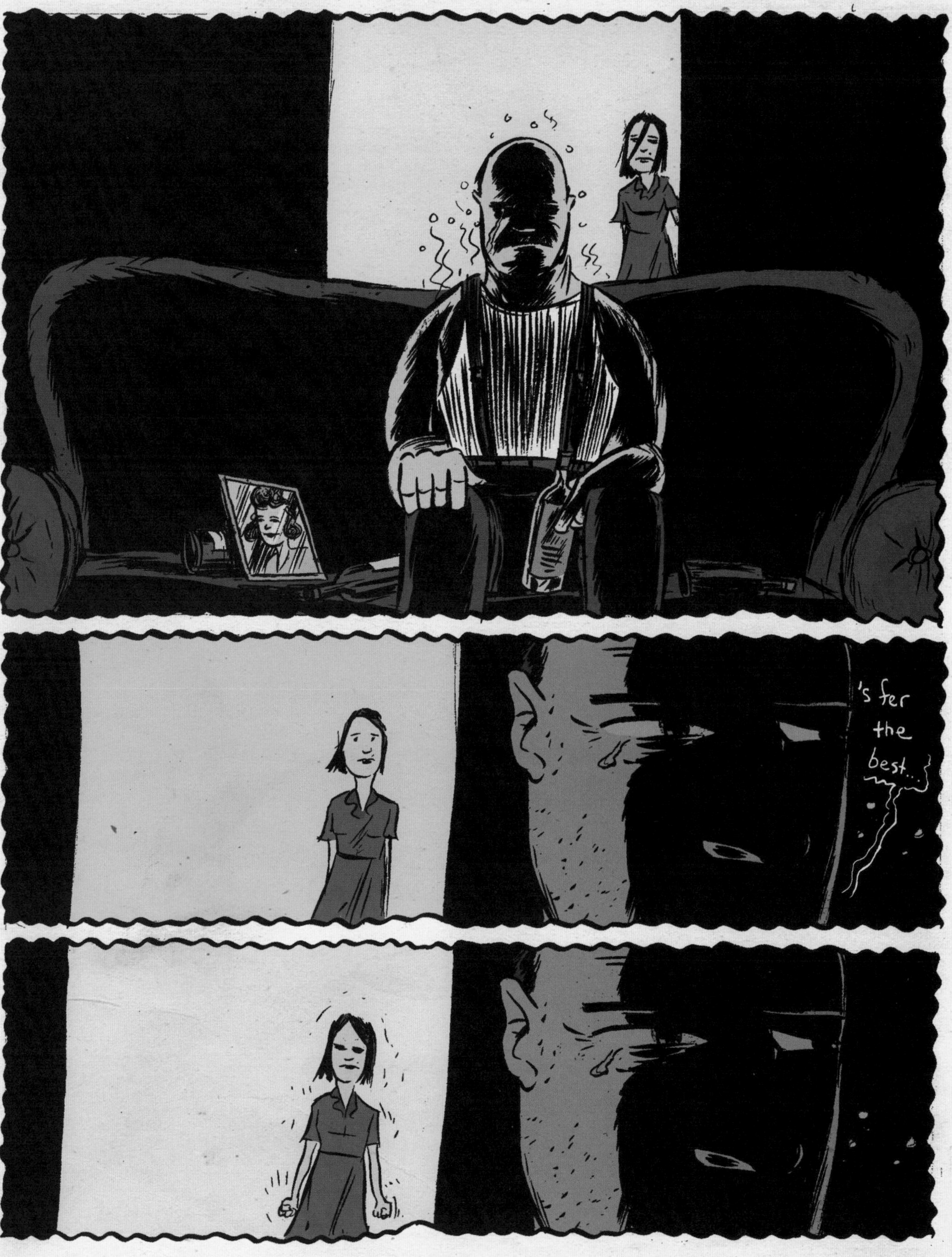
's fer the best...

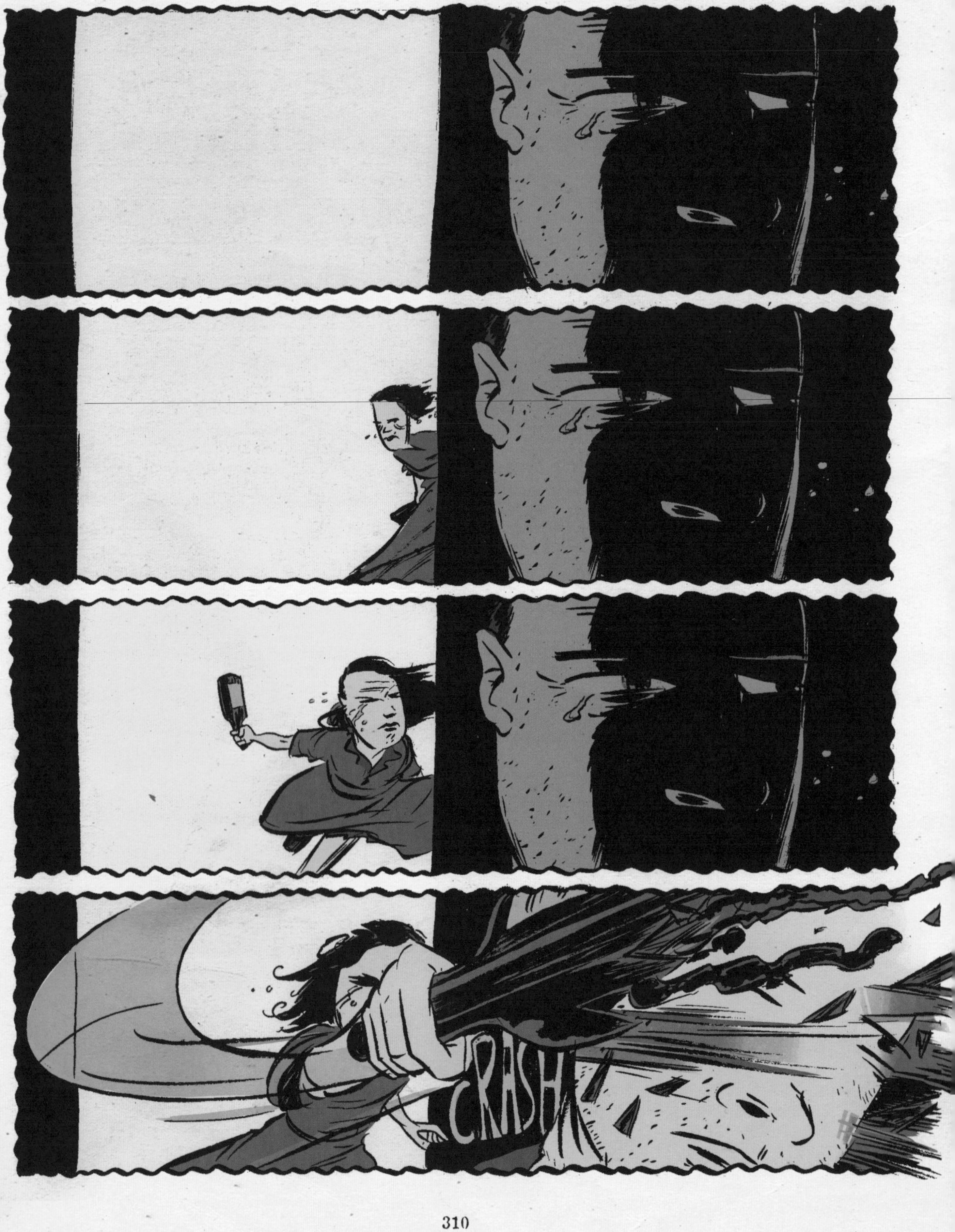
CRASH

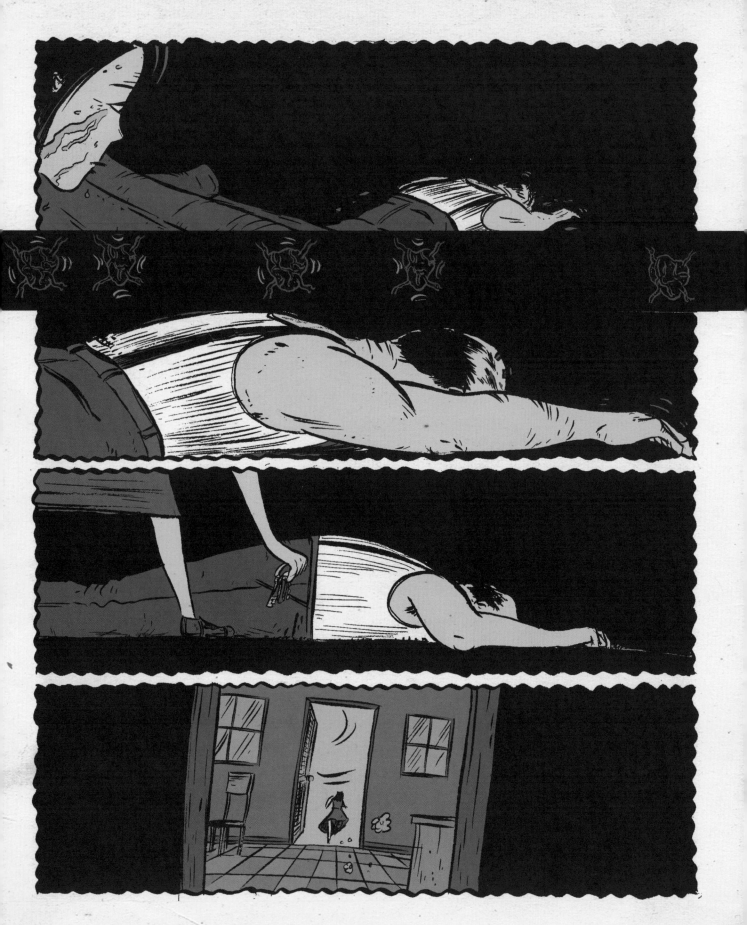

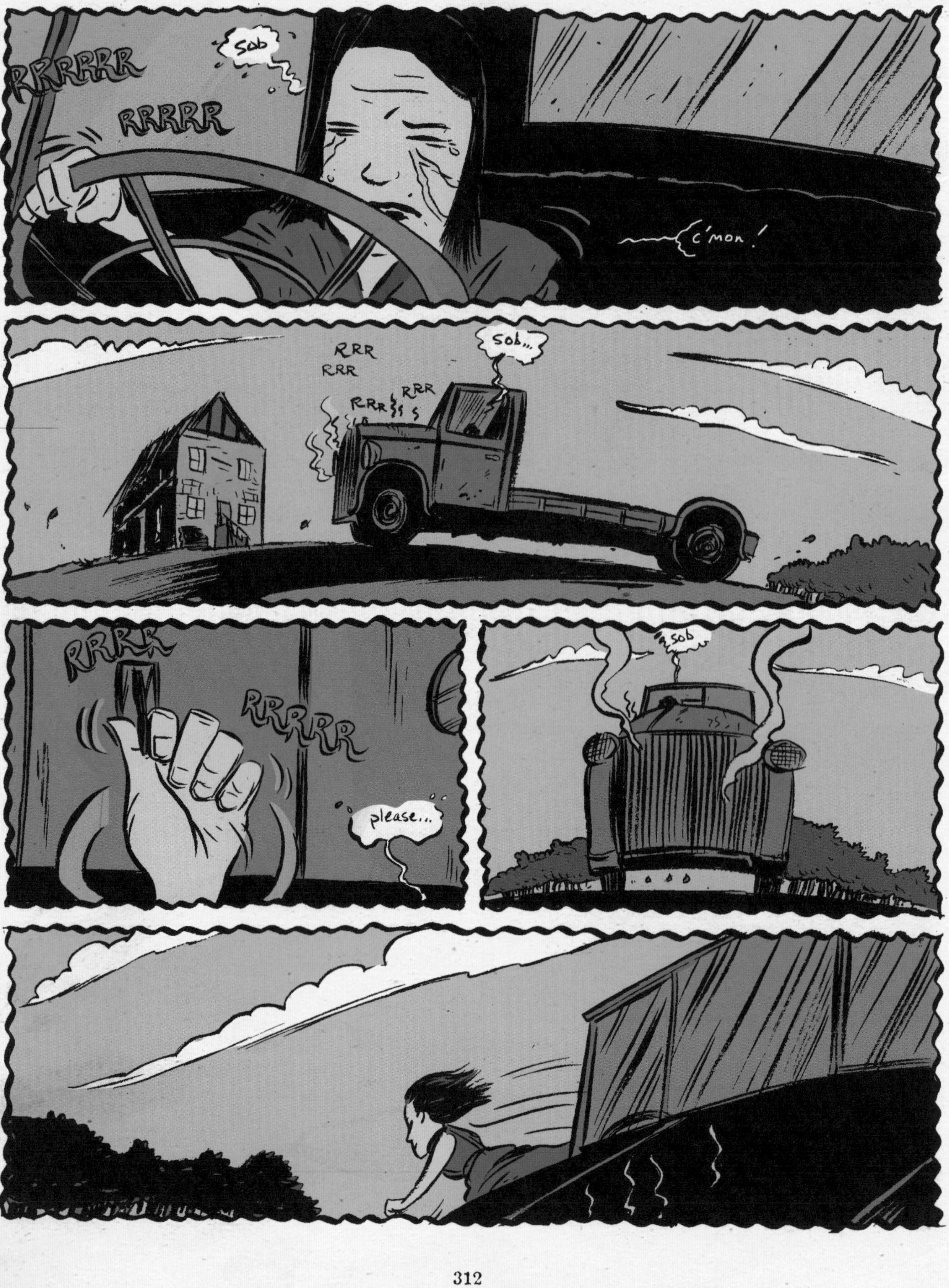
RRRRRR
RRRRR
sob
c'mon!
RRR
RRR
RRR
RRR
sob...
RRRR
RRRRR
please...
sob

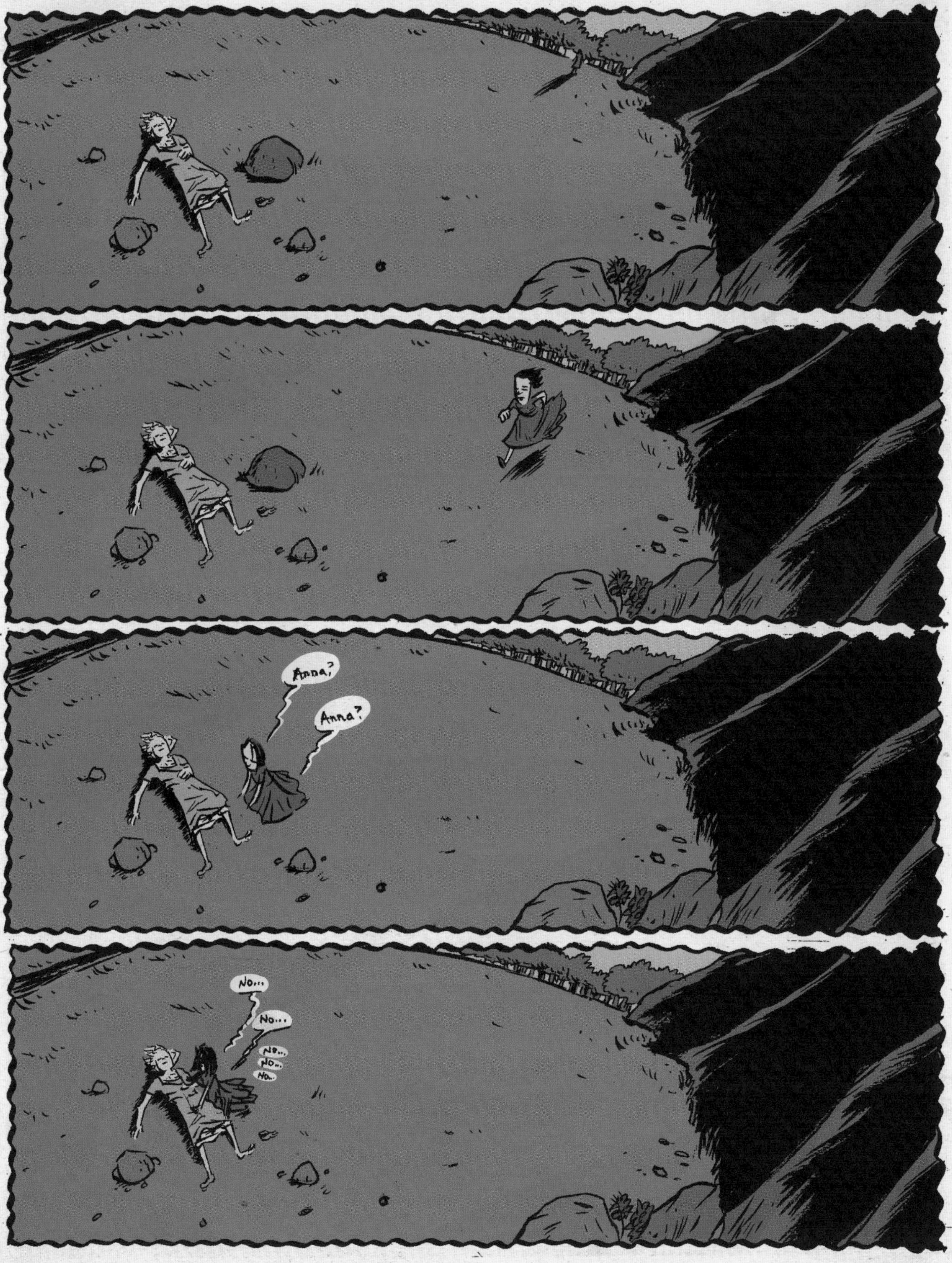
Anna?
Anna?
No...
No...
No...
No...
No...

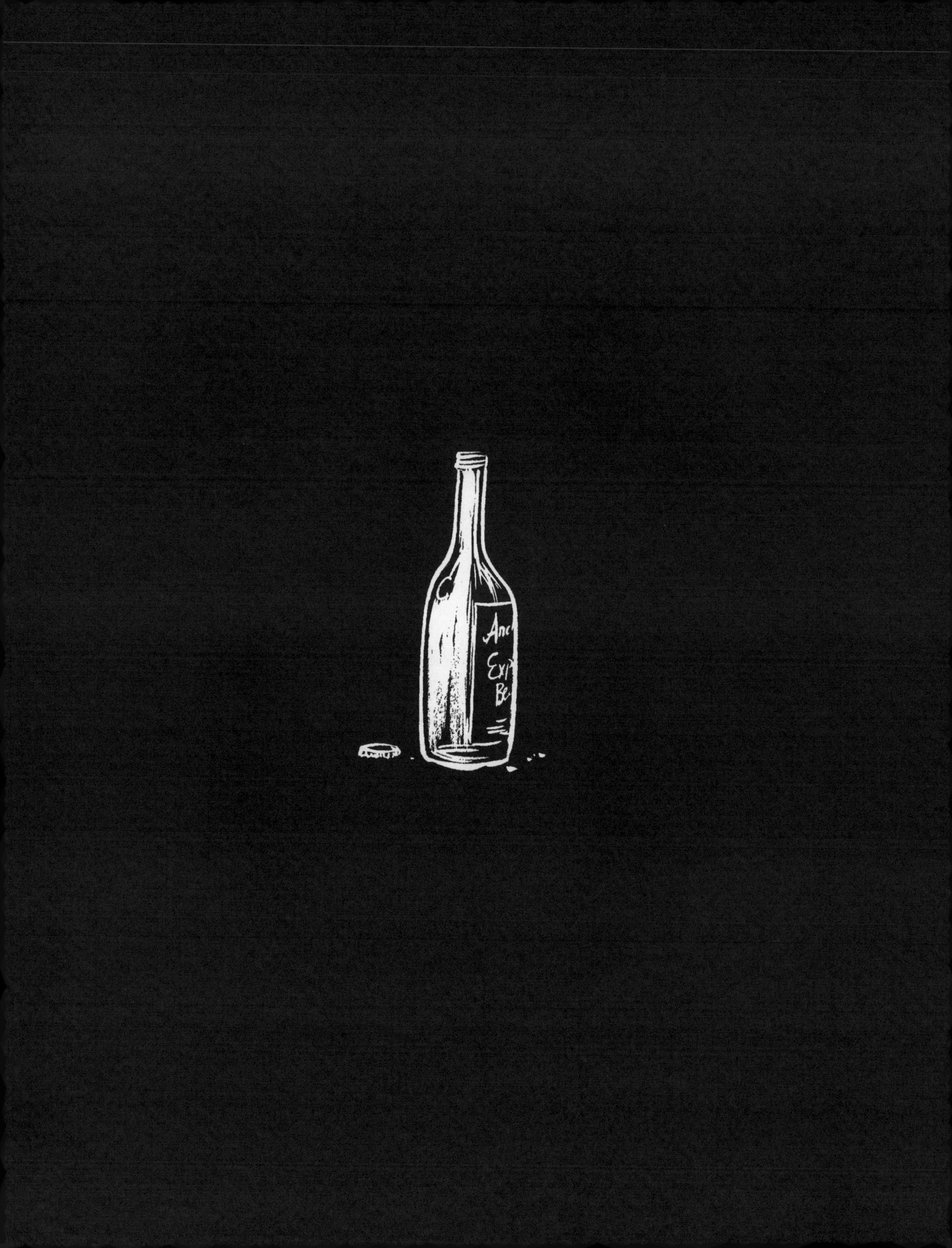

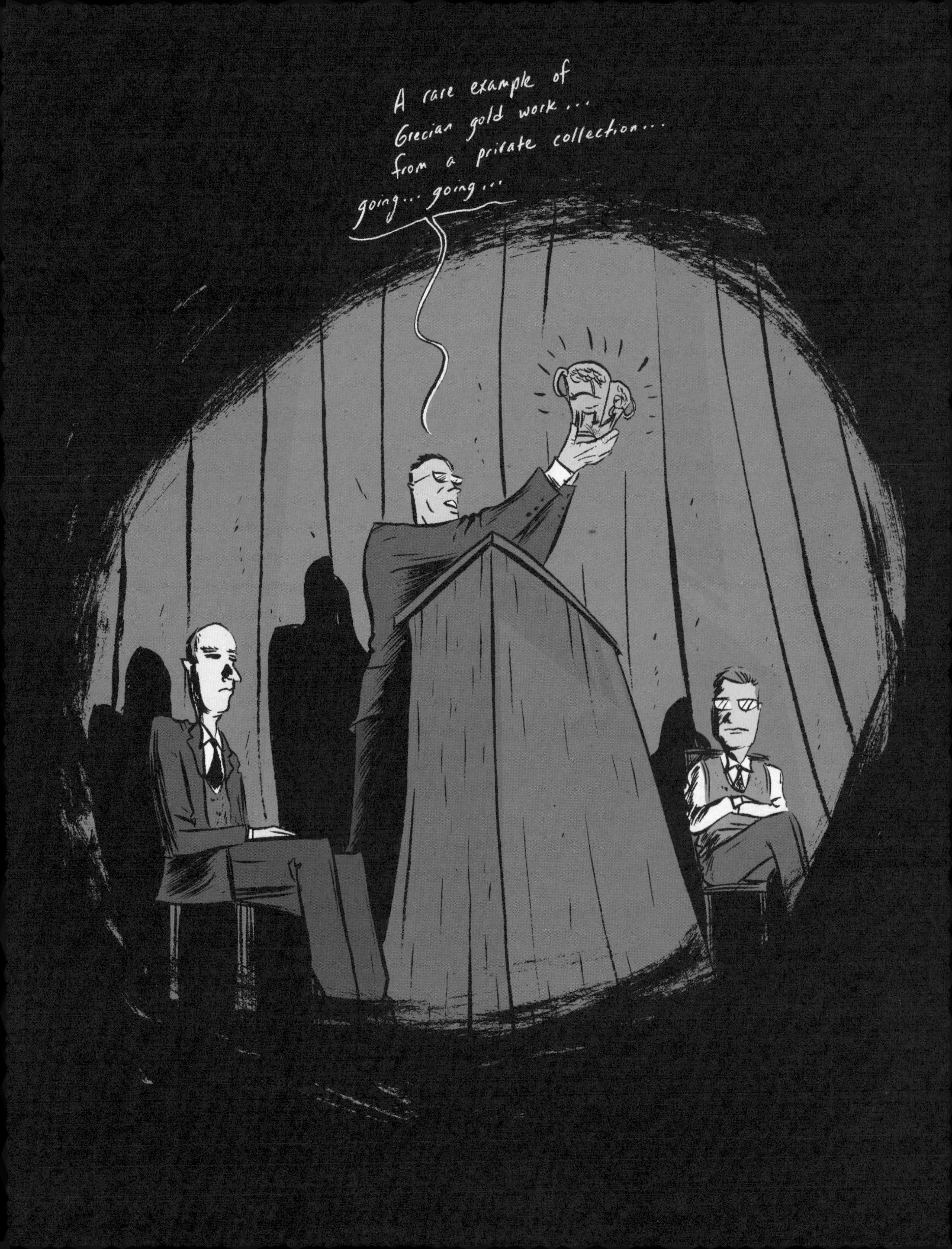
A rare example of
Grecian gold work...
from a private collection...
going... going...

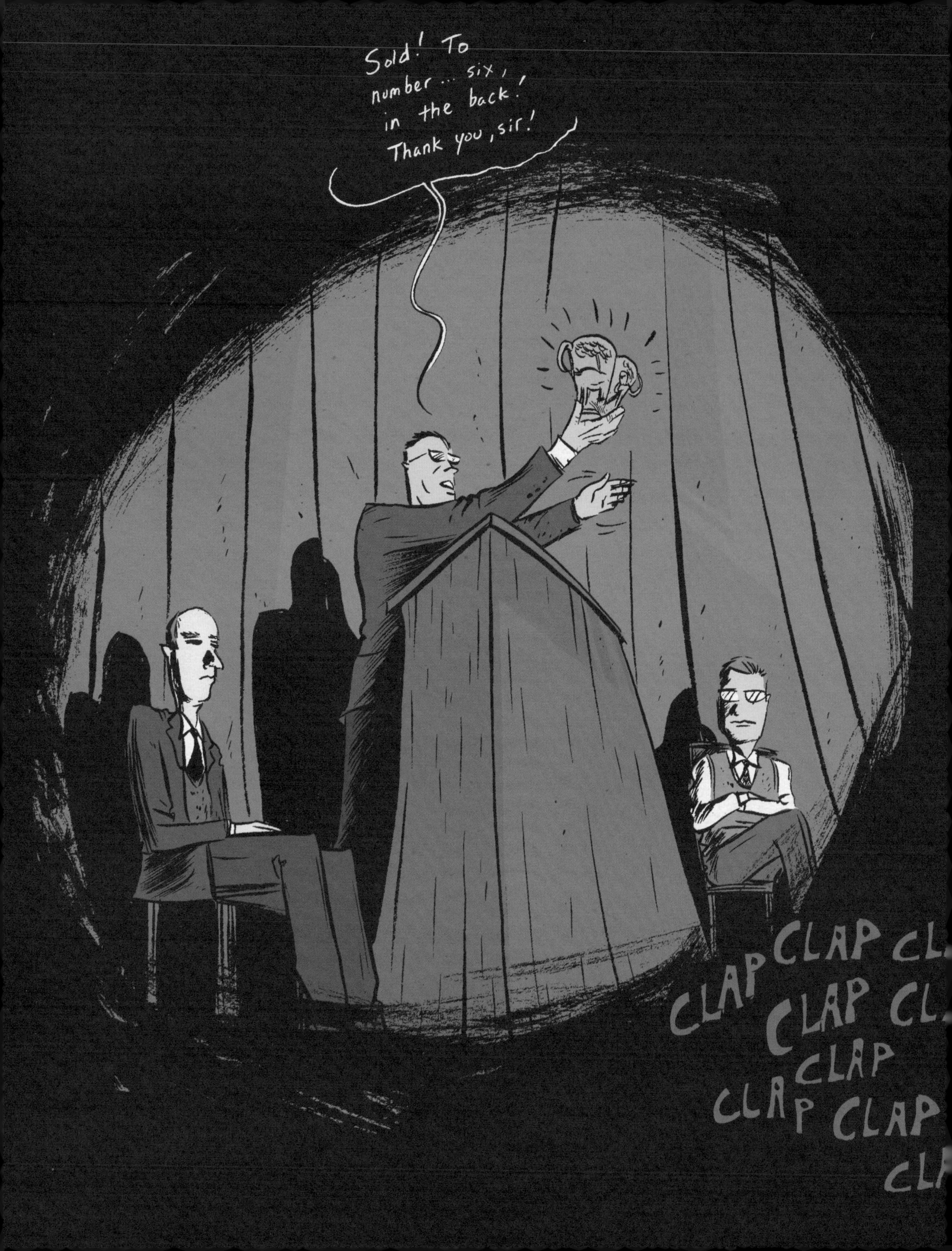
Sold! To number... six, in the back! Thank you, sir!
CLAP CLAP CLAP CLAP CLAP CLAP CLAP CLAP

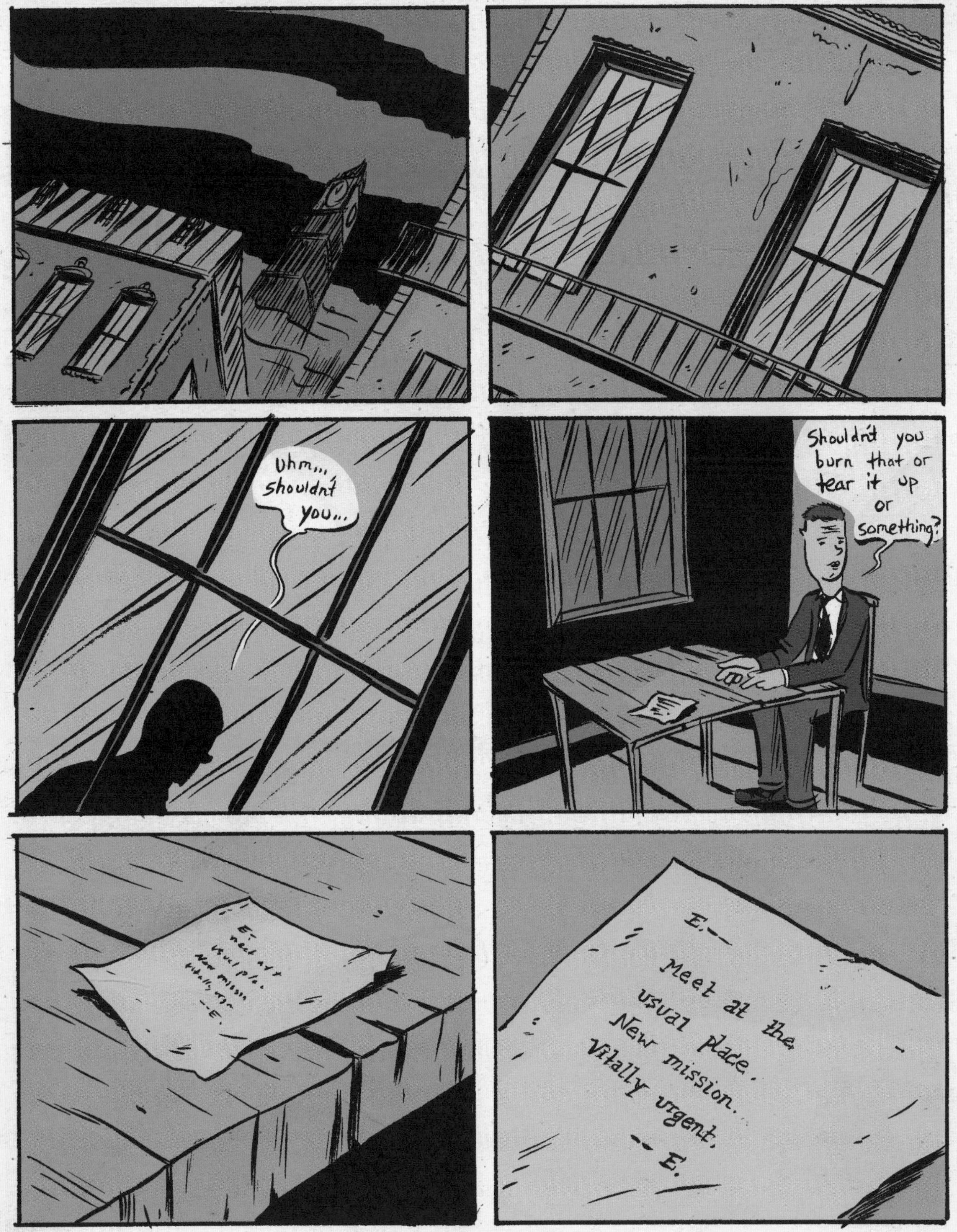
Uhm... shouldn't you...
Shouldn't you burn that or tear it up or something?
E.--
Meet at the usual place. New mission. Vitally urgent.
-- E.

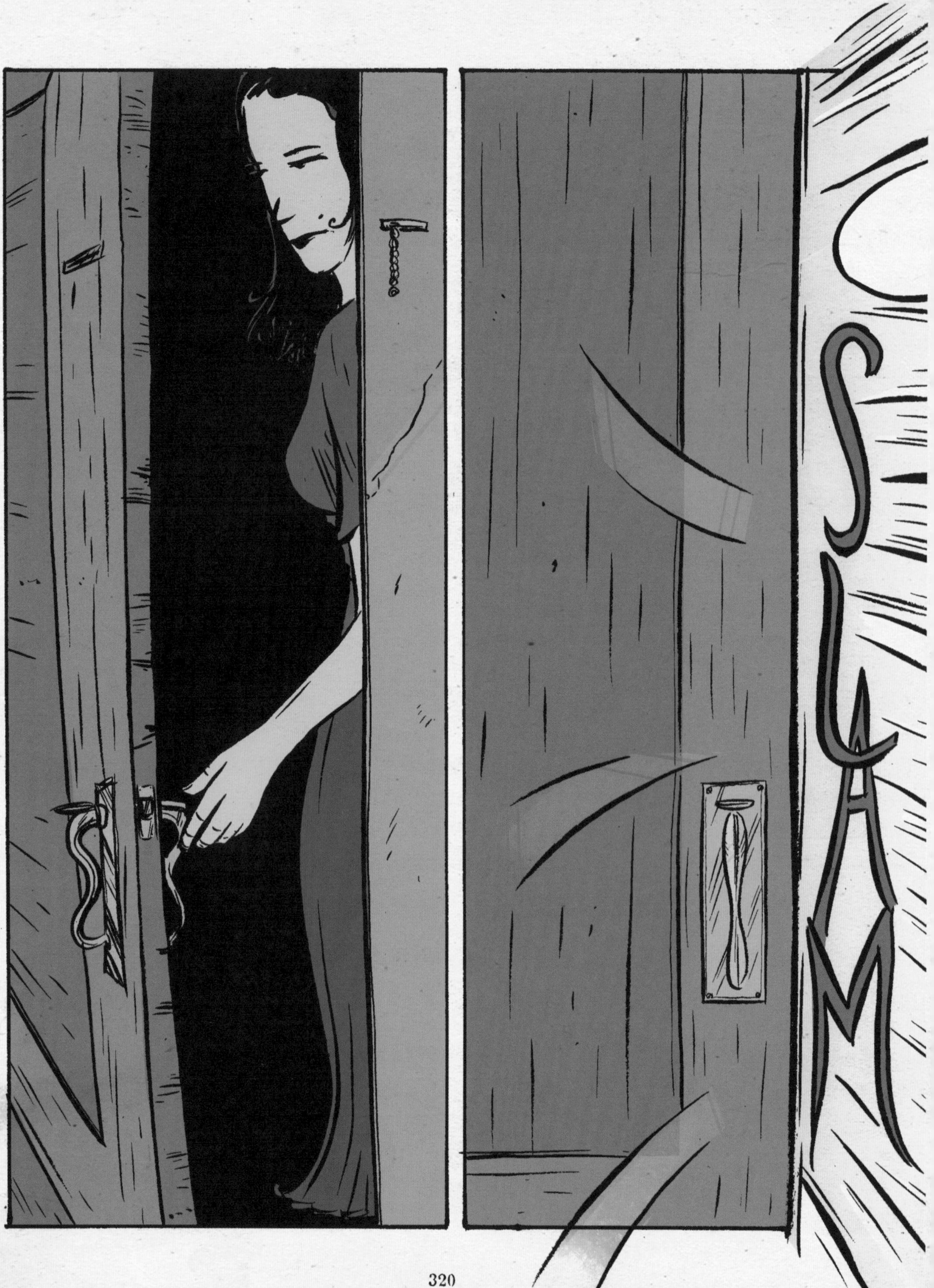
SLAM

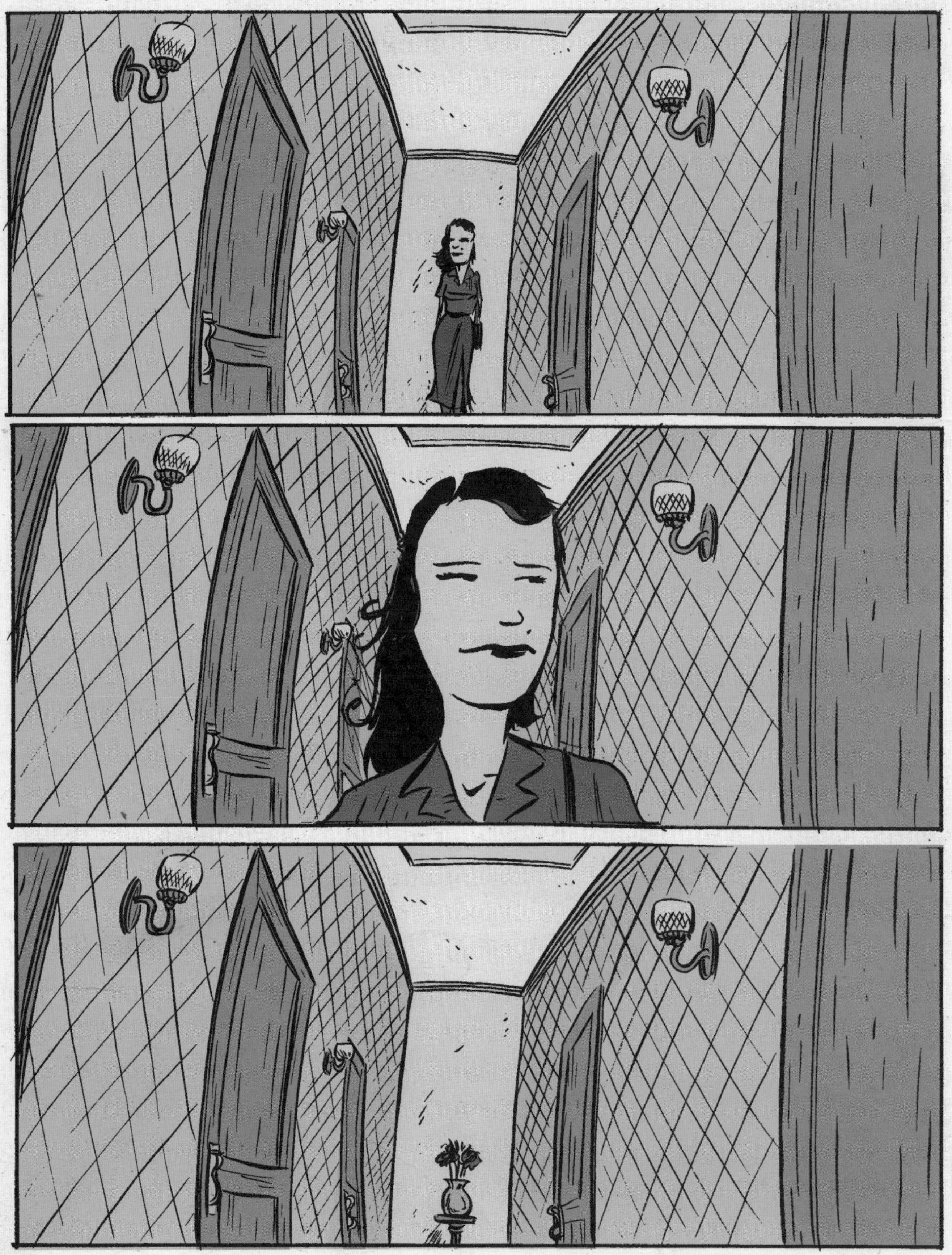

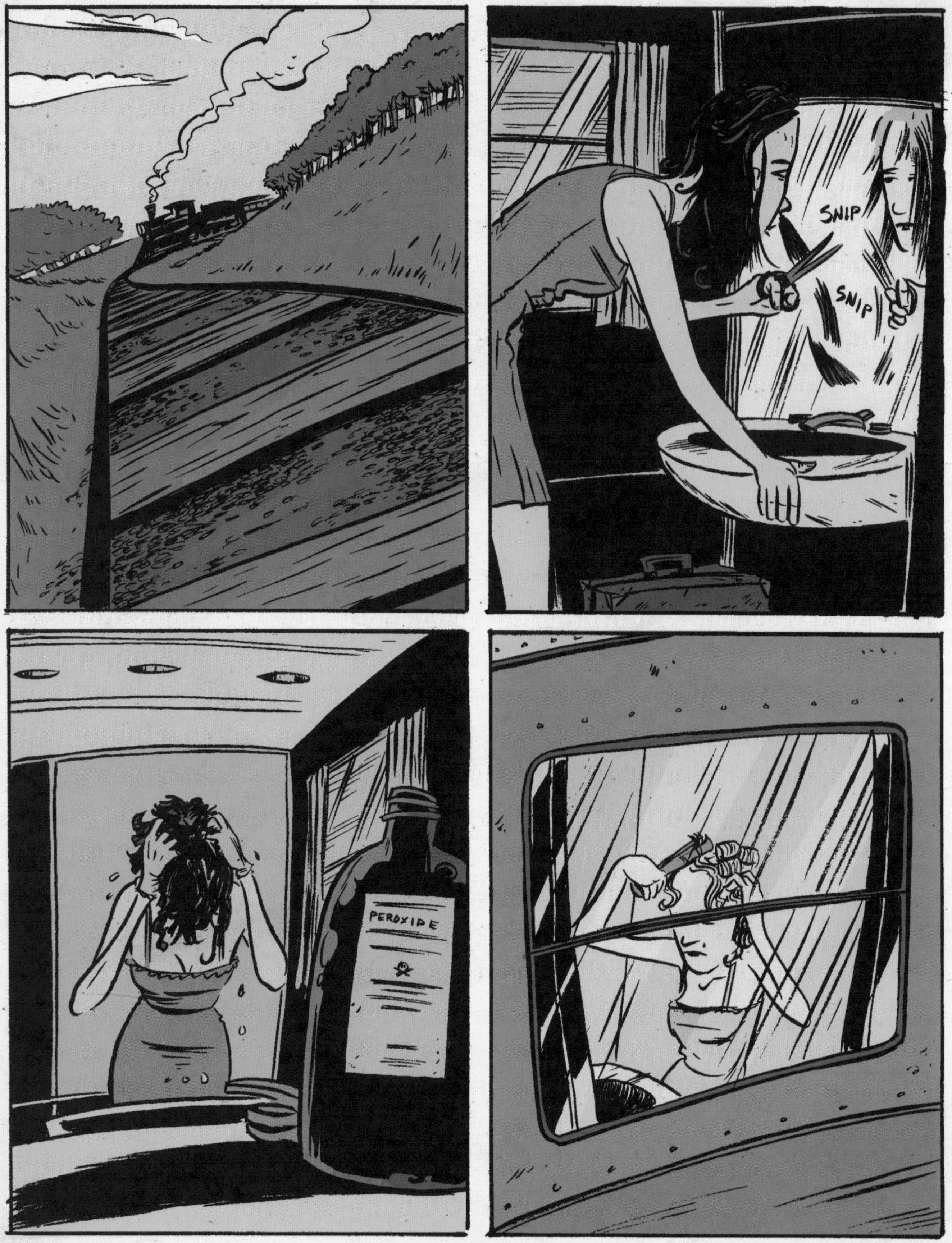
SNIP
SNIP
PEROXIDE

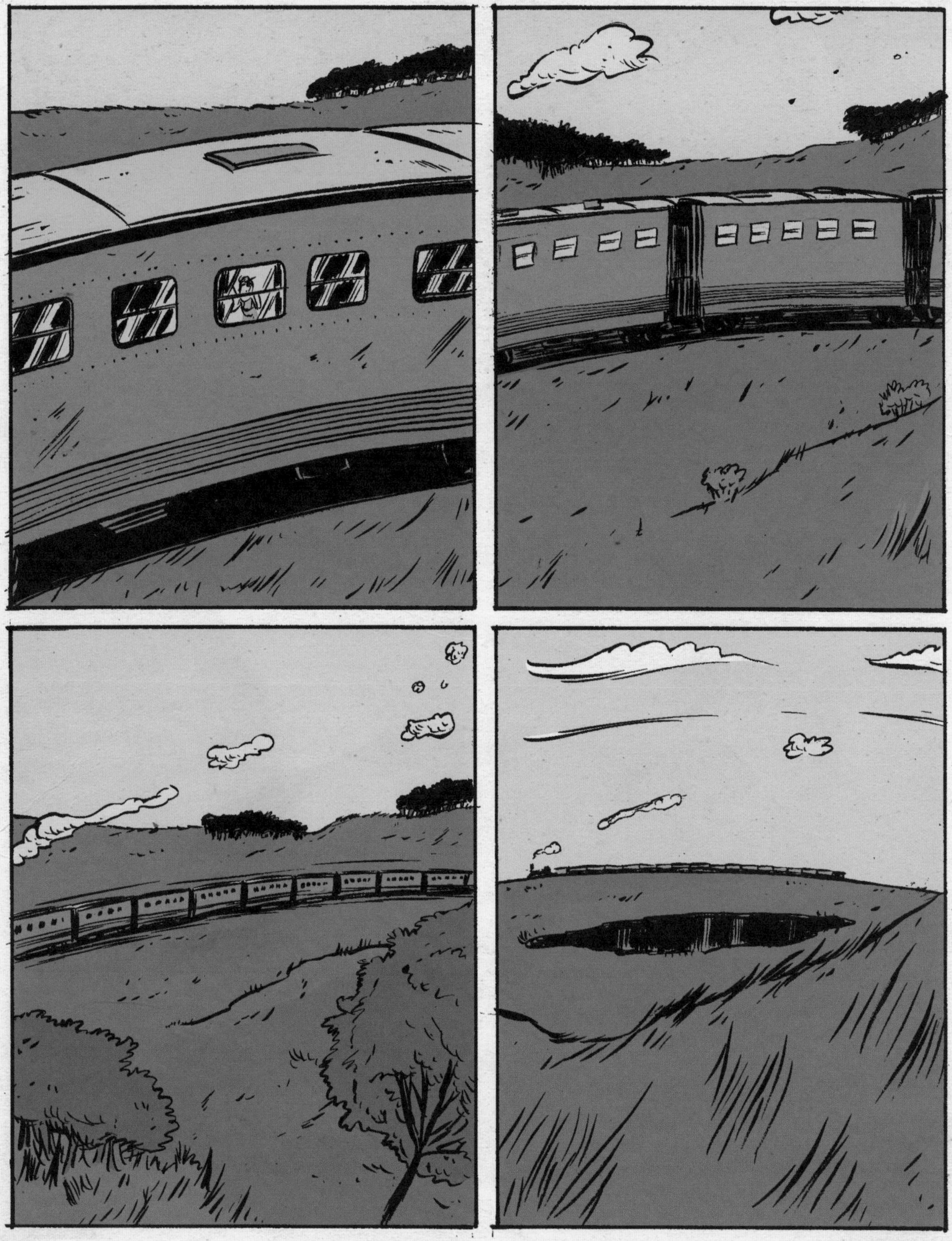

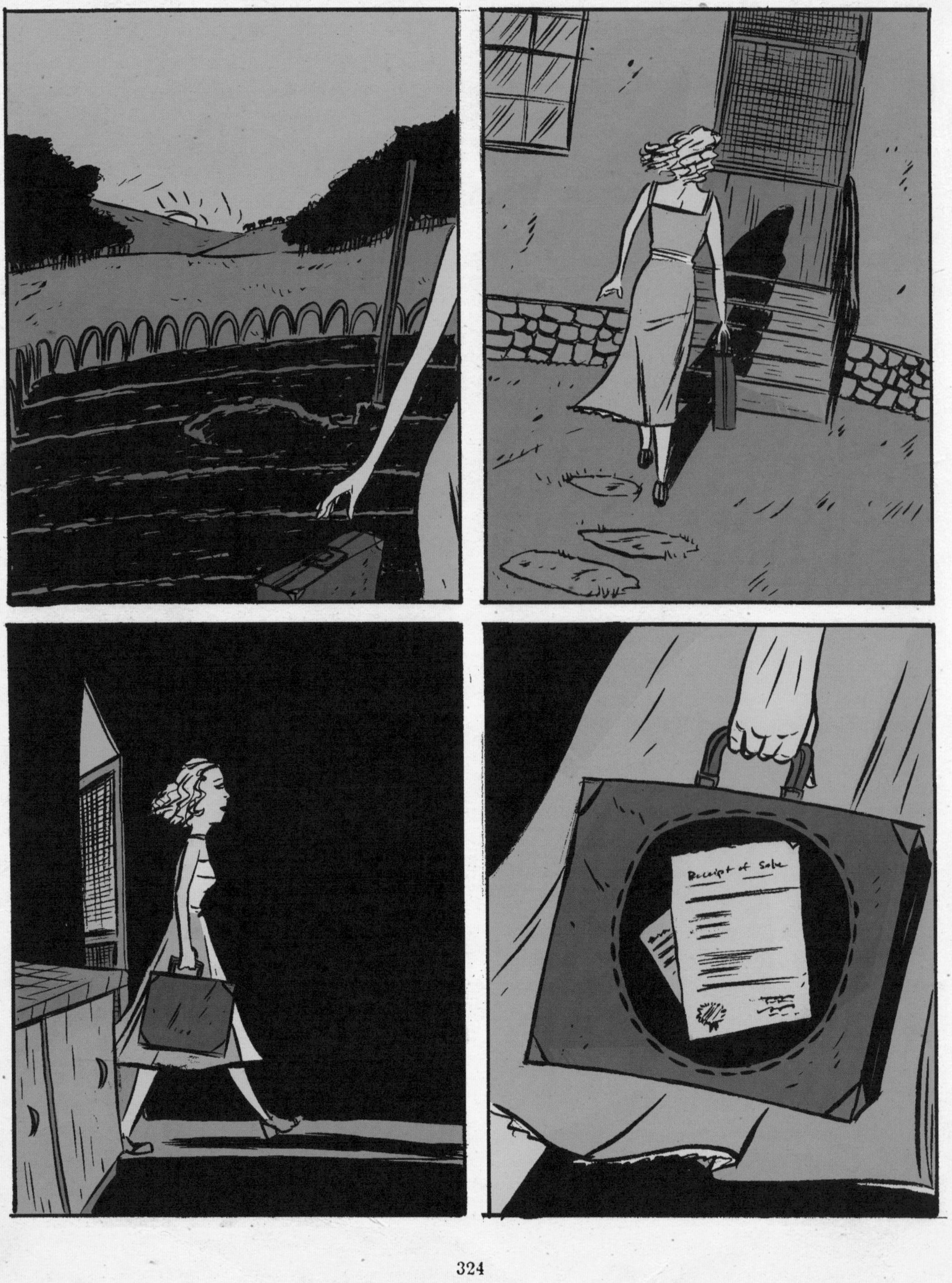
Receipt of Sale

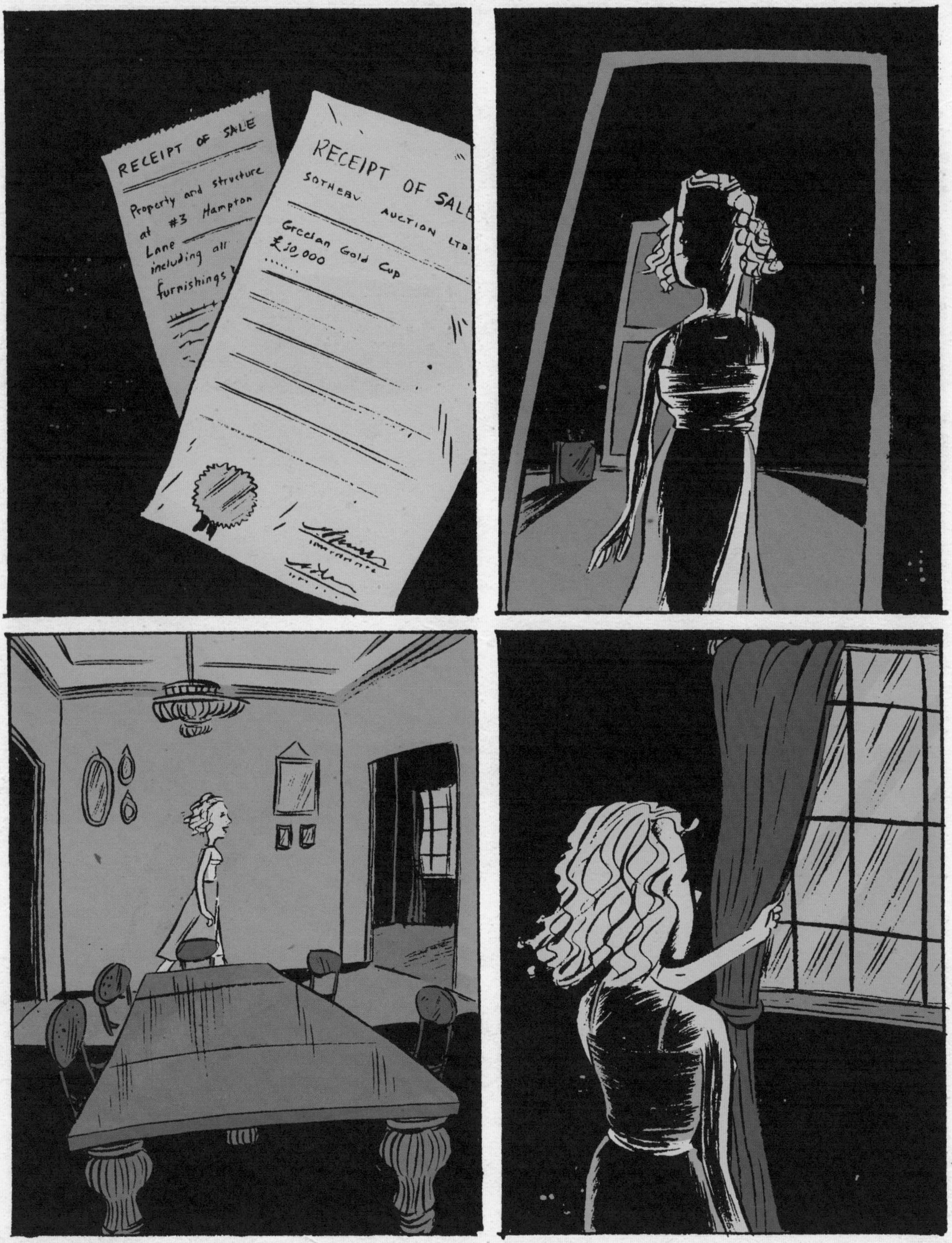
RECEIPT OF SALE
Property and structure at #3 Hampton Lane including all furnishings
RECEIPT OF SALE
SOTHEBV AUCTION LTD.
Grecian Gold Cup
£10,000

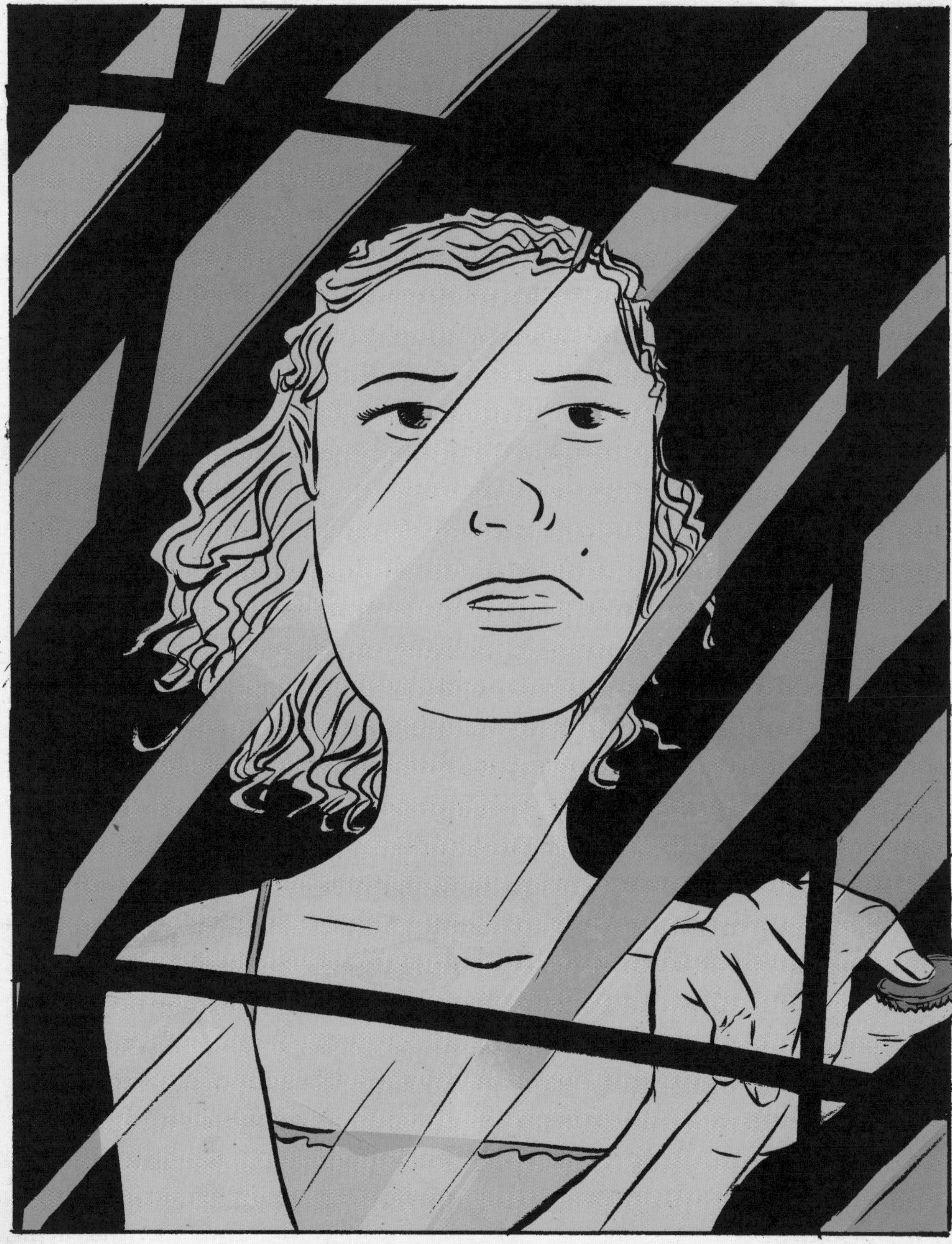

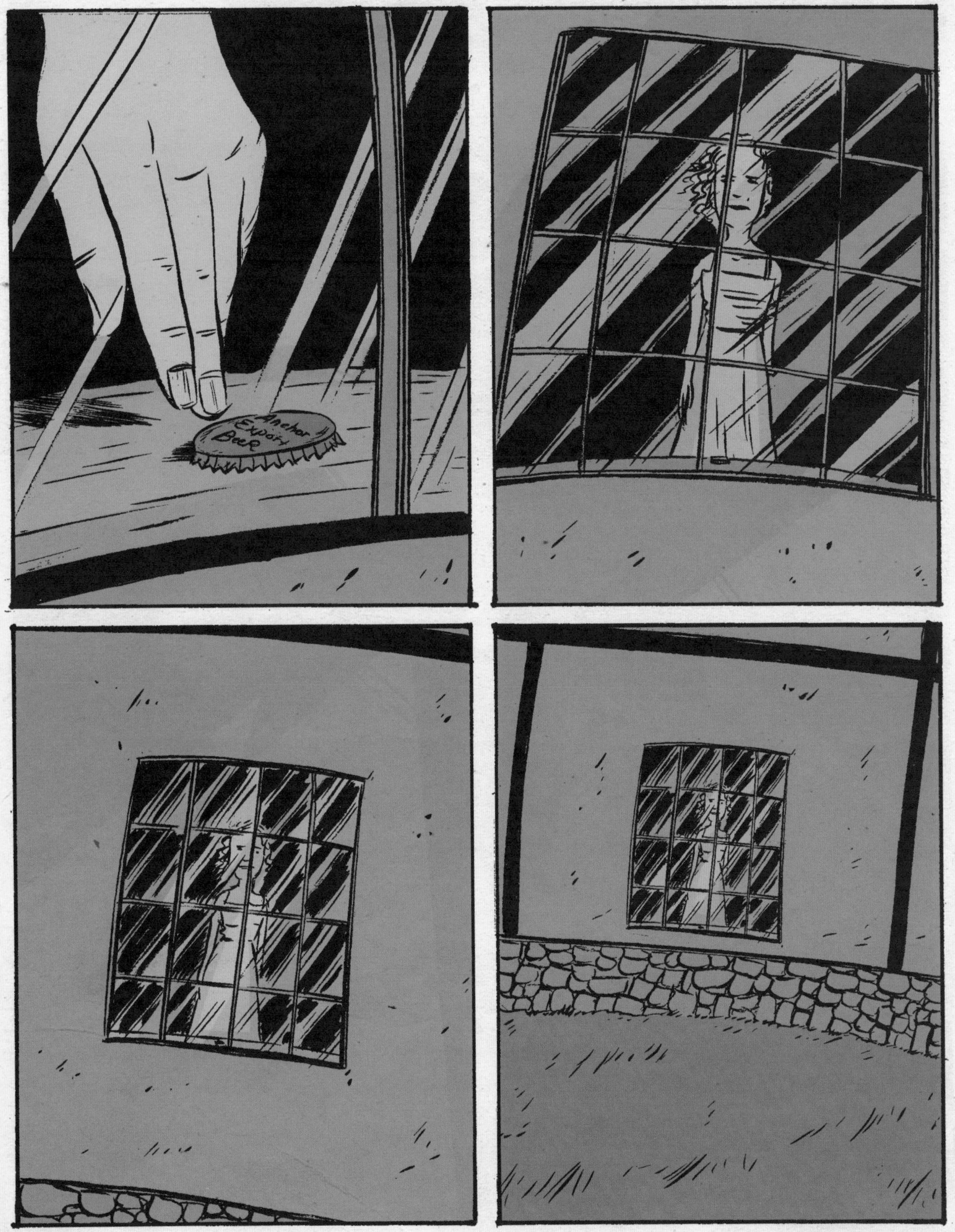
Anchor
Export
BeeR

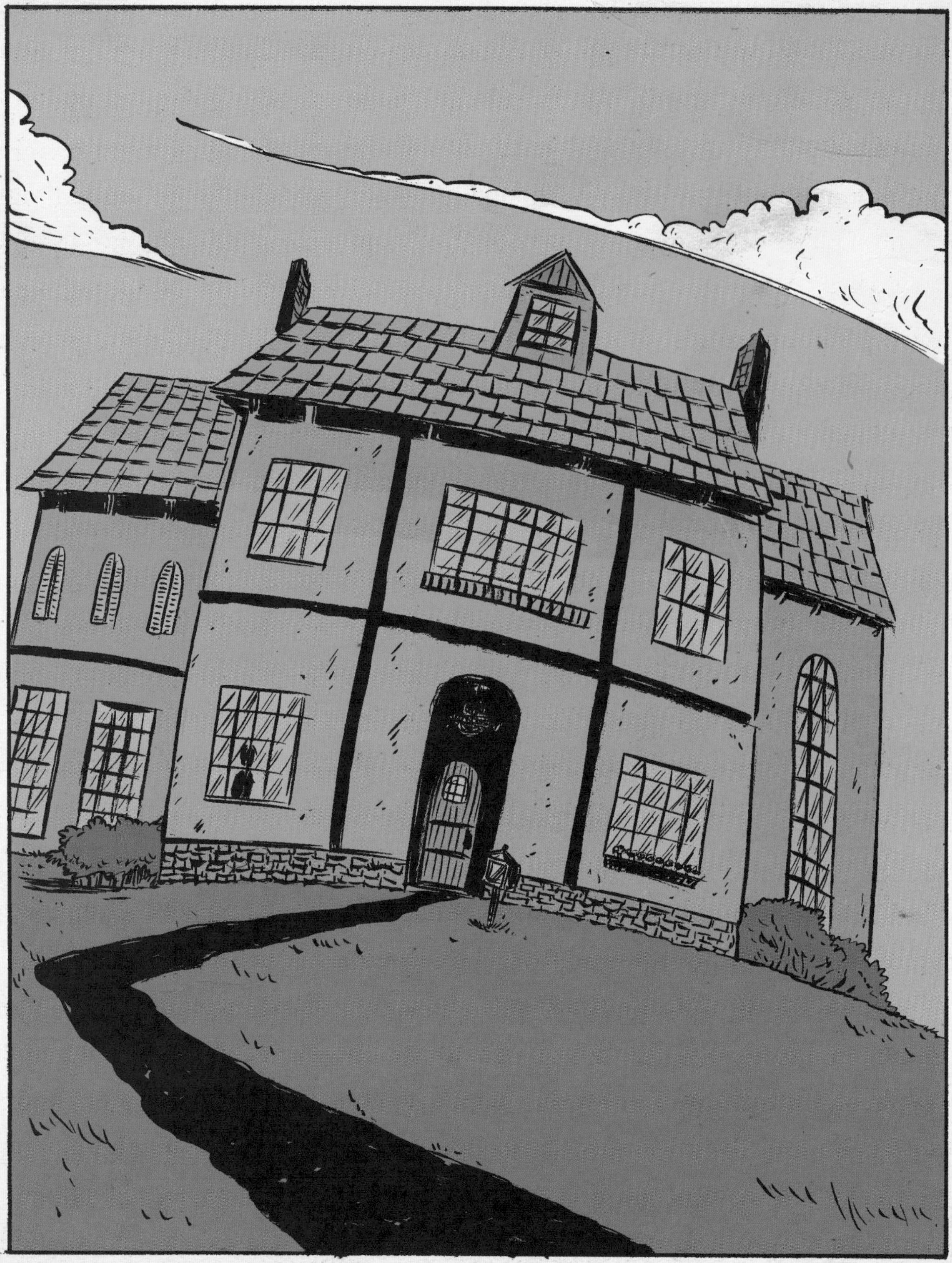

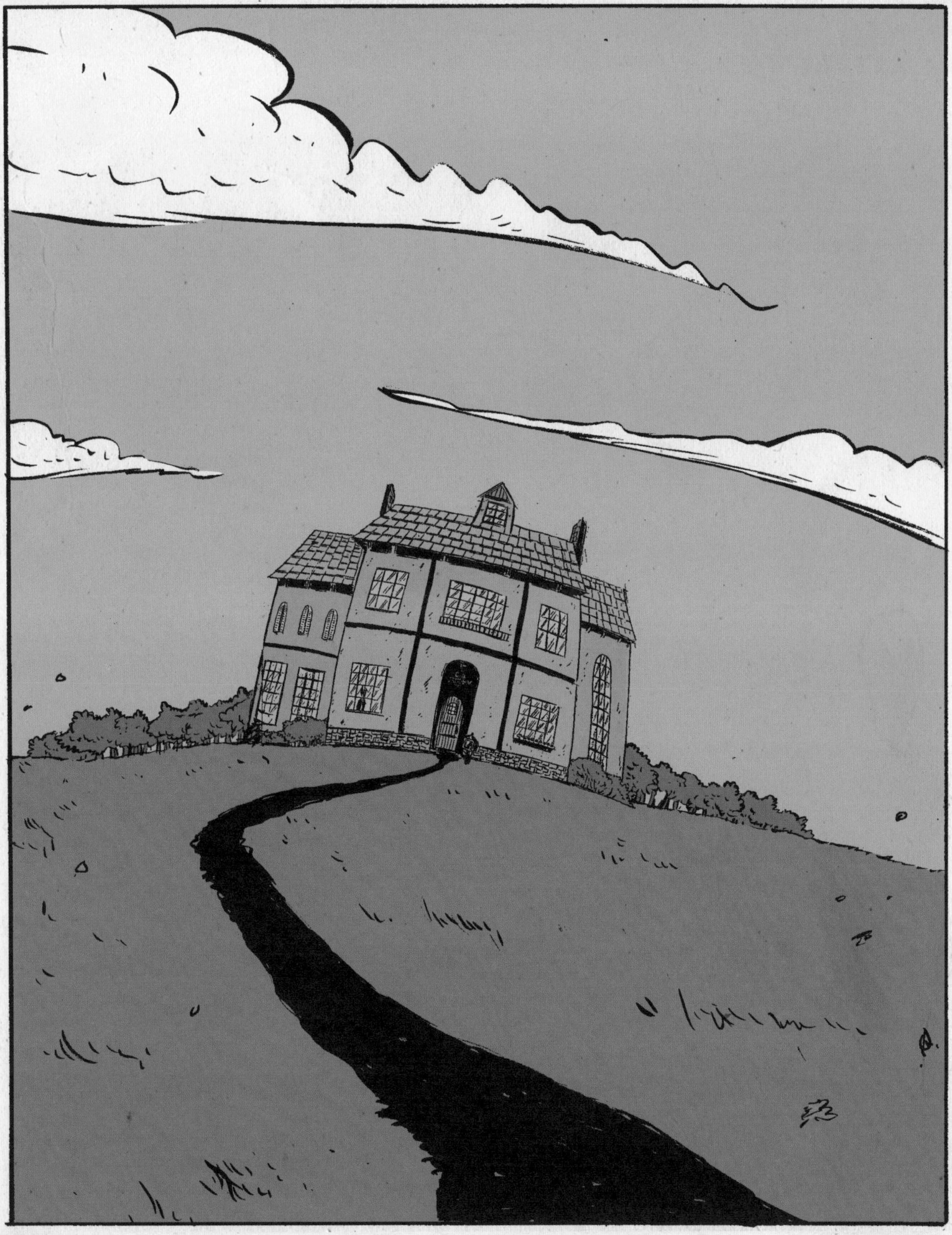

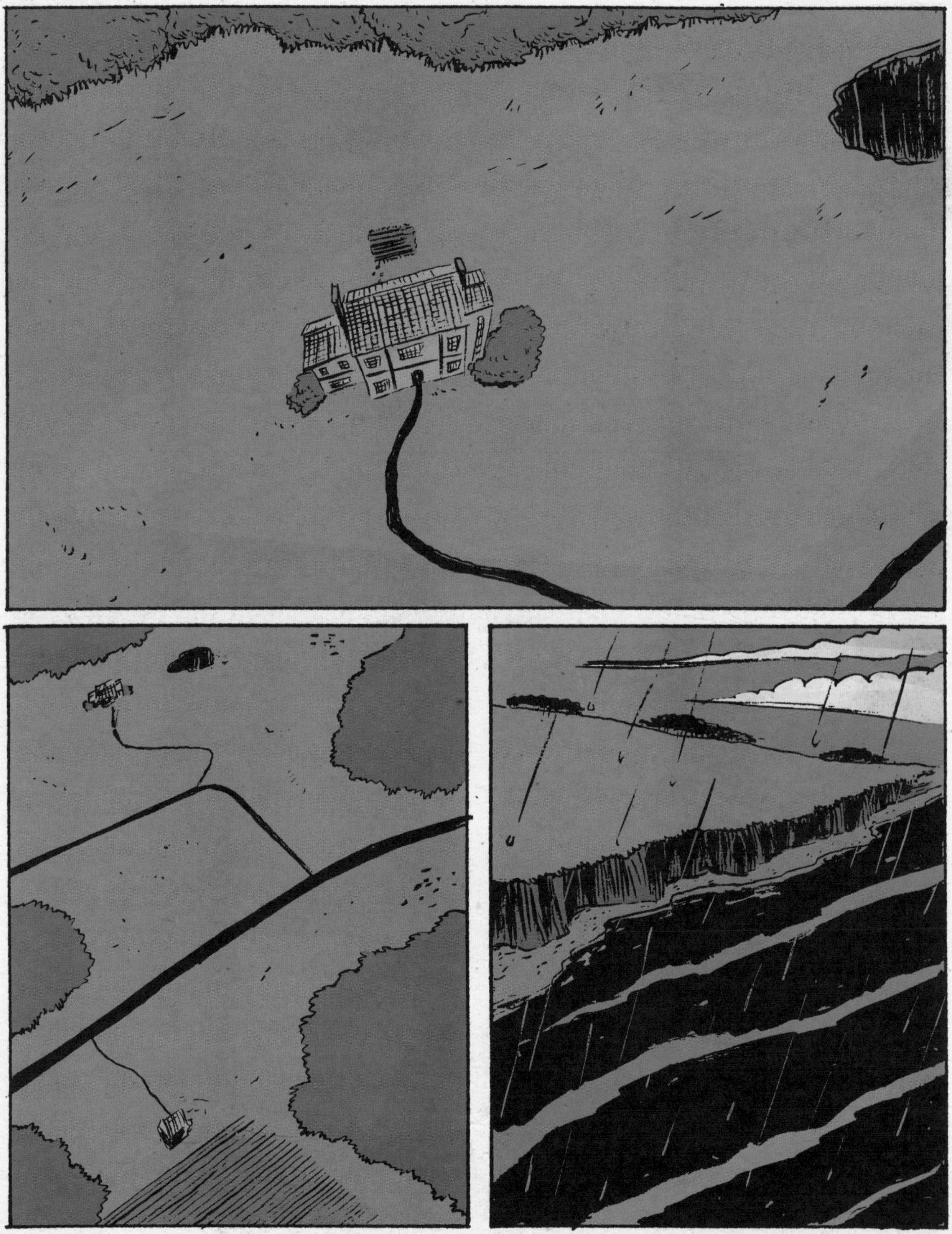

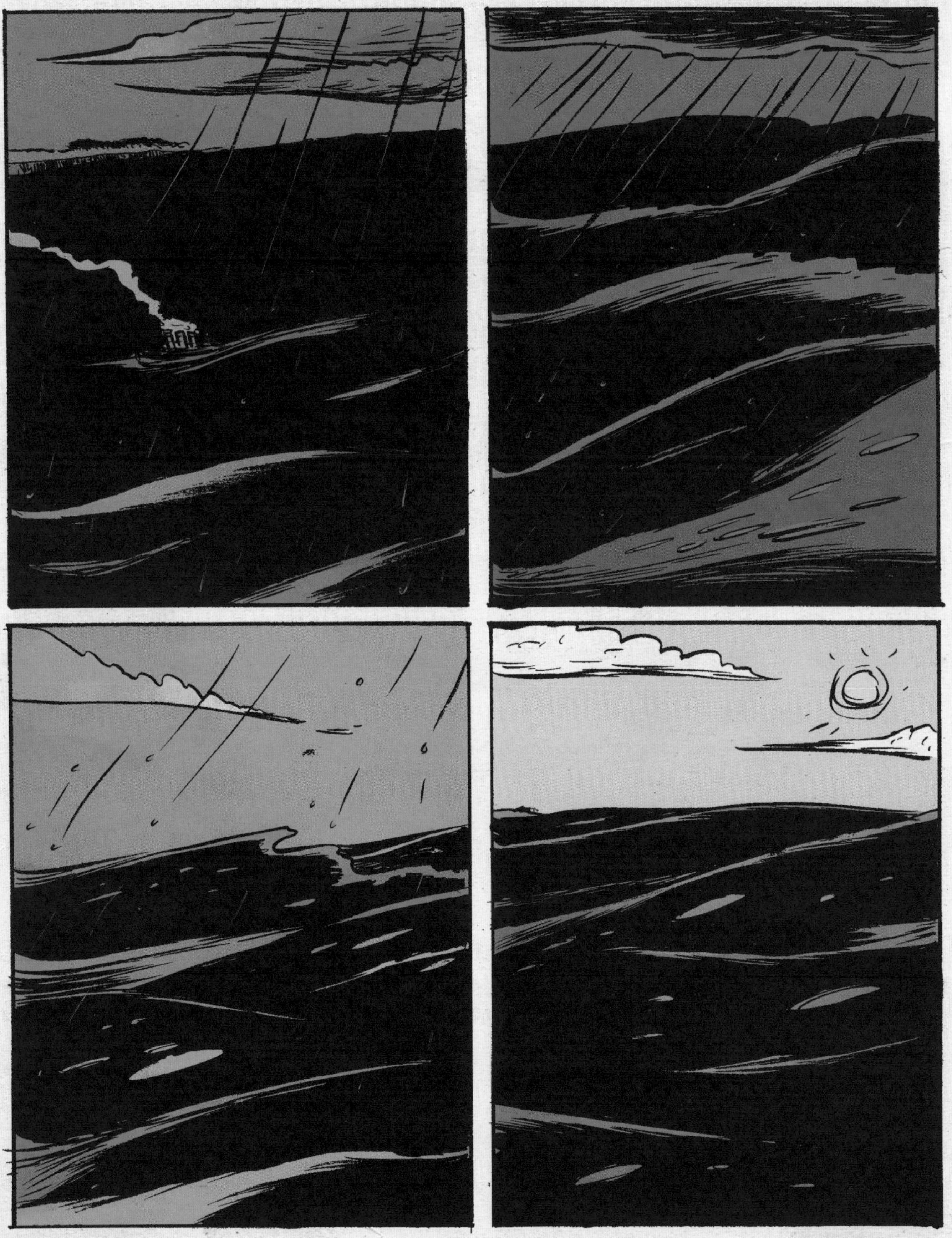

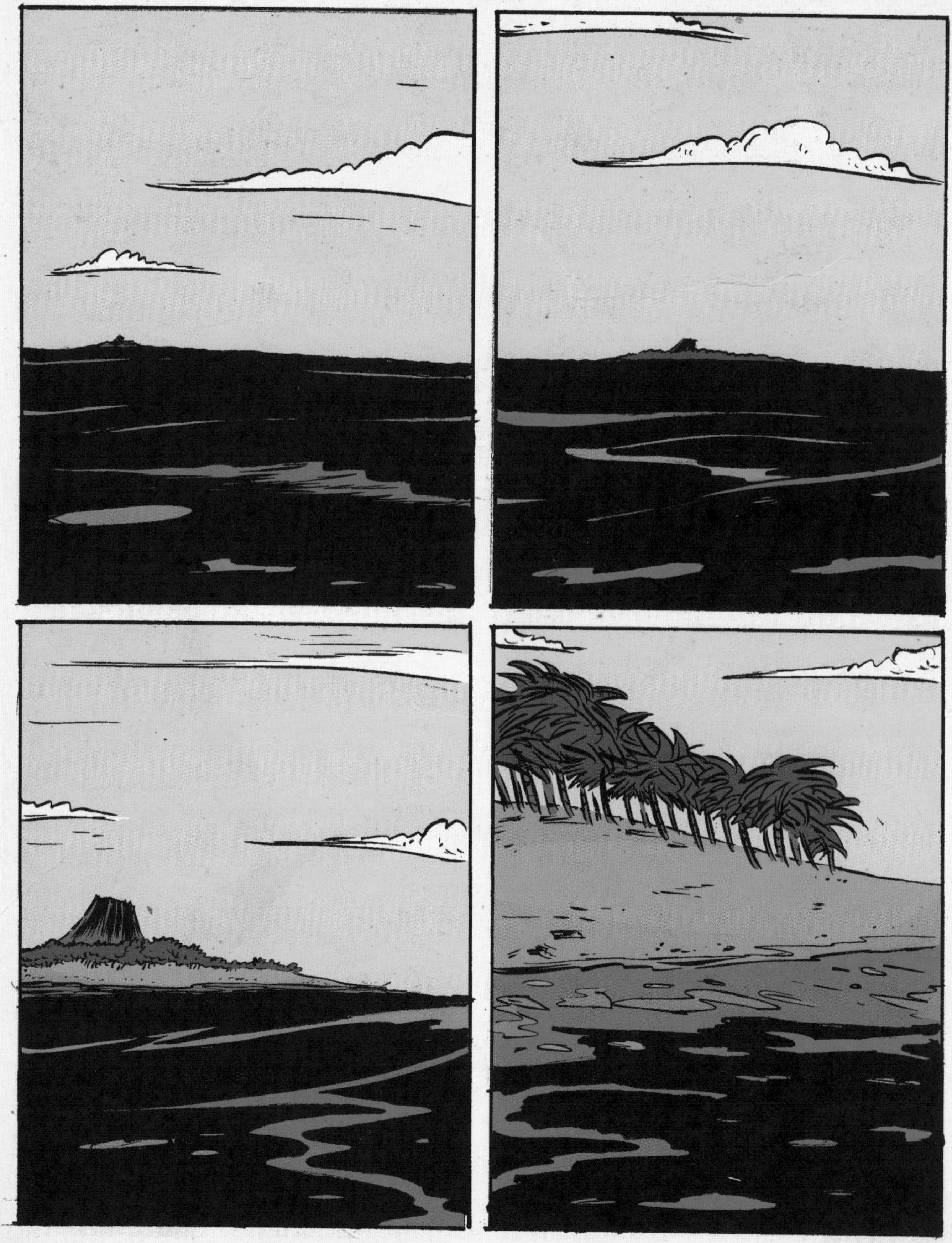

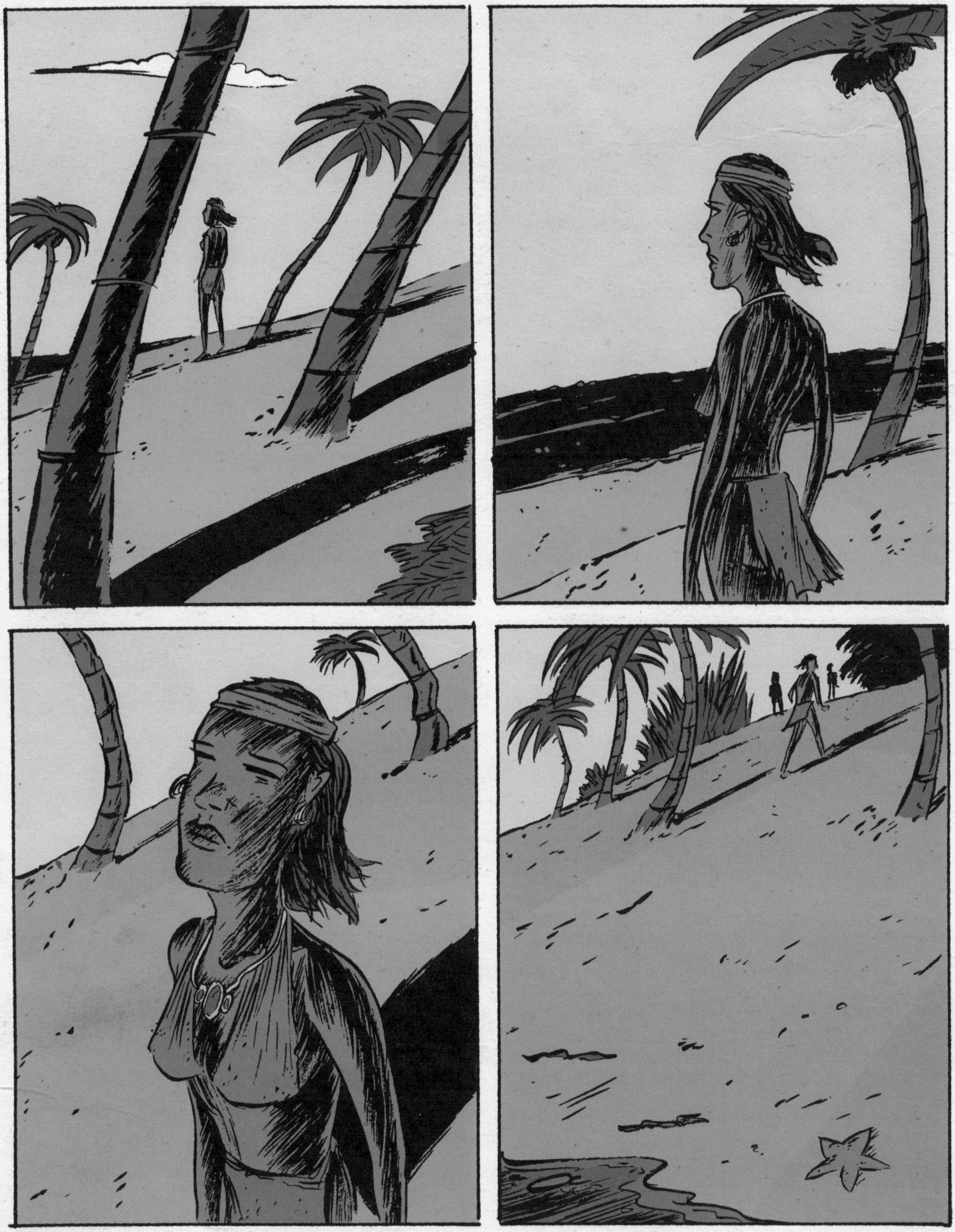

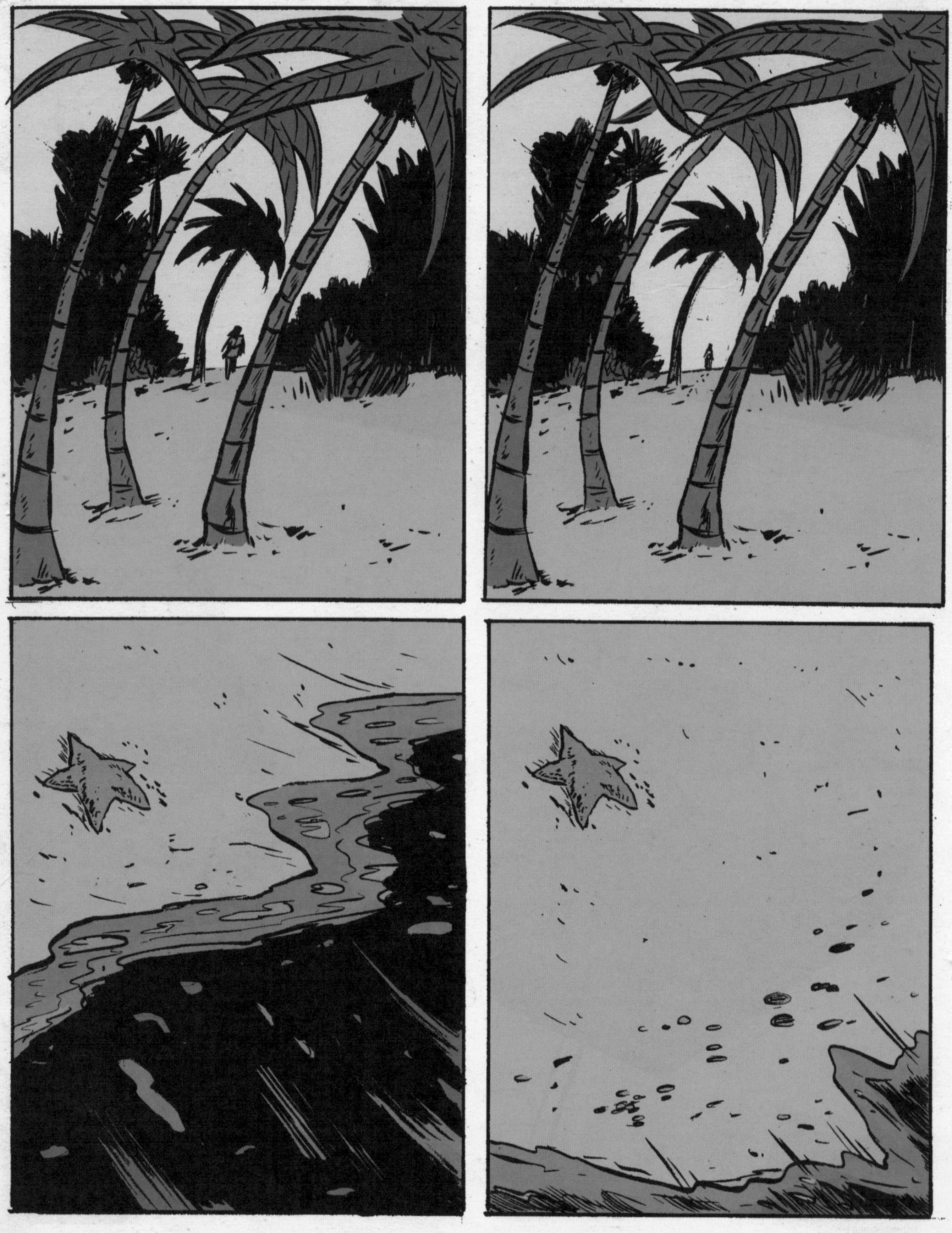

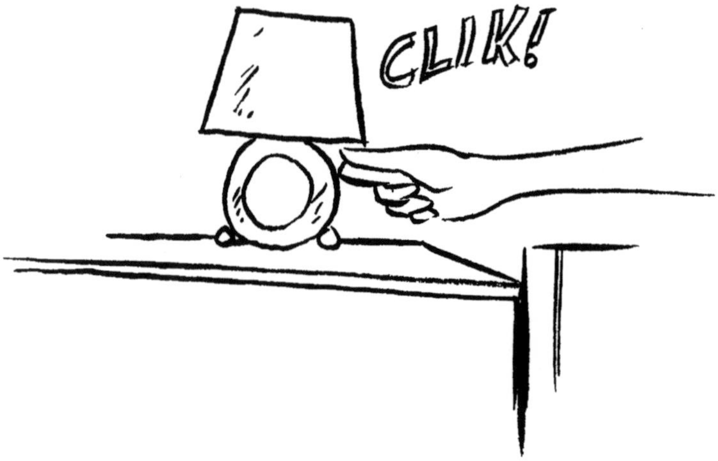
CLIK!